Perspectives on Personality

fourth edition

Perspectives on Personality

CHARLES S. CARVER
University of Miami

MICHAEL F. SCHEIER
Carnegie Mellon University

ALLYN and BACON
Boston   London   Toronto   Sydney   Tokyo   Singapore

Editor in Chief, Social Sciences: Karen Hanson
Executive Editor: Carolyn Merrill
Editorial Assistant: Lara M. Zeises
Executive Marketing Manager: Joyce Nilsen
Editorial Production Service: Chestnut Hill Enterprises, Inc.
Manufacturing Buyer: Megan Cochran
Cover Administrator: Linda Knowles
Text Designer: Carol Somberg/Omegatype Typography, Inc.

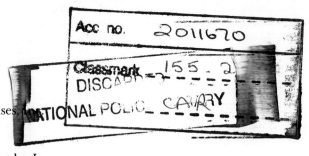

Internet: www.abacon.com

Between the time Website information is gathered and published, some sites may have closed. Also, the transcription of URLs can result in typographical errors. The publisher would appreciate notification where these occur so that they may be corrected in subsequent editions.

Library of Congress Cataloging-in-Publication Data

Carver, Charles S.
    Perspectives on personality / Charles S. Carver, Michael F.
Scheier.—4th ed.
      p. cm.
    Includes bibliographical references and indexes.
    ISBN 0–205–29394–8 (alk. paper)
    1. Personality.   I. Scheier, Michael.   II. Title.
BF698.C22   2000
155.2—dc21   99–26281
                                  CIP

Photo Credits: Photo credits can be found on p. 602, which should be considered an extension of the copyright page.

Printed in the United States of America

10 9 8 7 6 5 4 3 2   VHP   04 03 02 01

For my favorite young ladies in all the world:
Alexandra Carver and Julia Carver
CSC

For my brother, Stephen P. Scheier
MFS

contents

14 Humanistic Psychology: Self-Actualization and Self-Determination 378

15 Personal Constructs 410

preface

Perspectives on Personality, Fourth Edition, examines one of life's most fascinating and mysterious topics: human personality. As the title implies, there are many perspectives a person might take on personality, many ways to think about how people function in life. In this book, we present a range of viewpoints that are used by personality psychologists today.

What's the Same in This Edition?

As in the three earlier editions of *Perspectives on Personality,* the book's content reflects two of our firm beliefs. The first is that theoretical concepts are the most important part of a first course on personality. For this reason, we stress concepts throughout the book. Our first priority has been to present as clearly as we can the ideas that form each theoretical viewpoint.

A second belief reflected in the book is that research is important in personality psychology. Ideas and intuitions are valuable, but an idea shouldn't lie around too long before someone checks to see whether it actually works. For this reason, along with each theory we discuss research that bears on the theory. This emphasis on the role of research stresses that personality psychology is a living, dynamic process of ongoing scientific exploration.

As in previous editions, we present the theories in groups, which we've labeled *perspectives*. Each group of theories depends on a particular sort of orienting viewpoint, an angle from which the theorists proceeded. Within a given perspective there often are several theories, which differ from one another. In each case, however, the theories of a given perspective share fundamental assumptions about human nature.

Each perspective on personality is presented in a pair of chapters, introduced by a prologue. The prologue provides an overview of that perspective's orienting assumptions and major themes. By starting with these orienting assumptions, you'll be right inside the thought processes of the theorists, as you go on to read the chapters themselves. Each chapter concludes with a discussion of current problems within that theoretical viewpoint and our own best guess about its future prospects.

The perspectives are discussed in an order that makes sense to us, but they can easily be read in other orders. Each theoretical section of the book is intended to stand on its own, with no assumptions about previous exposure to other parts of the book. Thus, instructors can move through the perspectives in whatever order they prefer.

As in previous editions, the final chapter takes up the question of how different views relate to each other. The main goal of this chapter is to tie together ideas from theories that were discussed separately in earlier chapters. A second goal is to consider the usefulness of blending theoretical viewpoints, treating theories as complementary to each other rather than as competitors.

This edition also continues our use of the box feature "The Theorist and the Theory." These boxes focus on how the personal experiences of some of the theorists have influenced the form of their theories. In more than one case, theorists almost literally took events from their own lives as models of human affairs more generally, deriving an entire theory from those personal experiences. Not all cases are quite this striking, but personal experience does appear to have played a role in the development of several views on personality.

In this revision we've tried hard to make the content accessible to readers. We've continued to use a conversational style, to try to draw you into the ideas. We've also included examples of how the ideas under discussion can apply to your own life. We hope these qualities will make the book enjoyable as well as informative.

What's Different in This Edition?

This edition retains the third edition's structure (the same chapters, in the same perspectives). However, the content of the fourth edition differs in several important ways from that of the third edition. Most of these changes in content reflect four years of change in the continually evolving research literature of personality psychology. We've made updates to every substantive chapter. Two of them are important enough that we should note them explicitly.

First, work has continued apace on the trait structure of personality. Much of it is taking place within the framework of the five-factor model of personality. Indeed, there have also been efforts to link that model to several other views of personality. This evolution has resulted in considerable change in Chapter 4 (Types, Trait, and Interactionism). It's also resulted in the inclusion of material bearing on the five-factor model in several other chapters.

Second, there continues to be rapid evolution in work concerning biological processes and their influence on personality. Theorists have approached this question from new directions, and there have been shifts in how certain biological processes are viewed. As a result, Chapter 7 (Biological Processes and Personality) has undergone a major reorganization. We've made a special effort in that chapter to pull the ideas of several theorists together into a coherent story.

A minor structural change in this edition is the relocation of the "Problems and Prospects" sections. In previous editions, they were epilogues. Each epilogue addressed criticisms raised about the perspective as a whole and evaluated its future prospects. In this edition, problems and prospects have been considered in individual chapters, with specific criticisms now presented closer to the theory to which they pertain. This, we hope, will create a greater sense of immediacy, making it easier for readers to keep the theory in mind while considering its remaining problems.

A final change that's worth noting, although more prosaic, concerns chapter length. In preparing this edition, we've shortened several of the previous edition's longer chapters. We did this partly by trimming the writing and partly by thinning the detail. We hope the result is more readable, but without loss of clarity.

For more on *Perspectives on Personality,* Fourth Edition, consult its web page: www.abacon.com/carver.

Acknowledgments

We'd both like to express our thanks to some of the people who were important in the creation of this edition, starting with Carolyn Merrill, our editor at Allyn and Bacon and her assistant, Lara Zeises. We also thank Peter Miene, Winona State University; Barbara Rybski Beaver, University of Wisconsin at Whitewater; Andrea A. Zevenbergen, University of North Dakota; Scott Dickman, University of Massachusetts, Dartmouth; and Lynn Friedman, for comments and suggestions on the previous edition.

We also have some more personal acknowledgments:

From Coral Gables, my thanks to those who've been part of my life during this period, particularly Linda Cahan, Janine Shelby, Allison Wilcox and Adrian Voorhies, Linda Nilsson, Rod Gillis, André Perwin, Jessica Lehman, Stacie Spencer, Barbara Wolfsdorf, Jennifer Strauss, Susan Alferi, Bonnie McGregor, Björn Meyer, Mike Antoni, Adele Hayes, and Caroline Willi. Thanks also to my family—Jeff, Allysen, Alexandra, and Julia; Carol; Nancy Lorey; all the Sherricks; and Mike, Karen, Meredith, and Jeremy. Finally, a very special note of appreciation goes to my shag terrier Calvin, who continues to amaze me with his deep insights and his ability to sleep upside down.

From Pittsburgh, thanks go first to the other members of the Matthews/Scheier clan: Karen, Meredith, and Jeremy (the last two, in part, for making the morning school bus at least some of the time). Thanks also to the following group of friends and colleagues: Andy Baum, Mike Bridges, Chuck Carver, Peggy Clark, Ed Gerrard, Vicki Helgeson, David Klahr, Ken Kotovsky, Ginger Placone, Rich Schulz, and Jim Staszewski. Finally, a special "thank you" to my brother, Steve, for helping me adjust to the changes that have occurred over the past few years to our original family group.

Chuck Carver
Michael Scheier

About the Authors

The authors met in graduate school at the University of Texas at Austin, where they both earned Ph.D. degrees in personality psychology. After graduation, they took jobs at the University of Miami and Carnegie Mellon University, where they've remained throughout their careers. They have collaborated for two and a half decades in work that spans personality, social, motivational, clinical, and health psychology—with a particular emphasis on personality and coping as influences on well-being under stress. In 1998, they received awards for Outstanding Scientific Contribution (Senior Level) from the Division of Health Psychology of the American Psychological Association. Along with the four editions of *Perspectives on Personality*, they have published two books on self-regulation (the most recent being *On the Self-Regulation of Behavior*, in 1998) and over 170 articles and chapters. Mike is an avid outdoorsman, hunter, and fisherman. Chuck keeps intending to take up painting but gets distracted by other things.

www.psy.miami.edu/faculty/ccarver/
www.psy.cmu.edu/~scheier/mscheier/html

Perspectives
on Personality

PART *one*

An Introduction

What Is Personality Psychology?

■ Sue met Rick in a philosophy class when both were starting their sopho-more year of college. They started to date casually a couple of months later. Their relationship gradually deepened until now, two years later, they're talk-ing seriously of marriage. Here's Sue talking about Rick: "He's attractive to me in so many ways it's hard to know which ones matter most. He's good-looking, and athletic, and smart—and he likes the same music I like. He knows how to do lots of things you don't expect a guy to know, like cooking and even sewing. But the best thing about him I don't even know how to put into words, except to say he has a really great personality."

Every now and then someone does a survey to find out what qualities people value in a potential husband or wife. The surveys usually find that most people want their mate to have a sense of humor, good looks, a streak of romance, and so on. Almost always, though, a high priority is "personality." If you're like most people, you want someone who has a "good personality."

A good personality. What does that phrase mean to you? If you were to describe a friend of yours who *does* have a good personality, what would you say about that per-son? "Rick has a terrific personality. . . ." But then what?

Describing someone's personality is trying to capture the person's essence. It in-volves crystallizing something from the bits of knowledge you have about the person. Describing someone's personality almost always means taking a large number of characteristics and reducing them to a smaller set of qualities. Evidence about per-sonality comes partly from what people do and say at various times, but it's partly a matter of *how* people do what they do—the style that brings a unique and personal touch to their actions.

Defining Personality

Trying to describe someone's personality is an exercise in being a psychologist. Everyone is a psychologist at least part of the time, because everyone spends part of his or her life trying to decide what other people are like. When you think about the qualities that describe someone, and when you think about what reveals those qual-ities to you, you're informally doing part of what personality psychologists do.

There's a difference in focus, though, between what you do in daily life and what personality psychologists do. Everyday use of the word *personality* tends to focus on *specific* personalities, belonging to specific persons (Rick, for instance). The psy-chologist is more likely to focus on personality in general, personality as an abstrac-tion. When psychologists talk about personality, they usually have in mind a conception of personality that can apply to everyone.

What *is* personality, when viewed this way? This question is hard to answer. Per-sonality psychologists have disagreed for a long time about exactly how to define personality. Many definitions have been offered, but none is universally accepted. Personality is, in fact, quite an elusive concept.

Why Do People Use Personality as a Concept?

In trying to come to a definition for the concept of personality, one way to start is to think about why the word is used. Understanding why people use it should help

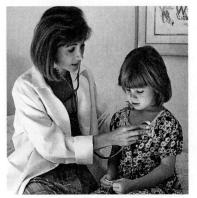

Personality produces consistencies in behavior across different contexts. Although this woman finds herself in different situations, her warm and caring nature comes through in all of them.

decide what it means. The reasons for using the word converge on an implicit definition for it.

When *you* use the word personality, why do you use it? What makes you pick that word instead of another one?

One reason for using the word personality appears to be the desire to convey a sense of *consistency* or *continuity* about a person. There are several kinds of consistency, all of which bring the concept of personality to mind. You may see consistency in a person across time (Sue talked a lot when you first met her, and years later she still dominates conversations). You may see consistency across similar situations (André is especially polite to waiters in restaurants and has been that way every time you've had dinner with him). You may even see consistency across situations that are fairly different from each other (Barbara tends to order people around in stores, at work, even at *parties*). In each case, you feel the sense that it's undeniably the same person from one instance to another, because the person acts (or talks, or thinks, or feels) in consistent ways from time to time and from setting to setting. One reason for using the word personality, then, is to imply this consistency or continuity within the person.

A second reason people use the word personality is to convey the sense that whatever the person is doing (or thinking or feeling) is *originating from within*. The idea that behavior arises from inside the person may seem so obvious that it hardly deserves mention, but not everyone sees it that way. There are philosophical and theoretical disagreements on this issue. Still, use of the term personality conveys the sense that there's a causal force *within* the person influencing how the person acts.

These two reasons for using the concept of personality join with each other when you try to predict and understand people's behavior (even your own). Predicting behavior is important to psychologists. It can be important to you, as well. When you choose a new roommate for next year, you're predicting you'll get along well. When you tell a chronically late friend that the movie starts at 8, when it really starts at 8:30, you're predicting that this means he'll arrive more or less on time. An important source of information in these predictions is your judgment about what the other person's personality is like.

The term personality is also used for another reason. It often conveys the sense that a few salient characteristics can serve as a summary for what a person is like. Saying that Karen has an outgoing personality, for example, implies that the quality of outgoingness is prominent in her. Saying that Tanya has a hostile personality implies that hostility influences many of her actions. The qualities that first come to mind when you try to describe someone are those that (from your point of view) seem important or central to that person. The more central the quality is, the more useful it is for predicting his behavior, and the more it distinguishes him from others. Thinking about these highly prominent characteristics of a person brings to mind the concept of personality.

These, then, are some reasons why people use the term personality. This patchwork of reasons for using the term moves us closer to having a definition for it. That is, the word personality conveys a sense of consistency, internal causality, and personal distinctiveness. These qualities, as it happens, are incorporated into almost all definitions of personality.

A Working Definition

We're tempted to leave it at that, creating the sense of a definition but not making it explicit. We won't, though. Here's an explicit definition. We're not saying that this is the "correct" one, but we think it comes close. We've adapted it slightly from one written some time ago, by Gordon Allport (1961): **Personality** *is a dynamic organization, inside the person, of psychophysical systems that create the person's characteristic patterns of behavior, thoughts, and feelings.*

This definition makes several points:

- Personality isn't just an accumulation of bits and pieces; it has *organization.*
- Personality doesn't just lie there; it's active, it has *processes* of some sort.
- Personality is a *psychological* concept, but it's tied to the *physical* body.
- Personality is a *causal force;* it helps determine how the person relates to the world.
- Personality shows up in *patterns*—recurrences, consistencies.
- Personality is displayed not just in one way but in *many ways,* in behaviors, thoughts, and feelings.

This definition covers a lot of ground, pointing to several elements that ought to be part of any theoretical conceptualization of personality. As good as it is, though, it isn't perfect. Even this careful definition seems to let something about the concept slip through your fingers. This elusiveness is something that personality psychologists have struggled with for many years.

Individual differences in behavior and reactions are an important part of personality.

Two Fundamental Issues in Personality Psychology

Two ideas implicit in what we've said so far represent core issues in thinking about personality. One issue concerns the existence of **individual differences.** Each person who ever lived is different from everyone else. No two personalities are quite alike—not even those of identical twins. Some people are happy, some are sad. Some people are sociable, some are shy, reclusive, or even antisocial. As we noted earlier, one reason for using the word personality in the first place is to capture features that summarize a person. This certainly wouldn't happen if the features didn't differ from one person to another. Thus, the notion of individual differences is important in everyday use of the term personality.

Individual differences are also important to the theorist who tries to understand personality. To be useful, any approach to personality has to have something to say about these individual differences. A complete account of personality should devote some attention to the question of where the differences come from. A complete account should also consider the questions of how and why these differences among people matter.

The other issue concerns something we'll call **intrapersonal functioning.** By this phrase we mean a set of processes taking place within the person, the processes that Allport called a "dynamic organization" of systems. The idea here is that personality isn't like a rubber stamp that you pound onto each situation you enter. Instead, there are mechanisms or processes that go on inside you, leading you to act in the ways you do. Such processes can create a sense of continuity within the person, even if the person acts in different ways in different circumstances. That is, you can feel the same processes engaged, even if the results differ in different situations.

Here's an illustration. Some psychologists believe that people's behavior is a product of their motives. Motivational tendencies rise and fall over time and across changes in situations. Which motives are strongest at any given time determines what the person does at that time. A person may work in isolation for several hours, then spend a couple of hours socializing, then go eat dinner, followed by some reading. Although the behaviors differ, they all stem from motives within the person that vary in strength over the course of the day. In this view on personality, the motives are critical variables. The processes by which motives vary in strength and by which they influence behavior are the processes of intrapersonal functioning.

This is just one example of an intrapersonal process. It's not the only kind of process you might assume is going on inside people. Regardless of what processes you assume, though, the idea of process is important. A complete account of personality should say what kinds of processes underlie personality and how they work.

Different approaches to personality place different amounts of emphasis on these two issues. Some approaches emphasize process and consist largely of a view of intrapersonal functioning, dealing less with differences among people. Other approaches treat individual uniqueness as the most important aspect of personality and are more vague about what processes occur inside. These differences of emphasis contribute to the diversity among personality theories.

Why have we gone on so long in describing what personality psychology is about and what issues its theorists focus on? We've done this to give you a feel for the content and breadth of the field. Salvatore Maddi, a commentator on issues in personality, has said that "theorizing about the nature of personality without keeping in mind just what you want to understand about human behavior is like building a boat in the absence of knowledge of what water is like" (1980, p. 645). He's right. Theorists have to keep in mind what aspects of human life they want to understand. If you're going to understand why theories are the way they are, you'll have to do so too.

Theory in Personality Psychology

Theoretical principles are a large part of what's in this book. Because theories are so important, we should devote a little attention to what they are, what they do, and how to evaluate them.

What Do Theories Do?

What *is* a theory? A **theory** is a sort of summary statement, a general principle or set of principles pertaining to a class of events. A theory can apply to a highly specific class of events, or it can be broader. Some theories in psychology concern processes within a single nerve cell. Others concern more complex behaviors that form a particular category (such as maintaining close relationships or playing chess). Still other theories are intended to pertain to all the behaviors a person engages in (personality).

Theories are used for two purposes (and this is true no matter what the theory pertains to). The first purpose is to *explain* the phenomena it addresses. A theory always provides a way of explaining some things that are known to be true. For example, some biological personality theories hold that heredity influences personality. This idea provides a way to explain why children often resemble their parents in how they act or react to events.

Every theory about personality provides an account of at least some phenomena of personality. This first purpose of the theory—explanation—is absolutely fundamental. Without providing an explanation for at least some of what's already known, a theory would be useless.

Theories also have a second purpose, though. A theory should also suggest possibilities you don't yet know for sure are true. To put it differently, a theory should allow you to *predict new information.* A theory of personality should allow you to predict things about people that you haven't thought to look for yet—maybe things *nobody* has thought to look for yet. For the psychologist, this is where much of the excitement lies.

The psychologist generally wants to make predictions about large numbers of people, but the same principle holds when you make predictions in your own life. It's exciting to take some idea about how personality works and use it to predict how your roommate will react to a situation you haven't seen her in before. It's particularly exciting when your prediction is right!

The predictive function of theories is more subtle and more difficult than is the explanatory function. The difficulty lies partly in the fact that most theories contain a little ambiguity. This often makes it unclear just exactly what the prediction should be. In fact, the broader the theory (the more things it has to account for), the more likely it is to be ambiguous. As you've seen, personality is a very broad and abstract concept, covering a wide range of phenomena. As a result, most theories of personality are complex. They're often intended to handle many variables more or less at once. As a result, it's sometimes hard to tell what they predict.

Evaluating Theories: The Role of Research

In talking about making predictions from theories, we've begun to drift into considering another issue: how to decide whether a theory is any good. In describing the predictive function of theories, we've revealed a bias that many personality psychologists hold. The bias is this: Theories should be *testable* and they should be *tested*. It's important to find out whether a theory makes predictions that receive support.

We want to be very specific here about what we're saying. Personality is such an important part of life that many people besides psychologists think and write about it. Personality has been a topic for theologians, philosophers, artists, poets, novelists, and songwriters, and many of them have had important insights about it. We don't mean to diminish the contribution of these insights. But is that enough?

People have different opinions on this question. Many believe that insight stands on its own and requires no further evidence. Even some personality theorists have believed this. Sigmund Freud, who's often viewed as the father of personality psychology, wasn't much interested in whether his ideas were supported by the research of others. He saw his own observations and insights as sufficient in themselves.

The view that dominates today's psychology, however, is that ideas—even brilliant ideas—have to be tested before they can be trusted. Too often things that *seem* true turn out not to be true after all. Unfortunately, you never know which ideas are brilliant and right—and which are brilliant but wrong—unless you test them. Because of this, today's personality psychology is a scientific field, in which evidence counts for a lot. Studies on personality provide information about how accurate or useful the ideas of a theory are. The information collected in these studies can either confirm or disconfirm the prediction, and thereby support or undermine the theory.

When theories are used to generate predictions for research, a continuous interplay develops (see Figure 1.1). If a theory makes predictions, the result is research—scientific studies—to test the predictions. Research often yields support for the predictions. Sometimes, however, the research either fails to support the theory

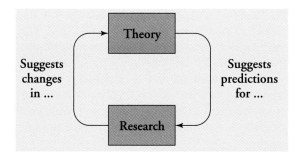

FIGURE 1.1

In a scientific approach to personality psychology, there is a continuous cycling between theory and research. Theory suggests predictions to be tested; the results of studies suggest the need for new or modified theory.

or provides only partial support. The outcome of the study may suggest limitations on the theory—perhaps it predicts accurately under some conditions but not others. Such a finding leads to revision or modification of the theory.

Once modified, the theory must be tested again, because it's no longer quite the same theory as it was. Its new or altered elements must be examined for other predictions to which they might lead. This sequence of prediction, testing, revision or refinement, and additional prediction and testing can be a virtually never-ending cycle.

What Else Makes a Theory Good?

To the scientist, then, an important basis for deciding whether a theory is good, or useful, is the extent to which it does what a theory's supposed to do: explain and predict. But this isn't the only way people evaluate theories. There are several other grounds on which theories are judged, other reasons why one theory is taken as preferable to another.

A theory shouldn't be based on too narrow a base of information (Maddi, 1980). Some theories are criticized because they're based heavily on the theorists' experiences in conducting therapy. Other theories are criticized because they rely heavily on the behavior of laboratory animals in highly restricted situations. Yet others are criticized because they rest largely on information from long sets of rating scales. None of these sources of information is bad in itself. But to base a theory on only one source of information weakens the theory.

A theory should also have the quality of **parsimony**—that is, it should use as few assumptions (or concepts) as possible. To put it a different way, things should be kept as simple as possible. This criterion is important, but it can't be applied too rigidly to personality theories, because knowledge on this topic is far from complete. A theory that looks parsimonious today may be unable to account for something that will be discovered tomorrow. A theory that looks too complex today may be the *only* one that can handle tomorrow's discovery. Nevertheless, excess theoretical baggage is a cause for concern.

Another way people judge theories is highly subjective. To put it bluntly, some theories just "feel" better than others. Some of the theories you'll read about will fit your personal worldview better than others. You're not the only one who reacts this way. So do psychologists. There's even evidence that behavioral scientists choose theories that fit with their images of *themselves* (Johnson, Germer, Efran, & Overton, 1988). William James, an important figure in the early years of psychology, said people will prefer theories that "are most interesting, . . . appeal most urgently to our aesthetic, emotional, and active needs" (James, 1890, p. 312). Which theories will feel best to you, then, will depend partly on who you are and how you see the world. This shouldn't be the only criterion you rely on, but it can be an important one.

Finally, a theory should be *stimulating* (Maddi, 1980). Being stimulating may mean provoking enthusiasm, interest, or excitement. A theory can also be stimulating by provoking outrage and efforts to show how wrong it is. Provoking either reaction is good, because the reaction leads to efforts at finding out whether the theory is useful or not. Theories so dull they provoke no reaction are less useful, because no one bothers to study their implications.

Perspectives on Personality

Now that we've talked about theory in the abstract, let's preview the kinds of theories people have developed in order to talk about personality. The theories range considerably in what they take as their starting points, which can make matters a little confusing. To sort out the confusion a little, let's back up one more step and consider how the various theorists decided *where to start*.

The starting point, in some sense, is always a vague conception of human nature. How often have you heard the expression "It's just human nature"? Use of the phrase "human nature" implies a way of thinking about what people are like. But what *is* human nature? *In what terms* should we think about people? As you will see, different theorists have come up with very different answers to these questions, ranging from human nature as primitive beast to human nature as robot.

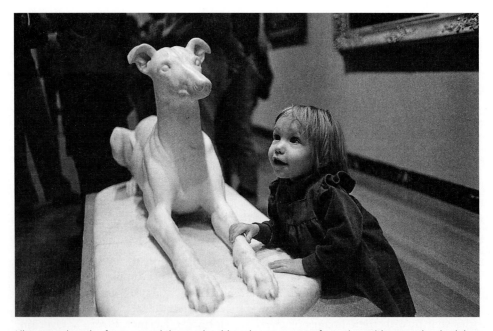

Like a good work of art, a good theory should evoke some sort of reaction, either good or bad, but not indifferent.

Groupings Among Theories

Theories of personality can be seen as falling into several groups. Each group is characterized by a general viewpoint on how best to think of human nature. Each group's orientation toward human nature differs (sometimes slightly, sometimes radically) from those of the other groups. Throughout the book we refer to each of these orientations as a "perspective" on personality.

Another term that means much the same as the word *perspective,* as we're using it here, is **metatheory.** A metatheory is a set of orienting assumptions *within which* theories are devised. These orienting assumptions are more general than are the assumptions of a particular theory. Metatheories are guides to the kinds of concepts that make sense to even think about putting into theories. For example, the assumption that life involves competition among energy systems is a metatheory. There are lots of ways of thinking about energy systems, which might lead to many theories. But all of them would be grounded in the idea that life is about energy systems. Each perspective, or metatheory, in this way provides a sort of core metaphor for human nature, and the metaphor becomes a guide used in the development of specific theories.

We think that placing each theory in a metatheoretical context provides you a clearer picture than if we treated each theory as a totally distinct approach. That's what we've done here. In this book we discuss seven perspectives on personality, which we've labeled dispositional, biological, psychoanalytic, neoanalytic, learning, phenomenological, and cognitive self-regulation. Almost every perspective is reflected in the work of several different theorists. The theories within a given perspective sometimes differ substantially from one another. Within a given perspective, however, they seem to share the orienting assumptions provided by that metatheory.

Each perspective is taken up in a separate section of the book, organized as follows: A brief prologue opens the section, describing basic themes and core assumptions of that section's metatheory. This description indicates the metaphor of human nature that stands as the bedrock for that perspective on personality. This prologue is followed by content chapters, each focusing on a particular theoretical view of personality within that perspective. Each of these chapters ends with a statement on the problems that that type of theory faces, and our guesses about its prospects for future development. To foreshadow what comes later, here are brief characterizations of the perspectives you'll be reading about.

The *dispositional perspective* is based on the idea that people have relatively stable qualities (dispositions) that are displayed in diverse settings. These dispositions are shown outwardly in different ways, but they're deeply embedded in the person. Human nature, from this point of view, is a set of relatively permanent qualities built into the person. Dispositional theorists vary in how they view dispositions. Some simply emphasize that dispositions exist, and don't say much about how they influence behavior. Others focus on the idea that dispositions influence behavior through motive forces. These two sets of ideas are described in separate chapters in the dispositional section.

Another way of thinking about human nature, which we've called the *biological perspective,* emphasizes the fact that humans are biological creatures. One biological viewpoint resembles dispositional theories, but with a different emphasis. This approach says personality is genetically based: Dispositions are inherited. Indeed, some theorists take this idea a step further, to suggest that many qualities of human behavior exist precisely because they had evolutionary purposes. Another part of today's biological perspective stems from the idea that understanding personality means understanding the workings of the body we inhabit. This biological view focuses on how the nervous system and hormones influence the kind of person you become.

The *psychoanalytic perspective,* which is taken up next, is a very different view of the world. It's based on the idea that personality is a set of internal forces that compete and conflict with one another. The internal dynamics of these forces (and the way behavior emerges from them) are the focus of this perpective. Human nature, from this viewpoint, is a set of pressures inside the person that sometimes work with each other and sometimes are at war with each other. This perspective is perhaps the most tightly focused of all, in the sense that one theory dominates it—the psychoanalytic theory of Sigmund Freud.

The next perspective we've labeled *neoanalytic.* In a sense, neoanalytic theories aren't really a distinct perspective: They all derive in one way or another from psychoanalytic theory (thus the name "neoanalytic"). One might argue that this makes them all variations on the psychoanalytic perspective (indeed, we said so ourselves in the first edition of this book). On the other hand, the theories evolved in ways that make them very different from Freud's theory. For this reason, we believe they no longer share the worldview assumed in Freud's theory. The ideas that form the core of the neoanalytic perspective concern the ego and its development, and the importance of social relationships in personality and its functioning.

The next perspective, the *learning perspective,* begins with a conception of human nature in which *change,* rather than consistency, is paramount. That is, the most obvious quality of human nature, from this perspective, is that behavior changes systematically as a result of experience. Since there are several aspects of learning, there are distinct theories that relate learning to personality, although they share a single metatheory. In this view, a person's personality is the integrated sum of whatever the person has learned up till now.

The next section focuses on the *phenomenological perspective.* The roots of this perspective trace to two ideas. The first is that everyone's subjective experience is important, valuable, meaningful—and unique. The second is that people tend naturally toward self-perfection and that all people can move themselves in that direction by exercising their free will to do so. Self-determination is an important element in this perspective, and the sense of self-determination is central to this view of human nature. A person's personality, in this view, is partly a matter of the uniqueness hidden within, and partly a matter of what the person chooses to make of it.

The final perspective is labeled *cognitive self-regulation.* This view holds that cognitive processes are the underpinnings of personality. Many who study cognitive processes assume a metaphor in which humans are seen as machinelike. In this metaphor, the nervous system is a giant organic computer with decision rules and patterns of information use that, in some ways, resemble those of silicon-and-metal computers. Another aspect of this viewpoint is that people are self-regulating systems, setting goals and checking on progress toward those goals. The metaphor in this case is less the computer and more the robot or guided missile.

How Distinct Are the Perspectives?

It should be apparent from even this brief description that each perspective on personality starts with a different orientation to human nature. There are also links among the perspectives, though, that may not have been as obvious. For example, phenomenological theories emphasize the concept of self and the need for the self to grow and develop naturally. The concept of self isn't too different from the concept of ego, which is a focus of neoanalytic theories. Thus, there's a link between neoanalytic and phenomenological theories. As another example, George Kelly, a phenomenological theorist, developed ideas that later became important in today's cognitive theories. This creates a link between the phenomenological and cognitive self-regulation views.

Is linking of theories to perspectives arbitrary, then? No, but it's imperfect. An analogy may help. Think of theories as hot-air balloons (perhaps a dangerous metaphor). All are attached by mooring ropes to posts in the ground. Each post represents a metatheory. Each balloon is tied firmly to one post, with a boarding ramp for this balloon's passengers. However, most also have second ropes (and sometimes third and fourth ones) attached to other posts. Some posts have many balloons tied to them, others have only one or two. Some of the mooring ropes are thick and heavy, some are lighter. In an analogous way, each theory in this book is placed according to the metatheory it's tied to most firmly, but each often has secondary ties to other metatheories.

Another Kind of "Perspective"

There's one more thing to say about our use of the term *perspective,* which involves a different shade of meaning of the word. There was a time when personality psychologists created grand theories aimed at the total complexity of personality. Freud's theory is the clearest example of this (some would say the only good example). However, this has become less common as psychology evolved. More common today are theories that deal with some *aspect* of what personality is about. Most of these weren't really intended to be full models of personality, and it's somewhat misleading to present them (and judge them) as though they were.

The fact that these aren't grand-scale theories doesn't mean they have nothing important to say about personality. It does mean, though, that a theory of this type won't tell us everything about personality. It gives us a particular viewing angle on the subject (a more literal meaning of the word perspective). This viewing angle may be special and may yield insights you can't find in other views, but it illuminates only part of the picture. This limitation is important to keep in mind as you think about the various theories and what they have to say.

Today's pattern of theory development also has another implication. Many people who have contributed to today's understanding of personality have made contributions to *several* points of view. Don't be surprised when you see the same names show up in two or three different places in the book. In today's personality psychology, people whose work informs us about psychoanalytic concepts may also have had useful things to say about principles of self-regulation. People who have helped us to understand learning may also have contributed to trait psychology.

This is one reason why, in general, we haven't focused the book's chapters on particular individuals. Rather, in each chapter we've emphasized the conceptual *themes* emphasized by a given theoretical viewpoint.

Organization Within Chapters

Each chapter within a given perspective addresses a specific type of theory. Most of the content of each chapter is a description of the basic elements and processes of personality, viewed from that theoretical vantage point. Each chapter thus tells you something about how intrapersonal functioning and individual differences are construed within that theory.

Each chapter also addresses two more subjects. One is assessment, the process of measuring personality. The other is the potential for problems to arise in human experience, and the processes by which behavior is changed for the better through therapy. Here's a brief preview of what these sections will be like.

Assessment

Personality psychologists give considerable attention to the process of measuring personality, for at least three reasons. First, psychologists are interested in portraying the personalities of specific individuals, in much the same way as you would characterize the personalities of people you know. To be confident that these pictures are accurate, psychologists need good ways to measure personality.

A second reason for assessing personality concerns the effort to conduct research on personality. To study qualities of personality, psychologists have to be able to measure those qualities. Without good ways to assess individual differences or intrapersonal functioning, it's impossible to study them. Good assessment, then, lies at the heart of personality research.

A third important reason to measure personality strays a bit from the main focus of this book. Specifically, determining the personality characteristics of individuals is an important part of applied psychology. For example, organizational psychologists use personality as a basis for making hiring decisions (you might want to be sure, for example, that you're hiring someone with a particular pattern of motives). Clinical psychologists also use personality assessment in making a diagnosis of pathology (it can be important to know whether a person's personality shows signs of poor functioning).

Assessment is a goal that's important throughout personality psychology. This goal is viewed somewhat differently, however, from different perspectives on personality (though some issues, addressed in Chapter 3, are common to all approaches). As a result, the theoretical viewpoints often differ in the assessment techniques they emphasize. In discussing assessment in each later chapter, we focus on how assessment from that viewpoint has its own special character.

Problems in Behavior, and Behavior Change

The other topic incorporated into each theory chapter concerns the fact that people's lives don't always go smoothly. Each viewpoint on normal personality functioning also suggests a way to think about problems. Indeed, it's easily argued that a theory of personality gains in credibility from being able to say useful things about personal problems. To clarify how each approach to personality would view such problems, we briefly take up this issue in each chapter, from that chapter's viewpoint. As with assessment, our emphasis is on the special contribution made by that theoretical orientation to thinking about problems.

Finally, we address the contributions that the theoretical orientation under discussion makes to understanding the therapeutic management of problems. If each viewpoint has a way of thinking about normal processes and about how things can go wrong, each viewpoint also has a way of thinking about how to try to deal with the problems. Each suggests ways to turn problematic functioning back into effective and satisfying functioning.

Personality does not always function smoothly. Each perspective on personality has its own view about why problems occur.

SUMMARY

Personality is a difficult concept to define, and even the best definitions are quite abstract. Thinking about how people use the concept, however, suggests three reasons for its use. People use it to convey a sense of consistency or continuity within a person, to convey the sense that the person is the origin of behavior, and to convey the sense that the essence of a person can be summarized or captured in a few salient qualities.

The field of personality addresses two fundamental issues. One is the existence of differences among people. The other is how best to conceptualize intrapersonal functioning—the processes that take place within all persons, giving form and continuity to behavior.

Much of this book deals with theories. Theories are summary statements, sets of principles that pertain to some class of events. Theories have two purposes: to explain things that are known and to predict possibilities that haven't yet been examined. One way to evaluate the worth of a theory is to ask what research supports its predictions. In scientific psychology there is a continuing cycle between theory and research, as theories are tested, modified on the basis of results, and tested again.

Theories can be evaluated on several grounds other than research support. For example, a theory shouldn't be based on a single kind of information. Theories also benefit from being parsimonious—from needing relatively few assumptions (or concepts). Apart from these considerations, theories are given greater weight when they fit well with one's intuitions, and they have a greater impact if they stimulate interest (and thus efforts to test them).

The theories addressed in this book are based on seven different perspectives, or viewpoints, on human nature. They are identified with the terms *dispositional, biological, psychoanalytic, neoanalytic, learning, phenomenological,* and *cognitive self-regulation.* Each theory chapter focuses on the assumptions about the nature of personality within a particular theoretical framework. Also included are a discussion of assessment from the viewpoint of the theory under discussion, and a discussion of problems in behavior and how they can be remedied.

GLOSSARY

Individual differences Differences in personality from one person to another.

Intrapersonal functioning The psychological processes that take place within the person.

Metatheory Sets of orienting assumptions about reality, which provide guidelines for what kinds of ideas should be used to create theories.

Parsimony The quality of requiring few assumptions; simplicity.

Personality A dynamic organization, inside the person, of psychophysical systems that create the person's characteristic patterns of behavior, thoughts, and feelings.

Theory An abstract statement that summarizes a relationship of some sort.

Methods in the Study of Personality

■   Sam and Dave are at the cafeteria taking a break from studying. Sam says "My roommate got a letter yesterday from his girlfriend at home saying she's breaking up with him. People around here better watch out 'cause he's gonna be looking for some serious partying to help him forget her."

"What makes you think so?"

"What kind of question is that? I thought it over, and it's obvious. That's what *I'd* do."

"Oh? I know several people who've gotten dumped by their hometown girlfriends, and *none* of them did that. Actually, they did the opposite, didn't go out much at all for a few weeks. I think you're wrong about how people react to this kind of thing."

People have tried for centuries to grasp the nature of personality. But when you try, where do you start? When people create theories, where do the theories come from? How are theories confirmed or disconfirmed? How do psychologists decide what to believe and what not to believe about personality? These are questions about the methods of science. They can be asked in all areas of study, astronomy to zoology. They are particularly challenging, though, when applied to the subject matter of personality.

Gathering Information

Sources: Observe Yourself and Observe Others

One simple way to gather information about personality is to look inward to your own experience. This technique (used by Sam in the opening example) is available to everyone. Try it. After all, you have a personality. If you want to understand personality in general, perhaps you should take a look at yours as an example. Sit back and think about some events that took place in your life recently, think about what you did and how you felt, and try to pull from those recollections a thread of continuity. From this might come a theory—a set of principles to help explain the processes behind those events.

Examining your own experience is an easy beginning, and it can be a useful one, but it has a drawback. Specifically, your own consciousness has a special relationship to your memories (and even to your present actions). It's hard to be sure that this special relationship doesn't create a distortion in what you're seeing. For instance, you can misrecall something you experienced, yet feel sure your memory is correct.

This problem diminishes when you look at someone else instead of yourself (as did Dave in the opening example). This is the second method of gathering information: Observe somone else. This method has its own problem, though, which is the reverse of introspection's problem. Specifically, it's impossible to be "inside another person's head," to really know what that person is thinking and feeling. This difference in perspective can create vast differences in understanding (cf. Jones & Nisbett, 1971). It can lead to misinterpretation.

Which starting point is better? Most psychologists would agree that each of these ways of getting insights has a place in the search for truth, though each also has problems. Each can lead to theories and hypotheses, and research follows from both starting points.

Seeking Depth: Case Studies

Some psychologists interested in personality seek to understand the whole person, rather than just part of the person. Henry Murray (1938) coined the term **personology** to refer to the effort to understand the whole person. Murray strongly emphasized the need to study persons as coherent entities. Many other early personality theorists took a similar view.

Such an orientation leads to the use of a technique called the **case study.** A case study involves repeated, in-depth examination of one person. It usually takes place over an extended period of repeated observation, and typically involves unstructured interviews as well as more standardized procedures. Sometimes it involves spending a day or two with the person, either interacting directly or just being around the person to see how he or she interacts with others. The repeated observations allow the observer to confirm initial impressions or to find out that the impressions were incomplete or misleading. Confirming or disconfirming an impression is hard to do, of course, when you make only brief observations. The depth of probing that's possible in a case study can also reveal detail about the person's life that otherwise wouldn't be apparent. This, in turn, can yield important insights.

Case studies are rich in detail and can create vivid descriptions of the person under study. Particularly compelling incidents or examples are often viewed as illustrating broader themes in the person's life. There are other advantages to case studies, as well. Because they examine the person in his or her life situation instead of settings created by the researcher, the information pertains directly to normal life. Because they're open-ended, they let the observer follow whatever leads seem interesting, rather than posing only questions chosen ahead of time.

Many case studies (though not all) are also clinical studies. That is, often people who do case studies focus on those with some kind of problem in their lives. Most taking this focus have been therapists, studying people they were treating. Clinical case studies give information about ways personality goes awry, as well as information about the normal workings of the person. Indeed, several theories of personality arose primarily from case-study observations made in the context of therapy.

As an illustration of how a case study might be used to generate broader conclusions about personality, consider this excerpt from a brief case study of a college student who's having personal difficulties: John is 19 years old, slender, and of medium height. His typical manner of dress conveys no particular style other than "average college student." The middle of three sons, John grew up in a small city in the Midwest. His father is a factory worker, and his mother works as an aide in a nursing home. Their combined income provides a modest living and lets the sons plan to attend the state university, but does not permit many luxuries. John's older brother (four years older) had been a stellar athlete in high school, but his college career ended with an injury, and he now works in the same factory as his father. John's younger brother (three years younger) shows a talent for math and science, and his father refers to him as "the engineer," clearly reflecting his hope for the boy's future.

Asked to talk about what his high school years were like, John said that he felt they had been mostly good, but maybe not as good for him as for others. Asked to clarify this, he related several minor disappointments he'd experienced in high school, none of which seemed to carry much weight by itself. Then he described an incident in which he had done poorly on a test for which he'd felt fully prepared. He shrugged, as if to suggest that the event wasn't important, but he seemed more tense than at other times during the conversation (or in other interviews).

John has had consistent academic difficulties at the university, despite having higher than average SAT scores. Academic Services referred him to the university's counseling center in the hope of resolving the difficulties. At first John was the picture of bravado with his counselor, but he didn't maintain that picture for long. In their second meeting, John said to his counselor that he didn't want to disappoint his parents, but he had doubts about whether he belonged in college. Although other people in his dorm never seemed to question their abilities, John felt a constant nagging sense that he wasn't up to the challenge.

After just a few discussions it became apparent to his counselor that John is lacking in self-esteem. As the counselor updated her notes on his case, she thought again about an idea that had crossed her mind more than once before: Students low in self-esteem don't seem to perform up to their academic potential in college. This is an idea that has many implications, and the counselor made some more notes on it.

Thus, a series of observations—even brief observations—made in the course of examining one person's life situation can lead an observer to conclusions about how personality is involved in important classes of events.

Seeking Generality: Studies of Many People

Case studies can provide revealing insights into the human experience. They provide useful information for researchers and often serve as an important source of ideas. But currently they aren't the major source of information on personality. In large part, this is because a case study, no matter how thorough, is lacking in an important respect. It deals with just one person. When you're forming theories or drawing conclusions from observations, you want them to be applicable to many people—if possible, to *all* people.

The breadth of applicability of a conclusion is called its **generality,** or its **generalizability.** If a conclusion is to be generalizable, it must be based on the observation of many people, not just one or two. The more people you look at, the more convinced you can be that what you see is true of people in general, instead of only a few people. In most studies of personality done today, researchers look at tens—even hundreds—of persons to increase the generality of their conclusions.

To truly ensure generality, researchers should study people of many ages and from all walks of life—indeed, from all cultures. For various reasons, however, this isn't always done. As a matter of convenience, much of the research on personality over the last several decades has examined college students. Do college students provide a reasonably good cross-section of the kinds of processes that are important in personality? Maybe yes, maybe no. College students differ from older adults in several ways, including having a less fully formulated sense of self (Sears, 1986). This may make a difference in the research findings. How big a difference is a matter of conjecture. It does seem clear, though, that we should be cautious in assuming that conclusions drawn from research on college students are always applicable to "people in general."

Similarly, most observations on personality come from research done in the United States and Europe. Most of that research has been done with middle- to upper-

The generality of a conclusion can be established only by studying a mix of people from different backgrounds.

middle-class persons. Some of it has used only men or only women. One must be cautious in assuming that the conclusions of a study are applicable to people from other cultures, other socioeconomic groups, and (sometimes) both genders. Generalizability, then, represents a kind of continuum. Rarely do studies range broadly enough to ensure total generalizability, but some are better than others. This issue should always be kept in mind in evaluating the results of studies.

The desire for generality and the desire for in-depth understanding of a person represent competing pressures for observers of personality, and they lead to a trade-off. That is, given the same investment of time and energy, you can know a great deal about the life of one person (or a small number of people), or you can know a little bit about the lives of a much larger number of people. It's very hard to do both at once. As a result, researchers tend to choose one path or the other according to which pressure they find more important.

Establishing Relationships Among Variables

Insights gained by self-examination, casual observation, or systematic examination of a person through a case study can suggest conclusions about relationships between variables. A **variable** is a dimension along which variations exist. There must be at least two values or levels on that dimension, though some variables have an infinite number of values. For example, "sex" is a variable with values of male and female. Self-esteem is a variable that has a virtually limitless number of values (from very low to very high) as you make finer discriminations among people.

It's important to see the difference between a variable and the values that form it, because conclusions about relationships between variables involve the entire

FIGURE 2.1

Whether or not a relationship exists between variables can be determined only by looking at more than one value on each variable. Knowing that people low in self-esteem have poor academic performances leaves open the question of whether everyone else has performances that are just as poor. This question is critically important in establishing a relationship between the two variables.

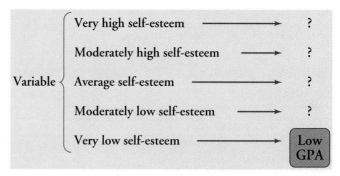

dimension, not just one end of it. For this reason, researchers always examine at least two levels of the variable they're interested in, if not the whole dimension. For example, you can't see the effects of low self-esteem by looking only at people with low self-esteem. If there's a relationship between self-esteem and academic performance, the only way to find out is to look at people with *different levels* of self-esteem (Figure 2.1). If the relationship does exist, people with very low self-esteem should have poor grades, and people with higher self-esteem should have better grades.

The last part of that statement is every bit as important as the first part. Knowing that people low in self-esteem have poor grades isn't informative if it turns out that people high in self-esteem also have poor grades. It can be hard to keep this in mind. In fact, people often fail to realize how important it is. If you don't keep it in mind, though, you can make serious errors in the conclusions you reach (for illustrations see Chapman, 1967; Crocker, 1981).

The need to examine people across a range of variability before drawing conclusions is another reason why it's important to go beyond case studies (the issue of generality was the first reason). Indeed, the importance of examining a range of variability is what leads to the methods on which we focus for the remainder of this chapter. Only by doing this can relationships between variables be verified.

Correlation Between Variables

There are two kinds of relationships that can be found between variables. The first is called **correlation.** A correlation between two dimensions means that as you examine them across many examples or instances, the values you observe tend to go together in a systematic way. There are two aspects of this relationship, which are entirely separate from each other. These are the *direction* of the correlation and the *strength* of the correlation. To clarify what these terms mean, let's reconsider the question of self-esteem and academic performance.

Suppose you've decided to investigate whether these two variables go together. You've gone out and found 40 students to study, and they've completed a measure of self-esteem and given you their current grade point average (GPA). You now have two pieces of information on each subject (Figure 2.2, A). One way to organize this information is to create a kind of graph called a scatterplot (Figure 2.2, B). In a scatterplot the two variables are represented by lines placed at right angles to each other (the axes of the graph). The point where the lines meet is the zero point for both variables. Being farther away from the zero point on either line means having a higher value on that variable. Since the two lines are at right angles, the combina-

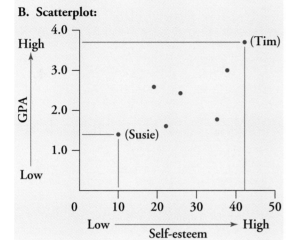

A. Raw data:

Subject	Self-esteem score	GPA
Tim D	42	3.8
Susie L	10	1.4
Warren M	15	2.5
Ronald X	22	3.1
... (etc.)		

B. Scatterplot:

FIGURE 2.2

Thinking about the meaning of correlation (with hypothetical data): (A) For each person (subject), there are two pieces of information, a self-esteem score and a grade point average (GPA). (B) The data can be arranged to form a scatterplot by plotting each person's self-esteem score along the horizontal dimension and GPA along the vertical dimension, thereby locating the combination in a two-dimensional space.

tion of any score on one variable and any score on the other variable can be portrayed as a point in a two-dimensional space. For example, in Figure 2.2, Tim has a self-esteem score of 42 (thus being to the right side on the horizontal line) and a GPA of 3.8 (thus being toward the top on the vertical line). The scatterplot for your study would consist of the points that represent the combinations of self-esteem scores and GPA for each person in the study.

To ask whether the two variables are correlated means (essentially) asking this question about the scatterplot: When you look at points that represent low versus high values on the *horizontal* dimension, do they differ in how they line up regarding the *vertical* dimension? If low values tend to go with low values and high values tend to go with high values (as in Figure 2.3, A), the two variables are said to be *positively* correlated. If people low in self-esteem tended to have low GPAs, and people high in self-esteem tended to have high GPAs, you would say that self-esteem correlates positively with GPA. This finding has, in fact, emerged from actual studies of these variables (for reviews see Scheirer & Kraut, 1979; Wylie, 1979).

Sometimes, however, a different kind of correlation occurs. Sometimes high values on one dimension tend to go along with low values on the other dimension (and vice versa). When this happens (Figure 2.3, B), the correlation between the variables is termed *inverse*, or *negative*. This kind of correlation might have emerged if you had studied the relationship between GPA and the frequency of going to parties. That is, you might have found that students who party the most tend to have lower GPAs, whereas those who party the least tend to have higher GPAs.

The *direction* of the association between variables (positive versus negative) is one aspect of correlation. The second aspect—entirely separate from the first—is the *strength* of the association. Think of strength as the "sloppiness" of the relationship

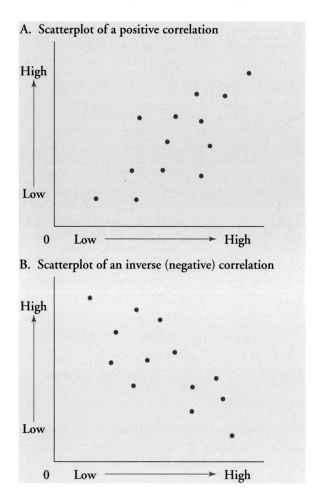

FIGURE 2.3

(A) If high numbers on one dimension tend to go with high numbers on the other dimension (and low with low), there is a positive correlation. (B) If high numbers on one dimension tend to go with low numbers on the other dimension, there is an inverse, or negative, correlation.

between the variables. More formally, it refers to the degree of accuracy with which you can predict values on one dimension from values on the other dimension. That is, assume a positive correlation between self-esteem and GPA. Suppose that you knew that Victoria had the second highest score on self-esteem in your study. How accurate a guess could you make about Victoria's GPA?

The answer to this question is determined by how strong the correlation is. Since the correlation is positive, knowing that Victoria is on the high end of the self-esteem dimension would lead you to predict a high GPA. If the correlation is *strong*, you're very likely to be right. If the correlation is weaker, you're less likely to be right. A perfect positive correlation—the strongest possible—means that the person who has the very highest value on one variable also has the very highest value on the other, the person next highest on one is also next highest on the other, and on so, throughout the list (see Figure 2.4, A).

The strength of a correlation is often expressed by a numerical index (which is often labeled with a lowercase r). An absolutely perfect positive correlation (as in Figure 2.4, A) is expressed with the number 1.0. This is the largest numerical value a correlation can take. It indicates a totally accurate prediction from one dimension to the other. If you know where the person is on one variable, you can tell with complete confidence where he or she is on the other.

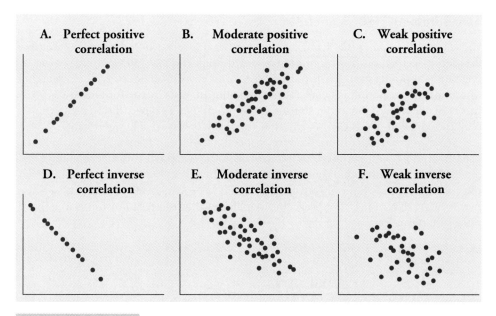

FIGURE 2.4

Six correlations: (A) A perfect positive correlation. (B) A moderately strong positive correlation. (C) A weak positive correlation. (D) A perfect inverse correlation. (E) A moderately strong inverse correlation. (F) A weak inverse correlation. The weaker the correlation, the more "scatter" in the scatterplot.

The scatterplot of a somewhat weaker correlation is shown in Figure 2.4, B. As you can see, there's more "scatter" among the points than in the first case. There's still a noticeable tendency for higher values on one dimension to match up with higher ones on the other, and for lows to match up with lows, but the tendency is much weaker. As the correlation becomes weaker, the number representing it becomes smaller (thus virtually all correlations are decimal values). Correlations of .6 to .8 are regarded as strong. Correlations of .3 to .5 are weaker but moderately strong. Below .3 or .2, the prediction from one variable to the other is getting poorer. As you can see in Figure 2.4, C, weak correlations have even more scatter. The tendency toward a positive relation is discernable, but it definitely isn't strong. A correlation of .0 means that the two variables aren't related to each other at all.

As we said before, a correlation's strength is entirely separate from its direction. Strength refers only to degree of accuracy in prediction. Thus, it is eminently sensible to talk about a perfect inverse (or negative) correlation as well as a perfect positive correlation. A perfect inverse correlation (Figure 2.4, D) means that the person who had the highest value on one variable also had the very lowest value on the other variable, the person with the next highest value on one had the next-to-lowest value on the other, and so on.

Negative correlations are expressed in numbers, just as are positive correlations. But to show that the relationship is an inverse one, a minus sign is placed in front of the number. Thus an *r* value of -.75 is precisely as strong as an *r* value of .75. The first describes an inverse correlation, though, whereas the second describes a positive correlation.

Two Kinds of Significance

We've been describing the strength of correlations in terms of the size of the number that serves as its statistical representation. Although the size of the number gives information about its strength, the size of the number by itself doesn't tell a researcher whether the correlation is believable or meaningful. This is true for all statistics. You can't tell just by looking at the statistic, or by looking at a graph, whether the result is real. Instead, you need to know whether the result is **statistically significant.**

Significant in this context has a very specific meaning: It means the correlation (or whatever) is large enough to be unlikely to have been a product of chance factors. When the probability that it was an accident is small enough (just under 5%), the correlation (or whatever statistic it is) is said to be statistically significant (see also Box 2.1). At that point, the researcher concludes that the relationship is a real one rather than random.

BOX 2.1

TWO KINDS OF STATISTICS:
Description Versus Inference

When people think about statistics, they often think about how statistics describe characteristics of a set of people or events, as in statements such as "The average American now earns $22,000 a year" and "She averaged 21.6 points per game over the last three years." These figures are called **descriptive statistics** because their purpose is to give a description.

Psychologists also use statistics in a different way, as indicated in the body of the chapter. This second kind of statistics is called **inferential statistics** because they allow the researcher to make inferences. The information they convey guides the scientist in deciding whether or not to believe something is true. Interestingly enough, it isn't possible to *prove* that something is true. What the statistics do is show how unlikely it is that the effect was caused by chance or random factors. If it can be shown that the effect was unlikely to have occurred by chance, the researcher infers that it's real.

Inferential statistics have been used even in courts of law. An interesting example (described by Zeisel & Kalven, 1977) comes from the 1968 trial of Dr. Benjamin Spock, who had urged men not to let themselves be drafted during the Vietnam War. During the trial, Spock's lawyer questioned the fairness of the judge's method of jury selection, claiming the method was biased against women (no women were on the jury). The lawyer argued that the absence of women was unfair to his case, because women favored Spock's position more than did men.

Was the judge biased against having women as jurors in his trials? Or was the lack of women on this particular jury an accident? Inferential statistics helped give an answer. They showed that there was only 1 chance in 1,000,000,000,000,000,000 (1 quintillion) that the low rate of female jurors chosen by this judge over the years would occur through the "luck of the draw." The inference thus was clear. The judge apparently was doing something over a long period that biased the composition of his juries.

We say "apparently" to emphasize something about the nature of inferential statistics. Whenever you use them to help make a judgment, the conclusion is always probabilistic. The odds that the inference was an error in this case were *extremely* small. But the possibility does exist—even here. Inferential statistics thus are best viewed as procedures that allow us to attach "confidence units" to our judgments, rather than procedures that lead infallibly to correct choices.

A correlation between two variables means they covary in some systematic way. Here there is a correlation between height and place in line.

A second use of the word significant has also become common in psychology. This use more closely resembles the use of the word in day-to-day language. Researchers say that an association is **clinically significant,** or **practically significant** if the effect is both statistically significant (so it's believable) and large enough to have some practical importance. How large that has to be varies from case to case. It's possible, though, for an association to be statistically significant but to account for only a tiny part of the behavior under study. The practical significance of such an association wouldn't be very great.

Causality and a Limitation on Inference

Correlations tell us whether or not two variables go together (and in what direction and how strongly). But they don't allow us to know *why* the variables go together. The "why" question takes us beyond the realm of correlation into a second kind of relationship. This relationship is called **causality**—the relationship between a cause and its effect. Correlational research isn't able to provide evidence on this second kind of relationship. A correlational study often gives people strong *intuitions* about causality, but it can't be definitive.

Why is this so? The answer is illustrated in Figure 2.5. In this figure, each arrow represents a possible path of causal influence. What this figure shows is that there are always three ways to account for the results of a correlational study. Consider the correlation between self-esteem and academic performance. What do you think causes that association? Your own intuition may say the best explanation is that having bad academic outcomes causes people to develop lower self-esteem, whereas good outcomes cause people to feel good about themselves (arrow 1 in Figure 2.5). Or maybe you think the best explanation is that having low self-esteem causes people not to try

FIGURE 2.5

Correlation does not imply cause and effect, because there are always three possibilities: (1) variations in one variable (academic performance) may be causing variations in the second (self-esteem); (2) variations in the second may be causing variations in the first; or (3) a third variable may actually be causing both observed effects. Knowing only the single correlation between self-esteem and GPA doesn't allow you to distinguish among these possibilities.

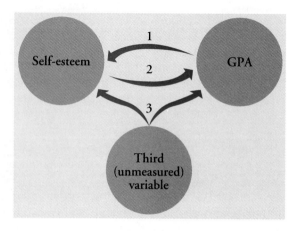

as hard in their courses, thereby resulting in poorer performances (arrow 2). Although they differ in direction of causal influence, either explanation is quite reasonable.

It could just as well be, however, that a third variable—not measured, perhaps not even thought of—actually exerts a causal influence over both variables that were measured (the pair of arrows labeled 3). Perhaps having a high level of intelligence causes a positive sense of self-esteem and also causes better academic performance. In this scenario, both self-esteem and academic performance are effects, and something else is the cause.

The possible involvement of another variable in the existence of a correlation is sometimes referred to as the **third variable problem.** It's a problem that can't be handled by the methods of correlational research. Those methods cannot tell which of the three possibilities shown in Figure 2.5 is actually correct.

Search for Causality: Experimental Research

There *is* a method that allows one to determine cause and effect, however. It's called the **experimental method,** and you can think of it as having two defining characteristics. The first is that in an experiment the researcher "manipulates" one variable—that is, creates the existence of at least two levels of that variable. The variable the experimenter is manipulating is called the **independent variable.** This is the one the experimenter is testing as the possible *cause* in the cause-effect relationship. When we say that the experimenter is "creating" two (or more) levels of this variable, we mean exactly that. There's some kind of event that *actively creates* a difference between the treatment given to some people and the treatment given to other people.

Sometimes researchers do experiments in order to better understand what they've observed in correlational studies. Let's illustrate the experimental method by doing just that—pursuing the correlational example just discussed. Suppose you have a hunch that variations in academic performance have a causal effect on self-esteem (because poor performance makes people get down on themselves). To study this possibility, you conduct an experiment, in which you hypothesize (predict) that academic outcomes cause an effect on self-esteem.

You can't manipulate GPA in this experiment, but it's fairly easy to manipulate something else with overtones of academic performance. For instance, you could arrange to have some people experience a success and others a failure, using a task rigged to be either easy or impossible. By arranging this, you would be *creating* the difference yourself between success and failure. You'd be manipulating it—not just measuring it. You're sure that a difference now exists between the two sets of people in your experiment, because you *made* it exist.

As in all research, you'd do your best to treat every participant in your experiment exactly the same in all other ways. You'd standardize all your procedures. Treating everyone the same—in fact, making everything be exactly the same except for what you manipulated—is called **experimental control.** Exerting a high degree of experimental control is important to the logic of the experimental method, as you'll see momentarily.

Although control is important, you can't control everything. It's rarely possible to have every person participate in the research at the same time of day or on the same day of the week. More obviously, perhaps, it's impossible to ensure that the people in the experiment are exactly alike. One of the main points of this book, after all, is that people differ. Some people in your experiment are just naturally going to have higher self-esteem when they walk in the door than will others. How can these differences be handled?

This question brings us to the experimental method's second defining characteristic: Any variable that can't be controlled—such as individual differences—is treated by **random assignment.** In your experiment, you would deal with individual differences by randomly assigning each participant to have either the success experience or the failure experience. Random assignment is often done by such means as tossing a coin or using a list of random numbers to determine assignment to a treatment.

The use of random assignment rests on a specific assumption: If you study enough people in the experiment, any important differences between people (and from other sources as well) will balance out between the groups. Each group is likely to have as many tall people, fat people, depressed people, and confident people as

Random assignment is an important hallmark of the experimental method. The experimenter randomly assigns participants to a condition, much as a roulette wheel randomly catches the ball in a black or red slot.

the other group—*if* you have a fairly large number of participants and use random assignment. Anything that matters should balance out.

So you've brought people to your research laboratory one at a time, randomly assigned them to the two conditions, manipulated the independent variable, and exerted experimental control over everything else. At some point in the experiment, you would then measure the variable you think represents the effect in the cause-and-effect relationship. This variable is termed the **dependent variable.**

In this experiment your hypothesis was that differences in success and failure cause people to differ in their sense of self-esteem. Thus, the dependent measure would be some sort of measure of self-esteem (for example, self-report items asking people how they feel about themselves). After getting this measure for each person in your experiment, you would then compare the groups to each other (through statistical procedures that need not concern us here). If the difference between groups was statistically significant, you could confidently conclude that the experience of success and failure *causes* people to differ in self-esteem.

What would make you so confident in that cause-and-effect conclusion? The answer, despite all the details we've gone through, is really quite simple. The logic is displayed graphically in Figure 2.6. At the beginning of the experiment, you separated people into two groups. (By the way, the reasoning applies even if the independent variable has more than two levels.) If the assumption about the effect of random assignment is correct, the two groups don't differ from each other at this point. Because you exercise experimental control throughout your procedures, the groups still don't differ as the experiment unfolds.

At one point, however, a difference between groups is introduced—the point at which you manipulate the independent variable. As we said before, you know there's a difference at this point, and you know *what* the difference is, because you created

FIGURE 2.6

The logic of the experimental method: (A) Because of random assignment and experimental control, there is no systematic difference between groups at first. (B) The experimental manipulation creates—for the first time—a specific difference. (C) If the groups then are found to differ in another fashion, the manipulation must have caused this difference.

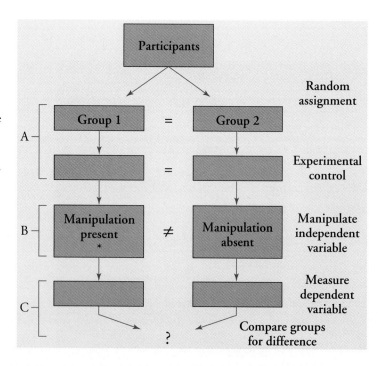

it yourself. For this reason, if you find that the groups differ from each other on the dependent measure at the end of the experiment, you know there's only one thing that could have caused the difference (Figure 2.6). It *had* to have been caused by the manipulation of the independent variable. That was the only place where a difference between groups was introduced during the experiment. It was the only thing that could have been responsible for causing the effect.

This reasoning is straightforward. We should note, however, that this method isn't entirely perfect. Its problem is this: When you do an experiment, you show that the *manipulation* causes the difference on the dependent measure—but you can't always be completely sure *what it was* about the manipulation that did the causing. Maybe it was the aspect of the manipulation that you as researcher were focused on, but maybe it was something else.

For example, in the experiment we've been considering, low self-esteem may have been caused by the failure and the self-doubt to which it led. But it *might* have been caused by other things about the manipulation. Maybe the people were worried that they had spoiled the results of your experiment by not solving the problems. They didn't feel a sense of *failure* but were unhappy with themselves for creating a problem for you. This interpretation of the result wouldn't mean quite the same thing as your first interpretation of it. This issue requires us always to be a bit cautious in how we view results even from experiments.

Recognizing Types of Study

When you read about correlational studies and experiments in later chapters of this book, how easy is it going to be for you to tell them apart? At first glance, it seems simple. An experiment involves a comparison between groups; a correlational study gives you a correlation. Actually, no. Results of correlational studies aren't always reported as correlations. Sometimes the study compares two (or more) groups with each other on a dependent measure, and the word *correlation* is never even mentioned.

Suppose you studied some people who were 20% overweight and some who were 20% underweight. You interviewed them individually and judged how sociable they were, and you found that fat people were more sociable than skinny people. Would this be an experiment or a correlational study? The way to tell is to recall the two defining characteristics of the experiment: manipulation of the independent variable, and random assignment of people to groups. Since you didn't randomly assign people to be fat or skinny (and didn't *create* these differences), this study is correlational. The limitation on correlational research (the inability to conclude cause and effect) applies to it.

A good rule of thumb is that any time groups reflect a *naturally occurring difference* or are formed on the basis of a *characteristic that you measure,* the study is correlational. This means that all studies of personality differences are by definition correlational.

Why do personality researchers make their correlational studies look like experiments? Sometimes it's because they selected participants from the extreme ends of some personality variable—people who are very low and very high, respectively, on some dimension of personality. This strategy maximizes the chances of finding differences. That is, removing the people who are average on that dimension helps to remove clutter and make the picture clearer. It has the side effect, however, of making it hard to express the finding as a correlation. The result is correlational studies that look at first glance like experiments.

What Kind of Research Is Best?

Another question that's often asked is which kind of research is better, experiments or correlational studies? The answer is that both have advantages, and the advantage of each is the disadvantage of the other. The advantage of the experimental method, of course, is its ability to show cause and effect, which the correlational method cannot do.

But experiments also have drawbacks. For one (as we noted), there's sometimes uncertainty about which aspect of the manipulation was important. For another, experiments on people are usually limited to events of relatively short duration, under conditions that must be carefully controlled. The correlational method, on the other hand, lets you examine events that take place over long periods (even decades) and events that are much more elaborate. Correlational studies also let us get information about events in which experimental manipulation would be unethical—for example, the effects of being raised by a divorced parent or the effects of cigarette smoking.

Many personality psychologists also criticize experiments on the grounds that the kinds of relationships they reveal often have little to do with the central issues of personality. Even experiments that seem to bear on important issues in personality may tell less than they first seem to. Consider the hypothetical experiment described previously, in which success and failure were manipulated and self-esteem was measured. Accept for the moment the hypothetical finding that subjects given a failure had lower self-esteem afterward than subjects given a success. You might be tempted to infer from this experiment that having poor academic outcomes over the course of one's life causes people to develop low self-esteem.

This conclusion, however, may not be justified. The experiment dealt with a brief task outcome, manipulated in a particular way. The broader conclusion you're tempted to draw deals with a basic quality of personality. This latter quality may differ in many ways from the momentary state you manipulated. The "reasoning by analogy" you're tempted to engage in is dangerous, and it can be misleading.

To many personality psychologists, then, the only way to really understand personality is to look at naturally occurring differences between people. These psychologists are willing to accept the limitation on causal inference that's inherent in the correlational approach; they regard it as an acceptable price to pay. On the other hand, many of these same psychologists are comfortable *combining* the correlational strategy with experimental techniques, as described in the next section.

Multifactor Studies

We've been talking about studies as though they always involved predicting a dependent variable from a single predictor variable (either an experimental manipulation or an individual difference). In fact, however, studies often look at the effects of several predictors at a time. Often such research involves use of a multifactor design. In this sort of study, two (or more) variables are varied *separately*, which means creating all combinations of the various levels of the predictor variables (Figure 2.7). The study shown in Figure 2.7 involves two factors, but more than two can be used. The more factors in a study, of course, the larger is the resulting array of combinations, and the trickier it is to keep track of things.

Sometimes the factors in a multifactor study are all experimental manipulations. Sometimes they're all personality variables. Often, though, studies involve mixed

	Low self-esteem	High self-esteem
Initial success		
Initial failure		

Dependent measure: performance on a second task

Diagram of a hypothetical two-factor study. Each square represents the combination of the value listed above it and the value listed to the left. In multifactor studies, all combinations of values of the predictor variables are created in this fashion.

or crossed designs, where experimental manipulations are crossed by individual-difference variables. The example shown in Figure 2.7 is a mixed design. The self-esteem factor is the level of self-esteem people had when they came to the research session. This is a personality dimension (thus correlational). The success-failure factor is an experimental manipulation, which takes place during the session. In this particular experiment, the dependent measure is performance on a second task, which the subjects work on after the experimental manipulation.

Crossed designs allow researchers to examine how different types of people respond to variations in situations, thus offering a glimpse into the underlying dynamics of the individual difference variable. Because this type of study combines experimental procedures and individual differences, it is often referred to as **experimental personality research.**

Reading Figures from Multifactor Research

Because multifactor designs are more complex than a single-factor study, what they can tell you is also more complex. Indeed, people who do experimental personality research use these designs precisely for this reason.

You don't *always* get a complex result from a multifactor study. Sometimes you find only the same outcomes you would have found if you had studied each predictor variable separately. When you find that a predictor variable is linked to the outcome variable in a systematic way, completely separate from the other predictor, it's referred to as a **main effect.** For example, the study outlined in Figure 2.7 might find only that people of both self-esteem levels perform worse after a failure than after a success.

The complexity in multifactor research occurs when a study finds what's termed an **interaction.** Figure 2.8 portrays two interactions, each a possible outcome of the hypothetical study of Figure 2.7. In each case, the vertical dimension portrays the dependent measure, performance on the second task. The two marks on the horizontal line represent the two values of the manipulated variable, initial success versus failure. The color of the line depicts the other predictor variable: the green line represents participants high in self-esteem, the black line represents those low in self-esteem.

We stress that these graphs show *hypothetical* outcomes. They are intended only to give you a clearer understanding of what interactions are about. Figure 2.8, A portrays the finding that people who are low in self-esteem perform worse after an initial failure than after a success. Among people high in self-esteem, however, this result doesn't occur. The failure apparently has no effect on them. Thus, the effect of one variable (success vs. failure) differs across the two levels of the other variable (degree of self-esteem). This is the meaning of the term *interaction.* In the case

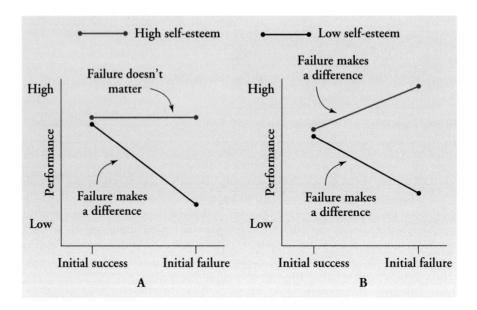

FIGURE 2.8

Two hypothetical outcomes of a two-factor study looking at self-esteem and an initial success-versus-failure experience as predictors of performance on a second task. (A) This graph indicates that experiencing a failure causes people low in self-esteem to perform worse later on than if they had experienced a success, but that the failure does not have any effect at all on people high in self-esteem. (B) This graph indicates that experiencing a failure causes people low in self-esteem to perform worse later on, but that the failure causes people high in self-esteem to perform *better* later on. Thus, the failure influences both kinds of people but does so in opposite ways.

shown in Figure 2.8, A, failure has an effect at one level of the second variable (the low self-esteem group) but has no effect at the other level of the second variable (the high self-esteem group).

There are two more points to make about interactions. First, to find an interaction, it's *absolutely necessary* to study more than one factor at a time. You simply can't find an interaction unless both contributors to it are being studied at once. This is one reason why researchers often use complex designs: They allow the possibility for interactions to emerge.

The second point is revealed by comparing Figure 2.8, A with 2.8, B. Specifically, interactions can take many forms. In contrast to the interaction we just described, the graph in panel B says that failure has effects on both sets of people, but opposite effects. People low in self-esteem perform worse after failure (as in the first graph), but people high in self-esteem actually perform better after a failure than after a success, perhaps because the failure motivated them to try harder.

These two graphs aren't the only forms interactions can take. Exactly what an interaction means depends on the form it takes. Thus, exploring interactions always requires checking to see in what manner each group was influenced by the other variable under study.

SUMMARY

Research in personality relies on observations of both the self and others. The desire to understand a person as an integrated whole led to case studies—in-depth examinations of specific individuals. The desire for generalizability—that is, conclusions that would apply to many rather than to a few people—led to studies involving systematic examination of a large number of people.

Gathering information is only the first step toward examining relationships between and among variables. Relationships among variables are examined in two ways, corresponding to two kinds of relationships. Correlational research determines the degree to which two variables tend to go together in a predictable way when measured at different levels along the dimension. This technique determines two aspects of the relationship: its direction and its strength. The special relationship of cause and effect cannot be determined by this kind of study, however.

A second technique, called the experimental method, allows one to test for cause and effect. In an experiment, an independent variable is manipulated, other variables are controlled (made constant), and anything that cannot be controlled is treated by random assignment. An effect caused by the manipulation is measured in the dependent variable. Experimental and correlational techniques are often combined in multifactor studies, termed experimental personality research.

GLOSSARY

Case study An in-depth study of one individual.

Causality A relationship such that variation in one dimension produces variation in another.

Clinically significant An association that is large enough to have some practical importance.

Correlation A relationship in which two variables or dimensions covary when measured repeatedly.

Dependent variable The variable measured as the outcome of an experiment; the "effect" in a cause-effect relation.

Descriptive statistics Statistics used to describe or characterize some group.

Experimental control The holding constant of variables that are not being manipulated.

Experimental method The method in which one variable is manipulated to test for causal influence on another variable.

Experimental personality research A study involving a personality factor and an experimental factor.

Generality (**generalizability**) The degree to which a conclusion applies to many persons.

Independent variable The variable manipulated in an experiment, tested as the "cause" in a cause-effect relation.

Inferential statistics Statistics used to judge whether a relationship exists between variables.

Interaction A finding in which the effect of one predictor variable differs, depending on the level of another predictor variable.

Main effect A finding in which the effect of one predictor variable is independent of other variables.

Personology The study of the whole person, as opposed to studying only one aspect of the person.

Practically significant An association that is large enough to have some practical importance.

Random assignment The process of putting people randomly into groups of an experiment so their characteristics balance out across groups.

Statistically significant Unlikely to have occurred by chance; believable as real.

Third variable problem The possibility that an unmeasured variable caused variations in both of two correlated variables.

Variable A dimension along which two or more variations exist.

chapter

3

Issues in Personality Assessment

■ On the first day of personality class Jeff saw a woman he didn't know, and he's been trying ever since to get an idea of what she's like. He observes how she acts, how she dresses, what she says to people. He asks friends if they know anything about her. After a while he starts to wonder how "good" the information is he's gathering. Pat always sees things in a slanted way, so what she says has to be taken with a grain of salt. Jennifer hardly notices things that are right in front of her, so who knows what to make of what she says? When the stranger raises her hand and gives opinions in class, do they reflect who she is, or is she just trying to convince the teacher she's an intellectual? When she turned down a date with Chris after class the other day, was that a trace of haughtiness in her voice? Or was she just flustered?

The measuring of personality is called **assessment.** It's something we all do in an informal way all the time. We all want to have a sense of the personalities of the people we interact with, so we know what to expect of them. For this reason we develop ways of gauging people, judging what they're like. Although you probably don't think of this as "assessment," what you're doing informally is much the same in principle as what psychologists do more formally.

Forming impressions of what other people are like can be difficult. It's easy to get misleading impressions. Personality assessment is also difficult for psychologists. All the problems you have, they have too. But personality psychologists work hard to deal with those problems (for a more extensive discussion, see Anastasi, 1988).

Sources of Information

Just as informal assessment takes information from many sources, so does formal assessment. In fact, as you'll see momentarily, each of the ways of getting information mentioned in the opening example has a counterpart in a formal assessment technique.

Many measures of personality come from someone other than the person being assessed (e.g., Funder, 1991; Paunonen, 1989). The broad name for this technique is **observer ratings.** There are many kinds of observer ratings, because there are many kinds of information that observers can provide. Sometimes observers make judgments about the person being assessed without interacting with the person. In some cases these judgments are based on observation of the person's actions. In other cases, the judgments are opinions coded on rating scales by people who know the person well enough to say what he or she is like.

Some observer assessments involve interviews. People being assessed may talk in their own words about themselves and the interviewer draws conclusions from what's said and how it's said. Sometimes the people being interviewed talk about something *other than* themselves, and in so doing reveal something indirectly to the interviewer about what they're like.

Though many techniques of assessment rely on the impressions of outside observers, not all do. A great many measures of personality—indeed, the vast majority—are **self-reports.** In self-reports people themselves indicate what they think they're like or how they feel or act. Self-reports thus resemble the process of self-observation described in the last chapter. Although self-reporting can be done in an unstructured descriptive way, usually it's not. Most self-report scales ask people to respond to a specific set of items.

Self-report scales can be created in many formats. An example is the true-false format, in which you read statements and decide whether each one is true or false for you. Another common format is a multipoint rating scale, in which a wider range of response options is available—for example, ranging from "strongly agree" to "strongly disagree."

Some self-reports focus on a single quality of personality. Often, though, people developing tests are interested in assessing *several* aspects of personality in the same test (as distinct scales). A device that assesses several dimensions of personality is termed an **inventory.** The process of developing an inventory is intrinsically no different from the process of developing a single scale. The only difference is that in developing an inventory, you must go through each step of development for *each scale of the inventory,* rather than just one.

As you can see, the arsenal of possible assessment techniques is large. All incorporate two processes, though. First, in each case, the person who's being assessed produces a sample of "behavior" of some sort. This may literally be action, which someone else observes, it may be internal behaviors such as changes in heart rate, or it may be the behavior of answering a set of self-report items. Second, someone then uses the behavior sample to try to determine some aspect of the person's personality.

Some measures are termed **subjective,** whereas others are termed **objective.** Subjective measures are those in which an interpretation is part of the measure. An example would be an observer's judgment that the person being watched looks nervous. The judgment makes the measure subjective, because it is an *interpretation* of the person's behavior. If the measure instead focuses on some concrete physical reality that requires no interpretation, it's said to be objective. For example, to count the number of times the person stammers while talking involves no interpretation yet. Although this count might later be used to infer nervousness, the measure itself is objective.

To some extent, this issue cuts across the distinction between observer ratings and self-reports. An observer can make objective counts of occurrences of acts, or can develop a subjective impression of the person. In the same way, a person making a self-report can report occurrences of concrete events, or can give a subjective impression of what he or she is like as a person. It should be apparent, though, that self-reports are particularly vulnerable to incorporating subjectivity. Even reports of concrete events, if they're retrospective, permit unintentional biases of interpretation to creep in.

Reliability of Measurement

All of these techniques of assessment confront several kinds of problems, or issues. One issue is termed **reliability** of measurement. The sense of this issue can be conveyed by putting it as a question: Once you've made an observation about someone, how confident can you be that if you made the same observation a second or third time you'd see about the same thing? When an observation is reliable, it shows a high degree of *consistency,* or *repeatability.* Low reliability means the observation or measurement is less consistent. The measure isn't just reflecting the person being measured. It's somehow also including a lot of randomness, termed **error.**

All measurement procedures have sources of error (error can be reduced, but it can't be entirely eliminated). When you use a telescope to look at the moon, a little dust on the lens, minor imperfections in the glass, flickering lights from the city nearby, and swirling air currents can all contribute error to what you see. When you

There are many different types of observer ratings. Here an observer is directly rating a research participant's overt behavior.

use a rating scale to measure how "independent" people think they are, the way you phrase the item can be a source of error, because it can lead to different interpretations. When you have an observer watching a child's behavior, the observer is a source of error, because of variations in how closely he's paying attention, thinking about what he's seeing, or being influenced by a thousand other things.

How do you deal with the issue of reliability in measurement? The general answer is to repeat the measurement, make the observation more than once. Usually this means measuring the same quality from a slightly different angle or using a slightly different "measuring device." This lets the multiple sources of error in the different devices cancel each other out.

Reliability actually is a family of problems, rather than a single problem, because it crops up in several different contexts. Each version of the problem has a separate name, and the tactic used to treat each version differs slightly from the tactics used on the others.

Internal Consistency

The simplest case is the single observation or measurement. How can you be sure it doesn't include too much error? An intuitive illustration of this problem and how people deal with it comes from ability assessment. Think about what you'd do if you wanted to know how good someone was at a particular type of problem—for example, math problems or word puzzles. You wouldn't give the person just a *single* problem to solve, because whether he or she solved it easily might depend too much on some quirk of that particular problem. If you want to know (reliably) how well the person solves that kind of problem, you'd give a *series* of problems.

The same strategy applies to personality assessment. If you were using a self-report to ask people how independent they think they are, you wouldn't ask just once. You'd ask several times, using different items that all reflect independence, but do so in different words. In this example, *each item* is a "measuring device." When you shift to a new item, you're shifting to a different measuring device, trying to measure the same quality in the same person. In effect, you're putting down one telescope and picking up another. The question is whether you see about the same thing through the different telescopes.

Human judges are not infallible. They sometimes perceive things inaccurately.

The kind of reliability we're discussing here is termed **internal reliability** or **internal consistency.** This is reliability within a set of observations of the same aspect of personality. Since different items have different sources of random error, using many items should tend to balance out the error. The more observations, the more likely it is that the random error will cancel out across them. Because people using self-report scales want to have good reliability, most scales contain fairly large numbers of items. If the items are reliable enough, they're then used together as a single index of the personality quality.

How do you find out whether the items you're using have good internal reliability? A large number of observations doesn't guarantee reliability. The degree of reliability among observations is a question about the correlations among people's responses. Saying that the items are highly reliable means that people's responses to the items are highly intercorrelated.

In practical terms, there are several ways to investigate internal consistency, all of which examine correlations among people's responses to the items. Perhaps the best way (although it's cumbersome) is to look at the average correlation between each pair of items taken separately. A simpler approach is to separate the items into two subsets (often odd- versus even-numbered items), add up people's scores for each subset, and correlate the two subtotals with each other. This correlation provides an index called **split-half reliability.** If the two halves of the original set are measuring the same quality of personality, people who score high on one half should also score high on the other half, and people who score low on one half should also score low on the other half. Thus, a strong positive correlation between halves is evidence of internal consistency.

Inter-Rater Reliability

As indicated earlier, personality isn't always measured by self-reports. Some observations are *literally* observations, made by one person watching and assessing someone else. Observer ratings are an important source of information in personality assessment, whether they consist of counts of behaviors or ratings of aspects of someone else's personality. Use of observer ratings gives rise to a slightly different reliability problem than occurs in self-report scales. In an observer rating, the *person making the observation* is a "measuring device." There are sources of error in this device, just as in other devices. How can you judge the extent of reliability in this case?

Conceptually, the answer is the same as it was in the preceding section. You need to put down one telescope and pick up another one. In the case of observer ratings, you need to check this observer against another observer. To the extent that both see about the same thing when they look at the same event, reliability is high. This double observation is logically the same as using two questionnaire items rather than one. Raters whose judgments correlate highly with each other across many ratings are said to have high **inter-rater reliability.**

In many cases, obtaining high inter-rater reliability requires the judges to be thoroughly trained in how to observe what they're observing. Judges of Olympic diving competitions, for example, have witnessed many thousands of dives and know precisely what to look for. As a result, their inter-rater reliability is high. Similarly, when observers assess qualities of personality, they often are given considerable instruction and practice before turning to the "real thing," so that their reliability will be high.

Stability Across Time

There's one more kind of reliability that's important in the measurement of personality. This type of reliability concerns stability across time. That is, assessment at one time should agree fairly well with assessment done at a different time.

If all judges are seeing the same thing when they rate an event, then inter-rater reliability will be high.

TABLE 3.1

Comparison among three kinds of reliability. Each assesses the consistency or "repeatability" of an observation by looking a second time, either with the same "measuring device" or with a slightly different one.

Type of reliability	"Measuring device"	Type of consistency
Internal reliability	Test item	Consistency within the test
Inter-rater reliability	Rater	Agreement between raters
Test-retest reliability	Entire test	Consistency across time

Why is this important? Remember, personality is supposed to be stable—that's one reason why people use the word, to convey the sense of stability. If personality is really *stable*—something that doesn't fluctuate from minute to minute or from day to day—then *measures* of personality should be reliable across time: People's scores should stay roughly the same when measured a week later, a month later, or four months later.

This kind of reliability is termed **test-retest reliability.** It is determined by giving the test to the same people at two different times. A measure with high test-retest reliability will yield scores the second time (the retest) that are fairly similar to those from the first time. People with high scores the first time will have high scores the second time, those with lower scores at first will have lower scores later on. (For a summary of these three types of reliability, see Table 3.1.)

Validity of Measurement

Reliability is the starting point in measurement, but it isn't the only issue that matters. It's possible for measurements to be highly reliable but completely meaningless. Another important issue here is termed **validity.** This issue concerns whether what you're measuring is what you *think* you're measuring (or what you're *trying* to measure) when you make an observation. Earlier the concept of reliability was illustrated in terms of random influences on the image in a telescope as you look through it at the moon. To extend the same analogy, the validity issue is whether the image you're seeing is the moon that you're looking for, or just a street light (see also Figure 3.1).

How do you decide whether you're measuring what you want to measure? There are two ways to answer this question, one an "in-principle" answer, the other a set of tactics. The in-principle answer is that people decide by comparing two kinds of "definitions" with each other. When you hear the word *definition*, what probably comes to mind is a conceptual definition (a dictionary definition). This is an abstract definition that spells out the meaning of a word in terms of conceptual qualities or attributes. It tells us the information that the users of a language have agreed is conveyed by the word. Psychologists also talk about another kind of definition, however, called an **operational definition.** These definitions are descriptions of physical events.

To illustrate the difference between the two kinds of definition, consider the concept of love. The conceptual (dictionary) definition of the word *love* might be

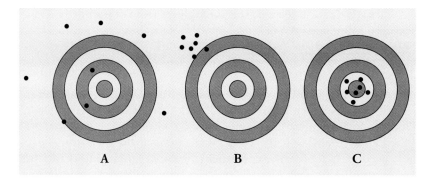

A B C

FIGURE 3.1

A simple way to think about the difference between reliability and validity is to use the metaphor of target shooting. (A) Sometimes when people shoot at a target their shots go all over. This result corresponds to measurement that's neither reliable nor valid. (B) Reliability is higher as the shots are closer together. Shots that miss the mark, however, are not valid. (C) Good measurement means that the shots are close together (reliable) *and* near the bull's-eye (valid).

something like "a strong affection for another." There are many ways, however, to define love operationally. For example, you might ask the person you're assessing to indicate on rating scales how much she loves someone. You might measure how often she looks into that person's eyes when interacting with him. You might measure how willing she is to give up events she enjoys in order to be with him. These three measures differ considerably from one another. Yet each may plausibly be taken as an operational definition, or operationalization, of love.

The essence of the validity issue in measurement is summarized in this question: How well does the *operational* definition being used (the events) match the *conceptual* definition (the abstract quality that you have in mind to measure)? If the two are close, the measure has high validity. If they aren't close, validity is low. How do you decide whether the two are close? In principle, this usually means poking at the conceptual definition until it's clear what the critical components are and then looking to see whether the same components are present in the operationalization. If they aren't (at least by strong implication), the validity of the operationalization is questionable.

The validity issue is both tricky and important. It is the subject of continual debate in psychology as researchers try to think of better and better ways to look at human behavior. The reason this issue is important is that the conclusions of researchers and assessors of personality are going to be formed in terms of what they *think* they're measuring. If what they're measuring isn't what they think they're measuring, the researcher will draw false conclusions. Likewise, the clinician may draw the wrong conclusion about the person being assessed if the device isn't measuring what the clinician thinks it's measuring.

Validity as an issue is important whenever anything is being observed. In personality assessment, however, the validity question is so important that it's been examined closely for a long time. In trying to ensure that personality tests are valid, theorists have come to distinguish several aspects of validity from one another. These distinctions have also influenced the practical process of establishing validity.

Construct Validity

The idea of validity you have in mind at this point is technically called **construct validity** (Campbell, 1960; Cronbach & Meehl, 1955). Construct validity is an all-encompassing kind of validity, and it thus is the most important kind (cf. Hogan & Nicholson, 1988; Landy, 1986). Construct validity means that the measure (the assessment device) accurately reflects the construct (the conceptual quality) that the psychologist has in mind. Although the word *construct* sounds abstract, a construct is simply a concept. Any trait quality, for example, is a construct.

Establishing construct validity for a measure is a long and complex process. It requires several kinds of information, each of which is treated as a separate aspect of the validation process. For this reason, the various qualities that contribute to construct validity have separate names of their own. They are described in the following paragraphs.

Criterion Validity

A particularly important part of showing that an assessment device has construct validity is showing that it relates to other manifestations of the personality quality the device is supposed to measure (Campbell, 1960). This usually means using a behavioral index (or the judgment of a carefully trained observer) as an external *criterion* (a standard of comparison) and seeing how well the assessment device correlates with it. This aspect of validity is sometimes referred to as **criterion validity** (because it uses an external criterion) or **predictive validity** (because it tests how well the measure predicts the other manifestation of personality).

As an example, suppose you wanted to establish criterion validity for a measure of dominance you were developing. One way to approach this problem would be to select people who score high and low on your measure and bring them to a laboratory (one at a time) to work on a task with two other people. You could record each group's discussion and score the tape for the number of times each person made suggestions, gave instructions, took charge of the situation, and so on. These behaviors would represent criteria of dominance. If people who scored high on your measure did these things more than people who scored low, it would indicate that the measure had a kind of criterion validity.

Another way to approach the problem would be to have a trained interviewer spend 20 minutes with each of the high and low scorers on your scale and rate each person's level of dominance after the interview. The interviewer's impression of the person would be a different kind of criterion of dominance. If the impressions proved to be related to the scores on your measure, it would indicate a different kind of criterion validity for the measure.

Criterion validity is usually regarded as the most important indicator of construct validity. In recent years, though, a controversy has arisen over the process of establishing it. Howard (1990; Howard et al., 1980) pointed out that people often assume the behavioral criterion chosen is a perfect reflection of the construct. In reality, though, this is almost never true. In fact, Howard argued that far too often researchers choose criterion measures that are *poor* reflections of the construct. We raise this point to emphasize how critical it is to be careful in deciding what criterion to use.

Unless the criterion is a good one, associations with it are meaningless. Despite this caution, however, criterion validity remains the keystone of construct validation.

Convergent Validity

Another aspect of trying to show construct validity involves getting evidence that's less direct concerning what the assessment device is measuring. It's useful to show that the measure relates to characteristics that are similar to—but not the same as—what it's supposed to measure. What makes this different from criterion validation is that in this case you know the second measure aims at assessing something a little different from what your measure assesses. Because trying to get this sort of evidence often proceeds from several directions, it is often termed **convergent validation** (Campbell & Fiske, 1959). That is, the findings "converge" on the construct you're interested in, even though any single finding by itself won't clearly reflect the construct.

For example, a scale intended to measure dominance should be somewhat related to measures of characteristics such as leadership (positively) or shyness (inversely). The correlations should be far from perfect because these aren't quite the same constructs, but the correlations shouldn't be zero. If you developed a measure intended to assess dominance and it didn't correlate at all with measures of leadership and shyness, you'd have to start wondering whether your measure was really assessing dominance.

Discriminant Validity

It's important to show that an assessment device measures what it's intended to measure. But it's also important to show that it does *not* measure qualities it *wasn't* intended to measure—especially qualities that don't fit with what the researcher had in mind as a construct (Campbell, 1960). This aspect of the overall construct validation process is termed **discriminant validation** (Campbell & Fiske, 1959).

The importance of discriminant validation can be easy to overlook, but discriminant validation is a major line of defense against the "third variable" problem in correlational research as discussed in Chapter 2. Recall that you can't be sure why two correlated variables correlate. It may be that one has an influence on the other. But it may also be that a third variable, correlated with the two you've studied, is really responsible for their correlation. In principle, it's always possible to attribute the effect of a personality dimension on behavior to some other personality dimension. In practice, however, this can be made much harder by evidence of discriminant validity. That is, if research shows that the dimension you're interested in is unrelated to another variable, then that variable can't be invoked as an alternative explanation for the effect of the first.

To illustrate this, let's return to an example used in discussing the third variable problem in Chapter 2, a correlation between self-esteem and academic performance. This association *might* reflect the effect of an unmeasured variable, for instance, IQ. Suppose, though, that we know this measure of self-esteem isn't correlated with IQ, because someone checked on that during the process of its validation. This information would make it difficult to claim that IQ is what really underlies the correlation between self-esteem and academic performance.

The process of discriminant validation is never-ending because new possibilities for third variables always suggest themselves. Ruling out alternative explanations thus is a challenging task, but it's also a necessary one.

Face Validity

Establishing construct validity is a long-term process that's of great importance. There is, however, one more kind of validity that should be mentioned. It is much simpler, a little more intuitive, and less important. It's called **face validity.** Face validity means that the assessment device appears, on its "face," to be measuring the construct it was intended to measure. It *looks* right. A test of sociability that included many items such as "I prefer to spend time alone rather than with friends" and "I would rather socialize than read books" would have a high degree of face validity. A test of sociability made up of such items as "Green is my favorite color" and "I prefer imports to American-made cars" would have a low degree of face validity.

Face validity is regarded as a convenience by researchers, for two reasons. First, some researchers believe that face valid instruments are easier for people to respond to than instruments that don't have face validity. Second, researchers are sometimes interested in distinctions between qualities of personality that differ in subtle ways. It often seems as though there's no other way to separate these qualities from each other than to use instruments that are high in face validity.

On the other hand, face validity can occasionally be a detriment. This is true of cases in which the assessment device is intended to measure something that the person being assessed would find threatening or undesirable to admit. In these cases the test developer usually tries to obscure the measure's face validity.

Whether face validity is good, bad, or neither, it should be clear that it is less important than other kinds of validity. If an assessment device is to be useful in the long run, it must undergo the laborious process of construct validation. The "bottom line" is always construct validity.

Culture and Validity

Another important issue in assessment is cultural differences. In a sense this is a validity issue, in a sense it's an issue of generalizability. The issue might be framed as a question: Do the scores on a personality test have the same meaning for a person from an Asian culture or a Latino culture or an African American culture as they do for a middle-American European culture?

There are at least two aspects to the question. The first is whether the pyschological construct itself has the same meaning from one culture to another. This is a fundamental question about the nature of personality. Are the elements of personality the same from one human group to another? Although many people assume the elements of personality are universal, that may in fact be a dangerous assumption.

The second aspect of the question concerns how the items of the personality measure are interpreted by people from different cultures. If an item has one meaning or implication for middle Americans, but a different meaning in some other culture, people's responses to the item will also have different meanings in the different cultures. A similar issue arises when a measure is translated into a different language. This involves translation into the new language, then translation back into the original language by someone who's never seen the original items. This process sometimes reveals that items contain idiomatic or metaphorical meaning that's hard to translate to an equivalent form. The process of adapting a measure developed in one culture for use in another culture is a complex one with many difficulties (Butcher, 1996). It must be done very carefully, if the measure is to be valid in the new culture.

Response Sets and Loss of Validity

Any discussion of validity must also point to the fact that there are problems in self-report assessment that can interfere with the validity of the information collected. We've already mentioned the fact that biases in recall of information can produce a distorted picture. This can render the information invalid. In the same way, people's motivational tendencies can also get in the way of accurate reporting.

There are at least two biases in the way people respond in assessment. These biases are called **response sets.** A response set is a psychological orientation, a kind of readiness to answer in a particular way (Berg, 1967; Jackson & Messick, 1967; Rorer, 1965). Response sets create distortions in the information assessed. Since personality psychologists want their assessments to provide information that's free from contamination, response sets are problems.

Two response sets are of particular importance in personality assessment. One of them emerges most clearly when the assessment device is a self-report instrument that in one fashion or another asks the person questions that require a yes-or-no response (or a response on a rating scale with agree and disagree as the opposite ends of the scale). This response set, called **acquiescence,** is nothing more than the tendency to say yes (Couch & Keniston, 1960).

Everyone presumably has this tendency to a degree, but people vary greatly in this respect. That's what causes the problem. If the set isn't counteracted, the scores of people who are highly acquiescent become inflated. Their high scores reflect the response set instead of their personality. People who have extreme personalities but not much acquiescence will also have high scores. But you won't know whose scores are due to personality and whose are due to acquiescence.

Acquiescence is usually viewed as a straightforward problem to counter. The way it's handled for self-reports is to write only half the items so that a *yes* response indicates being high on the personality characteristic. Write the other half of the items so that a *no* response means the person is high on the personality characteristic. In the process of scoring the test, then, any bias coming from the simple tendency to say yes is canceled out.

Although this procedure takes care of the problem of overagreement, not everyone is convinced it's a good idea. Negatively worded items often turn out to be harder to understand or more complicated to answer than positively worded items. The result can be responses that are less accurate (Converse & Presser, 1986; Schriesheim & Hill, 1981). For this reason, some people feel it's better to live with the acquiescence problem than to introduce a different kind of error by complex wordings.

There's a second response set that's perhaps more important than acquiescence and also more troublesome. It's called **social desirability,** referring to the fact that people tend to portray themselves in a good light (in socially desirable ways) whenever possible. Once again, this tendency is stronger among some people than others (see Crowne & Marlowe, 1964; Edwards, 1957). As with acquiescence, if it isn't counteracted, people with strong concerns about social desirability will produce scores that reflect the response set rather than their personalities.

For some personality dimensions this problem is minimal. That is, some personality qualities imply no social approval or disapproval at either end of the dimension. In other cases, though, there's a consensus that it's better to be one way (for example, honest or likable) than the other (dishonest or unlikable). Here assessment becomes tricky.

The tendency to provide socially desirable responses can sometimes mask a person's true characteristics or feelings.

In general, psychologists deal with this problem by trying to phrase questions (or whatever the assessment device uses) so that the issue of social desirability isn't salient. As much as anything else, this is a process of trying to avoid even bringing up the idea that one kind of person is better liked than the other. Sometimes this means phrasing the undesirable response in a way that makes it more acceptable. Sometimes it means looking for ways to let people admit the undesirable quality indirectly. Another way to deal with the problem is to include items that assess the person's degree of concern about social desirability and to use this information as a correction factor in evaluating the person's responses to other items. In any event, it should be clear that this problem is one that personality psychologists must be constantly aware of and constantly guarding against in trying to measure what people are like.

Two Rationales behind the Development of Assessment Devices

Thus far this chapter has considered issues that arise in attempts to measure any quality of personality. What hasn't been taken up yet is how people decide what qualities to measure in the first place. This question won't be answered completely here, because the answer depends partly on the theoretical perspective from which the assessor is proceeding. There is, however, a general issue to address. In particular, development of personality measures usually follows one of two paths. Each path has a certain kind of logic, but the logics differ from each other.

Rational, or Theoretical, Approach

One strategy is termed a **rational,** or **theoretical, approach** to assessment. This strategy is based on theoretical considerations from the very beginning. The psychologist first develops a rational basis for believing that a particular dimension of personality is important. The next task is to create a test in which this dimension is reflected validly and reliably in people's answers. This approach to test development often leads to assessment devices that have a high degree of face validity.

It's important to recognize that the work doesn't stop once a set of items has been developed. Instruments developed from the theoretical starting point must also be shown to be reliable, to predict behavioral criteria, and to have good construct validity. Until these steps are taken, the scale shouldn't be considered a useful measure of anything.

It's probably safe to say that the majority of personality measurement devices that now exist were developed using the theoretical path. Some of these measure are single scales, others are inventories. Most of the measures that will be discussed in later chapters were created by first deciding *what* to measure and then figuring out *how* to measure it.

Empirical Approaches

The theoretical approach isn't the only way to start in scale development, though. A second strategy is usually characterized as an **empirical,** or data-based, **approach.** The basic characteristic of this approach is that it relies on data rather than on theory to decide what items make up the assessment device.

There are two important variations on this theme. One of them is an inductive approach whereby the person developing the measure uses the data to decide what qualities of personality exist and are worth measuring at all (Cattell, 1947, 1965, 1979). Because this line of thought is an important contributor to trait psychology, we're going to defer our discussion of it until the chapter on trait psychology. Instead we'll focus here on another empirical approach. This one reflects a very pragmatic orientation to the process of assessment. That is, it's guided less by a desire to understand personality than by a practical aim of sorting people into categories. If a quick or inexpensive technique can be found to do this, the technique provides an important benefit.

Instead of developing the test first and then validating it against a criterion, this approach works in the opposite direction. The groups into which people are to be sorted represent the criteria for the test. Developing the test is a matter of starting out with many possible items and finding out which items tend to be answered differently by members of one criterion group than by other people. For this reason, this approach to test development is termed the **criterion keying** approach. This label comes from the fact that the items that are kept empirically distinguish between the *criterion* group and other people. If an item set with those characteristics can be found for each criterion group, then the entire test (all the item sets together) can be used to tell who belongs to which group.

In the point of view reflected in this approach, it doesn't matter at all what the items of the assessment device look like, as long as they distinguish persons who fit a criterion from those who don't. Every aspect of the scale's development is tied to successful prediction of the criterion. The items in a scale deriving from this approach are chosen because members of a specific group (defined on some other basis) tend to answer them differently than other people.

The best illustration of the use of this method is the Minnesota Multiphasic Personality Inventory, better known as the MMPI (Hathaway & McKinley, 1943) and revised in 1989 as the MMPI-2 (Butcher, Dahlstrom, Graham, Tellegen, & Kaemmer, 1989). The MMPI was a very long true-false inventory developed as a measure of abnormality in personality. The first step in its development was to collect a large number of self-descriptive statements. The statements then were given to a group of normal persons and to groups of previously diagnosed psychiatric patients—people already judged by a clinician to have a specific disorder. Thus, the criterion already existed. The next step was to test the usefulness of each item. Do people with one psychiatric diagnosis agree or disagree with the item more often than normal people? If so, that item was included in the scale that pertains to that psychiatric diagnosis.

The original MMPI was developed long ago on a sample that was narrow ethnically and geographically (most people involved were from Minnesota), and had a narrow age range. There was concern that scores from other populations might not be interpreted properly. In addition, many items were out of date, and some were difficult to understand. The people developing the MMPI-2 reworded about 20% of the original items for clarity, and wrote 154 new ones. This larger total then was distilled down to 567. The researchers collected responses from people who varied more widely in ethnicity, age, and gender. Thus, the interpretation of responses has been made more consistent with the contemporary U.S. populace.

As did the original, the MMPI-2 has 10 basic content scales (Table 3.2). It also has 6 validity scales. The content scales indicate how similar a person's responses are to those of patients with a particular diagnosis. The validity scales provide an estimate

TABLE 3.2

Content scales of the MMPI-2 and interpretation of each scale's meaning.

Clinical scales	Interpretation
Hypochondriasis	High scorers are cynical, defeatist, overconcerned with physical health
Depression	High scorers are despondent, distressed, depressed
Hysteria	High scorers report frequent symptoms with no apparent organic cause
Psychopathic deviate	High scorers are adventurous, have disregard for social or moral standards
Masculinity/femininity	Scores provide indication of level of "traditional" male/female interests
Paranoia	High scorers are guarded and suspicious, feel persecuted
Psychasthenia	High scorers are anxious, rigid, tense, and worrying
Schizophrenia	High scorers exhibit social alienation, bizarreness in thinking
Hypomania	High scorers are emotionally excitable, impulsive, hyperactive
Social introversion	High scorers are shy, withdrawn, uninvolved in social relationships

of how meaningful the person's entire response profile is. For example, the Lie scale is a measure of people's tendencies to present themselves too favorably to be true. As another example, frequent "cannot say" responses—an inability to choose the true or false option—may mean that the person is being evasive. If too many of these responses are made, the meaning of the other responses is called into question.

Better Assessment: A Never-Ending Search

As is indicated in the preceding section, even one of the most widely used tests in the world isn't considered "finished." It was subjected to further refinement, further data gathering, and a continuing examination of how people respond to its items. The result was a further improvement in what the test can tell the people who use it.

The MMPI isn't the only measure to be reexamined and revised in this way. Most personality scales in widespread use have been revised once or more and restandardized periodically so it's always clear what people's responses mean. The process of establishing construct validity requires not just a single study but many. It thus takes time. The process of establishing discriminant validity is virtually never-ending. There is a tremendous amount of effort invested in the process of creating and improving tests of personality. This investment of effort is necessary if people are to feel confident of knowing what the tests are measuring. Having that confidence is an important part of the assessment of personality.

The characteristics of personality tests that have been discussed in this chapter distinguish these tests from the kinds of tests you see from time to time in newspapers, magazines, on TV, and so forth. In some cases, the items in a magazine article were written specifically for that article. It is unlikely that anyone checked on their reliability. It's even less likely that anyone checked on their validity. Even if the items were taken from a carefully developed instrument, the entire set of items usually doesn't appear; it can be hard to be sure how well the ones that do appear reflect the entire scale. Unless the right steps have been taken to create an instrument, you should be careful about putting your faith in the results that come from it.

SUMMARY

Assessment (measurement of personality) is something that people constantly do informally. Psychologists formalize this process into several distinct techniques. Observer ratings are judgments made about people who are being assessed by an observer—an interviewer, someone who just watches, or someone who knows the people well enough to make ratings of what they are like. Observer ratings often are somewhat subjective, involving interpretations of the person's behavior. Self-reports are made by the people being assessed, about themselves. Self-reports can be single scales or multiscale inventories. All assessment device can be subjective or objective. Objective techniques require no interpretation as the assessment is made. Subjective techniques involve some sort of interpretation as an intrinsic part of the measure.

One issue for all assessment techniques is reliability (the reproducibility of the measurement). Reliability is determined by checking one measurement against another (or several others). Self-report scales usually have many items (each a measurement), leading to indices of internal reliability, or internal consistency. Observer judgments are checked by inter-rater reliability. Test-retest reliability assesses the reproducibility of the measure over time. In all cases, high correlation among measures means good reliability.

Another important issue is validity (whether what you're measuring is what you want to measure). The attempt to determine whether the operational definition (the assessment device) matches the concept you set out to measure is called construct validation. Contributors to construct validity are evidence of criterion, convergent, and discriminant validity. Face validity is not usually taken as an important element of construct validity. Validity is further threatened by the fact that people have response sets (acquiescence and social desirability) that bias their responses.

Development of assessment devices proceeds along one of two paths. The rational path uses a theory to decide what should be measured and then figures out the best way to measure it. Most assessment devices developed this way. The empirical path involves using data to determine what items should be in a scale. The MMPI was developed this way, using a technique called criterion keying, in which the test developers let people's reponses tell them which items to use. Test items that members of a diagnostic category answered differently from other people were retained.

GLOSSARY

Acquiesence The response set of tending to agree, to say yes in response to any question.

Assessment The measuring of personality.

Construct validity The accuracy with which a measure reflects the underlying concept.

Convergent validity The degree to which a measure relates to other characteristics that are conceptually similar to what it's supposed to assess.

Criterion keying (also *Empirical keying*) The developing of a test by seeing which items distinguish between groups.

Criterion validity The degree to which the measure correlates with a separate criterion of the same concept.

Discriminant validity The degree to which a scale does *not* measure unintended qualities.

Empirical approach (to scale development) The use of data instead of theory to decide what should go into the measure.

Error Random influences incorporated in measurements.

Face validity The scale "looking" as if it measures what it's supposed to measure.

Internal reliability (**internal consistency**) The agreement among responses made to the items of a measure.

Inter-rater reliability The consistent agreement between observers of the same events.

Inventory A personality test measuring several aspects of personality on distinct subscales.

Observer ratings An assessment in which someone else produces information on the person being assessed.

Objective measure A measure that incorporates no interpretation.

Operational definition The defining of a concept by the events through which it is measured (or manipulated).

Predictive validity The degree to which the measure predicts other manifestations of personality.

Rational approach (to scale development) The use of a theory to decide what you want to measure, then deciding how to measure it.

Reliability Consistency across repeated measurements.

Response set A biased orientation to answering.

Self-report An assessment in which people make ratings pertaining to themselves.

Social desirability The response set or style of tending to portray oneself favorably.

Split-half reliability One way of assessing internal consistency among responses to items of a measure.

Subjective measure A measure incorporating personal interpretation.

Test-retest reliability The stability of measurements across time.

Theoretical approach See *Rational approach.*

Validity A measure's "truthfulness," or the degree to which it actually measures what it is intended to measure.

PART two

The Dispositional Perspective

THE DISPOSITIONAL PERSPECTIVE: Major Themes and Underlying Assumptions

A major theme that underlies the dispositional perspective on personality is the idea that people display consistency or continuity in their actions, thoughts, and feelings. A human being's dispositional nature doesn't shift aimlessly from moment to moment—it endures across changes in time and place. Indeed, the very concept of disposition arose as a way of conceptualizing the fact that people remain the same people, even through passage of time and even as they move from situation to situation. Dispositions are qualities that people carry around with them, that belong to them, that are somehow part of them.

Certainly we all experience occasional periods in which we're unpredictable, in which we may feel buffeted by the psychological winds around us. But for most people that experience of unpredictability is the exception rather than the rule. It certainly isn't what defines the essence of personality. Rather, personality implies stability, constancy, something that doesn't vary much from one time to another. You—like most people—undoubtedly feel within yourself a sense of coherence, a kind of

permanence across time, events, and experiences. You're the person you are, and you'll still be that person tomorrow, and next week, and next year. This is the essence of dispositions.

A second major theme of the dispositional perspective derives from the fact that people differ from each other in many ways. As indicated in Chapter 1, the entire field of personality psychology is guided in part by an emphasis on differences among people. This emphasis is particularly central, however, to the dispositional perspective. From this perspective, each person's personality consists of a pattern of dispositional qualities, and the composition of the pattern differs from one person to another. The intersection that these dispositions form in any given person constitutes the defining nature of that person's personality.

These assumptions are important throughout the dispositional perspective. They're dealt with in different ways, however, by different kinds of theorists. One approach to dispositions emphasizes their mere existence. It focuses primarily on trying to measure and catalog them in better ways, to obtain a clearer understanding of what dimensions are most important in personality and to develop better ways of placing people on those dimensions. This "trait and type" approach is discussed in Chapter 4. In some ways, this trait approach most clearly exemplifies the dispositional perspective.

This isn't the only way to approach the concept of disposition, though. A second way is to think of dispositions as enduring motivational characteristics that vary in strength from person to person. These differences in the motives that underlie people's actions are reflected in differences in the qualities that the people display in their behavior. This "needs and motives" approach to dispositions is examined in Chapter 5.

4

Types, Traits, and Interactionism

■ "I want you to meet a friend of mine from high school. He's a real outgoing sort of person. He's friendly, but he's not the type who goes along with the crowd all the time. You might say he's sociable, but he's also independent."

■ "Why do you keep *doing* things like that? I tell you over and over I don't like you to act that way, and you keep saying you'll change, but you never do. You just keep doing the same thing. Won't you *ever* change?"

■ "My psychology professor is *so* predictable. He's smart, I suppose, but he's *such* a nerd. He must spend all his time locked up in his office. I can't imagine him doing anything interesting or adventurous. He can't help it, I guess. It's just his personality."

These quotes illustrate a broad and important theme in personality psychology. In particular, you often assume that everyone you meet has a set of dispositions that a little observation will reveal to you fairly easily. When you find out what people around you are like, you can rely on that knowledge as a guide for what to expect of them in the future. This theme, of course, applies to personality psychology as a whole. But it's particularly prominent in the trait and type view of personality. The words *trait* and *type* convey slightly different meanings. They converge, though, on the idea that people have stable characteristics that they exhibit across various circumstances and across time.

Types and Traits

The notion that people could be divided into different types, or categories, goes back at least to the time of Hippocrates (about 400 BC), whose ideas were later embellished by Galen (about AD 150). In those early times, people were thought to form four groups: *choleric* (irritable), *melancholic* (depressed), *sanguine* (optimistic), and *phlegmatic* (calm). Each personality type was thought to reflect an excess of one of four bodily fluids.

A typology of more recent origin is Carl Jung's (1933) argument that people are either introverts or extraverts. An **introvert** tends to be alone a lot, behaves as if shy, and prefers solitary activities to those involving social interaction. When confronted by stress in their lives, introverts tend to withdraw into themselves. An **extravert** is the opposite: someone who isn't at all shy and prefers to spend time with others rather than be alone. When confronted by stress, extraverts are likely to seek a group to talk things over.

In typologies, the **types** are usually regarded as categories of membership that are distinct and discontinuous. An example of a discontinuous category is gender, with people being either male or female. Jung often portrayed the categories of introvert and extravert as discontinuous in the same way, so that a person is either one or the other (Figure 4.1). Any appearance to the contrary simply reflects distortion of the person's basic personality.

In contrast to this picture, discussions of **traits** usually assume that people differ on variables or dimensions that are continuous (Figure 4.1). As a result, this sort of theory is sometimes referred to as a "dimensional" approach. In trait theories, people differ from each other in the *amounts* of the various characteristics they have in

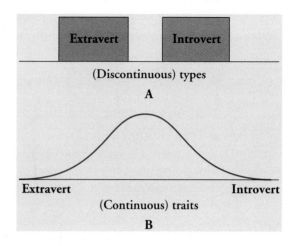

FIGURE 4.1

Early type theories (A) assumed a discontinuity between or among categories of people. Trait theories (B) assume that traits are continuous dimensions of variability on some characteristic and that the degree of presence versus absence of the characteristic is distributed across a population.

their personality. To put it another way, in this view differences among people are *quantitative* rather than qualitative.

Type theories have generally fallen by the wayside in personality psychology. Even Jung wasn't really a type theorist—he used type labels as a convenience. Today, theorists of this group tend to think of people in terms of continuous trait dimensions (for a differing view, however, see Gangestad & Snyder, 1985; Meehl, 1992; Robins et al., 1996; Strube, 1989; York & John, 1992; for a typology that's widely used in business, see Blake & Mouton, 1980).

As true typologies became less prominent, the term *type* began to be used in a way that differed from earlier usage. This second use comes from Eysenck (1967, 1970, 1975). He used the word type not to imply discontinuity, but to refer to a kind of "supertrait"—a trait that's very broad and important.

Nomothetic and Idiographic Views of Traits

The ideas we've discussed thus far incorporate an implicit assumption: that traits are qualities of personality that are relevant to everyone. People simply vary in how much of that quality they have. Is this assumption warranted?

The idea that traits exist and have the same psychological meaning in everyone is known as a **nomothetic** approach to personality (Allport, 1961). The term *nomothetic* derives from the Greek word meaning "law." This view emphasizes comparisons among people, which can't be made unless a trait has the same meaning for all concerned. The nomothetic view has dominated trait psychology for at least the past 40 years, and it still does.

In contrast is the **idiographic** approach to personality (Allport, 1961), which emphasizes that each person is unique (see also Lamiell, 1981). The term *idiographic* has the same source as the word *idiosyncratic*. This approach suggests that traits are individualized. Some are possessed by only one person. Indeed, there may be as many traits as there are people. This view suggests there are times when it's impossible to compare people because everyone is, in effect, on a different scale. Even if the same trait term is relevant to two people, its meaning or connotations may differ between people (Dunning & McElwee, 1995). Even if people agree about the meaning, the trait may differ so much in importance between people that they really can't be compared meaningfully with each other.

Introverts want to be alone and prefer solitary activities to activities involving interaction with others.

This idea recently reemerged in a slightly different form. Baumeister and Tice (1988) coined the term **metatrait** to refer to the quality of possessing or not possessing a given trait. They produced evidence that specific traits are meaningful to some people but irrelevant to others. Similar findings were reported by Britt (1993), who argued that the findings reflect the presence versus absence of a trait structure in personality.

Thus, the nomothetic view emphasizes comparability among persons, whereas the idiographic view emphasizes uniqueness. Don't overinterpret this difference, though. Psychologists who favor the nomothetic approach believe that everyone is unique. However, they think the uniqueness reflects a unique *combination* of levels on many trait dimensions, with the dimensions being the same for everyone. As Eysenck once put it, "To the scientist, the unique individual is simply the point of intersection of a number of quantitative variables" (1952, p. 18).

Even psychologists who emphasize the idiographic approach don't entirely reject the nomothetic approach (see, e.g., Pelham, 1993). Indeed, Allport was nomothetic in most of his own work. He believed, though, that the nomothetic view always produces approximations or oversimplifications. In his opinion personality psychologists should never lose sight of this fact: Even the traits that people seem to share always have a personal flavor (maybe from differences in how the trait is expressed) that varies from individual to individual (Allport, 1961).

Most contemporary trait psychologists do keep this point in the back of their minds. But most disregard the strong version of the idiographic approach—the idea that traits themselves differ from person to person.

What Traits Matter?

When you think of personality in terms of types or traits, a question you quickly confront is this: *What are the traits that are basic* to personality?

This is a hard question to answer. In fact, there have been serious disagreements about where to *start* in answering it. Thus, different people approached it in different ways. We'll turn to some of these approaches momentarily. First, though, let's consider a logical problem that all trait theorists share and a tool that helps immensely with it.

A Tool to Use Along the Way: Factor Analysis

Personality is reflected in many ways—for example, in descriptive words. A huge number of words describe personality. If each word represented a different trait, and all the traits mattered equally, a trait psychologist would go crazy trying to organize things. That, in a nutshell, is a problem every trait psychologist faces: bringing order to diversity. A solution to this problem derives from the widely shared belief that the huge number of words reflect a small number of underlying dimensions. What's needed is a way to sort out what the dimensions are.

A tool that's often used for this is a statistical technique called **factor analysis.** The basic idea is simple: If two or more characteristics covary (vary along with each other) when assessed across many people, they may reflect an underlying trait. By examining *patterns* of covariation, you can discover the trait dimensions that underlie the measured qualities.

You already know that covariation between two qualities is computed as a correlation. Factor analysis is a more complex version of a correlation. Instead of looking at a correlation between *two* variables, a factor analysis integrates a matrix of correlations among *many* variables. Because the process is very complex, factor analysis has been widely used only since the invention of computers. Indeed, the sharp rise in computing power in recent years has led to increasing sophistication in these procedures (Bentler, 1990; Jöreskog & Sörbom, 1979).

What happens in a factor analysis? You start by collecting measurements on many variables, across large numbers of people. The measurements can take any form. They can be self-reports, observer ratings, or observer codings of behavior. You can even use several forms of data in the same analysis. The same measurements must be used for all subjects, though (you can't use self-reports for some people, behavioral observations for others).

Once the data have been collected, correlations are computed between every pair of variables (see also Box 4.1). The correlation matrix is then subjected to a procedure called *factor extraction*. In this procedure the patterns of correlations are distilled to a smaller set of factors. Each factor represents shared variations among several of the measures in the data set (e.g., test items, if the data came from a self-report scale). Thus, one way of thinking about the factors is that they are an attempt to "account" statistically for covariations in the original data.

Once the factors have been extracted, each can be described in terms of a set of factor loadings. These can be thought of as correlations between the factor and each item (or whatever measures are used) that contributes to its existence. Items that correlate strongly with the factor (usually higher than .30 or so) are said to "load on" that factor. Items that don't correlate well with the factor are said not to load on it. What the factor *is* is revealed by which items load on it.

The final step in the factor analysis—in many respects the most delicate part of the whole process—is labeling the factors. Because a factor is defined by items that load on it, you choose a label to reflect as closely as possible the content of the items—particularly items with the highest loadings. In factor analyses bearing on personality, at this point the factor is being thought of as the statistical reflection of a trait.

It should be clear that the act of naming or labeling the factor is highly subjective. Several different names might seem equally good. Which name is chosen, however, can have important consequences. That is, people often forget that the label is an inference from the pattern of data. As a result, people rely on the label to tell them what the trait is. If the label you choose is misleading, it can create problems of interpretation later on.

Factor analysis as a tool in trait psychology does three things. Most important, it reduces the multiple reflections of personality to a smaller set of traits, by telling you what traits lie behind the reflections. It also provides a basis for arguing that some traits matter more than others. That is, if a factor accounts for a lot of the variability in the data, it reflects an important trait. A factor that accounts for less variability is less important. Finally, factor analysis helps you decide how to create an assessment device. That is, you keep items (or ratings) that load high on the factor corresponding to the trait. Items that don't load are discarded, or they're revised and tried out again. Through repeated analyses, items that don't do a good job of measuring any particular trait are replaced by better ones.

Factor analysis is a very useful tool. It's only a tool, though. What we've told you has a major hole in it. We haven't said anything about *what measures to collect in the first place*. A factor analysis can tell you only about what you put into it. Thus, the decision about what to measure and analyze has a huge impact on the traits that emerge.

How do you decide what measures to collect? As we said a bit earlier, different theorists have answered this question differently.

Let Reality Reveal Itself: Cattell's Approach

One answer is that researchers must determine *empirically* what traits make up personality, not impose their own preconceptions. If you start with preconceptions, you're in danger of leading yourself astray. Raymond Cattell, an early contributor to trait psychology and one of the first users of factor analysis, made this argument (Cattell, 1947, 1965, 1978; Cattell & Kline, 1977). This reasoning had a strong influence on many other trait researchers (e.g., Goldberg, 1993a).

How do you determine the structure of personality empirically? One source of information is language (see Goldberg, 1982). That is, a language that's evolved over thousands of years has words to describe virtually every human quality there is. Presumably the importance of a trait is reflected by there being words to describe it. A quality of personality that's described by lots of words is likely to be more important than one described by just a few. This principle is called the **lexical criterion** of importance.

In line with this lexical approach, Cattell (1947, 1965) took a set of 4,500 trait names (already reduced from a larger number by Allport & Odbert, 1936) and removed obvious synonyms, leaving 171 trait names. He then collected ratings on these words and factor analyzed the ratings. The resulting factors were the traits he believed are important.

Though Cattell used the lexical strategy as a starting point, he also emphasized the need to use data of different sorts as well. To Cattell, self-report data, observer ratings, and objective behavioral data should all be used. All kinds of data

BOX 4.1

A CLOSER LOOK:
The Process of Factor Analysis

The process of factor analysis is complex, but its underlying logic is fairly simple. It's an attempt to find regularities or patterns of association among a set of variables.

The process has several distinct steps. The first step is collecting data. This is more complicated than it might seem. First you have to decide what *kinds* of data to include. Should you use self-reports, observer ratings, or a combination? Even more fundamentally, what aspects of behavior do you want to measure? Should your analysis be guided strictly by "what's out there," or do you want theory to play a role? As you can see, the first step—"collecting data"—involves many decisions.

Let's use an example in which we let theory play a role. Imagine you're interested in how people cope with stress (see Lazarus & Folkman, 1984). You've decided to use self-reports: people's ratings of how much they did particular things during the most stressful event they can recall from the past 2 months. To "collect data," you get 300 or so of your friends to recall their stressful event and rate each of a set of items (which list things that people sometimes do when under stress). The items are things like these:

1. Took action quickly, before things could get out of hand.
2. Refused to believe that it was real.
3. Did something concrete to make the situation better.
4. Tried to convince myself that it wasn't happening.
5. Went on thinking things were just like they were.
6. Changed or grew as a person in a new way.
7. Tried to look on the bright side of things.

The second step is to compute the correlation of every item with every other item (see panel A, opposite). Each correlation reflects the degree to which your 300 people tended to answer one item the same way as they answered the other item. As you can see, there are strong correlations between items 1 and 3, between items 6 and 7, and between item 2 and items 4 and 5 (which are also strongly related to each other). The other correlations are very weak.

Since you had people respond to 78 items (instead of just these 7), your correlation matrix is quite large. Interpreting the pattern of correlations (and absence of correlations) from that matrix would be a big chore. The size of this chore is diminished by the third step in the analysis, called factor extraction. Through a small mathematical miracle (Comrey, 1973), your matrix is reduced to a smaller number of underlying dimensions (for example, the associations among items 2, 4, and 5 would contribute to one dimension). These dimensions of underlying commonality are called **factors.** At this point, factors are hazy hypothetical entities you can't see.

Now that the factors are extracted, the next step is to compute the **factor loadings** of each item on each factor. Factor loadings tell you the relations between the item and the factor (panel B, opposite). Each indicates the degree to which the item reflects the underlying dimension. As with any correlation, factor loadings can range from +1.00 to −1.00, and larger numbers mean stronger associations. Thus, a large number (a high loading) means the item is related to that dimension, a small number means it's not. As shown in panel B, items 1 and 3 load on factor A (but not on any other factor), items 6 and 7 load on factor B (but not any other factor), and items 2, 4, and 5 load on factor C (but not any other factor). Similar loadings are produced for all the items, letting you know which items go together to establish the underlying dimensions.

Once it's clear which items form which factors, you've reached the final step: naming the factors. This is tricky. In naming the factor, you want to convey the essence of the underlying dimension as well as you can, but your only guide is the items loading on the factor. Often the items are ambiguous or of mixed content. It's a judgment call what the underlying quality really is. In this example, a couple of the factors are fairly easy. The items loading on Factor A reflect a tendency to take action to try to resolve the problem. This factor might be called "problem-focused coping." Given the content of Items 2, 4, and 5, Factor C might be labelled "denial." Factor B seems to reflect "positive reinterpretation" or "post-traumatic growth" or "looking on the bright side," but it's hard to be sure which name is best. It's important to be careful in this step, though, because the name you choose to call the factor will guide your future thinking.

A.   Hypothetical Correlation Matrix

Item	1	2	3	4	5	6	7
1	*	.10	.75	−.05	.03	.12	.00
2		*	−.02	.52	.61	−.07	−.08
3			*	.17	.00	.09	.15
4				*	.71	.11	.08
5					*	.06	−.04
6						*	.59
7							*

B.   Hypothetical Factor Loadings

Factor	A	B	C
Item 1	(.62)	.15	.01
Item 2	.03	−.08	(.49)
Item 3	(.54)	.04	−.20
Item 4	.10	.11	(.56)
Item 5	.07	.08	(.50)
Item 6	−.02	(.72)	.12
Item 7	.08	(.48)	.08

have problems, but the problems differ from one kind to another. Using several types of data tends to balance the problems of each type. Cattell called this a **multivariate** approach, because it takes into account many manifestations of personality simultaneously.

After conducting many analyses on various kinds of data, Cattell came to believe that personality is captured in a set of 16 dimensions (Table 4.1). The dimensions reemerged in analyses across the various types of data he was using, and he saw them as the primary traits in personality. These 16 primary factors of personality provide a name for the inventory that measures them: the 16 Personality Factor inventory or 16PF (Cattell, Eber, & Tatsuoka, 1977).

Recall the statement earlier that labeling of factors is highly subjective and that the content of a factor can be hard to pin down. Cattell dealt with this problem at first by inventing names (alaxia, praxernia, threctia, parmia). Because these words had no connotations, they weren't as likely to be misleading as would more intuitive labels that might not fit the factors perfectly. Eventually, though, he shifted to the labels used in Table 4.1, which convey some of the psychological sense of the 16 factors.

TABLE 4.1

The 16 factors in Cattell's analysis of personality, as defined by the characteristics of high and low scorers on each trait dimension. The factors are listed in order of variance accounted for by each factor. The labels listed are the currently used verbal approximations for the content of each factor. Copyright © 1993 by the Institute for Personality and Ability Testing, Inc., Champaign, IL 61824-1188. Reproduced by permission.

1. Reserved	versus	Warm
2. Concrete-reasoning	versus	Abstract-reasoning
3. Reactive	versus	Emotionally stable
4. Deferential	versus	Dominant
5. Serious	versus	Lively
6. Expedient	versus	Rule-conscientious
7. Shy	versus	Socially bold
8. Utilitarian	versus	Sensitive
9. Trusting	versus	Vigilant
10. Practical	versus	Imaginative
11. Forthright	versus	Private
12. Self-assured	versus	Apprehensive
13. Traditional	versus	Open to change
14. Group-oriented	versus	Self-reliant
15. Tolerates disorder	versus	Perfectionist
16. Relaxed	versus	Tense

Start from a Theory: Eysenck's Approach

Though many believe an empirical origin is best, not all agree. Another argument is that theorists should begin with well-developed ideas about what qualities they want to measure. Then they should set about measuring those qualities well. Another important contributor to trait psychology, Hans Eysenck, advocated this approach (e.g., 1967, 1970, 1975, 1986; Eysenck & Eysenck, 1985).

Eysenck didn't entirely disregard the observation of reality. He made use of observations made recurrently by others over a period of centuries. In particular, he began with the typology of Hippocrates and Galen, and related observations made by Jung and Wundt (Eysenck, 1967). He set out to investigate the idea that the four types identified by Hippocrates and Galen (and re-identified by others) could be created by combining high and low levels of two supertraits.

The two supertraits Eysenck posed as the underlying dimensions of personality are introversion-extraversion and emotionality-stability (or neuroticism). The extraversion dimension concerns tendencies toward sociability, craving excitement, liveliness, activeness, and dominance (all of which characterize the extravert). The

TABLE 4.2

Traits that are common among four categories of people deriving from the two major personality dimensions proposed by Eysenck. Each category results from combining introversion or extraversion with either a high or a low level of emotional stability (adapted from Eysenck, 1975).

	Emotionally stable		**Emotionally unstable**	
Introvert	Passive careful thoughtful peaceful controlled reliable even-tempered calm	**Phlegmatic**	Quiet pessimistic unsociable sober rigid moody anxious reserved	**Melancholic**
Extravert	Sociable outgoing talkative responsive easygoing lively carefree leaderly	**Sanguine**	Active optimistic impulsive changeable excitable aggressive restless touchy	**Choleric**

emotional stability dimension concerns the ease and frequency with which the person becomes upset and distressed. Greater moodiness, anxiety, and depression reflect greater emotional instability.

Table 4.2 portrays four sets of people, with various combinations of highs and lows on these two dimensions. The ancient type label for each group described is printed in color. In considering the nature of these four groups, keep two things in mind: First, although the form of Table 4.2 suggests a discontinuity, both dimensions are continuous. Second, the descriptions in Table 4.2 apply to relatively extreme and clear-cut cases. Most people are closer to the midpoint on both dimensions and thus have less extreme characteristics.

Look first at the introvert groups. As can be seen in Table 4.2, people who are introverted *and emotionally stable* tend to be careful, controlled, calm, and thoughtful in their actions. The combination of introversion and emotional *in*stability, on the other hand, tends to create a more moody sense of unsociable reserve, a pessimistic and anxious quality in behavior. Thus introverts can differ, depending on their emotional stability or instability.

So can extraverts. When extraversion is combined with emotional stability, the result is an easygoing carefree sociability. Emotional *in*stability among extraverts introduces an excitable aggressive quality into behavior. Thus the impact of one dimension (introversion-extraversion) can differ as a result of what other traits the person has (emotional stability).

Eysenck assessed these two dimensions by a self-report device called the Eysenck Personality Questionnaire, or EPQ (Eysenck & Eysenck, 1975). He used factor analysis as a tool to help create it, but with a different goal than Cattell had. Cattell used factor analysis to find out what dimensions *exist*. Eysenck used it to refine his scales (by seeing which items didn't load well) and to confirm that the scales measure two factors, as intended.

Eysenck and Cattell started out in very different ways, but the trait structures they produced have distinct similarities. The two dimensions Eysenck saw as supertraits resemble two of the first three factors of Cattell's 16PF (Table 4.1). The similarities are even stronger when you look at **second-order factors** from the 16PF. A second-order factor analysis tells whether the factors *themselves* form factors (correlate in clusters). One second-order factor from the 16PF is virtually identical to extraversion (Cattell & Kline, 1977). Another, which Cattell calls *anxiety*, is similar to emotional stability. Thus, the factor structures have much in common.

Indeed, a further reflection of the resemblance between structures can be seen in Eysenck's view that the dimensions of extraversion and emotional stability are at the top of an unfolding hierarchy of qualities that combine to create personality (Figure 4.2). Each supertrait is made of component traits (similar to Cattell's primary traits). These are either superficial manifestations of the superordinate trait, or specific qualities that contribute to it. Component traits, in turn, reflect habits, which derive from sets of specific responses. Eysenck believed all levels are involved in behavior, but he saw the type level as the most important.

There are two further points to make here about Eysenck's analysis. First, he believed that extraversion and emotional stability relate to aspects of nervous system

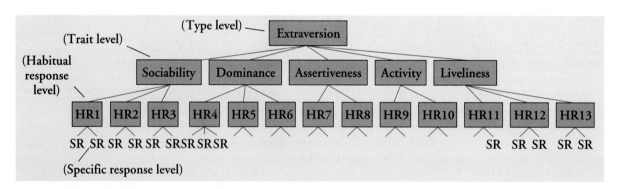

FIGURE 4.2

Eysenck's hierarchical view of personality. The superordinate level of the model (types) subsumes the elements represented at the next-lower level (traits). These elements, in turn, are made up of yet lower-order qualities (habits), which are made up of associations between stimulus and response. Adapted from *The Biological Basis of Personality* (1967, p. 36) by H. J. Eysenck. Reprinted courtesy of Charles C. Thomas, Publisher, Springfield, IL.

functioning. That biological aspect of his theory is discussed in Chapter 7. Second, there's another dimension in Eysenck's analysis, which has had less attention than the other two. The third dimension, called *psychoticism* (Eysenck & Eysenck, 1976), is a predisposition toward disorders involving psychological detachment from other people. Psychoticism has been studied far less than Eysenck's other dimensions, and less is known about it. According to Eysenck, however, people high in psychoticism tend to be hostile, manipulative, impulsive, and tend to seek out unusual experiences (Eysenck, 1992).

Other Theoretical Starting Points: Folk Concepts and the Interpersonal Circle

Eysenck's theoretically based approach to the dimensions of personality is not the only one. Here are two others.

Harrison Gough (1968) argued that certain aspects of behavior are common to every culture and society, because they arise naturally out of social interaction. He calls them **folk concepts.** For example, all cultures seem to incorporate a notion of social responsibility—a tendency to keep in mind the good of the group and to try not to act out of pure self-interest. This tendency, of course, varies across people. Gough saw folk concepts as forming basic aspects of personality.

Gough developed the California Psychological Inventory, or CPI (Gough, 1956, 1968), using these folk concepts as his theoretical base. For example, the socialization scale measures a kind of social maturity related to social responsibility. It involves a tendency to sense and interpret subtle aspects of social situations and to modify one's actions on the basis of those cues (Gough, 1960).

One more illustration of a theoretical starting point is also a theory that emphasizes interpersonal issues. Based on earlier work by Leary (1957) and others, Jerry Wiggins and his colleagues (Wiggins, 1979; Wiggins, Phillips, & Trapnell, 1989) argue that traits influencing the quality of interpersonal experiences are basic to personality. Wiggins proposed a set of eight patterns, which he calls the **interpersonal circle,** arrayed around two dimensions that underlie human relations (see Figure 4.3). The core dimensions in this view are dominance (or status) and love.

Wiggins argued (much as did Eysenck) that diverse personalities arise from combinations of values on these two dimensions. For example, a person who's high in

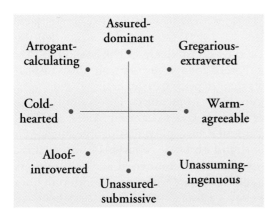

FIGURE 4.3

The interpersonal circle, a set of personality patterns portrayed in terms of their relative prevalence of two traits: love (the horizontal dimension) and dominance (the vertical dimension). The midpoint of each trait is the point where the lines cross. Adapted from Wiggins, Phillips, and Trapnell (1989).

dominance and toward the cold-hearted end of love will seem arrogant and calculating. Put the same amount of dominance together with warmth on the love dimension, though, and you get a person who's gregarious and extraverted. Both introversion and extraversion appear on this interpersonal circle (in lower left and upper right corners), but they aren't seen here as being a fundamental dimension. Instead, they are seen as resulting from the intersection of two other qualities.

The Five-Factor Model: The Basic Dimensions of Personality?

Thus far we've emphasized that people started to address the question of what traits are basic in diverse ways. Despite these diverse starting points, however, a remarkably strong consensus on what traits are basic has begun to emerge. The consensus has overtones of several ideas we've already presented, but it goes beyond them. The emerging consensus is that the basic structure of personality may consist of five superordinate factors, which are often referred to as the 5-factor model, or the "big five" (Goldberg, 1981; Wiggins, 1996).

The evidence in support of a five-factor view of personality structure has been accumulating for 45 years, but it's received wide attention only within the past two decades. John Digman (1990) chronicled the history of this work (see also Goldberg, 1993a; John, 1990). He argued that the five-factor view emerged early on, but it was ignored at first because most trait theorists were pursuing other ideas. Later it was ignored because other issues had arisen, removing the spotlight from the issue of what traits are basic. Now, however, the question has reemerged, and evidence has been mounting in support of the five-factor view.

Very early evidence for the five-factor model was published in 1949, when D. W. Fiske reported being unable to reproduce Cattell's 16-factor structure. Instead, he found a five-factor solution. The findings sat in obscurity until the early 1960s, when Norman (1963), Borgatta (1964), and Smith (1967) all addressed the same question with different measures. Each reached the same conclusion: Five factors provided the best account of the data.

During the decades of the 80s and 90s, there was a virtual explosion of work on this topic. Data from earlier studies have been reanalyzed in new ways (Digman & Takemoto-Chock, 1981). New and diverse samples have also been collected—for example, teachers' ratings of children (Digman & Inouye, 1986), children's ratings (Donahue, 1994), peer ratings (McCrae & Costa, 1987), and data from multiple cultures and languages (McCrae & Costa, 1997; McCrae et al., 1996; Paunonen, Jackson, Trzebinski, & Forsterling, 1992; Stumpf, 1993). Other studies expanded the data base in other ways. For example, Peabody and Goldberg (1989; Peabody, 1984) used a set of scales chosen to be sure there were enough *common* trait words instead of terms that mean more to psychologists than to people in general.

Others tested the model with different kinds of measures. For example, some studies have used a self-rating measure called a *Q-sort* (Lanning, 1994; McCrae, Costa, & Busch, 1986); others assessed frequencies with which people engage in particular kinds of actions (by self-report and observer reports [Botwin & Buss, 1989]); others conducted nonverbal assessments (Paunonen et al., 1992); others tested the model against measures originally developed from entirely different lines of thought (Costa & McCrae, 1988a; McCrae & Costa, 1989a). There have been exceptions (e.g., Benet & Waller, 1995; Zuckerman, Kuhlman, & Camac, 1988) and some imperfections in the findings (Church & Burke, 1994; Lanning, 1994); yet the body of literature as a whole is impressive in the extent to which it fits the five-factor model (Digman, 1990; John, 1990; McCrae & Costa, 1997; McCrae & John, 1992; Ozer & Reise, 1994).

What *Are* the Five Factors?

Given what we've said about the emerging consensus on the five-factor model, what comes next may surprise you. Specifically, there's still a fair amount of disagreement as to exactly what the five dimensions *are* (Briggs, 1989; John, 1990; Johnson & Ostendorf, 1993; Saucier, 1992).

The disagreement traces to two sources. First, recall that one of the hardest steps in factor analysis is naming the factors. You do it by looking at the items that load and trying to characterize what they mean—what underlying thread connects them. This can be very hard to do. Words have multiple connotations, and trait terms often represent blends of factors rather than pure reflections of one factor per word (Hofstee, de Raad, & Goldberg, 1992). Naturally, then, there are disagreements in interpretation.

Second, exactly what a factor looks like depends on what measures were included in the study. If a particular quality is left out or isn't well represented in the items, its involvement in a trait will be missed (cf. Peabody & Goldberg, 1989). Thus, different analyses with different measures can lead to different conclusions about the meaning of the factors, even when there's agreement that more or less the same factors have appeared.

Table 4.3 displays the five traits we've been discussing, using a variety of names for each. Peabody and Goldberg (1989) suggested that the big five factors are the metaphorical equivalent of a piece of classical music in which there's a theme and a series of variations on it. That's pretty much what you see in Table 4.3. The labels listed under each factor all share a theme, but there are also variations. Some of the

TABLE 4.3

Labels used by various authors to refer to the big five factors in personality. Labels in the rows are from (in order) Fiske (1949), Norman (1963), Borgatta (1964), Digman (1990), and Costa and McCrae (1985). The final row provides a characterization by Peabody and Goldberg (1989) of the life domain to which the trait pertains.

1	2	3	4	5
Social adaptability	Conformity	Will to achieve	Emotional control	Inquiring intellect
Surgency	Agreeableness	Conscientiousness	Emotionality	Culture
Assertiveness	Likeability	Responsibility	Emotionality	Intelligence
Extraversion	Friendly compliance	Will to achieve	Neuroticism	Intellect
Extraversion	Agreeableness	Conscientiousness	Neuroticism	Openness to experience
Power	Love	Work	Affect	Intellect

TABLE 4.4

Bipolar and unipolar adjective scales reflective of the five major personality factors. Taken from Digman and Inouye (1986), McCrae and Costa (1987), Norman (1963), Peabody and Goldberg (1989).

Factor	Item	
Extraversion	Bold–timid	Gregarious
	Forceful–submissive	Outspoken
	Self-confident–unassured	Energetic
	Talkative–silent	Happy
	Spontaneous–inhibited	Seclusive (inverse)
Agreeableness	Friendly–unfriendly	Jealous (inverse)
	Warm–cold	Considerate
	Kind–unkind	Spiteful (inverse)
	Polite–rude	Touchy (inverse)
	Good-natured–irritable	Complaining (inverse)
Conscientiousness	Cautious–rash	Neat
	Serious–frivolous	Persevering
	Responsible–irresponsible	Planful
	Thorough–careless	Careful
	Hardworking–lazy	Eccentric (inverse)
Emotionality	Nervous–poised	Concerned
	Anxious–calm	Nervous
	Excitable–composed	Fearful
	Relaxed–high strung	Tense
Intellect	Imaginative–simple	Knowledgeable
	Intellectual–unreflective	Perceptive
	Polished–crude	Imaginative
	Uncurious–curious	Verbal
	Uncreative–creative	Original

basis for the variation is displayed in Table 4.4, which lists examples of the descriptive terms that loaded on the five factors in one study or another.

The first factor is usually termed *extraversion,* but there's a good deal of variation in what makes up this factor (McCrae & Costa, 1987). This accounts in part for the different labels. Sometimes what characterizes this factor is assertiveness, an open expression of impulses. Sometimes it's a kind of dominance and confident assurance, sometimes a quality of happiness. Extraversion is usually thought of as also incorporating a sense of sociability, however (Watson, Clark, McIntyre, & Hamaker, 1992), which isn't always strongly represented in this factor.

The second factor is most commonly called *agreeableness*. Digman and his colleagues (Digman, 1990; Digman & Inouye, 1986; Digman & Takemoto-Chock, 1981) have argued that this trait isn't just a quality of being warm and likeable versus being cold. Agreeableness (at least in some conceptualizations) can include a kind of docile compliance. It can also include a sense of nurturance and emotional supportiveness. At the other end, disagreeableness often has an oppositional or antagonistic quality that can easily become hostility toward others. Digman (1990) suggests that this factor might also be thought of as friendliness/hostility, and McCrae and Costa (1987) have begun to call it agreeableness/antagonism. Consistent with this, there's evidence that people low in agreeableness choose displays of power as a way of resolving social conflict more than people higher in agreeableness (Graziano, Jensen-Campbell, & Hair, 1996). There's also evidence that they *experience* more conflicts (Asendorpf & Wilpers, 1998).

The essence of the third factor is also a little hard to capture. The most commonly used label is *conscientiousness*. However, this label doesn't fully reflect qualities such as planning, persistence, and purposeful striving toward goals, which often load on this factor (Digman & Inouye, 1986). (Indeed, because the word conscientious itself has two shades of meaning, that word loads on both this factor and the agreeableness factor—suggesting that conscientiousness may not be a perfect name for this factor.) Digman (1990), noting that several studies have linked this personality quality to educational achievement (see also Dollinger & Orf, 1991), has suggested that it be thought of as will to achieve, or simply *will*. Other suggested names include *constraint* and *responsibility*.

There's more agreement (though still not unanimity) about the meaning of the fourth factor. *Neuroticism*, or *emotionality*, is regarded by most as being what Eysenck had in mind by those terms. Yet Digman and Takemoto-Chock (1981) wanted to label this factor emotional disorganization, because the scales contributing to it convey more than the mere presence of emotion. What's at the heart of this factor, though, seems to be the experience of anxiety.

Factor five provides the largest disagreement of them all. The disagreement appears to stem from differences among studies in what's measured. Early on, Cattell measured qualities relevant to intelligence, but he stopped doing so and has used the term culture to refer to a set of qualities that remained. The label stuck. Peabody and Goldberg (1989) point out, though, that when intelligence-related measures are reintroduced, they join with the culture scales, and the factor seems more properly labeled *intellect*.

Costa and McCrae (1985) favor yet another label for this fifth factor: *openness* to experience. On the other hand, Peabody and Goldberg (1989) suggest that the Costa and McCrae measure taps one aspect of intellect (the imaginative side) but doesn't touch on the other side (the logical side). Peabody and Goldberg say when both sides are measured, they merge, thus supporting the idea that this factor is really intellect. McCrae and Costa (1987) disagree, and argue that intelligence may simply provide a basis for a broader sense of openness (see also John, 1990). The concept of openness to experience is less established in psychology than the concept of intelligence. However, McCrae (1996) has reviewed a wide range of ways in which this quality is relevant to social experience, suggesting that it may be more important than most people realize.

The Five-Factor Model in Relation to Other Models

As we said a bit earlier, the five-factor model of personality has important similarities to elements of several other trait models. Because theorists sometimes focus on less than the full picture of personality, other models often have fewer than five components. Yet the components that they do have often resemble elements of the five-factor model.

The easiest comparison is to Eysenck's theory. It's obvious from Table 4.3 that two of the five factors resemble Eysenck's supertraits, extraversion and emotional stability. It's also been suggested that Eysenck's third dimension, psychoticism, is a blending of the characteristics that contribute in other data sets to the factors of agreeableness and conscientiousness (Goldberg, 1993a; Zuckerman, Kuhlman, Joireman, Teta, & Kraft, 1993).

A second comparison to Eysenck is also noteworthy. Although we haven't emphasized it until now, the five factors are generally viewed as superordinate traits, incorporating narrower traits. For example, Paul Costa and Robert McCrae's (1985, 1992) NEO Personality Inventory (NEO-PI) includes measures of six narrow traits for each domain of the five-factor model (NEO stands for neuroticism, extraversion, and openness). The six traits are combined into a score for that factor. Thus, people using the five-factor model share with Eysenck the assumption that the important traits are supertraits, which in turn are composed of more specific facet traits.

Another useful comparison is with the interpersonal circle of Wiggins and his colleagues. Again there are similarities to aspects of the five-factor model. The basic dimensions in the interpersonal circle are dominance and love (agreeableness). If dominance is taken as roughly equivalent to the first factor of the big five, then the interpersonal circle would seem to comprise the first two factors of the five-factor model. This, at least, is the conclusion reached by Peabody and Goldberg (1989) and by McCrae and Costa (1989b). Trapnell and Wiggins (1990) have recently expanded the interpersonal measure to include additional scales, providing an even better fit to the five-factor model (see also Saucier, 1992).

Once again, though, a question arises as to whether the first factor of the big five is dominance and assertiveness or whether it's more properly viewed as extraversion. As noted earlier (Figure 4.3), Wiggins sees extraversion as a combination of qualities in the interpersonal circle, rather than as a basic dimension (some of this tone appears in some versions of the five-factor model as well).

Another theoretical approach mentioned earlier was based on folk concepts. Gough (1987) factor analyzed the folk-concept scales and obtained four factors. These factors, in Gough's view, resemble four of the components of the five-factor model (although emotionality merges with other qualities, rather than forming a factor of its own). McCrae, Costa, and Piedmont (1993) concluded from additional research that there are good links from the CPI to the five-factor model, except for agreeableness. This seems to provide yet one more indication of the possible ubiquity of the five factors.

In sum, the five-factor model of the structure of personality has emerged as a candidate to integrate a variety of earlier conceptual models. The data now available make this set of broad traits look very much as though they represent universal domains of personality (McCrae & Costa, 1997). Keep in mind that what comes out of a factor analysis depends on what goes into it. It can be dangerous to draw solid conclusions too quickly. At present, however, the five-factor model seems to offer the best promise of a consensus on the dimensions of personality that trait psychology has yet seen.

Further Variations

Consensus is not the same as unanimity, however. A number of people have offered dissenting opinions (e.g., Eysenck, 1992, 1993; Zuckerman, 1992), which have a variety of focuses (for a review of issues that go beyond the points made here, see Block, 1995, and the articles following it). One dissenting opinion asserts that previous work using the lexical approach omitted an important set of words that *shouldn't* have been omitted—words that are strictly evaluative (e.g., excellent, evil). When these words are included, two more factors emerge: *positive valence* and *negative valence* (Almagor, Tellegen, & Waller, 1995; Benet & Waller, 1995). Maybe, then, it should be the "big seven" instead of the "big five."

One more point that's been made about the five-factor model is that it appears to be possible to distill it further, into two dimensions (Digman, 1997). That is, using the five factors as data for a higher-order analysis yields two higher-order factors. The first factor is defined by agreeableness, conscientiousness, and emotional stability. Digman characterized it as reflecting *socialization,* because all these qualities influence whether people get along in social units. The second factor is defined by extraversion (or surgency) and intellect (or openness). Digman characterized it as reflecting *personal growth,* because these qualities influence whether people expose themselves to new things, thereby fostering growth.

These characterizations are provocative, suggesting important functions behind these clusters of traits. This picture of why these traits are important may be worth keeping in mind, as you read about other approaches to personality in later chapters.

Are Superordinate Traits the Best Level to Use?

There remains one more question about the five-factor model that should receive attention. It stems from the fact that this is a model of superordinate traits. Measures of these supertraits often incorporate facets traits within them. For example, as noted earlier, Costa and McCrae's NEO-PI has measures of six different facets of each of the factors of the model. Those who use the five-factor model sometimes emphasize the utility of examining patterns of traits within each factor (Costa & McCrae, 1995; Goldberg, 1993b), but this isn't always done.

This raises the question of whether anything is lost when lower-level traits are combined with each other to create the supertraits. This is essentially the same question as Cattell asked of Eysenck when the two disagreed over the meaning of the second-order factors (see also Briggs, 1989; Carver, 1989; H. Cattell, 1993; Funder, 1991; John, 1990). The question hasn't received much attention thus far, but the evidence seems to suggest that something is indeed lost when separate scales are merged.

For example, Mershon and Gorsuch (1988) reexamined the data from four studies relating the 16PF to real-life criteria (such as pay, job tenure, change in psychiatric status). In each case, they did a test in which the outcome variable was predicted from the 16 scales, and another in which the outcome variable was predicted from second-order factors. The two sets of analyses were compared, to see whether one accounted for more of the outcome variable than the other. In most cases, prediction from the 16 scales was better than prediction from second-order factors. In fact, the basic scales accounted for twice the variance in outcomes as did the composites.

Better prediction comes at a cost, though. Specifically, to understand those findings you have to hold 16 traits in mind at once instead of six. In general terms, here's the tradeoff: Using supertraits creates a picture that's more intuitive and easier to hold in mind. Using the narrower traits may produce greater accuracy (see also Paunonen, 1998; Wolfe & Kasmer, 1988).

Traits, Situations, and Interactionism

The trait approach to personality was the subject of an important controversy over a period of two decades, from about 1970 to about 1990 (for a different theoretical controversy, see Box 4.2). The ways researchers reacted to this controversy had a strong impact on today's trait psychology, although this impact is separate from anything we've discussed thus far.

Is Behavior Actually Traitlike?

The issue that shook the foundations of trait theory in the early 1970s concerns whether behavior actually does show traitlike consistency. That is, traits are assumed to be *stable* aspects of personality that influence behavior in a *wide range of settings*. The reason for believing in traits in the first place was to account for consistency in people's thoughts and actions across time and circumstances. It follows that differences on a trait should predict differences in trait-related behaviors.

It was somewhat surprising, then, that such measures often didn't correlate well (Mischel, 1968; P. E. Vernon, 1964). Walter Mischel (1968) coined the phrase **personality coefficient** to characterize the modest correlations between trait self-reports and behavior, which he said typically fell in the range of .20 to .30. This range of correlation means that the trait accounts for less than 10% of the variation in the behavior, with the remaining 90% unaccounted for. Later estimates ranged a little higher (Nisbett, 1980, suggested a correlation of .40). Even so, the proportion of variance accounted for isn't all that high.

What, then, are we to think about traits? If traits don't predict people's actions, then why should the trait concept be considered useful? (Indeed, some people went so far as to ask why the concept of *personality* should be considered useful.)

Situationism

An extreme form of the attack on traits was termed **situationism.** This is the idea that situational variables matter more than personality in determining how people act. This view is often identified with social psychologists, who traditionally emphasize the impact of the social environment rather than personality as a determinant of actions.

The situational approach was a first reaction to the low correlations between traits and behavior. As is true of many first reactions, it was too simple. That is, many people assumed that correlations between traits and behavior were low because situational variables were overwhelming the effect of personality. This turned out to be quite wrong.

Funder and Ozer (1983) pointed out that effects of situations and effects of traits usually are reported with different kinds of statistics. This makes it hard to compare the effects with one another. They returned to several famous studies of situational variables on behavior and converted the original statistics to correlations To the surprise of many, these correlations were *just about the same size* as the personality coefficients that had been criticized so sharply.

Low Reliability in Measurement of Behavior

Seymour Epstein (1979, 1980) responded to the criticism of traits by arguing that the apparent problem really isn't a problem. It's an issue of measurement. He pointed out that measurement error can be large when something is measured only once. That's

BOX 4.2

THEORETICAL CONTROVERSY:
Is Personality in the Person or in the Mind of the Observer?

Trait theorists assume that traits are the building blocks of personality, the best way to account for consistency in behavior. There is, however, a body of thought that calls into question the very existence of traits.

As indicated elsewhere in this chapter, factor analytic studies of personality have yielded a consistent pattern of factors over many studies of self-reports and observer ratings. The fact that these factors emerge over and over is one reason personality psychologists believe the factors reflect the basic structure of personality.

A simple but striking finding, however, questions the meaning of this picture. The finding first occurred in a study in which students made ratings of other students on personality scales (Passini & Norman, 1966). So far, this is like any other study of personality using observer ratings. The students in this study, however, were completely unacquainted with each other. They'd never even *spoken* to one another. They were told to imagine what the other person was like. Factor analysis of the ratings yielded a factor structure nearly identical to those from other studies using the same set of scales for self-ratings.

This finding raises an intriguing question. Does the structure revealed by factor analyses reside in *personality*? Or does it reside in the minds of the people making the ratings? Findings such as this have led some to suggest that factor analyses of personality scales tell us more about cognitive processes than about personality (D'Andrade, 1974; Shweder, 1982). The argument goes as follows: If there's a semantic connection between words (between *sincere* and *kind* or between *aggressive* and *masculine*), raters assume a *behavioral* association between the qualities the words refer to (Shweder, 1975). In reality, the behavioral qualities

may be unrelated. Thus a personality factor may emerge in ratings when none exists in reality.

In this view, people develop a set of assumptions about the structure of personality, which they apply uncritically when they make judgments about other people. This pattern of assumed associations is termed an **implicit personality theory** (Bruner & Tagiuri, 1954; Schneider, 1973; Sternberg, 1985). It's often suggested that once people know of one trait a person has, they use their implicit theories to infer other traits (e.g., Berman & Kenny, 1976).

This criticism has not gone unanswered by trait theorists. The studies on which critics based their strongest assertions (D'Andrade, 1974; Shweder, 1975) have been challenged on methodological grounds (Block, Weiss, & Thorne, 1979, but see Shweder & D'Andrade, 1979, for a reply). Another study found that the pattern of trait ratings stayed the same even under procedures to prevent subjects from relying on semantic similarities (Weiss & Mendelsohn, 1986). There's also evidence that self-reports correlate well with raters' reports (McCrae & Costa, 1989c), and that certain aspects of personality can be picked up on quickly (Watson, 1989), even from nonverbal cues (Borkenau & Liebler, 1992, 1993). These findings seem to indicate that the dimensions of personality aren't just in the minds of the raters.

The issues in this debate are complex (see Kenrick & Funder, 1988). For now, let us simply say that the matter is not yet completely resolved. Whenever measurement requires interpretation, there's a potential for distortion. Yet only people can observe psychological qualities in other people. This creates a problem of interpretation that's hard to avoid.

why personality scales use more than one item to assess whatever they're measuring—to increase reliability (Chapter 3). But people pay less attention to this issue when they measure behavior. A single measurement of a person's action is, in effect, a one-item test. Maybe correlations are poor because of the error in the one-item test.

Epstein argued that correlations between personality measures and behavior would be stronger if the behavior was measured more than once and the measures combined, a process called **aggregation.** In a test of this reasoning (Epstein, 1979), participants completed personality scales, then kept detailed records of relevant feelings and behaviors for 2 weeks. The feelings and actions varied a lot from day to day, but differences between people became quite stable when condensed over a longer period. More important, the condensed indices (but not the separate measures) were closely related to the personality qualities measured earlier. Similar findings have been reported by others (Cheek, 1982; Rushton, Brainerd, & Pressley, 1983).

There's a good deal of stability in behavior, then, once it's aggregated across measurements. This approach has not always been well received, though (e.g., Mischel & Peake, 1982; see Epstein, 1986, for a reply). Most relevant here is that when people think of consistency, they're usually thinking of consistency across day-to-day events. If traits really do have a big influence on behavior, you shouldn't have to condense a week's worth of events to be able to see it. Even while Epstein pointed out a lot of consistency in the long run (see also Box 4.3), he was also implying there's little consistency in the short run.

Interactionism

Another approach to this problem has been termed **interactionism** (e.g., Ekehammer, 1974; Endler & Magnusson, 1976; Magnusson & Endler, 1977; Ozer, 1986; Pervin, 1985). Interactionism is the idea that personality traits and situations interact with each other to influence behavior. Neither the setting alone nor the person alone provides a complete account.

The term *interactionism* is tied in part to an "analysis of variance" understanding of how two variables (or in this case, two classes of variables) influence an outcome. To make this clear, we return to an idea from Chapter 2. We described there how experimental personality research often combines two variables as factors in a single study. We now restate that point, but in terms of people and situations.

When a situation and a trait are examined in the same study, there are three systematic sources of influence on behavior. Sometimes variations in the *situation* have an overall effect—for example, stressful situations may induce depression. Sometimes variations on a *trait* have an overall effect—for example, people who are susceptible to depression may be generally more depressed than people who are less susceptible. It's also possible, however, for the situation and trait to *interact* (Figure 4.4).

FIGURE 4.4

Sometimes there is an interaction between a situation and a trait variable, such that variations in the situation affect some people but not others. This particular interaction is one that has, in fact, been hypothesized by Abramson, Seligman, and Teasdale (1978). The type of interaction displayed here is only one type of interaction between people and situations (see text).

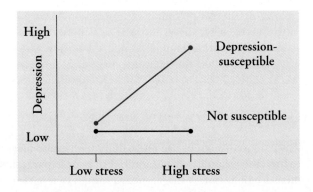

BOX 4.3

HOW STABLE IS PERSONALITY OVER *LONG* PERIODS OF TIME?

Discussions of consistency in personality usually focus on relatively short periods or across a few situations. Another kind of consistency implied by the trait concept is stability over long periods. As we consider consistency in behavior, we should also ask what evidence there is that people's personalities themselves are the same years later as they were earlier.

Researchers have addressed this question using several measures of personality. Helson and Moane (1987) reported on women who were first studied as college seniors, then at age 27, and again at age 43. One measure collected was the CPI. During the span from ages 21 to 27, eight CPI scales showed test-retest correlations of better than .50 (the other two were .49 and .39). During the span from 27 to 43, seven scales correlated at .50 or better (the other three ranged from .40 to .48). It's clear that the women changed some over the years—becoming more dominant and independent from age 27 to age 43. There was also evidence that those with the most change were those who'd begun families or had career development during this period. The authors noted that this is just what one would expect, since both activities produced changing role demands, which caused shifts in how the women saw themselves. Subsequent assessment at age 52 (Wink & Helson, 1993) found that the change toward more competence and self-confidence also continued over the next 9 years (see also Agronick & Duncan, 1998).

The idea that some people's personalities shift more than other people's is also confirmed in other studies (Block, 1971; Ozer & Gjerde, 1989). This research adopted "person-centered" methods of examining stability, that is, looking at the pattern within each person one at a time across the period of the study. These procedures reveal that some people remain quite stable over extensive periods, whereas others experience relatively large and abrupt changes. It's not clear, though, what determines which pattern a person displays.

Another project focused on two fairly specific qualities of childhood personality—shyness and temper—and how they predict adult behavior (Caspi, Elder, & Bem, 1987, 1988). The study started with mothers of 8- to 10-year-old children talking about what the children were like. The children themselves were interviewed when they were 30 and 40, along with their spouses and their own children. The interviews revealed that boys with frequent temper tantrums in childhood grew up to be ill-tempered men. Girls with frequent tantrums didn't look that way when interviewed later, but their *families* saw them as ill-tempered mothers. Effects of childhood shyness also occurred in later life. Shy boys were married later and were slower to establish stable careers than the less shy. Shy girls weren't slower to marry but were more likely to follow a conventional pattern of family and homemaking than were less-shy girls.

It's apparent from these studies that aspects of personality can remain fairly consistent over long periods, despite pressures from the person's environment. Indeed, this stability appears to be even greater during the person's adult years than earlier (Costa & McCrae, 1988b, 1989; McCrae, 1993). This kind of consistency is one more reason to believe that traits are real.

An interaction means that variations in situation affect some people in one way and affect others in a different way. For example, stress may cause an increase in depression among those who are prone to depression but not among others. This interaction may occur in addition to one or both of the overall effects, or it may occur *instead of* them, thereby creating a picture of weak overall effects for both the trait and the situation.

Some situations act to constrain behavior and hide individual differences. Other situations allow personality free expression.

In this "analysis of variance" account, situations and dispositions can interact in several ways to determine behavior. Perhaps most obvious (the case shown in Figure 4.4) is that a situation may have an impact on one kind of person but not others (stress influences depression-prone people but not others). Sometimes a situational variable induces one behavior in one kind of person and a *different* behavior in another kind of person. For example, a stressful situation may cause extraverts to seek out others and cause introverts to withdraw from others.

Another way to describe interactions between person and situation (which creates a different sense of what the interaction is) is to say that some situations permit an easy expression of personality, whereas other situations force behavior into specific channels, thus preventing expression of personality (Monson, Hesley, & Chernick, 1982; Schutte, Kenrick, & Sadalla, 1985). The first are termed *weak* situations, the second *strong* situations (Mischel, 1977). As an example, the lawns and

Knowing that someone likes active sports may tell us little about whether the person prefers tennis to swimming.

walks of a college campus on a Sunday afternoon constitute a weak situation, letting individual differences be expressed easily. An army boot camp is a strong situation, which dampens the expression of individual differences.

Individual Differences in Consistency

Apparently dispositions are also strong and weak (in the same sense). That is, some people are very consistent (overwhelming the situations they're in), others are less so (letting situational influences guide them). This has been shown in several ways.

Some of the evidence pertains to the construct of self-monitoring (Snyder, 1974, 1987). People high in self-monitoring like to fit smoothly into whatever situation they encounter. They look to others for cues about what actions are appropriate, and they accommodate to the needs of the situation. People low in self-monitoring behave the way they think they *are*. It follows that the behavior of high self-monitors should be less consistent from one situation to another than the behavior of low self-monitors. This turns out to be true (see Snyder, 1987).

The idea that people vary in their consistency regarding *specific* traits has also been studied. Bem and Allen (1974) found that people who saw themselves as inconsistent on a trait acted in ways that were not well predicted by their trait self-reports. Among those who said they were very consistent, however, the self-reports predicted their actions quite well. Similar results have been reported by several others (Kenrick & Stringfield, 1980; Woodruffe, 1985; Zuckerman et al., 1989; Zuckerman, Koestner, et al., 1988).

Beyond Analysis of Variance in Interactionism

The body of thought known as interactionism also has additional aspects. The analysis of variance model derives from lab research, a context in which researchers place people into identical situations. It tends to imply that people outside the lab also enter identical situations.

This assumption, of course, is wrong—a point made by a number of researchers (e.g., D. M. Buss, 1984; Emmons & Diener, 1986; Emmons, Diener, & Larsen, 1986; Magnus, Diener, Fujita, & Pavot, 1993; Plomin, DeFries, & Loehlin, 1977; Scarr & McCartney, 1983; Snyder & Gangestad, 1982). In life outside the lab (and rarely, but occasionally, even in the lab, see Gormly, 1983), people exercise considerable choice over which environments they enter.

Some people choose to go to church, others choose not to. Some people choose to go to basketball games, some to rock concerts, some to country meadows. By exercising choice over the settings they enter, people thereby influence the behaviors they display. Indeed, there's even evidence that people choose their *marriage partners* partly by whether the partner lets them be who they are (Caspi & Herbener, 1990). Because the choices that people make about which situations to enter depend partly on personality differences (Brandstätter, 1983; Emmons & Diener, 1986; Emmons et al., 1986), choosing situations represents a kind of interaction between person and situation.

Another way persons and situations interact is that people differ in the kinds of responses they bring out in others (Scarr & McCartney, 1983). Some people naturally bring a smile to your face, others can make you frown just by entering the room. Introverts tend to steer conversations in one direction, extraverts in another (Thorne, 1987). Indeed, people actively manipulate each other, using such tactics as charm, coercion, and the silent treatment (Buss, Gomes, Higgins, & Lauterbach, 1987). Being in various social roles causes different aspects of our personalities to emerge (Donahue & Harary, 1998). All these effects of people serve to change the situation, so *the situation is different for one person than for another.* This reciprocal influence is another way persons and situations interact.

Was the Problem Ever Really as Bad as it Seemed?

The various attempts to understand poor prediction from trait to behavior have provided a wealth of information about how the two relate. We should note, however, that some doubt has also arisen that poor prediction was ever as bad a problem as it seemed to be.

After Mischel (1968) said that personality correlated with behavior around .30, others pointed out that the studies leading to that conclusion weren't really the best of studies (Block, 1977; Hogan, DeSoto, & Solano, 1977). This argument seems to have had some truth to it. More recent studies (e.g., Conley, 1985; Deluty, 1985; Funder & Block, 1989; Funder & Colvin, 1991; Moskowitz, 1994; Woodruffe, 1985) found much stronger relationships than those Mischel had summarized.

There also turn out to be statistical reasons why a correlation of .30 isn't really so bad. Many actions are influenced by more than one trait. For example, when you get to a party where you don't know anyone, what you'll do will probably depend on how extraverted you are, but it will also depend on how anxiety prone you are. As it happens, whenever a behavior is influenced by several traits at once, the *mere fact of multiple influence* places limitations on how strong a correlation can be for a single trait (Ahadi & Diener, 1989). This limit looks, in fact, very nearly the same as the much maligned personality coefficient.

Maybe the core problem really wasn't ever as bad as it seemed to be in 1968. But the work aimed at addressing the problem has been very informative about how behavior works. Indeed, this work has led many people to hold a more elaborated view of the trait construct than they might otherwise hold. We consider an example of such a view in the next section.

Interactionism Extended: Context-Dependent Expression of Personality

Psychologists put a lot of effort into developing the ideas known as interactionism. People outside the lab, however, seem naturally to approach traits with what seems an interactionist mentality. That is, people seem to recognize intuitively that whether a trait influences behavior varies from setting to setting. A given trait shouldn't be expected to operate all the time—only in situations to which it's relevant.

Why do we think people think this way? Because in discussing personality they often use verbal "hedges" (Wright & Mischel, 1988). A hedge, in this case, is a word or phrase that limits a trait's applicability. As examples, you might describe someone as being "shy *with strangers*" or "aggressive *when teased.*" The ultimate hedge for traits is the word *sometimes*. Use of a hedge implies you think the trait-based behaviors occur only in particular kinds of situations (see also Shoda, Mischel, & Wright, 1989).

Such evidence, along with the insights of interactionism more generally, have led Mischel and Shoda (1995) to a more elaborated analysis of how traits influence behavior (see also Cervone, 1997). They argued that traits represent patterns of situation–behavior linkages. These linkages are different from one person to another. The key to individuality is the pattern of situation–behavior linkages the person has established over time and experience. Even if two people tend toward the same kind of behavior, the situations that elicit that behavior may be very different from one person to the other. The people act differently, even though they have the same trait.

The tendency to do that particular kind of behavior is a trait. But the linking of the behavior to classes of situations does two things that influence the trait's impact. First, this pattern of links creates a uniqueness to the trait's expression (this, in fact, may be a mechanism for the existence of idiographic traits). Second, this linkage means that the behavior in question won't always be displayed, because the situation won't always be present.

We noted earlier that aggregating behavior across time creates better correspondence between personality self-reports and behavior (Epstein, 1979, 1980). The error of measurement is reduced when the acts are aggregated. This observation left many people wondering about the *source* of that short-term measurement error. Is it random, or can it be identified and accounted for? Mischel and Shoda's (1995) position is that it's not random at all. It comes from the fact that the behavior is context-dependent. The behavior emerges only when you encounter a relevant situation. The context may not be there every day, but if you aggregate over a long enough period, it will show up eventually, and the trait-related behavior will occur.

This view seems to deal well with some problems people have had in thinking about traits. It doesn't really distort the trait concept, though it adds something to the concept as it was discussed in the first part of this chapter. The Mischel and Shoda view has elements that we'll discuss more thoroughly in Chapter 16. For now, the point is that the impact of traits seems to be context-dependent. This conclusion is very much an interactionist view of personality.

Older and Contemporary Views of Traits and Behavior

If you had read only the first half of this chapter, you might have been tempted to think that trait theorists hold the view in Figure 4.5, panel A or B, in which traits have a *constant* influence on behavior. Theorists who discuss the five-factor model tend not to talk much about how traits and situations interact, and it can be easy to get such a misimpression from their statements.

FIGURE 4.5

Three different models of the effects of traits on behavior (portrayed using the trait of gregariousness). (A) A naive model, in which people are assumed to display their traits at a relatively constant level, no matter what situation they are in (what Magnusson & Endler, 1977, called absolute consistency). (B) A model in which situations influence the *overall* levels at which the trait is displayed, but people retain the same ordering in what they display (relative consistency). (C) An interactionist model, in which some situations (2 and 4) permit or even elicit individual differences, whereas others (1 and 3) don't do so.

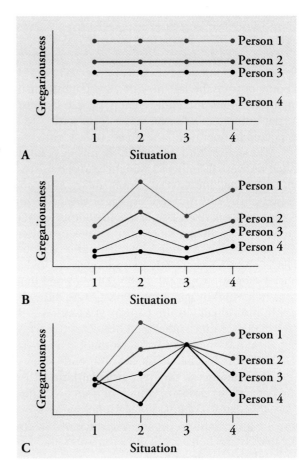

But traits don't really work that way. The kind of work described in the previous sections makes that clear. Rather, traits sometimes influence behavior a lot, and sometimes not at all. Whether the trait matters depends on the situation (Figure 4.5, C). People also display traits by choosing and influencing situations, not just by reacting to situations forced on them. This dynamic approach to understanding the role of traits in the constantly varying social environment recognizes complexities in the creation of behavior.

This picture is certainly more compelling than the simpler ones. But interestingly enough, the core idea is not really all that new. At least some trait theorists of earlier years said much the same thing. They just didn't say it in as much detail as it's being said today.

As early as 1937 Gordon Allport wrote that "traits are often aroused in one situation and not in another" (p. 331). His conception of a trait explicitly included the assumption that the trait doesn't influence all behaviors and may not influence a given category of behavior at all times (see Zuroff, 1986). Rather, the effect of the trait depends on whether it's evoked in that situation. Allport even believed that people have *contradictory* traits, and that what keeps this from being a problem is that the different traits are aroused by different situations. Allport also anticipated another contemporary theme, when he pointed out that people choose the situations they enter and actively change the situations they're in (Zuroff, 1986). Thus, the essence of the ideas that would become known as interactionism has a considerable history.

Assessment

More than is true of most viewpoints on personality, the trait approach focuses a great deal on the process of assessment. Indeed, the first part of this chapter incorporated a discussion of how various theorists developed assessment instruments. In this section we consider briefly how the instruments are used.

Comparing Individuals: Personality Profiles

The trait approach makes extensive use of self-report inventories as an assessment technique. These self-reports ask people to describe their view of themselves by making ratings of one kind or another. The most common ratings involve indicating whether a descriptive adjective applies to you or not, or where on a dimension (anchored by opposing adjectives) you'd fall, or whether you agree with a set of statements. The ratings may be made as yes-no or agree-disagree decisions, or they may be made on multipoint scales.

Recall that traits are thought of as fundamental qualities of personality, reflected in diverse behaviors. For this reason, self-reports of traits usually include ratings for several reflections of each trait being measured. A test using adjectives would have several adjectives for each trait; a questionnaire made up of statements would include statements suggesting diverse ways the trait might be expressed.

Regardless of the exact form of the inventory, the nomothetic version of trait psychology assumes that anyone can be placed somewhere along whatever trait dimensions are assessed. Inventories measuring these traits are used to create "profiles" of individuals. A personality profile is a summary description of a person's place on each trait dimension the inventory measures (Figure 4.6). Knowing the dimensions and the person's place on each can create a sense of what the person is like and how the person is likely to behave in a variety of situations.

The profile in Figure 4.6 illustrates the kind of information a personality inventory gives. At first glance, a profile can seem like nothing more than a string of beads (Allport once said that's exactly what these profiles are, 1961). Perhaps a better comparison, suggested by one of our students, is a bar code, like the ones supermarkets use to identify an almost infinite variety of products. Nomothetic theorists believe that the profile is where individual uniqueness lies. You can see from Figure 4.6 that a shift on any single trait changes the balance of a person's characteristics. It can thereby change how the person will act in various settings and how the person will seem to someone else. Since everyone has a unique combination of levels of traits, everyone is different from everyone else.

That isn't the whole story, though. Most trait theorists believe traits can *interact* with one another. To put it differently, how a given level of a trait is expressed may differ from person to person, as a function of where the two people are on other traits. For example, two adventuresome people may display their boldness differently as a function of how sociable they are. The highly sociable one may engage in exciting and risky interpersonal exchanges, whereas the less sociable one may climb mountains. Thus, a given trait quality can be reflected in unique ways

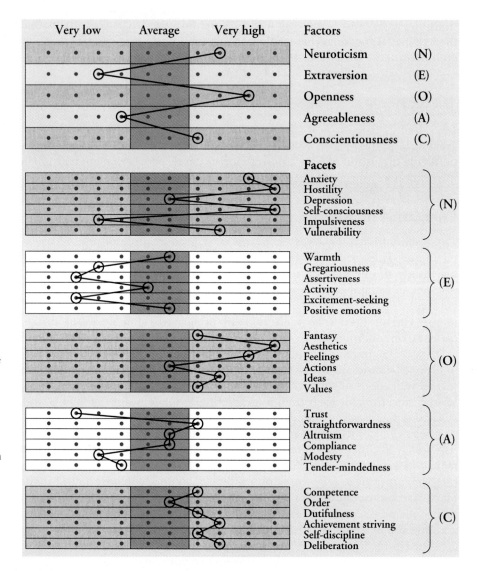

FIGURE 4.6

An illustration of a personality profile, adapted from the NEO-PI-R. The NEO-PI-R provides both an overall profile of the five major factors (top portion), and a profile of the facets within each of the "big five" (lower portion). The top profile provides a quick and simple summary for the person's personality, the other provides a more detailed picture. Reproduced by special permission of the Publisher, Psychological Assessment Resources, Inc., Odessa, FL, from the *NEO Personality Inventory*–Revised, by P. T. Costa, Jr., and R. R. McCrae. Copyright 1978, 1985, 1989, 1992 by PAR, Inc. Further reproduction is prohibited without permission of PAR, Inc.

for each person because of the modifying effect of differences on *other* traits (recall our earlier discussion of extraversion and emotionality). This is true even though the trait dimensions themselves are the same from one person to another.

Problems in Behavior, and Behavior Change

The trait approach to personality hasn't had much to say over the decades about problems in personality or the process of therapy. This is a little ironic, since the trait approach was the starting point for some of the earliest efforts to assess disorder. Those efforts were based on the assumption that problems directly reflect a person's traits. Differences among categories of problems reflect the fact that each trait (or group of traits) relates to a different kind of problem.

The attempt to understand psychopathology from this trait-based point of view was largely an attempt to categorize it. Categorizing, in turn, was a matter of determining the **signs** (trait indicators) in people's behavior that relate to a given class of problem. This process led to a taxonomy for identifying and labeling problems (Wiggins, 1973), which has been revised several times.

The taxonomy provides a set of categories in which to place people, but not much more. It amounts to little more than saying certain kinds of traits are tied to certain kinds of problems. This association can occur in two ways. First, a person may be at an extreme on a dimension, rather than nearer the middle of the range. Just being so deviant or unusual can potentially create problems, no matter what the trait is.

Other traits relate to problems because the trait *defines* abnormality. As mentioned earlier in the chapter, Eysenck's model includes a dimension termed psychoticism. Psychoticism is a predisposition toward certain psychological disorders. Since people vary in psychoticism, they vary in the degree to which they can be expected to display symptoms of disorder.

The emerging influence of the five-factor model of personality has led to a renewed interest in the patterns of traits associated with personality disorders (see Watson & Clark, 1994). Using measures of personality problems that were developed independent of the five-factor model, Wiggins and Pincus (1989) found that the five factors were well represented in the measures of pathology. A similar conclusion has been reached by Costa and McCrae (1990). A broader treatment of how the five-factor model relates to a range of personality problems was published by Costa and Widiger (1994). This area of work would seem to be an important focus for further exploration in future years by proponents of the five-factor model.

Interactionism in Behavior Problems

As described earlier in the chapter, the idea that traits are reflected directly in overt behavior was challenged two decades ago, resulting in a more elaborate position, termed interactionism. The logic of interactionism has been useful not just for understanding normal behavior, but also for understanding problems.

A basic idea of interactionism is that individual differences are important in some situations but not in others. As applied to problems, the idea takes on slightly different connotations. The connotations are easiest to understand if you think of a trait as a *vulnerability* or *susceptibility* to a problem. Saying a person is susceptible to a problem doesn't mean that the person has the problem. It means the problem will occur more easily for this person than for someone else. To put it in terms of interactionism, there are situations in which the susceptibility matters and others in which it doesn't.

The situations in which the susceptibility matters usually are those in which the person is under a lot of stress. Therefore, this approach to problems is called a **diathesis-stress model.** (The word *diathesis* means a predisposition or susceptibility.) In this model, an interaction is required between the diathesis and some stress before the problem will become manifest (Meehl, 1962). In recent years, diathesis-stress models have been especially prominent in thinking about the processes underlying depression (e.g., Abramson, Seligman, & Teasdale, 1978; Peterson & Seligman, 1984).

Behavior Change

What of the process of therapeutic behavior change? The trait approach is inherently a little pessimistic about such change. If traits define a person's personality, how much can problems be resolved without changing the person's personality? Traits are stable. Any change that therapy produces is likely to be in how traits are displayed in behavior, rather than in the traits themselves.

Even a person prone to experiencing fear will not experience fear unless a fear-producing situation is encountered.

On the other hand, the interactionist approach also has an implication regarding this issue. If problems arise through an interaction between susceptibilities and difficult situations, it should be helpful for the susceptible person to avoid entering situations in which the relevant stresses are likely to occur. Avoiding such situations should prevent the problems from arising.

This, of course, is something that people often do on their own. As we said earlier in the chapter, people exercise some degree of control over the situations they choose to enter. Just as some people choose to go to church and some do not, some people choose to avoid situations in which their vulnerabilities place them at risk. Shy people may avoid singles bars. People with short tempers may try to avoid arguments. Avoidance as a strategy isn't always possible. Yet if people learn which stressors they can and cannot handle, this knowledge should make them more effective in managing their lives.

Trait Psychology: Problems and Prospects

The trait view is in many respects the most basic approach to personality that ever existed. The very concepts of type and trait arose literally thousands of years ago, to account for consistency in behavior across time and circumstances. The concepts have been elaborated and embellished over the years, but in some ways their core has remained the same.

Although the trait view on personality is the most basic, some people find it unsatisfying. It's been criticized on several grounds in recent years (for opinions on both sides, see Pervin, 1994, and the commentaries that follow it). One problem is that trait theories have had extraordinarily little to say about how personality works (Block, 1995) or how it influences behavior, how the person gets from trait to action (Pervin, 1994).

To put it differently, the trait approach has little to say about intrapersonal functioning, resulting in a picture of personality that feels static and empty. McAdams (1992) called trait psychology the "psychology of the stranger," because it provides information that you'd need to know if you knew nothing about people yet, but it doesn't go farther in portraying the dynamic aspects of personality. Labeling a person as friendly, or sociable, or dominant provides a name for what you see. But it doesn't tell you anything about how or why the person acts that way. This is one major criticism of the trait concept.

The idea that the trait viewpoint says little about the process side of personality is often made jointly with a second, related criticism. This second criticism is that trait theories sometimes resort to circular explanation in trying to deal with causality. As an example, imagine a woman who acts in a dominant manner—not just occasionally, but often; not just in one situation, or with one set of people, but in many situations, with whoever else is around. You might be tempted to conclude from this that she has a high level of the trait of dominance.

But that can be a hollow conclusion. Ask yourself two questions and think about your natural responses. Question: Why does she behave that way? (Answer: Because she's dominant.) Question: How do you know she's dominant? (Answer: Because she behaves that way.) The problem here is that the information about behavior is being used to infer the existence of a trait, which is being used in turn to explain the behavior. This is called circular reasoning, because it can go around and around in an endless circle. There's no point here at which the presumed trait is used to predict anything but the evidence that was used to hypothesize it initially. The circularity can be broken if the trait is used to predict something new, and sometimes trait theorists do this. However, this view on personality is more vulnerable than most to the criticism of circularity.

A third criticism that's sometimes made of the trait view is that its decisions about what personality dimensions are important to measure and study are arbitrary. The factor analytic approach is defensible (the more variance accounted for in people's ratings, the more important a trait is). The lexical approach is also defensible (the more words there are that refer to a trait, the more important that trait must be). Other approaches have their own appeal—Eysenck's use of the observations of ancient scholars, Gough's study of folk concepts. Each of these bases for deciding, though, is arbitrary.

A reasonable reply is that there is always some arbitrariness in deciding what dimensions personality consists of, no matter which view you adopt. There's no particular reason why theorists with other views have a better basis for deciding which traits are basic. Furthermore, it's quite striking that many psychologists working in the trait tradition—using very different conceptual starting points and different measures—have arrived at similar conclusions about what constitute the basic dimensions of personality. This fact lends additional credence to the importance of those dimensions.

A final problem with the trait perspective, discussed earlier but worth restating, concerns the issue of consistency. As we just noted, the concepts of trait psychology were developed to account for stability in behavior across time and situations. The discovery that people's behavior sometimes fails to display this consistency created a crisis of confidence among trait theorists. Although there have been many creative and thoughtful responses to this discovery, the issue continues to pose a challenge to the concepts and assumptions of trait psychology.

Ironically, that challenge provided one impetus to a revitalization of work within the trait viewpoint. This "problem" thus also served as a basis for a favorable "prospect" for this viewpoint. There has been a growing awareness among trait theorists that to view traits as having a constant impact on behavior is too simple. This view has been replaced by approaches in which situational forces and the interaction between situations and dispositions are explicitly taken into account. These insights hold additional promise for the future of this approach.

A final point in support of the future of the trait approach is this: No matter how hard various people have tried over the years to dispense with the use of traits as explanatory mechanisms, the trait concept has retained an active place in the working vocabulary of the personality psychologist. The long history of these concepts attests to their hardiness. Somehow it appears as though the personality psychologist needs them (A. H. Buss, 1989). The fact that they've endured the test of time seems to imply a fundamental correctness that is difficult to deny.

SUMMARY

The trait and type approach begins with the assumption that personality consists of stable inner qualities, which are reflected in behavior. Types are discontinuous categories of personalities, with each person falling into one category or another. This concept has largely disappeared from contemporary psychology. Traits are continuous dimensions of variability, along which any person can be placed. Most approaches are nomothetic—emphasizing how people differ but assuming that the trait dimensions are the same for everyone. The idiographic approach emphasizes persons' uniqueness and treats some dimensions as unique to specific persons.

Factor analysis is a tool used by many trait psychologists (and others). Factor analysis tells what items (or ratings, etc.) go together. Further, the more variability in ratings a factor accounts for, the more important the factor. Factor analysis also lets you tell which observations do and don't reflect a factor well, thus helping refine scales.

An important question in trait psychology is what traits are basic and important. Cattell, who believed we must let reality tell us the structure of personality, took an empirical approach. He saw personality as consisting of 16 dimensions. Eysenck, who believed we must start with a theory, saw two major factors as critically important in personality: extraversion and emotional stability. Other theoretical views have also been developed, including one that relies on folk concepts and one that emphasizes traits relevant to social interaction (the interpersonal circle).

More attention is increasingly being given to the idea that there are five major factors in personality. Evidence to that effect is mounting, and a relatively successful attempt has also been made to fit these five factors to the models of personality structure already mentioned. There is disagreement about the precise nature of the five factors, but commonly used labels for them are extraversion, agreeableness, conscientiousness, emotionality, and openness.

A question about the usefulness of the trait concept was raised by the finding that people's behavior often isn't well predicted from trait self-reports. The question is whether traits actually influence behavior. Situationism, the idea that behavior is controlled by situational influences instead of dispositions, was an inadequate alternative. The idea that individual differences in behavior become consistent over time if measurements are aggregated over several instances appears correct, but it implies that behavior is inconsistent over the short term. Interactionism holds that personality and situations interact with one another in several ways to determine behavior. For example, some situations permit or even elicit individual differences, whereas other situations don't. People also choose which situations to enter, and then they influence the nature of situations by their own actions. Indeed, people also vary in how consistent they are. Those who know they're inconsistent don't act consistently, those who say they are consistent act more consistently. The idea that the influence of traits on behavior is dependent on situations has also been extrapolated into a broader view of personality structure.

Personality assessment from the viewpoint of trait psychology is a matter of developing a personality profile of the person being assessed—a description of where the person falls on all the dimensions being measured by the inventory. To these psychologists, the profile holds the key to understanding the person's uniqueness.

The trait approach to personality focuses primarily on normal behavior. Trait theorists say that problems in behavior result either from having an extreme position on some trait dimension or from having a trait that is intrinsically problematic. The interactionist position suggests the following possibility (termed a diathesis-stress model): Certain dispositions may create a susceptibility to some kind of problem, but the problem occurs only under certain conditions, usually involving stress. Therapeutic behavior change, from the trait perspective, may mean changing how a trait is reflected in behavior, since a person's traits are not easily altered.

GLOSSARY

Aggregation The process of combining a variable across several measurements.

Diathesis-stress model A theory holding that a vulnerability plus stress creates problems in behavior.

Extravert A person who prefers social and outgoing activities.

Factor A dimension that underlies a set of interrelated ratings.

Factor analysis A statistical procedure used to find commonality across measurements.

Factor loading A correlation between a single measure and the factor to which it is being related.

Folk concept An aspect of interpersonal behavior common to every society and culture.

Idiographic Pertaining to an approach that focuses on an individual person's uniqueness.

Implicit personality theory The idea that people have implicit beliefs about which traits go together in personality.

Interactionism The idea that situations and personality interact to determine behavior.

Interpersonal circle Personality patterns deriving from varying levels of dominance and love.

Introvert A person who prefers solitary activities.

Lexical criterion An index of the importance of a trait based on the number of words that refer to it.

Metatrait The quality of possessing or not possessing a given trait.

Multivariate Pertaining to an analysis that takes into account several dimensions simultaneously.

Nomothetic Pertaining to an approach that focuses on norms and on variations among persons.

Personality coefficient A stereotypic correlation between personality and behavior of about .30.

Second-order factor A factor that merges two or more basic factors that correlate with each other.

Sign A trait indicator that is associated with a given category of psychopathology.

Situationism The idea that situations are the primary determinants of behavior.

Traits The dimensions of personality on which people vary.

Types Distinct and discontinuous categories of persons.

chapter

5

Needs and Motives

■ I'm in the pre-med program here, and I really want to get into a good medical school. The courses aren't that easy for me, so I have to study more than some people. I can't even take time off on weekends because I'm taking an extra heavy load. I don't mind, though, because I'm really motivated to go to med school, and that makes it worth the effort.

■ I've been going with my boyfriend for over two years now. I care for him a lot, really I do. But lately I've been wondering if this is really the right relationship for me. It's hard to describe what's wrong. It's not anything about *him*, exactly, but it's like the relationship isn't meeting my needs. I don't know how else to put it.

Think for a moment about the major concerns of your life. One issue that stands out as important in the minds of many college students is what to do after graduation. Some people have ambitions they're already pursuing full speed (as with the pre-med student quoted above). Others know they want to do *something*, and can tell you some qualities they want their work to have, but they aren't sure exactly what that work will be. To some people, on the other hand, what they'll do doesn't seem too big a deal one way or another.

Another topic that may occupy a place in your thoughts is your relationships. Some college-age people are in close relationships, thinking about marriage and trying to decide whether the person they're with is the right one for such a big commitment. Some don't have close attachments of this kind but wish they did. For some, having this kind of relationship is the most demanding issue of their lives. For others, it matters less.

These sets of concerns are probably familiar to you, because work and love as aspects of human existence are part of everyone's life. They aren't everything, of course, and some people have other things on their mind. Some are preoccupied with trying to find order and meaning in life's experiences. Some seek truth; some seek beauty. For others, what really matters isn't truth *or* beauty but having the laundry done, the kitchen clean, or new high-performance tires on their sport utility vehicle.

Looking at the concerns we've touched on here, you'll see a lot of diversity. Despite the diversity, these concerns (and others) have something in common. They imply the existence of needs and motives behind people's thoughts and actions. Think about how people describe their preoccupations. I *need* to find a lover. I *need* to have a direction for my future. I *want* to do well in school. I *need* to find a sense of purpose in life. I *want* to get caught up on my chores. I *need* to get an A on this test. For any aspect of life you might imagine, some people feel a deep need behind it, others feel it less.

The idea that needs and motives can influence people's thoughts and actions this way suggests that they are important. It might even be argued that they define who a person is. This idea forms the basis for the approach to personality that's examined in this chapter.

Basic Theoretical Elements

Needs

The fundamental principle of this approach is the idea that human behavior is best understood as a reflection of underlying needs. A **need** is an internal state that's less

BOX 5.1

THE THEORIST AND THE THEORY:
Henry Murray and Human Motives

The history of Henry Murray, the father of the motive view of personality, contains tantalizing suggestions about how his theory drew on his life's experiences, but clear links are harder to specify. Murray was born into a wealthy family in New York in 1893. He got on well with his father but had a poor relationship with his mother. He reports feeling that his mother gave him less attention than his sister and brother. The emotional separation he felt between his mother and himself created a deep-seated need to stand on his own, which became a central part of his personality. It's tempting to speculate that this experience led Murray to be especially aware of social needs, and may have led his thinking toward the idea that such needs are the underlying determinants of personality.

Murray's education was varied. Interestingly enough, however, none of it was in psychology (he disliked his only undergraduate psychology course). He majored in history, but shifted to biomedical studies. He finished medical school, got a master's degree in biology, completed an internship in surgery, and then a Ph.D. in biochemistry. A common thread past college was a focus on the biology of human functioning. This biological emphasis is also there in Murray's thinking about personality. As noted elsewhere, the ideas behind his theory are most easily illustrated by biological motives. Indeed, Murray believed that even psychological motives have biological roots.

Murray's medical background also influenced his approach to research. The program he led at the Harvard Psychological Clinic was very much a team approach. This seems to reflect the view that personality is best assessed by a team of specialists working together, much as a team of physicians collaborates on diagnosing patients.

A turning point in Murray's life occurred seven years into his marriage, when he met and fell in love with Christiana Morgan. This was a turning point in at least two ways. First, Murray was faced with a serious conflict. He didn't want to leave his wife, but neither did he want to give up his lover. He wanted both women in his life, which surely made Murray acutely aware of the conflicting pressures that differing motives exert on a person.

The experience was a turning point in a second way, as well. Morgan was fascinated by the psychology of Carl Jung. At Morgan's urging, Murray visited Jung in Switzerland. Jung, it turned out, was living in much the same situation as Murray, but with no discomfort. Jung's advice was to continue with both relationships, which Murray proceeded to do for 40 years (for biographies of Murray and Morgan, see Robinson, 1992, and Douglas, 1993). The experience of bringing a problem to a psychologist and receiving an answer that seemed to work had a great impact on Murray, leading him to seriously consider psychology as a career (J. W. Anderson, 1988). When given the opportunity to assist in founding the Harvard Psychological Clinic, which was being set up specifically to study personality, he jumped at the chance.

than satisfactory. It's a lack of something necessary for well-being. Henry Murray (1938), whose work began this approach to personality, defined a need as an internal directional force that determines how people seek out or respond to objects or situations in the environment.

Some needs are based in our biological nature (such as needs for food, water, air, sex, and avoidance of pain). Murray called these **primary,** or **viscerogenic, needs.** Others, such as the need for power and the need for achievement, either *derive* from biological needs or are inherent in our *psychological* makeup. Murray called these **secondary,** or **psychogenic, needs.**

Every need has associated with it some category of "goal objects." When thirsty, you need water, not food.

When you start to examine need theories, it's easiest to start with biological needs, because biology provides a good model for how needs work (see also Box 5.1). Biological needs must be satisfied repeatedly over time. As time passes, need states gradually become more intense, and the person comes to act in a way that causes the need to be satisfied. For example, with the passage of time your body starts to need food. Eventually, when the need gets strong enough, you'll do something to get food. That will diminish the need state.

The strength of a need influences the intensity of the behavior to which it relates. The stronger the need, the more intense the action. The idea of intensity covers several qualities—the vigor, enthusiasm, or thoroughness with which a behavior is done. But intensity can also be expressed in less obvious ways. For example, need strength can determine priorities—which action you take first versus which you put off until later. The stronger the need, the sooner it's reflected in action. Figure 5.1 shows how this prioritizing can result in a continually changing stream of actions as need strengths build and subside. The need that's greatest at any given point (highest on the graph) is the one that appears in your behavior.

Needs are directive. They help determine which of many possible actions occurs at a given time. Needs are directive in two senses. First, when you have a need, it's a need for something in particular. When you need water, you don't just need, you

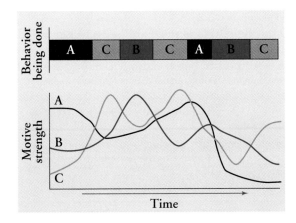

FIGURE 5.1

A graphic display of how changes in behavior over time can be explained by variations in the relative strengths of several motives over the same time. The letters at the top of the diagram indicate which of three activities the person is engaged in at any given time (shifting from one to the other). The three lines indicate the levels of the three motives related to these three activities. As one motive rises above the other two, the behavior changes (adapted from Seltzer, 1973).

need *water*. Needs thus pertain to classes of goal objects or events. Needs are also directive in specifying whether to move *toward* the object or *away* from it. When you have a need, it's a need either to get something or to avoid something. Thirst reflects a water-related need, but it's more than just water-*related*. After all, fear of swimming also reflects a water-related need. Thirst reflects a need to *get* water. Moving toward versus moving away is part of the directionality of all needs.

Motives

Many theorists assume that needs operate through another construct called a **motive.** Motives take the underlying need and move it a step closer to behavior. David McClelland (1984), an important contributor to this view on personality, said that motives are clusters of *cognitions with affective overtones, organized around preferred experiences and goals*. Motives appear in people's thoughts and preoccupations. The thoughts pertain to goals that are either desired or undesired. Thus, they are affectively toned. Motives are eventually reflected in actions.

To illustrate, the need for food occurs in the tissues of the body. But it gives rise to a motivational state called hunger. Unlike the need for food, hunger is experienced directly. It produces mental preoccupation and it leads to behavior that will reduce the hunger (along with the need for food). Thus, people who distinguish between needs and motives do so partly by whether there's a subjective experience. The need is a physical condition you don't sense directly. This condition creates a motivational state that you *do* experience subjectively.

Although needs and motives *can* be distinguished from each other this way, people don't always do so. One reason is that it's harder to make this distinction for psychogenic needs than for biological needs. A need for achievement isn't like a need for water, because it involves no deficit in the body. It's hard to say how the need for achievement differs from the motive to achieve. For this reason, it's common for people writing about needs and motives in personality to use the two terms somewhat interchangeably.

Press

There is, however, a reason to keep the motive concept distinct from the need concept, even for psychogenic needs. In particular, although needs influence motives, motives are also influenced by external events. Murray (1938) used the term **press** to refer to these external influences. A press (the plural is also press) is an external condition that creates a desire to obtain (or avoid) something. It thus exerts a motivational influence, just as does a need (Figure 5.2).

It's probably easiest to get a feel for the effects of need and press by looking at a biological motive. Imagine that your need for food created a hunger motive, to which you responded by eating lunch. Your peanut butter sandwich, though dry and

FIGURE 5.2

Internal need states and external press can both influence motives to engage in particular kinds of action, which in turn become realized in overt behavior.

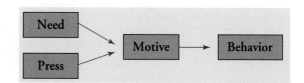

TABLE 5.1

Examples of press during childhood that can influence motives and thereby behavior (adapted from Murray, 1938).

Press	Resulting motive
Lack of companionship	Desire to make new friends
Family discord	Desire to be comforted
Lack of variety	Desire to seek out new experiences
Betrayal of trust	Desire for revenge
Inconsistent discipline	Desire for predictability
Friendships	Desire to be nurturant
Confinement	Desire for freedom

crumbly, satisfied the need for food. But now, just as you finish, someone walks in with an extra-large pizza (or whatever you personally find irresistible). Suddenly you don't seem as satisfied as you did a moment before. The motive to eat has been rekindled—not by a need, but by a press.

The concept of press also applies to motives stemming from secondary needs. For instance, when you see someone else receive an honor, it can increase your own motive for recognition. Being around someone who's in a close relationship may increase your motive to be with someone. A woman once told us that being around expectant mothers brings out caretaking motives, and she finds herself wishing she had a baby to care for. These are all examples of motivational states brought on by press from the environment. Table 5.1 lists additional examples of press, which Murray saw as important influences during childhood.

Needs, Motives, and Personality

Motive theories of personality suggest that when needs and motives are strong, they're reflected in the behaviors we commonly think of as relating to personality. The effects have two facets, though, because there are both temporary variations in needs and deeper patterns of needs.

Motivational States and Motive Dispositions

Everyone's needs vary across time and circumstances. People also vary in their *dispositional* needs. Some people just naturally have more of a particular need (pretty much all the time) than do others. Just as some people are always hungry, some are always motivated to achieve, or to be close to others.

We've already shown how to think about temporary fluctuations of needs (Figure 5.1, earlier). People shift from doing one thing to doing something else, as one need is satisfied and others build up. Ongoing behavior reflects whichever need is greatest. This model gives a sensible portrayal of how people shift from one action to another over time.

FIGURE 5.3

John has a high dispositional need for achievement; Bill's is lower. Assume this need fluctuates for both of them in the same pattern (over time). John's and Bill's levels of two other needs are identical (and also fluctuate). The result of the difference in the dispositional need for achievement creates a great difference in the overt actions that John and Bill display (the bars across the lines).

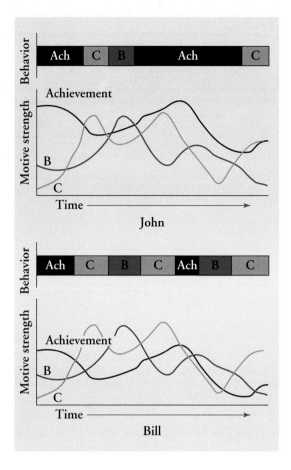

Now add in the idea that people differ from each other in their dispositional levels of needs. This would be reflected in differences in the height of the lines overall. Moment-to-moment consequences of this can be substantial. For example, John has a high dispositional need for achievement, Bill's dispositional need for achievement is lower. Assume both have the same experiences, so the achievement motive goes up and down in the same pattern for both. Assume further that they have identical patterns in all their other needs.

As Figure 5.3 indicates, John and Bill would display quite different patterns of behavior over time. Why? Because *even when John's other needs are up, his need for achievement is so high that it tends to remain above the others.* As a result, he tends to display achievement-related behavior a lot of the time. For Bill, the achievement motive rarely gets high enough to be the strongest influence. Thus, Bill doesn't display achievement-related behavior very often.

Murray's System of Needs

Murray (1938) developed a wide-ranging theory of personality that was organized in terms of needs, press, and motives. He and his colleagues developed a catalog of human needs, with emphasis on the secondary or psychogenic ones. Part of his list of secondary motives is in Table 5.2. These, to Murray, are the motives that underlie most important human behavior. These are the needs whose patterns describe people's personalities. Murray believed that everyone has all these needs, and also a dispositional tendency toward *some particular level* of each need.

Each need stands on its own, but Murray argued that needs can also be interrelated in several ways. Needs sometimes *fuse,* and are reflected in the same act. For

TABLE 5.2

Partial list of psychological needs (adapted and abridged from Murray, 1938)

Domain	Need for . . .	Representative behavior
Pertaining to ambition		
	Achievement*	Overcoming obstacles
	Recognition	Describing accomplishments
	Exhibition	Attempting to shock or thrill others
Pertaining to inanimate objects		
	Acquisition	Obtaining things
	Order	Making things neat and orderly
	Retention	Hoarding things
	Construction	Building something
Pertaining to defense of status		
	Infavoidance	Concealing a handicap or a failing
	Defendance	Giving an explanation or excuse
	Counteraction	Retaliating for something
Pertaining to human power		
	Dominance	Directing others' behavior
	Deference	Cooperating with or obeying someone
	Autonomy	Standing up to authority
	Contrariance	Being oppositional
	Aggression	Attacking or belittling others
	Abasement	Apologizing or confessing
	Blame avoidance	Stifling blameworthy impulses
Pertaining to affection between people		
	Affiliation	Spending time with others
	Rejection	Snubbing others
	Nurturance	Taking care of someone
	Succorance	Being helped by another
	Play	Seeking diversion through others
Pertaining to exchange of information		
	Cognizance	Asking questions of others
	Exposition	Delivering information to others

*Needs printed in boldface are those that have received the most research attention from other psychologists.

example, Sarah's mother has a high need to dominate and a high need to nurture. She often acts toward Sarah in a caring manner (nurturing) but does so in such a way that Sarah's wishes and preferences are disregarded (dominating). A single action thus satisfies two needs for her at the same time.

Needs can also act *in the service of* one another. For example, a person may have a need for order, which supports and works to the benefit of a more general need for achievement. Needs can *conflict* with one another, as well. For instance, the need for autonomy can conflict with the need for intimacy. Someone who has a strong need to be independent and a strong need to share experiences with someone else may feel conflict over these incompatible needs.

Just as needs can interrelate in complex ways, needs and press can interrelate. As one need can operate in the service of another, a press can operate in the service of a need. For example, Jane, who has a high need for achievement, works at an advertising firm. Her office surrounds her with new and challenging tasks, each of which is a press concerning achievement. Having this constant press at work facilitates and supplements her already high motive to achieve.

Measuring Motives: The Thematic Apperception Test

To study the motive view on personality, researchers have to measure motives. Motives turn out to be tricky to measure, because people don't always openly display their needs. **Manifest needs** can be observed in overt actions. These are easy to assess. **Latent needs** are those that aren't being openly displayed. This doesn't mean they aren't there. In fact, often it's the pattern of latent needs you really want to know about.

How do you measure latent needs? Morgan and Murray (1935) suggested that a strong latent need is likely to be "projected" into a person's fantasy, just as the image of a movie is projected onto a screen. (This idea derives from psychoanalytic theory; we'll say more about it in Chapter 9.) Murray applied the term **apperception** to the process of projecting imagery onto an outside stimulus. The assumption that people naturally engage in apperception provided the rationale behind the **Thematic Apperception Test,** or **TAT** (Morgan & Murray, 1935; Murray, 1938; Smith, 1992). This is the technique that's most frequently used to assess latent needs.

When your motives are being assessed by TAT (see Box 5.2), you view a set of ambiguous pictures, pictures in which it isn't clear what's going on. You're asked to tell or write a story about each one. Your story should describe what's happening in the picture, the characters' thoughts and feelings, the relationship among characters (if there are more than one), and the outcome of the situation. The principle of apperception says that the themes in your stories reflect your latent motivations. To put it another way, people put into their stories the motivational concerns that occupy their minds.

Do these fantasy responses really reflect people's needs? Yes. Several initial validation studies were done, one looking at a biological need—the need for food. Subjects were deprived of food for varying lengths of time, so they'd have different needs for food. They proved to differ in food-related TAT imagery (Atkinson & McClelland, 1948).

Other research manipulated people's achievement motive, by having some experience success and others experience failure. A failure should produce a temporary increase in the achievement motive because it creates an achievement deficit, much as the passage of time creates a deficit for food. A success should reduce

BOX 5.2

THE PROCESS BEHIND THE TAT

Take a good look at the picture on the right. Something's happening in the minds of these people, but what? Decide for yourself. Make up a story that fits the picture. Include the following specific information (and whatever else you want to include): *What's just happened to these people? What's the relationship between them? What are their present thoughts and feelings? What will be the outcome of the situation?* Take your time, and make your story as long and detailed as you wish.

What you've just experienced is similar to what people experience when completing the Thematic Apperception Test, or TAT (Morgan & Murray, 1935). The idea behind the TAT is that the needs people have will show up in the thoughts they generate from their imaginations when they try to make sense out of ambiguous stimuli such as this picture. The ambiguity in the stimulus makes it less likely that an environmental press will determine the story's content and more likely that your needs will influence what you write. When people complete the TAT, they write stories for 20 different pictures, including one that's completely blank (it could hardly get more ambiguous than that).

Scoring of people's responses can be complex, but here's a very simple version of what happens. Look to see what kinds of events take place in your story and what themes and images are in it. Events that involve overcoming obstacles, attaining goals, and positive feelings about these activities reflect the achievement motive. Events in which people choose to be with other people or

Illustration by Stephen P. Scheier. Reproduced by permission.

which emphasize building relationships among people reflect the affiliation motive. Stories that contain images of one person controlling another reflect the dominance, or power, motive. The themes in your story can be scored separately; thus the story can be used to assess several different motives. If you're interested in the motives of your own personality, look for evidence of each of the motives listed in Table 5.2.

It should be obvious that different pictures will prompt stories with different themes. Some pictures just naturally elicit achievement-related stories; others are more amenable to stories with affiliation themes. Over the course of several pictures, however, dispositional tendencies emerge in the fantasy narratives that people compose. Presumably these storytelling tendencies reflect the motives that characterize the person's personality.

achievement motivation because it satisfies the need to achieve. As predicted, after these experiences, subjects differed in TAT achievement imagery (McClelland, Atkinson, Clark, & Lowell, 1953). In the same way, people led to be concerned about their social acceptability displayed more affiliation imagery than did other subjects (Atkinson, Heyns, & Veroff, 1954).

Individual Differences in Specific Needs

Once validated by such studies, the TAT was used extensively to measure individual differences in *dispositional* needs. Since the TAT was responsive to experimentally created differences, it should also be sensitive to personality differences. Using this method, researchers have studied several dispositional needs in detail.

Need for Achievement

Of the needs identified by Murray, the first to receive research attention was the **need for achievement.** This motive plays a role in many human activities. It's been studied extensively for several decades by David McClelland, John Atkinson, and many other researchers and theorists (e.g., Atkinson & Birch, 1970; Atkinson & Raynor, 1974; Heckhausen, 1967; Heckhausen, Schmalt, & Schneider, 1985; McClelland et al., 1953).

Achievement motivation is *the desire to do things well, to feel pleasure in overcoming obstacles* (though see Box 5.3 concerning a subtle issue in thinking about this need). Need for achievement is reflected in TAT responses that mention performing well at something, goals or obstacles to goal attainment, positive feelings about success, or negative feelings about failure.

Persons high in achievement motivation have a strong need to succeed.

BOX 5.3

THE MOTIVE TO SUCCEED AND THE MOTIVE TO AVOID FAILURE

It seems straightforward to speak of achievement behavior as motivated by the desire to successfully attain goals. But whenever there's an achievement task, the possibility of *failing* is always present. As mentioned earlier in the chapter, a motive is either a tendency to approach something or a tendency to avoid something. Thus far, we've talked about achievement only in terms of approach: People with the desire to achieve try to move toward success. It seems likely, though, that the desire to avoid failure also plays a role in achievement behavior.

There are several ways this can happen. For example, people who want to avoid failing may to avoid achievement-related situations altogether. Never trying allows you to avoid failing. Another way to avoid failing, though, is *by the very act of succeeding*. It may well be that some of the people who do try hard to achieve don't care so much about gaining success as they do about the fact that by gaining success they're thereby avoiding failure.

Much early research on achievement actually included measures of both of motives. Following Atkinson (1957), most researchers classify people by simultaneously measuring the motive to approach success (through the TAT) and the motive to avoid failure (usually through a measure of test anxiety). An index is created from the two called **resultant achievement motivation** (**RAM**). People high in RAM have a high motive to approach success and a low motive to avoid failure. People low in RAM have a low motive to approach success and a high motive to avoid failure.

Atkinson's theory of achievement, which had a considerable influence on achievement research, makes its clearest predictions for people with high RAM and low RAM. For this reason, studies typically included only those two groups. This practice, though based in theory, has a distressing side effect: It creates a perfect confounding between the two motives. This causes ambiguity in interpreta-

tion (see Chapter 2). When high RAM subjects act differently from low RAM subjects, is it because of the difference in the motive to approach success, or is it because of the difference in the motive to avoid failure? In many studies there's no way to know, though most interpretations focus on the motive to approach success.

Research by Elliot and Sheldon (1997) indicates that the two motive tendencies have very different effects on people. Of particular interest, people who spend their time and effort trying to avoid failure report poorer well-being and less satisfaction with their performances than do people who are trying to approach success.

There's a more general point to be made here concerning motivation: Once you grasp the idea of separate approach and avoidance motives, you realize the idea has implications for *every* motive (see also Carver, Lawrence & Scheier, in press; Higgins, 1997; Ogilvie, 1987). Pick any motive in Table 5.2 and try it out. Acts of affiliation, for example, can be based in the desire to *be with others* (need for affiliation), but they can also be based in a desire to *avoid being alone* (Boyatzis, 1973; Pollak & Gilligan, 1982). These aren't identical. One is a motive to approach; the other is a motive to avoid. In the same way, the need to dominate is paralleled by a need to avoid domination. The same point can be made for any need on the list.

The idea that a given behavior can be based on either an approach motive or an avoidance motive (or some combination of the two) raises many questions about why people do the things they do. Are people generally moving toward goals, or are they trying to avoid or escape from things? Do the actions differ in any way, depending on which of these is more prominent? This general question has broad implications, complicating the picture of human behavior enormously.

Studies of people who differ in achievement motivation have found that they differ in several ways regarding achievement-related situations. Consider, for instance, the very act of choosing a task. Tasks (or problems within a task) can be easy, hard, or somewhere in the middle. Given a choice, which would you prefer? (When you're setting up your course schedule for next semester, for example, do you choose easy courses and professors, or hard ones, or ones in the middle?)

People low in need for achievement prefer tasks that are either very easy or very hard (Atkinson, 1957). It's easy to see why they might like easy ones, because there isn't much achievement pressure in an easy task, and it's nice to get something right, even if everyone else is getting it right too. Why, though, would people with low achievement needs want to work on a hard task? Apparently not for the challenge. It seems to have more to do with the fact that doing poorly on a hard problem doesn't reflect badly on you. And there's always the possibility (however remote) that you'll get lucky and get it right.

People high in need for achievement, in contrast, tend to prefer tasks of moderate difficulty. Consistent with this, people high in achievement motivation have been described as taking up occupational goals that are challenging but realistic, given their capabilities (Mahone, 1960; Morris, 1966). People high in need for achievement also work harder on moderately difficult tasks than on tasks that are either very hard or very easy (Clark & McClelland, 1956; French, 1955).

Why do people high in need for achievement prefer tasks of intermediate difficulty? These tasks provide the most information about ability (Trope, 1975, 1979). If you do well at an easy task, you don't learn much about your ability, because everyone does well. If you *fail* at a *hard* task, you don't learn much about your ability, because almost *no one* does well. In the middle, though, you can find out a lot. Perhaps people high in achievement motivation want to find out about their abilities. Trope (1975, 1980) tested this by having people choose test items. He figured out a way to manipulate (separately) the items' difficulty and their **diagnosticity** (how much they tell about ability). People with high achievement needs had a strong preference for diagnostic items (Figure 5.4), whereas difficulty in itself turned out not to be important.

Effects of achievement motivation have been studied in a variety of domains. For example, need for achievement is related to persistence in the face of failure (e.g., Feather, 1961). It's related to actual task performances (e.g., Lowell, 1952) and even to grades in school (Schultz & Pomerantz, 1976; see Atkinson & Birch, 1978, for a

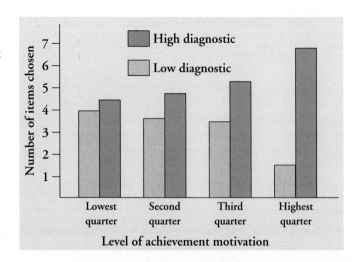

FIGURE 5.4

Subjects in this study chose items to work on that they expected to be either highly diagnostic of their abilities or not diagnostic. This figure divides subjects into four levels of achievement motive, ranging from very low to very high. There is an increasingly strong preference for highly diagnostic items among subjects with higher levels of achievement motivation (adapted from Trope, 1975).

more complete treatment of this research literature). This variable thus plays an important role in a variety of achievement-related behaviors.

Indeed, it's even been suggested that the need for achievement plays a major role in the economic rise and decline of entire cultures. This idea led to studies examining literature from several civilizations, at several distinct points in their history. The literature is interpreted for its themes, in much the same way as TAT responses are interpreted. The economic growth and decline of that civilization are then plotted over the same period.

One impressive study of this phenomenon was done by Bradburn and Berlew (1961), who examined the literature and economic history of England from 1500 to just after 1800. They divided this period into 50-year segments and coded achievement imagery and economic development in each. Achievement imagery was stable for about 100 years, fell off, and then rose sharply. The index of economic development followed a nearly identical pattern of falling then rising—but 50 years later. This suggests that shifts in achievement needs had economic consequences.

Another, even more complex study of this sort was done by McClelland (1961). This study focused on a much narrower period (1925 to 1950) but looked at 23 cultures across the world. McClelland coded achievement imagery from children's schoolbooks at both points in history. He developed two measures of economic growth over the intervening period, and compared the achievement imagery to economic growth. A moderately strong association emerged between achievement imagery in 1925 and economic growth from 1925 to 1950. As in the Bradburn and Berlew study, there was virtually no relation between economic growth and later achievement imagery. This pattern suggests that motivation (indirectly reflected in the imagery) produced the economic achievement, instead of vice versa.

Achievement motivation predicted economic success in these studies, but there are situations in which the need for achievement can work against people. For example, people who serve in high-level managerial or political positions don't usually have opportunities for personal achievement. Their task is to mobilize others, which depends on a different need altogether. If people in this situation try to do too much themselves, it can backfire, producing worse rather than better performance. Consistent with this idea, Spangler and House (1991) found that need for achievement related inversely to the effectiveness of U.S. presidents.

An interesting aspect of the literature on the achievement motive is that until recently far more was known about its effects among men than among women, since most early research studied only males. Eventually, however, researchers looked more closely at achievement motives among women. Much of this work suggests that achievement needs are expressed in varying ways among women, depending on where they see their lives as headed.

Elder and MacInnis (1983) recruited two sets of 17- to 18-year-old girls. Their scores on a vocational interest test indicated that one group was family oriented, the other group had a mix of family and career interests. Achievement motives were assessed at the same time. These motives predicted different things in the two groups, as they moved into adulthood. Among family-oriented women, those with high achievement needs invested energy in dating and other activities leading to marriage and family. In effect, these women defined achievement as creating and sustaining a strong family. Among the career-minded women, high achievement motivation led to later marriage and later families. Presumably this was because these women were focusing their energies on their careers. In a similar vein, Stewart (1980) found that high levels of need for achievement predicted women's career persistence across 14 years. This was true, however, only among women with no children. Thus, the behaviors that follow from achievement needs seem to depend on what the woman values as an achievement goal.

Another way of portraying these findings is to say that women with achievement needs pursue achievement in ways that fit their views of themselves and the world they live in. It seems reasonable that this principle also influences the careers women consider entering. A study of this (Jenkins, 1987) looked at career choices made by women who were college seniors in 1967. Those high in need for achievement were likely to become teachers, but they weren't likely to go into business. Why teaching but not business? Teaching is a profession that provides an outlet for achievement needs but doesn't conflict with traditional women's roles. This was less true of business careers back then. Thus, the achievement needs of these women apparently were channeled in expression by other aspects of their social environments.

These studies raise questions about whether achievement behavior promotes social acceptance for women, as it seems to do for men. Some have argued it doesn't (French & Lesser, 1964; Horner, 1973; Lesser, 1973; Tresemer, 1977). High-achieving women may risk being seen as having lost their femininity. Such possibilities can create conflicts for the woman who's motivated to achieve. She may even develop a motive to *avoid* success (Horner, 1973), as a way to avoid these adverse consequences of high levels of the achievement motive. The fear of success appears to be more rare than was once thought (Peplau, 1976), but the idea that women are threatened by achievement is still under investigation (Pollak & Gilligan, 1982).

Need for Power

Another motive that's been studied extensively is the **need for power.** The need for power, which has been studied by David Winter (e.g., 1973) and others, is *the motive to have impact on other people, to have prestige, to feel strong* compared to others. TAT responses that reflect the need for power have images of forceful, vigorous action—especially action that evokes strong emotional responses in other people. Responses expressing concern about status or position also reflect need for power.

What kinds of behavior reflect the power motive? Not surprisingly, people high in need for power seek out positions of authority and influence. Students high in the power motive are likely to be officeholders in student organizations (Greene & Winter, 1971). The power motive seems to be important in organizational effectiveness. For example, among U.S. presidents, those high in the power motive were more effective than those lower in the power motive (Spangler & House, 1991).

The need for power is often expressed in the tendency to acquire high-status possessions and to surround oneself with symbols of power.

When in positions of authority or responsibility, people with different levels of the power motive also differ in the way they respond to problems. In one study (Fodor, 1984), subjects were supervisors of work groups that were either efficient or inefficient. The question was how they'd respond to inefficiency. People high in the need for power (but not those low) reported becoming more aroused or activated when things went poorly. Thus, encountering leadership difficulties seems to engage the energies of people high in the need for power.

A different—and much less obvious—effect of the power motive occurs in friendship patterns. It's been found that people with high need for power tend to form friendships with others who aren't especially popular or well-known (Winter, 1973). At first this doesn't sound right. Wouldn't power-minded people want to seek each other out? After a little more thought, though, it makes sense. If your friends aren't popular or well-known, they won't compete with you for power. If what you want is power and influence, influential friends can get in the way.

A finding similar to this is that men with high power needs are more likely than those with lower power needs to say that the ideal wife is a woman who's dependent (Winter, 1973). An independent woman is a potential threat. A dependent woman allows a man to have feelings of superiority. Indeed, a later study confirmed that the wives of men high in the need for power were less likely to have careers of their own than were wives of men lower in this need (Winter, Stewart, & McClelland, 1977).

This isn't to say that the need for power is something that matters only among men. Women vary in this need as well, and it has proved to predict important outcomes among women. One study (Jenkins, 1994) found that women high in the need for power experience more power-related job satisfactions than women lower in this need—but also more job *dis*satisfactions. These women also made greater strides in career development over a 14-year period—but only if they were in power-relevant jobs.

The level of a person's need for power can influence how the person relates to others. In one study (McAdams, Healy, & Krause, 1984) subjects described episodes of peer interaction, and the descriptions were analyzed. Need for power related strongly to indications that the subject had taken an active, assertive, controlling orientation in the interaction. Another study (Mason & Blankenship, 1987) found evidence of a more extreme exercise of power, with more ominous overtones. This study found that men high in power needs were more likely than men with lower power needs to physically abuse their female partners during arguments.

There are many other ways the power motive can be manifest in behavior. For example, people high in the need for power surround themselves with symbols of power, including credit cards (Davis, 1969) and high-prestige possessions (Winter,1972). The tendency to surround oneself with the trappings of power occurs even among college students. Students high in the need for power are more likely to put their names on the doors of their dorm rooms, to portray their grades as better than they really are, and to put their term papers in fancy binders (Winter, 1973). Power-motivated students are also more argumentative in class and eager to convince others of their point of view (Veroff, 1957). This may be why they do particularly well in courses requiring classroom participation (McKeachie, 1961).

Many of these findings fit the idea that people with a high need for power are concerned about controlling the self-images they present to others around them (see McAdams, 1984). They're motivated to enhance their reputations. They want to create in others' minds images of themselves as authoritative and influential. It will be no surprise that they tend to be somewhat narcissistic, absorbed in their own importance (Carroll, 1987).

Winter has suggested that the power motive is manifested in different ways, depending on whether socialization has led to a sense of responsibility (Winter, 1988; Winter & Barenbaum, 1985). For those high in responsibility, the power motive is reflected in "conscientious" pursuit of prestige. In such cases, power is expressed in socially accepted ways. For those lower in responsibility, though, the need for power can lead to more problematic ways of influencing others—what Winter calls "profligate, impulsive" power. This includes impulsive aggressiveness, sexual exploitation, and alcohol and drug use.

In a series of reanalyses of earlier studies, Winter and Barenbaum (1985) found considerable support for this argument. For example, in one sample of men coded as low responsible, the need for power was related to drinking, fighting, and sexual possessiveness. Among men coded as high responsible, in contrast, need for power was inversely correlated with all of these tendencies. Similar findings emerged from other samples. The effect of need for power on behavior apparently does depend on people's sense of responsiblity.

Need for Affiliation

Another motive that's received a good deal of research attention is the motive to affiliate (see Boyatzis, 1973, for a review). The **need for affiliation** is *the motive to spend time with others*. This isn't a need to dominate others but to be in social relationships, to spend time interacting with others. These social interactions aren't a means to some other end—they're a goal in their own right. In TAT responses, need for affiliation is reflected in concern over acceptance by others, or active attempts to establish or maintain positive relations with others (Shipley & Veroff, 1952).

Studies have uncovered several implications of this motive. For example, people who want to affiliate should want to be thought of as agreeable. If a group exerts pressure on them, they should go along, compared to people with lower affiliation needs—and they do (Hardy, 1957). People high in need for affiliation also display their concern with being accepted and liked by other people in other ways. They get nervous if they think others are judging their interpersonal skills (Byrne, McDonald, & Mikawa, 1963). They show a strong preference for potential interaction partners who are warm over those who are more reserved (Hill, 1991). They're also more likely to initiate contacts and to try to establish friendships (Crouse & Mehrabian, 1977).

Actively making social contacts suggests that affiliative needs involve more than worrying about acceptance from others. They can also lead to active participation in social events. For example, Sorrentino and Field (1986) studied the emergence of leadership in discussion groups, which met in 5 weekly sessions. At the end, group members were asked to indicate whom they viewed as group leaders. As can be seen in Figure 5.5, people high in need for affiliation were nominated more often than people lower in need for affiliation.

As suggested by the Sorrentino and Field research, people with strong affiliation motive spend more time actively engaged in social activities than people lower in this motive. They make more phone calls (Lansing & Heyns, 1959); when randomly paged, they're more likely to be engaged in social activities—conversing or letter writing (Constantian, 1981; McAdams & Constantian, 1983). When they're alone, they're more likely to express a wish to be interacting with others (McAdams & Constantian, 1983; Wong & Csikszentmihalyi, 1991).

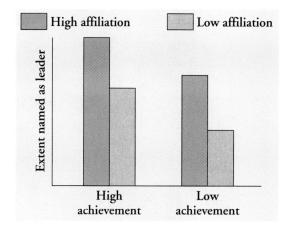

FIGURE 5.5

Subjects interacted informally in groups for 5 weeks, then indicated who they thought were the leaders in the group. Those with higher affiliation motivation were rated as showing more leadership, and a similar tendency also appeared for the achievement motive (adapted from Sorrentino & Field, 1986).

Another study suggests that the affiliation motive influences relationship satisfaction (Meyer & Pepper, 1997), though in a tricky way. Happiness depends partly on the balance of affiliation needs between partners. That is, well-adjusted husbands and wives had affiliation needs that were *correlated* with each other. Poorly adjusted couples had affiliation needs that were unrelated. To put it concretely, if you have low affiliation needs, you're best off with someone else with low affiliation needs. If your affiliation needs are high, you're best off with someone whose affiliation needs are also high.

We noted in Chapter 4 a difference of opinion about whether traits should be measured as broad supertraits, or as more narrow traits. A similar question has been raised about affiliation motivation, and by implication about the entire motive approach to personality. Hill (1987) pointed out that affiliation can occur for several reasons. Perhaps the reasons for affiliation should be considered as separate motives.

To do this, Hill developed self-report scales for four affiliation needs: social comparison, emotional support, positive stimulation, and attention from others. Consistent with the idea that the needs are at least somewhat separate, the scales correlated only moderately with each other. Of greater interest is how they predicted behavior. Hill created four hypothetical situations, each engaging a particular kind of affiliation need. One situation involved a job interview that was confusing and ambiguous, which should target a need for social comparison but not other needs for affiliation. As expected, the social comparison scale predicted subjects' responses to this situation better than any other scale. The same pattern held for each situation— in each case, the theoretically relevant scale was the best predictor of responses.

These findings suggest, more generally, that there is merit in focusing on specific rather than on global needs. Again, however, the question seems to be whether the enhanced prediction is worth the tradeoff of having to hold a great many variables in mind.

Need for Intimacy

Another motive that's emerged in recent years as a research focus is the **need for intimacy.** It's been studied intensively by Dan McAdams (1982, 1985, 1989) and his collaborators. Intimacy motivation is *the desire to experience warm, close, and communicative exchanges with another person, to feel close to another person.* Carried to an extreme, it's the desire to merge the self with another person. Intimacy motivation

Need for intimacy is the desire to experience warm, close, and meaningful relationships with others.

shares with affiliation motivation a wish to be with others as an end rather than as a means to an end. It goes beyond the need for affiliation, though, in its emphasis on closeness and open sharing with another person.

Interestingly enough, intimacy motivation wasn't on Murray's list of needs. McAdams proposed it as a new construct partly because he felt that assessment of the need for affiliation didn't focus enough on the positive, affirmative aspects of close relationships. Additionally, the need for affiliation is an active, striving, "doing" orientation toward relationships, whereas the need for intimacy as McAdams views it is a more passive, noncontrolling, "being" orientation (McAdams & Powers, 1981). The two aren't entirely distinct, of course. McAdams and Constantian (1983) reported a correlation between them of .58.

What kinds of behaviors derive from the intimacy motive? In one study, people high in need for intimacy reported having more one-to-one exchanges with other people (though not more large-group interaction) than those lower in the need for intimacy (McAdams, Healy, & Krause, 1984). The interactions reported by intimacy-motivated subjects involved more self-disclosure, as well. To put it differently, people with high intimacy needs are more likely to share with friends their hopes, fears, and fantasies. The sharing goes both ways: People with high intimacy needs report doing more *listening* than do people with low intimacy needs, perhaps because they are more concerned about their friends' well-being. Indeed, intimacy seems to entail both self-disclosure and partner disclosure (Laurenceau, Barrett, & Pietromonaco, 1998).

Because close interactions are important to people high in the need for intimacy, it should be no surprise that they define their lives partly in terms of such interactions. McAdams (1982) collected autobiographical recollections among students high and low in intimacy needs. They were asked to report a particularly joyful or transcendent experience from their past and then to report an important learning experience. The content of each was coded several ways. For instance, some events involved considerable psychological or physical intimacy with another person; others did not. Analysis revealed that intimacy motivation was strongly correlated with memory content that also implied intimacy.

How do people high in the intimacy motive act when they're with others? They laugh, smile, and make more eye contact when conversing than do people with lower intimacy needs (McAdams, Jackson, & Kirshnit, 1984). They don't try to dominate the social scene (people with the need for power do that). Instead, they seem to view group activities as chances for group members to be involved in a communal way (McAdams & Powers, 1981).

There's evidence that the desire for intimacy may be good for people (McAdams & Vaillant, 1982). Men in this study wrote narrative fantasies at age 30 and were assessed for psychosocial adjustment 17 years later. Men with higher intimacy motivation at 30 had greater marital and job satisfaction at 47 than did those with less intimacy motivation. Another study found that women high in the intimacy motive reported greater happiness and gratification in their lives than those low in the intimacy motive—unless they were living alone (McAdams & Bryant, 1987). On the other hand, intimacy needs (needing to be close) don't coexist well with power needs (needing to influence or dominate others). Persons high in both needs are often poorly adjusted (Zeldow, Daugherty, & McAdams, 1988).

Some have suggested that strong intimacy needs may threaten men's sense of masculinity (Helgeson & Sharpsteen, 1987; Pollak & Gilligan, 1982; Wong & Csikszentmihalyi, 1991). This idea has logical parallels to the idea, mentioned earlier in the chapter, that achievement threatens the sense of feminity. Both ideas are controversial (Benton et al., 1983); both surely will be investigated further.

Patterned Needs: Inhibited Power Motive

Thus far for the most part we've discussed needs individually. Indeed, for many years that's how researchers examined needs—one at a time. However, researchers have also examined patterns involving several needs at once, sometimes in combination with other characteristics. One well-known pattern combines a low need for affiliation with a high need for power, in conjunction with the tendency to inhibit the expression of the latter. This pattern is called **inhibited power motivation** (McClelland, 1979). Sometimes it's called "leadership motivation pattern" (McClelland, 1975). Why people find this pattern of interest depends on the context in which it's examined.

With regard to leadership, the theory goes as follows: A person high in need for power wants to influence people. Being low in need for affiliation lets the person make hard decisions without worrying about being disliked. Being high in self-control (inhibiting the use of power) means the person will want to follow orderly procedures and stay within the organizational framework. Such a person should do very well in the structure of a business organization.

This pattern does seem to relate to success in managerial ranks (McClelland & Boyatzis, 1982). Those with the inhibited power pattern moved to higher levels of management in a 16-year period than those without this pattern. Interestingly, this was true only of nontechnical managers. Among managers whose jobs rested on engineering skills, personality pattern didn't matter. This is reasonable, since the managerial value of those people depends heavily on their particular skills.

The pattern of high power motivation and low affiliation motivation may be good for getting others organized, but even this may be a mixed blessing. Winter (1993) has argued that this pattern is actually conducive to starting wars. Using historical data of various types, he found that high levels of power imagery and low levels of affiliation imagery in the statements of relevant politicians predicted entering wars. For example, speeches made by the sovereigns of Great Britain contained more

Balance of power motive imagery versus affiliation motive imagery in sovereign's speeches during the year before Great Britain entered a war (18 cases) compared to the year before Britain did not enter a war (36 cases; adapted from Winter, 1993, Table 3).

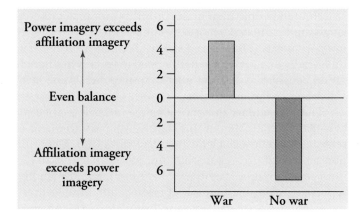

power than affiliation imagery in the year before Britain entered a war, whereas the reverse was true during years preceding a no-war year (Figure 5.6). In another case (the Cuban missile crisis of 1962), greater affiliation than power imagery preceded the *avoidance* of a war.

Further Determinants of Behavior

It should be clear that no single motive—no matter how interesting it is—is the only determinant of personality. From the motivational point of view, personality is a *system of multiple needs.* In this section we briefly reconsider how the continually changing stream of human behavior reflects the waxing and waning of many needs.

As indicated earlier, every human motive exists in every person. The behavior that takes place at a given time is determined partly by how *intense* various motives are. As one need becomes so intense that it outweighs the others, it's reflected in activity. As that need is satisfied and others grow more intense, the balance changes and the person shifts to another activity. The result is a flow of continually changing behavior (Atkinson & Birch, 1978).

Winter (1996) has recently suggested that needs for achievement, affiliation–intimacy, and power represent the fundamental dimensions underlying Murray's more elaborate list. In this view, although many needs wax and wane, they form three broad domains of needs. One might think of each domain as a superordinate need within which facets needs can vary somewhat independently.

Incentive Value

This analysis is reasonable, but it's missing something. If your need for affiliation is now more intense than your other needs, this analysis predicts you'll engage in an affiliative act. But what act in particular? Here the theory must use additional concepts. Indeed, motivational theorists do usually assume that behavior has other determinants (e.g., McClelland, 1985).

Another determinant is **incentive value,** the degree to which a given action is capable of satisfying a need for you. Incentive is sort of a personalized weighting of how relevant the act is to the need. These values determine how a motive is expressed in behavior. For example, a person with a high need for affiliation who likes long conversations with special friends but dislikes impersonal crowds will avoid parties. Avoiding parties may appear strange for a person with a high need for affiliation. But people don't just mindlessly engage in all conceivable types of need-related behavior. Rather, they choose ways to satisfy their needs. They do so based partly on the incentive values that various activities have for them.

We didn't emphasize the role of incentives earlier in the chapter. It should be clear, however, that something like this concept is needed to account for behavior's diversity. People differ considerably in the activities they engage in, even when trying to satisfy the same need. As we noted earlier in the chapter, evidence suggests some women satisfy their need for achievement through careers, and others do so by achieving strong family lives. These activities are different from one another, yet each can satisfy the need to achieve.

This principle is related to a point made in Chapter 4 in discussing interactionism: We said that people choose for themselves which situations to enter and which to avoid, thus creating an interaction between person and situation. We didn't say there *why* different people choose different situations. One obvious answer is that people have different needs, which relate to different situations. Another answer, though, is that various situations have different *incentive* values for a given person, even if the situations are fulfilling the same need.

Needs and incentives both influence behavior, but in different ways. McClelland (1985) suggested that measures of need strength are likely to predict long-term *frequencies of need-relevant actions of any type.* Measures of values, on the other hand, should predict *choices within a domain of action.* In his view, needs influence behavior primarily at a nonconscious level, whereas values influence the more conscious process of choice.

McClelland (1985) also noted that people's actions are influenced by at least two other factors. One is **expectancy**—the perceived probability of success. People who expect an action to be successful will continue to engage in it, even if it's going slowly. People who are doubtful about the outcome are more likely to think about alternative ways to satisfy the need. The second additional factor, which is a partial determinant of expectancy, is the presence or absence of skills or talents needed to do the action.

These additional variables obviously are important. To consider them all at once, however, creates a description that's very complex (for broader treatment see, e.g., Atkinson & Birch, 1978; McClelland, 1985). This is why we've focused this chapter on the central concepts of this approach: needs and motives.

The Methods of Personology

Research examining the effects of motive patterns has tended to take one of two forms. Some research examines how people respond to particular events, in the laboratory or in the field. Other research collects evidence of a dispositional motive (or set of motives) in stories composed at one time and relates it to some outcome that occurs considerably later.

These two ways of studying motives differ greatly from the approach favored by Murray, the father of this research area. Murray believed the only way to understand personality is to study the *whole person,* and to do so over an extended period. Indeed, the work on which he based his theory was an intensive study of 51 college men (Murray, 1938). Each was tested in many ways and interviewed by a staff of professionals with widely varying backgrounds. These people then presented their impressions to what Murray called the Diagnostic Council, the most experienced members of the team. After extensive discussions and interviews, the group came to know each subject's personality quite thoroughly.

This approach was idiographic in nature, focusing on the pattern of qualities that made each person unique. Murray disliked nomothetic methods, believing that their focus on comparison prevents them from probing deeply into a person's life. To Murray, the nomothetic approach yields only a superficial understanding of what individuals are like.

In fact, Murray's concern about the inadequacies of nomothetic approaches led him to coin the term **personology** to refer to the approach he preferred. He defined personology as the study of individual human lives and the factors that influence their course. He believed that personology was more meaningful than other approaches, because of its emphasis on the importance of the person's life history for understanding the person. According to Murray (1938, p. 604), "the history of a personality *is* the personality."

Murray was not alone in this belief. Another who took this position was Erik Erikson. Erikson was a member of the research team that Murray assembled, and the similarity in view doubtlessly relates to that shared experience. However, Erikson (whose ideas are discussed in Chapter 11) is usually seen as a neoanalytic theorist, partly due to his emphasis on the life course. Thus, in this emphasis on personal history Murray's thinking aligns more with themes of the neoanalytic perspective than with those of the dispositional perspective.

Recent years have seen a resurgence of interest in this way of thinking about personality. For example, McAdams, whose work on intimacy motivation was described earlier, has written extensively on the idea that identity takes the form of an extended narrative, a life story that each of us writes and lives out over time (McAdams, 1985). This narrative has chapters, heros, and thematic threads that recur and permeate the story line. Further contributions to this way of studying whole persons have been collected in a volume by Rabin, Zucker, Emmons, and Frank (1990). Whether this approach will be more prominent in personality psychology in the future remains to be seen, but it surely is a development that Murray would have applauded.

Assessment

Assessment of personality from this viewpoint is a matter of determining the dispositional levels of a person's needs. This approach to personality uses several techniques, including self-reports and interviews. The assessment technique most distinctly associated with assessment of needs, however, is the TAT (Smith, 1992; Winter, 1996).

Though the TAT is widely used to measure motives, it has also been criticized. Questions have been raised about its relatively low internal consistency and test-retest reliability (Entwisle, 1972). Defenders reply that there are reasons for both of these to be low. The pictures in the TAT vary considerably in content. It's not surprising that they bring out different kinds of stories. This reduces internal consistency. It is also arguable that being asked to tell multiple stories creates implicit pressure to avoid repetition. This can reduce both internal consistency and test-retest reliability (e.g., Atkinson & Raynor, 1974). There's evidence, though, that the reliability of the TAT need not be as low as was once believed (Lundy, 1985).

Another criticism of the TAT is more pragmatic: It takes a lot of time and effort to administer and score. This is an important reason why self-report measures of motives were developed.

There have been several attempts over the years to develop self-reports that would reflect the needs Murray saw as fundamental to personality. An early effort was the Edwards Personal Preference Schedule (Edwards, 1959). A more recent one is the Personality Research Form, or PRF (Jackson, 1984). The PRF measures 20 needs derived from Murray's list. As with any inventory, it can be used to create personality profiles. In this case, however, the traits being measured are motivational traits.

Self-Reports and the TAT May Not Measure the Same Thing

Although researchers such as Edwards and Jackson intended their self-report scales to measure motives, others have questioned whether they really do so. A reason for concern about this is that the self-report measures usually correlate poorly with TAT assessment. The critical question is why.

McClelland and his colleagues have argued that the two kinds of assessments are in fact measuring different things (McClelland, Koestner, & Weinberger, 1989). They used the term *implicit motive* to refer to what's measured by the TAT. They called these motives implicit because the person may or may not be aware of having them. They used the term *self-attributed motive* to refer to what's measured by self-reports.

McClelland et al. argued that implicit motives are basic. These are the recurrent preferences for particular kinds of affective experiences that McClelland believed define motives (the feeling of "doing better" for the achievement motive, of "being strong" for the power motive, of "feeling close" for the intimacy motive). Because these are basic, they're good predictors of behavioral trends over time.

In contrast, self-attributed motives are tied to specific action goals. They may be closer to reflecting incentive values than to reflecting basic needs. They tell how a person will act in a particular situation. For this reason, they're better at predicting responses in structured settings.

Further evidence that these qualities are distinct comes from research in which subjects completed TAT and self-report measures, then kept records of memorable experiences over 60 days (Woike, 1995). The records were coded for motive relevance and for feeling content. Implicit motive strength derived from TAT (but not self-report motive strength) related to frequency of recording feelings relevant to that motive. Self-report motives (but not TAT scores) related to frequency of recording motive-related events that had no feelings. It seems, then, that the two aspects of motivation link to different aspects of memory.

McClelland believed that both qualities are important, but that they should be viewed and treated separately. There are cases in which it makes sense to expect an implicit motive to predict an outcome but not a self-attributed motive. There are also cases in which the opposite is true. For this reason, it's important to be sure which one you want to measure, and to measure it appropriately (McClelland, 1989).

Motives and the Five-Factor Model

The PRF was developed from Murray's list of needs, measuring qualities related to Murray's theory. A reasonable question is whether the qualities the PRF measures resemble those measured by inventories with different starting points. Chapter 4 described a body of opinion holding that the fundamental traits of personality can be largely placed within the framework of five supertraits. Can this framework absorb the personality qualities Murray saw as important?

Several researchers have addressed this question. A starting point is the fact that several analyses of the PRF have yielded five factors (Stumpf, 1993). Stumpf concluded that all of the big five except neuroticism were captured in the PRF factors. Costa and McCrae (1988a) looked at associations of PRF scales with the NEO-PI, which was developed expressly to measure the big five. Their findings suggested two conclusions. First, many PRF scales do reflect underlying qualities of the five-factor model. For example, the scales measuring needs for affiliation, play, and exhibition all load with extraversion. Scales measuring needs for change, sentience, understanding, and (inversely) harmavoidance load with openness to experience.

On the other hand, several prominent PRF scales loaded on two or more factors rather than one. This appears to indicate that these motives are tied to several traits. For example, the need for dominance related to extraversion, openness, and (inversely) agreeableness. It seems, then, that the five-factor model doesn't perfectly absorb the needs reflected in the PRF. This general pattern of loadings has since been replicated by Paunonen et al. (1992). Somewhat better support for the five-factor model has been found in the Edwards measure of needs (Piedmont, McCrae, & Costa, 1992).

Traits and Motives as Distinct

The attempt to fit the motives identified by Murray and others to the five-factor model is viewed by some as an effort to integrate across theoretical boundaries. Some believe, however, that the effort is misguided, that traits and motives are fundamentally different from each other (Winter, John, Stewart, Klohnen, & Duncan, 1998). In taking this position, Winter et al. noted that all the evidence just reviewed dealt with self-attributed motives, rather than TAT-derived motives. Self-attributed and TAT-derived motives aren't strongly related. This limitation by itself is reason to be cautious about concluding that traits and motives are the same.

Winter et al. (1998) proposed that motives instead represent fundamental goals or desires, and that traits channel how those desires are expressed. Thus, they argued, motives and traits interact to produce behavior. In some respects, this resembles the argument described earlier about implicit motives and incentive values. In the view taken by Winter et al., traits act much as patterns of incentive preferences.

In support of their argument, Winter et al. presented two studies of the trait of introversion–extraversion and (TAT-derived) needs. The studies used data sets examining women's lives across a period of many decades. One prediction Winter et al. made is that intimacy needs would have different effects among introverts and extraverts (see Table 5.3). For women with low intimacy needs, it should hardly matter whether they are introverts or extraverts. Since intimacy isn't a big need for them, they're likely to have average levels on variables such as marital disruption and marital satisfaction.

For people with high intimacy needs, though, the picture is more complex. An extravert with intimacy needs should do just fine in relationships, because extraverts are comfortable with and good at various kinds of social interaction. Introverts with a high intimacy need should have more problems. Their inner-directed orientation should create more interference with relationships (their partners may see them as remote or withholding), and they should be more likely to experience marital problems. This is exactly what Winter et al. (1998) found.

TABLE 5.3

Sample hypothesis about interaction between the Affiliation–Intimacy motive and the trait of Introversion–Extraversion (adapted from Winter et al., 1998)

| | Affiliation–Intimacy Motive | |
	Low	High
Extravert	Intimate relationship not salient as a desire	Desire for intimate relationship leads to single stable relationship
Introvert	Intimate relationship not salient as a desire	Desire for intimate relationship, but difficulty maintaining it because focus on inner world is disruptive

Problems in Behavior, and Behavior Change

People working within the motive approach to personality have been interested in specific domains of human activity (e.g., achievement, affiliation, power, intimacy) and in the more general idea of motivation as a concept. They haven't addressed the question of problems in behavior in great detail, nor have they suggested a particular approach to therapy. Nevertheless, the literature in this area has at least tentative links to certain problems in behavior and to the processes of behavior change.

The Need for Power and Alcohol Abuse

It's been suggested that the need for power can play a role in development of problem drinking (McClelland, Davis, Kalin, & Wanner, 1972). This idea stems partly from the finding that drinking alcohol leads to increased feelings of power. Thus, a person with high need for power can satisfy that need, at least to a degree, by drinking. This isn't an effective way of satisfying the power motive for long, of course, because in this case the sense of power is illusory.

The notion that alcohol abuse may reflect the need for power leads to some recommendations for treatment. In particular, it suggests that people who are using alcohol this way aren't aware of doing so. They'd probably benefit from realizing that's what they're doing. By encouraging alternative ways to satisfy the power motive, therapists can treat the issue in a productive way, rather than simply treating a symptom. Evidence from one study (Cutter, Boyatzis, & Clancy, 1977) indicates that this approach can be more effective than traditional therapies, yielding nearly twice the rate of rehabilitation at one-year follow-up (see also McClelland, 1977).

Focusing On and Changing Motivation

Theorists who've contributed to the motive approach to personality have had relatively little to say about behavior change in therapy. Murray, the father of this approach, was a therapist but he didn't develop new therapy techniques. In general, he tended to apply the currently existing psychodynamically oriented techniques to people's problems.

It would seem, however, that one of the studies just discussed makes some suggestions concerning the process of behavior change. As was indicated, some people appear to use alcohol as a way of temporarily satisfying a desire for power. A treatment program developed for these people had two focuses. It made them more aware that this motive was behind their alcohol consumption. It also helped them to find other ways to satisfy the need for power, thus reducing the undesired drinking.

A broader implication of this discussion is that people may *often* be unaware of the motives that underlie their problem behaviors. That is, problem behaviors may often reflect needs that are being poorly channeled or expressed. If so, taking a close look at the person's motive tendencies might tell something about the source of the problem. Knowing the source may make it easier to make changes.

Another program of work with indirect implications for therapy has been conducted by McClelland and his colleagues. This research concerns a training program developed to raise people's levels of achievement motivation (McClelland, 1965; McClelland & Winter, 1969), which has been used mostly among business people (see also Lemann, 1994). The program has its roots in the idea that thinking a lot about achievement-related ideas increases your motive to achieve (see Box 5.4 for another look at this idea).

This program begins by describing the nature of the achievement motive and instructing people on how to score TAT protocols for achievement imagery. People then are taught to use achievement imagery in their thoughts as much as possible. By teaching themselves to think in terms of achievement, they increase the likelihood of taking an achieving orientation to whatever activity they engage in.

Achievement-related thinking is important. By itself, however, it isn't enough. A second purpose of the training is to link these thoughts to specific, concrete action patterns. It's also important to be sure that the patterns will work outside the train-

Motivation seminars are often used to enhance achievement motivation among people in business.

BOX 5.4

THEORETICAL CONTROVERSY:
Are Motives Biologically Based, or Are They Rooted in Cognition?

As discussed in the body of the chapter, McClelland and his colleagues developed a training program to increase people's achievement motivation. This program seems to produce the desired results. But its success raises fundamental questions about the nature of the need for achievement—indeed, about all psychogenic motivation.

Early motive theorists such as Murray assumed that even psychological or social needs derive from biological processes. Though biology is often used more as a metaphor than as an explanatory device, it's generally been assumed that individual differences in need profiles are relatively stable, determined by the person's basic nature.

McClelland (1965), on the other hand, came to believe that human motives are learned. Thus they can be altered relatively easily. The success of his program stands as a testament to this idea. The program is really very simple. Participants get a clear understanding of what the motive is and how it shows up in behavior and thought, and they're taught to think and act that way. Since McClelland knew a lot about how naturally occurring need for achievement is manifested, it was easy for him to tell people what to do.

Though these procedures produce the intended changes, they raise several questions. If motives are so easily altered—if motives are learned—why not dispense with the concept of motive altogether? There are, after all, psychologists from other per-

spectives who see concepts such as motive as being both misleading and useless (see Chapters 12 and 13). Isn't this, then, a case in which a motivational theorist is turning around and embracing a competing approach?

Another sort of question is raised by the training program's emphasis on cognitive processes. The procedures of the program include an elaborate process of coding in people's memory the nature of the motive they're trying to acquire. It also includes drawing explicit mental associations between that motive and concrete actions, along with an emphasis on the monitoring of outcomes. These various processes look suspiciously like the sort of things that would be emphasized by people who take a cognitive or self-regulation approach to personality (Chapters 16 and 17). Are the effects of the program, then, really motivational?

One possible response to these questions is that the program developed by McClelland may change motives but not needs. That is, recall from earlier in the chapter that motives are influenced by both needs and press. It's possible to think of McClelland's training program as teaching people how to surround themselves with situational press to evoke the achievement motive. This way of thinking would account for the fact that the motive seems to change, while still allowing the assumption that needs are enduring dispositions.

---

ing program. The person is encouraged to think in achievement terms everywhere—not just in the training sessions—and to put the action patterns into motion.

People who complete the course write down the plans they have for the next two years. They're encouraged to plan realistically and to set goals that are challenging but not out of reach. This description is a way of turning the achievement orientation they've learned into a self-prescription of an actual course of activity. This prescription then can be used in guiding actual achievement later on.

Is the course effective? The answer seems to be yes. During a two-year follow-up, participants had higher business-achievement ratings, were more likely to have started new business ventures, and were more likely to be employing more people than before, as compared to control subjects (McClelland & Winter, 1969).

This program suggests it's possible to change people's dispositional levels of basic motives, though a question remains as to whether needs themselves have changed. It also remains uncertain how much these results can be generalized to the broader domain of therapy. Nevertheless, the studies do seem to provide intriguing suggestions regarding behavior change, suggestions that deserve further attention.

Need and Motive Theories: Problems and Prospects

In the previous chapter we dealt with trait theorists. As a group, those theorists are more concerned about describing the structure of personality, the nature of the individual differences that underlie it, than they are in describing the mechanics by which personality traits are expressed. The theorists of this chapter, in contrast, look to motivational processes and the pressures they place on people, as a way to specify how dispositions influence behavior. By providing a way to think about how dispositions turn into behavior—by specifying a "process" within personality, a type of intrapersonal functioning—this approach to dispositions evades one of the major criticisms of trait theories.

A criticism of trait theories that's less readily evaded by need theorists is that the decision about what qualities to study is arbitrary. Murray developed his list of needs from his own intuition. The list was accepted uncritically by others working in that tradition. Although additions have been made to the list—for example, the intimacy motive—even these might be viewed as arbitrary. One response to such a criticism is that the motives that have been examined most closely reflect concepts that also appear elsewhere in psychology, including trait psychology. This convergence across views suggests that the needs in question really are fundamental.

Another criticism that's sometimes made of motive theories bears less on the theory itself than on its implementation. In particular, Murray was very explicit in his view that the dynamics of personality can be understood only by considering multiple needs at the same time. However, research on the motive approach to personality has very rarely done that. More typically people have studied one motive at a time, to examine its dynamics. Occasionally researchers have stretched to the point of looking at particular clusters of two or three needs, but this is relatively rare. Thus it will be important for future researchers interested in needs and motives to take multiple needs into account in the studies they conduct.

Despite these criticisms, work on personality from the point of view of motive dispositions has continued into the present. Indeed, such work has enjoyed a resurgence in the past 8 years or so. The idea that people vary in what motivates them has a good deal of intuitive appeal. Further appeal derives from the fact that this idea can be joined to the idea that motive states wax and wane across time and circumstances. This approach thus has a built-in way of incorporating both situational influences and dispositional influences in an integrated way. Given these strengths, and a growing interest in the relation between motive theories and trait theories, the future of this approach seems assured.

SUMMARY

The motive approach to personality assumes that behavior reflects a set of underlying needs. As a need becomes more intense, it is more likely to influence what behavior is done. Behavior is also influenced by press—external stimuli that elicit motivational tendencies. Needs (and press) vary in strength from moment to moment, but people also differ from each other in patterns of chronic need intensities. According to this viewpoint, this difference is the source of individual differences in personality.

Murray made an ambitious attempt to catalog human needs, listing both biological (primary) and psychogenic (secondary) needs. Several of the psychological motives later received systematic study by others. The first studied (by McClelland, Atkinson, and others) was the need for achievement: the motive to overcome obstacles and to attain goals. People with high levels of the achievement motive behave differently from those with lower levels in several ways: the kinds of tasks they prefer, the level of task difficulty they prefer, their degree of persistence, and their performance levels.

The need for power—the motive to be strong compared to other people—has also been studied extensively. People who score high in this need tend to seek out positions of influence, to surround themselves with the trappings of power, and to become aroused when the groups they are guiding experience difficulties. People with high levels of the power motive tend to choose as friends people who aren't influential or popular, thereby protecting themselves from undesired competition. Power-motivated men prefer wives who are dependent, and these wives tend not to have their own careers. The power motive can lead to unpleasant forms of social influence unless it's tempered by a sense of responsibility.

The need for affiliation, another need from Murray's list, is the desire to spend time with other people, to develop and maintain relationships. People who score high in this need are responsive to social influence, spend a relatively large proportion of their time communicating with other people, and when alone often think about being with others. A related motive that isn't represented in Murray's list but has received research attention in recent years is the need for intimacy. People high in this need want warm, close, and communicative relationships with other persons. People with strong intimacy needs tend to spend more time in one-to-one interaction and less in groups. They tend to engage in interactions that involve lots of self-disclosure and are especially concerned about their friends' well-being.

Recent research has also begun to investigate patterns of motives, such as inhibited power motive. This pattern is defined by having more of a need for power than a need for affiliation and by restraining the power need. People with this pattern do well in managerial careers, but the pattern has also been linked to political orientations preceding wars.

Most of the emphasis of this view on personality concerns needs and motives, but the theorists of this view also use other concepts in talking about behavior. Incentive value, the extent to which a given action will satisfy a given need for a person, helps to explain why people with the same need express the need in different ways. Expectancy, the apparent likelihood of success, helps determine whether people pursue incentives.

Although somewhat distinct from his emphasis on needs and motives in behavior, Murray also emphasized the study of individual lives over extended periods of time. He coined the term *personology* to refer to the study of the whole person, and he viewed personology as his goal. This emphasis has reemerged in the work of several other researchers.

Although many kinds of assessment devices are used in the motivational approach to personality, the contribution to assessment most identified with this approach is the Thematic Apperception Test (TAT). The TAT is based on the idea that a person's motives are reflected in the imagery that they "apperceive," that is, read into an ambiguous stimulus—in this case, a set of pictures depicting people in ambiguous situations. Although there are also self-report measures of needs, they appear to measure something (self-attributed motives) different from what the TAT measures (implicit motives). Some people have suggested that the five-factor model can be fit to the motives that Murray listed. Others point out that the evidence comes only from self-report measures, and view traits and motives as different.

The motivational approach to personality has largely ignored the issue of analyzing problems in behavior, although at least some evidence links the need for power to the misuse of alcohol. It's possible to infer from this evidence, however, that many problems in behavior may stem from inappropriate channeling of motives. It's also reasonable that people can be helped by increasing their awareness of the motive that underlies the problem, so the motive can be channeled in alternative ways. Research on increasing the need for achievement suggests that it's possible to alter people's dispositional levels of the motives that make up personality.

GLOSSARY

Apperception The projecting of a motive as imagery onto an external stimulus.

Diagnosticity The extent to which a task provides information about something.

Expectancy The anticipated probable outcome of an action.

Incentive value The degree to which an action can satisfy a particular need for a person.

Inhibited power motivation The condition of having more need for power than for affiliation, but restraining its use.

Latent need A motive that exists but presently isn't being openly displayed.

Manifest need A motive that presently is influencing a person's actions.

Motive Cognitive-affective clusters organized around readiness for a particular kind of experience.

Need An unsatisfactory internal condition that motivates behavior.

Need for achievement The need to overcome obstacles and attain a standard of excellence.

Need for affiliation The need to form and maintain relationships and to be with people.

Need for intimacy The need for close communication with someone else.

Need for power The need to have influence over other people.

Personology Study of the entire person.

Press An external stimulus that increases the level of a motive.

Primary (viscerogenic) need A biological need, such as the need for food.

Resultant Achievement Motivation (RAM) Motive to approach success minus motive to avoid failure.

Secondary (psychogenic) need A psychological or social need.

Thematic Apperception Test (TAT) A method of assessing the strength of a motive through narrative fantasy.

PART three

The Biological Perspective

THE BIOLOGICAL PERSPECTIVE: Major Themes and Underlying Assumptions

Human beings are biological creatures, of that there is no doubt. We're members of the animal kingdom, and we carry around all of the characteristics implied by citizenship in that kingdom. We eat, drink, breathe, void wastes, and engage in the sexual activities that ensure the continuation of our species. We're also affected by a number of more subtle forces that stem from our animal nature.

How deeply rooted are these biological pressures, and how pervasive is their influence on us? Are the qualities of personality determined by genetics? Is the existence of personality itself a product of evolution over the eons? How subtle and how pervasive an influence do biological processes have on personality, and what adaptive functions do these influences serve? These are some of the questions that underlie the biological perspective on personality.

Biological approaches to personality have varied widely in focus over the years. Some theories of this group are only vaguely biological. Other theories are tied to specific biological processes and structures. The nature of the research on the ideas also varies widely, from studies examining the nature of biological functions to studies of inheritance. In some respects, the biological orientation is a scattered approach to personality. There are, however, threads of thought that underlie the fragmented surface, linking many of the pieces back to one another.

The biological orientation to personality has two general thrusts, and people working from this point of view tend to have two separate sets of interests. Theorists of the first group focus on the idea that personality characteristics are genetically determined. The biological mechanisms by which inherited differences influence behavior usually aren't well understood, and have rarely even been explored. The interest of this group lies largely in knowing what characteristics of personality and social behavior are influenced by heredity. This set of theorists represents something of a cross between the biological perspective and the dispositional perspective.

Many of these same people are also interested in the broader idea that the human qualities that we term *personality* are consequences of the evolutionary pressures that produced the human species. This view of personality has been extended rapidly in recent years. It's now being suggested that far more of human social behavior is a product of our evolutionary heritage than anyone would have guessed two decades ago.

These two ideas—that many personality characteristics are genetically determined and that human behavioral tendencies derive from our evolutionary history—form the basis of Chapter 6.

The second aspect of the biological perspective is the idea that human behavior is produced by a complex biological system. The biological processes that make up this system reflect the way we're organized as living creatures. In this view, many biological processes can be expected to have an influence on people's behavior and experience. To understand these influences, the theorists first try to follow the biological systems that exist within the human organism, to see exactly what they're about and how they work. They then think about how the workings of these systems might influence the kinds of behavior that are identified with personality.

This idea has its roots in antiquity, but it's been revolutionized by methodological advances of the recent past. These advances mean that the component processes of the nervous system are now becoming better understood. It also means we're coming to understand how the system of hormones influences behavior. The viewpoint represented in this work is very much a "process" approach to personality, examining how biological functions influence human action. As you'll see, however, this focus on process doesn't mean ignoring individual differences. That is, the processes often operate to different degrees in different people, thereby creating the patterns of uniqueness we think of as personality. This type of biological approach to personality is considered in Chapter 7.

Inheritance, Evolution, and Personality

■ Two 3-day-old babies are lying in their cradles behind the glass window. One of them lies peacefully for hours at a time, rarely crying and moving only a little. The other thrashes his arms and legs, screws up his face, and frequently rends the air with piercing yowls. What could possibly have made two children be so thoroughly different from each other so soon in life?

■ A group of young men, 16 to 18 years old, have been hanging around the pool hall–bar all afternoon, acting cool, eyeing women who pass by, and trying to outdo one another with inventive insults. Occasionally tempers flare, the lines of faces harden, and there's pushing and taunting. This time, though, the one doing the taunting goes too far. There's a glint of dark steel, and the hot air is shattered by gunshots. Later, the dead one's grieving mother cries out, "Why must men do these things?"

Part of who you are is the body you walk around in every day. Some people have big bodies, some have small ones. Some bodies are strong, some are frail. Some bodies are coordinated, some are klutzy. Some bodies turn toward dolls at a certain stage of life, others are drawn instead to Legos.

Your body isn't your personality. But does it influence the kind of personality you have? The idea that our bodies determine our personalities goes back at least to Hippocrates and Galen. As mentioned in Chapter 4, Hippocrates proposed four personality types, and Galen added the idea that each type reflects an excess of some bodily humor. The idea that people's physical makeup determines their personalities has reemerged repeatedly ever since.

"Physical makeup" has meant different things at different times, however. As a result, the idea that physical makeup determines personality has taken different forms. This chapter starts with a brief look at an early version and then turns to a newer and more sophisticated one.

Physique and Personality

The idea that people's body shapes relate to their personalities shows in popular stereotypes: the easygoing, jolly fat man; the adventurous, strong, muscular hero; the frail intellectual. Is there any truth to these stereotypes?

Several theorists over the years have thought so. A psychiatrist named Kretschmer (1925), interested in psychological disorder, classified people into three groups: thin, muscular, and obese. His observations suggested that different body types were susceptible to different disorders. This line of thought was later taken up and expanded on by William Sheldon (1942). Sheldon focused on normal qualities of personality. Further, he proposed that Kretschmer's categories should be considered as dimensions of variability, not as discrete types. (Here's another case where the idea of categories gave way to the idea of dimensions.)

Somatotypes

A person's **somatotype** is defined by placing the person at some point along each dimension. The somatotype is designated by three numbers (each from 1 to 7) indicating the degree of each body characteristic. Sheldon described each dimension in

A.

B.

C.

FIGURE 6.1

Photographs illustrating Sheldon's three body types: left, the endomorph; middle, the mesomorph; and right, the ectomorph.

detail and developed a rationale for how each comes to exist. He believed that each reflects an emphasis during development on one of three layers of the embryo. For this reason, he named the characteristics after the layers.

Endomorphy (the first number of the somatotype) is the tendency toward plumpness. Sheldon viewed this as reflecting an emphasis on the digestive system. Endomorphic bodies are soft and round and not suited to hard physical effort. (They're the basis for the expression "built for comfort, not for speed.") An example of endomorphic bodies shown in Figure 6.1, A.

Mesomorphy (the second number) is the tendency toward muscularity. It reflects a predominance of bone, muscle, and connective tissue. Bodies that are mesomorphic are hard and rectangular. They're strong, resistant to injury, and suited to hard exertion (Figure 6.1, B).

Ectomorphy (the third number) is the tendency toward thinness. This quality reflects predominance of the skin and nervous system. Bodies that are ectomorphic are delicate, linear, and frail (Figure 6.1, C). They have large brains compared with their bodies, but they're easily overwhelmed by stimulation and aren't well suited to physical labor.

It's possible (although rare) for a person to be a perfect example of a single category. For instance, a total mesomorph would be a 1-7-1. Most people, however, have a little of each quality. Someone who's generally muscular, but tends also to be a little pudgy, might be classified as a 4-6-2. A person who's very narrow and frail but has a potbelly might be a 6-1-7. A person who's absolutely average would be a 4-4-4.

Temperament

In parallel with these physical dimensions, Sheldon proposed three aspects of "temperament," each reflected in personality (Table 6.1). **Viscerotonia** relates to such

TABLE 6.1

Some characteristics of the temperaments described by Sheldon (adapted from Sheldon, 1942)

Viscerotonia	Somatotonia	Cerebrotonia
Relaxed posture and movement	Assertive posture and movement	Restrained posture and movement
Love of physical comfort	Love of physical adventure	Love of privacy
Sociability and warmth	Competitive aggressiveness	Social avoidance
Emotional evenness	Bold directness of manner	Emotional restraint
Tolerance, complacency	Energetic quality	Mental overintensity, apprehension
Love of polite ceremony	Need for physical exertion	Inhibited social address
Indiscriminant good will	Indifference to pain	Hypersensitivity to pain

qualities as relaxation, tolerance (even complacency), sociability, love of comfort, and easygoingness. **Somatotonia** includes qualities such as courage, assertiveness, and a desire for adventure, risk, and physical activity. **Cerebrotonia** includes a mental intensity approaching apprehensiveness, avoidance of social interaction, physical and emotional restraint, and a tendency toward privacy (even secretiveness). As with somatotypes, most people have some degree of each quality of temperament.

The name of each temperament is linked to an aspect of the somatotype. This was no accident. Sheldon believed temperament qualities and somatotype qualities go together. He conducted a study over 5 years, involving 200 men, to assess relations between the temperament qualities and the components of the somatotype (Sheldon, 1942). The results were startling. He found extremely high correlations between each aspect of physique and the temperament it was expected to fit. Mesomorphy related strongly to somatotonia, endomorphy to viscerotonia, and ectomorphy to cerebrotonia. Correlations between all other combinations of temperament and physique were inverse.

Thus, Sheldon found exactly what he'd hoped to find. The findings were so good, though, as to suggest that he'd inadvertently biased his ratings. This was possible, because he knew his hypothesis and when making most ratings he already knew a lot about the person he was rating. Later studies also supported his ideas, however, in ratings of children (Walker, 1962) in self-reports (e.g., Cortes & Gatti, 1965; Yates & Taylor, 1978), and in other ways (Davidson, McInnes, & Parnell, 1957; Glueck & Glueck, 1956; Parnell, 1957).

What should be made of these findings? The studies indicate that body types relate to differences in personality. But what's the path of influence? Does physique create personality directly? Or is the process more roundabout? For example, the somatotypes relate to well-known stereotypes. The stereotypes include expectations about how people act. If we carry the expectations into social encounters, we can induce people to behave in the "expected" way (Gacsaly & Borges, 1979). The result would be an association between somatotype and behavior. It would be based on social pressure, though, rather than on body type per se.

It's hard to be sure why associations exist between body type and personality. In part for this reason, many people remained skeptical of Sheldon's theory, and interest in it waned. Although his ideas themselves are no longer influential in personality psychology, Sheldon stressed a theme that reemerged later on. He was convinced that personality, along with body type, was inherited. He believed it, but he didn't test it. Indeed, in his era it wasn't widely understood *how* to test it. Others found ways, however.

Determining the Role of Inheritance in Personality

How do researchers decide whether traits are inherited? Relying on something such as family resemblances would have serious problems. Most important, knowing that family members have similar personalities doesn't allow you to separate two possibilities: They may be similar because of inheritance. Or they may be similar because they're around each other all the time and have learned to act the same way (see Chapter 13).

To get a clearer picture requires better methods. Psychologists turned to the discipline of genetics for ideas. The result was a mix of psychology and genetics called **behavioral genetics.** This is the study of genetic influences on behavioral qualities, including action tendencies, personality dispositions, psychological abnormalities, and even cognitive or emotional processes (Plomin, 1997; Plomin, DeFries, & McClearn, 1990; Plomin & Rende, 1991).

Twin Study Method

A method that's been widely used in behavioral genetics is the **twin study.** It takes advantage of two naturally occurring accidents in reproduction, which result in two types of twins. One kind of accident occurs shortly after conception. A fertilized egg normally divides into two cells, each of which continues to divide, eventually yielding a person. Sometimes, though, the first two cells become separated, and each develops *separately* into a person. The two persons are identical twins, or **monozygotic (MZ) twins.** Because they came from what was initially a single cell, they are 100% alike genetically.

The second kind of accident occurs in conception itself. Usually only one egg is released from the mother's ovary, but occasionally two are. If both happen to be fertilized and begin to develop simultaneously, the result is fraternal twins, or **dizygotic (DZ) twins.** (Any opposite-sexed pair obviously are DZ twins.) Genetically, DZ twins are like any pair of brothers, pair of sisters, or brother and sister. They just happened to be born at the same time rather than separately. As with any pair of **siblings** (brothers or sisters), they are on the average 50% alike genetically (though the overlap of specific pairs ranges from zero to 100). Interestingly enough, many twins are wrong about which kind they are, and errors are just as common for MZ as DZ twins. One study found that in about 30% of pairs one twin was wrong; in about 12% of pairs *both* twins were wrong (Scarr & Carter-Saltzman, 1979).

In a twin study (Figure 6.2), pairs of identical twins are related to each other on the characteristic of interest by a correlation, and pairs of same-sex fraternal twins are also related to each other. These two *correlations* are then compared. If identical twins are more similar to each other than fraternal twins, it must be because of the difference in genetic similarity.

The index of genetic influence on personality is termed a **heritability** estimate. This index is considered to be the amount of variance accounted for by inheritance, in the trait under study. The higher the heritability, the stronger the evidence that genes matter.

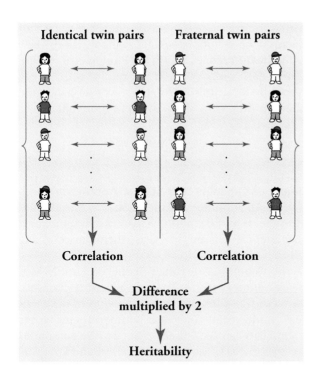

Identical twin pairs | Fraternal twin pairs

Correlation | Correlation

Difference multiplied by 2

Heritability

FIGURE 6.2

The twin study method examines pairs of identical and same-sex fraternal twins. The members of each pair are compared on the variable of interest, and a separate correlation is computed for each type of twin. One of these correlations is then subtracted from the other. Multiplying this difference by 2 gives an index of the heritability of the characteristic, an estimate of the variance in it that is accounted for by inheritance.

The twin study method is based on the assumption that co-twins who are raised together are exposed to much the same life experiences as each other, *whether they are identical or fraternal twins.* This assumption is critical (Figure 6.2). You couldn't conclude that a difference between correlations stems from heredity if parents treated DZ twins differently from MZ twins. The difference in genetic overlap would be confounded with the difference in treatment.

Comparisons between identical and fraternal twins can provide information about the heritability of characteristics.

Are the two kinds of twins treated more or less the same? The evidence is surprisingly limited, but the answer seems to be a cautious yes. MZ twins are more likely than DZ twins to be dressed alike, but the differences are slight (Plomin et al., 1990). MZ twins also don't seem to resemble each other more in personality if they were treated alike than if they weren't (Loehlin & Nichols, 1976). On the other hand, one study found that DZ twins who thought they were MZ twins were more alike than other DZ twins (Scarr & Carter-Saltzman, 1979).

Adoption Research

The twin study method isn't the only way to study inheritance. Another method, termed the **adoption study,** is also used. An adoption study looks at how the adopted child resembles both the biological parents and the adoptive parents. Resemblance to biological parents is viewed as genetically based, whereas resemblance to the adoptive parents is environmentally based.

Another methodological variation combines features of the twin study with features of the adoption study. It's sometimes possible to study MZ twins who were adopted and raised separately (see also Box 6.1). Since they grew up in different homes, any environmental impact should create *differences* between them, rather than similarities. The degree of similarity between these pairs can be compared with similarities of two comparison groups: MZ twins raised together and DZ twins raised together. If heredity is important to the trait under study, MZ twins—even if they were raised apart—should be more similar than DZ twins. If heredity's *really* important, MZ twins raised apart should be nearly as similar as MZ twins raised together.

What Personality Qualities are Inherited?

The methods just described have been used for three decades to study genetic influences on personality. They've been applied to many personality qualities, chosen for study in a variety of ways.

One approach focuses on **temperaments.** This term is used differently by various people (see Buss & Plomin, 1984). Sheldon used it to refer to the aspects of personality he measured. Others have used the singular form *temperament*, rather than the plural, to refer to a person's overall "emotional nature" (e.g., Allport, 1961; Gallagher, 1994; Kagan, 1994).

Today's use of the word may be best exemplified in the work of Arnold Buss and Robert Plomin (1984, p. 84), who use the plural *temperaments* to refer to "inherited personality traits present in early childhood." What distinguishes temperaments from other traits, in their view, is that temperaments are genetically based. Also implicit in their view is that temperaments are more pervasive in their influence than other traits. They're deeper and more far-reaching (A. Buss, 1995). Temperaments affect *what* people do, and *how* people do what they do.

A feature that Buss and Plomin also regard as important is that temperaments should affect adult personality, not just early childhood. Temperaments should show continuity over the life span. Buss and Plomin caution not to expect this continuity to be perfect, however, for two reasons. First, genes don't operate continuously. They turn on and off during development, which may disrupt continuity (Plomin, 1983). Second, despite their genetic base, temperaments can be modified by experience.

> ## BOX 6.1

TWINS SEPARATED AT BIRTH, REUNITED AS ADULTS:
The Resemblances Can Be Startling

Our emphasis in this part of the chapter is on systematic studies of genetics and personality. However, some of the most striking indications that personality can be inherited are more anecdotal. The information comes from the experiences of identical twins who were separated early in life and raised in different homes, only to be reunited later on.

This combination of circumstances occurs when identical twins are put up for adoption separately as newborns, a practice that once was fairly common in this country, but no longer is. In some cases these twins were reunited as adults when they set out to find their co-twins. In many cases, however, the infants grew into adults who had no idea that they were twins. Imagine the surprise of discovering someone else who looks just like you!

What's it like to discover your identical twin after you're both grown? Reunited twins sometimes discover astonishing similarities (Rosen, 1987). Fascinating stories have emerged from projects studying twins raised apart, such as the Minnesota Center for Twin and Adoption Research. Two of their subjects, brothers from New Jersey, didn't meet—didn't even know the other existed—until they were adults. At that time both were volunteer firefighters, both held their beer bottles in the same unusual way, both drank the same brand, and both tended to make the same remarks and gestures when joking, which both did frequently. Another pair of twins discovered that they both smoked the same brand of cigarettes, drove the same kind of car, and did woodworking as a hobby.

A pair of women from Finland provide another amazing example. They were raised in economic circumstances that were very different from each other, but both grew up to be penny pinchers. Each had a fear of heights, each had had a miscarriage, then three healthy children. Not long after they first met, they were so in tune with each other that they began finishing each other's sentences—all this despite being raised totally separated from each other.

Examples such as these are striking, but it's hard to say how much they capitalize on chance. That is, although reunited twins do tend to be similar in many ways, not every pair of twins displays such dramatic patterns of unlikely similarities. Nonetheless, dramatic examples such as these do tend to stick in people's minds and influence their thinking about the nature of personality. Such illustrations convey the impression that inheritance not only influences broad qualities such as activity level and emotionality but also affects personality in more subtle ways.

Temperaments: Activity, Sociability, and Emotionality

Buss and Plomin (1984) argued that three normal personality dispositions deserve to be called temperaments. These are *activity level, sociability,* and *emotionality.* As with all trait dimensions, each is a range of individual differences.

Activity level is the person's overall output of energy or behavior. This temperament has two aspects that differ conceptually from each other, although they're highly correlated. One aspect is *vigor*—the intensity, or amplitude, of behavior. Vigorous acts involve a lot of energy, and people high in vigor prefer high-intensity action (e.g., they may choose to play tennis instead of shuffleboard). The second facet of activity level is *tempo*—speed. People whose tempo is high prefer fast-paced activities, and they tend to do quickly whatever they're doing. People whose tempo is lower take a more leisurely approach to life's activities.

Sociability is the tendency to prefer being with other people rather than alone. Sociability involves a desire for other people's attention, a desire to share activities, and a desire for the responsiveness and stimulation that are part of social interaction. According to Buss and Plomin, sociability is *not* a matter of desiring social rewards such as praise, respect, or sympathy—these rewards are of similar value to everyone. Rather, to be sociable is to value intrinsically the process of interacting with others.

Emotionality is defined by Buss and Plomin as the tendency to become physiologically aroused—easily and intensely—in upsetting situations. They argue that this temperament pertains to only three emotions: distress, anger, and fear. In their view, other emotions don't involve enough arousal to be relevant to this temperament (though see Box 6.2 for a different view). Their temperament survey for adults (Table 6.2) has three subscales, which measure general emotionality (undifferentiated distress), anger proneness, and fear proneness. It's of interest that anger proneness isn't highly correlated with the other two (Buss & Plomin, 1984). Perhaps the temperament of emotionality is actually two distinct traits.

It's of interest that the temperaments proposed by Buss and Plomin resemble those of Sheldon more than is usually recognized. Activity level, and the impact on the world that this concept implies, is similar to somatotonia (take a look back at

---

BOX 6.2

THEORETICAL ISSUE:
How Should Emotionality Be Conceptualized?

In Buss and Plomin's view the temperament of emotionality concerns the joint *ease* and *intensity* of arousal of negative emotions. However, the items by which they assess emotionality pertain primarily to easy arousability (Table 6.2). Consequently, what they've been measuring probably relates primarily to the *frequency* of negative emotions.

Larsen and Diener (1985, 1987) took a different approach. Their focus is the *intensity* of emotional feelings, rather than the frequency with which the feelings occur. Larsen and Diener suggest that people differ on affect intensity in a general way—across all feeling qualities, not just fear, anger, and distress. Measuring mood over several weeks, they found that people who report having strongly positive moods are the same people who report having strongly negative moods. People whose positive feelings tended to be weak also tended to have weak negative feelings (*r* values range from .70 to .77). Larsen and Diener contend that *intensity* of feelings is separate from the *frequency* of feelings, and have provided support (Larsen, Diener, & Emmons, 1986).

Thus the two pairs of theorists focus on different aspects of the experience of emotion—Larsen

and Diener on intensity, Buss and Plomin on ease or frequency of arousal. Which view is more useful? It's hard to be sure. Larsen and Diener have gathered evidence that the affect-intensity construct is a good tool for understanding and predicting people's behaviors and experiences in day-to-day life, which hasn't been done with the Buss and Plomin construct. On the other hand, there's strong evidence that the qualities Buss and Plomin measure are inherited. Evidence on this point for the Larsen and Diener construct is far less direct (see Larsen & Diener, 1987).

For our present purpose, what's most important is that there are two fundamental issues separating these theories. One issue is whether theorists and researchers should be focusing on intensity of feelings, on frequency of feelings, or on both. This important question has far-reaching research implications. The other issue, also important, is whether the word *emotionality* should refer to the arousal of distress-related emotions only or should refer instead to a more general tendency to experience *any* emotions. This second issue doesn't go away. It comes up again in the biological approach to personality, discussed in the next chapter.

TABLE 6.2

Items from the EAS temperament survey for adults (Buss & Plomin, 1984). The EAS (which stands for Emotionality, Activity, and Sociability) measures the temperaments of emotionality, activity level, and sociability. Emotionality has three component scales measuring fear, anger, and general distress. Response choices are on a five-point scale ranging from "not at all typical of me" to "very typical of me."

Emotionality

I am easily frightened.	[fear]
There are many things that annoy me.	[anger]
Everyday events make me troubled and fretful.	[distress]
I often feel insecure.	[fear]
I am known as hot-blooded and quick tempered.	[anger]
I get emotionally upset easily.	[distress]

Activity

I usually seem to be in a hurry.

My life is fast paced.

I often feel as if I'm bursting with energy.

Sociability

I like to be with people.

I prefer working with others rather than alone.

I find people more stimulating than anything else.

From *Temperament: Early developing personality traits* by A. H. Buss and R. Plomin, 1984, Hillsdale, NJ: Erlbaum. Copyright 1984 by Lawrence Erlbaum Associates, Inc. Reprinted by permission.

Table 6.1). Sociability was an important part of viscerotonia. Emotionality (apprehensiveness) was part of cerebrotonia. This resemblance, though far from perfect, is certainly intriguing.

What's the evidence that these three temperaments are inherited? Consider twin studies of parents' ratings of their children (Buss & Plomin, 1975; Plomin, 1974; Plomin & Rowe, 1977; Plomin, described in Plomin & Foch, 1980). In these studies, associations between parent ratings of emotionality, activity, and sociability were strong for MZ twins (average correlations are graphed in Figure 6.3). The correlations were next to nonexistent and sometimes even inverse for DZ twins. Thus, the data seem clear in indicating a powerful role for heredity in these three characteristics (see also Thomas & Chess, 1977).

On the other hand, concerns have been raised about possible rater biases when parents rate their children (Neale & Stevenson, 1989; Saudino, McGuire, Reiss, Hetherington, & Plomin, 1995). Parents of DZ twins that don't resemble each other closely apparently tend to contrast the two, amplifying the differences they see. Parents of MZ twins, seeing more similarity, don't seem to do this. Further, there's evidence that mothers (of very young children) aren't very good reporters of their children's behavior (Seifer, Sameroff, Barrett, & Krafchuk, 1994).

It's important, then, that other sources of evidence exist. Several studies have examined the heritability of emotionality with Eysenck's self-report scales. These

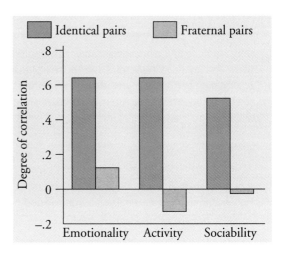

FIGURE 6.3

Average correlations for parental ratings of identical and fraternal twins on temperaments of emotionality, activity level, and sociability. (Correlations are averaged across 4 samples, totaling 228 pairs of identical twins and 172 pairs of fraternal twins, with an average age of 5 years 1 month) (adapted from Buss & Plomin, 1984).

studies uniformly found that MZ twins are more alike by self-report than DZ twins (Floderus-Myrhed, Pedersen, & Rasmuson, 1980; Loehlin & Nichols, 1976; Viken, Rose, Kaprio, & Koskenvuo, 1994; Young, Eaves, & Eysenck, 1980; see also Loehlin, Willerman, & Horn, 1985; Eysenck & Eysenck, 1985). One recent study even found the same relation when using co-twin ratings rather than self-reports (Heath, Neale, Kessler, Eaves, & Kendler, 1992). These findings give added weight to the conclusion that emotionality is genetically influenced.

Adoption research (Loehlin et al., 1985) also supports a genetic influence for activity level and sociability. This study compared adopted children with their biological parents and their adoptive parents. The measures were two self-report inventories, the California Psychological Inventory (CPI) and the Thurstone Temperament Schedule (TTS). The CPI has two scales that reflect sociability (sociability and social presence), and the TTS also has a sociability scale. The TTS also has scales that reflect activity level (called active and vigorous).

Table 6.3 displays some of the correlations from this study. Although these children had spent their lives with adoptive parents (from a few days after birth), there was remarkably little resemblance between them (column A). On the other hand, despite the separation from their biological parents, there was a pattern of moderate correlations between them (column B).

The data also allowed comparisons between the adopted children and both biological and adoptive siblings (columns C and D). Though the pattern is less consistent than for parents, the same general picture emerges: The adopted children are more like their biological brothers and sisters than their adoptive brothers and sisters.

Are There Other Temperaments?

Two other dimensions merit mention in our discussion of temperaments: impulsivity and intelligence. In an earlier statement of their theory, Buss and Plomin (1975) viewed impulsivity as a possible temperament. Evidence collected between then and 1984 was inconclusive, and they dropped impulsivity. Later on, a new study found a genetic influence on impulsiveness (Pedersen et al., 1988). This study was unusual in that it examined older adults (average age 58), whereas Buss and Plomin had relied mostly on parent ratings of children. Pedersen et al.'s finding might reopen the question of whether impulsiveness is a temperament.

TABLE 6.3

Correlations between adopted children and (A) their adoptive parents, (B) their biological parents, (C) their adoptive siblings, and (D) their biological siblings, on three measures of sociability and two measures of activity (data adapted from Loehlin, Willerman, & Horn, 1985)*

Measure	(A) Adoptive parent	(B) Biological parent	(C) Adoptive siblings	(D) Biological siblings
Sociability (CPI)[†]	.04	.17	.04	.22
Social presence (CPI)	.12	.34	−.08	.70
Sociable (TTS)[‡]	.02	.18	−.13	.38
Active (TTS)	.02	.16	−.12	.06
Vigorous (TTS)	.06	.33	.18	.42

*Parent correlations are averages of child–father and child–mother correlations; sibling correlations are also averaged.

[†]CPI is the California Psychological Inventory.

[‡]TTS is the Thurstone Temperament Schedule.

Intelligence is a different case. Although intelligence is an important variable, it's not usually regarded as a *personality* trait (for a dissenting opinion see Eysenck & Eysenck, 1985). For this reason, it's rarely discussed in this context. However, there's substantial evidence that intelligence has all the characteristics that Buss and Plomin used to define temperaments. That is, it's genetically influenced (Bouchard, Lykken, McGue, Segal, & Tellegen, 1990; Loehlin et al., 1988; Plomin, 1989), and its effects on behavior are broad, manifest early in life, and continue throughout the life span.

Inheritance of Traits

We began this discussion with temperaments: broad, pervasive qualities that underlie a wide range of behaviors. Are other traits also influenced by inheritance?

Twin studies have looked at the heritability of a variety of traits, using personality inventories. An early twin study (Loehlin & Nichols, 1976) found correlations among MZ twins consistently higher than among DZ twins across a wide range of characteristics (an average of about .50 vs. an average of about .30, respectively). A later study of twins raised apart (Bouchard & McGue, 1990) found similar patterns. Several other studies (reviewed by Carey, Goldsmith, Tellegen, & Gottesman, 1978) concurred.

These studies were done some time ago, before trait theorists began to converge on the idea that personality is described by five basic traits. Since the emergence of the big five model, researchers have begun to ask whether the five dimensions outlined in the last chapter are genetically influenced. The answer appears to be yes.

At least three twin studies have explicitly studied the five-factor model (Bergeman et al., 1993; Jang et al., 1996; Jang et al., 1998), and a fourth used a measure that incorporates elements of the big five (Tellegen et al., 1988). These studies all found evidence of heritability for conscientiousness. Agreeableness was found to be heritable in the three studies in which it was measured (Bergeman et al., 1993; Jang et

Temperaments influence many kinds of behavior; for example, activity level expresses itself through the kinds of leisure activities people choose to engage in. Some activities are more laid back, others are more fast paced and require lots of energy.

al., 1996). With respect to both neuroticism and extraversion (which have been studied over a much longer period), the evidence of heritability has been quite strong and consistent (e.g., Heath et al., 1992; Jang et al., 1996; Tellegen et al., 1988; Viken et al., 1994).

As noted in Chapter 4, the last of the big five is the one that's been the hardest to characterize and name. Some call it openness to experience, others call it intellect, culture, and even intelligence. As indicated just earlier, there's lots of evidence of a genetic contribution to intelligence. There's now also evidence of a genetic contribution to openness to experience (Bergeman et al., 1993; Jang et al., 1996; Jang et al., 1998; see also Loehlin, 1992).

Temperaments and the Five-Factor Model

The supertraits that make up the five-factor model are broad and pervasive in influence. In that respect they're a lot like temperaments. This suggests some further questions, which may have already arisen in your own mind. What's the relationship between the five-factor model and the temperament model discussed earlier in this chapter? Do the big five *derive from* the temperaments? Are they *the same* as the temperaments?

Let's consider how the big five relate to the temperaments (for more extensive discussions, see Digman & Shmelyov, 1996; Halverson, Kohnstamm, & Martin, 1994; Loehlin, 1992). An obvious similarity is that Buss and Plomin's (1984) emotionality closely resembles neuroticism, or emotional instability. Although the labels *emotionality* and *emotional instability* are more neutral than is *neuroticism,* the dimension clearly focuses on *negative* emotions, particularly anxiety. Thus, in this case temperament and trait are quite similar.

Another of the big five is extraversion. This trait has overtones of not one but two temperaments (plus some other qualities). Extraversion suggests a preference for being with others, implying a possible link to sociability. Eysenck (1986) has also included a quality of activity in his portayal of extraversion. This suggests that extraversion may blend sociability with activity. On the other hand, extraversion has come to be viewed partly in terms of social dominance, which isn't directly implied either by sociability or by activity.

Another of the five factors also has overtones of sociability, although again not being identical to it. In particular, agreeableness suggests liking to be with people. It goes beyond that, however, in having connotations of being easy to get along with. Whether agreeableness can plausibly be seen as deriving from sociability is something of an open question.

What of conscientiousness? Examination of this supertrait suggests that it's defined partly by an absence of impulsiveness. That is, conscientiousness is partly a planful, persistent, focused orientation toward life's activities. Given earlier discussion of the possibility that impulsiveness is a temperament (Pedersen et al., 1988), this would suggest another link between temperaments and the five-factor model.

The last of the big five is openness to experience, or intellect, culture, or intelligence. Given the diversity of labels for this factor, it isn't clear whether this is the same quality as the intelligence mentioned earlier as a potential temperament. (Indeed, it isn't all that clear exactly what intelligence is—cf. Sternberg, 1982.) But if this part of the five-factor model did reflect the same quality as intelligence tests measure, there'd be yet another link between temperament and trait models.

In sum, although the fit is far less than perfect, the set of qualities proposed as biologically based temperaments bears more than just a slight resemblance to the five-factor model. The places where the resemblance is less clear serve partly to raise interesting questions. For example, why should activity and sociability be considered fundamental, rather than extraversion? There are many ways to divide the qualities of behavior, and it's hard to decide which is best.

It seems likely that these questions will continue to spur interest. More specifically, it seems likely that the five-factor model will continue to have an increasing influence on how behavioral genetics researchers decide which qualities of personality to study.

Genetics of Other Qualities: How Distinct Are They?

Studies of traditional traits aren't the only evidence that inheritance influences personality. A number of other effects have emerged, some of which relate fairly readily to personality.

An example is the evidence of a genetic influence on risk of divorce (McGue & Lykken, 1992). Not only is personality a plausible basis for this, there's now evidence that the effect operates *through* personality (Jockin, McGue, & Lykken, 1996). A particularly unlikely finding is a genetic influence on people's likelihood of experiencing impactful life events. Not only is this true, but evidence again indicates that the effect operates via personality (Saudino et al., 1997). Heredity also influences how much social support people have (Kessler, Kendler, Heath, Neale, & Eaves, 1992), which again might reflect personality differences. There's also a genetic contribution to people's attitudes on various topics (Eaves, Eysenck, & Martin, 1989; Tesser, 1993), which seems likely to reflect broader personality qualities.

Findings such as these raise a question: To what extent are these effects distinct and separate? The temperaments discussed earlier are broad and relate to many traits. Whenever evidence is found that a quality is genetically influenced, it raises a question. Is this a *separate* effect? Or is the effect emerging only because the quality under study relates to a temperament?

The question of how many distinct qualities are *separately* influenced by inheritance is one that hasn't been explored much. However, it's an important question in understanding how inheritance influences personality. A very recent study has begun to explore it, within the framework of the five-factor model (Jang et al., 1998). This study found that not only were the five supertraits heritable, so were most of the facet traits that underlie them. Indeed, the latter genetic influences were separate from the genetic influences on the overall traits. This suggests that many distinct qualities may be genetically influenced, rather than just a few broad ones.

Two Further Issues

There are two more issues to raise in this part of the chapter. One of them concerns the "other" effect of twin studies, the part we haven't emphasized until now, the fact that nonhereditary factors also contribute to personality. The issue concerns what kind of contribution they make.

The Nature of Environmental Influences

The studies that establish a powerful role for inheritance in personality also show an important role for nonhereditary factors. Surprisingly, however, families don't operate to make children alike, as most people assume. The environment has an impact on personality, but the impact takes place primarily on an *individual* level (Plomin & Daniels, 1987).

What might be the sources of nonshared environmental influence? Several guesses sound reasonable (Dunn & Plomin, 1990; Plomin & Daniels, 1987; Rowe, 1994), although there isn't a lot of information on the question. For example, siblings often have different sets of friends—sometimes totally different. Peers have an important influence on growing children—some think an even greater influence than parents (Harris, 1995). Differences in peer groups may cause children's personalities to become different. If that happens, it's an environmental influence, but it's one that's not shared by the siblings.

Another point is that siblings in families don't exist side by side. In their interactions with each other, they develop roles that play off each other (e.g., Daniels, 1986; Hoffman, 1991). For example, if one child frequently helps another child with schoolwork and so on, the two are developing styles of interacting that are different from each other. As another example, parents sometimes favor one child over another. This can influence the children's relationship, perhaps inducing differences between them. Again, such effects would be environmental, but they would differ from one child to the other.

The exact manner in which the environment influences personality development remains to be fully explored. It seems likely, however, that this is an area that will receive increased attention in the future.

Inheritance and Sexual Orientation

Another topic about which there's been much discussion in recent years is the possible role of genetics in determining a person's sexual orientation. Some would regard this topic as outside the realm of personality, but others would say it's very much a part of personality.

Evidence regarding the possibility of a genetic role in sexual orientation goes back over 30 years, with the report of a higher incidence of homosexuality among men whose MZ twin was gay than among men whose DZ twin was gay (Eysenck, 1964b). More recent twin studies have also looked at homosexual men (Bailey & Pillard, 1991) and homosexual women (Bailey, Pillard, Neale, & Agyei, 1993). In each case, the co-twin was more than twice as likely to be homosexual if the twins were MZ than if they were DZ (similar findings were also reported by Whitam, Diamond, & Martin, 1993).

Another article has reported evidence of a genetic basis for male homosexuality using an entirely different approach (Hamer, Hu, Magnuson, Hu, & Pattatucci, 1993). These researchers carefully examined families of gay men for patterns of similarity. They found more gay relatives on the mother's side of the family (maternal uncles and sons of maternal aunts) than on the father's side. This suggested to them that the homosexual gene might be on the X chromosome (which a son always receives from his mother).

Examination of subjects' genetic material revealed a region of the X chromosome that was similar among most of the gay subjects. This suggests a genetic basis for some instances of homosexuality. The evidence also suggest that other instances have another basis, since this region *wasn't* similar for some men in the study (see also Pool, 1993). It's long been wondered why homosexuality hasn't died out over generations, because gay men don't reproduce at the same rate as other men. If the gene is on the X chromosome, that would account for it. That is, the X chromosome is carried by women as well as men. Thus, the gene can be passed on without being reflected in behavior. All involved in this research caution that the finding must be replicated before its implications are pursued too far, but the finding does have far-reaching implications.

Evolution and Human Behavior

Evidence that inheritance plays a role in personality is one contributor to the emergence of a broader current of thought in psychology. The broader current is the idea that evolutionary processes have a stronger influence on present-day human behavior than is generally realized. This line of thought is tied to several labels, including behavioral ecology, sociobiology, and most recently evolutionary psychology (Barkow, Cosmides, & Tooby, 1992; D. Buss, 1991, 1995; Segal, 1993; Tooby & Cosmides, 1989, 1990).

Sociobiology and Evolutionary Psychology

Sociobiology (Alexander, 1979; Barash, 1977, 1986; Crawford, 1989; Crawford, Smith, & Krebs, 1987; Dawkins, 1976b; Lumsden & Wilson, 1981; Wilson, 1975) was defined as the study of the biological basis of social behavior. The assumption that underlies sociobiology is that many—perhaps all—of the basic elements of social interaction in human society are products of evolution. That is, these patterns were retained in our species genetically, because at some point in prehistory they conferred an adaptive advantage.

In some respects the sociobiological viewpoint resembles that presented earlier by a group working in **ethology,** the study of the behavior of animals in their natural environment. Two topics in ethology are commonly mentioned in psychology

Evolutionary psychologists believe that even acts of altruism, such as doing disaster relief work for the Red Cross, may have a genetic basis.

courses. One is imprinting, by which the young of many species become attached to their mothers (Hess, 1973). Another is the idea that animals mark off and defend territories (cf. Ardrey, 1966).

Ethologists suggested we can learn much about human behavior by studying other species. For example, the things in your room can be seen as territorial markers. It may be a mess, but it's *your* mess. As another example, attachment of infants to their mothers may involve the same processes as imprinting. Psychologists have been wary of adopting such ideas too quickly. Drawing parallels to other animals gets risky when the animals aren't closely related to people—for example, the birds in which imprinting is so clear.

Ethologists influenced thinking about human behavior mostly by making analogies. Sociobiologists, in contrast, focused more on evolutionary genetics and the question of how behavior patterns might get built in (see also Box 6.3). This view is in some ways more radical than that of the ethologists. To a sociobiologist, a behavior pattern might exist in humans *but in no other species*, because of a unique adaptation among humans.

The reasoning of sociobiology has sometimes led in surprising directions. For example, it's led to a way to account for a tendency that seems particularly hard to justify in evolutionary terms. The tendency is altruism—concern for the welfare of others, to the point of sacrificing one's own well-being (potentially one's life) for someone else. From a narrow biological view, altruism would seem to have adaptive *dis*advantage. That is, acting altruistically may help someone, but it also might get you killed. This, in turn, prevents your genes from being passed on to the next generation. If the genes aren't passed on, a genetically based tendency toward altruism should disappear very quickly.

Sociobiologists point out, however, that the process of evolution isn't really a matter of individual survival. What matters concerns a "gene pool," distributed across a population. If one *group* in a population survives, prospers, and reproduces at a high rate, its genes move onward into subsequent generations more than other groups' genes.

BOX 6.3

THEORETICAL ISSUE:
Population Genetics and the Existence of Individual Differences

The basic concepts of natural selection and population genetics are simple: For any characteristic that's genetically influenced, there's a range of values for that characteristic. Each value is held by some people. For example, eye color varies, as do height and weight. Variations stem from the fact that there are different "versions"—termed **alleles**— of any gene that influences the characteristic.

The pattern of differences among people is influenced over generations by a process called selection. Selection means that one version of the characteristic (or one end of a dimension) is represented in the next generation either more (because it's helpful in survival or reproduction), or less (because it *interferes* with survival or reproduction). This is called **directional selection.** It follows a more-is-better principle, causing shifts toward presence of the adaptive quality in the next generation. If it goes on long enough, directional selection reduces individual differences because (over generations) more and more of the population wind up with the adaptive characteristic.

It's hard to imagine a variable like eye color influencing survival. It isn't all that hard, though, to think of characteristics that might do so. For example, in a world where strength matters (which probably was true during human evolution), strength makes it more likely that a person will survive long enough to reproduce, thereby sending genes for strength onward into the next generation. As long as these genes are well represented in the population, the population will tend to survive and create yet another generation.

But wait. If some characteristics are more adaptive than others, why are there individual dif-

ferences? Why aren't we all large and strong and wise and healthy and whatever else is a "good" thing to be? One of the tricky things about selection is that whether a particular value is adaptive or not depends on where the population lives. Sometimes a value that's useful in one environment is not just useless—but fatal—in another.

In the long run, genetic variability is important for a population to survive in a changing world. Thus population geneticists have come to recognize the importance of another kind of selection, termed **stabilizing selection,** which serves to maintain genetic variability (Plomin, 1981). Stabilizing selection occurs when an intermediate value of some characteristic is more adaptive than the value at either end of the distribution. Presumably, intermediate values reflect combinations of alleles, rather than a specific allele. Predominance of intermediate values thus implies genetic variability rather than uniformity.

To illustrate how an intermediate value of a characteristic can be more adaptive than an extreme value, consider this example. It's important for people to have some sociability, given that we are such a social species. Having too little sociability isn't adaptive. But neither is it adaptive to have too *much* sociability. A person with extremely high sociability could hardly bear to be alone, and life sometimes requires people to be alone.

Stabilizing selection thus is extremely important. It's what causes genetically influenced differences in personality to exist. Without it, there'd be only a single biologically influenced character, which everyone would have.

This means there are ways to get your genes carried forward besides individual reproduction. In particular, your genes are helped to move into the next generation by anything that helps *your part of the gene pool* reproduce, an idea called **inclusive fitness** (W. D. Hamilton, 1964). If you do an altruistic act for a relative, it helps the relative survive. If an extremely altruistic act (in which you die) saves a great many of your relatives, it helps aspects of your genetic makeup be passed on because your relatives are genetically similar to you. This process is sometimes called "kin selection."

Thus, it's argued, the tendency to be altruistic may be genetically based. This argument also implies that people will be more altruistic toward those in their kinship group than toward strangers (especially competitors). This seems to be true (Burnstein, Crandall, & Kitayama, 1994). Also consistent with this view, there seems to be a genetic contribution to empathic concern for others, which may underlie altruistism (Burnstein, Crandall, & Kitayama, 1994; Matthews, Batson, Horn, & Rosenman, 1981; Rushton, Fulker, Neale, Nias, & Eysenck, 1986).

The idea that altruistic tendencies are part of human nature has been extended to suggest an evolutionary basis for cooperation among nonrelatives. The idea is essentially that having survived better by cooperating than by being individualists and competitors, our ancestors acquired a tendency toward being helpful more generally. One person helps the other in the expectation that the help will be returned, an idea termed **reciprocal altruism** (Trivers, 1971).

Can this possibly have happened? Wouldn't people cheat, and take without giving? From an evolutionary view, the question is whether reciprocation works—leads to better outcomes for those involved. There's evidence that it does, at least in the cooperative situations studied by psychologists (Axelrod & Hamilton, 1981). This has led some to conclude that a tendency to cooperate is part of human nature (Guisinger & Blatt, 1994; Kriegman & Knight, 1988).

Genetic Similarity and Attraction

The idea that people act altruistically toward relatives has also been extended by Philippe Rushton and his colleagues (Rushton, 1989a; Rushton, Russell, & Wells, 1984) to what he calls **genetic similarity theory.** The basic idea is similar to what's come before: A gene "survives" (is represented in the next generation) by any action that brings about reproduction of any organism in which copies of itself exist. That may mean being altruistic to your kinship group, but Rushton suggests it means other things as well.

Rushton and his colleagues (1984) argued that genetic similarity has an influence on who attracts you. Specifically, you're more attracted to strangers who resemble you genetically than to those who don't. How does this help the survival of the gene? If you're attracted to someone, you may become sexually involved, which may result in offspring. Offspring have genes from both parents. By making you attracted to someone with genes like yours, your genes increase the odds that genes like themselves will be copied (from one parent or the other) into a new person, surviving into the next generation.

Are people attracted to others whose genes resemble their own? Maybe so. Rushton (1988) has had couples take blood tests that give a rough index of genetic similarity. He found that sexually involved couples had in common 50% of the genetic markers. When he took the data and paired people randomly (instead of letting them select their own mates), the pairs shared only 43% of the markers, a significantly lower proportion. Rushton went on to compare couples who'd had children with those who hadn't. Those with a child shared 52% of the genetic markers; those with no child shared only 44%. Thus, among sexually active couples, those most similar were also most likely to have reproduced.

This attraction effect isn't limited to the opposite sex. People also tend to form friendships with others who are genetically similar to them. Rushton (1989b) repeated his study with pairs of men who were close friends (all were heterosexual, so the friendships had no sexual aspect). The pairs of friends shared 54% of the genetic markers, random pairs shared only 48%. Again, it appears that genetic similarity resulted somehow in attraction.

How would forming friendships with genetically similar people of the same sex be adaptive? The point is to get the genes into the next generation. Having same-sex friends doesn't do that directly. There are two ways it can help, though. The first is similar to the idea discussed earlier about altruism and kin selection. You're more likely to be altruistic for a close friend than a stranger, making it more likely that the friend will live to reproduce. The second possibility is that you may meet the same-sex friend's opposite-sex sibling. If the sibling is also genetically similar to you, an attraction may develop, with potential sexual activity, resulting in offspring.

How do people detect genetic similarity? That's hard to say. One possibility is that people are drawn to others who share their facial and body features. That is, people who look like you seem like family and therefore attract you. Another possibility is that genetic similarity is conveyed by smell (cf. Monmaney, 1987). Thus, outside your awareness, you may recognize those who are like you by subtle physical cues.

The general idea that people choose mates on the basis of particular characteristics is called **assortative mating** (Thiessen & Gregg, 1980). It's clear that human mating isn't random. People select their mates on the basis of a variety of characteristics, though there are limitations on how fine-grained this selection is (Lykken & Tellegen, 1993). Often the features that influence mate selection are similarities to the self (Buss, 1985).

Mate Selection and Competition for Mates

We've talked at length about the all-importance of conveying genes onward to the next generation. (From this view, it's sometimes said, a person is just a gene's way of creating another [identical] gene.) Obviously, then, the evolutionary view on personality focuses closely on mating. Indeed, from this view, mating is what life's all about (although other issues do arise when you think about the complexities involved in mating). Just as certain qualities confer survival advantage, certain qualities also confer reproductive advantage.

Mating involves competition. Males compete with one another; so do females. But what's being competed for differs between the sexes. Trivers (1972) has argued that males and females evolved different strategies, based on differences in their roles in reproduction. Female humans have greater investment in offspring than males—they carry them for 9 months, and they're more tied to caring for them after birth. The general rule across species is that the sex with the greater investment can generate fewer offspring over the life span, and thus is choosier about a mate (though not everyone agrees on this point; see Small, 1993). The sex with less investment can generate more offspring, and thus is less discriminating.

Given the difference in biological investment, the strategy for women is to tend to hold back from mating until they identify the best available male. "Best" under this strategy is defined in terms of quality of genetic contribution, parental care, or material support for the mate and offspring. In contrast, the strategy for males is to maximize sexual opportunities, copulating as often as possible. This means seeking partners who are available and fertile (Buss, 1994a, 1994b). In this view, men tend to view women as *sex objects,* whereas women tend to view men as *success objects.*

These differences in orientation should produce different strategies for trying to get the opportunity to mate (which both males and females want). David Buss and David Schmitt (1993) examined differences in how men and women compete for and select mates, and how the strategies differ from short term to long term (see also Buss, 1994a, 1994b; Feingold, 1992; Schmitt & Buss, 1996). Because men are interested in finding fertile partners, women should compete by emphasizing their qualities that relate to fertility—youth and beauty. Because women want to find partners that will provide for them and their babies, men should compete by emphasizing their status, personal dominance and ambition, and wealth or potential for acquiring wealth (Sidanius, Pratto, & Bobo, 1994; Sprecher, Sullivan, & Hatfield, 1994).

What do men and women actually *do* to compete for mates? College students report doing pretty much that (Buss, 1988). Men brag about their accomplishments and earning potential, display expensive possessions, and flex their muscles. Women enhance their beauty through makeup, jewelry, clothing, and hairstyles. Women also play hard to get. This seems intended to incite widespread interest among many males. This permits the women to be choosy once candidates are identified (see also Kenrick, Sadalla, Groth, & Trost, 1990).

Buss (1989) also examined aspects of mate preferences in 37 different cultures around the world. Cultural differences were surprisingly rare. The preferences of U.S. college students didn't differ much from those of people elsewhere. Females (more than males) are drawn to cues indicating availability of resources (see also Singh, 1995). Females are also drawn to cues of dominance and high status (Cunningham, Barbee, & Pike, 1990; Feingold, 1992; Sadalla et al., 1987; Kenrick et al., 1990), especially when the dominance is expressed in socially positive ways (Jensen-Campbell, Graziano, & West, 1995). The cross-cultural data indicate that males (more than females) are drawn to cues indicating reproductive capacity.

Evidence from other research shows that men prefer younger women, especially as they themselves grow older, consistent with the seeking of reproductive capacity. This comes from a study of the age ranges specified in singles' ads (Kenrick & Keefe, 1992). As can be seen in Figure 6.4, men past age 25 specified a range that extended increasingly below their own age. Women, in contrast, tended to express a preference for men slightly older than themselves.

Also consistent with predictions from the evolutionary model are results from several other studies of gender differences (see also Table 6.4). Men are more interested in casual sex than are women (Bailey, Gaulin, Agyei, & Gladue, 1994; Buss & Schmitt, 1993; Clark & Hatfield, 1989; Oliver & Hyde, 1993) and are less selective in their criteria for one-night stands (Kenrick, Groth, Trost, & Sadalla, 1993). Men are also more readily excited by visual erotica than are women (Bailey et al., 1994). Men's confidence in their commitment to their relationship is shaken by exposure to a very attractive woman, whereas women's confidence is shaken by exposure to a very dominant man (Kenrick, Neuberg, Zierk, & Krones, 1994).

Both men and women experience jealousy, but there seems to be a difference in what creates this emotion. In theory, it's evolutionarily important for men to be concerned about paternity (they want to support their *own* children, not someone else's). Thus, men should be especially jealous about acts of sexual infidelity. In theory, women are most concerned about whether the man will continue to support her

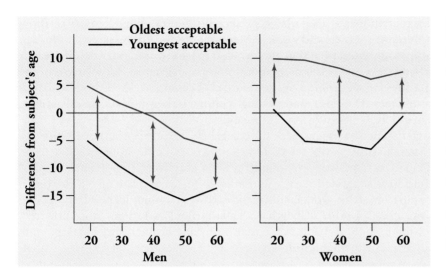

FIGURE 6.4

Singles' ads by men and women often specify age ranges of persons of the opposite sex the ad's placer would like to meet. In this sample of ads, men expressed an increasing preference for younger women. Women tended to prefer men slightly older than they were, and the extent of that preference didn't change over time. (adapted from Kendrick & Keefe, 1992).

and the children. Thus, women should be especially jealous about a man's having emotional bonds with another woman, rather than about sex per se. Data from several studies support this view: Men were more disturbed by thoughts of sexual infidelity and women were more disturbed by thoughts of emotional infidelity (Buss, Larsen, Westen, & Semmelroth, 1992; see also Bailey et al., 1994).

Mate Retention and Other Issues

The first challenge in mating is attracting a potential mate. The next challenge is retaining the mate. Both men and women have the potential to stray, and people use various tactics to prevent that from happening (Buss & Shackelford, 1997). Some tactics are used by both men and women, but use of others differs by gender. For example, men reported being more likely to spend a lot of money and give in to their wives' wishes; women were more likely to make themselves look extra attractive and to let others know their mate is already taken.

TABLE 6.4

Summary of predictions from evolutionary psychology for sex differences in mating tendencies

Issue	Females	Males
Reproductive constraints	Can produce only a limited number of children over life	Can reproduce without limit through life
Optimal reproductive strategy	Locate and hold onto best quality mate	Mate as widely and often as possible
Desired quality in potential mate	Resources to protect and support them and offspring	Childbearing capability
Basis for evaluating mate potential	Earning capacity, status, possessions, generosity	Physical attractiveness, health, youth
Most likely basis for jealousy	Partner's sexual infidelity with another	Partner's emotional attachment to another

Use of retention tactics also related predictably to other factors in the relationship, but differently for men and women. Men used more of these tactics if they saw the wife as physically attractive. Men also devoted more effort to retention if the wife was young—an effect that was independent of the man's age and the length of the relationship. In contrast, women worked harder at retention when their husbands had higher incomes. They also made stronger efforts if their husbands were striving for high status (independent of current income).

Although mating strategies per se have been the starting point for much of this research on gender differences, others have applied the theme more broadly. (As we noted earlier, issues involved in mating lead to several other complexities in life.) Several writers have suggested that evolutionary differences cause men and women to have very different styles—indeed different *needs*—in communication (e.g., J. Gray, 1992; Tannen, 1990). Men are seen as having an individualistic, dominance-oriented, problem-solving approach. Women are seen as having an inclusive, sharing, communal approach. The further argument is often made that these differences in goals and patterns of communication can result in a good deal of misunderstanding between men and women.

We should note that our discussion in this section has emphasized gender differences rather than similarities. There are in fact many similarities. Both genders are looking for partners who have a good sense of humor and a pleasing personality (Feingold, 1992), who are agreeable and emotionally stable (Kenrick et al., 1993), and who are kind and loving (Buss, 1994b). Both also seem to prefer partners whose faces are symmetrical (Grammer & Thornhill, 1994). Clearly the way men and women look at each other goes beyond seeing each other as sex objects and success objects (Buss, 1994b). Nevertheless, the gender differences also seem important.

Aggression and the Young Male Syndrome

Competition for mating opportunities leads to posturing on the part of males, but it can lead to more. Another aspect of the evolutionary view is that in certain periods of life male humans behave in ways evolved by primates in prehistory. When there is competition for scarce resources (females), the result is confrontational behavior and potentially serious violence.

This pattern has been referred to as the "young male syndrome" (Wilson & Daly, 1985). It's viewed as partly an effect of evolutionary pressures from long ago and partly a response to situations that elicit the pattern. That is, although the pattern of behavior may be coded in every man's genes, it's most likely to emerge when present situations predict reproductive failure. The worst case would be single men who are unemployed and thus poor candidates as mates.

In line with this analysis, there's clear evidence that homicide between competitors is primarily a male affair (Daly & Wilson, 1990). Figure 6.5 displays the homicide rates in Chicago during a 16-year period, omitting cases in which the person killed was a relative. Males are far more likely to kill one another than are females. It's also obvious that the prime ages for killing are the prime ages for mating. According to Daly and Wilson, these killings come largely from conflicts over "face" and status (see also Wilson & Daly, 1996). Trivial events escalate into violence, and someone is killed.

Why killing instead of ritualized displays of aggressiveness? No one knows for sure, but one guess rests on the easy access to guns in the United States. When weapons aren't part of the context, the same pressures for status are more likely to

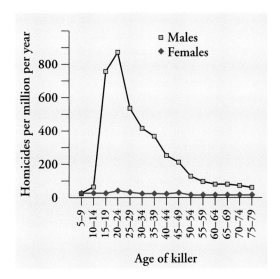

FIGURE 6.5

Homicide rates for males and females killing nonrelatives of the same sex in Chicago during the period 1965-1981 (adapted from Daly & Wilson, 1990).

result in pushing and shouting. Deadly violence certainly is possible without weapons. But when weapons are a part of the scene, death is far more likely.

We should point out explicitly that the theory underlying this area of study is very different from ideas about aggression and human nature of only a few years ago. The current view isn't that aggression is part of human nature, expressed indiscriminately. Rather, aggression is seen as largely a male phenomenon, which occurs as a result of sexual selection pressures in the competition for mates.

Our focus here is on violence by young men toward their genetic competitors. It's worth noting that genetic competition also appears to play a role in violence within family units. In particular, as shown in Figure 6.6, children—especially very young children—are far more likely to be killed by stepparents than by genetic parents (Daly & Wilson, 1988, 1996). The overall frequency of this event is low; most parents don't inflict this kind of harm on their children. Yet if it happens, a stepparent is far more likely to be involved than a biological parent. As is true of the young male

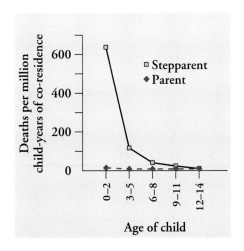

FIGURE 6.6

Risk of a child's being killed by a stepparent versus a genetic parent as a function of the child's age. Risk is expressed in terms of deaths per million child-years of co-residence of child and parent or stepparent (adapted from Daly & Wilson, 1988).

syndrome, this finding appears to reflect a deep-rooted desire to pass one's own genes into the next generation, rather than the genes of a competitor.

We noted earlier that part of mating is retaining one's mate. People have a variety of tactics for discouraging infidelity. Most of these are quite benign in character. Some can even be viewed as efforts at solidifying the relationship to make it resistant to temptation. However, some tactics of mate retention are coercive. Some men, in particular, are so concerned about losing their mates—or about unknowingly supporting a rival's child—that they become quite controlling. Tactics sharply limiting the woman's autonomy sometimes escalate to violence against the woman (Wilson & Daly, 1996). Sometimes that violence is a warning: Don't stray. Sometimes the result is murder. Of killings *within* families, most victims are wives.

Assessment

The orientation to personality that was discussed in the first part of this chapter evolved as a branch of the dispositional perspective. In general, its ways of assessing personality reflect the dispositional view. What it offers primarily is content—indications of which traits to assess. As we said earlier, theorists who take the genetic view on personality feel that certain dispositions are inherited as a biological substrate of personality. By implication, these are the personality qualities that are most worthy of attention.

A second point made by this approach to personality concerns a more general issue regarding assessment in research. The issue is what kind of data to collect to measure the trait you want to study (an issue discussed in Chapter 3). For example, in some twin studies, participants filled out self-report scales. In other studies, children were rated by their parents or by teachers. Occasionally, behavioral observations have been made of children at play.

It turns out that it may matter considerably which of these sources of data is used in the research, because different types of data don't always give the same answers about degree of genetic influence (Plomin & Foch, 1980). In general, parent ratings of children and self-ratings indicate genetic influence more reliably than do behavioral observations (in fact, they may overestimate the size of genetic effects—Saudino et al., 1995). This raises questions about which kind of data to have most confidence in. The importance of deciding which kind of measure to use is not unique to the biological approach, of course. It may be particularly important here, though, because of the fact that twin studies are difficult and expensive.

Problems in Behavior, and Behavior Change

Let's turn now to problems in behavior. The genetic approach has made a major contribution here. Behavior geneticists have examined the possibility that several kinds of vulnerabilities to serious disorder may be influenced by inheritance.

Behavior Genetics and Disorders

The inheritance of pathology has been studied in the same way as the inheritance of normal personality dispositions (for a broad review see Vandenberg, Singer, & Pauls, 1986). For a number of years, research on the behavior genetics of problems has focused mainly on two categories of disorder: schizophrenia and manic-depressive disorder. Most of this research is on schizophrenia, a disorder characterized by disorientation, confusion, cognitive disturbances, and a separation from reality.

One well-known study of genetic influence on schizophrenia was conducted by Gottesman and Shields (1972). Their study began by recruiting twins who'd been admitted to a hospital with a diagnosis of schizophrenia. They then sought out each such person's co-twin and independently evaluated the co-twin's psychiatric status.

The term **concordance** is used to describe similarity of diagnosis. A pair of twins were concordant if they were both diagnosed as schizophrenic. Gottesman and Shields (1972) found a concordance rate of 50% among identical twins and a rate of 9% among fraternal twins. They also found an association (among identical twins) between severity of the initial case and the likelihood that the co-twin was also schizophrenic.

It appears from these data that inheritance plays an important role in the development of schizophrenia. Indeed, this is a conclusion that follows from over a dozen studies similar to this one. Nevertheless, the data from these studies also indicate that life circumstances play a role in determining who shows schizophrenic symptoms openly (see Plomin & Rende, 1991). Some people have the genetic susceptibility but don't develop the disorder. This interaction between a susceptibility and a context that touches it off reflects the diathesis-stress view of disorder, which we discussed in Chapter 4.

A second disorder that may be influenced by heredity is called bipolar (manic-depressive) disorder. Bipolar disorder is characterized by severe depressions, alternating with episodes that involve frenetic, hyperactive, grandiose, and talkative behavior, accompanied by a rush of ideas. Often this manic pattern is accompanied by elevated mood, but there can be irritability if the person's desires aren't met. The onset of this disorder is usually sudden and usually begins with a manic episode. As with schizophrenia, twin studies reveal a tendency toward a genetic contribution (M. G. Allen, 1976; Loehlin et al., 1988; Tsuang & Faraone, 1990).

More recently, bipolar disorder was linked to a specific dominant gene on chromosome 11 in a group of Amish families (Egeland et al., 1987). Two other studies, however, found no link between the disorder and that chromosome, meaning that this gene can't always be responsible for the disorder (Detera-Wadleigh et al., 1987; Hodgkinson et al., 1987). This set of studies reflects a new twist in the effort to understand the genetics of disorder—indeed, the genetics of personality. The researchers used the techniques of molecular genetics to examine genetic markers (see also Box 6.4). This procedure probably will be used increasingly in the future in the effort to track down single-gene effects on pathology (McGuffin, 1987; Plomin, 1995).

Although most research on the genetics of problems in behavior has focused on schizophrenia and bipolar disorder, at least some research has gone beyond these boundaries (Vandenberg et al., 1986; Rowe, 1994). For instance, Eysenck (1964b) found that MZ twins were more likely to share tendencies toward alcoholism than DZ twins. For an identical twin who was alcoholic, the probability was 65% that his co-twin also was alcoholic. For fraternal twins the probability was only 30%. Similar findings, with information about mediating metabolic processes, have since been reported by Schuckit and Rayses (1979). In a Swedish adoption study, 22% of biological sons of alcohol-abusing men were alcoholic, further supporting a genetic role in alcoholism (Bohman et al., 1987).

Eysenck (1964b) also reported higher concordance rates among MZ than DZ twins on antisocial characteristics, in the form of childhood behavior problems and

BOX 6.4

MAPPING THE HUMAN GENOME:
What Are the Implications for the Future?

Researchers today are more knowledgeable than ever about the genetic makeup of the human body and the functions of some of the genes. The technology that's made this possible is continuing its rapid development and shows no signs of slowing down.

In fact, this technology has led to a project, now underway: a hugely ambitious effort to map the human **genome.** The genome is the full set of genes on the human chromosomes, and the task is to understand the full sequencing of their codes (e.g., Jaroff, 1989; Kevles & Hood, 1992). The job is almost unbelievably complicated and will take many years to complete. When it's finished, though, the instructions by which the human body is formed will have been spelled out.

What are the implications of having such a map of the human organism? One benefit is clear. Some disorders are caused by single genes. Knowing the map will make it easier to locate the genes that cause the disorder (for example, the gene for cystic fibrosis is in the middle of chromosome 7). This information can be used in genetic counseling, to warn people when they carry a gene for a disorder, which they may pass on to a child. Another benefit will be genetically based therapies, which even now exist for certain disorders—for example, correcting defects in production of blood cells. Researchers also hold out the possibility of "germ-line gene therapy," altering genetic instructions prior to conception, to eliminate defects. Some people argue that the map of the genome, by permitting identification of genetic weaknesses, will usher in a new era of preventive medicine, dramatically changing the way we deal with disease (see Lewin, 1990).

Don't expect this project to revolutionize our understanding of human behavior next year. No one knows whether the qualities that form personality are created by effects of single genes (though one such effect has been identified, a case we take up in Chapter 7). Many behavior geneticists (e.g., Plomin, 1989) warn not to expect easy solutions for disorders such as schizophrenia or bipolar disorder—despite the promise of studies that seemed to implicate a single gene. It almost certainly won't be that simple. Nevertheless, the potential is there for a revolution in our understanding of how personality is created (Plomin, 1995).

The project to map the genome has excited the imagination of many, but has also raised many concerns. Suppose it were known which genes controlled characteristics of personality, body, or behavior. This knowledge would raise serious moral and ethical issues. For example, a great deal of pressure would doubtlessly arise to modify genes to create specific characteristics in new generations of children, creating "boutique" babies (Landers, 1993). Should this be permitted? Who is to decide which characteristics should be created? What happens to people whose genetic characteristics are viewed by society as inferior?

Even knowledge about disorders raises many ethical issues. Will people with particular genetic profiles experience social and employment discrimination? What happens to the cost of medical insurance when it's possible to know who is susceptible to what diseases? Will insurance even remain *available* to people with disease susceptibilities? This isn't an idle question. Already, insurance policies have been cancelled for entire families because of genetic problems in specific family members (Stolberg, 1994).

In short, the project to map the genome holds out much promise, but it also raises very difficult issues that will have to be addressed (Hubbard, 1995). You might want to start thinking about them, because they're issues that are in your future—and the future of your children.

adult crime. Other research has also found support for the idea that antisocial personality may be genetically influenced (Rowe, 1994; Vandenberg et al., 1986; Willerman, Loehlin, & Horn, 1992). Further research on adult criminality has tended to fit the hypothesis of a genetic influence (DiLalla & Gottesman, 1991; Wilson & Herrnstein, 1985), though several studies of juvenile delinquency have failed to support the genetic view (Gottesman, Carey, & Hanson, 1983).

Evolution and Problems in Behavior

A somewhat different view of certain problems in behavior is suggested by sociobiology. Barash (1986) suggested that many of the difficulties in human life stem from the fact that two kinds of evolution influence people and their behavior. There is biological evolution, a very slow process that occurs over millenia. There is also cultural evolution, which is much faster. Your experiences in life are partly a product of what biological evolution has shaped humans to be during prehistory, and partly a product of the cultural circumstances in which you live.

According to Barash, the problem is that biological evolution prepared us for life in a world very different from the one we now inhabit. Cultural evolution has raced far ahead, outstripping the ability of biological evolution to keep up. Inhabiting a world in which they don't quite belong, people experience conflict and alienation. Barash's point is a general one, rather than being specific to a particular disorder, but it's an interesting point to consider: That is, problems result when behavioral tendencies that are built in as part of human nature are countermanded by pressures that are built into contemporary culture.

Behavior Change: How Much Is Possible?

A major theoretical question about therapeutic behavior change is raised by the view under discussion in this chapter. This question concerns the fact that biologically based personality dispositions—whether they are fully legitimate temperaments or not—are by definition firmly anchored in the person's constitutional functioning.

Some people believe that our cultural evolution has outstripped the ability of our biological evolution to keep up.

One has to ask how easy it can be to alter these aspects of personality in any major way, through *whatever* therapeutic processes are brought to bear on the problem. Psychotherapy may change the person somewhat, but how far against his or her biological nature can a person be expected to bend?

This is an interesting problem, about which little is known. It's been suggested that even true temperaments can be modified, within limits (Buss & Plomin, 1984). But what are the limits? It seems likely that some kinds of therapeutic change are far more difficult to create and sustain for some people than for others. For example, it will be harder for a therapy aimed at reducing emotional reactions to be effective for a person with high emotionality than for a person lower in that temperament. There may be, in fact, some people whose constitutions make certain kinds of therapy attempts so difficult as to be impractical.

On the other hand, it should also be recognized that the heritability of personality, though strong, is not overwhelming. There remains a good deal of influence from individual experiences. Thus, the data that establish a genetic influence on personality also indicate that genetic determination is not total. The extent to which behavior change is hampered by genetically coded tendencies is an important issue raised by this view on personality. Unfortunately, little concrete is thus far known about the answer to the question.

Inheritance and Evolution: Problems and Prospects

The biological view on personality has roots that go far back in the history of ideas. Yet the views of today are in many ways quite new. For example, research on heritability of personality is still fairly recent in origin. Application of the ideas of evolutionary psychology is even more recent. With the advent of advances in molecular genetics, people are now trying to link particular genes with qualities of personality—an approach that's newer still.

In considering the usefulness of these biological ideas in thinking about personality, several issues arise. For example, temperaments are broad tendencies regarding fundamental aspects of behavior. For this reason, temperaments are thought to be pervasive in influence. The fact that temperaments are so basic, however, raises a question about how to view their role in personality. It's undeniable that activity level, emotionality, and sociability are important. By themselves, though, they don't seem to constitute a very complete picture of personality. The question, then, is this: Does it make more sense to think of temperaments as all of personality, as part of personality, or perhaps as the bedrock on which personality is constructed?

It's hard to answer this question, partly because there hasn't been much research on how temperaments influence people's day-to-day lives. That is, do combinations of high and low activity, emotionality, and sociability have direct influences on the kinds of experiences that are usually thought of as implying personality? Or is the effect of temperaments more indirect? Perhaps they provide a basis for development of more-specialized traits, and these traits influence behavior more directly. Attention to questions such as this would provide more clarity about exactly how temperaments fit into the total picture of personality.

Another important question for clarifying the picture of heredity and personality concerns the fact that a large number of personality traits seem to be at least somewhat heritable. Many of these traits are tied conceptually to the temperaments. An unresolved question is how to think about the relations between the specific traits and the temperaments. The general question is "how many qualities underlying personality are genetically influenced, and how many *look like* they're heritable because they derive from the former?" Recent evidence suggests that facets of the five supertraits are separately heritable. This puts a different twist on the question. Now maybe we should be asking whether the temperaments are really unitary, broad qualities, or whether instead they are aggregates of separate traits.

A final question concerns the methods of behavioral genetics as a discipline. Although we didn't address this point in discussing the research, questions have been raised about whether the methods used in this research really tell the investigators what they believe they are being told (e.g., Haviland, McGuire, & Rothbaum, 1983; Wahlsten, 1990). The issues here are very technical, and it's difficult to know how they will be resolved. But until they *are* resolved, there will remain at least a small cloud on the horizon of the behavioral genetics approach to personality.

Another aspect of the viewpoint discussed in this chapter is the work making up sociobiology, or evolutionary psychology. This view on personality has been controversial during its relatively brief existence and has been criticized on several grounds. The early arguments of sociobiology were heavily theoretical, with little evidence to support them. During that stage of its development, sociobiology was seen by some as more a game of speculation than a serious science. More than a few people scorned the ideas under discussion as unfalsifiable and indeed untestable.

In the past decade, however, this situation changed dramatically. As more precise ideas were developed about the implications of evolutionary theory, this way of thinking led to a surge of studies. Evolutionary psychology is increasingly an area of vigorous research activity (see D. Buss, 1991, 1995). It seems clear that evolutionary thinking provides a wealth of hypotheses for researchers who are willing to pursue them. Moreover, the hypotheses are becoming more and more sophisticated. For example, evolutionary psychologists are seriously pursuing the idea that the cognitive structures of the human mind are products of evolutionary pressures (Cosmides, 1989; Cosmides & Tooby, 1989).

Nevertheless, there remains concern about whether the hypotheses being studied by these researchers really *depend on* evolutionary theory, as opposed to merely being *consistent* with it. A major problem of evolutionary psychology today may be that of making clear predictions that are resistant to alternative interpretations. This problem, of course, is faced by all views on personality, not just this one. The issue, however, seems likely to remain an important one for this approach for some time. (Those interested in this problem are referred to an article by Rushton, 1989a, and the commentaries that follow it.)

A very different criticism of sociobiologists has been that their statements sometimes have disturbing political and social overtones. Arguments about how human nature evolved seem to some to be thinly veiled justifications for unfair social conditions and prejudices in today's world (e.g., Kitcher, 1987, and the succeeding commentaries; see also Lewontin, Rose, & Kamin, 1984). That is, sociobiological ideas have been used to explain why men are bullies, why there's a double standard of sexual behavior for men and women, and why race and class differences exist. These explanations provide a basis for considering such conditions to be natural. This is only a small step from saying they should continue to exist. These overtones of evolutionary thinking are construed by some as racist and sexist, and among some people have prompted considerable hostility toward the theories.

One response to this sort of criticism is to point out that evolution is a natural force that works dispassionately, based on the principles of reproduction and survival.

In the arena of evolution, issues of equal rights and equal opportunities have no meaning. It may well be that in today's world some of the results of evolution work against some people because evolution prepared us to fit not this world but the world of prehistory. If people are disadvantaged by the consequences of evolution, though, it's something that should be dealt with by the cultures that people have built. The fact that the theory explains why inequity exists can't be used as an argument that the theory is wrong. As you might expect, this response is not entirely satisfying to critics.

Despite controversies such as these, there remains a great deal of interest in evolutionary ideas in today's personality psychology. This is a set of ideas that will not be going away any time soon.

SUMMARY

The approach to personality rooted in inheritance and evolution has two facets. One of them emphasizes the idea that your personality is tied to the biological body you inherit. An early version of this was Sheldon's analysis of somatotypes. He hypothesized and found that the relative presence of endomorphy (obesity), mesomorphy (muscularity), and ectomorphy (thin frailness) predicted the relative presence of three corresponding dispositions.

Sheldon believed that personality is inherited, but didn't test the idea. Behavior genetics, a newer field of study, provides ways to find out whether personality differences are inherited. In twin studies, correlations among identical twins are compared with correlations among fraternal twins; in adoption studies, children are compared with their biological and adoptive families. Studies of identical twins raised apart provide yet a different look at the effects of inheritance and environment.

Twin research has been used to look at genetic contributions to a variety of dispositions. Recent theorists define temperaments as broad inherited traits that appear early in life. At least three seem to be genetically influenced: activity level, emotionality, and sociability. There also is evidence of genetic influence in the big five supertraits and other variables. It's unclear whether the big five derive from (or duplicate) the temperaments studied under other names. It is also unclear whether other hereditary influences depend on associations between the other variable and a temperament. Somewhat surprisingly, the environmental effects found in twin studies seem not to occur at the shared (family) level but at the individual level.

The idea that dispositions are genetically influenced can be extended a step farther, to the suggestion that many aspects of human social behavior are products of evolution. This idea is behind an area of work termed evolutionary psychology or sociobiology. It draws in part from ethology, which earlier suggested analogies between humans and other species. Sociobiologists propose ways to account for various aspects of human behavior, even behavior that on the face of it seems not to provide an evolutionary advantage. Altruism, for example, is understood as people acting for the benefit of their family groups, so that the family's genes are more likely to be continued (kin selection). This idea has been extended to the notion that people are attracted to other people who share their genetic makeup. People exhibit assortative mating (selective choice of mates) on several variables, some of which do seem genetically influenced.

The evolutionary view also makes some other suggestions about mate selection, including the idea that males and females have different strategies. The male strategy is to mate whenever possible, and males are drawn to signs of reproductive capability. The female strategy is to seek the best male available, and females are drawn to signs of resources. People use the relevant strategies and act in ways that make us seem better candidates as mates. Mating pressures also may lead to aggression among young men. Theory suggests that violence is most likely among men of reproductive age who are in poor reproductive circumstances. Evidence seems to bear this out, along with the idea that much violence concerns conflicts over status.

The genetic approach to personality says little about assessment except to suggest what dispositions are particularly important to assess—those that have biological links. With regard to problems in behavior, this view says little about minor adjustment problems. There is, however, substantial evidence that schizophrenia and manic-depressive disorder are affected by heredity.

With regard to therapeutic behavior change, this approach raises a question on the basis of studies of temperament: How much can people be expected to change, even with therapy, in directions that deviate from their biological makeup?

GLOSSARY

Activity level The overall intensity, speed, and vigor of a person's behavior.

Adoption study A study of resemblances between children and their adoptive and biological parents.

Allele Some version of a particular gene.

Assortative mating Mating based on choice of some characteristic rather than on random choice.

Behavioral genetics The study of inheritance of behavioral qualities.

Cerebrotonia A mental overintensity that promotes apprehensiveness and social inhibition.

Concordance Agreement in diagnosis between a twin and a co-twin.

Directional selection Evolution in which one extreme of a dimension is more adaptive than the other.

Dizygotic (DZ) twins Fraternal twins.

Ectomorphy A tendency toward frail thinness.

Emotionality The tendency to become emotionally aroused easily.

Endomorphy A tendency toward obesity.

Ethology The study of animals in their natural environment.

Genetic similarity theory The idea that people work toward reproduction of genes similar to their own.

Genome The sequence of the genes contained in the full complement of chromosomes.

Heritability An estimate of how much variance of some characteristic is accounted for by inheritance.

Inclusive fitness The passing on of genes through the survival of relatives.

Mesomorphy A tendency toward muscularity.

Monozygotic (MZ) twins Identical twins.

Reciprocal altruism Helping others with the expectation the help will be returned.

Siblings Brothers and sisters.

Sociability The tendency to prefer being with people over being alone.

Sociobiology The study of the evolutionary basis for social behavior.

Somatotonia The energetic desire for adventure and physical activity.

Somatotype The description of a person's body configuration along three dimensions.

Stabilizing selection Evolution in which intermediate values of a dimension are most adaptive.

Temperaments Inherited traits that appear early in life.

Twin study A study comparing similarity between MZ twins against similarity between DZ twins.

Viscerotonia A relaxed sociability and love of comfort.

Biological Processes and Personality

■ Janine craves excitement. She always seems to be pushing herself into more activities, widening her circle of acquaintances and partying. It's as though she needs the stimulation to keep her alive and happy. Her boyfriend Leo shies away from parties. It isn't that he dislikes Janine's friends, but all the noise and action seem to be too much for him. He's just more comfortable when things are less intense. Oddly enough, both feel their bodies are telling them what's best for them, even though "what's best" is so different from the one to the other.

The idea that people's personalities are somehow embedded in the makeup of their bodies was the point of departure for Chapter 6. Our explorations there focused on the idea that genetics play a big role in determining what people are like. That idea accounts for people being different from one another (people inherit different temperaments). It also accounts for how people are the same (evolution shaped certain tendencies into the human species as a whole).

The ideas discussed in Chapter 6 are definitely biological. That is, if something is genetically influenced, the influence occurs through a biological process. But the ideas discussed in Chapter 6 say little about how the effects are *exerted*. That is, knowing that temperaments are inherited says nothing about the process by which genes influence the behaviors that eventually emerge.

In this chapter, we take the same point of departure: the idea that personality is embedded in people's bodies. This time, though, we focus on the idea that personality is influenced by the *workings* of the body. No more unspecified processes. Now we consider aspects of physiology whose purposes are beginning to be understood. The point of view taken here is that personality is a reflection of these biological processes.

As in the last chapter, there's room for both similarities across people and individual differences. The similarities reflect the fact that everyone has a nervous system and an endocrine system, with the same basic structure and functions from one person to another. Differences reflect the fact that aspects of the nervous system and endocrine system are more active in some people than in others.

Eysenck: Extraversion, Neuroticism, and Brain Functions

One of the first modern attempts to link personality to biological functions was that of Hans Eysenck (see also Box 7.1). Recall from Chapter 4 that Eysenck saw personality as composed largely of two supertraits: emotional stability (or neuroticism) and extraversion. In Chapter 4 our focus was on the nature of the dimensions. Now we consider how they influence behavior.

Extraversion and Cortical Arousal

As described earlier, introverts are quiet, asocial, and introspective, whereas extraverts are outgoing, uninhibited, dominant, and immersed in social activity. Eysenck (1967) suggested that this difference depends on a part of the brain called the **ascending reticular activating system (ARAS).** As its name suggests, the ARAS activates (and deactivates) higher parts of the brain (the cerebral cortex). It's involved in maintaining alertness and concentration and in controlling the sleep cycle. When

BOX 7.1

THE THEORIST AND THE THEORY:
The Many-Faceted Contributions of Hans Eysenck

One of the more eclectic theorists in personality psychology was Hans Eysenck. As described in Chapter 4, Eysenck played a major role in the dispositional approach to personality. He also studied inheritance in personality, and he has worked to understand how the nervous system relates to personality. Nor do his interests stop there. Eysenck wrote about topics as diverse as intelligence, politics, the link between personality and health, parapsychology, and astrology. He published more than 50 books and hundreds of articles and has often been embroiled in controversy (which he appeared to relish).

Eysenck would seem to have been destined for the stage. His parents were successful actors in Germany, where he was born in 1916. It has been suggested (Gibson, 1981) that this theatrical background contributed to Eysenck's enjoyment of public appearances. If so, the effect took hold quickly, because his parents divorced when he was two years old, and he lived with his grandmother for years afterward. Given his own theoretical leanings, Eysenck would probably ascribe his personality more to biological dispositions. The fact that his parents were actors may say something about their genetic makeup, which in turn was passed on to him.

Regardless of the source of his temperament, Eysenck grew quickly into a self-confident and strong-willed young man. Two anecdotes vividly illustrate his tenacity (Gibson, 1981). When he was about eight, he was called on during singing class to sing a solo passage. He declined on the grounds that his voice wasn't any good, but the teacher insisted. He finally went ahead, but sang so poorly the teacher thought he was mocking the lesson. The teacher was about to punish him for this, but Eysenck struck first, taking the teacher's thumb in his teeth and holding on like a bulldog, not letting go until the headmaster intervened.

The second incident occurred as the Nazis were coming into power, when Eysenck was in high school. Eysenck's teacher once said that Jews were known to be lacking in military valor. Eysenck set off to explore this question and returned with the fact that Jewish soldiers had earned an extra-high proportion of military honors during World War I. This incident didn't endear him to his teacher, but it illustrates Eysenck's tendency to take on controversy willingly. It also illustrates his dedication to scientific evidence.

Eysenck's strong will later took him to England for university studies. He had decided to study physics and astronomy, but in starting out he made an error that changed the path of his life. Prospective students had to take a series of exams in the areas of their intended study. Eysenck inadvertently took the wrong set of exams, making himself eligible to major only in subjects other than his chosen ones. Because psychology was the most scientific of the majors available to him at that point, he decided to study psychology. One wonders how much this series of events provoked his later interests in astrology and parapsychology.

In short, the qualities that mark Eysenck's contributions to personality psychology include an extremely diverse range of interests, a tenacity about sticking with what he believes, and an enjoyment of controversy and of being the center of attention. All those qualities were apparent early in Eysenck's life. These same qualities also play a role in the central construct of his theory: extraversion.

the ARAS is functioning at a high level, the person feels sharp and alert; when it's functioning at a low level, the person feels sluggish and drowsy.

Eysenck proposed that the typical (resting) levels of ARAS activity among introverts are higher than those of extraverts (Eysenck, 1981). Thus, the higher brain

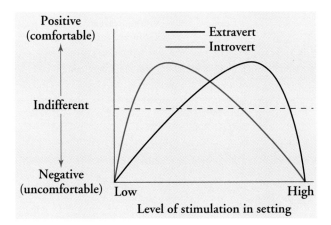

Positive (comfortable)

— Extravert
— Introvert

Indifferent

Negative (uncomfortable)

Low   High

Level of stimulation in setting

FIGURE 7.1

Comfort and discomfort theoretically experienced by introverts and extraverts in situations of varying stimulation. If introverts naturally are more aroused cortically than are extraverts, introverts are more likely to be overwhelmed by too much stimulation than are extraverts. The result is that introverts should feel more comfortable at lower levels of stimulation (up to a point) than at higher levels. The low level of arousal of extraverts should lead them to be more comfortable at higher levels of stimulation (again, up to a point) than at lower levels (after Eysenck, 1971).

centers of introverts are more aroused than those of extraverts. To put it differently, when nothing's going on, introverts are more alert than extraverts. This idea has many implications.

Because introverts have higher base levels of arousal, they're easily overaroused. They become "stimulus shy," perhaps withdrawing from social interaction because they're sensitive to being overstimulated. Extraverts are "stimulus hungry," because their base level of cortical arousal is lower. This causes them to seek social stimulation to bring their arousal level up.

One implication of this difference concerns the kinds of situations introverts and extraverts should prefer. People should be most comfortable when the situation has the right amount of stimulation (not too much, not too little). Different situations stimulate at different levels. The situation adds cortical arousal on top of whatever your baseline is. If everyone is comfortable at the same level of arousal, and if introverts and extraverts differ in how much they start out with, they should differ in the situations they prefer (Figure 7.1). Introverts should prefer situations with lower levels of stimulation—but not *too* low, or it gets boring even to them. Extraverts should prefer higher levels—but not *too* high, or it gets overwhelming even for them. In this theory, then, it's natural for these two types of people to prefer different kinds of situations.

Cortical Arousal Differences

What's the evidence for this theory? Extensive animal research shows that the ARAS does control alertness. There's also evidence that introverts and extraverts prefer different levels of stimulation—even in the context of a psychology experiment. In one study (Geen, 1984), the research ostensibly concerned the effects of random noises on a learning task. Some subjects were to choose the noise intensities they'd hear. Others were assigned to hear specific levels. Each of the latter group was assigned a level that was chosen by someone in the former group.

This research had three important findings, all of which fit the idea that introverts prefer less outside stimulation than extraverts. First, extraverts spontaneously chose to hear louder noises than introverts. Second, physical arousal suggested that extraverts and introverts were comfortable in different situations. When they had the levels of noise they'd chosen (which, remember, were different levels), their heart

FIGURE 7.2

Heart rate among six groups of subjects working on a task while being exposed to random noises. On the left are groups hearing the quieter noises chosen by introverts; on the right are groups hearing the louder noises chosen by extraverts. Introverts and extraverts who chose freely (the two diamonds) don't differ in their arousal. Arousal goes up among introverts who have to hear louder noise (red line), and arousal goes down among extraverts who have to hear quieter noise (black line). The findings fit the picture that introverts are more aroused than extraverts at lower levels of stimulation (adapted from Geen, 1984).

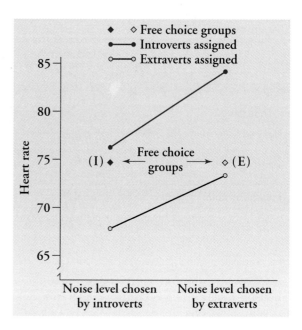

rates were about the same (the unconnected diamonds in Figure 7.2). This suggests that being at their preferred level resulted in about the same level of arousal for the two groups, although the preferred levels differed.

But recall that some subjects had no choice—they were just given either the level chosen by introverts or the level chosen by extraverts. When introverts were assigned to hear the noise chosen by other introverts, their heart rate was the same as the free-choice introverts. However, introverts forced to listen to the louder noise chosen by extraverts had higher heart rates. In the same way, extraverts assigned to hear the noise level chosen by other extraverts had heart rates that matched the free-choice extraverts. But those assigned to hear the quieter noise chosen by introverts had lower heart rates.

The third finding was that performance on the task was affected by the noise to which subjects were exposed. Introverts performed better at the level chosen by introverts (even if they'd been assigned it) than at the level chosen by extraverts. Extraverts performed best at the level chosen by extraverts. It seems, then, that the two groups really do function better at different levels of stimulation.

It's easy to relate these findings to life outside the lab. Imagine that the university's housing office assigns an introvert and an extravert to room together. The extravert always wants the stereo louder than the introvert. Each feels that life is right when the stereo's set the way he likes it. When the extravert sets the volume, the introvert feels keyed up and can't study. When the introvert sets the volume, the extravert feels as though the room's too dead and he can't get going. Each knows what level is "right," but each one's "right" is different from the other's.

Other evidence also suggests that introverts and extraverts maintain different levels of cortical arousal. In boring, repetitious tasks, you eventually pause involuntarily. This occurs because you've lost alertness. An obvious prediction is that extraverts should display these pauses more than introverts, and they do (Eysenck, 1964a). Another way this difference is reflected is in a vigilance task. This requires being alert for a specific stimulus embedded in other stimuli. For example, you

Laboratory studies suggest that introverts may do better then extraverts at tasks that require the monitoring of slowly changing visual displays, as is required in the work of air traffic controllers.

might have to listen to a long series of numbers and press a button whenever you hear three odd numbers in a row. If your mind wanders, you'll miss some of what you're listening for. Because introverts are apparently more alert than extraverts, introverts miss less (Claridge, 1967).

Another kind of evidence that introverts have higher cortical arousal than extraverts comes from research on the effects of drugs (Eysenck, 1983). If introverts are cortically aroused, they shouldn't require as much of a stimulant as extraverts to reach a given level of behavioral arousal. On the other hand, introverts should require more of a depressant drug than extraverts to reach a predefined index of "unalertness." This reasoning was supported in studies in which subjects gradually received drugs intravenously (Claridge, 1967; Shagass & Kerenyi, 1958; see Eysenck, 1983, for review). Thus, given the same amount of alcohol (a depressant), the extravert—the "party animal"—gets more drunk than the introvert.

Biological Basis of Emotionality

Eysenck also proposed a neural basis for his second trait, emotional stability (neuroticism). He said people who are emotionally unstable are easily aroused in the *emotion centers* of the brain. This arousal is very different from cortical arousal, relying on different brain structures. On the other hand, because there are neural projections from the emotion structures to the ARAS, emotional arousal can cause an increase in cortical arousal.

Emotional arousal has two important "process" implications, both related to the interaction between emotionality and extraversion. First, Eysenck sometimes held that emotional arousal causes the behavioral reflections of both extraverts and introverts to emerge more fully. It makes both kinds of people become "more what they are."

A second and more subtle point is that emotional arousal sets the stage for conditioning to occur, because conditioning sometimes *follows from* emotional reactions.

This leads to a complicated line of reasoning. Introverts, being cortically aroused, are easily conditioned. If they're also *emotionally* reactive, they'll have many *opportunities* for conditioning (because of the many emotional reactions) and thus many *instances* of conditioning. Since conditioning during socialization often arises from punishment and frustration, the emotions conditioned are mostly unpleasant ones. The result is a lot of conditioned anxiety and depression. Thus, Eysenck argues, emotional introverts should be vulnerable to anxiety and depression.

What happens when emotionality combines with extraversion? Here high levels of emotionality have different consequences. Extraverts, less cortically aroused, don't condition well. They don't learn from punishment, and show a pattern of poorly socialized and impulsive behavior. Extraverts who are highly *emotional* respond to those emotions impulsively.

A Different View of Brain Functions: Approach and Inhibition

Eysenck's attempt to link these two dimensions to specific qualities of brain function is often praised as a groundbreaking effort. However, the ideas came at a time when the functioning of the brain was not as well understood as it is today. Given the changing picture, some of the same people who applaud Eysenck's effort also believe his ideas were wrong.

Within the past 10 to 15 years, several theorists have proposed newer ideas about how the nervous system relates to personality. The ideas vary in focus. Some concern what parts of the brain are involved in certain kinds of actions. Some concern what brain chemicals are involved in certain kinds of activities. All of them incorporate what might be called a "functional" analysis. That is, they ask questions such as "What functions do particular behaviors serve?" "How many classes of behavior should be distinguished from each other?" The various classes of behavior that emerge from this analytic effort then are linked back to ideas about brain processes and chemical processes. Both sets of ideas are also linked to personality.

Many people are working hard on this set of problems. The good news is that there are broad areas of agreement among them. The bad news is that there are also disagreements. In many respects the situation resembles that faced by trait psychologists. There is much agreement about the major elements in the personality pie. But there are lots of ways to slice the pie. People differ in where they draw the lines for slicing. They also differ in what they think is contained within a particular segment of the pie.

Behavioral Approach, Activation, Engagement, or Facilitation

The theorists of this group all believe there's a set of brain structures that cause animals to move toward **incentives:** things they desire. Several theorists have made assertions about which parts of the brain are involved in this system, though they're not in complete agreement with one another (for discussions see Cloninger, 1988; Davidson, 1992a, 1992b, 1995; Depue & Collins, in press; Depue & Iacono, 1989; Gray, 1982, 1991).

This set of structures has been given several names: the behavioral approach system (J. A. Gray, 1981, 1987, 1990, 1994a, 1994b), behavioral activation system (Cloninger, 1987; Fowles, 1980), behavioral engagement system (Depue, Krauss, & Spoont, 1987), and behavioral facilitation system (Depue & Iacono, 1989). We will refer to it here as the **BAS,** for **behavioral approach system.** You might think of this system as regulating the psychic gas pedal, moving you toward things you want. It's a "go" system. Fowles (1980) described it as reward-seeking.

The theorists of this group assume that this set of brain structures is involved any time a person is pursuing an incentive—any incentive. Certainly specific bits of the brain are involved in the pursuit of food, others in the pursuit of sex, and others in the pursuit of shade on a hot summer day. But the assumption is that all these separate bits involve the more general BAS once the incentive is identified. Thus, the BAS is a general mechanism to go after things you desire. The BAS doesn't rev you up "in neutral," though, with no incentive in mind (Depue & Collins, in press). It's relevant only to an approach: the active pursuit of an incentive.

The BAS is also held to be responsible for creating positive emotions (hope, eagerness, and excitement). These emotions reflect the anticipation of attaining incentives. Researchers who study brain activity in emotional experience have also adopted this idea. Richard Davidson and his colleagues have studied the biology of emotions by recording the electrical activity from people's brains (Davidson, 1984, 1988, 1992a, 1992b, 1995; Davidson & Sutton, 1995). While that's happening, the people are exposed to stimuli such as video clips chosen to create specific kinds of emotional reactions. The question is which parts of the brain become more active in various circumstances.

A variety of evidence suggests that positive feelings involve activity in the left frontal lobe of the cortex. Higher levels of left frontal activity occurred in adults presented with an incentive (Sobotka et al., 1992) or with positive emotional adjectives (Cacioppo & Petty, 1980). Similar effects were obtained when 10-month olds viewed their approaching mothers, presumably an incentive for them (Fox & Davidson, 1988). Higher *resting* levels in the left frontal area have predicted more positive responses to happy films (Wheeler, Davidson, & Tomarken, 1993). They've also been related to self-reported BAS sensitivity (Harmon-Jones & Allen, 1997; Sutton & Davidson, 1997). Findings such as these have led Davidson and his colleagues to make two assertions: First, the tendency to experience happiness relates to a behavioral approach system. Second, that system is based partly in the left frontal cortex.

Another recent project has linked BAS sensitivity to conditioning. Recall Eysenck argued that introverts condition more readily than extraverts, regardless of the kind of association being formed. Thinking in terms of BAS functioning, however, suggests a different hypothesis. Because BAS is responsive to incentives, BAS should relate to conditioning involving *positive* outcomes. It shouldn't relate to conditioning involving negative outcomes. Recent work by Zinbarg and Mohlman (1998) found support for this idea. A BAS-based self-report measure of reward responsiveness predicted people's speed at learning cues of reward in a conditioning task. This scale was unrelated to people's speed at learning cues of punishment.

In sum, people with reactive approach systems are highly sensitive to incentives, or cues of good things about to happen. Those whose approach systems are less reactive don't respond as much (either behaviorally or emotionally) to such cues. To give you a sense of how this relates to ordinary behavior, consider two people with tickets to an upcoming concert by a band they like. Melanie gets excited whenever she thinks about the concert (although it isn't until next week). Every time she thinks about it she's ready to jump in the car. Melanie is very high in incentive responsivity, or BAS sensitivity. Barbara, on the other hand, is far more calm about the whole thing. She knows she'll enjoy the concert, but when she thinks about it she's not so responsive to the thoughts of potential reward. Barbara has less incentive responsivity.

Neurotransmitters and the Approach System

Recent work links the functioning of the approach system to a particular **neurotransmitter** in the brain. A neurotransmitter is a chemical involved in sending messages along nerve pathways. There are several different neurotransmitters, and they seem to have different functions. Several theorists have argued that a neurotransmitter called **dopamine** is critically involved in the functioning of the system that engages in the pursuit of incentives (Cloninger, 1988; Depue, in press; Depue & Collins, in press; Zuckerman, 1994).

Although we won't review evidence on this hypothesis in detail (see Depue & Collins, in press), we note a couple of interesting points briefly. One of them creates a link between this topic and the ideas of the last chapter. In particular, geneticists have identified a gene that's involved in dopamine production. That gene has several alleles (versions), one of which is longer than the others. Two independent research teams (Benjamin et al., 1996; Ebstein et al., 1996) have found that people with the long allele have higher scores on personality scales that relate to the approach tendency. This finding is interesting in part because it links a biological *process* variable (dopamaine activity) with *inheritance* (the location of a particular gene).

Another research team has produced converging evidence on this point using a very different methodology. Depue et al. (1994) looked at individual differences in dopamine reactivity, using biomedical indicators of response to chemical challenges. They found that dopamine reactivity related to a personality measure related to the approach tendency.

Behavioral Inhibition, Withdrawal, or Avoidance

The preceding section dealt with an approach system. Most of the theorists of this group (though not all—see Depue & Collins, in press; Depue & Iacono, 1989) also assume a second system. This system is responsive to punishers. Gray (1981, 1987, 1990, 1994a, 1994b) calls it the **behavioral inhibition system (BIS).** It's sometimes also referred to as a withdrawal system (Davidson, 1984, 1988, 1992a, 1992b, 1995) or an avoidance system (Cloninger, 1987). Activity in these parts of the brain causes people to *inhibit* movement, or to pull back from the stimulus they just encountered. You might think of the BIS as a psychic brake pedal. It's a "stop" system (sometimes more of a "stop-and-throw-it-into-reverse" system).

The BIS is responsive to cues of punishment or danger. It's involved any time a person displays an avoidance or inhibition tendency. When the BIS is operating, the person may stop whatever's going on and scan the environment for further cues. The person may also pull back from what's being confronted. Gray links the operation of this system to specific parts of the brain that he's studied in considerable detail (Gray, 1982, 1991).

As a system that's responsive to cues of threat or danger, the BIS is also responsible for feelings such as anxiety. Once again, research on cortical activity in response to emotional stimuli converges on this conclusion. We said earlier there's an increase in activity in the left frontal lobe when people are feeling happy. Related work shows there's an increase in activity in the *right* frontal areas when people are experiencing feelings of anxiety or aversion.

For example, right frontal activation occurs when people view film clips that induce fear and disgust (Davidson, Ekman, Saron, Senulis, & Friesen, 1990). Higher resting levels in the right frontal area also predict more intense negative feelings in response to such films. Higher right frontal resting levels also relate to greater self-reported BIS sensitivity (Harmon-Jones & Allen, 1997; Sutton & Davidson, 1997). Findings such as these led Davidson and his colleagues to propose that the tendency to experience fear relates to a behavioral withdrawal system, which is based partly in the right frontal cortex.

Research on conditioning has also examined the role of BIS sensitivity. Because BIS is responsive to punishments rather than incentives, BIS sensitivity should relate to conditioning for *negative* outcomes. It should be unrelated to conditioning of positive outcomes. This idea found support in a project by Zinbarg and Mohlman (1998) mentioned earlier. A self-report measure of BIS sensitivity predicted people's speed at learning cues of punishment (but not cues of reward). Conceptually similar results were reported by Corr, Pickering, and Gray (1997).

In sum, people with reactive inhibition systems are highly sensitive to cues of threat. People whose inhibition systems are less reactive aren't as responsive to such cues. It's pretty apparent that this dimension reflects the trait of anxiety proneness. To get a sense of how this dimension relates to ordinary behavior, think of two people who just had a psychology test and suspect they did poorly. Anxiety-prone Randy is almost in a panic about it. Jessica, less anxiety prone, is bothered hardly at all. One of them is reacting emotionally to the cues of threat, the other isn't.

As with the BAS, there have been efforts to link the functioning of the BIS to a particular neurotransmitter, but they've been somewhat less successful. Cloninger (1987) has argued that harm avoidance, his BIS-equivalent system, is mediated by **serotonin.** Low levels of serotonin functioning are believed to relate to greater sensitivity of harm avoidance. Gray (1987, 1990) sees a link from the BIS to serotonin as well, but he thinks its role is smaller than Cloninger does. One research group reported that an allele related to serotonin functioning also relates to anxiety proneness (Lesch et al., 1996). However, several other groups have failed to confirm the finding (Jorm et al., 1998).

Anxiety proneness and incentive sensitivity are thought to be separate and distinct. People presumably vary on both characteristics. As a result, all combinations of high and low BAS and BIS responsiveness probably exist. To some theorists, then, some of the important individual differences in personality derive from these two basic qualities: how susceptible the people are to cues of impending danger or punishment, and how drawn they are to anticipated rewards.

The idea that feelings separate into positive and negative qualities that are relatively independent of each other has also been pursued by Auke Tellegen (1985) and David Watson and their colleagues (Watson & Clark, 1984; Watson & Tellegen, 1985). Tellegen argues that some people are predisposed to have frequent positive emotional experiences, whereas others are less so. This dimension of differences is termed **positive emotionality.** Independently, some people are predisposed to frequent negative emotional experiences, others less so. This dimension is termed **negative emotionality.** This description is very consistent with the idea that people have approach and avoidance systems (respectively) of varying sensitivities.

Relating These Systems to Temperaments or Traits

Let's stop for a moment and consider what we've said thus far. Many theorists have converged on the idea that one brain system manages the approach of incentives, and another manages the withdrawal from unpleasant stimuli. The system that manages approach also creates excitement and positive feelings, the system that manages avoidance or withdrawal creates anxiety. How do these ideas fit with other conceptions described in previous chapters?

The easiest link to make is from BIS sensitivity to the temperament of emotionality, or the supertrait of emotional instability–neuroticism. As we noted in Chapter 6, despite the fact that some of these labels are neutral about the emotion involved, in reality it's always anxiety that's at the core of this trait. Consistent with this, Larsen and Ketelaar (1991) found that neuroticism predicts susceptibility to an experimental manipulation of anxiety. Carver and White (1994) found the same for their measure of BIS sensitivity. In sum, neuroticism and anxiety proneness have a great deal in common. In fact, we'd go so far as to say there's little doubt that the brain system we've been calling the BIS is a critical determinant of neuroticism.

Several theorists have also suggested a link between what we've been calling the BAS and extraversion. The fit between these two is a little trickier than that between neuroticism and BIS. What makes it trickier is partly that various theorists differ about what qualities define extraversion. Indeed, Eysenck himself took two different positions during two different periods. As we said in Chapter 4, definitions of extraversion usually incorporate a sense of activity and a sense of sociability. Sometimes there's also a quality of social dominance or potency (leading to the use of the label surgency). Sometimes there's a quality of impulsiveness. Most definitions also incorporate a tendency to experience positive emotions.

How well do these various extraversion packages relate to the BAS? Pretty well, especially regarding positive feelings. Positive emotionality, as measured by Tellegen, relates closely to extraversion (Costa & McCrae, 1980; Diener, Sandvik, Pavot, & Fujita, 1992); extraversion also relates to a BAS-based measure of incentive sensitivity (Carver & White, 1994). Extraverts are susceptible to positive mood manipulations (Larsen & Ketelaar, 1991). In the same way, self-reported BAS sensitivity relates to positive feelings that arise in response to cues of impending reward (Carver & White, 1994).

There are, however, a couple of qualifications. Table 7.1 lists several theorists who have written about extraversion, or traits resembling extraversion, including BAS sen-

TABLE 7.1

Several theorists and qualities that they believe belong to extraversion (and alternative traits closely related to extraversion). All incorporate pursuit of incentives and a tendency to experience positive emotions. Many, though not all, include a quality of sociability. A few, but again not all, include impulsiveness.

Theorist	Preferred term	Pursuit of incentives	Sociability	Impulsivity	Positive emotions
Eysenck	Extraversion	X	X		X
Costa & McCrae	Extraversion	X	X		X
Depue	Extraversion	X	X	X	X
Zuckerman	Sociability	X	X		X
Tellegen	Positive emotionality	X	X		X
Cloninger	Novelty seeking	X		X	X
Gray	BAS–Impulsivity	X		X	X

sitivity. The table also lists some of the qualities the theorists see as belonging to these extraversion-like traits. As you can see, there are two places where questions arise.

One disagreement concerns the social quality that's part of extraversion. Of particular concern is the absence of that quality from Gray's view of the BAS. Gray's theory ignores sociability altogether. One way to resolve this issue, although it doesn't appear to be exactly what Gray has in mind, would be to think of BAS sensitivity as sensitivity to *social* incentives. Given that humans are a very social species, it might be plausible to think of human behavioral approach primarily in terms of approaching social interaction.

The second issue concerns the role of impulsivity. Eysenck included that quality in his view of extraversion for years, but later moved it from extraversion to his third supertrait. Gray uses the word *impulsivity* as his label for incentive sensitivity, but his writing doesn't really indicate that he's referring to issues of impulse control per se. Depue and Collins (in press) note there's controversy about where impulsivity should be placed. They also note that impulsivity has multiple facets. In their view, positive affect is the hallmark of the engagement trait (which they say is extraversion). They say that impulsivity incorporating positive affect belongs there, but impulsivity without positive affect doesn't.

This issue—where to place impulsiveness—begins to raise another very broad question. Is there perhaps another biological dimension, besides BAS and BIS? Many believe the answer is yes and that impulsiveness is an important reflection of it.

Sensation Seeking: A Third Biological System?

Another long-standing effort to link personality with the functioning of the nervous system is represented in the work of Marvin Zuckerman (e.g., 1971, 1985, 1991a, 1991b, 1992, 1993, 1994). The variable that he and his colleagues have studied is **sensation seeking.**

People high in sensation seeking are in search of new, complex, varied, and exciting experiences. Compared to people lower on this dimension, sensation seekers are faster drivers (Zuckerman & Neeb, 1980), more likely to use various drugs (Zuckerman, 1979), more likely to increase their use of alcohol over time (Newcomb & McGee, 1991), more likely to engage in high-risk sports such as sky-diving (Hymbaugh & Garrett, 1974), and more likely to engage in antisocial sorts of risky behavior (Horvath & Zuckerman, 1993). In the army they're more likely to volunteer for combat units (Hobfoll, Rom, & Segal, 1989).

Sensation seekers are also more sexually experienced and sexually responsive than persons low in sensation seeking (Fisher, 1973). When in relationships, though, they tend to be more dissatisfied (Thronquist, Zuckerman, & Exline, 1991). Sensation seekers enjoy paintings with lots of tension, and they're drawn to expressionism; low sensation seekers prefer pastoral landscapes (Zuckerman, Ulrich, & McLaughlin, 1993).

It would be a mistake to assume that sensation seekers are always after high-intensity experiences, though that's what they're known for. Sensation seekers also volunteer for experiences such as learning to meditate (Myers & Eisner, 1974) or undergoing sensory deprivation (Zuckerman, Schultz, & Hopkins, 1967). These findings are paradoxical in that they involve the *removal* of stimuli. They show, though, that sensation seeking isn't just the seeking of high stimulation. It's a tendency to seek novel and unusual experiences.

Sensation seekers like to seek out new, varied, and exciting experiences.

Sensation Seeking, Impulsiveness, and Other Theories

We got to the topic of sensation seeking by raising a general question about impulsiveness. Now that we've given you a little sense of what high versus low sensation seekers are like, let's go back to that question. Is sensation seeking the source of impulsiveness?

Zuckerman has said several times that sensation seeking is fairly closely related to the third supertrait in Eysenck's theory: psychoticism (Eysenck & Eysenck, 1976). As we said earlier, years ago Eysenck moved impulsiveness from extraversion to psychoticism. This shift would fit with the idea that this trait (whatever it should be called) may be the source of impulsiveness.

We should call attention, by the way, to a point Zuckerman has made, with which we agree. The label of psychoticism was an unfortunate choice on Eysenck's part. It's misleading. A better choice would have been *psychopathy* (later known as *sociopathy* and now as *antisocial personality*). That is, this trait revolves around a disregard of social convention in pursuit of intense sensations. Behavior of that sort is seen in psychopaths, rather than psychotics.

Zuckerman (1991a, 1991b, 1993) actually prefers a different term altogether—one that's more descriptive, though a bit cumbersome. He prefers **impulsive unsocialized sensation seeking** (IUSS). He thinks this trait concerns *the capacity to inhibit behavior in the service of social adaptation.* Those very high on sensation seeking have trouble doing this. The result is impulsive action, a lack of social integration, and a core tendency to seek sensations. Consistent with this view, sensation seeking relates

BOX 7.2

THEORETICAL CONTROVERSY:
Is Impulsiveness a Basic or Resultant Property?

There is considerable consensus that impulsivity is an important dimension of human behavior. Issues of impulse control emerge throughout personality psychology in various forms, as you will see in later chapters. Both ends of this dimension can relate to problems. People who have lives of total constraint fail to experience a broad assortment of experiences from which they might profit. Those who are completely unable to control their impulses are a threat to society. Understanding how this aspect of personality is regulated would seem to be a paramount goal.

Although there's widespread agreement that it's important to understand impulsiveness, there's far less consensus on how impulsiveness works. As indicated in the main text, many theorists assume a third biological system that regulates this quality. However, it can be hard to disentangle the workings of this system from the workings of BAS and BIS. Indeed, some theorists think there's no third system for impulsiveness. Rather, they see impulsive behavior as emerging from the joint actions of the BAS and BIS (Depue & Collins, in press).

Indeed, there are several ways to conceptualize the dimension of impulsiveness as being a resultant of BIS and BAS sensitivities. A person with a highly active BAS pursues incentives with great vigor. Maybe that's the real source of impulsiveness

(Gray's position; see also Arnett, Smith, & Newman, 1997). Alternatively, a person with a weak BIS doesn't experience much anxiety in the face of threats. Maybe this interferes with punishment-based learning, creating a person who hasn't learned to restrain the pursuit of incentives.

Or maybe impulsiveness derives from a *combination* of BIS and BAS qualities. Maybe both a strong BAS and a weak BIS are required to produce impulsivity. Maybe there's no third *system*, but another factor (a hormone or a neurotransmitter or an enzyme) that causes the balance of influence between BIS and BAS to shift.

From a personality point of view (as opposed to a neurological one), separating these possibilities from each other will require an inventive research strategy. An attempt must be made to assess personality on BIS and BAS sensitivities (in one form or another) along with the dimension that's believed to be the third system. If the third dimension really matters in impulsive behavior, it will predict that behavior when BIS, BAS, and their interaction are all taken into account. Such work remains yet to be done. In the meantime, however, most observers continue to argue for a more complex path to impulsiveness, involving a third biological system.

inversely to conscientiousness of the five-factor model (Zuckerman, 1996). It also relates to Zuckerman's own scales measuring both sociability and aggressiveness, suggesting a kind of social dominance (Zuckerman et al., 1993).

How does this view of the third system relate to what we said earlier about the first two systems? It can be tricky to fit the three together. High IUSS involves seeking events that are expected to be positive (e.g., Zuckerman, 1985)—a quality that's shared with high BAS functioning. High IUSS also involves lack of inhibition—a quality that's shared with low BIS functioning. But high IUSS isn't viewed as a combination of high BAS and low BIS. It's distinct and separate from both of them.

You might think of it like this: If you have a sensitive BIS, cues of impending punishment cause you distress. But if you're also high in IUSS, any distress you experience doesn't stop you from doing what you're about to do. Furthermore, if you're high in IUSS, you may not think ahead to the *possibility* of punishment until it's already there.

Two other theoretical views deserve mention with regard to this issue. The first is Tellegen's (1985), in which positive emotionality is roughly equivalent to extraversion and negative emotionality is roughly equivalent to neuroticism. Tellegen also assesses a third major trait, which he calls constraint. Constraint is essentially the opposite of sensation seeking. It's the holding back of impulses. It has facets called control, harm avoidance, and traditionalism. This sounds very much like a reverse description of the same dimension as Zuckerman assumes.

A second view that deserves further attention is that of Depue and Collins (in press). We described earlier how Depue and Collins view extraversion as a combination of sociability and happy impulsiveness. They noted that impulsive behavior sometimes is joined by happiness and sometimes not. They argued that the latter may stem from a different trait. Depue and Collins prefer to think a trait resembling BIS serves this role, rather than a trait of impulsivity or sensation seeking. They see impulsiveness and sensation seeking as emerging from the interactions of this BIS-like trait with extraversion (see also Box 7.2).

Brain Chemicals and Sensation Seeking

Earlier we said that dopamine seems to be the brain chemical behind the approach tendency. We said there that a genetic marker for dopamine has been related to measures of personality dealing with approach. As it happens, one of the studies showing this used Cloninger's measure of novelty seeking. What happens to the dopamine–approach idea, if novelty seeking is partly approach and partly impulsiveness?

The answer isn't fully clear, but here's the current evidence. Ebstein et al. (1996) used Cloninger's measure. They found the genetic marker related to novelty seeking but no other Cloninger scale. They didn't test any facet scales, though—just the overall scales. Benjamin et al. (1996) used the NEO-PI. They found that the genetic marker related to overall extraversion, and to its facets of warmth, excitement seeking, and positive emotion. They then did something that's harder to describe (and harder to trust). They used previous information about how the NEO-PI relates to Cloninger's scales to extrapolate (from NEO scores) what subjects' Cloninger scores would be if they'd taken Cloninger's measure. Using the extrapolated scores, they found the genetic marker related to novelty seeking, and to all its facets *except impulsivity*.

This evidence as a whole seems consistent with the idea that dopamine is related to approach, after all, rather than to impulsiveness. Also consistent with that conclusion are the findings by Depue et al. (1994) mentioned earlier. They looked at individual differences in dopamine reactivity (a different biological indicator), but using Tellegen's scales. They found dopamine reactivity related to positive emotionality, but not to negative emotionality or to constraint (the reverse of impulsiveness).

Is there a particular brain chemical for sensation seeking or constraint? Opinions and evidence both are mixed. There's sketchy evidence that serotonin is involved in constraint (Netter, Hennig, & Roed, 1996) and dominance (Madsen, 1985). Zuckerman (1994, 1995) has also suggested a role for an enzyme called monoamine oxidase (MAO). MAO regulates levels of various neurotransmitters, including both serotonin and dopamine. Sensation seeking relates to low MAO levels (Zuckerman, 1994). Low MAO levels also relate to social dominance, sociability, and aggression (Zuckerman, 1995). Maybe MAO is the key, then, to this system.

Many people are now trying to link particular qualities of behavior (and thus personality) to specific neurotransmitters. This view has an appealing simplicity, a kind of parsimony. Zuckerman (1995), however, cautions against this view. He believes that behavioral systems probably involve neurotransmitters, enzymes, and hormones interacting in complex ways. Here is a region where it may be wise to tread lightly and suspend conclusions for a little longer.

Biological Function of Sensation Seeking

Earlier in the chapter we said that people who take a biological view of personality tend to use a functional approach—that is, look for the purpose that a given biological system might serve. Let's return to that approach and ask what might be the point of a sensation-seeking system. Zuckerman's view (1979, 1991a, 1991b, 1994) is that sensation seeking relates to a biological mechanism that regulates exposure to stimulation, particularly intense stimulation. People high in sensation seeking seem to be opening themselves to stimulation, whereas low sensation seekers are protecting themselves from overstimulation (see also Aron & Aron, 1997). This produces the behavioral differences between low and high sensation seekers.

Some of the evidence leading to this view concerns reflexive reactions to new or unexpected stimuli. The *orienting response* increases sensory intake and knowledge of the stimulus. People high in sensation seeking show the orienting response more than people low in sensation seeking (Feij, Orlebeke, Gazendam, & van Zuilen, 1985; Neary & Zuckerman, 1976).

Another source of evidence on this point is the pattern of brain activity that occurs when a person is exposed to a series of stimuli varying in intensity. Some people (called augmenters) show an increase in brain-wave response as the stimuli become more intense. Other people (reducers) show a decrease in response as the stimuli become more intense. As can be seen in Figure 7.3, high sensation seekers tend to be augmenters, and low sensation seekers tend to be reducers (e.g., Coursey, Buchsbaum, & Frankel, 1975; Zuckerman, Murtaugh, & Siegel, 1974; Zuckerman, 1991a). The implication is that high sensation seekers are opening themselves to stimulation, whereas low sensation seekers are protecting themselves from overstimulation.

Animal research provides more support for this idea. Cats are also augmenters or reducers. Augmenter cats are more curious, active, exploratory, and quicker to approach new stimuli than reducer cats (see Zuckerman, 1993). These behavioral qualities look as though the cats are opening versus closing themselves to information. They also look like feline differences in sensation seeking. A similar pattern has been found in rats (Siegel & Driscoll, 1996).

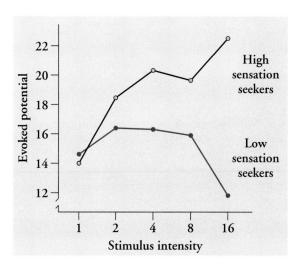

FIGURE 7.3

Average evoked potential (cortical activity in response to stimuli) among subjects who scored high versus those who scored low on a subscale of the Sensation Seeking scale. Low evoked potentials are sometimes interpreted as a screening out of the stimulation. This difference between high and low sensation seekers suggests that the lows are acting (at some level) to screen away the stimulation they're receiving (adapted from Zuckerman, Murtaugh, & Siegel, 1974).

Taken together, these and other findings fit the idea that low sensation seekers have strong defense mechanisms against overstimulation. High sensation seekers have weaker defenses. Both patterns have advantages and disadvantages (Zuckerman, 1991a). People high in sensation seeking should be able to function well in overstimulating conditions such as combat. But they can display antisocial and even manic behavior when the situation is less demanding. People lower in sensation seeking are better adapted to most circumstances of life, but they may "shut down" psychologically when things get too intense.

Hormones and Personality

We turn now to a different aspect of biological process and personality. Now we consider effects of sex hormones—testosterone, estrogen, and progesterone—on behavior. These hormones determine a developing embryo's physical sexual characteristics. They also influence physical sexual characteristics at other stages of development. We won't explore all the ways these hormones can influence behavior (see, e.g., Le Vay, 1993; Rubin, Reinisch, & Haskett, 1981; Tavris & Wade, 1984), but we'll examine a few of them.

Hormones, the Body, and the Brain

The sex hormones are important in a variety of ways from very early in life. Normal males have higher testosterone than normal females from week 8 to week 24 of gestation, from approximately the first through the fifth month of life after birth, and again after puberty (Le Vay, 1993). Early differences appear to be essential to the cre-

Recent research suggests a link between testosterone level and aggression.

ation of certain changes in the nervous system that result in normal male and female physical development. Many believe that the hormonal effects also change the brain in ways that result in behavioral differences between the genders later on (Breedlove, 1994; Le Vay, 1993).

The basic template for a human body is female. Only if hormones cause specific changes to take place does a body emerge that looks like a male. If a genetic male isn't exposed to the proper androgen ("male-making") hormones at critical points in development, the result is an exterior that looks female. If a genetic female is exposed to testosterone at the same points, the result is an exterior that looks male (Breedlove, 1994). During typical fetal development, of course, only males are exposed to enough androgen to be masculinized.

The same hormonal signals that guide the body in its sexual development have effects on nerve cells (Breedlove, 1992; Le Vay, 1993). As a result, the brains of males and females differ in subtle ways. There are differences in linkages among synapses and even in the size of some brain structures. For example, there's evidence that the two sides of the cortex are more richly interconnected in women than in men (Le Vay, 1993). Interestingly, there's also evidence that the brains of gay men are structurally more similar to those of women than to those of heterosexual men (Allen & Gorski, 1992; Le Vay, 1991).

A challenging question is how these differences in the nervous system may relate to personality. Exposure to androgens is believed to "masculinize" the nervous system. Several effects are hypothesized to follow from this.

Early Hormonal Exposure and Behavior

Some information exists on the effects of early exposure to hormones—even prenatal exposure—on later behavior. One study (Reinisch, 1981) looked at children (average age 11) whose mothers had received synthetic hormones (which act like testosterone) during treatment for complications in their pregnancies. Each child thus was exposed to the hormones prenatally, years earlier, during a critical phase of development. The other group was their same-sex siblings (to match them as closely as possible on both genetic and environmental variables).

Each child completed a self-report measure in which six situations are described, involving interpersonal conflict. The children made decisions about what they would do in each situation. The decisions assessed the likelihood of responding with physical aggression, verbal aggression, withdrawal, and nonaggressive coping.

The study yielded two separate effects, both bearing on the choice of physical aggression as a response to conflict (see Figure 7.4). The first was a sex difference: boys chose this response more than girls. There was also an effect of prenatal exposure to the hormone. Children who'd been exposed chose physical aggression more than did those who hadn't been exposed. This was true both for boys and for girls (Figure 7.4).

This study is intriguing for a couple of reasons. It's clear that a biological variable—the hormone—influenced the behavior. It's less clear, however, *how* it did so. Evidence from animal research (reviewed in Reinisch, 1981) indicates that exposure to male hormones during early development can increase aggressive displays. But the behavior measured here wasn't comparable to that in the animal research. That is, Reinisch measured no aggressive acts, just self-reports indicating the choice of an aggressive act. Thus any masculinizing influence on the nervous system had to filter through a good deal of cognition to be displayed.

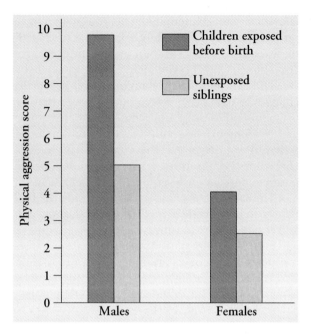

FIGURE 7.4

Average (self-report) physical aggression scores during childhood for boys and girls who had been exposed to synthetic hormones before birth and for their sex-matched siblings who had not been exposed. Exposure to the hormone produced elevated aggression scores for both boys and girls (adapted from Reinisch, 1981).

In another project, Berenbaum and Hines (1992) studied children with a genetic disorder that causes high levels of androgens (masculinizing hormones) prenatally and in early postnatal periods. Years later (ages 3 to 8), these children (and unaffected same-sex relatives) were observed as they played individually with toys that had been predetermined to be generally preferred by boys and by girls. The question was who played with which toys.

The androgen-exposed girls spent more time with the boys' toys and less time with the girls' toys than did the unexposed girls (Figure 7.5). In fact, they displayed a preference pattern similar to that of boys. In contrast, preferences among the boys in the study were unaffected by exposure to the androgens. These findings suggest that a masculinizing hormone can have an impact on the activities in which children spend their time in play later on.

Other research also provides support for the idea that hormones influence play styles. Jacklin, Maccoby, and Doering (1983) found that hormone levels at birth were

FIGURE 7.5

Amount of time two groups of girls played in a free-play setting with toys generally preferred by boys and toys generally preferred by girls. Some of the girls had been exposed to masculinizing hormones before birth and shortly afterward, the others had not been exposed (adapted from Berenbaum & Hines, 1992).

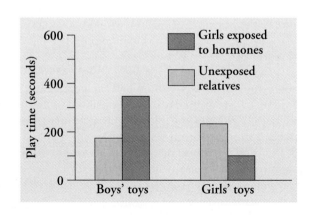

related to the boldness versus timidity that infant boys displayed over the next 18 months. Boldness was assessed by exposing children to novel (and thus somewhat scary) toys. Higher testosterone levels at birth predicted more boldness among boys. So did higher birth levels of progesterone (which has some effects that resemble those of androgens). In contrast to this, higher estradiol (an estrogen) was related to more timidity. No association with any hormone was significant among the girls in the study, however.

The findings thus are somewhat mixed, but they appear to be generally consistent with the idea that early exposure to masculinizing hormones can influence behavior in several ways (see Collaer & Hines, 1995, for a review). Such exposure can increase the potential for aggression, lead to preference for masculine toys, and enhance boldness.

Testosterone and Adult Personality

Most research on sex hormones and personality focuses on current levels of testosterone and how these levels relate to behavior. This, of course, is several steps away from the idea that exposure to testosterone masculinizes the nervous system. Yet it shares with that idea the theme that testosterone is involved in the regulation of certain important qualities of human behavior. Much of the research in this area has been conducted by James Dabbs and his colleagues.

Although testosterone is a sex hormone, testosterone levels are more often tied to antisocial and dominance behavior than to sexual behavior. One study of men in prison (Dabbs, Frady, Carr, & Besch, 1987) found that inmates high in testosterone had violated prison rules more often and were more dominant in prison than inmates lower in testosterone. They were also more likely to have committed violent crimes. Similar results have also come from studies of female inmates (Dabbs et al., 1988) and adolescent males (Dabbs, Jurkovic, & Frady, 1991).

Other research examined testosterone and antisocial behaviors in a noncriminal population (Dabbs & Morris, 1990). Subjects were U.S. military veterans (average age 37). They were asked questions about antisocial behaviors during childhood and in the recent past. Dabbs and Morris found that men higher in testosterone were more likely to have gone AWOL while in the military, assaulted other adults, had large numbers of sex partners, and abused alcohol and other drugs. They were also more likely to have had trouble with parents, teachers, and classmates while growing up (see also Box 7.3). These effects were far stronger among men who were lower in socioeconomic status (SES) than among those of higher SES. In low-SES men, all the associations were significant. In high-SES men, only one was significant: Higher testosterone men were more likely to smoke marijuana.

Although being high-SES can diminish the ill effects of high testosterone, research also suggests that high testosterone tends to lead men *into* lower-status occupations (Dabbs, 1992a). This seems to occur because high testosterone promotes antisocial behavior and less education; both of these factors then lead people away from white-collar occupations.

Differences in testosterone relate to occupational differences in other ways, as well, fitting a picture in which testosterone is related to social dominance (for a review see Mazur & Booth, 1998). For example, trial lawyers are higher in testosterone than non-trial lawyers, and this is true of lawyers of both genders (Dabbs, Alford, & Fielden, 1998). Actors and NFL football players have high levels of testosterone (Dabbs, de La Rue, & Williams, 1990), ministers low levels (college professors, if you must know, were intermediate).

BOX 7.3

STEROIDS: An Unintended Path to Aggression

Discussion of the effects of testosterone on behavior brings to mind a related topic. The desire to have a strong body has led many people to exercise programs. One exercise is body building, lifting weights to increase the size and strength of muscles. Part of the appeal of body building comes from the final result: a body that looks as though it's chiseled from rock.

The desire for a well-formed body has led to a variety of training techniques. It's also led many people into a world of illegal drugs called **anabolic steroids.** The word *anabolic* means "building up." Anabolic steroids are chemicals that mimic the body's tendency to rebuild muscle tissues that have been stressed or exercised. Normally, your body gives you small doses of such chemicals, producing growth in muscle size. Using steroids gives you a much bigger dose. Steroids thus permit you to speed up and exaggerate the building of muscles in ways that exercise alone can't do. That's why people use them.

What many users fail to realize is that steroids are synthetic hormones. Their effects go far beyond the building of muscles. Anabolic steroids are chemically related to testosterone (that's why men's muscles tend to be larger than women's). Testosterone is involved in many things, not just building of muscle tissue. Consequently, people who use steroids for larger muscles are in for a surprise: Steroids can have unintended and unpleasant side effects.

Some of these effects are physical. If you're a man, part of your body sees the steroids as testosterone and reacts to what looks like too much testosterone by shutting down production of more. The results are a lowered sperm count and a decreased sex drive (the steroids don't act like testosterone in

these respects). If you're a woman, steroids cause masculinizing effects: shrinking breasts, deepening voice, and growth in facial and body hair.

Other effects of steroids are behavioral, and those are of most interest here. As you've read in the main text, several studies have linked testosterone to dominance and aggressiveness. Steroids produce much the same effect. Moreover, since the doses tend to be large, so are the behavioral effects. Heavy steroid use can result in irrational bursts of anger that are popularly referred to as "roid rages." Here are actual cases from the *Miami Herald:* A 21-year-old man punched someone at a shopping mall who looked at him the wrong way, and another time punched 20 holes in his walls at home. A 45-year-old man reported, "I'd ask for lamb chops for dinner, and my wife would make steak. The walls would eat the steak." Another young man, as described by his mother, "would put holes in the walls . . . would rip the phone off the wall. He would take bricks and throw them at [his brothers' and sisters'] cars. He would fight with them. He would look for any excuse."

These effects are bad enough in the average person. But body building and steroid use aren't confined to any one group of people. Body building is a sport that has considerable appeal for someone who already has a strong streak of dominance and aggressiveness. Add steroids to an already aggressive personality, and the result is a potential for serious violence.

In sum, the use of synthetic hormones for muscle building has created a sort of natural laboratory. It's opened an unexpected window on how hormones influence behavior. The view, although educational, is not necessarily pretty.

Why are actors so different from ministers? After all, they're both on stage. Dabbs et al. suggested that actors must be constantly dominant, because their reputation is only as good as their last show. Ministers operate in a framework that tolerates more variability. Further, whereas the actor's role is to seek and hold onto glory, a minister's role is to be self-effacing.

The dominance that's linked to high testosterone is useful in some contexts, but it can interfere with relationships. Booth and Dabbs (1993) found that men with higher testosterone were less likely to have married. If they did marry, they were more likely to divorce. They were also more likely to have had extramarital sex and to commit domestic abuse. Men high in testosterone have unfriendlier smiles than those lower in testosterone, and they express more dominance in their gaze when in conversation (Dabbs, 1992b, 1997). Members of low-testosterone fraternities are friendly and smile a lot, whereas members of high-testosterone fraternities are wilder and more unruly (Dabbs, Hargrove, & Heusel, 1996).

Several studies have related testosterone levels to personality as measured through inventories. In two of these studies, the personality data were factor analyzed along with the testosterone data, forming a factor around testosterone (Daitzman & Zuckerman, 1980; Udry & Talbert, 1988). In both cases, the emerging factor had overtones of sensation seeking and dominance. Udry and Talbert's (1988) factor included ratings on these adjectives: cynical, dominant, original, robust, sarcastic, spontaneous, persistent, and uninhibited. The similarity of some of these adjectives to impulsivity and sensation seeking also suggests that these findings may tie into the work on brain functions discussed earlier in the chapter.

Cycles of Hormones and Action

It may be most obvious to think about testosterone in terms of stable individual differences. However, Dabbs (1992b) has pointed out that testosterone is also part of a dynamic system that changes over time and events. Levels of testosterone shift in response to social situations of several types. These shifts may, in turn, go on to influence the person's later behavior.

Testosterone levels rise after certain kinds of positive experiences, and the experience doesn't have to involve great exertion. As shown in Figure 7.6, testosterone rises after success at a competitive event (Mazur, Booth, & Dabbs, 1992) and falls after a failure or humiliation. It rises when your team wins and falls when your team loses (Bernhardt, Dabbs, Fielden, & Lutter, 1998). It rises when you are confronted with the challenge of an insult (Nisbett & Cohen, 1996). And it rises (for both men and women) after sexual intercourse (Dabbs & Mohammed, 1992).

Such changes in testosterone also have implications for subsequent behavior. Increases in testosterone make people more sexually active (Dabbs, 1992b). An increase in testosterone can also make a person feel more assertive—may lead him to

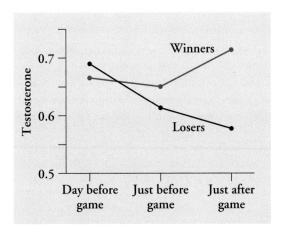

FIGURE 7.6

Testosterone levels among chess players who won or lost close matches in a citywide tournament (adapted from Mazur et al., 1992).

seek out new competitive challenges and opportunities to be dominant (Mazur, 1985; Mazur et al., 1992). Decreases in testosterone after a failure may cause a person to feel less assertive and to avoid new competition. Thus, in either case (success or failure) there is a tendency toward a spiraling effect, with a given outcome tending to promote more instances of the same outcome.

Hormones, Dominance, and Evolutionary Psychology

This research was done to gain a better understanding of the role of a hormone in behavior. Let's step back from the studies to consider their broader implications. Specifically, the findings seem to fit with one of the themes of evolutionary psychology, discussed in Chapter 6.

Recall that evolutionary thinking includes the idea that selection pressures led to certain gender differences. These differences stem from the fact that human females have greater investment than males in offspring (through the extensive period of pregnancy and mothering). Females are believed to be choosy about mates for this reason, trying to find one who will provide resources for her children. Another consequence of the differing selection pressures is believed to be a gender difference in dominance and aggression.

In particular, the evolutionary view suggests that aggression can increase males' opportunities to mate. Aggressiveness helps males establish dominance and status. Overt aggressiveness in females doesn't confer an advantage and may even confer a disadvantage. That is, it can create the potential for damage to an unborn or young child. It also creates a drain on the woman that interferes with her more important activities (bearing and raising children). The research discussed in this second part of the chapter suggests that this difference in the behavior of men and women occurs partly via differences in levels of testosterone.

Dabbs (1992b, 1998) has noted an interesting irony here. In the evolutionary view, males are high in dominance and in the testosterone that supports it because physical domination over other males brought access to mates. In recent millenia, however, the rules have changed somewhat. Success is now defined partly in socioeconomic terms, rather than by physical dominance. A man who's too preoccupied with displays and posturing may have difficulty acquiring the skills needed for economic and social power. Thus, a quality that was important in prehistory may actually interfere with success in today's world.

Assessment

The biological view on personality discussed in this chapter assumes that personality derives from events taking place in the nervous system and hormonal system. If personality is biological, then why not just assess the biological characteristics that are relevant to personality? Rather than self-reports, observer ratings, or any traditional psychological assessment, why not just isolate the biological function and measure it?

There are a couple of problems with this. In many cases no one's quite sure how the biological influences are mediated, so it's hard to know what index to focus on. It's also hard to assess biological functions in a way that's not invasive—doesn't require a sensor somewhere in the body. Despite these problems, some biological methods of assessment are now in use.

Electroencephalograms

An indirect indication of what's going on in someone's brain can be obtained by recording electrical activity from the skin over the skull. The record is called an **electroencephalogram, or EEG.** The reasoning behind it is that neurons throughout the brain fire at various intervals, creating continuous fluctuations in voltage. Electrodes on the person's scalp can sense these changes, giving a view on aspects of the activity taking place in the cerebral cortex. Cortical activity is very complex, but it forms patterns that relate to different subjective states.

One pattern, called an alpha wave, occurs when the person is awake but resting. When the person becomes more alert (for example, when attending to something), a higher frequency pattern occurs, called a beta rhythm. When the person's in deep sleep, a very slow wave form occurs, called a delta rhythm. Looking at this set of patterns as a group suggests that, in general, higher frequency waves mean greater cortical arousal or activity.

EEG procedures are increasingly being used as a way of investigating normal personality processes. In fact, the work discussed earlier in the chapter by Davidson and his colleagues used the EEG. Studying personality this way used to be hampered by the diffuseness of the information from the EEG. It's always been fairly easy to tell when a person has abnormal brain rhythms, but it's been harder to make more subtle distinctions.

It's been found, however, that various regions of the cortex are active to different degrees when people experience various psychological states. This realization is leading to a more focused effort to assess what areas of the brain are involved in what kinds of mental activity. This is being done by mapping EEG activities in different locations. For example, it's now possible to identify a person who's dominated by incentive motivation or by avoidance motivation, by looking at left versus right frontal activation levels at rest (Harmon-Jones & Allen, 1997; Sutton & Davidson, 1997).

Computer-Assisted Imaging

Recent developments have permitted the mapping of brain activities to move further inside the brain. One technique is called **positron emission tomography (PET).** PET derives a picture of brain functioning from metabolic activity. The person being assessed receives a radioactive form of glucose (the brain's energy source). Later on, radioactivity in different areas of the brain is recorded. Presumably the more active areas of the brain use more glucose, resulting in higher radioactivity there. A computer color-codes the intensities in different areas, producing a brain map in which colors represent levels of brain activity.

The major application of the PET procedure is measuring neurotransmitter function. To do this, a radioactively labeled drug with known effects is given. The person's brain activity is then compared to its activity when in a nondrugged condition. Differences between the PET scans provide information about the receptor systems involved in the drug's effects. This technique is likely to be used more in the future, given the links suggested between certain neurotransmitters (such as dopamine) and certain aspects of personality (such as heightened sensitivity to reward).

Another technique, called **magnetic resonance imaging (MRI),** relies on a very subtle property of nerve activity. Functioning nerve cells create magnetic fields. With a good deal of computer assistance, the magnetic resonances of a person's brain can be translated into a visual image. Typically, the image is of a slice across the brain, as seen from above or from the side. Different slices give different information, because they show different parts of the brain.

At first, these images were used primarily to look for structural problems in the brain. For example, if you were having blackouts after an auto accident, you might be asked to have an MRI to look for possible damage. Researchers are also examining MRIs for clues about whether serious psychiatric disorders might involve brain abnormalities.

Given EEG evidence that different parts of the brain are involved in different kinds of activities, MRIs are also now being used in a different way. People are being studied to assess levels of activation in different parts of the cortex, both at rest and in other mental states. The picture from this sort of study, called *functional MRI,* is much more detailed than what comes from EEG recordings. Of particular importance is that the brain can be viewed at different levels. The result is a detailed three-dimensional picture about what brain centers are active. As with PET scans, the images are usually created in multiple colors, with each color representing a different level of activity.

Diagnosing Depression Chemically

One more case of biological assessment deserves mention. It's related not to normal personality but to depression. It's long been suspected that many cases of depression are biological in origin, and other cases aren't. It might be useful to be able to separate depressed people into subgroups, so that biologically based depression could be handled differently from depressions that have purely psychological causes. Some people believe that a way to do this has been found: the **dexamethasone suppression test (DST).**

The DST is based on the fact that a chemical called dexamethasone suppresses the production of the hormone cortisol in the cortex. Ordinarily this effect lasts about 24 hours. Among some depressed people, though, it doesn't last nearly that long. It's been suggested that people whose suppression is short may have a biological predisposition toward depression (Carroll, 1982). Research on this question and on the more general question of whether the DST should be used as a biological assessment procedure has continued for several years. The procedure is regarded by many as useful, and some have become excited about its potential, but it has also been noted that caution is needed in interpreting the test results (Carroll, 1985). As a result, the test is still regarded as experimental but promising, and it is used mostly in research.

Problems in Behavior, and Behavior Change

Let's now consider problems in behavior. The biological approach has made large contributions to the understanding of disorders, particularly serious ones. A full treatment of that literature is well beyond the scope of this chapter. We'll focus here on contributions that relate to the ideas discussed earlier in the chapter.

Biological Bases of Anxiety, Depression, and Antisocial Personality

Recall that a fundamental assumption of today's biological models is that two motivational systems in the brain manage approach of incentives and avoidance of threats, respectively. People presumably vary in the strength or sensitivity of these systems. As is often the case, being at an extreme on one or the other system may set a person up for problems.

Perhaps the easiest problem to link to this view is anxiety disorders. The BIS creates anxiety when there are cues of impending punishment. A person with a very sensitive BIS will experience anxiety easily and frequently. This creates fertile ground for an anxiety disorder to develop. If these people are exposed to frequent punishments during childhood socialization, they learn anxiety responses to many stimuli. The result may be the development of such clinical symptoms as phobias, anxiety attacks, and obsessive-compulsive disorders.

Another problem related to this is depression. There is somewhat less of a consensus on the biological roots of depression than those of anxiety. In some views, depression is a variant of anxiety, stemming from an oversensitive BIS. Other views tie depression to a failure of the BAS, rather than to an oversensitive BIS (e.g., Allen, Iacono, Depue, & Arbisi, 1993; Carver & Scheier, 1998; Henriques & Davidson, 1990, 1991). With minimal BAS activation, the person has little or no motivation to approach incentives, resulting in the leaden behavioral qualities that typify depression.

Another problem that's often discussed in terms of these biological systems is **antisocial personality.** As noted earlier, this is a pattern of behavior involving impulsivity and an inability to restrain antisocial urges. It's sometimes argued that the BAS in these people is overactive (Arnett et al., 1997). Thus they pursue whatever incentive comes to mind. It's sometimes argued that these people have BIS deficits (Fowles, 1980). Thus they fail to learn from punishment. Some think their failures to learn from punishment stem not from a deficient BIS, but from a failure to stop and think before plowing ahead (Patterson & Newman, 1993). Some views of antisocial personality involve a third system—the one underlying sensation seeking (Zuckerman, 1994) or constraint (Krueger et al., 1994).

Medication in Therapy

This biological approach to personality also has a relatively straightforward implication for therapy. This orientation suggests that many manifestations of personality, and of problems in personality, reflect biological functions. It follows that changing these biological functions should influence the manifestation of the disorder. There are several disorders for which this approach seems effective. Because the treatment typically involves administering drugs, the therapies are often termed **pharmacotherapy.**

It has long been known that manic-depressive, or bipolar, disorder can be relieved by doses of lithium. About 80% of persons with bipolar disorder respond to lithium (Depue, 1979). Besides treating existing symptoms, repeated doses can ward off new symptoms. Unfortunately, lithium has serious side effects. Nevertheless, its effectiveness supports two ideas: that the disorder is biological and that its treatment should also be biologically based.

A similar case has also been made for treatment of schizophrenia. Research on the biological basis of schizophrenia has looked for ways to treat its symptoms. One hypothesis is that the symptoms reflect too much dopamine (see Walker & Diforio, 1997). As we said earlier, dopamine is a neurotransmitter. With too much dopamine, transmission in certain parts of the nervous system is too easy. With too many messages being sent, communication is disrupted.

This hypothesis, though speculative, is supported by studies of biochemical treatments for schizophrenic symptoms. Drugs that remove the symptoms of schizophrenia also turn out to lower the levels of usable dopamine in the brain. Apparently the effectiveness of these drugs is related to their ability to block the use of dopamine. Once again, this finding suggests that the disorder is biological and that treatment should also be biologically based.

Pharmacological treatments are also used for disorders that are far less extreme than the two just discussed. Antianxiety drugs are among the most often prescribed of all medications. The most recent generation of antidepressants—called selective serotonin reuptake inhibitors (SSRIs)—are used by many people with moderate to mild depression. Indeed, development of this generation of antidepressants (such as Prozac) has led to a far wider use of mood-altering medication than ever before.

The widespread use of these drugs raises a number of questions and issues, many of which were addressed in a book called *Listening to Prozac* (Kramer, 1993). One issue concerns the fact that responses to this class of medication often are much broader than the mere lifting of a depressed mood. People's personalities undergo subtle but profound and pervasive changes in response to the treatment. People often become more confident, more resilient, more decisive—almost more dominant—than they were before. In a sense, they aren't quite the same people as they were before taking the medication. Their very personalities have changed.

Seeing these changes in personality take place as a function of a slight alteration in brain chemistry caused Kramer to question for himself (as a psychiatrist) where personality resides. No longer was it obvious to him that the personality is a fixed and stable entity lying beneath the symptoms that brought people to him. The personality, in the form of the person's biological processes, was now seen as the *source* of the symptoms. No longer was it even obvious that the medication was acting to treat an illness. In the view that Kramer began to adopt, treatment of an illness had become indistinguishable from treatment of personality. In that view, personality may *be* the person's biological functioning and the experiences to which it gives rise.

The descriptions in Kramer's book were anecdotal, from his experiences with people in therapy. Since then, however, researchers have investigated whether drugs such as Prozac have an influence on people who don't have a disorder. This study (Knutson et al., 1998) involved giving volunteer subjects either an SSRI or a placebo for 4 weeks, and assessing them both before and after. Those given the medication later reported less hostility and less negative feelings in general (but no greater positive feelings). They also displayed more positive social behavior while working on a cooperative task.

The availability of drugs that have these broad effects on personality raises many questions. How widely should such therapies be prescribed? Should people whose problems are not severe be given medication if it will make their lives more enjoyable? Should people be given the option of changing their personalities by taking a daily pill? Questions such as these are complex, involving many further issues. They are associated with considerable controversy that is a long way from being resolved.

Biological Processes and Personality: Problems and Prospects

In this chapter we've discussed the idea that patterns of biological processes have important things to tell us about personality. We wouldn't blame you if you came away feeling that the presentation was a little fragmented. In truth, the ideas themselves are somewhat fragmented. The pieces are coming together, but they aren't quite there yet. As a result, this way of thinking about personality has something of a disjointed feel.

One reason for this is that theories about how the nervous system and hormones influence behavior rely in part on knowledge from other sciences. Ideas in those sciences are continually evolving, causing changes in these ideas about personality. Further, work on these topics is as new as the methodological advances that permit closer looks at how the biological systems function. These methodological advances continue to march forward. The result is a kaleidoscope of new looks at biological functioning that sometimes have unexpected implications for personality.

For example, psychologists now have access to PET scans and functional MRIs that illuminate brain functioning in ways only dreamed of a few years ago. Some of what's been found out has raised as many questions as it has answered. There is likely to be a good deal of complexity in sorting out the picture that such devices reveal.

It's clear that there's been progress in these areas of research and thought. To a large extent the theorists agree about what they're trying to account for. There's general consensus that approach and avoidance (and positive and negative feelings) are important focal points for biological theory building. Almost everyone seems to feel the need to include something more than that, but there's been a little less consensus about what else to include. Partly for this reason, this way of thinking doesn't yet stand as a fully developed personality theory. It's more of a vantage point, a place to stand and from which to look at and consider the nature of personality.

Lest you be tempted to conclude from the disagreements that these theorists aren't doing their homework carefully enough, let us point out that it's not easy to tell what's going on in the nervous system. To really know what connects to what in the brain means tracing neural pathways, which can't be done in human subjects. The animals used as subjects in these studies can't report directly on the psychological effects of what the researcher is doing. Thus information often is indirect, and progress can be slow. The functions of the nervous system are being sorted out by research of several types, but there's a long way to go. Until the nature of the organization of the nervous system becomes clearer, personality psychologists of this orientation won't have definitive models.

Although criticisms can be made of various aspects of this way of thinking about personality, this line of work is among the more active areas of personality psychology. Many people believe that the mysteries of the mind will be revealed by a better understanding of the brain. They are committed to unraveling those mysteries and their implications for personality. At the moment, the prospects of this viewpoint seem quite bright indeed.

SUMMARY

The idea that personality is tied to the biological functions of the body leads to a variety of possibilities involving the functions of the nervous system and the endocrine (hormone) system. An initial approach of this sort was Eysenck's theory that brain processes underlie extraversion. He argued that introverts are more cortically aroused than extraverts. Thus introverts avoid overstimulation, whereas extraverts seek out stimulation.

Others have taken issue with this, arguing that personality rests on an approach system (BAS) that responds to incentives and an inhibition system (BIS) that responds to threats. Work on emotions suggests that the approach system, which produces positive feelings, involves the left frontal cortex, and that the withdrawal system, which produces feelings such as fear, involves the right frontal cortex. The

BIS seems to represent the biological basis for the supertrait of neuroticism. Some suggest that the BAS represents the biological basis for the supertrait of extraversion. Differences of opinion about extraversion relate to the involvement of sociability (which isn't intrinsically part of BAS theories) and the placement of impulsivity.

Questions about impulsiveness introduce another biological variable: sensation seeking, the tendency to seek out novel, complex, and exciting stimuli. Sensation seeking relates to Eysenck's dimension of psychoticism. Research suggests that sensation seeking relates to biological systems that regulate exposure to stimulation (as a defense process), with people scoring low in sensation seeking being those who show defense responses.

Another aspect of the biological view on personality focuses on the role in behavior played by male hormones. Exposure to such substances before birth can increase aggressive responses to conflict years later, and increases girls' preference for boys' toys. Testosterone in adults is related to dominance behavior, sometimes expressed in antisocial ways. Testosterone also fluctuates, increasing with challenges and victories, decreasing with failures.

This approach to personality suggests it may be possible to assess personality through biological functions. Although the attempt to do this is in its infancy, some believe recordings of brain activity—EEGs and MRIs—hold great promise for the future.

With regard to problems in behavior, high levels of BIS activity promote disorders involving anxiety. Either high BIS or low BAS may contribute to depression. High BAS function, or low BIS, can yield symptoms of antisocial personality. This orientation to personality also suggests that therapy based on medication is a means to bring about behavioral change. The idea is that medication can influence the underlying biological system, thereby altering the person's behavior and subjective experience.

GLOSSARY

Anabolic steroids Chemicals that mimic the body's tendency to rebuild muscle tissues.

Antisocial personality (also **sociopath**) A person who displays impulsive action with little thought to consequences.

Ascending reticular activating system (ARAS) The part of the brain that activates the cerebral cortex into alertness.

Behavioral approach system (BAS) The part of the brain that regulates pursuit of incentives.

Behavioral inhibition system (BIS) The part of the brain that regulates anticipation of punishment.

Dopamine A neurotransmitter believed to be especially important to approach regulation.

Dexamethasone suppression test (DST) A test that may diagnose biologically based depression.

Electroencephalogram (EEG) A record of overall electrical activity in higher regions of the brain.

Impulsive unsocialized sensation seeking (IUSS) Trait involving the capacity to inhibit behavior in the service of social adaptation.

Incentives Things that people desire.

Magnetic resonance imaging (MRI) A picture of activity inside the brain based on the brain's electromagnetic energy.

Negative emotionality The predisposition to experience negative feelings frequently.

Neurotransmitter A chemical involved in sending messages along nerve pathways.

Pharmacotherapy A therapy based on use of medication.

Positive emotionality The predisposition to experience positive feelings frequently.

Positron emission tomography (PET) A picture of activity in the brain based on the brain's metabolism

Sensation seeking The tendency to seek out varied, unusual, and exciting stimuli.

Serotonin A neurotransmitter that some believe is involved in behavioral inhibition.

PART four

The Psychoanalytic Perspective

THE PSYCHOANALYTIC PERSPECTIVE: Major Themes and Underlying Assumptions

The psychoanalytic perspective originated in the writings of Sigmund Freud. His impact on thought in personality psychology was so strong that his ideas form the essence of a distinct perspective on personality, although others have since contributed to it. The psychoanalytic view on personality is the subject of Chapters 8 and 9.

One theme of this perspective, which gave rise to the term *psychodynamic,* is the idea that personality is a dynamic set of processes, always in motion. They sometimes work in harmony with one another and sometimes against one another, but rarely or never are they still. Personality is a dynamo—or a bubbling spring—from which emerge forces that can be set free, channeled, modified, or transformed. As long as you're alive, these forces never come to rest.

An important implication of this dynamic quality in personality is that the forces sometimes work against each other. The processes of personality sometimes compete or wrestle with each other for control over the person's behavior. The assumption that competing pressures within the personality *conflict* with each other is another theme that's very prominent in the psychoanalytic perspective.

An additional assumption goes hand in hand with this one. Specifically, psychoanalytic thinking emphasizes the role of the unconscious in determining behavior. The conflicts that take place among the elements of personality are often unconscious. Many of the motivations that people have are also unconscious. The idea of unconscious influence wasn't unique to Freud, but the emphasis on the unconscious is a theme that permeates this perspective on personality.

Another theme in the psychoanalytic perspective is the idea that human experience is suffused with qualities of lust and aggression, sexuality and death. These assumptions tie psychoanalytic thinking to Darwin's theory of evolution (for more detail see Ritvo, 1990). They serve as a reminder that humans are, first of all, animals whose purpose in life is reproduction. Although this idea doesn't seem so odd today, the extent to which Freud emphasized the role of sexuality in human life was very unusual at the time.

Indeed, Freud's emphasis on sexuality even extended to his ideas about the development of personality. A sixth theme of the psychoanalytic perspective is that personality is greatly influenced by early experiences. Freud argued more specifically that human sexuality must be taken into account at all stages of development—even infancy. Many people found the idea of infantile sexuality absurd or shocking. Nevertheless, the idea that the fundamentals of personality emerge from the crucible of early experience is deeply embedded in psychoanalytic thought.

Another theme that characterizes psychoanalytic thought is the idea that defense is an important aspect of human functioning. An assumption underlying this idea is that there are things about every person that are threatening to him or her. Maybe you have what you regard as shameful desires or impulses; maybe you secretly feel you're unworthy or inadequate as a human being; or maybe you're afraid the social world will reject you. Whatever it is that most threatens you, you have psychological processes that keep these impulses or elements of self-knowledge from overpowering you. The notion of defense is an important aspect of psychoanalytic thought.

The psychoanalytic perspective on personality is extremely metaphorical in nature. Oddly enough, given this emphasis on metaphor and analogy, it's difficult to point to a single metaphor for human nature that dominates this perspective. Rather, the perspective uses multiple metaphors. Freud was a physician, and the idea of biological processes underlying mental processes often appeared in his writing. Similarly, his concepts of life instincts and death instincts resemble the dual processes of metabolic functioning—continually tearing down and building up.

Freud didn't limit himself to the biological metaphor, however, but used many others as well. Sometimes he likened the human psyche to a sociopolitical system, making reference to censors, economics, compromises, and repression. Sometimes his analogies were from physics, with personality described as an energy system, and the competition among forces compared to hydraulic systems in which energy focused at one point had an inevitable consequence at another point. At other times, he treated psychological phenomena almost as though they were the products of the person's artistic or literary efforts.

Despite the lack of a single orienting point, or perhaps because of it, the psychoanalytic viewpoint on personality may be characterized fairly as one in which the *quality* of analogy or metaphor figures prominently. Human behavior is to be understood not as the product of any one process but as a reflection of multiple processes whose functioning can be captured only imperfectly by any one metaphor.

A final theme of the psychoanalytic perspective is the idea that mental health depends on a balance of forces in one's life. It's good to express your deep desires, but not to let them control your life. It's good to act morally, but a constant effort to be perfect can cripple your personality. It's good to have self-control, but not to be overcontrolled. Moderation and balance among these forces provide the healthiest experience of life.

chapter

8

Psychoanalytic Structure and Process

■ John and his girlfriend Ann go to different colleges, located a thousand miles apart. It's been hard for them both to be separated for long periods of time, and John has finally decided that he can't go on this way. He's decided to call Ann on the phone and break off their relationship. He picks up the phone, dials a number, and hears a voice on the other end of the line say hello—at the residence hall where Ann lived last year, before she moved off campus. "Now why'd I dial *that* number?" John wonders to himself.

Why did you do that? Most people, most of the time, find it easy to answer this question without the slightest doubt that their answer is correct. Most of us assume a direct link between our conscious intentions and our actions. Accidents sometimes interfere with those intentions, but accidents are just random events.

There's a viewpoint on the nature of personality that sharply challenges these assumptions. It sees behavior as determined partly by inner forces that lie outside your awareness and control. As for accidents, this view holds that most accidents really aren't accidents: What seems accidental, you've done on purpose—you just aren't *aware* of the purpose.

The approach to personality that takes this view is psychoanalytic theory, or psychoanalysis. Psychoanalytic theory is closely identified with a single theorist (although it rests on more historical precedents than is widely realized—Ellenberger, 1970; Erdelyi, 1985). The theorist was an Austrian physician named Sigmund Freud. The theory, which evolved over the period from 1895 to 1940, stunned the scientific world when it was proposed (Box 8.1). Since then, it's been one of the most influential views ever developed. Its effects have been felt not just in psychology but also in anthropology, political science, sociology, and even art and literature. Indeed, it's hard to think of a single aspect of modern-day thought in Western civilization that hasn't been touched in some way by psychoanalytic ideas.

Perhaps the greatest testament to the impact of psychoanalytic ideas is the extent to which they've crept into our everyday language and experiences. For example, people often use the phrase "Freudian slip" to refer to errors in speech that seem to suggest hidden (unconscious) feelings or desires. Such slips imply that behavior is caused by forces outside our awareness, an idea that traces directly to psychoanalysis.

Before describing the elements of psychoanalytic theory, we note two aspects of this view that make it different from any other in personality psychology. First, Freud was fascinated by symbols, metaphors, and analogies. This fascination is reflected both in the form of the theory and in its content. In its form, the theory uses many analogies. Freud constantly sought new metaphors. He used different ones at different times, and the metaphor in use often had a major impact on the form the theory took. As a result, it can be hard to be sure which ideas are basic and which are only metaphors (Erdelyi, 1985).

Freud's fascination with symbol and metaphor is also reflected in the theory's content. Specifically, Freud came to believe that human behavior itself is highly symbolic. People's acts are rarely quite what they seem to be. Instead, qualities of each act symbolize other, more hidden qualities. This is an idea that permeates psychoanalytic theory.

A second point is that it's hard to separate Freud's theory from the therapy procedures on which he based it or from the assessment process that occurs continually

BOX 8.1

PSYCHOANALYSIS IN HISTORICAL CONTEXT

The concepts of psychoanalytic theory were developed earlier than any other theory in this book (at the start of the twentieth century and for several decades thereafter). The cultural and scientific context in which the theory was created differed greatly from that of today, and the context had a big impact on the theory's form. To get a better idea of why Freud's ideas took the form they did (and why they had the impact they had), consider the world in which he lived.

Freud did his early writing during the latter part of the Victorian era (late 1800s), a time in which middle- and upper-class society had come to view humans as having reached a lofty state of rational self-control, civilization, and even near perfection. It was a smug and self-satisfied society. By today's standards it would be viewed as stuffy and hypocritical. For example, human sexuality was rarely even acknowledged publicly, never mind openly discussed.

Into this calm society, Freud dropped a cultural bomb. Instead of seeing people as rational, he argued that people are driven by forces of which they are unaware. Instead of godlike, people are primitive animals. Instead of intellectual beings, people—even in infancy—are motivated primarily by sexual and aggressive urges.

Freud observed that humanity's admiration of itself had suffered three traumatic shocks: The first was the discovery by Copernicus that the Earth is not the center of the universe. The second was the assertion by Darwin that humans evolved as animals just as did other animals. The third was Freud's own assertion that people are at the mercy of forces that are unconscious and uncontrollable. For good measure, the horror of World War I showed conclusively that the veneer of civilization was far thinner than most assumed.

Freud's ideas jolted the scientific world when they were proposed, partly because they conflicted so sharply with widely held assumptions. Another reason was Freud's emphasis on sexuality, particularly infantile sexuality. This caused many to view him as a pervert, obscene and wicked. The fact that

he was a Jew in an anti-Semitic society raised additional suspicion. Further, he presented his theories without much evidence, which didn't sit well in the scientific community. All these factors raised controversy over Freud's theory. Ironically, the controversy only brought his ideas greater attention.

Although Freud's ideas sharply contradicted the assumptions of Victorian society, they didn't arise in an intellectual vacuum. Darwin's earlier assertion that humans were just one sort of animal inhabiting the Earth carried several other assumptions. Darwin saw all creatures as driven by instincts to survive and reproduce. Freud's sexual and life instincts are similar to these. Although society at large viewed humanity as rational, philosophers such as Schopenhauer and Nietzsche were arguing that human behavior is often impelled by unconscious and irrational forces. This idea is also echoed in Freud's work.

Freud was also influenced by the ideas of scientists in other areas, and he often assimilated these ideas into his own theories (Ellenberger, 1970). For example, Freud's view of the human being as an energy system drew directly from then-current ideas in the physics and chemistry. Nineteenth-century physicists had also developed the principle of conservation—the idea that matter and energy can be transformed but not destroyed. This led scientists in many areas to ponder how various physical systems could be viewed in terms of transformations of energy. Among them was Freud. This conservation principle is reflected in his belief that instinctive impulses must eventually be expressed, in one form or another.

If Freud had lived in a different time, his metaphors may well have been different. But the fact is that psychoanalysis lives on in the terms Freud used. As you read this chapter, keep in mind the cultural and scientific context in which the theory was constructed. We've tried to present the theory as it applies to you, in today's world. If aspects of the concepts seem out of date metaphorically, try to keep in mind the world in which they were conceived.

within that therapy. Indeed, the very word *psychoanalysis* is used indiscriminately to refer to Freudian therapy, Freud's method of research, and his theory of personality. The entanglement of theory with therapy is far greater here than in any other approach to personality, and it tends to color all aspects of the theory.

When viewed in its entirety, psychoanalytic theory is very complex. Underlying this complexity, however, is a fairly small number of principles. The theory can be confusing, because its concepts are deeply interwoven. For this reason it's hard to talk about any aspect of the theory separate from other aspects. Perhaps the best place to start, though, is Freud's view of how the mind is organized, a view that's often termed Freud's **topographical model** of mind.

The Topographical Model of Mind

A common description of the mind says it has two regions. One region holds conscious experience—the thoughts, feelings, and behaviors you're aware of at the moment. The other contains memories, now outside awareness but able to enter awareness easily. Drawing on the work of other theorists of his time (see Ellenberger, 1970), Freud added a third region to this list. Taken together, the three regions form what Freud thought of as the mind's topography, or surface configuration.

Freud used the term **conscious** in much the way we use it today to mean the part of the mind that holds what you're now aware of. People can verbalize about their conscious experience and think about it in a logical way. The part of the mind that represents ordinary memory is termed **preconscious.** Elements in the preconscious, although now outside awareness, can be brought to awareness easily. For example, if you think of your phone number or the name of the last movie you saw, you're bringing that information from the preconscious to consciousness.

Freud used the term **unconscious** in a way that's considerably different from the way it's used in everyday language. He reserved this word to stand for a portion of the mind that's not directly accessible to awareness (see also Box 8.2). Freud viewed the unconscious as being (in part) a repository for urges, feelings, and ideas that are tied to anxiety, conflict, or pain (e.g., Rhawn, 1980). Being unconscious doesn't mean they're gone, though. *They exert a continuing influence* on later actions and conscious experience.

Freud often compared the mind to an iceberg (an idea he borrowed from Theodor Lipps—see Ellenberger, 1970). The tip of the iceberg corresponds to consciousness. The much larger part, the part below water, is outside awareness. Part of that submerged portion (the part you can see through the water) is the preconscious. The vast majority of it, however—the part you can't see—is the unconscious. Although the conscious and preconscious influence behavior, Freud saw them as less important than the unconscious. The unconscious is where Freud thought the truly important operations of personality take place.

The three levels of consciousness constitute the topographical model of the mind (Figure 8.1). Material passes easily from conscious to preconscious and back again. Material from both of these can slip into the unconscious. Truly unconscious material, however, can't be brought voluntarily to awareness, because of psychological forces that keep it hidden. These regions of the mind constitute the theater in which the dynamics of personality are played out.

BOX 8.2

TODAY'S VIEWS ON THE UNCONSCIOUS

Psychologists have long had an interest in the nature of consciousness. In pursuing this interest, it was apparent almost immediately that events outside awareness have an influence on what happens in awareness. Hardly anyone has gone on to assume an unconscious as contentious and conflicted as Freud assumed. But many have found it necessary to make assumptions about what's going on in the unconscious.

In recent years, interest in how the mind works has grown dramatically, along with the field of cognitive psychology (we say more about cognitive processes in Chapter 16). Today's theorists use the concept of the unconscious with different connotations than did Freud (Bargh, 1997; Brody, 1987; Epstein, 1994; Kihlstrom, 1987; Loftus, 1992). The unconscious is still seen as a part of mind to which we don't have ready access, but for different reasons than Freud assumed. Reflecting this difference, today's theorists sometimes talk of the *cognitive unconscious,* as opposed to the psychodynamic unconscious

From today's point of view, consciousness is viewed as a sort of workspace where you consider information and make judgments, come to decisions, and form intentions. If these processes become sufficiently routine, they begin to occur automatically, outside awareness. What makes things routine? Some processes are innately routine. You don't have to decide to start digestive juices flowing or to have your heart beat, and you'd probably have trouble bringing to consciousness the processes by which those events take place.

Other processes become routine from practice. As you practice anything (a tennis stroke, a new recipe, typing, forming a first impression), what goes on changes over repeated instances. The first few times, you devote lots of attention to whatever actions you're engaged in. As you do it over and over, the event starts to feel more fluid and go more smoothly (and quickly). The more you practice, the less attention it requires. When you've practiced it enough, you can disregard it almost totally—it occurs without your notice. When an activity has be-

come *very* automatic, the processes that underlie it have become unconscious. You no longer have access to them as you did when just starting out. One well-known study, for example, showed that people weren't able to accurately report the basis of a decision they'd made; instead they fell back on stereotypes (Nisbett & Wilson, 1977).

Other evidence of an unconscious part of mind comes from studies of hypnosis (Hilgard & Hilgard, 1983; Kihlstrom, 1987). Hypnotic suggestion can cause people not to experience subjective discomfort from a normally painful stimulus. At the same time there's evidence that the stimulus has registered on the person's perceptual system, and that part of the person's mind is aware of the pain. Although the hypnotist can reach that part of the mind to verify the pain, participants themselves apparently can not.

Seymour Epstein (1994) argues that all of these phenomena and more are reflections of what he calls an *experiential* mode of processing events. This mode of processing occurs in parallel to, but distinct from, more rational processing. The experiential system is emotional, intuitive, and nonverbal, rather than deliberative and verbal. Its functioning is largely out of awareness. It creates biases, but in most circumstances these biases don't create problems. Epstein argues that an unconscious as chaotic as the one Freud assumed would have been very unlikely to evolve. Being so poorly fit to reality, it couldn't possibly have survived. On the other hand, an unconscious such as Epstein envisions has much more adaptive value.

In sum, researchers have found that many aspects of people's experience are influenced by processes that occur outside awareness. Such influences occur when you're forming perceptions and impressions of other people, and when you're making judgments about how likely something is to happen. Such influences can also affect your mood states and your actions. Whether you agree with Freud about what defines the *contents* of the unconscious, it's clear that he was right about its existence.

FIGURE 8.1

Graphic representation of Freud's topographical model of the mind. (a) Material can pass easily back and forth between the conscious and preconscious portions of the mind. (b) Material can also move from the conscious and preconscious into the unconscious. But once material is in the unconscious, the person is prevented from having conscious access to it because (c) a mental gate prevents retrieval.

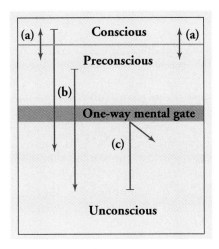

Aspects of Personality: The Structural Model

Freud (1962/1923) also developed a **structural model** of personality, which complements the topographical model. He came to see personality as having three aspects, which work with each other to produce the complexity of human behavior. They aren't physical entities in the body but labels for three aspects of functioning. They are known as id, ego, and superego.

Id

The **id** is the original component of personality, the only one present at birth. *Id* (the Latin word meaning "it") encompasses all the inherited, instinctive, primitive aspects of personality. The id functions *entirely in the unconscious.* It's closely tied to basic biological processes, from which it draws energy. Indeed, Freud believed that *all* psychic energy comes through the id. Thus the id is the "engine" of personality.

The id conforms to what's called the **pleasure principle.** The pleasure principle is the idea that needs should be satisfied immediately (Freud, 1949/1940). Unsatisfied needs constitute an aversive tension state. Thus people want to gratify needs whenever they arise. According to the pleasure principle, any increase in hunger should produce an attempt to eat. Any twinge of sexual desire should produce an effort to obtain sexual gratification.

At first glance, this sounds great. Who wants to walk around with unmet needs? There's a problem, though. The pleasure principle doesn't say *how* needs are to be met. It does *not* say needs should be met in a way that's rational or appropriate or takes into account risks or potential problems. It just says needs are to be met at once.

Being ruled totally by the pleasure principle would soon get you into a lot of trouble. There's a complex and often threatening world out there. A hungry person can't rush across a street filled with moving cars to get to food. Social reality also limits behavior. For example, if you grab your roommate's pizza before he can get to it (or if you get too friendly with his girlfriend), you may find yourself with an angry roommate on your hands.

Nonetheless, the pleasure principle means that when any tension arises the id tries to discharge it. The id's mechanism for doing this is called the **primary process.**

This entails forming a mental image (whether by fantasy, dream, hallucination, or delusion) of an object or event that would satisfy the need, and becoming involved with that image. In the case of a hungry infant, the primary process might conjure up an image of the mother's breast or a bottle. When you're separated from someone you love, the primary process produces fantasy images of that person. The experience of generating such an image is called **wish fulfillment.**

Tension reduction by primary process has a major drawback. The primary process can't distinguish between a mental image and reality. Thus, although primary-process thought may reduce tension in the short run, it can't do so in the long run (Zern, 1973). The hungry infant imagining sucking at a nipple won't be satisfied for long. The person who misses a loved one won't be content with fantasies of being together, no matter how real they seem. This illustrates once again how the id doesn't take reality into account. It's in a world of its own, a world with no rules beyond the pleasure principle.

Ego

Because the id can't deal with objective reality, a second set of psychological functions develops, termed **ego** (the Latin word for "I"). The ego evolves from the id and harnesses part of id's energy for its own use. Ego processes focus on ensuring that id impulses are expressed *effectively,* by taking into account the external world. Because of these transactions with the outside world, most ego functioning occurs in the conscious and preconscious. Given the ego's ties to the id, however, it also functions in the unconscious.

The ego is said to conform to the **reality principle** (G. S. Klein, 1972). This is the taking into account of the external world in addition to internal needs and urges. The reality principle introduces a sense of rationality into behavior (Zern, 1973). Because it orients you toward the world, it leads you to consider the risks associated with various options before acting. If the risks of an action seem too high, you'll consider another way to meet the need. If there's no safe way to reduce tension immediately, you'll delay it to a later, safer, or more sensible time.

Thus, one goal of the ego is to delay the discharge of id energy until an object or activity appropriate to the tension can be found (Box 8.3). More concretely, the ego tries through what's called the **secondary process** to match the image of a tension-reducing object (from the id's primary process) to a perception of that object in the world. It's important to realize that the ego's goal is *not* to block the id's desires permanently. The ego wants the id's urges to be satisfied, but to be satisfied at an appropriate time and in a realistic manner (Bergmann, 1980).

The ego, functioning primarily under the reality principle and using secondary-process thought, is the source of intellectual processes and problem solving. The capacity for realistic thought allows the ego to form plans of action to satisfy needs and test the plans to see whether they'll work. This is called **reality testing.** The ego is often described as having an "executive" role in personality, mediating between the desires of the id and constraints of the external world.

It's easy to see how the pleasure and reality principles, and thus id and ego, inevitably come into conflict (Figure 8.2). The pleasure principle dictates that needs be met *now;* the reality principle leads to delay. The pleasure principle orients to the press of internal tension states; the reality principle orients to environmental constraints. The ego's function, in the short run, is to prevent the id from operating—to hold it up, so its needs can be met in a realistic and rational way. Thus there's a

BOX 8.3

EGO CONTROL AND DELAY OF GRATIFICATION

A major function of the ego is to delay gratification of impulses and urges until a later time (Block & Block, 1980). Delay of gratification is a mark of a mature personality; it's a major goal of socialization. Children must learn to wait for rewards (e.g., to work now but be paid later) if they're to become contributing members of society. The *in*ability to delay gratification may play an important role in the development of criminal behavior. For all these reasons, delay of gratification has been studied over the years from a variety of angles (in fact, it comes up several more times in this textbook). Much of the research was prompted by ideas other than psychoanalytic theory, but the findings are relevant to psychodynamic processes.

In most laboratory studies of this phenomenon, children are given the following choice. They can have a smaller, less desired reward now, or they can wait for a while and then get a larger, more desired reward. One focus of research using this paradigm is on the determinants of delay of gratification (for reviews, see Mischel, 1966, 1974). It's harder for children to delay when the desired objects are right in front of them (Mischel & Ebbesen, 1970). Delay becomes easier if the children can mentally transform the situation to make it seem the objects aren't really there. For example, they might imagine that the objects are only "color pictures in their heads" (Mischel & Baker, 1975; Moore, Mischel, & Zeiss, 1976). More generally,

delay of gratification seems to be enhanced when children distract themselves, shifting attention away from the desired rewards (Mischel, Ebbesen, & Zeiss, 1973). In effect, the ego tricks the id by getting it involved in something else.

A second line of research on delay of gratification concerns personality correlates of the ability to delay. Ability to delay relates to certain aspects of intelligence (Mischel & Metzner, 1962), perhaps because brighter children are better able to mentally transform the situation. Children who are better able to delay also seem more concerned with achievement and social responsibility (Mischel, 1961), fitting the idea that they have well-defined egos.

More recent longitudinal research by Funder, Block, and Block (1983) suggests that the basis for delay differs slightly from boys to girls. Among boys, delay seems to be closely related to the ability to control emotional and motivational impulses, to concentrate deeply, and to be deliberate in action. This fits the psychoanalytic position that delay of gratification is an ego function, aimed at deliberate control over id impulse expression. Delay among girls, in contrast, appears most strongly related to intelligence, resourcefulness, and competence. According to Funder et al. (1983), these gender differences stem from differences in the manner in which boys and girls are socialized (see also Block, von der Lippe, & Block, 1973; Block, 1973, 1979).

vast potential for conflict within the personality. This theme runs deep in psychoanalytic theory.

Freud (1933) used the metaphor of a horse and rider to refer to this pulling of forces within the personality. The id is the horse, providing the power for movement; the ego is the rider, trying to direct that movement. Often the rider is successful in directing the horse's energy in appropriate directions, but sometimes the rider can do no more than guide the horse more or less in the direction the horse wants to go.

Although the ego can appear to be a positive force because it exercises restraint over the id, that's somewhat misleading. The ego has no moral sense. It's entirely pragmatic, concerned with getting by as well as possible, given the constraints of reality. The ego wouldn't be bothered by cheating or stealing, or giving free rein to the

FIGURE 8.2

Graphic representation of the basis of conflict between the id (which follows the pleasure principle) and the ego (which follows the reality principle).

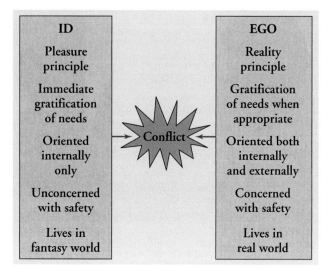

pleasure principle, as long as there's no chance of being caught and no danger involved. The moral sense resides in the third and final part of personality.

Superego

The final aspect of personality—the last to develop—is the **superego** (a joining of two Latin words meaning "over-I"). The superego develops while the person resolves a particular conflict during personality development (discussed later in the chapter).

The superego is the embodiment of parental and societal values. It decides what's right and wrong and strives for perfection rather than pleasure. The values in your superego depend on the values of your parents. To obtain the parents' love and affection, the child comes to do what the parents think is right. To avoid pain, punishment, and rejection, the child avoids what the parents think is wrong. Although other authority figures can influence the superego, Freud viewed the superego as deriving largely from parents. The process of "taking in," or incorporating, the values of parents (and wider society) is called **introjection.**

The superego is further divided into two subsystems. One facet of the superego, called **ego-ideal,** is rules for good behavior, standards of excellence toward which the ego must strive. What the parents approve or value is in the ego-ideal. Conforming to those standards makes you feel proud. The other aspect of the superego, the **conscience,** is rules about what behaviors are bad. Prohibitions against actions that parents disapprove of and punish are in the conscience (Sederer & Seidenberg, 1976). Engaging in bad acts or thoughts causes the conscience to punish you with guilt feelings.

The superego has three interrelated goals. First, it tries to inhibit completely (rather than just postpone) any id impulse that would be frowned on by society (your parents). Second, it tries to force the ego to act morally rather than rationally. Third, it tries to guide the person toward absolute perfection in thought, word, and deed. The superego exerts a "civilizing" influence on the person, but its perfectionism is quite removed from reality.

Like the ego, the superego operates at all three levels of consciousness. This has important implications for how you experience the superego's effects. When superego processes are conscious, you're aware of your feelings and where they're com-

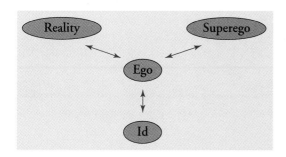

DENNIS THE MENACE

" MOM TELLS ME THE STUFF I SHOULDN'T DO AND MY DAD TELLS ME THE STUFF I *SHOULD* DO !"

The superego has two parts. The conscience holds an image of undesirable behavior, and the ego-ideal holds an image of desirable behavior.

DENNIS THE MENACE® used by permission of Hank Ketcham and © by North America Syndicate.

ing from. If, for example, you're aware you've just insulted someone, despite your belief that doing that is inexcusable, the origin of your guilt is obvious. However, when the superego operates unconsciously to punish an urge of the id (also unconscious), the experience is different. You feel guilty but you don't know why. Because guilt can be set off by primary-process thought, the guilt may even be completely irrational.

Balancing the Forces

Once the superego develops, the ego has a hard road to travel (see Stolar & Fromm, 1974). The ego must deal simultaneously with the desires of the id, the moral dictates of the superego, and the constraints of reality (Figure 8.3). To satisfy all these demands, the ego would have to find a way to release all tension immediately in a way that's both socially acceptable and realistic. This, of course, is highly unlikely. It's much more likely that repeated conflicts will occur among these forces. To Freud, such conflicts are an intrinsic part of life.

FIGURE 8.3

Graphic representation of how the ego must mediate among the often-conflicting demands of the id, the superego, and the constraints of outside reality.

The term **ego strength** refers to the ego's ability to function effectively despite the demands of these conflicting forces (Barron, 1953). With little ego strength, the person is torn among competing pressures. With more ego strength, the person can manage the pressures without serious problems. However, it's possible for the ego to be too strong. A person whose ego is too strong is very rational and efficient but may also be very boring, or cold and distant.

In fact, there's a more general point here. Freud didn't hold that any aspect of personality is intrinsically "better" than the others. Rather, there should be a balance among them. A person whose superego is too strong may feel guilty all the time or may act in an insufferably "saintly" way. A person whose id is too strong may be so bound up in self-gratification as to be completely uninterested in other people. The healthiest personality is one in which the influences of the three aspects are well-balanced.

Motivation: The Drives of Personality

At several points we've talked in general terms about energy, impulses, tension states, drives, and urges. Let's now consider these motivational forces more explicitly.

In thinking about motivation, Freud borrowed heavily from prevailing views in the biological and physical sciences. He saw people as complex energy systems, in which the energy used in psychological work (thinking, perceiving, remembering, planning, dreaming) is released through biological processes. These biological processes, which operate through the id, have received the labels *instinct* and *drive*. These two terms are used in distinct ways in other contexts (see also Box 8.4), but they are used interchangeably here.

A drive has two interrelated elements: a biological need state and its inborn psychological representation (or wish). The need state in the experience of thirst is an

Ego strength refers to a person's ability to deal effectively with competing demands and taxing situations.

imbalance in chemical composition of cells within the body. Psychologically, thirst is the desire for water. These elements combine to form a drive to drink water when water is needed. (This portrayal isn't much different from the picture of motives presented in Chapter 5.)

One further feature of drives must be mentioned. The processes underlying personality operate continuously. Drive states build up until an action causes their tension to be released. If a drive isn't expressed, pressure continues to build. This view of motives is called a "hydraulic" model. In this view, trying to prevent a drive from being expressed only creates greater pressure toward its expression. This idea has important implications a little farther along.

Cathexes and the Utilization of Energy

Freud believed that psychic energy is generated continuously, but that only so much is available at any given time. (Recent research with a different starting point has tended to confirm this latter belief—Baumeister, Bratslavsky, Muraven, & Tice, 1998; Muraven, Tice, & Baumeister, 1998). Given the limited supply at any given time, how energy gets distributed becomes an important issue. The three aspects of personality—id, ego, and superego—compete for this energy. Each gains power only at the expense of the other two.

At first, of course, the id has all the energy. The energy is used to satisfy the id's needs and to operate the primary process. Investing energy in an activity or an image is called forming a **cathexis.** The more important an object or activity, the more energy invested (cathected) in it. As we said earlier, the id doesn't distinguish between reality and unreality. As far as the id is concerned, cathecting an image is as good as cathecting the object. This limitation allows the ego to capture part of the id's energy for its own use.

The ego uses secondary-process thought to identify objects in the world that match the images of the id. Since real objects satisfy needs better than images, the ego gradually comes to control more and more of the id's energy. Over time and experience, the ego controls enough energy that a surplus is available for uses other than gratifying id urges. The ego uses the surplus to bring intellectual functioning to a higher level and to form cathexes of its own. These **ego cathexes** form with objects and activities *associated with* satisfying needs. Regarding hunger, for example, ego cathexes might form with reading *Gourmet* magazine or restaurant reviews, shopping for food, or watching cooking shows on TV.

Another way the ego uses energy is to restrain or counteract the id from acting irrationally or immorally. The restraining forces are called **anticathexes,** because they prevent cathexes from being expressed. The clearest illustration of anticathexis is **repression.** Repression is investing energy to keep an upsetting idea or impulse in the unconscious. The harder it pushes to emerge, the more energy must be used in the anticathexis that keeps it hidden.

In the short run, anticathectic forces are useful because they prevent troubling urges from being expressed. They're less useful in the long run, though, because they continue to drain energy from the ego that could be used more positively in other ways. Remember, there's only so much energy to go around at any given time. If there are too many anticathexes, the ego has little energy left for anything else.

The superego also gathers energy from the id, through a process of *identification.* It goes like this: Initially, children depend on parents for need satisfaction.

BOX 8.4

HAVE FREUD'S IDEAS BEEN DISTORTED BY TRANSLATION AND CULTURAL DISTANCE?

Freud wrote in German and lived in a culture different from ours. His ideas were later translated into English. Translation of any complex or subtle idea from one language into another is hard, and there is great potential for error. Even less than perfect word choices can greatly distort meaning. It's hard for any translator to know precisely what the original writer intended to convey, and it's likely that no translation is entirely faithful to the original.

How faithful are the translations of Freud's writings? Not very, according to Bruno Bettelheim (1982), an important analyst in his own right. Bettelheim had the background to judge this question. He came from a Jewish family of Vienna, spoke German from childhood, and lived in exactly the same cultural context as Freud. Fluent in both English and German, he was distressed by many aspects of the English translations of Freud. Here are some examples.

Whenever possible, Freud tried to communicate his ideas in words that his readers had used since childhood, adding new insights to those common words. Two names he chose for aspects of personality are among the first words learned by every

German-speaking child. In the original, the words are personal pronouns, used as nouns. In the pronoun *I* (*Ich*), Freud chose a word that virtually forces you to think of yourself, eliciting the emotional qualities associated with your assertive affirmation of your own existence. The translated *ego*, in contrast, is lifeless and sterile. Why use such an empty word?

In the pronoun *it* (*Es*), Freud made an allusion that's completely lost to people who speak only English. In German, the word meaning "child" is neuter. For this reason, during early childhood virtually every German child is referred to as an "it." This word, as applied to a part of the self, has clear emotional overtones: It's what you were called when you were so young you hadn't learned to stifle your impulses or to feel guilty about them. A sense of personalized infancy is conveyed in the original, whereas the translated *id* has no intrinsic associations at all.

Another common word used by Freud was *Trieb,* which is commonly translated as *instinct.* Bettelheim says that *drive* is better, because Freud used a different word when he wanted to refer to inborn instincts of animals. Thus, Freud distinguished be-

This leads the child into id-based cathexes toward the parents. As parents impose rules of conduct—punish bad behavior and reward good behavior—the child determines which behaviors maximize need satisfaction. The child's affection for the parents (its cathexis to them) leads the child to act in ways the parents value and to *hold* those values. Cathected parental ideals thereby become part of the ego-ideal, and cathected prohibitions become part of the conscience.

The competition for psychic energy among the three aspects of personality is never-ending. It's yet one more way in which the aspects conflict with one another. Energy, after all, is the power to exert control. As one aspect of personality gains control, the influence of the others diminishes.

Two Classes of Drives: Life and Death Instincts

As with many aspects of Freud's work, his ideas about the nature and number of drives changed over time. Ultimately, he contended that all the basic instincts fit into two classes (Freud, 1933). The first class is termed **life** or **sexual instincts** (collectively termed **Eros**). Eros is a set of drives that deal with survival, reproduction, and plea-

tween these concepts. By *Trieb,* he meant to convey an inner propulsion, a basic urge, an impulse, but not the sense that the drive was the same as an animal instinct—inborn and unalterable.

Among the few non-German terms Freud used in his theory are Eros and Psyche. These are the names of two characters in a Greek myth, characters Freud knew intimately, as did most of the people to whom he was writing (educated people at that time read the classics). When Freud wrote of "erotic" qualities, he meant to evoke these two characters and their qualities—Eros's charm and cunning, and the deep love he had for Psyche. Psyche had at first been tricked into believing that Eros was disgusting, and the message of the myth is that this is an error. For sexual love to be an experience of true erotic pleasure, it must be imbued with beauty (symbolized by Eros himself) and also express the longings of the soul (symbolized by Psyche). These are some of the connotations Freud wanted to convey when he used the word *erotic.* When those connotations are stripped away (because readers don't know the myth), the word not only loses its proper mean-

ing, but even takes on connotations opposite to Freud's intention.

Indeed, Bettelheim argued that the word *psyche* itself has also been misrepresented. We're accustomed to think of the psyche as the mind, because that's how it's been translated. The German word for psyche, however, is *Seele,* which means soul. Thus, said Bettelheim, Freud's focus was on the metaphysical, but this has been misread as a focus on mental organizations.

In sum, Bettelheim argued that much of the sense of Freud's ideas has been misportrayed. Freud chose his language to evoke responses not just at an intellectual level but at an emotional level, which is lost in translation. Since we don't live in the cultural context in which Freud wrote, we miss many of his nods to ideas that were common at the time.

Bettelheim also argued, however, that Freud was aware of the distortions and chose to let them stand. Why? Freud, never an admirer of the United States, was annoyed at the U.S. medical establishment, which seemed intent on making psychoanalysis part of medicine, which Freud opposed. Apparently he simply didn't care enough to correct them.

sure. Despite the label Eros, not all life instincts deal with erotic urges per se. Hunger and pain avoidance, as well as sex, are life instincts. Collectively, the energy produced by the life instincts is known as **libido.**

Although not all life instincts are explicitly sexual, sexuality plays an important role in psychoanalytic theory (Freud, 1953a/1905). According to Freud, there's not one sex drive, but many. Each is associated with a different area of the body, called an **erogenous zone.** The erogenous zones identified by psychoanalytic theory are the mouth, the anus, and the genitals. Erogenous zones are potential sources of tension. Manipulating these areas relieves the tension and produces pleasure. Thus sucking or smoking produces oral pleasure, emptying the bowels produces anal pleasure, and rubbing of the vagina or penis produces genital pleasure.

A second set of instincts is **death instincts** (also termed **Thanatos**). Freud's view of these instincts is reflected in his statement that "the goal of all life is death" (Freud, 1955/1920). He believed that life provides a vehicle for death and that people desire (unconsciously) to return to the inanimate state from which they came. Because the expression of death instincts is usually held back by the life instincts, the effects of the death instincts aren't as visible.

Freud never coined a specific term for the energy associated with death instincts, and the death drive has received less attention than Eros. Today's biology, however, holds that a death instinct does exist in human physiology. That is, an active gene-directed suicide process occurs in human cells in certain circumstances. This suicide process, which is termed *apoptosis* (e.g., Clark, 1996), is a critical element in human development. Indeed, the cell-death machinery exists right now in most of your cells (Hopkin, 1995). This phenomenon suggests that death is an ultimate goal for elements of the body. Perhaps the principle extends more broadly into the personality as well.

One aspect of the death instinct that *has* received attention from psychologists concerns aggression. Freud believed that aggression isn't a basic drive, but stems from the thwarting of the death drive. That is, if Eros blocks expression of the death drive, tension remains—energy is left unspent. It can be dissipated in aggressive or destructive actions against others. Thus, in this view, acts of aggression express *self*-destructive urges, but turned outward onto others.

Coming Together of Libidinal and Aggressive Energies

Usually libidinal and aggressive energies are released in separate activities. Sometimes, however, sexual and aggressive drives exist side by side, with one expressed first, then the other. This pattern is termed *ambivalence*. Sometimes the two even fuse and jointly energize a single activity (Freud, 1933). This merging of sex and aggression is termed *sadism*.

Several research areas bear on Freud's ideas concerning the interplay between sexual and aggressive energies. One of the more interesting areas derived from a desire to examine the effects of pornography on aggression, rather than to test psychoanalytic theory (for reviews, see Donnerstein, 1983, or Malamuth & Donnerstein, 1984). Nevertheless, some of the findings are instructive regarding the competition between these energies and their possible blending.

The major point made in this literature is that sexual arousal can facilitate or inhibit aggression, depending on other factors. When a person is angry, exposure to *mild* sexual stimuli typically reduces aggression (e.g., Baron, 1974a, 1974b, 1979; Baron & Bell, 1977; Donnerstein, Donnerstein, & Evans, 1975; Frodi, 1977). In one study (Baron, 1974a), men were angered (or not) and later retaliated. Before retaliation, half viewed pictures of nude women, and the rest saw a set of neutral stimuli (pictures of scenery, furniture, and abstract art). As can be seen in Figure 8.4, exposure to erotica significantly reduced aggression among the angry subjects.

FIGURE 8.4

Influence of mild sexual arousal on aggression. Exposure to mildly erotic pictures reduced aggressiveness among men who had previously been angered but had no effect on men who had not been angered (adapted from Baron, 1974a).

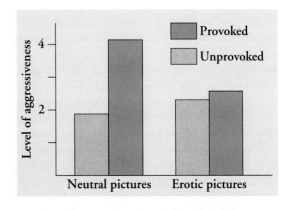

In contrast to this, creation of *intense* sexual arousal *increases* aggression among angered persons. In one study (Zillmann, 1971), male subjects were angered (or not) and later retaliated. Just beforehand, they viewed either a neutral film or a highly erotic, explicitly sexual film. The highly erotic film increased the aggression of angry subjects to a level even higher than that created by watching a violent fight film. Other research shows that highly erotic material increases aggression toward women (Donnerstein & Hallam, 1978), especially when the erotic stimuli are also aggressive (Donnerstein, 1980) and regardless of whether the aggressive-erotic material has a pleasant or an unpleasant ending (Donnerstein & Berkowitz, 1981). In sum, the evidence suggests that sexual and aggressive urges are sometimes antagonistic to each other but sometimes combine with each other (for broader discussion see Zillmann, 1998).

Catharsis

We said earlier that if a drive's tension isn't released, the pressure of the drive remains and grows. At some point, the buildup of energy may become so great that it can't be restrained any longer. At this point, impulse control is lost and the impulse is unleashed. The term **catharsis** is used to refer to the release of emotional tension that may occur in such an experience. (The term also has a second use that's discussed in Chapter 9.)

The concept of catharsis in the context of motive forces has been studied mostly with respect to aggression. The principle of catharsis leads to two predictions there. First, engaging in aggression should reduce tension, because the aggressive drive is no longer being stifled. Second, because doing this dissipates the drive's energy, the person should be less likely to aggress again in the near future.

This view of aggressive energy and its release is echoed in the ideas of more-recent theorists. For example, Megargee has analyzed acts of extreme violence (1966, 1971; Megargee, Cook, & Mendelsohn, 1967). He argues that people with strong inhibitions against aggressing rarely blow off steam, even when provoked. Over time, though, their feelings build until their restraints can no longer hold. Since so much energy has built up, the aggression released may be quite brutal. Ironically, the final provocation is often trivial, "the straw that broke the camel's back." Once the aggressive episode is over, these people (whom Megargee terms *overcontrolled aggressors*) tend to revert to overcontrolled, passive ways.

This portrayal is consistent with the psychoanalytic view of aggression, if one assumes the id impulses of these people are overcontrolled by ego and superego processes. The dynamics of overcontrolled aggression have also received a fair amount of verification (see, e.g., Megargee, 1966; Blackburn, 1968a, 1968b). Note, though, that overcontrolled aggressors are a rather select group of people.

How accurate is the catharsis hypothesis for aggression in *most* people? The evidence is mixed (Baron & Richardson, 1994). Aggression can help dissipate arousal (Baker & Schaie, 1969; Geen, Stonner, & Shope, 1975; Hokanson & Burgess, 1962a, 1962b; Hokanson, Burgess, & Cohen, 1963; Hokanson & Shetler, 1961), but it's less clear why. For example, in one study (Hokanson & Burgess, 1962b) subjects working on a task were harrassed by the experimenter, which raised their blood pressure. Later, some could retaliate physically, others verbally, others in fantasy (writing an aggressive story in response to a TAT picture), and some couldn't retaliate at all. As can be seen in Figure 8.5, the results supported the idea that true retaliation produces emotional catharsis. Subjects who retaliated physically or verbally showed decreases in blood pressure, though fantasy aggression had little effect.

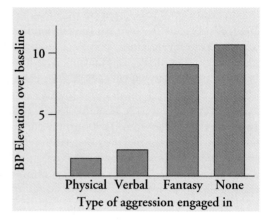

FIGURE 8.5

Tension-reducing effects of aggressive acts. This figure portrays elevations in systolic blood pressure after being provoked and then engaging in various kinds of aggression, in comparison with levels before provocation. Both physical and verbal aggression were relatively effective in returning subjects to their initial levels, whereas fantasy aggression was not (adapted from Hokanson & Burgess, 1962b).

Although this general pattern of effects has been obtained many times, there are important limiting conditions. The target of the aggression can't be high in status (Hokanson & Burgess, 1962a; Hokanson & Shetler, 1961) and must either be the instigator or linked to the instigator (Hokanson, Burgess, & Cohen, 1963). Moreover, tension reduction doesn't require aggression per se. Experiments have shown that virtually *any* active response that stops a provocation can reduce arousal (e.g., Hokanson & Edelman, 1966; Hokanson, Willers, & Koropsak, 1968; Stone & Hokanson, 1969). There's even evidence that, at least for women, responding to provocation in a friendly fashion reduces arousal more than does responding aggressively (Hokanson & Edelman, 1966). This finding isn't very consistent with the catharsis hypothesis.

What about the other reflection of catharsis? Does aggression make the person less aggressive in the near future? The findings are even more mixed here. Baron and Richardson (1994) concluded that such effects occur only under very specific conditions. Aggression reduces later aggression only if it's a response to an instigation (e.g., Bramel, Taub, & Blum, 1968; Doob, 1970; Konečni, 1975) and the retaliation is both toward the instigator and roughly equivalent to the instigation (e.g., Berkowitz & Alioto, 1973; Ebbesen, Duncan, & Konečni, 1975; Goldstein & Arms, 1971; Goranson, 1970; Mallick & McCandless, 1966). Interestingly enough, the retaliation itself may be done by someone else and still reduce aggression (E. J. Murray, 1985). On the other hand, sometimes engaging in aggression actually *increases* later aggression (Geen, Stonner, & Shope, 1975), which seems to contradict the catharsis hypothesis.

In sum, although some evidence is consistent with catharsis effects, the effects occur only under very specific circumstances. Moreover, other evidence seems to contradict the principle of catharsis. Taken together, this body of evidence doesn't seem easy to reconcile with psychoanalytic theory.

Displacement and Sublimation of Motive Forces

The life and death instincts provide for a wide range of behavior. Behavior is rendered even more complex by two additional processes that influence how these drives are expressed. One, called **displacement,** is a change in how energy's used or in the object toward which it's used. As people grow or circumstances change, old ways of

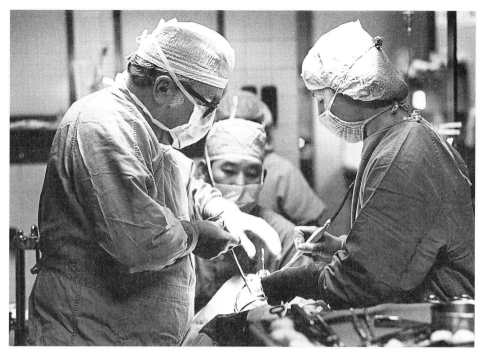

One view of surgery is that it allows unacceptable aggressive energy to be sublimated and released through a more socially acceptable form of activity.

satisfying desires are sometimes no longer acceptable or available. Displacement allows the blocked energy to be released in other ways or in other object choices. Energy will be shifted from one object to another until a suitable outlet for tension reduction is found.

Strictly speaking, the word displacement applies to any shift in object choice. There's a special type of displacement, however, that's important enough to get a special term—**sublimation.** In sublimation, a shift occurs from a socially unacceptable to a socially acceptable form of action.

As an illustration, consider two students who are angry over criticisms a professor wrote on their term papers. Both would love to hit the professor with a baseball bat. Neither does, though. One goes home, kicks his dog, and yells at his roommates. The other writes a letter to the editor of the campus newspaper, criticizing a policy of the university's administration. In both cases, aggressive energy is released through an activity that substitutes for the desired act (hitting the professor). The one who wrote the letter, however, did a more acceptable activity than the one who took out his anger on the dog and roommates. The one who kicked the dog was displacing. The one who wrote the letter was both displacing and sublimating.

As another example, consider two women who are experiencing sexual urges toward their best friend's boyfriend. One of them displaces this impulse by acting out the sexual impulses toward the person she happens to be dating. The other one sublimates the sexual energy by composing a poem.

Although displacement is presumed to occur for both sexual and aggressive energy, most research on displacement looks at aggression. The studies focus on how people choose a target for hostile impulses. Displacement of aggression clearly does occur (e.g., Berkowitz & Holmes, 1960; Fenigstein & Buss, 1974; Holmes, 1972). For example, Fenigstein and Buss (1974) found that people who'd been provoked acted more aggressively in a research task, even though the person on the receiving end was just an innocent bystander.

The concepts of displacement and sublimation are very important in psychoanalytic theory. They provide it with the kind of flexibility needed to account for the diversity of human behavior. From the psychoanalytic view, such wide-ranging phenomena as works of art and music, altruism, creativity, critical thinking, and excellence in sports can all be attributed to patterns of displaced and sublimated sexual and aggressive energy.

Indeed, the concept of sublimation is even more important than this. It's sublimation that permits humans to be civilized. Freud believed that without this process, people would act wholly from self-interest and their own primitive desires. Thanks to sublimation, people are capable of acts of altruism and cooperation. Sublimation, then, is the path by which humans are able to transcend their animal nature and develop as a society.

Psychosexual Development

Freud derived his ideas primarily from a few case histories of adults in therapy, but he wrote a great deal about how personality develops during childhood. He believed that early experiences play a critical role in determining what a person's adult personality is like. To understand the difficulties of adulthood, one must know the difficulties of childhood. Indeed, Freud thought that personality is largely determined by age five. During later life, personality stabilizes further, and its expression becomes more symbolic and less literal.

Freud viewed personality development as moving through a series of stages. Each stage reflects the body area through which libido, or sexual energy, is discharged during that period. For this reason, they're called *psychosexual stages*. In Freud's view, the child confronts conflicts at three stages. If the conflict isn't well resolved, too much libido gets permanently invested in that stage, a process termed **fixation.** This means that less energy is then available to handle conflicts during later stages. As a result, it's harder to successfully resolve the conflict in the later stages. In this sense, each stage builds on previous ones.

Fixation can occur for two reasons. A person who is overindulged in a stage may be reluctant to leave it and move on. A person whose needs are deeply frustrated *can't* move on until the needs are met. In either case, personality becomes partly arrested at this stage as a portion of the libido becomes invested in that cathexis. The stronger the fixation, the greater is the amount of libido invested in it. In a very strong fixation, one is so preoccupied—unconsciously—that one has little energy left for anything else.

The Oral Stage

The **oral stage** extends from birth to roughly 18 months. During this time, much of the infant's interaction with the world occurs through the mouth and lips, and libidinal gratification focuses in that area. The mouth is the source of tension reduction (eating) and pleasurable sensations (tasting, licking, and sucking). Infants are also completely dependent on others for their security and survival. The basic conflict of this stage concerns the process of weaning—literally and figuratively. That is, toward the end of this stage children are under increasing pressure to let go of their mother and become less reliant on her.

The oral stage has two substages. During the first phase (lasting roughly 6 months) the baby is particularly helpless and dependent. Because the infant is more or less limited to taking things in (both in terms of food and in other ways), the first part of the oral stage is called the *oral incorporative phase.* Freud thought that several traits that will last throughout life develop during this time. These traits include a general sense of optimism versus pessimism, trust versus mistrust, and dependency on others. Recall Freud's fascination with symbolism and the idea that literal events become transformed into symbolic versions. He felt that gullibility—the tendency to be "taken in" easily or to "swallow" everything you're told—also arises from events during the oral incorporative phase.

The second part of the oral stage, which starts with teething, is called the *oral sadistic phase.* Sexual pleasure now comes from biting and chewing. During this time the infant is weaned from the bottle or breast and begins to bite and chew food. The adult personality traits arising during the oral sadistic phase can be traced to this newly acquired ability. This phase is thought to determine who is verbally aggressive later in life, and who tends to use "biting" sarcasm in conversation.

In general terms, then, oral characters should relate to the world orally. They should be more preoccupied than others with food and drink. When stressed, they should be more likely than others to reduce tension through activities involving the mouth, such as smoking, drinking, or nail biting. When angry, they should engage in verbal aggression. Oral characters should be concerned with receiving support from others, and should do things to ease interactions with people rather than alienate them.

Although oral gratification may be most important during infancy, the pleasure of oral stimulation continues throughout life.

Is this characterization accurate? Perhaps. Joseph Masling and his colleagues have found that tests of oral imagery relate to both obesity (Masling, Rabie, & Blondheim, 1967; Weiss & Masling, 1970) and alcoholism (Bertrand & Masling, 1969). Orality has also been related to measures of interpersonal interest and social skills. For example, use of oral imagery was correlated with the need to nurture others (Holt, 1966) and with interpersonal effectiveness (Masling, Johnson, & Saturansky, 1974). Persons high in oral imagery also volunteer readily for interpersonal tasks (Bornstein & Masling, 1985; Masling, O'Neill, & Jayne, 1981) and rely on other people's judgments during ambiguous tasks (Masling, Weiss, & Rothschild, 1968).

More generally, people who display oral imagery seem to be highly motivated to gain closeness and support from others and are sensitive to how others react to them. They have greater physiological reactivity to social isolation (Masling, Price, Goldband, & Katkin, 1981) and to subtle cues of rejection from others (Masling, O'Neill, & Katkin, 1982) than do people who display less oral imagery. They also use more physical contact during social interaction (Juni, Masling, & Brannon, 1979) and are more self-disclosing (Juni, 1981) than less oral people (see also Blum & Miller, 1952; Fisher & Greenberg, 1977).

We should point out that you don't have to be an extremely oral character to seek oral gratification. Lots of people chew gum. Nor is the expression of sexual energy through oral contact limited to early childhood. Indeed, there's evidence all around you that seeking of oral pleasure continues into adulthood. After all, what is serious kissing but an oral expression of sexuality? Nor is that the only way sexuality is expressed orally among adults. In sum, it seems true that the mouth is an important part of the body through which the human's sexual nature is expressed and pleasure obtained.

The Anal Stage

The **anal stage** of psychosexual development begins at about 18 months and continues into the third year of life. During this period the anus is the focal erogenous zone, and sexual pleasure comes from the stimulation that occurs when defecating. The major event of this period is the start of toilet training. For many children, toilet training is the first time that external constraints are systematically imposed on satisfaction of internal urges. When toilet training starts, children can't relieve themselves whenever and wherever they want, but must learn instead that there's an appropriate time and place for everything.

The personality characteristics that arise from fixations during this period depend on how toilet training is approached by parents and caretakers. Two general orientations are typical. One involves urging the child to eliminate at a desired time and place and praising the child lavishly for success. This approach places a lot of attention on the elimination process and reward for the child. The child is thereby convinced of the value of producing "things" (in this case urine and feces) at the "right" time and place, by whatever means possible. To Freud, this experience provides a basis for adult productivity and creativity.

The second approach to toilet training is harsher. Rather than praise for a job well done, emphasis is on punishment, ridicule, and shame for failures. These practices yield two patterns of characteristics, depending on how the child reacts. If the child adopts an active pattern of rebellion, eliminating forcefully when the parents least want it, a set of *anal expulsive traits* develop. These are tendencies to be messy, cruel, destructive, and overtly hostile.

If the child attempts to get even by withholding feces and urine, a set of *anal retentive* traits develops. The anal retentive personality is a rigid, obsessive style of interacting with the world (Shapiro, 1965). The personality characteristics that make up this pattern are sometimes known as the *anal triad:* stinginess, obstinacy, and orderliness or cleanliness. Stinginess stems from the desire to retain feces. Obstinacy stems from the struggle of wills over toilet training. Orderliness is a reaction against the messiness of defecating.

Research suggests that such a pattern does exist. In one study (Rosenwald, 1972) male undergraduates assessed as having the greatest anal anxiety were also the most obstinate and the most compulsively neat. Conceptually similar results were reported by Juni and Rubenstein (1982). They had subjects work on a monotonous task with an ostensible cosubject who interrupted the subject frequently. The dependent measures were liking for the experimental task and hostility toward the confederate. Anal subjects reported less annoyance with the tedious task (suggesting obsessiveness) and more hostility toward the disruptive confederate than did persons who had been categorized as less anal (see also Juni & Fischer, 1985; Juni & Lo Cascio, 1985).

The Phallic Stage

The **phallic stage** begins during the third year and continues through the fifth year. During this period the focus of libidinal excitation shifts to the genital organs. This is also the period when most children begin to masturbate, as they become aware of the sensory pleasure that arises from genital manipulation.

At first the awakening sexual desires are completely *autoerotic* in nature. That is, sexual pleasure is totally derived from, and satisfied by, self-stimulation. Gradually, however, libido begins to shift toward the opposite-sex parent, as boys develop an interest in their mothers and girls develop an interest in their fathers. At the same time the child becomes hostile toward the same-sex parent because of the perceived competition between them over the affection of the other parent.

The desire on the part of boys to possess their mothers and replace their fathers is termed the **Oedipus complex** (after the character in Sophocles' play *Oedipus Rex* who unwittingly marries his mother after killing his father). Comparable feelings in girls are sometimes called an Oedipus complex and sometimes an *Electra* complex (after the Greek character Electra, who persuades her brother to kill both their mother and their mother's lover in revenge for the death of their father). Although these complexes reflect forces that are similar in many ways, the forces become manifest differently for boys and girls. Both enter this period loving their mothers, but girls' affection shifts toward their fathers. With this shift, the developmental pattern for boys and girls diverges.

Let's consider first what happens to boys. For a boy, the changes are that his initial love for his mother transforms into a strong sexual desire. His feelings for his father shift toward hostility and hatred, because his father is a rival for his mother's affection. Over time, the boy's competitiveness and jealousy toward his father may become so extreme that he may want the father out of the family, or even dead. Such thoughts may induce strong feelings of guilt. At the same time, the boy is threatened by the fear his father will retaliate against him for his desire toward his mother. In traditional psychoanalytic theory, the boy's fear is quite specific: that his father will castrate him to eliminate the source of his lust. Freud termed this fear **castration anxiety.**

Ultimately, castration anxiety causes the boy to push his sexual desire for his mother into the unconscious. Castration anxiety also causes the boy to **identify** with his father (a term that takes on a somewhat different meaning here than earlier in the chapter). Identification, as used here, means to develop feelings of similarity to and connectedness with someone else. This serves several functions. First, it gives the boy a kind of "protective coloration." Being like his father makes it seem less likely that his father will harm him. Second, by identifying with desirable aspects of the father, the boy reduces his ambivalence toward him. The process of identification thus paves the way for the development of the superego, as the boy introjects his father's values.

Finally, by identifying with the father, he gains a vicarious outlet for his sexual urges toward his mother. That is, the boy gains symbolic access to his mother *through* his father. Presumably, the more the boy resembles the father, the more easily the boy can unconsciously fantasize himself in his father's place.

For girls, the conflict of the phallic stage is more complicated. As we said earlier, girls abandon their love relationship with their mother for a new one with their father. This shift occurs when the girl realizes she has no penis. She withdraws love from her mother because she blames her mother for her castrated condition (after discovering that her mother has no penis either). At the same time, the girl's affection is drawn to her father, who does have a penis. Ultimately the girl comes to wish that her father would share his penis with her through sexual union or that he would provide her with the symbolic equivalent of a penis—a baby.

Freud referred to these feelings as **penis envy** (though see Box 8.5). Penis envy is the female counterpart of castration anxiety in boys. As for boys, the emotional conflict is resolved through identification. By becoming more like her mother, the girl gains vicarious access to her father and increases the chances that she'll marry someone just like him.

Several studies have sought evidence of penis envy among girls and castration anxiety among boys. Hall and Van de Castle (1963) found that women's dreams have more symbols of penis envy, whereas men's dreams include more symbols of castration anxiety. Johnson (1966) studied penis envy by seeing whether or not subjects returned a pencil (a penis symbol) after borrowing it for an exam. Women kept the pencils more often than did men. Unfortunately, this dependent measure is pretty far removed from the concept of penis envy. The results may simply reflect a tendency for women to become absorbed in test taking, or an automatic tendency to return pencils to purses.

Fixations that develop during the phallic stage result in personalities that, in effect, continue to wrestle with Oedipal conflicts. Men may go to great lengths to demonstrate that they haven't been castrated, seducing as many women as they can, or fathering many children. The attempt to assert their masculinity may also be expressed symbolically by attaining great success in their career. Alternatively, they may fail in their sexual and occupational lives (purposely, but unconsciously so) because of the guilt they feel over competing with their fathers for their mothers' love.

Among women, the continuation of the Oedipal conflict results in a way of relating to men that is excessively seductive and flirtatious, but with a denial of the underlying sexuality. This style of relating first develops toward the woman's father, since she was drawn to him first and has by this point repressed the sexual desire that first drew her. The pattern is then carried over to her later social interactions. This is a woman who excites men with her seductive behavior and then is surprised when the men want sexual contact with her.

BOX 8.5

PENIS ENVY OR VAGINA ENVY?

As discussed in the body of the chapter, Freud assumed that developing girls eventually confront the fact that they don't have a penis, and he believed this discovery has shattering implications. Girls feel castrated—betrayed—and they blame their mothers for it. This feeling of castration and incompleteness haunts them for the rest of their lives. In his view, the envy women develop for men—penis envy—motivates much of their later behavior, both directly and symbolically.

Examples of this come from many domains. Women try to recover their lost penises symbolically by incorporating one into their bodies through sexual intercourse and by giving birth to male children. In today's society, they also seek to obtain the power that the penis confers by entering business, law, and other power-related pursuits. Manifestations of penis envy aren't limited to efforts to regain the missing organ. Envy can also be expressed by desiring others to share the same fate. Thus women sometimes try to reduce men to the same pitiful state as they occupy themselves, castrating men symbolically by being "sharp" and "cutting" in social interactions.

This characterization is entirely compatible with psychoanalytic thought. And a case can be made that at least some girls experience in their childhood a sense that they're missing something that boys have—something that may be important. But the idea that penis envy is a prime source of women's motivation is not exactly calculated to win friends among women, particularly women with feminist leanings. To many, this position is condescending and demeaning toward women and presents a gross distortion of reality (Horney, 1939, 1967).

To point out the arbitrariness of Freud's assumptions, Peterson (1980) set forth a different hypothesis. According to Peterson, Freud was on the right track, but he got things backward (perhaps because the truth was too threatening to him). It's not women who are envious of men; it's men who are envious of women. Young boys, growing up, sooner or later confront the fact that they have no vagina. This shattering discovery leads to a sense of envy from which they never recover. The resentment that stems from this envy influences all subsequent male behavior.

As did Freud, Peterson assumed that the manifestations of this envy are primarily symbolic. This, suggested Peterson, is why men insist on having pockets in their pants. Lots of pockets. Indeed, the three-piece suit (commonly worn by businessmen and others making vain, pathetic attempts to convey an image of power) is a virtual orgy of symbolic wish fulfillment. It has pants pockets, vest pockets, jacket pockets, even an *internal* jacket pocket—symbolism on top of symbolism!

It should be obvious that Peterson's argument was made tongue in cheek (although we're not about to tell you which of us requires four pockets in every pair of pants he buys). However, she also was making a more serious point about psychoanalytic theory, and about theory more generally. There are places in psychoanalytic theory (as in any theory) where assumptions are made that are somewhat arbitrary and seem based on societal preconceptions rather than theoretical necessity. It's always important to think about the basis for these assumptions in order to decide for yourself whether or not they're sensible.

Freud felt that identifying the Oedipus complex was one of his most significant theoretical contributions. This brief span involves considerable emotional turmoil filled with love, hate, guilt, jealousy, and fear. He believed that how the child negotiates the conflicts and difficulties of the phallic stage determines fundamental attitudes toward sexuality, interpersonal competitiveness, and personal adequacy (see also Box 8.6).

THE THEORIST AND THE THEORY:
Freud's Own Oedipal Crisis

The idea that personal experiences of personality theorists influenced the very form taken by their theories is vividly illustrated by the life of Sigmund Freud. In fact it's widely believed that several aspects of Freud's life had a direct impact on his theories.

Freud's father Jakob, a merchant, was 40 years old at the time of Sigmund's birth (1856). By all accounts he was a strict and authoritarian father. Given this, it would be no surprise that Freud's feelings about his father were ambivalent. Freud's memories later in life were, in fact, of hating his father as well as loving him. A hint of scandal concerning Sigmund's birth may also have had a bearing on his relationship with his father. Two different dates are indicated in various places as his birthdate. This may have been a clerical error. Some believe, however, that the later date was an effort to disguise the fact that Freud's mother was pregnant when she and his father married (Balmary, 1979).

Jakob Freud had had two sons in a prior marriage and was himself a grandfather when Sigmund was born. His wife Amalie, on the other hand, was only 20. Sigmund was her first child and her special favorite. Sigmund responded to this maternal affection by developing and maintaining a highly idealized image of his mother and a strong affection for her. By all accounts, they had a very close relationship throughout her life.

In short, the relationships of Freud's childhood had all the elements of what he would later call the Oedipal conflict. There was a deep attachment to his mother, which some have said had sexual overtones. There was also a strong ambivalence toward his father (the depths of which are reflected in the fact that Freud was late for his father's funeral, an act he later saw as having been unconsciously motivated). It seems hard to ignore the possibility that Freud used his own experiences as a model for what he came to argue were universal aspects of development.

Nor was the Oedipal crisis the only aspect of Freud's thinking to be influenced by events in his own life. The experience of World War I, in which 10 million people were killed, deeply disillusioned Freud, along with many other Europeans. Newspapers were filled with accounts of the slaughter, which seemed truly purposeless. Two of Freud's sons fought in the war, and his fears for their safety must have been a great strain on him. Shortly after the end of the war Freud wrote his statement on the death instinct. It seems likely that this concept—that people have an unconscious wish to die, which they turn outward toward others in murderous actions such as war—was partly Freud's attempt to understand how the atrocities of that war could have come to happen. Thus, once again, the elements of the theory seem formed by the experiences of the theorist.

Fixations that develop during these first three stages of development presumably form much of the basis of adult personality. Some of the traits deriving from fixations during these stages are summarized in Table 8.1.

The Latency Period

At the close of the phallic stage, the child enters a period of relative calm, termed the **latency period.** This period, from approximately age 6 to the early teens, is a time when sexual and aggressive drives become less active. The lessening of these urges results partly from changes in the body and partly from the emergence of the ego and superego aspects of personality. During this period, children turn their atten-

TABLE 8.1

Personality qualities that follow from fixations in the first three stages of psychosexual development.

Stage of fixation	Personality qualities
Oral	Incorporative: Dependent, gullible, jealous
	Sadistic: Sarcastic and verbally aggressive
Anal	Expulsive: messy, cruel, destructive
	Retentive: obstinate, neat and orderly, stingy
Phallic	Among males: macho aggressive sexuality, excessive striving for career potency; alternatively, sexual and occupational impotence
	Among females: flirtatious, seductive behavior that doesn't lead to sexual interaction

tion to other pursuits, often of an intellectual or social nature. Thus the latency period is a time when the child's experiences broaden, rather than a time when new conflicts are confronted and new traits emerge. As an example, parental identifications adopted during the phallic stage may be supplemented by identifications with other figures of authority, perhaps religious figures or teachers.

With the onset of puberty (toward the end of the latency period), libidinal and aggressive urges again intensify. In addition, conflicts of previous periods may be reencountered. This is a time when the coping skills of the ego are severely taxed. Although adolescents experience adult sexual desires, the release of sexual energy through intercourse isn't socially sanctioned. As a consequence, sexual gratification is sought in other ways—for instance, through fantasy or masturbation.

The Genital Stage

In later adolescence and adulthood the person moves into the final stage of psychosexual development—the **genital stage.** If earlier psychosexual stages have been negotiated well, the person enters this stage with libido still organized around the genitals, and it remains focused there throughout life. The sexual gratification during the genital stage differs, however, from that of earlier stages. Specifically, earlier attachments were narcissistic. The child was interested only in his or her own sexual pleasure. Others were of interest only insofar as they furthered the child's own pleasure. In the genital stage, a desire develops to share mutual sexual gratification with someone else. Thus the person becomes capable of loving others not only for selfish reasons but also for altruistic reasons.

Ideally, the person is able to achieve full and free orgasm on an equal basis. Indeed, this ability to share with others in a warm and caring way, and to be concerned with their welfare, is the hallmark of the genital stage. Persons in this stage also have better control over their impulses, both sexual and aggressive, and are able to release them in smaller amounts (although more frequently) in sublimated, socially acceptable ways. In this manner the person becomes transformed from a self-centered pleasure-seeking infant into a well-socialized caring adult.

Freud believed that people don't enter the genital stage automatically and that this transition is rarely achieved in its entirety (see Fenichel, 1945). Most people have less control over their impulses than they should, and most have difficulty in gratifying sexual desires in a completely satisfying and acceptable way. In this sense the genital personality is an ideal to strive for, rather than an end to be taken for granted. It is the perfect culmination of psychosexual development, from the analytic point of view.

Psychoanalytic Structure and Process: Problems and Prospects

The psychoanalytic view on how personality is organized and how it functions has been influential since its development, but it has also been controversial. From the start, people were reluctant to accept aspects of the theory. Many were incensed by the prominence of its sexual themes. They couldn't understand how anyone could suggest that the behavior of young children is sexually motivated. It also was difficult for many to believe that behavior is determined largely by forces outside awareness.

The scientific community has faulted psychodynamic theory on other grounds. The primary problem from a scientific standpoint is that the theory is very hard to test. One reason is that many psychoanalytic concepts are defined ambiguously. An example of this is provided by the term *libido*. Freud used this term to refer to sexual energy, a psychological quality that arises from physiological processes. We know little else about it. Where exactly does it come from? What is it that makes it sexual in nature? Most important of all, how do you measure it? Without some way to measure it, you can't study it. By implication, other ideas to which libido is linked (e.g., psychosexual development, fixation) are also hard to examine.

Nor is this problem limited to the concept of libido. Other psychoanalytic concepts—cathexis, transference, the death wish, id, ego—are also problematic from a research point of view. When a theory's concepts can't be defined operationally, the theory can't be tested.

Part of the ambiguity of psychoanalytic concepts comes from Freud's tendency to describe concepts differently from one time to another. Even more ambiguity comes from the fact that Freud thought about personality in highly metaphorical ways. This metaphorical approach is deeply embedded in descriptions of the theory. As a result, it's difficult to know when Freud should be read literally and when he should be read metaphorically.

Consider, for example, his description of the Oedipal complex. Should we take Freud to mean literally that he thought every boy comes to desire his mother sexually at around age 4? Or should we take it metaphorically and assume he was using the Oedipal theme as a graphic way of describing the conflict between young children and their parents? Freud wrote at one point that many of the specific explanatory devices he used could be replaced or discarded without damaging the theory (see Silverman, 1976). It's apparent, then, that parts of what he wrote shouldn't be taken literally. Unfortunately, he didn't specify which parts.

As a metaphorical statement, the Oedipal theme makes a good deal of sense. As a literal statement, it doesn't hold up so well. Sears (1943, p. 136) wrote, "Freud's notion of the universal Oedipus complex stands as a sharply etched grotesquerie against his otherwise informative description of sexual development."

Scientific psychologists also criticize the evidence base on which psychoanalytic theory rests. One focus of this criticism is Freud's heavy reliance on case studies in developing his ideas, particularly the ideas involving infantile sexuality. The case study method has several problems. It's inherently subjective, influenced as much by what the researcher brings to the situation as by what the subject brings. It's hard to be sure whether the insights gained by one researcher would be gained by another person looking at the same case.

The problem of reliability is even further compounded in this case. Freud acted both as theorist-researcher and as therapist. Thus he took an active role in the development of the case history, becoming involved in interpretation of what was said and done. Freud's actions as a participant-observer may have biased the kinds of things his patients said even more than usual (Powell & Boer, 1994). For example, more sexually toned material came from the patient across the course of therapy. Was this because repression was weakening, or because the patient learned over time that this was the kind of information Freud was interested in? Indeed, there is evidence that Freud was sometimes highly directive with patients (Esterton, 1998).

Freud allowed himself to be biased in another way, as well, by relying so much on patients. He carefully screened potential patients and allowed into therapy only those he thought were very good candidates. Thus he developed his ideas from observations of a biased set of cases. We can't be sure how much or in what ways these people differed from the overall population, but it's clear they weren't chosen randomly.

Moreover, the number of cases Freud relied on for a data base was distressingly small. In fact, in all his writings and works Freud described case histories of only a dozen or so people. Yet, from this very narrow data base—a dozen or so people, all of whom had been carefully chosen and all of whom were in therapy—he went on to formulate what he regarded as universal rules about personality functioning in general. Many find this very problematic.

Another criticism of psychoanalytic ideas is the tendency to confuse facts with inferences. For example, certain observations led Freud to infer the existence (and universality) of an Oedipal complex. He then went on to discuss the Oedipal complex as though its existence were a fact, with no need to test the inference. A general tendency to mix fact with inference has contributed to an intellectual climate in psychoanalytic circles in which basic concepts have gone untested—because it apparently was thought they didn't *need* to be tested (Crews, 1996; Esterton, 1993).

Despite these problems, there's been a resurgence of interest in the ideas that make up both the topographic model of mind and the structural model of personality (Bargh, 1997; Carver, 1996). With respect to the topography of the mind, many people who start from different perspectives now argue that important aspects of memory can't be brought to consciousness voluntarily. In some cases, this is because the elements are too small, or too hard to locate. Sometimes it apparently is because the thing we're looking for (by its very nature) can be used but not "viewed." Sometimes it's because the thing we might be looking for has become so automatic that, in effect, it's fallen out of our mental address book and become lost. Although these phenomena aren't quite the same as those Freud emphasized, they represent new interest in the idea that the mind has more than two regions.

With respect to the structural model, observers have begun to reemphasize that we shouldn't get distracted by the idea that the mind has three components. Think of them instead as three modes of functioning. Take the descriptions a little less literally. The id is simply the psychological nature of the infant. Infantile qualities are overlaid in all of us by effects of our socialization. But those infantile qualities remain in some sense the basic structure from which we grew. Id is the part that *wants,* without regard to obstacles, dangers, or disapprovals—wants as the 1-year-old wants. We still have that part, and it still makes its presence known. Ego is the set of restraints we learn, restraints that diminish the pain we experience from grabbing too fast for what we want without thinking of dangers. Superego is the abstract rules we learn, to become part of a society in which we can't always have our way, even by waiting.

The idea that humans begin life grabbing for what they want at the moment they really want it, and only gradually learn to restrain themselves, makes a lot of sense. The idea that people later learn abstractions concerning morality also makes sense. So does the idea that those abstractions can conflict with the wants. In sum, the structural model expresses a fair amount of truth about the human experience.

What is the future of these ideas? Some see them as being of historical interest only. Others see them as valuable. They remain an important part of the course you're taking. We suspect they'll remain there for a long time.

SUMMARY

Freud's topographical model holds that there are three regions of mind: the conscious, the preconscious (ordinary memory), and the unconscious (a part of mind that isn't accessible to consciousness). The unconscious is a repository for threatening or unacceptable material and urges.

Freud also assumed that personality has three component structures. The id (the original part of personality) is the source of all psychic energy. It follows the pleasure principle (the idea that all needs should be immediately gratified), exists wholly in the unconscious, and uses primary-process thinking (which is primitive, instinctual, and separate from reality).

The ego eventually develops from the id because the id cannot deal effectively with the demands of the external world. The ego follows the reality principle (the idea that behavior must take into account external reality), operates in all three regions of the mind, and tries to see that id impulses are gratified in a realistic and appropriate manner. The ego uses secondary-process (reality-based) thought.

The third component of personality, superego, is a representation of rules by which parents reward and punish the child. It has two parts: Ego ideal consists of standards of moral perfection. Conscience holds a representation of all behaviors that are considered reprehensible. Both function in all three regions of the mind. Once the superego develops, the ego must mediate among id, superego, and reality.

The investment of energy in a need is called a cathexis. Restraining forces (from the ego) are called anticathexes. Id impulses form two categories: Life instincts (Eros) aim for self-preservation and sexual pleasure. Death instincts (Thanatos) are self-destructive and may be turned outward as aggression. Catharsis in aggression is the releasing of an aggressive desire, which leads to tension reduction and a decreased need to aggress. Impulses can be displaced—released onto a different target from that initially intended. Impulses can also be sublimated—that is, transformed into socially acceptable acts.

Freud argued that child development proceeds through psychosexual stages and that adult personality is influenced by how crises are resolved at each stage. In the oral stage, sexuality centers on the mouth, and the crisis involves being weaned from the mother. In the anal stage, sexuality centers on the anus, and the crisis involves toilet training. In the phallic stage, sexuality centers on the genitals, and the crisis (creating Oedipal and Electra complexes) involves lust for the opposite-sex parent and fear of or hatred for the same-sex parent. The latency period is a calm interval with no serious conflict. The genital period is maturity, in which genital sexuality shifts from selfish narcissism to mutual sharing.

GLOSSARY

Anal stage The second stage of development, in which anal needs create a crisis over toilet training.

Anticathexis The investment of energy in suppressing an impulse or image.

Castration anxiety A boy's fear (from the phallic stage) that his father will perceive him as a rival and castrate him.

Catharsis The release of emotional tension.

Cathexis The investment of psychic energy in a desired activity or image.

Conscience The part of the superego that punishes violations of moral standards.

Conscious The part of the mind that holds what one is currently aware of.

Death instincts (Thanatos) Self-destructive instincts, often turned outward as aggression.

Displacement The shifting of an impulse from its original target to a different target.

Ego The rational part of the personality that deals pragmatically with reality.

Ego catharsis Binding psychic energy in an ego-guided activity.

Ego-ideal The part of the superego that represents perfection and rewards for good behavior.

Ego strength The ability of the ego to function despite competing demands of id, superego, and reality.

Erogenous zone A sexually responsive area of the body.

Fixation The condition of being partly stuck in some early stage of psychosexual development.

Genital stage The final stage of development, mature and mutual sexual involvement with another.

Id The original, primitive component of personality, the source of all energy.

Identify Develop feelings of similarity to, and connectedness with, another person.

Introjection Absorbing the values of one's parents into one's superego.

Latency period The period in which the crises of the phallic stage give way to a temporary calm.

Libido The collective energy of the life instincts.

Life instincts or **sexual instincts (Eros)** Survival and sexual instincts.

Oedipus complex The mix of desire for the opposite-sex parent and fear of or hatred for the other parent.

Oral stage The first stage of psychosexual development, in which oral needs create a crisis over weaning.

Penis envy A girl's envy of males, from feelings of having been castrated.

Phallic stage The third stage of development, in which a crisis occurs over sexual desire for the opposite-sex parent.

Pleasure principle The idea that impulses should be gratified immediately.

Preconscious The region of the mind that corresponds to ordinary memory.

Primary process The id process that creates an unconscious image of a desired object.

Reality principle The idea that actions must take into account the constraints of external reality.

Reality testing The ego's checking to see whether plans will work before they are put into action.

Repression The preventing of an idea or impulse from becoming conscious.

Secondary process The ego process of rationally seeking an object to satisfy a desire.

Structural model Freud's model of three components of personality.

Sublimation The altering of an unacceptable id impulse into an activity that's more socially acceptable.

Superego The component of personality that seeks moral perfection.

Topographical model Freud's model of three regions, or areas, of the mind.

Unconscious The region of the mind that's not accessible to consciousness.

Wish fulfillment The creation of an unconscious image of a desired object.

Anxiety, Defense, and Self-Protection

■ Dan and Jamie are standing in the cafeteria talking about a party they'd been to last weekend, at which one of their friends had gotten flagrantly, ostentatiously drunk—something she's done weekly for the past year. "Man, I can't believe how much Robin *drinks*," says Jamie. "She soaks it up like a sponge." At this moment Robin rounds the corner, practically running into them. "Hey Robin, watch it, are you still high from last weekend?" Jamie asks. "What are you talking about?" replies Robin, "I didn't drink that much." "Seriously, Robin," Dan throws in, "aren't you concerned about how much you've been drinking lately?" Robin's face takes on a perplexed and somewhat offended look. "Look, guys, I don't have a problem, so just stay off my back," she says, as she turns and walks away. Dan and Jamie look at each other and shrug.

■ Robert and Hillary have been dating for several months. They're at a party. Also there is Tim, a very good-looking guy who has the reputation of being friendly to everyone, but also a little inaccessible. Toward the end of the evening (after Tim and his date have left), Hillary is talking about him with Robert and several of their friends. "Didn't you see the way he was coming on to me? I wish he wouldn't do that, but he does it all the time." Later, on the way home, Robert says to her, "Hillary, you just made a fool of yourself—and me—in front of all those people. Tim didn't come on to you at all. I can't imagine where you got such an idea."

Chapter 8 described the basic elements of the psychoanalytic view on human nature. In this chapter we consider more deeply some of the ways in which that nature plays itself out in behavior. In many respects the points to be made here are direct extensions of the logic of Sigmund Freud's theory. Some of the ideas we'll be discussing, however, were developed by people other than him. Most prominent among them was his daughter, Anna Freud (1966).

Anxiety

Much of the process within personality—in people who are perfectly normal, as well as people with difficulties—is linked to the concept of **anxiety.** Anxiety is an aversive inner state that people seek to avoid or escape. Freud initially thought anxiety was a way of releasing libidinal energy that had been blocked from direct release (e.g., Breuer & Freud, 1955/1895). He later changed his view (e.g., Freud, 1936/1926) to the position that anxiety is a warning signal to the ego that something bad is about to happen.

Freud (1959/1926) distinguished among three different types of anxiety, which reflect three different categories of bad things. The most basic is **reality anxiety,** which arises from a threat or danger in the world. It's the kind of fear you experience when you realize you're about to be bit by a dog, crash your car, be yelled at for a big mistake at work, or fail an exam. Reality anxiety is the most basic form of anxiety because it's rooted in objective reality. One way to deal with it is to avoid or escape from the situation that's producing the feeling.

The second type of anxiety is **neurotic anxiety.** This is unconscious fear that your id impulses will get out of control and lead you to do something that will get you punished. The person experiencing a lot of neurotic anxiety is constantly worried about the id's escaping from the ego's control (though the worry is unconscious). The anxiety isn't a fear of the id's impulses and urges per se. It's a fear of the punishment that may result from expressing them.

Since people are often punished for impulsive behavior, particularly if it's behavior that's disapproved of by society, this type of anxiety has a sort of basis in reality. Unlike reality anxiety, however, the danger originates within the person, from the urges of the id. For this reason, neurotic anxiety is harder to deal with than is reality anxiety. That is, you can drive carefully, prepare for your exams, and avoid dangerous dogs, but you can't escape from your id. It always has the potential to get out of control.

The third type of anxiety is called **moral anxiety.** This is the fear people have when they've violated (or are about to violate) their introjected moral codes. If your moral sense forbids cheating and you're tempted to cheat on something, you feel moral anxiety. If your moral sense forbids sexual intercourse before marriage and you're just about to have sex with someone, you experience moral anxiety. Subjectively, moral anxiety is felt as guilt or shame.

Moral anxiety is fear of the conscience that's part of your superego. The stronger your superego, the more likely you'll have moral anxiety. As with neurotic anxiety, it's important to be clear about the difference between this and reality anxiety. People are often punished by society for transgressing moral standards, but the threat of punishment from society isn't the basis of moral anxiety. Its source is internal, in your conscience. As with neurotic anxiety, it's hard to deal with. Just as you can't escape your id, you can't run away from your conscience.

Mechanisms of Defense

If your ego were doing its job perfectly, you'd never feel any anxiety of any sort. External dangers would be avoided or dealt with, thereby preventing reality anxiety. Id impulses would be released in acceptable degrees at appropriate times, preventing neurotic anxiety. You'd never let yourself do anything (or even *want* to do anything) that your superego disapproves of, thereby preventing moral anxiety. No one's ego works this well, however. As a result, most people, at one time or another, experience some anxiety, and many people experience a lot. This is a part of normal human life.

When anxiety occurs, the ego responds in one of two ways. First, it increases rational problem-oriented coping efforts in an attempt to deal better, consciously, with the source of the threat. This works best for reality anxiety. The second way is to employ a **defense mechanism.** Defense mechanisms are tactics the ego develops to help it deal with anxiety. When defenses are well established, they can even prevent anxiety from arising. All defense mechanisms share two characteristics: They can operate unconsciously and they distort, transform, or falsify reality in one way or another.

Various theorists have postulated varying numbers of defense mechanisms. Anna Freud (1966), in what is generally considered to be the most influential work done on ego defenses, identified ten mechanisms available to the ego to ward off anxiety. The following sections outline several of these strategies.

Repression

The fundamental mechanism of defense is called **repression.** Indeed, Sigmund Freud often used the terms *defense* and *repression* interchangeably. Repression sometimes is undertaken consciously (being thereby equivalent to *suppression*) as the person tries to force an idea from entering consciousness (see also Box 9.1). Most discussions of repression, however, assume that its operation is usually unconscious.

As was said in Chapter 8, repression is keeping things out of consciousness—particularly id impulses. By creating an anticathexis with the impulse, the ego restrains

BOX 9.1

UNINTENDED EFFECTS OF THOUGHT SUPPRESSION

As discussed in the body of the chapter, people sometimes exert conscious effort to try to keep particular thoughts out of their minds. If you're trying to quit smoking, you want to avoid thinking about cigarettes. If you're trying to lose weight, you want to avoid thoughts of food. If you've just broken up with someone, you want to avoid thinking about the things you used to do together. So you try to keep these ideas out of your consciousness.

Sometimes this suppression works, but sometimes trying not to think of something has unintended side effects. Dan Wegner (1989, 1994) and his colleagues have conducted a program of studies on thought suppression, and their conclusions may surprise you. Trying not to think about something can actually make that thought become more likely later on, especially if the thought's an emotionally arousing one (Wegner, Shortt, Blake, & Page, 1990).

Theoretically, the idea of conscious thought suppression contains a paradox. Thought suppression requires two steps: deciding to suppress the thought, and then getting rid of all manifestations of the thought—including the plan to suppress it. This seems to require you to be conscious of your intent and not conscious of it, all at the same time. (If repression occurs unconsciously, of course, this problem is avoided, because the plan to get rid of the thought is unconscious.)

So what happens when people try to suppress a thought? Research on this question (e.g., Wegner, Schneider, Carter, & White, 1987) began by teaching subjects a think-aloud technique in which they report in a continuous stream of consciousness all thoughts that come to mind. Subjects were then asked to do this for periods of 5 minutes under two different conditions. In one condition they're to try not to think of a white bear. Every time a white bear comes to mind, they're to ring a bell in front of them. In the other condition

they're to *think* of a white bear and to ring the bell when they do. For some people the suppression came first, then the thinking. For other subjects the order was reversed.

Two findings emerged from this study. First, it was hard to avoid thinking of a white bear (the most effective strategy used was to concentrate on something else). Interestingly, most intrusions of the unwanted thought occurred when the subject had just finished a sentence or thought and was silent. It was as though the thought could be kept out as long as the mental machinery was fully occupied, but when an opening came up the thought leaped in. Wegner et al. argued that suppression is hard unless you have a specific distractor to think of instead (and additional evidence supports this idea). To put this idea in psychoanalytic terms, it's apparently easier to form an alternative cathexis than to form an anticathexis.

The second finding was that subjects who suppressed showed a rebound effect. That is, when they were later asked to think of the bear, they did so more frequently and consistently than did the other people. Their reports of the white bear were stable over the 5-minute period. In contrast, those who'd started by thinking of the bear apparently wore out fairly quickly, and their reports fell off over the 5-minute period.

In practical terms, what are the implications of findings such as these? What should you do when you want not to think about something? Wegner (1989) argues that, as odd as it may sound, the best medicine is to let the thoughts in. Experience the feelings associated with the intrusion and let the experience run its course. Only by relaxing our mental control, he says, can we regain it. By lowering your defenses, you eventually reduce the pressure of the unwanted thought, and it will go away on its own (perhaps through the mechanisms of the unconscious).

it from being expressed. If you have the impulse to fondle the leg of the person next to you in class, your ego (presumably) takes action to keep the impulse out of your awareness. If you did something last week you're utterly ashamed of, you try not to think about it and eventually may even be unable to recall doing it.

Though repression is particularly important with respect to id impulses, it also applies more generally to information that's painful or upsetting. You may, for example, repress an event in which you acted irresponsibly, but not in a way that obviously derives from id impulses. For example, maybe you forgot to turn off the stove, thereby causing a fire, or forgot to lock your apartment, thereby letting someone walk off with your new TV. You may repress things about yourself you think are inadequate—for example, the fact that you're unpopular, or the fact that you can't dance. You may repress your awareness of things in life that conflict with what's in your superego—for example, the fact that people in some parts of the world are starving and you aren't doing anything about it, or the fact that your parents have an active sex life with certain preferred coital positions.

Some people, of course, do think about their parents' sex lives (or the fact that they can't dance or the fact that they let somebody walk off with their TV). This illustrates two more points about repression. First, what's repressed depends on what acts are punished and what values are in your superego. What gets people punished varies across cultures. In the same way, the content of people's superegos also presumably varies. When Freud began writing, society was very conflicted over sex. That's less true today, and the values introjected today into superegos probably focus less on sex than was true 90 years ago. As the values of societies shift, what's repressed also shifts. Instead of repressing sexual feelings, perhaps you repress memories of behavior that harms the environment.

The second point is that repression need not be total. It's easiest to talk about defenses in all-or-nothing terms, but this can be misleading. You may partly repress a moderately distressing memory so you don't think about it often. You haven't forgotten it altogether. If reminded of it, you're still aware it's there, but you'd just as soon not be reminded of it. This would represent a partial repression (for more on repression see Box 9.2).

Denial

Another relatively simple defense occurs when people are overwhelmed by a threatening reality. The defense is **denial:** refusal to believe that the event took place or that the condition exists. An example is the mother who refuses to believe the message that her son has been killed in combat and acts as though he's still alive. A less extreme example is a college student who refuses to believe the grade by her name on the sheet outside her professor's door and assumes instead that there's been some sort of mistake. Denial also is implicit when a young boy at play assumes a role of power, thereby hiding the reality of his weakness.

As people mature and the ego gets better and better at assessing reality accurately, denial becomes harder to engage in. That is, reality stares you in the face more clearly as you get older and more experienced. Denial remains possible at any age, though. It's common for people who have serious problems with alcohol or drugs to deny the problem (as in the first example opening the chapter). It's common for someone whose lover is straying to deny that it's happening, despite signs to the contrary. Many victims of Nazi persecution failed to flee to safe havens while there was still time because of denial. Indeed, it has been argued that self-report measures of mental health can be untrustworthy because some

BOX 9.2

RECALL OF TRAUMATIC CHILDHOOD MEMORIES:
Breakdown of Repression, or Events That Never Happened?

Repression can keep memories of past traumas from reaching awareness. If the events can't be recalled, the person is spared any anxiety, anguish, or guilt associated with the experience. It's possible, however, for repression to break down. If that happens, people can recall episodes from their lives they might prefer not to recall.

Consider, for example, the following case reported by Elizabeth Loftus (1997). Nadean Cool sought psychiatric help to deal with her reactions to a trauma experienced by her daughter. Through hypnosis and other techniques, the therapist assisted her in recalling repressed memories of abuse she herself had endured. She became convinced she had repressed memories of having been in a satanic cult, eating babies, being raped, having sex with animals, and being forced to watch the murder of her eight-year-old friend.

In fact, none of these events had ever happened. The therapist's procedures simply induced her to think they had. When she realized this was so, she sued the psychiatrist for malpractice and eventually won a $2.4 million settlement. Nor is this the only case of "memories" being planted by therapists (see Loftus, 1997, for other examples).

Indeed, evidence suggests that false memories are surprisingly easy to induce. In one method of study, researchers ask people to recall childhood events mentioned by relatives (e.g., Loftus, Coan, & Pickrell, 1996; Loftus & Pickrell, 1995). A few events that weren't mentioned—because they never happened—are embedded among the real ones. Not surprisingly, most people (80% or so) recall something about the real events. More surprising is the percentage who report memories about

the events that never happened. Twenty to 30% of people typically report memories of nonexistent events, and the rate sometimes exceeds 60%!

False memories seem to depend partly on the false event's being plausible. However, even events that are unusual or highly unlikely can produce false recall (Hyman, Husband, & Billings, 1995; Spanos, 1996). Another important variable seems to be the extent to which the events are verifiable. False memories are more likely for events that can't be easily verified (Lynn, Myers, & Malinoski, 1997).

Interest in "recovered" memories runs high today, partly because the memories often lead to accusations of terrible acts that had been repressed. Many persons have been accused of acts of physical and sexual abuse on the basis of such newly recovered memories. Some of them have been shown to be innocent. Yet they've undergone public humiliation in ways that permanently changed their lives.

It's very important to bear in mind that the occurrence of false memories doesn't mean that the spontaneous recall of traumatic events is never true (see also Box 9.5, later in this chapter). Children are sometimes the victims of sexual, physical, and emotional abuse. Sometimes those events are repressed, to avoid distress associated with them. However, it does seem clear that not all cases of recalled trauma are real. Sometimes people are misled into remembering things that never happened. It can be very hard to tell whether a vivid memory is true or false. But given the consequences of such memories, a great deal can depend on deciding which it is.

---

people deny to themselves the distress that they're experiencing (Shedler, Mayman, & Manis, 1993).

Denial is similar in many ways to repression. Both keep hidden from awareness things the person feels unable to cope with. They differ from each other in the source of the threat they're combating. Repression deals with threats that in one fashion or another originate within the dynamics of the mind. Denial is aimed at threats that have other sources.

Denial prevents us from becoming aware of unpleasant things in our lives.

Everyone uses repression and denial, because they work. They save you from pain or anxiety. But too much repression or denial has a cost. The anticathexes they represent (holding back the unacceptable) require energy. Energy tied up this way is unavailable for other uses. If an act of repression holds for long, the investment of energy is more or less permanent. Thus, despite the fact that repression and denial are sometimes necessary, they can eventually work against you.

Perhaps for this reason, other defenses also develop. These other mechanisms of defense operate in combination with repression (and in combination with one another). They free some of the energy from anticathexes, while still keeping unacceptable thoughts or feelings from registering on consciousness. How they do so varies from one defense to another.

Projection

Another defense is called **projection.** In projection, anxiety is reduced by ascribing your own unacceptable impulses, wishes, desires, or qualities to someone else. Thus, projection provides a way to hide your knowledge of an unacceptable aspect of yourself, while still expressing the unacceptable quality (though in a highly distorted form).

For example, if you have feelings of hostility toward others, you remove the feelings from awareness through repression. The feelings are still there, however, trying to gain expression. You project them by developing the belief that others hate you and are out to get you. In this way, your original hostile impulse gains expression, but in a way that's not threatening to you. Another example is a woman who has sexual urges toward a man she's not supposed to have those feelings for, who accuses him of being seductive toward her (as in the second example opening the chapter). The impulse gets to the surface in a distorted form, while the woman remains unaware of her own desires.

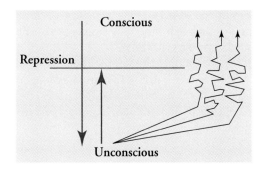

Conscious

Repression

Unconscious

FIGURE 9.1

Defenses begin with repression, removing threatening material from the conscious region of the mind to the unconscious. What has been repressed cannot be brought out directly because it's too anxiety provoking. Repressed material can sneak around the barrier, however, by being transformed so as to make it less recognizable. Though these distortions permit the repressed urges to gain expression, the expression is weaker and less effective than the initial urge. Thus, pressure to express the urge still remains.

Thus, projection serves two purposes, as do the more elaborate ego defenses. It helps to get the id's desires into the open in some form or other, thereby releasing some of the energy required to repress them. That is, when you project, you recognize that the threatening quality exists. Just as importantly, though, the desire emerges in such a form that the ego and superego don't recognize it. In this way, the threat from the impulse is diminished (see Figure 9.1).

Rationalization

Another important defense mechanism is **rationalization.** In rationalization the person reduces anxiety by finding a rational explanation (or excuse) for a behavior that really was done for unacceptable reasons. For example, the man who cheats on his income tax may rationalize his behavior as reducing the amount of money spent on weapons in the world.

Rationalization also protects against other kinds of threats. For example, after a failure, rationalization maintains your self-esteem. If you don't get into medical school, you may convince yourself that you really didn't want to be a doctor anyway. A man who's snubbed when asking for a date may convince himself that the woman really wasn't so interesting after all. Rationalization seems very common in people's responses to success and failure. It's been demonstrated repeatedly that people tend to take credit for good performances and blame bad performances on forces outside their control (e.g., Ross & Fletcher, 1985).

Intellectualization

Another defense is the tendency to think about threats in cold, analytical, and detached terms, a process called **intellectualization.** Thinking about events in such a clinical fashion allows people to dissociate their thoughts from the feelings involved, thereby insulating themselves from anxiety. Through this process the threatening event is separated and isolated from the feeling that normally would accompany it.

For example, the woman who finds out that her husband is dying of cancer may try to learn as much about cancer and its treatment as she can. By focusing on the disease intellectually and compartmentalizing that information, she shields herself from her distress. As another example, the man who is sexually aroused by a coworker may analyze in great detail the qualities that make her attractive, considering her from the point of view of an uninvolved connoisseur of beauty. Doing this permits him to distance himself from his desires.

Freud (1961/1915) made a more general point about this aspect of defense when discussing the separation of the unconscious from the conscious part of the mind. He suggested that an idea can exist in both parts of the mind at once, but in different forms. The intellectual aspect of the idea can exist in consciousness, even if it's a potentially threatening idea such as hating your father. This can be managed if the emotional quality attached to the idea, the deeply personal part that makes the idea psychologically meaningful, remains repressed. This sounds like a perfect description of intellectualization.

Reaction Formation

One way to guard against the release of an unacceptable impulse is to make a point of emphasizing its *opposite*. Doing this is termed **reaction formation.** For example, a child may deal with hostile feelings toward a new baby in the family by repressing her hostile feelings and replacing them with effusive positive displays.

Freud believed that it's often hard to tell whether an act stems from its apparent motivation or from the opposite impulse. Reaction formation is sometimes inferred on the basis of the appropriateness of the response. If the person seems to "go overboard," or the response seems out of proportion to the context, you may be seeing reaction formation. Another clue is that the act may incorporate tinges of the impulse being defended against. For example, the child in the last example may attempt to "love her new brother to death" by hugging him so hard he begins to hurt. Another example is "friendly advice" that is subtly disparaging.

It's also possible to point to more adult forms of reaction formation. For example, an adult male who appears to be a super-stud, sleeping with one woman after another, may be doing so to hide from himself fears about his sexual adequacy. As another illustration, cases have been reported in which the very legislators who worked to pass laws against homosexual rights were rumored to be homosexual themselves. It's arguable that the people in question were trying to prevent themselves from confronting their true nature by behaving in a way that is its opposite.

You can also display reaction formation in interpreting the behaviors of people close to you. For example, people confronting evidence that their romantic partners have important faults may distort their perceptions of the evidence. The result is to turn the faults into virtues (Murray & Holmes, 1993).

Regression

In Chapter 8 we described the stages of psychosexual development and indicated how people can become fixated along the way. The fixation means that libidinal energy remains bound up in the cathexes of that stage. Anna Freud believed that physical and emotional stress often causes people to abandon mature coping strategies and instead use patterns of the stages in which they are fixated. She called this process **regression,** because it means giving up a more advanced form of coping in favor of one that's more primitive and infantile.

For example, an adult who's fixated at the oral stage of development might smoke more cigarettes or eat or drink more when stressed at work. Someone who has an anal fixation may respond to stress by becoming even more obstinate and compulsive than usual. The stronger a fixation, the more likely the person is to regress (under stress) to the mode of functioning that characterizes that stage. Recall that fixations can develop because needs were gratified so well in an early stage of development. Thus, regression often represents a return to a way of relating to the world that used to be very effective (A. Freud, 1966).

Regression can occur at any point in development. An older child can regress to patterns of earlier childhood; adults can also regress. It should be clear that in adult regression people don't always behave literally as they did during the earlier stage of development (although this may sometimes occur). Rather, the person's thoughts and behaviors become permeated with the concerns and interests of the earlier stage. The manifestation of these concerns thus is often symbolic rather than literal.

Displacement and Sublimation

Two final defense mechanisms were introduced in Chapter 8: displacement and sublimation. These defenses are generally considered less neurotic than the others we've described and more adaptive. **Displacement** is shifting an impulse from one target to another. This often (though not always) happens when the intended target is threatening. Displacement is a defense mechanism in such cases because substituting a less threatening target for the original one reduces anxiety.

For example, the student who's angry with her professor and takes out her hostility on her very understanding boyfriend avoids the anxiety that would arise from attacking her professor directly. The person with an inappropriate lust who displaces that urge onto a more permissible target avoids the anxiety that would arise from expressing the desires toward the true target.

Sublimation also allows impulses to be expressed behaviorally, in this case by transforming the impulse into a more acceptable form. In this case it's not something about the target that creates the threat, but something about the impulse itself. Sublimation serves as a defense because anxiety is reduced when a transformed impulse is gratified instead of the initial one. Freud felt that sublimation, more than any other mechanism of defense, reflects maturity and normalcy. Sublimation is

People often express impulses in symbolic form. Sometimes people live out their impulses through their children—or even their pets!

viewed as a mechanism that prevents problems from occurring, as opposed to a tactic that people turn to after anxiety is aroused.

Research on Defenses

What's the scientific status of the defense mechanisms? A fair amount of research has been conducted on them, but the research is controversial. As an example of the research that's been done, consider a study of projection by Halpern (1977). In this research, people who did or did not seem sexually defensive (on a self-report scale) either were or were not exposed to erotic photographs before making ratings of someone else. Those classed as sexually defensive rated the other person as more "lustful" if they'd seen erotic photographs than if they hadn't. Those who weren't defensive about sexual issues didn't display projection. This makes sense from a psychodynamic perspective. You project only about things that threaten you.

More recent research has investigated the idea that projection occurs when people actively try to suppress thoughts about something they don't like about themselves (Newman, Duff, & Baumeister, 1997). This active attempt to suppress seems to cause thoughts about the unwanted trait to push back and become extra accessible. This in turn causes the thoughts to be ready for use when someone else's behavior even remotely fits it.

These studies seem supportive of the idea of defense. But the literature as a whole is ambiguous, and alternative interpretations are often easy to construct. As a result, different readers draw different conclusions. For example, to Sherwood (1981) there's substantial evidence of projection, whereas to Holmes (1981) there isn't. Many researchers are convinced that repression occurs in the short term (e.g., Erdelyi, 1985; Paulhus & Suedfeld, 1988), although in the longer term there are more questions.

Recent research has begun to take a different angle on the study of repression. This research looks at individual differences in the tendency to repress and asks whether repressors differ in important ways from people who repress less. In one study, subjects did a task that required them to make associations to phrases with sexual and aggressive content (Weinberger, Schwartz, & Davidson, 1979). Repressors reported the lowest level of distress during this task, but they also showed the most physical arousal. In other research, repressors were less able to recall emotional memories from childhood and from their day-to-day experiences than were other subjects (Davis, 1987; Davis & Schwartz, 1987). These findings suggest that the search for evidence of repression may be coming closer to fruition.

Evidence of Unconscious Conflict

Much of the preceding discussion of ego defenses assumes that conflicts are buried in the unconscious through repression to avoid neurotic or moral anxiety. Although unconscious, the conflicts presumably continue to influence behavior. Some of those influences are reflected in the defenses we've been discussing. That is, repressed desires leak out through such processes as projection, reaction formation, or sublimation.

Sometimes, though, the conflicts emerge through symptoms such as depression. Because the conflicts are inaccessible, the person doesn't know what's causing the symptoms, making them all the more distressing. The idea that unconscious conflicts influence symptoms has received support from research by Lloyd Silverman and his colleagues (reviewed by Silverman, 1976, 1983; Weinberger & Silverman, 1987). This idea is hard to test experimentally, because it requires arousing the conflict in the unconscious but not letting it reach consciousness. Silverman's solution was to present material subliminally—at exposures so brief the subjects couldn't tell what they were seeing.

Subliminal stimuli apparently do register on the unconscious, however. That is, when susceptible people were presented with material designed to stir up their unconscious conflicts, their pathological symptoms increased. This did *not* happen if the stimuli were allowed to enter consciousness (by using longer exposures). This supports the idea that it's the unconscious that's producing the symptoms.

An example of a susceptible group is depression-prone people. The psychoanalytic view is that depression occurs because of unconscious self-destructive wishes. These wishes could be stirred up by words (e.g., the words *Cannibal eats person*) or by pictures (e.g., one person stabbing another). In several studies (reviewed by Silverman, 1976), presenting such material subliminally to depression-prone people caused them to have deeper feelings of depression.

Another study in this series involved arousing or diminishing the Oedipal conflict among college men (Silverman, Ross, Adler, & Lustig, 1978). Subjects first completed a competitive dart-throwing task. Then they viewed subliminal stimuli. In one condition a message read "Beating Dad is wrong"; in another condition the message read "Beating Dad is OK"; in a third condition the stimuli were neutral on Oedipal issues. Finally, subjects repeated the dart-throwing task. Arousing Oedipal feelings (Beating Dad is OK) led to improved scores (Figure 9.2), presumably because the Oedipal wish translated into enhanced competition. Diminishing the Oedipal desires (Beating Dad is wrong) led to poorer scores.

In sum, there's evidence that surface displays of psychological characteristics, including symptoms of distress, can be influenced by arousing a conflict at an unconscious level. There are limitations on these effects, however. Some of them occur reliably only among people in whom the conflict is already well established. In the last study described, the effect occurred across the sample, presumably because *everyone* has experienced the Oedipal conflict.

We should also note that Silverman's research has been controversial, partly because others have found it hard to obtain some of the same effects (e.g., Heilbrun, 1980) and partly for other reasons. One problem is the lack of evidence for the

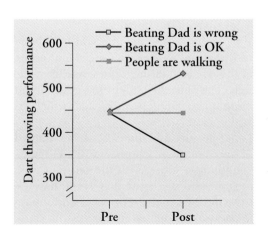

FIGURE 9.2

Effects of subliminal activation (or deactivation) of Oedipal feelings on competitive dart throwing. Subjects threw darts for one score before exposure to the subliminal stimuli (pre) and threw again afterward (post). Subjects exposed to "Beating Dad is wrong" got lower scores the second time. Those exposed to "Beating Dad is OK" got higher scores the second time. Those exposed to "People are walking" were not affected (adapted from Silverman et al., 1978).

processes presumed to underlie the effects (Weinberger & Hardaway, 1990). The controversy is complex (see Balay & Shevrin, 1988), and different reviewers of this research have reached different conclusions about its meaning (Hardaway, 1990). Despite the controversy—or perhaps even because of it—it seems likely that this technique will continue to be explored as a way to study unconscious conflict.

The Psychopathology of Everyday Life

We've been focusing on how the ego handles conflicts among the three aspects of the personality. To guard against neurotic and moral anxiety, the ego represses things that are threatening. The threatening material, now unconscious, continues to influence behavior through the operation of further ego defenses.

Freud believed that the unconscious is where the vital forces of human life are at work, influencing people in complex ways. It's there that the true motives lie. Gaining access to the conflicts and desires of the unconscious would seem to be a daunting task. Freud believed, though, that it's not as hard as it seems. He thought unconscious impulses constantly reveal themselves in everyday events. You just have to look for them. In this section, we discuss some ways in which unconscious motives are revealed to the careful observer.

One way such motives are revealed is in people's mistakes. We all make mistakes from time to time. We forget things, get our words jumbled, and have small and large accidents. Freud (1960b/1901) referred to such occurrences as the *psychopathology of everyday life* (a phrase which also conveys his belief that every normal life contains a little of the abnormal). He believed that such events, far from being random, stem from urges buried in the unconscious. These urges emerge in a distorted form, causing the mistakes. Thus memory lapses, slips of speech, and accidents provide indirect insights into the person's true desires (for a contrasting opinion on the question, however, see Reason & Mycielska, 1982).

Parapraxes

Collectively, these events are termed **parapraxes** (a literal translation from the German term is "faulty achievement"—Bettelheim, 1982). Perhaps the simplest parapraxis is forgetting. From the psychoanalytic perspective, forgetting reflects repression—an attempt to keep something from reaching consciousness. Sometimes it's easy to see why forgetting occurs (e.g., the student who forgets to return an important book to someone he doesn't really like). At other times, it's harder to see the underlying motive. Yet a motive can often be found, if enough is known about the situation.

Brenner (1957) gave a case history of a patient in therapy who said he'd been unable to remember the name of a friend when the two met at a social gathering. As the patient talked, it became clear that the friend had the same name as someone else the patient disliked. It also became clear that the patient felt guilty about the dislike. Finally, the patient mentioned that the friend was disabled, which reminded him of his wish to harm the disliked person.

Why, then, did he forget his friend's name? Presumably, the sight of the disabled friend had unconsciously reminded him of the other man, whom he wished to hurt. To prevent this impulse from becoming conscious—along with the sense of guilt that would have come with it—the patient repressed the name that would have established the link between the two. Since the motive for the repression and the repression itself were both unconscious, the patient was unable to identify the cause of the memory lapse.

Freud believed that accidents often result from an unconscious desire to cause harm.

If forgetting is a successful act of repression, slips of the tongue and pen are partially *un*successful acts of repression. That is, the person inadvertently expresses all or part of the unconscious thought or wish, despite the effort to keep it hidden. As with forgetting, the hidden meaning is sometimes obvious to observers. Consider the woman who reveals her ambivalent feelings toward her lover by telling him he's exactly the kind of person she'd like to "bury" (instead of "marry"). At other times the hidden meaning is hard to decipher and can be established only with the help of the person who makes the slip.

There's evidence that these verbal slips are related to anxiety, although the evidence falls short of indicating that the anxiety is unconscious. Motley (1985) and his colleagues have done studies in which they induce subjects to make a certain kind of slip. In this slip a pair of words is read incorrectly as a different word pair (for example, saying "flute fry" instead of "fruit fly"). The research requires having specific pairs that are easy to misread into slips with particular overtones. The experiments involve creating specific anxieties and then seeing whether those anxieties increase the relevant slips.

For example, in one case male subjects were made to feel anxious about receiving electric shocks. In another, the session was run by a provocatively dressed woman, which was expected to arouse anxiety over sexual issues. Both conditions included word pairs that could be misread as shock-related (e.g., "damn shock" instead of "sham dock") and pairs that could be misread as sex-related (e.g., "happy sex" instead of "sappy hex"). As can be seen in Figure 9.3, subjects led to be nervous about

FIGURE 9.3

Freudian slips, induced in the laboratory. When subjects expected to receive electric shocks, they made more shock-related slips (left side). When subjects had been exposed to a provocatively dressed experimenter, they made more sex-related slips (right side) (adapted from Motley, 1985).

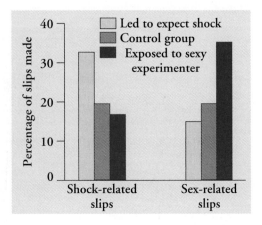

shocks made more shock-related slips than anyone else; subjects led to be thinking about sex made more slips with sexual connotations than anyone else. Another study found that sexual slips were most frequent among men high on a measure of sex guilt (Motley, 1985).

Most people, when accused of committing a slip, attribute it to factors such as fatigue, distraction, or haste. Freud held, however, that such factors facilitate but don't cause slips. The real cause always comes from the unconscious. A person is more likely to commit a slip of the tongue or pen when tired or inattentive, but the form of the slip depends on unconscious forces.

Accidents, on the other hand, are a bit more complicated. Accidents that are most interesting from a psychoanalytic point of view are those that stem from the carelessness of the victim (or the harm doer, if the accident injures someone else). To decide whether something is an accident, you must look at the circumstances. If you learn a man was struck by a motorboat while scuba diving, you might think it an accident. But if you learn that the man, an experienced diver, failed to put out a diving marker and didn't pause to listen for approaching motors before surfacing, you might be more inclined to conclude that (for whatever reason) he had the unconscious desire to do himself harm.

Accidents are complicated for another reason as well. Because they can involve injury, accidents can serve several functions at once. In harming yourself, you can also harm someone else—someone who cares for you. In this sense, an accident can serve both as crime (causing someone else to feel bad) and as punishment (causing you to suffer an injury).

Dreams

Freud (1953b/1900) believed that the unconscious also reveals itself through dreams. Indeed, he referred to dreams as "the royal road to the unconscious." Freud began by distinguishing between two kinds of dream content. The **manifest content** of a dream is the sensory images of the dreamer—what most of us think of as the dream. More interesting, to Freud, was the **latent content**—the unconscious thoughts, feelings, and wishes that give rise to manifest content. Latent content tells why a dream takes the form it takes (see Box 9.3 for another view).

Freud believed that latent content derives from three sources. The first is the *sensory stimulation* that bombards us as we sleep—the sound of a distant thunderstorm, a passing siren, or the barking of dog. These sounds can both prompt

BOX 9.3

FUNCTIONS OF SLEEP AND DREAMS

Sleep has long been a source of wonder and mystery. Each of us, willing or not, spends a substantial portion of each 24-hour day lost in a state suspended somewhere between life and death. Dreams are especially fascinating. What are they? Fragmented recollections of fantastic journeys taken while sleeping? Are they bits of truth whispered to us by gods (on the condition that we not remember them for long)? Are dreams, as Freud believed, reflections of the primary process—visual echoes of the snarling and lurid passions of the id? Or are they just a jumble of nonsense, the mutterings of a brain left to idle like a car at a red light?

In Freud's time, little was known about sleep and dreams. It seemed natural to him to think of dreams as the pathway to the unconscious, given the surreal and symbolic qualities that often are prominent in them. In recent years, though, scientists have probed sleep and dreaming, and more is now known about their patterns. Some think we're coming closer to an understanding of why people dream, although the answer isn't quite the same as Freud envisioned (Winson, 1985, 1990; see also Hobson, 1988).

What do we know? To begin with, everybody has dreams, although many people don't remember them. A pivotal finding (Aserinsky & Kleitman, 1953; Kleitman, 1963) was the discovery of a sleep state in which people's eyes move rapidly, breathing becomes irregular, heart rate increases, and most movement is suppressed. Because a key feature seems to be rapid eye movement (REM), the state is known as REM sleep. People awakened from REM sleep almost always report they were dreaming. People awakened from non-REM sleep rarely say they were dreaming. REM sleep occurs four or five times a night for adults; infants spend nearly 8 hours a day in REM sleep.

Several other things about REM sleep: First, REM occurs in other mammals as well as in hu-

mans. Second, it seems not to occur in animals *other than* mammals. Third, whatever's going on in REM sleep apparently is necessary. When people are kept out of REM sleep (by being awakened whenever REM starts), they show a stronger tendency to enter it.

Why is REM sleep necessary? And if REM sleep is dreaming, what in the world are *infants* dreaming so much about? After piecing together evidence about behavioral and brain properties of several different animals, Winson (1985) made the following argument. A basic problem in biological adaptation is how to integrate new experiences with old ones. Winson thinks the evolutionary solution to this problem among mammals was REM sleep. That is, he thinks the integration takes place during REM sleep. If this were so, a single set of neuronal structures could serve two purposes: guiding action when you're awake, consolidating and integrating knowledge when you're asleep. Thus, we can get the most out of our nervous system, since it's being used round the clock rather than just when we're awake.

Why then do infants dream so much? It may be that the same processes that produce consolidation also produce the final stage of cortical development (infants don't have fully developed cortexes). Or perhaps it's because the almost complete absence of a personal history means that infants have to do more integration and consolidation than adults.

Winson argues that the processes of REM sleep *are* the unconscious that Freud looked for in people's dreams. The paths of symbolic association that fascinated Freud reflect the fact that consolidation is a process of following mental associations, even associations that are odd and tangential. In this view, then, the brain is simply doing its homework in the dreaming state, sorting the experiences of the day (and the week) into all the categories to which they are potentially relevant.

dreams and be incorporated into them. When this happens, the stimulation is part of the dream's latent content. Dreams are said to be "guardians of sleep," because incorporating an outside stimulus into a dream prevents the stimulus from awakening the sleeper.

The second source of latent dream content is thoughts, ideas, and feelings connected to the sleeper's current waking life—**current concerns**—which remain active in your unconscious while you sleep. For example, during the day you may have been thinking about an upcoming exam, an unfinished project, an interesting person you'd just met, or a financial problem you've got. Incorporating thoughts about the same topic into dreams prevents them from waking you, just as with sensory stimuli.

The third important source of latent dream content is unconscious *id impulses* that the ego has blocked from gratification while you're awake. Often these impulses relate to childhood conflicts. For this reason, the impulse is often infantile in form and primitive in content. Freud believed that every dream incorporates some unconscious impulse or urge.

To understand how dreams offer insight into personality, you must understand the relationship between manifest and latent content. Manifest content consists of conscious sensory impressions (usually visual). Manifest content is a fantasy in which the latent wish or impulse is gratified. To use a term from Chapter 8, the dream is an attempt at *wish fulfillment* on the part of the id.

During early childhood, the tie between latent and manifest content is quite transparent. Consider the dream of a two-year-old boy a few days after his mother brought home a new baby from the hospital (Brenner, 1957). The boy reported as manifest content, "See baby go away." It takes little imagination to infer the latent content, especially as the mother felt the boy had been hostile toward the new baby's arrival from the moment he learned of the impending event. In this case, then, the dream's manifest content was a direct translation of the latent content—the boy's wish to have the new baby no longer a part of his life. The manifest content simply fulfilled this wish in the form of visual images.

During later childhood and adulthood, the relationship between latent and manifest content becomes less obvious. Indeed, dreams sometimes seem completely senseless. How can such dreams relate to wish fulfillment? The answer is that with increasing age it becomes more important to distort or disguise the latent content of the dream. The ego and the superego must remain unaware that an unacceptable impulse is being expressed, if wish fulfillment in manifest content is to occur. Keeping them unaware gets harder as people grow. Thus, even in dreams the defense mechanisms remain at work.

Two processes allow forbidden impulses to be represented in the manifest content of dreams. One is called **symbolization.** In symbolization, unacceptable latent content is expressed in manifest content directly but symbolically. The symbol is a form that's less recognizable to the ego and the superego and is thereby less threatening. Symbolization might be considered the dreaming equivalent of sublimation.

The second way in which latent content is translated into manifest content is called **dream work.** In dream work, latent content is disguised and distorted in other ways to make it more acceptable to the ego and the superego. Dream work involves several distinct mechanisms.

In **condensation,** separate thoughts are compressed and combined into a single unified thought. The consolidation is less threatening than having the thoughts exist separately. That is, a thought taken alone might be obvious enough to be threatening. When several thoughts are jumbled, however, it's harder to tell what's what, and the threat is reduced. When condensation occurs, the resulting manifest content is said to be "overdetermined" because it's based on more than one latent idea.

In the **mechanism of opposites** an unacceptable element of latent content is expressed manifestly as the reverse of its latent form. For example, a boy who fears that his dog will run away might dream of the dog's returning to him from a journey. A woman who secretly wishes her husband dead may dream of holding a celebration for him. The real meaning of dreams such as these is the opposite of what it appears to be. This distortion resembles the defense mechanism of reaction formation, employed during waking hours.

Another way in which the latent content of dreams is altered is a *reaction* to dream work (Freud, 1933). Because dream work operates according to primary-process thought, manifest content is often chaotic. To cause manifest content to make better sense, a dreamer will often fill in missing elements or build up a sketchy part of a dream. This part of the dream is actually unrelated to the latent content. The process of making dreams more understandable is called **secondary elaboration.** Secondary elaboration diminishes threat by further disguising the urges and desires that underlie the dream.

A major part of the interpretation of dreams involves examining the images of manifest content to understand their unconscious meaning. Freud believed that many of the symbols that appear in dreams are unique to the dreamer. He also believed, however, that there are certain categories of shared symbols that have similar meanings for everyone. The existence of universal symbols makes dream analysis somewhat easier to attempt (Box 9.4).

Humor

A final way in which the unconscious reveals itself is humor (Freud, 1960a/1905). Humor often rests on threatening desires or impulses that are transformed in amusing ways. Much humor, for example, reflects an underlying hostility. This hostility is blunted by its distortion into something ludicrous. Freud felt that many jokes depend on an underlying inhibited thought. The joke-telling technique slips around the inhibition, diverts attention and permits the internal censor of the ego to relax. When the punch line comes, the forbidden thought is abruptly expressed, too late for the censor to recover. The energy previously devoted to restraining the forbidden thought is released in laughter.

Humor is similar to dreams in certain respects, for example, in using condensation and symbolism. They differ, though, in important ways. Dreams permit the urges of the unconscious to emerge, but only in a symbolic and unrecognizable form. Humor, in contrast, is intentional communication from one person to another. Thus, whereas dreams conceal their latent content, joking tends to expose the underlying content more completely (Oring, 1984). There's protection from threat in the symbolism and the laughter, but the latent content is closer to the surface than in dreams.

Projective Techniques of Assessment

The preceding sections have focused on ways in which the unconscious reveals itself in everyday life. We now turn to ways in which the unconscious reveals itself in formal assessment as practiced from the psychoanalytic perspective.

Formal methods of assessing unconscious processes are called **projective techniques** (Frank, 1939). These devices confront people with stimuli for which there's no culturally defined way to respond. Since there's no obvious response to such ambiguous stimuli, people's responses are determined primarily by their own feelings,

BOX 9.4

DREAM ANALYSIS

As was said in the main text, Freud believed important insights could be gained about personality by analyzing dreams. One step in dream analysis is translating the manifest content of a dream into its latent (unconscious) content. Some symbols in dreams are idiosyncratic—to understand them you need to know something about the meaning the *dreamer* attaches to them. Others are more universal.

Freud believed that latent content concerns a relatively small number of things, which are symbolized in dreams in a wide variety of ways. The important elements underlying dreams are the human body, parents, children, siblings, birth, death, nakedness, and sexual activity. Here are some common dream symbols and their psychoanalytic interpretations:

- Authority figures—kings and queens, police officers, and so on—represent parents.

- Small animals—mice, squirrels, chipmunks—symbolize children.

- Reference to water signifies birth; going on a journey symbolizes dying.

- Uniforms and clothes stand for nakedness (through the mechanism of opposites).

- A house symbolizes the human body. If it has smooth walls, it's a man. If there are ledges, balconies, or other kinds of projections outward, it's a woman.

In keeping with other aspects of psychoanalytic theory, sexual activity is seen as most richly represented of all. There are many symbols of male and female genitalia. For example, the number 3 stands for male genitals as a group (penis and testicles). The penis itself is symbolized by a wide range of images. Some symbolize by their shape (e.g., sticks, umbrellas, poles, golf clubs), others by their penetrating function (e.g., knives, daggers, guns, pistols, rifles) or by their function as devices through which fluids flow (e.g., hypodermic needles, fire hoses, faucets). Yet others symbolize the penis by their capacity to lengthen or to rise up in defiance of gravity (e.g., airplanes, blimps, balloons, and expanding telescopes).

Female genitals are symbolized by objects that enclose spaces or serve as receptacles (e.g., pits, caves, bottles, jars, pockets, shoes). Rooms, cupboards, and ovens are symbols of the uterus. Things that can be opened and closed (e.g., gates, doors, windows) are symbols for the vagina. Breasts are symbolized by fruits (e.g., peaches, melons, apples). Verdant landscapes and gardens also represent female genitals. A host of other female symbols are also thought to exist, such as wood and paper, snails, oysters, clams, churches, and chapels.

Sexual pleasure is often symbolized by candy or sugar-covered fruit. Play—for example, playing musical instruments or group games—symbolizes masturbation. Masturbation is also represented by activities such as sliding or gliding or pulling something off something else. Sexual intercourse is implied in any kind of rhythmic activity—for example, dancing, riding, and jogging. It can also be symbolized by the image of being threatened by a weapon or by being the victim of violence—for example, being run over by a car or train.

A word of caution is in order here. We've listed some common symbols and their typical interpretations to give you a look at how dreams may give insight into unconscious processes. We emphasize, though, that dreams aren't interpreted strictly on the basis of "typical" meanings of their content. Since some of the meaning is unique to the dreamer, it's also essential to determine what personal significance the dream has for the dreamer. If you're tempted to try out these symbols on your own dreams, keep this point in mind.

attitudes, desires, and needs (recall our discussion of one projective technique, the TAT, in Chapter 5). These tests allow people to apply the defense mechanism of projection to those hidden feelings and put the feelings into their interpretations of what they see. What's projected presumably is beyond the person's conscious control and thus reflects the unconscious.

A number of projective techniques, forming several categories, have been developed over the years. In *associative* techniques, people respond to a stimulus with the first word, thought, or image that pops into their heads. *Constructive* techniques involve constructing stories. *Completion* techniques involve completing the thought begun in an incomplete stimulus, such as a sentence that begins, "I wish."

Although the techniques differ in format, they share several features. They all use stimuli that are ambiguous. The test taker is never told the purpose of the test or how responses will be interpreted. Instructions stress that there are no right or wrong answers and that the test taker can respond in whatever way seems appropriate. Finally, because of the open-ended and ambiguous nature of the technique, scoring relies heavily on subjective clinical judgments.

To give you a better understanding of projective techniques, we focus for the rest of this section on one device that's often used to assess unconscious processes—the **Rorschach inkblot test.**

Rorschach Inkblot Test

Swiss psychiatrist Hermann Rorschach is usually credited with systematizing the use of inkblots for assessing personality (Rorschach, 1942). He had tried geometric patterns but because he found them too structured he began to experiment with inkblots. He finally arrived at a set of ten blots, chosen for their ability to evoke different responses from different groups of psychiatric patients. (His strategy thus made use of the criterion-keying approach to test development, described in Chapter 3.)

The ten inkblots in the Rorschach set are all bilaterally symmetrical, meaning that they are approximately the same on both sides of an imaginary center line (Figure 9.4). The ink on five of them is all black, but the intensity is uneven, ranging from solid black to light gray. Two of the blots have both black and red ink. The remaining three are composed of brilliant shades of different hues—including variations of blue, green, yellow, and orange.

FIGURE 9.4

Example of inkblot similar to those used in the Rorschach test (courtesy of Jeremy and Meredith Scheier).

The Rorschach usually is administered to one person at a time in a two-stage procedure. First the person views the inkblots in a predetermined order and indicates what he or she sees in them, or what the inkblot resembles or suggests, while the examiner records what's being said. Then the person views all 10 cards again. The examiner provides reminders of what what was said earlier about the card and asks what it was about the card that made it look like that.

Several systems have been devised for scoring the Rorschach. The most popular (considered the standard by most people) was devised by Exner (1974, 1993). In Exner's system the responses are first compared against normative data (people with known personality characteristics). Then the person's own responses are examined in terms of the progression from one card to the next. Finally, content is analyzed in terms of location, determinants, and content. *Location* is where in the blot the response focuses (the whole blot, a commonly noted detail, an unusual detail, the space surrounding the blot, or some mixture). *Determinants* of the response include form, color, shading, or perceived movement in whatever location prompted the response. The *content* of the response is its subject matter. Table 9.1 gives examples of common interpretations of specific responses. You should be aware, however, that a given response is interpreted only in connection with the entire test profile.

Although it's interesting as a technique, the Rorschach has always had psychometric problems. Its internal consistency is low, its test-retest reliability and interrater reliability are low, and its validity has been hard to establish (Anastasi, 1988). Exner and his collaborators have worked to develop scoring schemes with better psychometric properties. Recently, however, their efforts have come under fire. Wood, Nezworski, and Stejskal (1996a, 1996b) criticized Exner's work on several method-

TABLE 9.1

Rorschach inkblot responses.

Here are three categories in which responses to the Rorschach are placed. In the left column is the category name, followed by its definition. The third column gives two examples of responses that would be placed into each category. The right column gives an interpretation for each of these examples and an indication of why this interpretation is made.

Name of Category	Nature of Category	Example Response	Possible Interpretation (with critical feature identified)
Location	Place on blot from which response arose	"Overall, it reminds me of a cornstalk."	Suggests ability to think conceptually (response is based on whole blot)
		"That thing there looks like a hammer."	Suggests need to be exact and precise (response is based on a commonly noted detail)
Determinant	Quality of blot that led to response	"It's a whale bleeding."	Suggests high degree of emotionality (response is based on color)
		"It's a bat flying."	Suggests high degree of imagination (response is based on perceived movement)
Content	Subject matter of response	"It's a man about to be beaten up by others."	Suggests anxiety over hostile feelings (response involves aggression)
		"It's a person diving into the ocean waves."	Suggests strong fantasy life (response involves *human* movement)

ological grounds that bear on issues of reliability and validity. One serious criticism is that most of the research has never been published. Another is that information reported on inter-rater reliability actually doesn't bear on reliability.

The issues raised are technical (and Wood et al.'s conclusions have been disputed by Exner, 1996), but it's clear that the argument over the psychometric adequacy of the Rorschach is far from over. On the other hand, Ganellen (1996a, 1996b) has reported evidence that the Rorschach does better at identifying depressed and psychotic persons than does the MMPI-2. Clearly there is some sorting out of information yet to be done.

Many who favor projective tests respond to these criticisms by saying that psychometric criteria are irrelevant to the Rorschach's usefulness. In their view, its value is in the insights it gives the examiner into the operation of the unconscious. Perhaps psychologists should stop treating the Rorschach as a test and think of it instead as a clinical tool. From this perspective the Rorschach would function as a supplementary interview aid in the hands of a trained clinician, giving clues and suggesting hypotheses worthy of further investigation.

It's too early to say how the Rorschach (and instruments like it) will come to be viewed. Continued efforts to standardize scoring procedures may yield better psychometric properties. Even if the Rorschach is viewed only as a clinical aid, though, one thing is certain. It will not soon be discarded as part of the psychoanalytic assessment battery.

Problems in Behavior, and Behavior Change

Throughout this chapter we've emphasized two ideas: First, people use a variety of ego defenses to protect themselves against anxiety. Second, repressed urges and memories continue to influence behavior in many ways, via these defenses. Psychoanalytic theorists believe that everyone uses defense mechanisms. Merely using defense mechanisms certainly isn't a sign that the person has a problem.

On the other hand, this is a viewpoint on personality in which normalcy shades easily into abnormality, with no clear boundary between the two. Theorists tend to distinguish between normal and abnormal functioning by the degree to which defense mechanisms dominate the person's life. Too much use of defenses is a sign of pathology. Heavy use of defenses can save the person from dealing with conflicts, but it ties up too much energy in anticathexes. This in turn leaves little energy for the person to use in dealing effectively with new challenges. As the person's level of functioning begins to deteriorate, it becomes clearer that this is someone with a problem.

Our discussion of such problems and how they can be dealt with emphasizes the themes we've emphasized all along. Freud believed that the unconscious holds the secrets of people's difficulties in life and that only by delving into the unconscious can those difficulties be identified and resolved. This section begins by considering the psychoanalytic perspective on ways in which problems arise.

Origins of Problems

Problems have several possible origins. One source is experiences in childhood. As stated in Chapter 8, Freud believed that adult personality is determined largely by experiences in early psychosexual development. If the person handles early stages successfully, relatively little residue from those stages is carried into adulthood.

However, it's rare for a person to enter the later stages of psychosexual development unmarked. Rather, most persons are fixated to a greater or lesser degree at earlier stages.

When fixations are strong, a great deal of energy is invested in them. In a very strong fixation, the preoccupation—albeit unconscious—leaves the person with little energy for anything else. This is one source of problems: overinvestment of energies in a fixation from early childhood. This works against effective adult functioning by depleting the energy that the ego requires.

Another source of problems is a broad repression of basic needs and urges. If an overly punitive superego or a harsh and unforgiving environment causes too many of these urges to be buried, it means that the person's fundamental nature is being distorted and denied. The person is cramped and can't function in the way he or she is supposed to function. The repressed needs and impulses can squeeze their way past the repression only in distorted forms. This isn't really effective in meeting the needs. Furthermore, the repression required to keep the needs hidden is a constant drain on the energy available to the ego.

A third source of problems is buried trauma. Although traumatic incidents can occur at any point in life, most discussion of trauma focuses on experiences of early childhood. Indeed, at one point early in the evolution of his thinking, Freud believed that the majority of his patients had suffered childhood sexual abuse, because their memories were filled with images of sexual encounters. The "seduction theory," as it came to be known, was later abandoned when Freud decided the seductions hadn't actually taken place.

It was this change in his thinking that led to his theory of the Oedipal conflict (Chapter 8), in which children deal with a developing sexual attraction to their opposite-sex parent. The Oedipal theory accounted for the sexual imagery of the patients, and it did so in a way that didn't require Freud to conclude that large numbers of parents had seduced their children. This was to remain Freud's view for the remainder of his career (though see Box 9.5).

Despite this change, Freud's theory clearly holds a place for traumatic experiences such as sexual or physical abuse. His altered view simply reflects his conclusion that such experiences aren't the norm. Still, a child who experiences physical abuse, especially repeated abuse, has a deeply unpleasant part of reality to deal with. The same is true of a child who experiences sexual abuse. Indeed, many events that are objectively far less traumatic can loom large in the experience of a young child: rejection by a parent, death of a person close to the child (or of a pet), exposure to venomous confrontations between parents. Children who experience traumatic events such as these have major threats to deal with. They're dealt with first and foremost by repression—as always, the first response to overwhelming anxiety. Once again, the energy invested in forgetting is a constant drain on psychic resources.

These three points of origin for problems are different, and the problems that result may also be very different. All three paths, however, share one mechanism. In each case the original fixation, urge, or trauma is repressed to ward off anxiety. This repression may protect the person, but it does so at a cost.

Behavior Change

What to do about this situation? The therapeutic methods of psychoanalysis developed through a period of trial and error in Freud's practice. His understanding of how to deal with problems evolved along with his views on the *bases* of those problems. Early on, he found that symptoms could be reduced by hypnotically inducing

BOX 9.5

SEDUCTION FANTASIES OR CHILD MOLESTATION?

A controversy arose in the 1980s over Freud's abandonment of his seduction theory of the origin of psychological disorder. As indicated in the main text, Freud eventually "realized" that the accounts he heard from patients weren't literally true. The women hadn't been seduced as children. Rather, they had unconsciously distorted their own sexual desires for their parents into a symbolic form and projected it outward.

That's the way Freud put it—that he'd realized the truth. In 1984, however, an analyst named Jeffrey Masson challenged this statement. Masson had reread a long series of letters between Freud and his friend and colleague Wilhelm Fliess (Masson was editing the letters for publication). Partly on the basis of previously unpublished parts of these letters, Masson argued that the seductions were in fact real, that Freud knew it, and that he'd chosen—eventually—to ignore their reality.

Masson holds that Freud lacked the courage to bring to light a shameful truth: that violent child sexual abuse was widespread. Freud apparently was in a position to know that this was so. He owned books from the literature of legal medicine on the subject of childhood rape (Masson, 1984). He had attended autopsies where he'd seen something "of which medical science preferred to take no notice." And Masson found that some of those autopsies may have been conducted on children who'd been raped and then murdered.

Why would Freud lack the courage to stand up for his belief? Two possible reasons stand out. One concerns Freud's professional reputation. His first presentation of the theory, in a speech to a professional society, was met with utter silence. He was later urged not to publish it. By pointing to upsetting realities, Freud risked becoming an outcast in his profession. He needed a way out, to salvage his fast-vanishing career prospects.

The second issue concerned Freud's friendship with Fliess. Masson claimed there's evidence that Fliess molested his own son. Thus, even as Freud was forming the view that psychological disturbance stems from sexual abuse, the person to whom he confided these ideas was guilty of precisely such abuse. Masson believed that Freud eventually came to realize this. Given these two pressures, said Masson, Freud was forced to banish the evidence of childhood seduction from his own consciousness.

Masson also argued that *seduction* is an extremely unfortunate label for this theory and that the word is not at all typical of Freud's first statement of the theory, in which he also used the terms *rape, abuse, attack, assault, aggression,* and *trauma.* It's ironic that even as the theory was being set aside, a preferential use of the term *seduction* made the theory's implications seem more benign. Perhaps this terminology represents yet one last defense against a truly unacceptable truth.

What really *was* the truth? We obviously can't return to Freud's era and investigate the rate of child abuse at that time. On the other hand, it has become clear that child sexual abuse today is far more common than once believed (Finkelhor & Dziuba-Leatherman, 1994; Trickett & Putnam, 1993). There remains controversy over how much credence to place in children's reports and accusations. There's danger in ignoring a child's plea, but children aren't always truthful or accurate. And don't forget that Freud's evidence came not from children, but from newly unearthed adult recollections of childhood, adding further potential for distortion (see Loftus, 1993, 1994). What, then, should be believed? The question pertains to today's recalled memories of child abuse, and it also pierces to the heart of psychoanalytic theory.

the person to relive highly emotional (and thus repressed) events—relive them fully and emotionally. This release of energy seemed to free the person from the problem by diminishing the energy investment in the repressed event. This experience is often referred to as a *catharsis,* because of the release of emotional energy.

Two discoveries radically changed the approach that Freud was to take in his later work. First, he found it wasn't necessary to hypnotize people (which he apparently wasn't very good at). If the person simply said aloud whatever came to mind—a procedure called **free association**—the secrets of the unconscious would gradually be revealed. In free association the person is encouraged not to censor any thoughts but to say immediately whatever thoughts arise, even if they seem trivial, illogical, embarrassing, or inappropriate. The therapist stays out of view during this procedure, to minimize the person's inhibitions against speaking.

Freud's second discovery was that what emerged from free association (and even from hypnotherapy) often wasn't literally true. As noted just earlier, much material from early cases suggested that patients had experienced childhood seductions. Eventually Freud concluded that those encounters had not actually taken place. This led to a drastic reorganization in how Freud viewed not only the content of free association but also childhood sexuality. Obviously free association was producing something important, but it wasn't quite what it had seemed to be.

In Freud's newer view, unconscious material emerges through free association in *symbolic* form. The symbolism renders it less threatening to the person than it otherwise would be, thus letting it escape from the unconscious. Images of seduction are less threatening than images of one's own carnal desire. Free association often creates a jumble of symbolic elements that may make no sense on the surface. Yet, as in a crossword puzzle, they provide an incomplete context from which missing elements may be inferred (Erdelyi, 1985).

As we said above, many problems that are serious enough to produce behavioral manifestations stem from repressed conflicts and urges and from suppressed libidinal energy. The goal of therapy is to uncover the conflicts and unleash the restrained libidinal energy (see also Box 9.6). Free association is a first step to this, because it allows symbolic access to the problem. Free association rarely reaches the heart of the problem, though, because of the high levels of threat in the repressed material.

Indeed, people in therapy actively fight against becoming aware of repressed conflicts and impulses, a struggle that's termed **resistance.** Resistance may be conscious—for instance when a person has an association that arouses anxiety but doesn't report it. Resistance also may occur unconsciously (the ego operates in both domains). Unconscious resistance reflects an automatic use of ego defenses against the possibility of anxiety. Its occurrence is usually a sign that something important is nearby, that the person is close to revealing something sensitive.

Whether conscious or unconscious, resistance provides a graphic illustration of how emotionally wrenching the psychoanalytic therapy process can be. The person in therapy is trying to uncover distressing truths, truths that have been buried in the unconscious precisely *because* they're too painful to acknowledge. It's no wonder that the process of uncovering them is difficult.

An important process in psychoanalytic therapy is **transference,** which is a set of *displacements.* Feelings toward the people who figure in the person's conflicts and repressed desires are displaced (transferred) onto the therapist. The feelings can be either of love or of hatred, depending on the underlying issue. Transference serves as a defense in therapy, in that the therapist provokes less anxiety than do the original objects of the feelings.

Transference can interfere with therapy because the client may become caught up in what's being felt toward the therapist. These feelings themselves don't reveal the fundamental conflict, because the conflict pertains to someone else. On the other hand, transference can point out the significance of the feelings that are be-

BOX 9.6

REPRESSION, DISCLOSURE, AND HEALTH

Our main discussion focuses on the idea that repression has a psychological cost. Recently, however, it's been argued that holding back memories, thoughts, and feelings about traumatic events can also have a *physical* cost. This is the conclusion drawn by James Pennebaker (1989, 1993) and his colleagues, who've conducted a series of studies of inhibition and confession of traumatic memories.

Subjects in this research are asked to describe (with complete anonymity, in most studies) their deepest thoughts and feelings either about a specific event, or about "the most upsetting or traumatic experience of your entire life." Ideally, the event the subject is to talk about (or write about, in some of the research) is one that he or she hasn't talked about much with other people. Thus, it's more likely to be something that's been repressed, at least partially. The disclosure of thoughts and feelings typically takes place for about 20 minutes at a time on 4 successive days.

Pennebaker reports that the way in which subjects disclose intimate information is different from the way they talk or write about mundane subjects. Across various studies, as subjects begin to describe their deepest feelings, they talk faster and in many cases lower their voices, to the point where they sound like different people. In studies in which the disclosures are written, subjects' handwriting changes, sometimes markedly, again reflecting a kind of urgency in the expression of the information. Pennebaker believes that these changes in presentation reflect a kind of "letting go," that the disclosures aren't simply a giving of information but involve more than that. In essence, Pennebaker thinks he's been observing catharsis.

The short-term effect of disclosing thoughts and feelings about traumatic events is, as you might expect, that subjects feel greater distress. In the longer term, however, Pennebaker and his colleagues have found evidence that self-disclosure confers health benefits. In one study, students who'd disclosed traumatic events were less likely to visit the student health center over the next 6 months than were other subjects (Pennebaker & Beall, 1986). Results of another study suggest that disclosure has an influence on the functioning of the immune system (Pennebaker, Kiecolt-Glaser, & Glaser, 1988). In a study of Holocaust survivors, those who seemed to let go most during their disclosures were least likely to visit their physicians in the following weeks (Pennebaker, 1989).

Why might disclosure of painful memories and the thoughts and feelings that accompany them have health benefits? Pennebaker (1993) is pursuing the idea that the mechanism lies partly in the expression of the feelings and partly in the cognitive changes that occur during and after the disclosures. He has found evidence that people who express more negative emotions and (independently) that people who come to organize their experiences into causal narratives benefit more than people who do not (Pennebaker, 1993). Interestingly enough, it apparently isn't *having* a coherent story that helps, but rather the process of *creating* the story.

Pennebaker (1993) suggests that the body expresses itself linguistically and biologically at the same time. As we struggle to create meaning from trauma, we create beneficial changes in our biological functions as well. The result is better biological functioning and ultimately better health. This perspective on the consequences of emotional expression is one that surely will evoke controversy and interest in the coming years. It is a viewpoint with many important implications. If it continues to be supported by research evidence, it will change the way many people think about therapy—and even about such activities as keeping a diary!

ing displaced. When transference occurs, then, its interpretation becomes an important part of the therapy process.

The goal of psychoanalytic psychology is **insight,** which is defined from this theoretical view as an emotional experiencing of previously unconscious parts of one's personality. More explicitly, insight in therapy isn't an intellectual understanding.

TABLE 9.2

Three origins of problems in personality and the goal of psychoanalysis in treating each.	
Origin	**Goal**
Fixation	Relive prior conflict to work through
Repressed trauma	Relive experience for catharsis of feelings
Repressed basic needs	Gain emotional insight into the needs and their acceptability

Rather, it implies the reexperiencing of the emotional reality of repressed conflicts, memories, or urges (see also Table 9.2). Intellectual understanding doesn't have the power to change the person. For a cognitive reorganization to be useful, it must come in the context of an emotional catharsis.

The development of true insight allows the person to see how the conflicts and unaccepted urges have influenced his or her functioning for years. The insight provides a basis to work from so that the person can attain greater acceptance of these previously unacceptable parts of the self. One result is that the person can get by with less defense in the future.

Does Psychoanalytic Therapy Work?

Psychoanalytic therapy is long (literally years) and usually painful. Given the costs involved, financial and emotional, an important question is whether it's effective. It's interesting that even Freud's view on this question changed over the years. Initially he was optimistic about psychoanalysis as a therapy technique. He believed that patients, particularly those who were bright and well educated, could benefit substantially from the insights they gained from therapy. He expected them to become better—and ultimately happier—people.

During the middle of his career, however, Freud's thinking on this matter began to shift. He became more and more convinced that the real value of his work was in his theory of the mind, not his therapy technique. By the end of his career he'd become pessimistic about the effectiveness of psychoanalytic therapy. He'd come to believe that most of what happens to a person is due to biological factors that are beyond anyone's control.

How effective *is* psychoanalytic therapy? Early reviews concluded that therapy in general—including psychoanalysis—isn't much help (Eysenck, 1961; Feldman, 1968; Wolpe, 1981). Other reviews, however, found that therapy works and that analytic therapy does about as well as other techniques (Smith & Glass, 1977; Smith, Glass, & Miller, 1980).

A problem in interpreting the studies stems from the fact that there are several ways to define success. Whether therapy is successful depends on how success is defined. It could be defined by a therapist's judgment of the patient's improvement. It could be defined by the patient's lower ratings of distress or symptoms such as anxiety or depression. These are, in fact, the ways in which success is typically defined in outcome research.

Psychoanalysts, however, tend to use different criteria of success. Although it's hard to find complete consensus, success in psychoanalytic therapy is often defined by how much insight patients gain into their conflicts and dynamics (a judgment that can be made from the perspective of either patient or therapist). This greater insight may or may not yield less distress. Some believe strongly, however, that the goal of psychoanalysis should be insight per se rather than reduced distress. Given this different goal, it's hard to be sure what negative findings say about the success of psychoanalytic therapy (for a more detailed discussion see Fisher & Greenberg, 1977).

This discussion also makes more understandable the fact that people continue to seek out and endure the painful effort of psychoanalysis. People who undergo this treatment must think that they're getting something out of it, or they wouldn't continue. It seems likely that people will find value in psychoanalysis if they believe the psychoanalytic perspective and believe that mature insight is of value. Perhaps the hope of a better life that this conviction can bring is a sufficient benefit in itself to warrant undertaking the therapy process.

Psychoanalytic Defense: Problems and Prospects

The ideas presented in this chapter extend and elaborate on those in Chapter 8. They thus add complexity to the theory with respect to its problems and it prospects. These ideas also can be evaluated on their own merits. How do these ideas fare in today's personality psychology? What are their implications for the broader usefulness of psychoanalytic theory?

We said at the end of Chapter 8 that a problem with psychoanalysis is that its concepts are hard to test. The ideas in this chapter create even more difficulty in that respect. Specifically, the defense mechanisms provide limitless flexibility. As a result, they can be used to explain virtually any pattern of behavior that might occur. Flexibility is an advantage because it allows a theory to account for a lot. However, it also makes prediction hard. If a theory's too flexible, you can reconcile *any* finding with the theory. To the extent that findings contrary to prediction can be "explained away" after the fact, the ideas being tested aren't tested at all.

Suppose, for example, you were interested in the idea that anal fixation is related to neatness. If the data show that neatness and anality are positively related, the idea is supported. But if the data show the opposite, that anal characters are the messiest of people, you just add a twist. You assume that the messiness is a type of defensive reaction, protecting these people against the anxiety that's created by their underlying need to be neat.

Given the range of defense mechanisms assumed by psychoanalytic theory and the mechanism behind them, such a twist can always be invoked. If a desire is too threatening, it's repressed. It emerges from the unconscious in a disguised or distorted form—even a complete opposite to its original form. If this is too threatening (perhaps because a reversal doesn't hide the threat well enough because it's too "obvious"), then a different distortion occurs. Thus the theory is amenable to virtually any outcome. As a result, predictions from it can never be disconfirmed. Unfortunately, when a theory can never be disconfirmed, it can never really be confirmed, either.

Other criticisms of elements of the psychoanalytic perspective that were introduced in this chapter concern its techniques for assessing personality and for therapy. Assessment in this perspective relies largely on projective techniques. As we said earlier, these techniques have received considerable criticism. There's a long way to go before projective tests live up to the psychometric standards set by most personality psychologists.

Regarding psychoanalytic therapy, disagreement about its efficacy reflects disagreement on its goals. A further difficulty in evaluating psychoanalysis as therapy is that information isn't always available to verify insights that emerge during therapy. If someone experiences a sudden realization that she's always resented her mother, who died 5 years ago, is this a "realization" or a self-deception? If you free associate long enough, eventually you'll recall bad feelings about almost anyone you know. But in many cases it's hard to tell how important the bad feelings actually were.

Given the various problems associated with psychoanalytic theory, why has it been so popular? Indeed, there's been a resurgence of interest in psychoanalytic theory in recent years, after a period of diminished influence. The American Psychoanalytic Association currently accredits 22 institutes and centers throughout the United States. There seem to be at least three reasons for this enduring popularity. One is that Freud's was the first comprehensive theory of personality. Whenever something comes first, its influence persists for a long time. Second, Freud spoke to questions and issues that lie at the heart of personality: How does childhood influence later life? What is mental health? To what extent are people's motives accessible to them? The questions he posed began to stake out in clear terms the territory of what would become personality psychology.

A final reason for the theory's popularity concerns the intuitive appeal of its major themes. Any metaphor that's incorporated into a language is adopted because it captures an element of reality in a striking and vivid way. Psychoanalytic theory uses many images and metaphors. Their scientific status aside, notions such as libido, unconscious motivation, psychosexual development, and the intrapsychic tug-of-war of conflicting pressures from id, ego, and superego have an emotional appeal. The ideas are novel, exciting, and interesting. In a word, they are seductive. Freud's theory undoubtedly established its foothold in part because it portrayed personality in a way that people found—and continue to find—interesting.

SUMMARY

Anxiety is a warning signal to the ego. Reality anxiety is fear of a threat in the world. Neurotic anxiety is fear that id impulses will get out of control and get you in trouble. Moral anxiety is fear of violating the superego's moral code. The ego deals with anxiety (and sometimes prevents it from arising) by employing defense mechanisms.

The basic defense is repression—forcing id impulses and other threatening material out of consciousness. Repression is useful, but it ties up energy. Denial is a refusal to acknowledge the reality of something that lies outside the mind. Other defenses, which typically operate along with repression, are projection (attributing your unacceptable impulse to someone else), rationalization (developing a plausible and acceptable but incorrect explanation for your action), intellectualization (separating your thoughts from your feelings and allowing the thoughts but not the feelings to enter awareness), reaction formation (behaving in a way opposite to the initial impulse), regression (returning to a mode of behavior characteristic of an earlier stage of development), displacement (shifting an impulse from one target to another, usually a safer one), and sublimation (transforming an unacceptable impulse to an acceptable one).

The psychoanalytic orientation holds that the unconscious is the key to personality. Freud believed that the unconscious reveals itself in many ways in day-to-day life. Parapraxes are slips of the tongue and pen that occur when unconscious desires cause you to act in a way other than you consciously intend. Similar processes are believed to underlie many accidents and also dreams. Dreams have manifest content (what's in the dream) and latent content (the determinants of the dream, many of which are unconscious). Manifest content usually is symbolic of latent content, which also may be distorted through other mechanisms termed dream work.

The unconscious can also be revealed more formally, through projective assessment techniques such as the Rorschach inkblot test. Projective techniques allow the person's unconscious to release symbolic versions of threatening material while describing ambiguous stimuli. The Rorschach is somewhat controversial in that its reliability and validity have not been strongly supported by research evidence.

In the psychoanalytic view, behavioral problems reflect an overuse of defenses. Problems may derive from fixations (unresolved conflicts at a pregenital stage of psychosexual development), from a general repression of libido, or from repressed traumas. In any case, too much energy is spent in confining the threatening material within the unconscious. The goal of therapy is to release some of the repression, thereby freeing some of the energy.

Psychoanalytic therapy begins with free association—saying whatever comes to mind without censoring it in any way. This approach typically produces an incomplete matrix of symbolic meanings from which other elements can be inferred. People in therapy often display resistance, which implies that the ego is trying to defend itself against something that the therapy is beginning to touch on. Eventually the person in therapy displays transference, displacing onto the therapist the feelings associated with the person about whom the conflicts exist. The goal of the therapy is insight—an emotional experiencing of previously unconscious parts of one's personality.

Freud came to believe that psychoanalysis was not as beneficial as he had first thought. This pessimistic view also emerged from some evaluation studies of the therapy process, although more recent studies have been more encouraging. Even in the absence of strong support for the usefulness of psychoanalytic therapy, many people continue to engage in it because they believe it provides benefits that are not adequately assessed by the measures used in outcome research.

GLOSSARY

Anxiety An aversive feeling warning the ego that something bad is about to happen.

Condensation The compression and combination of several thoughts in a dream.

Current concerns Preoccupations in one's current waking life.

Defense mechanism An ego-protective strategy to hide threats from yourself and thereby reduce anxiety.

Denial A refusal to believe that some real condition exists.

Displacement The shifting of an impulse from its original target to a different target.

Dream work Processes that distort latent dream content and transform it into manifest content.

Free association A therapy procedure of saying without hesitation whatever comes to mind.

Insight An emotional reexperiencing of earlier conflicts in one's life that occurs during therapy.

Intellectualization The process of thinking about something clinically and without emotion.

Latent content The underlying sources of symbolic dream images.

Manifest content The images that make up the dream experience as it is recalled.

Mechanism of opposites The dreaming of the opposite of what you fear.

Moral anxiety The fear of behaving in conflict with the superego's moral code.

Neurotic anxiety The fear that your id impulses will get out of control and get you into trouble.

Parapraxis A slip of the tongue, behavior, or memory.

Projection Ascribing a threatening urge or quality in yourself to someone else.

Projective techniques An assessment in which you project from the unconscious onto ambiguous stimuli.

Rationalization Finding an acceptable but incorrect explanation for an action or event.

Reaction formation Doing the opposite of what your impulses are.

Reality anxiety The fear of danger in the world.

Regression A return to a mode of coping from an earlier developmental stage.

Repression The process of keeping an idea or impulse in the unconscious.

Resistance An attempt to avoid becoming conscious of threatening material in therapy.

Rorschach inkblot test A projective test that uses inkblots as ambiguous stimuli.

Secondary elaboration The filling out of the content of a dream to make it be somewhat sensible.

Symbolization The transformation of unacceptable latent dream content into less threatening symbols.

Sublimation The alteration of an id impulse into a socially acceptable act.

Transference The displacement onto your therapist of feelings that are tied to some object of conflict.

PART five

The Neoanalytic Perspective

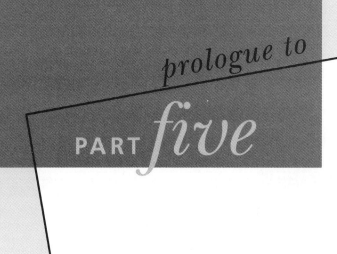

THE NEOANALYTIC PERSPECTIVE: Major Themes and Underlying Assumptions

As the term *neoanalytic* implies, the perspective on personality discussed in this section derives in part from the psychoanalytic perspective. Freud attracted a group of followers and colleagues. All of these people adopted aspects of his viewpoint, but most also differed from him in important ways. They dealt with their ambivalence about psychoanalysis by recasting and embellishing Freud's ideas in their own terms. In doing so, they deemphasized aspects of his theory they disliked, and they extended aspects they liked. Their disagreements with Freud are basic enough, however, that their views seem distinctly different from Freud's. For this reason, we've chosen to treat them as a distinct perspective on personality.

These "post-Freudian" psychodynamic theorists were fairly diverse in their thinking. As a result, there are as many different post-Freudian theories as there were theorists. Treatment of each theory by itself can create a jumble of ideas that's hard to keep straight. On the other hand, although the theories are distinct in some ways,

there are at least two themes that many of them share. As a result, the two chapters that form this section of the book don't simply discuss each theory of this group in isolation from the others. Rather, the focus is on several of the theories that most clearly reflect the two themes that are most salient in post-Freudian psychodynamic thinking. Points made by other theorists that supplement these core ideas are introduced where they seem most relevant.

The theorists who form the neoanalytic group differed from Freud on several grounds. Some neoanalytic theorists were bothered by Freud's emphasis on the importance of sexuality and the idea that sexual issues are important even in infancy. Others took issue with Freud's strong emphasis on the importance of unconscious processes. Perhaps the most frequent criticism among Freud's followers, however, was that he didn't give enough attention to the ego. Accordingly, many neoanalytic theories focus on the nature of the ego and how it functions. As a group, these theories emphasize the existence of certain ego processes and how they come to develop. This line of theory is the focus of Chapter 10.

Theorists who emphasize ego functioning and ego development tend to focus more on how the ego operates than on the content of the problems and situations the ego confronts. However, a second group of neoanalytic theories addresses more closely the question of what kinds of situations are central in the ego's transactions with the world. In general, the theorists of this second group have held that the ego's primary tasks revolve around the nature and quality of the person's relations with other people. The theories deriving from this assumption focus on how the ego interacts with, and is affected by, other individuals and the broader social and cultural matrix. The theories with this emphasis on social interaction are described in Chapter 11.

Ego Psychology

■ Jeremy has an apparently irresistible attraction to video and computer games. He will sit transfixed for hours at a time in front of any challenging game there is. When he isn't pumping quarters into an arcade machine, he's parked in front of his computer, trying out whatever new game has just been released. His scores so completely outstrip those of his friends that most of them have stopped playing with him at all. Often enough they don't even watch. It's just Jeremy and the machine, locked in combat. His friends aren't sure why he does it. It's obviously not that he wants to be best in his group, or even the best in town (he's long since owned all the top scores). When asked, Jeremy shrugs and replies that he simply feels a desire to be better than he already is. "It's hard to explain—I just want to be as good at it as I can be."

Why do people spend large amounts of their time becoming good at activities that have little or no practical significance? Name an activity, and people somewhere spend countless hours perfecting their skills at it: bowling, golf, cow-chip tossing, ballet, hog calling, and—yes—video games. Why? From the perspective of psychoanalysis there's an explanation for everything people do. You just need to search for a symbolic meaning behind the activity. But how do you feel about the idea that becoming proficient at video games is a symbolic reflection of, for example, Oedipal urges?

This question raises a more general issue. If you're like most people, you have a mixed reaction to psychoanalytic theory. Most people find some aspects of the theory compelling and believable. For example, many agree that early experience has a big effect on personality, many agree that conflict is inherent in personality functioning, and most agree that behavior is usually aimed at gaining pleasure and avoiding pain. Probably, though, there were aspects of the theory you found less convincing. Maybe you don't agree with Freud's stress on the unconscious. Or maybe you're put off by his insistence that so much of human behavior is sexually motivated.

If you have mixed feelings about psychoanalysis, you're not alone. Even Freud's followers were ambivalent. There were several areas of disagreement. Perhaps the most frequent criticism was that Freud didn't give enough attention to the ego and its functioning (see Box 10.1 for another disagreement). Interestingly enough, toward the end of his career Freud felt the same way himself. He began to wonder whether the ego might have a more important and autonomous status than he'd earlier believed.

Freud died before he could openly indicate his gradually changing position on this matter. Even his last formal publication (Freud, 1949/1940) gives no hint of this shift in his thinking. Others knew of Freud's informal statements, though, and found his shifting views to be more compatible with their own thinking. Encouraged by this change, they began to develop a set of ideas that collectively came to be called **ego psychology.** As the name implies, ego psychology is a psychodynamic framework in which ego functioning has greater status than Freud gave it.

The emergence of ego psychology was a subtle and gradual process that actually began well before Freud's death. Indeed, many would say that some of the ideas described in Chapter 9 are just as relevant to ego psychology as to psychoanalysis. It was Anna Freud who analyzed the process of defense so carefully, and her ideas weren't identical to those of her father. Recall that these defenses are used *by the ego* to protect itself. Thus, they're easily viewed as being ego functions and as a part of ego psychology.

BOX 10.1

ANOTHER KIND OF PSYCHODYNAMICS:
Jung's Analytical Psychology

This chapter focuses on people who modified Freud's ideas by emphasizing the ego and deemphasizing the unconscious. We should, however, note another theorist of the time whose ideas moved in the other direction: Carl Jung (e.g., 1960/1926, 1968). Jung was less a follower of Freud than a *contemporary* of Freud (though 20 years younger) who was influenced by many of the same currents of thought as molded Freud's work. Thus similarities in some of the ideas they advanced seemed initially to give them common ground.

Freud and Jung associated professionally and personally for 6 years, during which Freud began to view Jung as his "crown prince" and eventual successor (see McGuire, 1974). Two factors, however, drove a wedge between them. The first was a series of theoretical differences. The second was a growing interpersonal difficulty. Freud saw himself as a father figure to Jung, and he began to suspect that Jung wished to usurp his power and authority (note the Oedipal overtones). Jung found this attitude hard to tolerate, and he eventually broke away from Freud.

Jung's theory differs from Freud's in many ways. It's a theory of great complexity, and we can make only a couple of points about it here. Jung shared with the neoanalysts the view that Freud overemphasized sexuality as a motive. He differed from them, however, in saying that Freud had too limited a view of human spirituality. Unlike Freud, for whom spirituality reflected sublimation of sexual drives, Jung considered it a fundamental aspect of human existence.

Jung's thinking was also dominated by the **principle of opposites,** the idea that the human experience consists of polarities—qualities that oppose and tend to balance each other. Using this idea, he proposed a series of dichotomies in human functioning, each of which bears some resemblance to what others would view as aspects of ego functioning. Jung believed that people are dominated by one of two attitudes: introversion or extraversion. People dominated by extraversion are absorbed by external experiences and spend their time interacting with the world around them.

People dominated by introversion are preoccupied by their inner experiences and thus tend to be less outgoing. Both tendencies can facilitate adaptation. And even though you're dominated by one of them, the other remains inside you, opposing and balancing it.

Jung also assumed two more pairs of opposed functions in the ego's experience. One pair, *thinking* and *feeling,* are both rational, in that each involves a kind of judgment—which ideas are true (for thinking) or whether you like or dislike something (for feeling). The other pair, *sensing* and *intuiting,* are nonrational in that they don't rely on thought. Both are ways of perceiving, although one uses senses whereas the other uses the unconscious. It may be less apparent than with introversion-extraversion, but each of these pairs forms a polarity, with one of each pair tending to dominate the other. Indeed, a further polarization exists between the rational and irrational. Jung believed that combinations of dominance of the functions just named (plus introversion-extraversion) produce the wide range of individual differences in personality. Today these tendencies are measured by an instrument called the Myers-Briggs Type Indicator (Myers & McCaulley, 1985), which is widely used for assessment in settings such as businesses and career counseling (DeVito, 1985).

Although Jung's theory has certain similarities to ego psychology, there are also great differences. For example, instead of deemphasizing the unconscious, Jung emphasized it even more than Freud did. Jung believed that human beings share a **collective unconscious,** or "racial memory," a set of memories from our human and even prehuman ancestors. He believed that these memories, which aren't recalled consciously, go back for countless generations. They provide the basis for images called **archetypes,** aspects of the world that people have an inherited tendency to notice. Jung described many archetypes, including birth, death, power, magic, unity, God, and the self, which he believed are experienced by everyone. Each of these, in Jung's view, exists in the individual because it's been part of the experience of human and prehuman life for millennia.

Principles of Ego Psychology

Anna Freud's analysis of defense mechanisms is a transitional statement, in that it can be applied either to traditional psychoanalysis or to ego psychology. But other aspects of ego psychology depart more clearly from psychoanalysis. Freud had emphasized that the ego's primary task was to mediate among the id, the superego, and external reality. From the vantage point of ego psychology, the ego does far more than that. The ego is involved in the process of *adaptation,* of fitting better and better into the world. This view holds that adaptation and the conscious processes by which it takes place are more important to personality than is unconscious instinctive behavior (Wolberg, 1967).

Nor is this the only departure from Freud. Ego psychologists also widely assumed that the ego exists at birth, apart from the id, and has its own source of energy. One ego psychologist (Fairbairn, 1952) even went so far as to suggest that there is no id—only ego—and that what were once seen as id functions are simply reflections of an ego that's at a primitive stage of development. All these ideas follow from the core assumption of the ego psychologists—that ego processes are important in their own right.

Shifting the Emphasis from Id to Ego

Since many of the people who became known as ego psychologists began as followers of Freud, they confronted a dilemma in deciding how to proceed. They wanted to construct theories that emphasized the ego, but many also wanted not to undermine the central ideas of psychoanalysis. How could this be done? This problem was a hard one, because traditional psychoanalysis had given the ego a specific subservient role—to help the impulses of the id gain expression.

Heinz Hartmann (1958/1939, 1964) had an inventive and simple solution to this dilemma: He ignored it. More specifically, he proposed that the ego serves two roles simultaneously. On the one hand it reduces conflict between the id and superego and between the id and external reality, as Freud had said. On the other hand it acts through its cognitive processes to adapt the person better to the environment.

Hartmann held that the ego acts in two different modes to handle these different functions (see Figure 10.1). When it acts to reduce conflict, it's operating in what he called the *conflict sphere* of personality. When it acts to promote adaptation, it's operating in the *conflict-free sphere*. Thus, said Hartmann, Freud's view of the ego was right and so was the emerging view of ego psychology. Each view simply emphasizes different aspects of what the ego does.

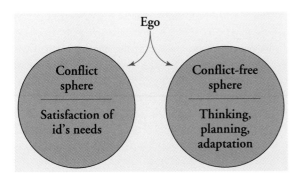

FIGURE 10.1

Hartmann assumed that the ego can operate in either of two modes. In the conflict sphere, it acts to see that the id's impulses are satisfied. In the conflict-free sphere, it engages in activities for its own purposes, aimed at better adaptation.

How can the ego function in two spheres? Hartmann assumed that ego and id have the same biological source. Given that, part of the ego stays in contact with the id throughout life. This part of the ego operates in the conflict sphere and works to satisfy the id's needs. The rest develops more independently and operates in the conflict-free sphere, working for its own purposes. This latter aspect of the ego is what Hartmann and other ego psychologists were interested in.

Having said that Freud was partly right (that is, that the ego functions in the conflict sphere), Hartmann then proceeded to ignore that aspect of the ego almost entirely. In that way he managed to remain connected to psychoanalysis, while heading off in a new direction.

Adaptation and Autonomy

In Hartmann's view, adaptation to the environment is the ultimate goal of behavior. This became an important theme throughout ego psychology. Adaptation occurs on several levels. Physically, people must learn to move their bodies to get where they want to go and do what they want to do. Psychologically, people must learn to gain control over their impulses, modifying them and channeling them into appropriate actions.

Hartmann agreed with Freud that sexual and aggressive energies provide the foundation of much of human behavior. He differed, however, in how he interpreted people's attempts to deal with their impulses. Freud saw the struggle to inhibit impulse expression in terms of avoiding anxiety (by eventually gratifying impulses in ways that avoid punishment or danger). Hartmann (and other ego psychologists) saw the effort to inhibit as part of a broader process of adaptation. The difference isn't so much in *what* happens as in *why* it happens. To Hartmann, the why of impulse control pertains to the ego's own goals.

Hartmann talked about two kinds of autonomy in describing the ego. First, ego processes exist on their own from birth and can function apart from the id (a principle called **primary ego autonomy**). An implication of this is that people get satisfaction directly from using ego processes to think, plan, imagine, integrate information, and so on (see also Box 10.2). In this view, just being effective is pleasurable in itself. As you exercise your ego, you become more adept, and thereby more efficient (better adapted) in dealing with the world.

The phrase **secondary ego autonomy** refers to the idea that an ego function originally done for one purpose may continue to be done long after that purpose has been satisfied. The original purpose may have been to fill some other need (even an id need), but the ego function is now gratifying in its own right. The meaning of the term *secondary ego autonomy* is similar to what Allport (1961) called **functional autonomy.** When a behavior that was originally done for a specific reason continues to occur after the original reason no longer applies, the behavior is said to have acquired functional autonomy. It's as though the behavior has now become an end in itself. As an illustration, think of a person who began an exercise program to lose weight. Even after she's lost the weight she continues to exercise because she now finds the exercise intrinsically satisfying.

The idea of an autonomous ego that has the goal of adaptation was widely adopted by other theorists, who extended it in a variety of ways. Among others, Rapaport (1960), Gill (1959), G. S. Klein (1970), and White (1959, 1963) were interested in how the ego goes about fitting itself better to the world. Although many ego psychologists view the exercise of ego processes as a source of pleasure and satisfaction, this idea has perhaps been elaborated most compellingly by Robert White (1959, 1963).

BOX 10.2

THE JOY OF THINKING:
Explorations in the Need for Cognition

The idea that ego processes are gratifying in their own right is consistent with a literature on a topic called the **need for cognition.** This is the need to think about and impose meaningful structure on one's experiences (Cohen, 1957; Cohen, Stotland, & Wolfe, 1955). People high in the need for cognition are more likely to spontaneously organize, elaborate on, and evaluate information to which they're exposed than are people lower in the need. They're less easily bored (Watt & Blanchard, 1994) and seem to attend more to the details of others' behavior (Lassiter, Briggs, & Bowman, 1991) and think more about its meaning (Lassiter, Briggs, & Slaw, 1991). People high in this need also aren't dogmatic and they tend to explain events in complex ways (Fletcher et al., 1986). They aren't necessarily smarter than people lower in this need—they just like to think things over (Cacioppo, Petty, Kao, & Rodriguez, 1986; Cacioppo, Petty, & Morris, 1983).

This ego function is reflected in several ways (for a review see Cacioppo, Petty, Feinstein, & Jarvis, 1996). Consider, for example, what happens when people try to persuade each other of something. It's known that persuasion affects people in two very different ways. When people get a persuasive message, some evaluate it and even *elaborate* on it in their minds. Others just take the message at face value. Cacioppo and Petty (1982, 1984) argued that this difference in responses rests on the need for cognition. People high in the need for cognition are those who evaluate and elaborate; people low in the need for cognition accept what they're given.

Cacioppo and associates examined this idea by finding subjects who held the same attitudes on a target issue but differed in their need for cognition (Cacioppo et al., 1983; Cacioppo et al., 1986, Experiment 1). Subjects received an essay intended to persuade them to change their opinion. Either the essay was full of weak arguments (which people resist, according to previous research), or it was full of strong arguments (which are more persuasive). As you might expect, people with high cognition needs reported thinking harder about the message than those with lower cognition needs. They also remembered more of the arguments in it.

Does thinking harder and remembering more result in more persuasion? Not always. Thinking about strong arguments produced more persuasion. Thinking about weak arguments, however, caused people to be more resistant to persuasion. In sum, people high in the need for cognition thought more about the value of the arguments they'd read, and they used the value of the arguments more as a guide for deciding whether to change their attitudes. Later research found that once the attitude changed, the change was also more persistent for those high in the need for cognition (Haugtvedt & Petty, 1992; Verplanken, 1991). This overall pattern seems much in line with the functions the ego psychologists emphasized, as people try to deal effectively and adaptively with external reality.

The Ego, Adaptation, and Competence Motivation

In discussing ego processes White used two motivational concepts. **Effectance motivation** is the motive to *have an effect* or an impact on one's surroundings. White believed that effectance motivation is a basic human motive. During early childhood it's the major outlet for the ego's energies. This motive gradually evolves into the more complex **competence motivation,** a motive *to be effective* when interacting with the environment. Because the goal of the competence motive is greater effectiveness, this motive underlies adaptive ego functioning. Competence motivation is endless in its potential because there are always new competencies (and higher

Children often seem driven to figure things out on their own. Successful mastery of the environment is important in developing feelings of competence.

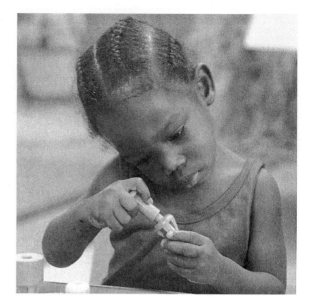

levels of competence) to attain. The competence motive thus moves the person toward ever-new masteries (recall Jeremy and his video games from the example that opened the chapter).

White pointed out that there are important differences between attaining goals and satisfying the competence motivation. Attaining a goal satisfies the desire to reach that goal, but the goal itself may or may not matter to your competence. For example, if you get a perfect exam score in a course you think is pointless, it won't enhance your sense of competence.

Consider for a moment how effectance and competence motives might be expressed in a child's behavior. Imagine an infant, surrounded by toys in her crib, who lunges at a dangling mobile and gives it a good whack with her fist. As the mobile jangles and bounces, the child has visible evidence of her impact on the environment. This gratifies her desire for effectance. Knocking things over, moving toys around, spreading stewed carrots all over her table tray—each of these actions has an effect on the world around her. Each satisfies the effectance motive. Infants clearly do these things, and they do seem to obtain pleasure from them.

What about competence? Suppose the child is just learning how to stand up. She struggles over and over to pull herself up against the wall of her crib, even though every attempt meets with failure and even though no one's there to encourage her. When success finally comes, she expresses her pleasure in giggles and shrieks. She's manifested a mastery over the environment, an increased competence in dealing with it. The motive to develop increasing mastery over the environment continues to be an important part of her life from now on.

In White's view, effectance and competence motives derive directly from the way the brain is organized. He held that people inherently seek stimulation from exploring the environment. This biological urge can be shown in many ways, but its most advanced form is the desire to be competent and feel competent in dealing with the world. This is an inherently adaptive urge because it causes people to be engaged in effective commerce with their environment to the greatest extent possible.

This theme has had reverberations in other perspectives on personality, as well as in ego psychology. As you'll see in Chapter 13, some learning theorists have come to believe that the sense of personal efficacy is a major determinant of people's actions. It can easily be argued that this line of thought traces to White's emphasis on an intrinsic human desire to master the environment. An additional theoretical similarity will become apparent when you read about humanistic views on personality in Chapter 14.

Is Competence Striving Automatic, or Is It Done to Remedy Inferiority?

White considered the desire for greater competence to be the major force behind people's attempts to be effective. This position differs somewhat from the view taken by another ego psychologist, Alfred Adler (1927, 1929, 1931). Adler also believed that people strive for greater competence, but he saw this as occurring for different reasons than White assumed.

Adler began his line of theory with an interest in a medical question—why one person develops heart trouble, a second respiratory problems, and a third ulcers. Adler's hypothesis was that people have an inferiority in some bodily region, which makes them vulnerable to illness at that site. He called this weakness an **organ inferiority** (Adler, 1917). Adler also argued that people try to *compensate* for their weakness by strengthening the inferior organ through exercise and training. He termed this effort a *striving for superiority*. No doubt Adler's belief in this principle of compensatory striving was influenced by his own life circumstances. He was a sickly

Feelings of inferiority can produce strivings for superiority.

child who nearly died in childhood, but through considerable effort he was able to overcome his health problems.

Support for this idea comes from a study of the performances of undersea divers engaged in a physically demanding task (Helmreich, LeFan, Bakeman, Wilhelm, & Radloff, 1972). This study found that the divers who performed best had had a serious illness during childhood. From Adler's perspective these divers were compensating behaviorally for earlier body inferiority.

Adler went on to expand his thinking to include *all* feelings of inferiority and to extend the principle to personality. He proposed that whenever a person has **feelings of inferiority** (any sense of physical or psychological inadequacy), a compensatory process is activated and the person strives for superiority (Adler, 1927, 1929, 1931). For example, consider a sprinter who feels inferior because she can't run 100 yards in 10 seconds. Because she feels inferior, she trains until she breaks the 10-second barrier. Her satisfaction, however, is short-lived. Feelings of inferiority set in again, as she realizes she could be even faster, and the struggle to improve begins anew.

Consider another example—the college freshman who arrives for his first semester knowing no one at school. He's a little shy, and a few minutes later he feels a sense of inferiority because people all around him are engaged in animated conversations with one another. What does he do? He grits his teeth and approaches a group of three people to introduce himself. Within a month, new friendships are sprouting like summer weeds. By now, though, just having friends isn't enough—he feels inferior because the friendships are a little superficial. He thinks he should know some people better than he does. As a result he gets involved in a church group that meets once a week to talk with others about personal reactions to the experience of college life.

There are many ways of responding to a feeling of inferiority. Adler coined the term **lifestyle** to refer to both a person's concerns over inferiority and the person's preferred way of striving for superiority. Healthy lifestyles move the person forward in an adaptive path of development in important domains of life. They allow people to attain meaningful goals and to get along well with others.

But there are also what Adler called **mistaken lifestyles.** Some people respond to feelings of inferiority by trying to dominate others, or becoming dependent and taking things from others instead of working toward them on their own. Other people respond to feelings of inferiority by trying to avoid situations in which such feelings can arise. They attempt to avoid a sense of inferiority by never trying. Yet other people respond to such feelings by being as useful as they can to others, thereby drawing their own attention away from their inferiorities. These people almost deny the validity of their own ego and their own feelings. Consistent with this view, people who are *excessively* concerned with the needs of others have been found to be lower in self-esteem and more likely to neglect their own needs than people whose concern with others is more moderate (Fritz & Helgeson, 1998: Helgeson & Fritz, 1998, in press).

Adler believed that inferiority feelings and superiority strivings continue to cycle with each other constantly. The result, unless the person has a mistaken lifestyle, is that people work to get better, more proficient at whatever it is they do (see also Box 10.3). Adler thus viewed the struggle for increased competence to be an important part of healthy ego functioning. He called it the "great upward drive," and he believed that healthy people continue to work in this way throughout life toward ever-greater integration and perfection.

BOX 10.3

BIRTH ORDER AND PERSONALITY

There are many influences on the development of a person's lifestyle. Adler saw birth order as one such influence. He believed that each child in a family is treated differently from every other child. The differences in treatment produce different adaptations, different personalities, and different choices of lifestyle (Adler, 1964/1933).

Adler argued that *firstborn* children begin life as the focus of the family's attention. Their parents place great expectations on them, which can motivate them to high achievement. The firstborn is vulnerable to feelings of being "dethroned" in favor of a successor, however, if a second child comes along. This loss of attention and power can be deeply distressing, and may give the firstborn a lifelong sensitivity to issues of power. If the first child isn't old enough to have begun to develop a cooperative lifestyle, the firstborn may resent the second-born forever.

Some firstborns are also *only children*. Only children are never dethroned and thus spend all of their lives as the center of family attention. As a result, only children often develop an exaggerated sense of their importance. This sense can be threatened as the child reaches school age, when a different sort of dethroning takes place. That is, they aren't as much the center of attention at school. Adler felt, however, that only children were likely not to develop a true social interest but rather to expect others to attend to their needs. They're often affectionate, but in a way that facilitates their continuing as the center of attention.

Second-born children are in a very different situation. They enter a family that already exists, with a rival already in place. Since they've never occupied a position of power, as did the firstborn, they tend to be less sensitive to power issues. On the other hand, second-borns have to "hit the ground running," because their lives will be a constant effort to catch up with the firstborn. Adler thought of second as the best place in the birth order, and his reasoning fits with his views on behavior in general. He saw the second-born as like a long-distance runner who's a few yards behind the leader. The sense of inferiority is there all the time because the firstborn is always just a little ahead. The result is a constant striving for superiority. This can work to your advantage if your striving produces good results. But second-borns sometimes develop the sense that they'll never be as good as the firstborns. Consequently, they may feel inferior to their older siblings throughout their lives.

The other place in the birth order that interested Adler was at the other end of the line—the *youngest child*. Adler believed that this is the worst position in the family, though it may not seem so on the surface. The youngest child tends to be spoiled. Although that may be fun, it can have bad effects. Adler (1958/1931) argued that such treatment undermines the child's desire to strive. There's irony here, in that the youngest child (by definition) has some of the same cues as does the second-born (by having an older rival) and thus should have the same strong striving for superiority. Adler argued, however, that the belief in attaining goals through your own efforts is damaged by having things given to you too easily, which can happen to the youngest. In order to avoid these bad consequences, youngest children sometimes break from the family mold to seek an identity in a different area. For example, if the father is a lawyer and the older siblings are all taking up law, the youngest may decide to become an artist or musician.

What evidence is there for the effects of birth order? There's much anecdotal evidence that firstborns are overrepresented in positions of power and prestige. For example, 21 of the first 23 American astronauts were firstborns. There's also evidence that firstborn and only children in the U.S. have higher levels of educational goals and achievements than later children (e.g., Belmont & Marolla, 1973; Breland, 1974; Falbo, 1981), though there are exceptions (see Zajonc, Markus, & Markus, 1979). This pattern of findings is consistent with the idea that the firstborn is the center of attention and that parents place the highest expectations on their first child. But the evidence doesn't seem to support the idea that it's the second-born who has the greatest urge to strive for superiority. Effects on other aspects of personality are less common. Ernst and Angst (1983) reviewed a large literature on birth order and found little support for the idea that birth order matters for most aspects of personality.

To Adler, this effort toward improvement begins with and stems from feelings of inferiority, which everyone confronts on a continuing or recurring basis. Adler believed that these feelings are part of being human. Since a major consequence of inferiority feelings is an effort to better oneself, the outward behavior is exactly the same as the pattern White described. But the two theorists proposed very different mechanisms for it. To White, competence strivings are a natural part of the ego's activity. To Adler they're a reaction to, and an attempt to replace, feelings of inferiority.

Ego-Control and Ego-Resiliency

The theorists named thus far all emphasized the idea that the primary goal of the ego is better adaptation to the world. Let's consider this concept of adaptation a little more closely. Adaptation can be seen as having two aspects. Part of adaptation is learning to *restrain impulses*. This lets you gain better command of your transactions with the world. Part of successful adapation, though, is being *flexible* in dealing with the world—knowing when to restrain yourself and when to behave more freely.

These issues surrounding restraint of impulses in the service of better adaptation lie at the heart of the work of contemporary ego psychologists Jeanne and Jack Block (1980). They and their colleagues examined two aspects of ego functioning. One aspect—called **ego-control**—concerns impulsiveness. It's the extent to which the person tends to inhibit the expression of impulses. At one extreme are people who undercontrol—people who can't delay gratification, who express their feelings and desires immediately. Block and Block described these impulsive people as having many-but-brief enthusiasms and interests, as distractible and exploratory, nonconforming and unconventional, and comfortable with ambiguity and inconsistency. They live an impromptu life.

At the other end are people who overcontrol—people who delay gratification endlessly, who inhibit their actions and feelings, and who insulate themselves from outside distractions. Block and Block describe them as conforming rather than exploratory, planful and organized, uneasy in ambiguous or inconsistent situations, and having narrow and unchanging interests. From their description of what these people are like, it's clear that high restraint doesn't always promote better adaptation.

In the middle of the dimension are people who inhibit and control impulses to a degree, but who don't overdo it. These people are less organized than those high in ego control, but less impromptu and chaotic than those low in ego control. These people are generally better adapted than are those at either extreme (Robins et al., 1996).

The other aspect of ego functioning that Block and Block focused on is called **ego-resiliency.** This is flexibility. It's *the capacity to modify your typical level of ego-control—* in either direction—to adapt to the demands of a given situation. People who are ego-resilient are resourceful in adapting to changing circumstances. If there's a situational reason to be organized, they can do it without trouble. If there's a reason to be crazy and impulsive, they can be that way too. People who are low in ego-resilience (ego-brittle) can't break out of their typical way of relating to the world, even when it's temporarily desirable to do so.

Having a high degree of ego-resiliency would seem to foster better adaptation, no matter what your level of ego-control. As Block and Kremen (1996) put it, the ego-resilient person's ultimate goal is to be "as undercontrolled as possible and as overcontrolled as necessary" (p. 351). To do this means being responsive to what's possible and what's necessary in any given situation.

The potential problems of being low in ego-resiliency are most obvious at the extremes of the ego-control dimension. A person who's low in ego-resiliency and *high* in ego-control behaves in a rigid and controlled manner even when it's obviously best to be impulsive. A person who's low in ego-resiliency and *low* in ego-control is impulsive even when there are obvious benefits to being organized and orderly.

Not surprisingly, there's evidence that people who are high in ego-resilience are better adjusted than people who are low (Klohnen, 1996). As an example, in two samples of women, those higher in ego-resiliency did better at negotiating menopause than those who were ego-brittle. They were more likely to continue their education or career-building, and had fewer health problems (Klohnen, Vandewater, & Young, 1996). Another project found that children high in ego resilience were faster to develop in their understanding of friendships and moral reasoning than children lower in ego resilience (Hart, Keller, Edelstein, & Hofmann, 1998).

It might be tempting to conclude that people with high ego-resilience are just smarter than people who are more ego-brittle. Thus they're quicker to recognize what the situation calls for. Although these variables are related, there are also important differences (Block & Kremen, 1996). Pure ego-resilience (controlling for effects of IQ) relates to competence in the world of interpersonal interaction. Indeed, close examination of the items that align with ego-resilience rather than IQ suggests a strong thread of extraversion.

Research has examined the role of ego-control and ego-resilience in behaviors bearing on restraint (Funder & Block, 1989). A typical way to study restraint examines decisions about delaying gratification. Participants in this case were 14-year-olds being paid $4 for each of 6 sessions in exchange for completing a large assessment battery. After each session, subjects were given the choice of being paid then or deferring payment until the end. Each time they deferred payment, they'd gain a small bonus in "interest." The dependent measure was how often (from five opportunities) subjects chose to delay their payment.

As expected, delay was related to observer ratings of participants' levels of ego-control ($r = .45$, after controlling for both ego-resiliency and intelligence). It was also expected that ego-resiliency would influence choices. That is, recall that delay is sometimes a good policy, sometimes not. Since this situation was set up so that delay produced an extra payoff, delay was adaptive. Flexible people should pick up on this and choose to delay, even if that's not their usual style. In line with this, ego-resiliency was also related to delay choices ($r = .41$, after controlling for both ego-control and intelligence).

These ego qualities have also been related to other kinds of behavior. One program of research has found that measures concerning ego-control relate to the age at which people first engage in sexual intercourse, with greater ego-control related to longer delays (Jessor & Jessor, 1975; Jessor, Costa, Jessor, & Donovan, 1983). Yet other studies found that ego-control has a similar relation to drinking. Undercontrol relates to problem drinking and overcontrol relates to total abstinence (M. C. Jones, 1968, 1971). Shedler and Block (1990) have recently reported similar results with respect to drug use (see Table 10.1).

TABLE 10.1

Observer-rating items that distinguished among three groups of 18-year-olds. Those of one group were total abstainers from drug use, those of the second group were occasional experimenters, and those of the third group were frequent users (adapted from Shedler & Block, 1990).

Items distinguishing frequent users from occasional experimenters

Is self-indulgent

Gives up and withdraws in the face of frustration, adversity

Thinks and associates to ideas in unusual ways

Is unpredictable and changeable in behavior, attitudes

Undercontrols needs and impulses; unable to delay gratification

Tends to be rebellious and nonconforming

Characteristically pushes and tries to stretch limits

Items distinguishing total abstainers from occasional experimenters

Is moralistic

Favors conservative values in a variety of areas

Prides self on being "objective," rational

Overcontrols needs and impulses; delays gratification unnecessarily

Is facially and/or gesturally expressive (lower score)

Is unpredictable and changeable in behavior, attitudes (lower score)

Enjoys sensuous experience (touch, taste, smell, physical contact) (lower score)

Ego Development

Thus far in the chapter we've emphasized the idea that a primary function of the ego is to establish better adaptation to the world. Now we turn to a slightly different viewpoint on the functions of the ego, although it's one that's fully compatible with these themes.

Jane Loevinger (1969, 1976) has argued that the ego is primarily a synthesizer and integrator of experience. This function is certainly consistent with the overall goal of enhancing adaptation. In her view the ego adapts to the world by making sense of the experiences the world supplies to it. She argues that this synthesizing function isn't just another of many things the ego does. Rather, this function is what the ego *is* . To Loevinger, this process of synthesis and integration is the essence of the ego.

Loevinger proposed a detailed account of the ego's development (Loevinger, 1966, 1976, 1987; Loevinger & Knoll, 1983). By ego development, she doesn't mean a process by which the ego comes to *exist*. Rather, she's referring to how the synthesizing function of the ego evolves across life. Her theory rests on ideas about cognitive development from theorists such as Piaget. A basic idea is that as cognitive capabilities grow, people organize and structure their experience in more elaborate ways. As a result, the integrating function of the ego acts in more elaborate ways.

Loevinger's is a stage theory. She believes that each shift in the nature of ego functioning derives from, and thus depends on, the nature of ego functioning in the preceding stage. Thus the person moves through the stages in a particular order. As you move to higher stages, the syntheses the ego makes become more differentiated and complex but also more integrated.

What makes people move forward into a different stage? It's generally assumed that both cognitive development and ego development are prompted because existing functions don't quite fit the reality with which they're trying to deal. That is, if an ego function works perfectly, there's no reason to change it. If it doesn't work perfectly, though, there's pressure to evolve in ways that work better (Baumeister, 1994; Block, 1982). Thus, ego development depends partly on having challenging circumstances in one's life (see also Helson & Roberts, 1994).

Are there limitations on this process? According to Loevinger, people move through the stages until they can go no further. Your adult level of ego development, then, is the highest of the stages you're able to attain as you grow to adulthood. How far you go will be influenced both by heredity and by life circumstances (Newman, Tellegen, & Bouchard, 1998). Loevinger does *not* assume that everyone goes through all the stages of ego development. It's possible for a person to remain fixed in even a fairly early stage. Such an adult would not be well adapted to certain complexities in life, but would get along adequately in many contexts.

We should point explicitly to two differences between this view and Freud's. First, Freud saw personality development as occurring fairly early in life. In contrast, Loevinger sees ego development as a process that continues well into adulthood. Second, in Freud's theory the ego's basic functioning remains much the same, though the issues it must deal with change over the years. Loevinger, however, argues that the synthesizing process that defines the ego changes over the course of life.

Early Ego Development

The stages Loevinger identified are summarized in Table 10.2. Initially the ego is primitive. Its major task is to acquire the ability to distinguish self from nonself. This ability emerges during the first stage of ego development, called the *Symbiotic* stage. This name comes from the fact that a young child's attachment to the mother is so strong the child has trouble distinguishing itself from mother. The process of consolidating a sense of being a separate person is assisted greatly by the emergence of language.

The next period of ego development is the *Impulsive* stage. Loevinger says that children of this stage purposely release impulses as a way of affirming their existence. In effect, the ego is acting in an unrestrained way to have an impact on the world. (This seems similar to exercising what White called effectance motivation.) This is a time when phrases such as "*I* do" and "by *myself*" emerge often (and often loudly) from the child. The child is oriented to the present, with little consideration of the future or broader implications of behavior. Although children's need for other people is high (they can't do everything for themselves), their relationships are exploitative: Others are valued only for what they can give the child.

It's of some interest that the behaviors that mark this period are those that a traditional psychoanalytic view would see as caused by the id. Behavior is impulsive and demanding, and the child doesn't *relate* to other people so much as *use* them. Yet Loevinger argues that these actions reflect not an id but a not-very-well developed ego struggling to assert itself. These quite different views of the same qualities of behavior illustrate a way in which the ego psychologists' perspective differs from the psychoanalytic perspective.

TABLE 10.2

Summary of Loevinger's portrayal of the stages of ego development (adapted from Loevinger, 1987).

Stage name	Behavioral manifestations
Symbiotic	Working to acquire sense of separation between self, nonself
Impulsive	Assertion of self through impulse expression; relationships with others are exploitive, for own needs
Self-protective	Begins to grasp rules, but only as guides to avoid punishment; no moral sense; personal expediency, opportunism
Conformist	Rules adopted because they are accepted by group; concerned with appearing properly to the social group
Self-aware	Realization that rules have exceptions; increased introspection, with increased awareness that own behavior isn't perfect
Conscientious	Use of self-evaluated standards rather than group's norm; realization that events have multiple meanings
Individualistic	Clearer sense of individuality; greater tolerance for individual differences
Autonomous	Realization of interdependency among people; awareness of conflicts among one's own needs; recognition of others' need for autonomy
Integrated	Conflicting demands have been resolved; not just tolerance, but intense appreciation of others' viewpoints

Middle Stages of Ego Development: Control of Impulses

The intentional releasing of impulses eventually gives way to a more restrained way of relating to the world. The *Self-protective* stage marks the first step toward self-control of impulses. During this stage children start to grasp the idea that there are rules about how to act, and that breaking the rules leads to punishment. Children still lack full appreciation of the meaning of rules, however. At this stage, rules simply provide information about how the world works—what you have to do to avoid punishment. As Loevinger (1976) put it, the main rule is "Don't get caught." The child's only morality at this stage is personal expediency.

The self-protective quality of this stage is reflected in the fact that children use the rules they've learned mostly for their own advantage. Behavior thus remains somewhat exploitive. On the other hand, Loevinger (1987) says this sort of behavior isn't a calculated opportunism, but just an open expression of self-interest and desire for gratification. In Loevinger's view, the clearest indicator of the self-protective mode of ego functioning isn't exploitiveness, but the absence of long-term goals and purposes.

Once again it seems useful to point to the relation between this theory and Freud's theory. It's in this stage that the two models bear the greatest resemblance in their views of the ego. Recall that to Freud the ego is amoral; it acts to satisfy the desires of the id as expeditiously as possible, without regard to right or wrong. The behavioral result looks much like what Loevinger is describing at the self-protective stage. Yet once again, there's a difference. Loevinger doesn't see this as reflecting a new structure in personality. Rather, it reflects a change in how the ego synthesizes and integrates experience in its efforts to adapt to the world.

The child attains the next stage of ego development, called the *Conformist* stage, by starting to link his or her own welfare and security to that of a social group (family or peers). This is when rules first start to be truly internalized. Doing this requires developing a sense of trust in the social group. Rules no longer are ways to avoid punishment. They're used because they reflect social consensus about how to act. Conformists obey the rules precisely because the group has adopted the rules. Little distinction is made between rules that are important and social norms that aren't. Rules are rules, at this stage. Consistent with the idea that the power of rules derives from their social basis, the punishments that are most effective during this stage involve social disapproval ("You let us down," or "We don't like what you did").

At this stage the ego is preoccupied with issues of reputation and social appearance, but the appearances are one-dimensional. Life is viewed in terms of stereotypes and cliches. People at the conformist level often appear highly conventional, but looking conventional isn't a good indicator of being at the conformist level. Indeed, conformists may give a surface appearance of being radically different from "most" people. At the same time, though, they're conforming quite closely to the norms of their own social group.

The next stage Loevinger identified was first thought of as a transitional one (Loevinger, 1976). It is now seen as a more stable stage (Loevinger, 1987), at least partly because it appears to be the most common level of ego development in the population of Americans between ages 16 and 26 (Holt, 1980). This stage is now termed the *Self-aware* level. Its name reflects the fact that the person in this stage is seeing for the first time multiple possibilities for the self.

Loevinger addresses this stage by asking what pressures might move a person beyond conformity. She suggests that this happens when people come to feel they don't quite fit the perfect-person stereotype held out to them by conformist thinking. Arriving at such a feeling seems to depend on developing a greater capacity for (or tendency toward) introspection. In line with this, Loevinger says that during this stage the person begins to differentiate "what I am" from "what I ought to be." People at this level realize that rules of conduct often have qualifications or exceptions. You can do this "if you're old enough." You can't do this "until you're married." Despite a richer inner life, however, people at this stage are still basically conformists in their behavior.

One more cognitive change seems to be needed for movement into the *Conscientious* stage: an awareness of the fact that events and situations have multiple meanings. This change makes it possible to understand and assimilate abstract moral imperatives. Abstract rules eventually seem more important than group-consensus rules. Because of the weakened influence of consensus, morality now is truly internalized. During this stage, guilt (a sense of having failed *oneself*) rather than shame (a sense of having looked bad to the group) keeps people from breaking moral codes. Loevinger (1987) says that the distinctive mark of having attained this stage is self-evaluated standards. That is, you approve or disapprove of your conduct because of what you personally feel, not because of the wishes of some social group.

The life of the person at the conscientious stage is richer and more complex than was possible at earlier stages. Instead of seeing other people as just good or bad, you see them as complicated, with good and bad qualities. Achievement is valued for its own sake rather than as a way to gain advantage over someone else (which would characterize the self-protective stage) or as a way to gain social recognition (which would characterize the conformist stage). Consistent with this, there's evidence that women who reach the conscientious stage by middle age also increase in the personality qualities of *achievement via independence* and *tolerance* during that period (Helson & Roberts, 1994).

Advanced Stages of Development: Taking More into Account

A transitional level comes between the Conscientious stage and the next full stage of development. This transition is called the *Individualistic* level of ego development. The person at this level has a heightened sense of individuality and of style of life. There is an emerging tolerance for differences among people with respect to these matters. People at the Individualistic level also have a greater appreciation of the fact that the same person is different when in different roles (e.g., wife, mother, daughter, lover, career woman, tennis partner).

These themes are elaborated even more fully as the person moves into the *Autonomous stage* of development. At this stage the ego is preoccupied with the interdependency among people and the search for self-fulfillment (as opposed to achievement). The person has the capacity to recognize and cope with conflicts among differing needs, differing duties, and combinations of needs and duties. For example, you may need to study all evening for an exam tomorrow, but you also have the duty to "be there" for your friend who's taking the recent death of her father very badly. At the Individualist stage, you'd view this conflict as being between your own need and an unyielding environment. In the Autonomous stage, you accept the fact that many such conflicts occur intrinsically, even among your own wishes and needs.

The term *autonomous* can be a confusing label for this stage, because the key isn't a desire for self-autonomy. It's an awareness of *others'* need for autonomy. Along with the ability to deal effectively with your own turmoil comes a greater tolerance for how others deal with their own conflicts. A mother who truly recognizes her children's need to learn from their own mistakes—and therefore lets them make mistakes without stopping them—is displaying this quality. Loevinger believes that full attainment of this level of ego development (i.e., the ability to use this mode of relating to the world in all of one's interactions) is relatively rare.

The final stage of ego development, which is even more rare (1% of the population), is called *Integrated*. Entry into this stage means the person has come to grips with internal conflict and has found a way to satisfy conflicting demands. If necessary, goals that are unattainable or unrealistic are abandoned. In the Integrated stage, tolerance for the others' viewpoints goes beyond mere tolerance to become an intense appreciation of those viewpoints. A conscious attempt is made in this stage to weave the threads of previous stages into an integrated whole.

In summary, Loevinger holds that as the ego passes through these stages of evolution, it acquires greater complexity in its functioning and in its ability to relate and adapt to the world around it. In developing her theory, Loevinger also argued that the ego plays the major role in acquiring moral character, impulse control, and internalization of rules of conduct. The ego gradually develops these capabilities over time and experience.

It seems useful at this point to make one last comparison between Loevinger's theory and Freud's. In Loevinger's theory, many of the qualities that the ego manifests in later stages of development resemble the functions of the superego in Freud's theory. Recall that Loevinger attributes even the *lack* of impulse control at an early age to the ego rather than to the id. From theories such as Loevinger's, it's clear that ego psychologists elevated the status of the ego in part by ascribing to it functions that Freud had assigned to the id or superego.

Research on Ego Development

Loevinger's analysis of ego development has been studied empirically, but the research is hard to conduct. One reason is that her model doesn't predict many clear relationships between ego development and overt behavior (Hauser, 1976). Its predictions have more to do with the mental dynamics that underlie a given behavior. Consequently, much of the research on this theory has been descriptive.

It's known, for example, that older adolescents score higher on a measure of ego development than younger adolescents, and adults score higher than adolescents (Avery & Ryan, 1988). This fits with the idea that the characteristics have a developmental progression. Girls seem to develop faster during middle and late childhood, though boys catch up by adulthood (Cohn, 1991). Ego development also relates to development of moral-reasoning capabilities (Lee & Snarey, 1988). This finding establishes convergent validity for both concepts, because there are certain logical similarities between changes in moral reasoning and changes in how the ego deals with reality. In a similar way, ego development has been found to be related to increasing maturity in thinking about interpersonal intimacy (White, Houlihan, Costos, & Speisman, 1990).

Another study obtained evidence on other psychological qualities that should be tied to variations in ego development. Rozsnafszky (1981) studied hospitalized veterans, collecting both self-ratings and observer ratings (made by nurses and therapists) of the participants' traits. These ratings then were related to participants' levels of ego development (Table 10.3). Those at the impulsive or self-protective level showed poor socialization and limited self-awareness. Those at the conformist and self-aware levels were seen as placing great values on rules, possessions, physical appearance, and social conventions. Those at higher levels displayed a pattern of greater insight into their own personality and motives. All of these findings are just as would be expected theoretically.

TABLE 10.3

Observer-rating items that were found to distinguish among three groups of male subjects. People of one group were at the impulsive or self-protective level of ego development, those of the second group were at the conformist or self-aware level, those of the third group were at higher levels (adapted from Rozsnafszky, 1981).

Impulsive / Self-protective

Exploitive; sees people as sources of supply; "good" seems to mean "good for me"

Sees what he can get away with; follows rules only to avoid punishment

Is self-defensive, manipulative, opportunistic

Impulsive; when he doesn't get what he wants, he may be self-destructive in an impulsive way

Self-aware

Tends to feel guilty if he has not done his duty

Behaves in a sympathetic, considerate, and helpful manner

Is concerned with the impression he makes on others; self-aware

Compares self to others; wants to be like others, i.e., "normal"

More advanced stages

Has insight into own motives and behavior

Behaves in an ethically consistent manner; is consistent with own behavior

Is comfortable with uncertainty and complexities; resists seeing the world as black and white

Values his own and others' individuality and uniqueness

Although studies of the behavioral reflections of ego development are somewhat rare, they aren't entirely lacking. There's evidence, for example, that social conformity is greatest among people who are at the conformist and self-aware stage of development and falls off among people whose development attains higher stages (Hoppe, 1972; Westenberg & Block, 1993). Research on peer judgments of women's maturity has also found that higher ego development was associated with higher ratings of maturity of functioning in careers and community involvement (Adams & Shea, 1979). Finally, there's evidence that adolescent inner-city delinquents have lower levels of ego development than nondelinquents (Frank & Quinlan, 1976).

Other research has examined variables that may influence advancement through the stages. It's been found that such progress is tied to having a clearer sense of identity (Adams & Shea, 1979) and to psychological mindedness (Helson & Roberts, 1994; Westenberg & Block, 1993). Another finding was that life challenge (in the form of having successful careers) predicted progression to higher levels of ego development in adult women (Helson & Roberts, 1994). Indeed, even the successful management of marital separation and divorce apparently can promote ego development (Bursik, 1991). It's also of interest that ego-resiliency (flexibility in degree of ego-control), which we discussed earlier in the chapter, is related to attaining higher ego development (Westenberg & Block, 1993).

Assessment

Throughout this chapter we've pointed to ways in which ego psychology differs from Freudian psychoanalysis. It's also informative to consider this question with respect to assessment. Assessment in ego psychology has two characteristics that make it different from assessment in psychoanalysis. The first is a difference in content. Specifically, ego psychologists aren't interested as much in unconscious conflict as they are in the ego. As a result, the assessment techniques they developed focus on assessing qualities of the ego.

A second difference (which goes hand in hand with the first) is a difference in technique. Given the theoretical de-emphasis in the role of the unconscious, it didn't seem so important to try to free information from the unconscious by projective techniques. Thus ego psychology shifted away from reliance on projective tests. Some ego psychologists moved all the way to objective self-report instruments, although most blend projective and objective methods.

One similarity does remain, however. Ego psychologists are willing (as was Freud) to draw on a wide range of formal and informal sources to obtain clues about personality. The next two sections describe two ways in which ego psychologists have approached assessment.

Assessment of Lifestyles

The first assessment technique to be considered is a highly informal one. Recall Adler's belief that people develop individualized lifestyles. Your lifestyle leads you to be especially attentive to certain kinds of inferiorities and to try to deal with them in a characteristic way. A reasonable question is how to identify a person's lifestyle.

Adler believed a person's lifestyle can be identified by asking the person about his or her earliest memories from childhood or infancy. In Adler's view, the nature of these memories gives a clue to the themes that are playing themselves out in the person's life. This idea has been borne out in research (Bruhn & Schiffman, 1982).

Many psychologists believe that birth order plays a significant role in the development of personality.

This research found that people who see themselves as having control over events in their lives reported early memories involving mastery over the environment. People who see themselves as having little control tended to recall experiences in which they were passive and events were beyond their control.

Interestingly enough, Adler didn't think it especially important whether the memories are accurate or not. What's important is how you view the experiences you recall. It's *how the person looks at the event* that gives insight into the person's concerns, the nature of the feelings of inferiority, and the domains in which the person is striving for superiority. Adler felt, in fact, that your memories are likely to be distorted by your lifestyle (cf. Ross, 1989). For example, if your lifestyle is organized around the idea that other people don't give you enough credit, then your memories—whether of recent or early events—will tend to reflect that theme. Although any memories can be revealing, Adler felt that a person's earliest memories reveal the most, because they reflect the person's fundamental view of life. "It offers us an opportunity to see at one glance what he has taken as the starting point for his development" (Adler, 1956, p. 351).

Adler collected interesting illustrations of the relationship between memories and lifestyle. An example is the case of a man whose life was filled with anxiety and jealousy over the possibility that others would be preferred to him. His earliest memory was of being held by his mother and then being put on the ground so she that could pick up his younger brother. Adler's own first memories were of illness and death, consistent with the fact that his lifestyle oriented around pursuit of a career in medicine (see also Box 10.4). Indeed, Adler found that among a group of medical doctors, memories of serious illness or a death in the family were frequently reported as first memories.

Assessment of Level of Ego Development

Another aspect of ego functioning that's important to assess is level of ego development. Loevinger's analysis of the stages of ego development has been used to create

BOX 10.4

THE THEORIST AND THE THEORY:
Adler's Lifestyle and the Ideas to Which It Led

The work of Alfred Adler provides an excellent illustration of how the elements of a theory often stem from the life experiences of the theorist (for a recent biography of Adler's career see Hoffman, 1994). Several themes that Adler contributed to ego psychology drew directly from his own life, something of which Adler himself was very well aware (Bottome, 1939). Let's consider a couple of these themes.

Perhaps the easiest point to make pertains to what we've just said in the main text concerning early memories. Adler's lifestyle, including his theory, was organized partly around his interest in medicine and the body, and his earliest memories were of illness. Adler's lifestyle also reflected personal anxiety and fear of inferiority—and for good reason. As was noted earlier, he was seriously ill as a child, and his parents were once told it was futile to try to educate him, yet he struggled against these obstacles.

This aspect of his lifestyle is deeply symbolized in another of his early memories. He recalled being about 5 years old and being frightened over the fact that the path to school led through a cemetery (Adler, 1927). The other children weren't afraid, which only exaggerated his feelings of inferiority. One day, in an effort to rid himself of his fear, he ran back and forth through the cemetery, over and over. From then on he was able to walk through it on his way to school without difficulty.

This memory neatly captures Adler's lifelong tendency to combat his fears by deliberately forcing himself to stand up to them. There's something else, though, that makes this example even more interesting. Many years later Adler met a former schoolmate and asked him something about the cemetery. The man was bewildered by the question, replying that there hadn't *been* a cemetery. After seeking out other former schoolmates and getting the same reply, Adler finally realized that his memory was wrong. This experience doubtlessly played a role in his view that it doesn't matter whether memories are accurate or not—they're still revealing.

As another illustration of how personal experience influenced Adler's views, consider his analysis of birth order (described earlier in Box 10.3). Adler saw the second-born as someone with a constant sense of inferiority by virtue of being developmentally behind the firstborn, who had greater capabilities right up until adulthood. This can work in the second-born's favor, because it serves as a constant spur to strivings. But if can also lead to lifelong competitiveness and jealousy. It's of considerable interest, in this regard, that Adler himself was second-born (1870) and throughout his life felt overshadowed by his older brother, a wealthy businessman (whose name, ironically, was Sigmund). It seems likely that this personal experience led Adler to argue more generally for the impact of birth order on personality.

Finally, and most generally, recall how Adler's theory focuses on how people experience repeated feelings of inferiority and engage in compensatory strivings for superiority, this pervasive theme reflects virtually all of the experiences of Adler's life. His feelings of inferiority in several domains—physical and psychological—led to a great upward drive in his own behavior. This experience, in turn, helped lead Adler to believe that these same processes characterize everyone.

a systematic measure called the Sentence Completion Test for Ego Development (Loevinger & Wessler, 1970), for which a revised scoring manual has recently been published (Hy & Loevinger, 1996). It consists of a series of partial sentences to which the person writes an ending. Thus its format is projective.

TABLE 10.4

Examples of responses to a sentence-completion item and the stage that they reflect. The item stem, "The thing I like about myself is—," is from the Washington University Sentence Completion Test (adapted from Hy & Loevinger, 1996).

Stage name	Response	Theme
Presocial	[not assessed]	
Symbiotic	[not assessed]	
Impulsive	. . . that I'm nice	Self-gratification
Self-protective	. . . that people like me	Exploitiveness
	. . . my grade in math	
Conformist	. . . that I'm athletic	Stereotypic thinking
	. . . that I don't hate other people	
Self-aware	. . . I'm very considerate of others	Modified stereotype
	. . . that I'm a straightforward person	
Conscientious	. . . that I can forgive and maintain caring feelings	Events in social context
	. . . my ability to look for the good in most things	
Individualistic	. . . that I'm different, but that's OK—I don't want to be like everyone else	Multiple viewpoints
	. . . that I'm really aware of others and how they relate to me	
Autonomous	. . . my personality, my constant striving to become more competent, and yet my ability to be patient	Recognition of mutual autonomy needs
	. . . my outlook on life, the fact that I can take people for who they are, and that I can stand by them while they deal with their problems	
Integrated	. . . the fact that I try to be honest with myself, even though I'm aware that that perception may be delusional	Fully integrated
	. . . that I can think independently and creatively, that I don't judge people I meet, and that I can still be a child when I feel like it	

Each response is classified as reflecting one of the stages in Loevinger's model, from the impulsive stage onward (the primitive earlier stages can't be measured with this instrument). Examples of responses reflecting various stages are in Table 10.4. The codings given to each response are entered into a formula, yielding an index of the person's overall ego development. Scorers who've been trained carefully show high inter-judge reliability, and there's evidence of high internal consistency and test-retest reliability as well (Redmore & Waldman, 1975). This test was used to assess stage of ego development in the research done on Loevinger's theory discussed earlier in the chapter.

Problems in Behavior, and Behavior Change

Different ego psychologists emphasized different aspects of the ego's functioning, but one theme runs through all the principles considered in this chapter: the ego's ability to adapt itself to and interact successfully with the surrounding world. Accordingly, problems in behavior are seen by most ego psychologists as reflecting deficiencies in this adaptation.

Ego psychologists view the process of adaptation as never ending. In a sense, then, problems are part of life. People struggle to make themselves better, and difficulties faced in that struggle are inherent in life. Problems become serious only if adaptational deficiencies are extreme. Thus well-being is judged not by whether you confront difficulties, but by how well you cope.

Inferiority and Superiority Complexes

Adler exemplifies this view. Recall his belief that inferiority feelings and superiority strivings cycle with each other throughout life. The result usually is that people continue trying to get more proficient at what they do. The issue of inferiority is confronted on a repeated basis. Problems arise only if feelings of inferiority are so strong that they're overwhelming, creating a barrier to striving. When feelings of inferiority are that strong, the person is said to have an **inferiority complex.**

Adler believed that inferiority complexes have two main sources. One of them is neglect (or rejection) during development. Being neglected may cause the person to feel unworthy and inferior in ways that are too large to overcome. This person may develop a mistaken lifestyle involving dependency or avoidance. Another source is pampering or spoiling during childhood. As was indicated earlier (Box 10.3), spoiling can undermine the child's desire to strive for superiority, again leading to a mistaken lifestyle.

Sometimes an inferiority complex leads to passiveness or avoidance, but sometimes it has different consequences. Strong feelings of inferiority can lead a person to *over*compensate, striving for superiority in inappropriate ways or to an exaggerated degree. An example of inappropriate striving is a lifestyle that involves efforts to dominate others. Sometimes the person's lifestyle involves a driven way of acting, in which the person has to excel at all costs. These exaggerated strivings are sometimes referred to by the term **superiority complex.**

Adler also believed that people with problems tend to use certain strategies to protect whatever small sense of superiority they're able to hold onto. These strategies, similar in some respects to the defense mechanisms discussed in Chapter 9, have the goal of diminishing at least temporarily the sense of inferiority. One such strategy is to blame others for your shortcomings or failures. A person using this strategy may spend all his or her time seeking revenge instead of making up the failure.

Another strategy is to deprecate the accomplishments or personal qualities of other people, thereby suggesting that your own qualities are better than they are. This strategy is most readily applied when others are implicit competitors with you, but it can also apply elsewhere. For example, adopting very high standards for a mate (you wouldn't consider someone who's not good looking, intelligent, a successful professional, and rich) may mean you're just trying to ease your own sense of inferiority. If no one out there is good enough for you, you must be *really* good.

Behavior Change

The process of therapeutic behavioral change from the viewpoint of ego psychology reflects the overall concerns of this line of thought. Therapies practiced by ego psychologists place greater emphasis than did Freud on current problems, as opposed to factors in the past that might have led to the problems. The emphasis on current problems fits with a point about assessment in ego psychology. Ego psychologists are more likely than Freudian psychologists to take the person's behavior at face value and not "overinterpret" it.

The therapist who operates from this viewpoint is more supportive than one who operates from the psychoanalytic viewpoint. On the other hand, the therapist is also clear about where the source of behavior change must lie. That is, behavioral problems are viewed as something patients have created in their own lives. The patient thus must take responsibility for dealing with the problems. This tendency to be direct with the patient is another way in which the two therapeutic approaches differ.

One consequence of this shift in emphasis is to draw the patient into the therapeutic process as a collaborator. This increased emphasis on patient involvement can be viewed as evolving directly from the core idea of ego psychology. That is, the major task of the ego is to promote adaptation to the world. If behavioral problems arise, it's because the ego isn't doing its job. For the ego to alter what it's doing, the patient must become involved.

Ego Psychology: Problems and Prospects

The group of neoanalysts who came to be known as ego psychologists includes a large number of people, who proposed a fairly diverse set of ideas. In all cases, however, the ideas reflect the theme that the ego is the most important aspect of personality. This theme is one of two that stand at the forefront of neoanalytic thinking.

Although ego psychology has had its adherents, it's fair to stand back and ask some questions about it. One reasonable question is whether these ideas really have anything to do with the psychoanalytic theory from which they evolved. Are these neoanalytic ideas really "analytic" at all? Or, despite the absorption with psychoanalytic traditions, do they actually have more in common with concepts from other parts of psychology?

Keep in mind the angle from which the neoanalysts proceeded. Most of them wanted to develop their own ideas, but at the same time they wanted not to stray too far from Freud. After all, these people were *analysts*. That was their professional identity, to themselves and to one another. As analysts, they thought of their ideas as amendments to Freud's theory rather than as separate and distinct theories.

All this orienting toward Freud, however, produced what was in some respects a very narrow view. As a result, the ideas can seem more revolutionary (to analysts) than they are. For example, it's widely believed that Freud created the concept of ego. Ego psychologists certainly saw themselves as building on a Freudian idea. But according to Loevinger (1976), Freud's theory was itself partly a reaction against an *already existing nineteenth-century ego psychology*. She also notes that her own theory of ego development was strongly foreshadowed in the writings of people who predated Freud (e.g., Bain, 1859; Mill, 1962/1859; Smith, 1969/1759).

Another comparison is also instructive. Aspects of ego psychology resemble ideas from a group of theorists (discussed later in the book) called humanistic. Though the latter group had a starting point very different from that of the neoanalysts, many humanistic themes resemble themes of ego psychology. Despite this, analytically oriented people tend to ignore humanists. Again, the analytically oriented have tended to view their ideas in relation to Freud's theory, rather than in relation to the broader spectrum of ideas in personality psychology.

It's easy to understand why the writings of the ego psychologists disregard nineteenth-century ideas. *Most* psychologists don't know much about nineteenth-century ideas. The failure to note other literatures may say something about the history of ego psychology. Psychoanalysis in the United States has a long medical tradition. Nearly all psychoanalysts begin their training with an MD degree and then do a psychoanalytic specialization. This also was true for early ego psychologists (Adler and Hartmann, for example, were MDs). There's a natural tendency to use ideas that are discussed within one's professional circle and to disregard ideas from outside. Since analytically oriented theorists were mostly medical people, it was the ideas of medical people that they took seriously.

To some extent, ego psychology began in relative isolation from the rest of psychology. It was a branch of psychoanalysis that was growing in the direction of psychology. This has changed over the years, as psychologists became more prominent in this group. Theorists such as the Blocks and Jane Loevinger have helped pull ego psychology toward academic personality psychology. This shift has served to integrate neoanalytic ideas more into the mainstream of academic thought. This integration has also yielded an increase in the tolerance and regard that many academic psychologists have had for psychodynamic conceptualizations.

The evolution of ego psychology appears, however, to carry with it the seeds of a more complete break with traditional psychoanalytic theory. What's unique about psychoanalysis is its emphasis on the dynamics of the unconscious and on the importance of powerful primitive impulses. In large part, ego psychologists have abandoned this conceptual heritage. Although the theories are still called psychodynamic, the dynamics that remain are very, very different from those that Freud asserted. In moving toward greater harmony with the rest of psychology, ego psychology is at the same time leaving Freud behind.

What are the prospects, then, for this view on human behavior? Some of the ideas of this group have already acquired a permanent place in personality psychology—for example, White's ideas about effectance and competence. We are also confident that Loevinger's theory and that of the Blocks will continue to stand as influential views of human development and behavior. If these two theories in particular continue to inspire active research activities as they do now, ego psychology will continue to remain an essential part of personality psychology.

SUMMARY

Neoanalytic theorists differed from Freud on several points. Many shared a feeling that Freud hadn't given enough emphasis to the ego and its functions. Accordingly, they devised ideas in which the ego plays a more central role. For this reason, they are commonly termed ego psychologists.

Hartmann argued that the ego can function to facilitate the id's impulses but can also function autonomously in the service of better adaptation to the environment. He believed that the ego has a separate existence at birth (primary ego autonomy) and that ego functions often continue long after their initial purposes are served (secondary ego autonomy). Others, such as White, emphasized that the ego strives for competence and mastery over the environment. The motive to become more competent serves the goal of better adaptation.

Adler also proposed that people strive for better adaptations, but he assumed a different underlying reason. Adler argued that people repeatedly experience feelings of inferiority in one or another aspect of life and that they respond to those feelings with a compensatory striving for superiority, that is, movement toward greater perfection. Adler used the term *lifestyle* to refer to the person's characteristic constellation of inferiority feelings and preferred way of dealing with them. Some lifestyles are effective, but others (called mistaken lifestyles) are not.

Block and Block examined the effects of two other kinds of individual differences: differences in ego-control (impulse control) and ego-resiliency (flexibility in ego-control). Too much ego-control is bad, as is too little. Ego-resiliency fosters better adaptation. Both qualities relate to behaviors that reflect restraint or impulsiveness, and ego-resilience relates to better social development.

Loevinger has examined how the ego's abilities grow and become more complex through a series of stages that extend into adulthood. In early stages the ego is focused on differentiating itself from others and on affirming its separate existence through expression of impulses. Later, the person begins to learn rules of conduct and to follow them to avoid group censure. Still later, the person begins to appreciate the diversity of viewpoints on existence and experience. People develop through these stages until they exhaust their ability to move further; not everyone goes through all stages.

Assessment from the point of view of ego psychology represents a shift away from projective techniques toward more objective techniques. The content of assessment focuses on the ego and the level at which it's functioning. From the viewpoint of ego psychology, problems in behavior always are a matter of degree, because no one is perfectly adapted to the world. Struggle is an intrinsic part of life, but serious feelings of inferiority can produce an inferiority complex (a paralyzing inability to strive) or a superiority complex (overcompensatory strivings), either of which is disruptive.

The approach that ego psychologists take to therapy is similar in some ways to the psychoanalytic approach, but it also differs in important ways. For one, it focuses on the here-and-now problems that the person has, rather than on buried fixations. There is much less of an attempt to probe for deep meanings and a stronger tendency to accept statements at face value. The person seeking treatment is also brought more into the treatment process, as a collaborator in the attempt to produce behavior change.

GLOSSARY

Archetypes Aspects of the world that people have an inherited tendency to notice or perceive.

Collective unconscious Memories everyone has from human and even prehuman ancestors.

Competence motivation The motive to be effective or adept in dealing with the environment.

Effectance motivation The need to have an impact on the environment.

Ego-control The extent to which a person modifies or inhibits impulse expression.

Ego psychology The neoanalytic theories that give ego functions central importance.

Ego-resiliency The capacity to modify one's usual level of ego-control to adapt to new situations.

Feelings of inferiority The realization that one is deficient in some way, minor or major.

Functional autonomy The continuance of an act even after its initial purpose no longer exists.

Inferiority complex Feelings of inferiority bad enough to suggest an inability to solve life's problems.

Lifestyle A person's pattern of inferiority feelings and manner of striving for superiority.

Mistaken lifestyle A lifestyle that isn't effective in adapting or attaining superiority.

Need for cognition A need to think about and impose meaningful structure on experiences.

Organ inferiority A weakness in an area of the body, making one vulnerable to illness there.

Primary ego autonomy The idea that the ego exists independently from the id from birth onward.

Principle of opposites The idea that life consists of polarities that oppose and balance each other.

Secondary ego autonomy The idea that an ego function can become satisfying in its own right.

Superiority complex Exaggerated strivings to excel to compensate for deep inferiority feelings.

chapter

11

Psychosocial Theories

■ Ever since she was in high school, Elizabeth has had a particular pattern in her love relationships with men. She tends to be close and clingy as the relationship is first being established—wanting almost to be joined to the man. Later on, an ambivalent quality emerges in her actions. She wants closeness, but at the same time she does things that drive her lover away—she gets upset with him, gets into arguments over nothing, and isn't satisfied by anything he does to calm her down. As he gets more and more irritated by this, and as their relationship becomes more and more strained, Elizabeth makes her final move—she breaks up. Even afterward there's ambivalence. Sometimes in thinking back she reflects that some former lover was too good for her. Sometimes, though, she thinks of them as no good at all. None of this makes her feel optimistic about the future of her personal life. "Why can't I ever seem to find the right kind of man?" she cries.

As the ego became more prominent in neoanalytic theories and as the functions of the ego were examined in more detail, another change was also taking place. There was an increasing emphasis on the idea that personality is inherently social. Theorists began to stress that many of the issues in personality concern one's relationships with other people.

This emphasis represents a substantial change of direction. As described in Chapters 8 and 9, Freud focused on the inner workings of personality. In his view, when conflict occurs it comes from within. People deal with external reality only to satisfy impulses more effectively. Even many ego psychologists tended to share this focus on internal processes, being more interested in how the ego works than in the interplay between it and the outside world.

This isn't true of all theories of ego psychology. For example, Adler (1930), who so strongly emphasized striving for superiority, also emphasized the importance of caring and concern for other people. He used the phrase **social interest** to refer to the need to live in harmony with others. Adler felt that social interest is important to being a complete person. He believed that everyone is born with this potential but that the potential must be nurtured.

Adler's ideas about the social nature of personality were relatively simple. Ideas that other theorists put forward on this theme, however, were more complex. Those ideas form the basis of this chapter.

Object Relations Theories

We begin with a group of theories that have diverse origins and terminologies but are also strikingly similar to one another. This group of theories is referred to by the phrase **object relations** (for overviews see J. Klein, 1987; Masling & Bornstein, 1994; St. Clair, 1986). In the term *object relations* the "object" is another *person*. Thus these theories focus on the individual's relations to other people.

The concept of object relations traces to an idea from Freud, but the idea was greatly transformed (Eagle, 1984). Freud saw an ego cathexis as the creation of a psychic bond from the ego to an external "object." The cathexis forms to release id energies effectively. Object relations theories focus on such bonds, but only for people as objects. Furthermore, the point isn't to enable the expression of id instincts, in this view. Instead, the bond to the other person is a *fundamental ego function*. It's the main focus for personality. As in other neoanalytic theories, the emphasis here is on the ego rather than id (e.g., Fairbairn, 1954).

Object relations theories were developed by several people in the neoanalytic movement, and they differ from one another in many ways (St. Clair, 1986; J. Klein, 1987). They share two broad themes, however. First, they all emphasize that a person's pattern of relating to others is laid down in the interactions of early childhood. Second, they all assume that patterns formed at that time tend to recur over and over again throughout later life.

One influential object relations theory is that of Margaret Mahler (1968; Mahler, Pine, & Bergman, 1975; see also Blanck & Blanck, 1986). She believed that newborns begin life in a state of psychological fusion with others. In her view personality development is a process of breaking down this fusion, of becoming an individual who's separate and distinct from others.

The period in which the infant is fused with its mother is called **symbiosis** (the same term as Loevinger used for early life). Boundaries between mother and self haven't been built yet (e.g., the infant doesn't distinguish well between its mother's nipple and its own thumb). Around 6 months of age, a shift away from this fusion begins. The child now starts the process of acquiring an awareness of its distinct existence, a process Mahler termed **separation-individuation.**

The process of individuation involves exploration away from mother, but the exploration must be done gradually. Remember that unity with the mother is all the infant has ever known. If the movement away from fusion comes too fast or goes too far, the child will experience *separation anxiety.* This renews the desire to be with and be loved by the mother. Thus there's a back-and-forth quality to the child's behavior—first moving away, then drawing close again.

It's important to recognize the built-in conflict here between two pressures in the child. The first is a wish to be taken care of by, and reunited with, the love object (mother). The second is a fear of being engulfed in a merger with the love object, and a desire to establish one's own selfhood. Thus, the child strives for individuation and separation but at the same time wants to return to the former sense of union. This conflict is important in adult behavior as well.

How the mother acts during this period determines the child's later adjustment. The mother should combine emotional availability with a gentle nudge toward independence. If the mother is ever present in the child's experience, the child can't establish a separate existence. If there's too much push toward individuation, the child will experience a sense of rejection and loss.

Eventually (at about age 3), the child develops a stable mental representation of the mother (incorporating feelings associated with her). Now the mother will be with the child all the time, symbolically. The "object relation" has been internalized. In the future the child will use the internalization in two ways. First, the image will be used as a lens through which the child will view mother in the future. Second, and perhaps even more important, this internal image will be generalized to other people. In many respects the child will act toward other people as though they were its mother and father.

Often the early years include some problems or stresses—for example, feeling either a sense of rejection from a parent or too much smothering fusion. If so, those problems are carried via your internal object representations onward into your later life. Indeed, because this internalization derives from infants' subjective experiences, there's a lot of potential for distortion. Object representations don't always accurately reflect the experiences of childhood. What matters, though, isn't what *happens* in childhood, but what the child *experiences* as happening.

You may not be very persuaded by the idea that you relate to others as though they were your mother and father. You think you treat everyone uniquely. An object relations theorist would reply that you think that because you're looking at yourself from *inside* your patterns. Being inside them, you don't notice them. You notice only variations within the framework of the patterns. You think the variations are big, but in some ways they're really minor.

In this view, the pattern of relating to others that you develop in early childhood forms the core of your way of relating to others for the rest of your life. Indeed, this pattern forms the very core of your personality. As such, you take it for granted as much as any other aspect of your personality. It's the lens through which you view not just your parents but the entire world.

Self Psychology

A neoanalyst who's often discussed in conjunction with object relations theorists is Heinz Kohut. Kohut was interested in the idea that relationships create the structure of the self. Partly for this reason his theory is identified with the label *self psychology* (e.g., A. Goldberg, 1985). Despite this different label, his theory focuses on the qualities of experience that others termed object relations.

Kohut based much of his thinking on the idea that people have narcissistic (self-centered) needs that have to be satisfied through others. He used the term **selfobject** to refer to someone who's important in satisfying your needs. In early childhood, self-objects (parents) are experienced literally as extensions of the self. Later on the term *selfobject* simply means any person *as he or she is experienced within the structure of the self.* Selfobjects still serve the self, since they exist from the self's point of view and to serve the self's needs.

According to Kohut, the child acquires a self through interaction with parents. Parents serve the important function of **mirroring:** responding to the child in a positive, empathic, and accepting way. Mirroring gratifies the child's narcissistic needs, because it makes the child temporarily the center of the universe. The child's developing sense of self is at first grandiose. This illusion of all-importance must be sustained to a degree throughout development, to create a continuing sense of self-importance to be carried into adulthood. It also must be tempered, though, so the child can deal with difficulties and frustrations later in life.

In a healthy personality the grandiosity is modified and channeled into realistic activities, turning into a sense of ambition and self-esteem. If there are severe failures of mirroring, though, the child never develops an adequate sense of self. This child will grow up with deeper narcissistic needs than other people (because the needs have been unmet). As a result, he or she will continue to relate to selfobjects (other people) immaturely (i.e., not distinguishing them from the self). A delicate balance is required here: The parents must give the child enough mirroring to nurture development, but not too much. This is similar to the balance between forces noted earlier in Mahler's theory regarding separation-individuation and fusion with the other.

Mirroring continues to be important in human relationships throughout life (see Tesser, 1991). After childhood, mirroring involves **transferences** from parents to other selfobjects. The use of the term *transference* here means that the orientation you've developed to your parents is now used as a frame of reference for symbolizing others. In effect, other people become substitutes for your parents and you expect them to mirror you just as your parents did. This is similar to Mahler's idea that the internal object relation regarding a parent is used in the formation of later relationships.

Kohut's conception of love provides an illustration of adult mirroring. He thought of a love relationship as one in which two people are selfobjects for each other, mirroring each other and enhancing each other's self-esteem (Kohut, 1977). Thus a healthy narcissism in normal adults—which Kohut saw as part of life—is satisfied and nurtured properly through mutual mirroring.

Basic Anxiety

Several themes we've been discussing were foreshadowed in the writings of Karen Horney (pronounced horn-eye), another post-Freudian analyst (see Box 11.1). Horney (1937, 1945) argued that from childhood onward, people have a sense of insecurity that she called **basic anxiety**—a feeling of being abandoned by one's parents, of be-

---

BOX 11.1

THE THEORIST AND THE THEORY:
Karen Horney's Feminism

Although much of Horney's work concerned such general themes as the role of basic anxiety in human behavior, she also had much to say regarding the psychoanalytic view of women. Horney was a vocal critic of Freud's position, believing that he'd managed to get nearly everything wrong.

Recall that, to Freud, a woman's life is deeply affected by the fact that she has no penis. According to him, women feel castrated and inferior, and they envy and resent men throughout their lives because of it. Partly on the basis of her own personal experiences, Horney came to a different view (for a biographical account see Quinn, 1987). Her tremendous feelings of pleasure and pride in childbirth and motherhood led her to realize how shallow were the comparable experiences of men. Men play a minor role in the creating and nurturing of new life, and Horney came to think that this leads to a deep sense of inferiority. This idea was also confirmed in her therapy experiences with men, who gave considerable evidence of envying women's ability to have children.

One result of men's feelings of inferiority is an attempt to compensate through achievement. The world of business and commerce is an attempt to *create*, although such creations can never compare to creating a baby. Besides these achievement efforts, men attempt to hide their inferiorities by disparaging and devaluing women. By denying women equal rights, men are able to hide from themselves the fact that they can never be as valuable to human society as women.

Horney argued forcefully that the tendency of women to feel inferior arises not from penis envy but from the cultural context in which they live. If women regard themselves as unworthy, it's only because men have treated them as unworthy for so long. It isn't penises that women want, but the ability to participate as full members of society (Horney was born in 1885, so the culture in which she lived was more restrictive than that of the present).

How did Freud (who was still living) feel about all this? He never responded directly to Horney's arguments, but late in his life he wrote something that probably was aimed in her direction. He wrote, "We shall not be very greatly surprised if a woman analyst who has not been sufficiently convinced of the intensity of her own wish for a penis also fails to attach proper importance to that factor in her patients" (Freud, 1949/1940). In short, to Freud, the source of Horney's theory was her own penis envy.

Horney took many positions that anticipated and foreshadowed later developments in psychological theory and in Western culture more broadly. Her early feminist stance was no exception. She did much to propose the outlines of a feminist agenda for the future. She argued that a woman's identity is not to be found in the mere reflection of her husband. Rather, women should seek their own identities by developing their abilities and pursuing careers. Truly, Karen Horney was a woman ahead of her time.

ing isolated and helpless in a hostile world. These feelings are stronger in some people than others. Basic anxiety is minimized by being raised in a home where there's security, trust, love, warmth, and tolerance.

Horney felt that people cope with basic anxiety by developing strategies to combat the feelings (Horney, 1937). A child may try to strike back against the people who've abandoned it. A person may try to win back love by being very submissive, never doing anything that could antagonize others. A third possibility is to develop an inflated self-conception to compensate for insecurity. A child who considers it impossible to win back the parent's love may try to gain power over others, to compensate for the feelings of helplessness.

Horney coined the term **vicious cycle** to refer to a pattern that can follow from basic anxiety. Feeling insecurity leads to an enhanced awareness of the need for love. If the need isn't met through whatever strategies are available (and often it isn't), the result is a further increase in the sense of anxiety and insecurity. Only if the need for affection is met is the cycle broken.

Attachment Theory and Personality

The ideas discussed in the preceding sections also fit in many ways with ideas proposed by theorists interested in the infant's **attachment** to its mother (e.g., Ainsworth, Blehar, Waters, & Wall, 1978; Bowlby, 1969, 1988; Sroufe & Fleeson, 1986). Attachment is an emotional connection to someone. The need for such a connection is a fundamental part of the human experience (for broader discussion of this idea see Baumeister & Leary, 1995).

The first attachment theorist was John Bowlby. Influenced by ethological studies of imprinting, Bowlby came to believe that the clinging and following of the infant serve an important biological purpose: They keep the infant close to the mother, helping to increase the infant's chances of survival.

A fundamental theme in attachment theory is that mothers (and others) who are responsive to the infant create a secure base for the child (Figure 11.1). The infant needs to know that the major person in his or her life is *dependable,* is there whenever needed. This sense of security gives the child a base from which to explore the world. It also provides a place of comfort (a safe haven) when the child is threatened.

A further theme is that the child builds implicit mental "working models" of relationships between self and others, and how those relationships work. These working models are later used to relate to the world (Bowlby, 1969). This conception is

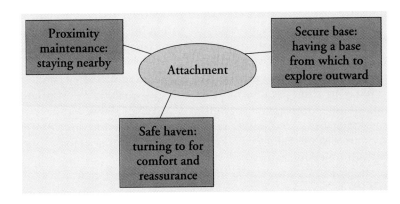

FIGURE 11.1

Three defining features of attachment and three functions of attachment: Attachment provides a secure base for exploration, keeps the infant nearby and safe, and provides a source of comfort (adapted from Hazan & Shaver, 1994).

Early attachment patterns can influence the quality of later social relationships.

similar both to Mahler's idea about internalized object representations guiding future experiences and to Kohut's view of selfobjects.

Much research has examined variations in infants' attachment. To assess attachment Mary Ainsworth and her colleagues devised a procedure called the **strange situation** (Ainsworth et al., 1978). This is an 8-minute series of events involving the infant's mother and a stranger. Of special significance are two times when the infant is left alone with the stranger, followed by the mother's return. The assessors carefully examine the infant's behavior throughout, paying special attention to its responses to the mother's return.

This procedure identified four patterns. *Secure attachment* is reflected by normal distress when mother leaves and a happy, enthusiastic response when she returns. There are also three types of *insecure attachment*. An *ambivalent* (or *resistant*) baby is clingy and becomes unusually upset when mother leaves. The response to mother's return mixes approach with rejection and anger. The infant seeks contact with its mother but then angrily resists all efforts to be soothed. In the *avoidant* pattern, the infant stays calm when mother leaves and responds to her return in an avoiding, rejecting way. It's as though this infant expects to be abandoned by its mother and is retaliating in kind.

At first it was believed that all infants fell into these three groups. Later a rarer group was identified, called *disorganized/disoriented* (Main & Solomon, 1986). These infants vary more. Their actions may be contradictory (for example, approaching but with its head turned away) or they may appear disoriented (for example, freezing as if dazed). This child's behavior often differs radically between parents (Main & Solomon, 1986). The child may seem secure with one parent but not with the other.

Observations made in the home suggest a basis for variations in attachment (Ainsworth, 1983; Ainsworth et al., 1978). Mothers of securely attached infants are very responsive to the crying of their infants and quick to return their smiles. They're also more likely to show "synchronous" behavior—making appropriate replies to a variety of infant actions (Isabella, Belsky, & von Eye, 1989). Mothers of ambivalent babies are inconsistent, sometimes responsive and sometimes not. Mothers of avoidant babies are distant, radiating a kind of emotional unavailability and sometimes being outright rejecting or neglectful.

Interestingly enough, it's not always the mothers' actions per se that differ between groups. For example, mothers of secure and avoidant infants don't differ in how much total time they spend holding their babies. Mothers of avoidant babies, however, are less likely to hold the baby *when it signals that it wants to be held*. Timing thus can be extremely important.

On the basis of findings such as these, Hazan and Shaver (1994) characterized the secure, ambivalent, and avoidant attachment patterns as reflecting the three possible answers to the question "Can I count on my attachment figure to be available and responsive when needed?" The possible answers—yes, no, and maybe—correspond to the secure, avoidant, and ambivalent patterns.

It's possible to get past an insecure attachment by forming a better one with someone else later on. Unfortunately this is often difficult, because insecure attachment leads to behaviors that alienate others. This interferes with creation of a new attachment. The clinginess mixed with rejection in the ambivalent pattern can be hard to handle (recall Elizabeth in the chapter opening, who displays an adult version of this). So can the aloofness and distance of the avoidant pattern. These patterns cause adverse reactions in others, which reconfirm the perceptions that led to patterns in the first place (i.e., that no one will be there for you when you need them). Insecure patterns thus have a self-perpetuating quality.

What are the consequences of these attachment patterns for later life? In the short term, the patterns of age 1 are still there at age 6, though in slightly different form (see Table 11.1). In one study, the earlier attachment pattern of 84% of the children was identifiable from current responses to parents (Main & Cassidy, 1988, Study 1). Secure children were still acting secure, avoidant ones were still being avoidant, and ambivalent ones were still being both dependent and sullen.

A surprise was what had happened to the disorganized/disoriented group. A kind of role reversal occurred, with the children controlling their parents. Some were punitive (embarrassing or humiliating the parent), some seemed to be doing caregiving. Other evidence suggests that parents of such children have in some cases

TABLE 11.1

Four forms of attachment-related behavior, viewed at 1 year and 6 years of age (adapted from Main & Cassidy, 1988).

Name of pattern at 1 year	Behavior at 1 year	Behavior at 6 years
Secure	Seeks interaction, closeness, contact with returning parent. Readily soothed by parent and returns to play.	Initiates conversation with returning parent or responds to parent's overture. Remains calm throughout.
Avoidant	Actively avoids and ignores returning parent, looks away, remains occupied with toys.	Minimizes opportunity for interaction with returning parent, looking and speaking only briefly, returns to toys.
Ambivalent	Distress over separation isn't soothed by parent. Child wants contact, but shows overt to subtle signs of anger.	Posture and voice exaggerate sense of intimacy and dependency. Shows some resistance, subtle signs of hostility.
Disorganized/ disoriented*	Shows one or several signs of disorganization (contradictory cues) or disorientation (freezing). Usually shows these cues to one parent only.	Assumes partial parental role toward parents. Attempts to control and direct parent behavior, by either humiliating parent or being overly solicitous.

*At age 6, this pattern is relabeled as Controlling

been abused. This gives a clue to what's going on in these children: A traumatized parent may give off cues that confuse and frighten an infant (Main & Hesse, 1990; Schuengel et al., 1999). This could produce disoriented behavior at age 1. At 6 the child's understanding is more organized, and the child is now starting to act as a parent to its own parent.

Attachment Patterns in Adult Behavior

Attachment behavior in childhood is interesting, but more relevant to our goals here is how these ideas relate to adult personality. Research on this question is guided by the idea that the working models of relationships developed in childhood are carried into adulthood (with modifications along the way). These working models influence the quality of the adult's social relationships. In effect, they represent the core of personality as it expresses itself in regard to other people.

Research on adult attachment patterns has mushroomed in recent years (for reviews see Ainsworth, 1989; Hazan & Shaver, 1994; Parkes, Stevenson-Hinde, & Marris, 1991; Simpson & Rholes, 1997; Sperling & Berman, 1994). The first study was done by Cindy Hazan and Phillip Shaver (1987). Subjects classified themselves as secure, ambivalent, or avoidant (most studies of adult attachment use these three categories, though Bartholomew & Horowitz, 1991, argued for a four-category model). They then described the most important romance of their life (past or current) on several scales (see Figure 11.2).

Secure adults described their most important love relationship as more happy, friendly, and trusting, compared with the other two groups. Their relationships also had lasted longer. Avoidant adults were less likely than the others to report accepting their lovers' imperfections. Ambivalents experienced love as an obsessive preoccupation, with a desire for reciprocation and union, extreme emotional highs and lows, and extremes of both sexual attraction and jealousy. These people were also more likely than others to report that the relationship had been love at first sight.

Hazan and Shaver also investigated the mental models that these people held on the nature of relationships (see Table 11.2). Again there were differences. Secure subjects said, in effect, love is real, and when it comes it stays. Avoidants were more cynical, saying that romantic love doesn't last. Ambivalent subjects showed their ambivalence. They said falling in love is easy and happens often to them, but they also agreed with avoidants that love doesn't last. Other research suggests that ambivalent

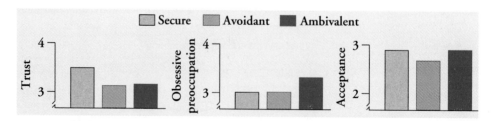

FIGURE 11.2

Adults with a secure attachment pattern report higher levels of trust in their romantic partner than do other groups, those with an ambivalent pattern report greater obsessive preoccupation, and those with an avoidant pattern report lower levels of acceptance of their partners' imperfections (adapted from Hazan & Shaver, 1987).

TABLE 11.2

Mental models of love held by adults of three attachment groups (adapted from Hazan & Shaver, 1987).

Endorsed *more* often by secure adults than others:

In some relationships, romantic love really lasts; it doesn't fade with time.

Endorsed *less* often by secure adults than others:

The kind of head-over-heels romantic love depicted in novels and movies doesn't exist in real life.

Endorsed *more* often by avoidant adults than others:

Intense romantic love is common at the beginning of a relationship, but it rarely lasts forever. It's rare to find someone you can really fall in love with.

Endorsed *more* often by ambivalent adults than others:

It's easy to fall in love.
I feel myself beginning to fall in love often.

college students are most likely to have obsessive and dependent love relationships (Collins & Read, 1990). Avoidants are the least likely group to report being in love either presently or in the past (Feeney & Noller, 1990). In contrast to these patterns, secure persons show the most interdependence, commitment, and trust (Mikulincer, 1998; Simpson, 1990).

Other Reflections of Adult Attachment

Adult attachment patterns are also reflected in a number of other ways. Hazan and Shaver (1990) examined the idea that attachment patterns influence people's orientations to their work. Recall that ambivalent attachment involves a sense of insecurity. Consistent with this, ambivalents report unhappiness with the recognition they get from others at work and with their degree of job security. They're also most likely to say their work is motivated by a desire for approval from others. Recall that avoidant attachment involves a lack of closeness. Consistent with this, avoidants report a desire to keep busy with work and are less likely to socialize during their leisure time. Hazan and Shaver suggested that avoidants use work as a way to escape from their lack of relationships.

Adult attachment patterns have also been related to differences in how people respond to stress. In one study (Simpson, Rholes, & Nelligan, 1992), women were told they were going to do a task that's known to create anxiety. They then waited for 5 minutes with their boyfriends, who expected to do a different task. How the women responded to this situation depended on their attachment pattern and on how anxious they were. As anxiety increased, secure women sought support from their partners, by mentioning what they'd been told, talking about their feelings, and so on. Avoidant women displayed the opposite pattern. The more anxious they got, the *less* they sought support.

The men also varied in the same way. Among secure men, the more anxiety their partners showed, the more reassuring they were. Among avoidant men, the more anxiety their partners showed, the *less* they offered reassurance (see also Kobak & Hazan, 1991). These findings resemble the behavior of infants in the *strange situation*.

Among secure individuals, stress led to making contact and both getting and providing reassurance. Among avoidant subjects, stress—even vicarious stress—led to a shutting down of contact on both sides.

Another study found similar differences in coping with the threat of a missile attack in Israel (Mikulincer, Florian, & Weller, 1993). Avoidants used more "distancing" coping (trying not to think about the situation) than did others. Ambivalents experienced more of a wide range of ineffective emotion-focused reactions (self-criticism, wishing they could change how they felt). Secure people used their social support more than did the other groups.

Also of interest is how people with the various patterns relate to one another. Unsurprisingly, secure partners are most desired, and they tend to wind up with each other (Collins & Read, 1990). Both partners are less satisfied in relationships where the man is avoidant and in relationships where the woman is ambivalent. On the other hand, there's evidence that avoidant men with ambivalent women tend to be stable pairings (Kirkpatrick & Davis, 1994) despite the dissatisfactions. Why? Avoident men also avoid conflict, which may help the relationship run smoothly. Ambivalent women may work harder at holding things together.

Pairings of avoidants with avoidants and of ambivalents with ambivalents are rare (Kirkpatrick & Davis, 1994). This fits with the idea that people with insecure attachment patterns steer away from partners who would treat them as they were treated in infancy. Avoidants avoid partners who will be emotionally inaccessible, and ambivalents avoid partners who will be inconsistent (Collins & Read, 1990; Kirkpatrick & Davis, 1994; Pietromonaco & Carnelley, 1994; Simpson, 1990).

This pattern of findings suggests that people are sensitive to the issue that was critical to them earlier. Perhaps in holding the mental model that people let them down, avoidants consider only people who display more closeness than they'd experienced earlier. Perhaps in holding the mental model that people are inconsistent, ambivalents consider only people who provide consistency—even if the consistency is consistent distance.

No one believes adult attachment pattern is a direct reflection of infant attachment (because so much has happened since then). However, the idea that events in childhood can have lingering effects has received some support. Mickelson, Kessler, and Shaver (1997) studied a very large national adult sample, asking many questions about events from the past. Reports of interpersonal trauma (ranging from abuse, to threat with a weapon, to parental violence) related to insecure adult attachment. So did a history of parental depression and anxiety.

Erikson's Theory of Psychosocial Development

We turn now to what is probably the most elaborate of psychosocial theories, that of Erik Erikson (1950, 1963, 1968). Erikson adopted Freud's view that personality develops in a sequence of stages, but the theories differ in major ways. Recall that Freud's is a theory of psychosexual development. Erikson's is a theory of psycho*social* development. It describes the impact of social phenomena across life.

Another difference pertains to the age span involved. The psychosexual stages that Freud described unfold within the first few years of life. In contrast, Erikson believed that personality evolves throughout life, from birth through maturity to death. He further believed that no part of life is intrinsically more important than any other part. Erikson thus was one of the first to advance the principle of **life-span development.** Many consider this concept to be one of his most important contributions to psychology.

According to the principle of life-span development, all periods of a person's life are important, infancy through adulthood—even old age.

Ego Identity, Competence, and the Experience of Crisis

The central theme of Erikson's theory is **ego identity** and its development (Erikson, 1968, 1974). Ego identity is the consciously experienced sense of self, which derives from transactions with one's social reality. A person's ego identity changes constantly in response to changes in the social environment. To Erikson, forming and maintaining a strong sense of ego identity is critical (thus linking him to ego psychology).

A second major theme in Erikson's theory concerns competence and personal adequacy. As you'll see shortly, his stages tend to focus on aspects of mastery (e.g., autonomy, initiative, industry). If a stage is managed well, the person comes away with feelings of competence. If the stage isn't managed well, the person acquires feelings of inadequacy. This theme in Erikson's theory—that a desire for competence is a motivating force behind people's actions—is similar in some ways to White's ideas about competence, discussed in Chapter 10.

Erikson viewed human development as a sequence of periods in which some issue is particularly prominent and important. In his view, people experience a **psychosocial crisis,** or **conflict,** during each stage. The terms *crisis* and *conflict* are interchangeable here. They have a special meaning, though, that differs from the ordinary use of either word in day-to-day speech.

To Erikson, a crisis is a *turning point*—a period when the potential for growth is high but when the person is also quite vulnerable. Each crisis period is relatively long (none is shorter than about a year) and some are quite long (perhaps 30 years). Thus, his use of the word *crisis* conveys more the sense of crucial importance than the sense of time pressure.

The "conflict" in each crisis isn't a confrontation between persons, nor is it a conflict within personality (as in Freud's theory). Rather, it's a struggle between attaining some psychological quality versus failing to attain it. To Erikson, this conflict never ends. Even handling the conflict in the period when it's most intense doesn't mean you've mastered it once and for all. The conflict is always there to a degree, and you reconfront it in different forms throughout life.

Erikson identified eight psychosocial stages. The first four parallel the first four periods of psychosexual development outlined by Freud. Each stage focuses on a particular aspect of one's transaction with the social environment, with some sort of conflict, or crisis. Each conflict pits two possibilities against each other, as a pair of opposing psychological qualities. One of the pair is obviously adaptive, the other appears less so. The labels that Erikson gave to the two qualities of each stage indicate the nature of the crisis.

People negotiate each stage by developing a balance between the two qualities for which the stage is named. The point isn't just to acquire the "good" quality. In fact, it's important that the developing ego incorporate *both* poles of the conflict, at least a little. Having too much of the quality that seems desirable can create problems. For example, if you had only "basic trust" and absolutely no sense of "basic mistrust" (from the conflict of the first stage), you'd be unable to deal effectively with a world that's sometimes *not* trustworthy.

Nonetheless, successful negotiation of a stage does imply that the balance is weighted more toward the positive value than the negative one. If this occurs, the person emerges from the crisis with a positive orientation toward future events pertaining to that conflict. Erikson used several terms to refer to the feeling quality that goes along with this positive orientation—terms such as **ego quality, ego strength,** and **virtue** (Erikson, 1964; Stevens, 1983). Once established, these ego qualities remain a part of your personality.

Erikson was extremely reluctant to specify age norms for his stages. He believed people pass through the eight stages in order, but he also believed each person has a unique timetable. Thus it's hard to say when each stage will begin and end for a person. The ages given here are only rough approximations.

Infancy

The first psychosocial stage in Erikson's theory (see Figure 11.3) is infancy, roughly the first year of life. The conflict at this stage—the first and most fundamental crisis of life—is between a sense of *basic trust versus basic mistrust.* In this period the infant is totally helpless and dependent on others to meet its basic needs. If the needs are met, the infant develops a sense of security and trust. The sense of trust is reflected by the infant's feeding easily, sleeping peacefully, and eliminating regularly. Caretakers can leave the infant alone for short periods without causing excessive distress, because the infant has learned to "trust" that they'll return. Mistrust is reflected by fitful sleep, fussiness in feeding, constipation, and greater distress when the infant is left alone.

The sense of trust provides the underlying basis for beliefs in the predictability of the world, including the self and especially relationships. It thus is extremely important. Trust is believed to be enhanced by interactions in which caregivers are attentive, affectionate, and responsive to the child. A sense of mistrust is created by inconsistent treatment, by emotional unavailability, or by rejection. This description closely resembles ideas that have emerged several times already in this chapter, regarding object relations, basic anxiety, and attachment patterns.

A predominance of trust over mistrust gives rise to the ego strength of *hope.* Hope is an enduring belief that wishes are attainable.

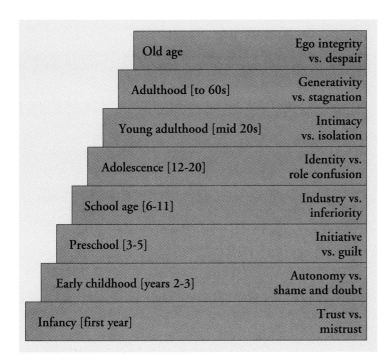

Old age	Ego integrity vs. despair
Adulthood [to 60s]	Generativity vs. stagnation
Young adulthood [mid 20s]	Intimacy vs. isolation
Adolescence [12-20]	Identity vs. role confusion
School age [6-11]	Industry vs. inferiority
Preschool [3-5]	Initiative vs. guilt
Early childhood [years 2-3]	Autonomy vs. shame and doubt
Infancy [first year]	Trust vs. mistrust

FIGURE 11.3

Erikson's eight psychosocial stages, the approximate age range in which each occurs, and the crisis that dominates each period.

Early Childhood

The second psychosocial stage is early childhood (the second and third years of life). Children's physical development is progressing, and the focus of their efforts begins to shift to developing a sense of control over their actions. The crisis of this stage concerns these efforts. It's about creating a sense of *autonomy* in one's actions *versus shame and doubt* about being able to act independently.

Erikson followed Freud in assuming that toilet training was an important event of this period, but not for the reasons Freud assumed. To Erikson, acquiring control over bladder and bowels is a chance to acquire feelings of autonomy (self-direction, or independence). Achieving control over these functions gives a sense of control, as opposed to being at the mercy of your body's impulses.

During this time children are also becoming more active in dealing with the world of objects and people. When children's interactions are effective, their feelings of autonomy and competence are strengthened. If their efforts meet with failure, ridicule, or criticism—or if overcontrolling parents prevent them from acting on their own—the result is feelings of shame and self-doubt. Erikson believed that successful management of this conflict leads to the ego quality of *will:* the determination to exercise free choice.

Much of the research bearing on Erikson's theory focuses on the idea that successful management of the crisis of one stage prepares you to deal well with the crisis of the next stage. Let's consider this idea as it applies to the first two stages. Children's sense of basic trust versus mistrust is reflected in the security of their attachment to their mothers. Infants with a sense of trust are distressed when their mother leaves the room, but greet her happily on her return and then resume their own activities. Children who are less securely attached show greater distress and resentment at the mother's leaving.

FIGURE 11.4

Children with a greater sense of basic trust and security at 1 year explore more at 2½ years of age than do less securely attached children, and a higher proportion of their exploration is self-initiated, or autonomous. This finding suggests that successful management of the first crisis prepares the child to do better with the second crisis (adapted from Hazen & Durrett, 1982).

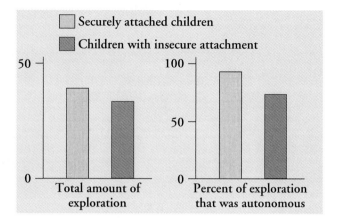

In a study by Hazen and Durrett (1982) children's sense of basic trust was assessed this way at 1 year. At 2½, the same children came to a laboratory with their mothers where they had a chance to explore a play area. Observers coded how many times the child went alone (or led the mother) to a new part of the area—action that reflects autonomy and self-initiation of behavior. They also coded how often the child was *led by* the mother into new parts of the area—action that's *not* autonomous.

As can be seen in Figure 11.4, children who'd been securely attached a year and a half earlier explored more than did those who'd been less securely attached. Further, a higher percentage of the exploration was self-initiated (autonomous) among the securely attached. Conceptually similar results have been reported by several others (e.g., Matas, Arend, & Sroufe, 1978). Thus, a sense of basic trust does seem to promote greater autonomy later on.

Preschool

Continued improvement of locomotor skills and the acquisition of language set the stage for the crisis of the next period, the preschool stage (from about 3 to 5). Being autonomous and capable of controlling your actions is an important start, but it's only a start. The increasing ability to manipulate objects in the world leads to an increasing desire to exert influence, to make things happen—in short, a desire for *power* (McAdams, 1985).

This is the period that corresponds to Freud's genital stage. Recall that this is the time when Freud saw Oedipal conflicts emerging. As we said earlier, people who are skeptical about the Oedipal conflict tend to treat Freud's depiction as a metaphor for the more extensive power struggle that takes place between the parents and the child—who by now has become so willful. It's this power struggle on which Erikson focused.

Accordingly, the conflict at this stage concerns *initiative versus guilt*. Children who take the initiative are actively seeking to impose their newly developed sense of will on their surroundings. They readily express and act on their curiosity as they explore and manipulate their world and ask questions about things going on around them. (This pattern resembles the impulsive stage in Loevinger's theory, described in Chapter 10.)

Acts and words can also be perilous, however. Action that's too powerful can cause others pain (grabbing a toy you want can be distressing to another child). Asking too many questions can become tiresome to adults. If taking the initiative often leads to punishment or disapproval, the result will be feelings of guilt. Because constantly exerting power does tend to produce some disapproval, initiative eventually must be tempered by restraint, to avoid the guilt. If this crisis is managed well, the child emerges with the ego quality of *purpose:* the courage to pursue valued goals without fear of punishment.

Research on initiative asks whether attaining a sense of basic trust during the first year fosters later initiative. In one study (Lütkenhaus, Grossmann, & Grossmann, 1985), infants' attachment was assessed at age 1, and the children were studied again (at home) at age 3. Children who'd been securely attached were quicker to show initiative in interacting with a stranger than were those who'd been insecurely attached. Furthermore, during a game in which the the child had a failure, securely attached children responded to failure by increasing their efforts, whereas the other children decreased their effort. Again, the sense of basic trust seems to provide the groundwork for a further quality, in this case, the sense of initiative and purpose.

School Age

The next stage corresponds to Freud's latency period (from about 5 to 11). Unlike Freud, Erikson assumed that this period also has a conflict. He called it *industry versus inferiority*. The term *industry* reflects the fact that the child's life remains focused on doing things that have an influence in the social and nonsocial world. But now the nature of those efforts acquires a different shade of meaning.

In particular, it's no longer enough just to take the initiative and assert your power to do things. Now you experience pressure to do things that others in the world acknowledge to be *good,* in two senses of that word. Industriousness isn't just *doing* things, it's doing things that others *value.* It's also doing things in ways that others regard as *appropriate* and *commendable.*

The crisis over this sense of industry begins about the time the child enters elementary school. This is no coincidence. After all, the entire experience of school is aimed at teaching children to become productive and responsible members of society. School years are also the period when intellectual and cognitive skills are tested for the first time. Children are expected to do well in their school subjects, and the adequacy of their performance is explicitly evaluated.

The school experience also involves learning social roles. Children are beginning to learn about the nature of adult work. They're also being exposed to some of the tools of adult work. In earlier times, this meant exposure to tools of farming, carpentry, and homemaking; today it may mean computers. Another social role that children are acquiring is the role of citizenship. Thus the child's industriousness is being judged partly on the basis of the acceptability of his or her behavior to the larger social group.

To emerge from this stage successfully children must feel that they're mastering the tasks set for them, in a fashion that's judged acceptable by those around them. The danger at this stage is the possibility of developing strong feelings of inferiority. Feelings of inferiority arise when children are led by others (parents, teachers, or peers) to view their performances either as inadequate or as morally wrong. Managing the conflict between industry and inferiority results in an ego quality that Erikson termed *competence:* the sense that one can do things that are valued by others.

Recent evidence suggests that children with a strong sense of industry differ in several ways from children with less of a sense of industry (Kowaz & Marcia, 1991). They're more likely to prefer reality-based activities over escapes into fantasy. They're more able to distinguish the role of effort from that of ability in producing outcomes. They get better grades. And they're more likely to agree with statements that are socially desirable.

Adolescence

The next stage of Erikson's theory is adolescence, a period that begins with the physical changes of puberty and lasts until roughly age 20. This stage represents a larger break with the past than has any stage up to this point. Part of the sense of separation comes from the physical changes of puberty. Your body doesn't just get larger during this period, it changes in ways it never did before. You're having desires you never had before. You're not quite the same person you used to be. But who *are* you?

Part of the break with the past reflects the fact that you're now beginning to think explicitly about yourself and your life in relation to the adult world. You have to find your place in that world, and doing so requires you to decide what roles fit with your identity. This, in turn, means knowing who you are.

The crisis of this stage thus is between developing feelings of *identity versus role confusion*. The concept of identity reflects an integrated sense of self. It's the answer to the question "who am I?" The words *role confusion* reflect, in part, the fact that every self has multiple facets that sometimes seem incompatible with one another. The greater the incompatibility, the harder it is to pull the facets together and the more confused you are. Worse yet, you can even be in a position where your roles are uncertain—where *no* role feels as though it's part of your identity.

To emerge from adolescence with a strong sense of identity requires the self-concept to evolve in two ways. First, you must consolidate the self-conceptions formed during the previous stages, merge them in a way that feels sensible. Second, this integrated self-view must itself be integrated with the conception of you that others hold. This second change reflects the fact that your identity is something you develop in a consensus with the people to whom you relate. Only by considering both views does a rounded sense of identity emerge.

Thus, from Erikson's perspective, identity derives from a melding of private and social self-conceptions. The outcome of this integration is a sense of personal continuity or inner congruence. Erikson placed great emphasis on the importance of developing a sense of identity. In many ways, he sees acquiring the sense of identity as the person's major life task (see also Box 11.2).

If the person fails to form a consolidated identity, the result is role confusion, an absence of direction in your sense of self. Role confusion is reflected in an inability to select a career (or a major in school that will make it possible to pursue a career). Role confusion can also lead a person to overidentify with popular heroes or groups, or even antiheroes, to try to fill the void.

The virtue associated with successful identity formation is *fidelity*. Fidelity means truthfulness. It's the ability to live up to who you are, despite the contradictions that inevitably occur among the values you hold.

A good deal of research has evolved from Erikson's ideas about the development of identity during adolescence. Much of this work has been conducted by James Marcia (1966, 1976, 1980) and his colleagues. He began by expanding a bit on Erikson's ideas. He argues that the balance between identity and role confusion depends on a sense of *commitment* to an identity, and also on the occurrence of an **identity crisis** in the person's life. Marcia's use of the word *crisis* is similar to Erikson's. An identity crisis involves actively exploring different ways of viewing oneself and giving serious thought to the implications of those views.

Marcia (1966) developed an interview method of measuring ego identity. It applies the two criteria of crisis and commitment to three areas of functioning: the person's occupation (intended work role), ideology (beliefs and values), and sexuality. He distinguishes among four **identity statuses** (see also Table 11.3).

BOX 11.2

THE THEORIST AND THE THEORY: Erikson's Lifelong Search for Identity

Erikson's life had a distinct impact on the form his theory took, particularly his emphasis on the importance of attaining a sense of identity. Erikson was born in Germany in 1902, of Danish parents. His father abandoned his mother before he was born, and three years later she married Theodor Homburger, a Jewish physician. Erik wasn't told for some years that Homburger wasn't his real father, which he later referred to as an act of "loving deceit."

He grew up as Erik Homburger, a Jew with the appearance of a Scandinavian. Jews saw him as a gentile, gentiles saw him as a Jew. For this reason he wasn't accepted by either group, and he began to form an image of himself as an outsider. By adolescence he'd been told of his adoption, and his identity confusion was further complicated by the realization that his ancestry was Danish rather than German.

As he wandered around Europe during his early 20s, his feelings of a lack of identity deepened. He worked as a portrait painter, but the work was irregular and not conducive to developing a clear sense of identity as an artist. Homburger interrupted periods of formal training in art to continue wandering, in search of his identity. Eventually he took a teaching job in Vienna, at a school created for children of Freud's patients and friends. There he became familiar with a number of psychoanalysts, including Anna Freud, with whom he went on to train as an analyst. In 1933 Homburger moved to the United States, where he established a practice as a child analyst. As Erik Homburger, he was also part of the research team that Henry Murray brought together, which led to development of the motive approach to personality that was described in Chapter 5.

In 1939 Homburger became naturalized as a U.S. citizen. At that time he took the name Erikson. This was an event—and, indeed, a choice of name—that unquestionably had much personal meaning, symbolizing his full attainment of the sense of identity.

In later years Erikson spent time studying methods of child rearing and other aspects of cultural life among the Sioux of South Dakota and the Yurok of northern California. These studies were important for two reasons. First, they established themes that would permeate Erikson's thinking, concerning the importance of culture and society in identity. Second, they revealed to him symptoms of dislocation, feelings of having been uprooted and separated from cultural traditions. The members of these tribes appeared to have lost their sense of identity, much as Erikson himself had done earlier in his life. Erikson also observed similar qualities in the lives of veterans of World War II who returned with emotional difficulties.

From all these experiences Erikson came to believe that the attainment and preservation of a sense of identity—not wholly separate from but rather embedded in one's own society—was the critical task of growing up. This idea was to stand as one of the major themes of his viewpoint on personality.

Identity achievement is the status of a person who's experienced a period of exploration and has made a commitment. *Moratorium* applies to a person who's now in crisis (exploring alternatives) but hasn't made commitments. *Foreclosure* is the status of a person who's made commitments, but with little evidence of a crisis. An example of someone who's foreclosed is a young man committed to becoming a surgeon because his father and grandfather were surgeons. In the fourth status, *identity diffusion*, there's no crisis and no commitment. Not surprisingly, either achieving or foreclosing on an identity has a benefit. People committed to identities (these two groups) feel better about themselves than people who haven't made commitments (Prager, 1982).

TABLE 11.3

Four identity statuses defined by Marcia.
This matrix of possibilities is derived by applying two criteria in the form of questions. Each possible pair of answers defines an identity status.

		Has an identity crisis been experienced?	
		Yes	**No**
Has a commitment been made?	Yes	Identity achievement	Foreclosure
	No	Moratorium	Identity diffusion

The existence of these four identity statuses is now well established, and researchers are beginning to learn what these people are like and how they come to exist (Bourne, 1978a, 1978b; Marcia, 1980; Waterman, 1982). Foreclosed persons seem to have closer relationships with their parents than do persons of any other status. Foreclosed men also are more willing than men of other statuses to involve their families in decisions about important life events. These close ties seem to prevent an identity crisis from occurring. Instead the person tends to make identity commitments without considering their implications.

People who've had identity crises (identity achievers and those in moratorium) are more critical of their parents and less concerned with living up to parents' wishes. They tend to turn inward rather than to their families when life decisions have to be made (this presumably facilitated their identity crises). Although neither group is closely tied to family (both are autonomous in that respect), they differ in how they view their parents. Compared with the identity achiever, people in moratorium feel more ambivalent about parents, sometimes thinking of them as examples of identities they want not to have. Presumably the ambivalence reflects the fact that for people in moratorium the crisis is ongoing.

Identity diffusers are perhaps the hardest group to characterize. They haven't entered the exploration of possible identities and have no commitment to one. They seem almost to have withdrawn from pursuit of an identity (e.g., Berzonsky & Neimeyer, 1994). Identity diffusers report feeling out of place and socially isolated (Donovan, 1975), which doesn't bode well for them in the next stage of development. They report seeing their parents as distant from them, which hints they may have had earlier problems in the development of basic trust.

One might expect that family stability would relate to attainment of a firm identity, but the evidence is mixed. In some studies, broken homes produce identity diffusers (e.g., Oshman & Manosevitz, 1976), in other studies they produce identity *achievers* (e.g., St. Clair & Day, 1979). Why might this be? The difference may lie in how severe the family situation is. Identity achievers are somewhat distant from their families, but people with a diffused sense of identity are even more distant. Two principles seem relevant here. Distance from your family is necessary if you are to arrive at your own identity. Too much distance, however, can impair development.

Young Adulthood

The next stage in Erikson's theory is young adulthood (through the mid-20s). The conflict here concerns the desire for *intimacy versus isolation*. Intimacy is a close, warm relationship with someone, in which there's a sense of commitment to that person. Erikson saw intimacy as an issue in relationships of all kinds—both sexual and nonsexual.

True intimacy requires you to approach relationships in a caring and open way and to be willing to share the most personal aspects of yourself with others. You also must be open and receptive to others' disclosures. Intimacy also requires the moral strength to live up to your commitments, even when it requires sacrifices. Erikson believed that people are capable of intimacy only if they already have a strong sense of identity. If you don't have a clear sense of who you are, it's impossible for you to share yourself in an intimate way with others.

The opposite pole at this stage of development is isolation, feeling apart from others and unable to make commitments to them. A person can drift into isolation if conditions aren't right for intimacy—if no one's there who fills your needs. Sometimes, though, people withdraw into isolation on their own—for instance, if they feel a relationship threatens their sense of separate identity. Withdrawing has other consequences, though. People can become self-absorbed to the point that they aren't able to establish intimate relationships in the future (Erikson, 1982). The ego quality associated with the ability to be intimate is *love:* a mutuality that subdues the antagonisms of separate identities.

The theme that handling one crisis prepares you for the next one continues here. Erikson said people need a strong sense of identity to be able to attain intimacy. Is this true? One study on this question looked at identity during college and intimacy in middle age (Kahn, Zimmerman, Csikszentmihalyi, & Getzels, 1985). Students completed a measure of identity strength in school and a measure of intimacy 18 years later. The capacity for intimacy was assessed in terms of whether subjects had married and, if so, whether the marriage had been disrupted by divorce.

The results showed a clear association between achieving a strong identity and a later capacity for intimacy. The effect differed slightly, however, between men and women (see Figure 11.5). Men with stronger identities were more likely to have married during the 18 years. Identity formation didn't predict whether women had married, but among those who *had* married, those with strong identity were less likely to divorce. Conceptually similar findings have also been obtained by others (e.g., Orlofsky, Marcia, & Lesser, 1973; Schiedel & Marcia, 1985; Tesch & Whitbourne, 1982).

The other pole of the conflict of this stage is isolation, a concept that's drawn interest in its own right (e.g., Peplau & Perlman, 1982; Shaver & Rubenstein, 1980; Weiss, 1973). Two aspects of isolation are distinguishable from each other. *Social isolation* is a failure to be integrated into a society. People who stand apart from social groups without belonging don't have people to confide in when they need to. In contrast to this, the failure to have intimacy in your life is termed *emotional isolation*—or, more simply, loneliness.

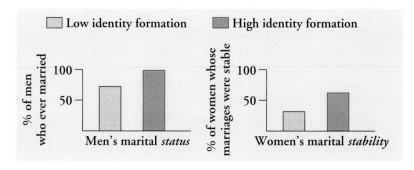

FIGURE 11.5

Percentage of men who had ever been married during the 18-year period after art school and percentage of women who had married and whose marriages remained intact during the same period, as a function of preassessed identity formation (adapted from Kahn et al., 1985).

Emotional isolation is a condition that feeds on itself. Recall Erikson's view that to experience intimacy requires a willingness to self-disclose, to open oneself to others. Lonely people don't do that (Jones, Hobbs, & Hockenberg, 1982). They're less responsive to people they're interacting with, they also ask fewer questions and seem less interested in what the other person is saying. As a result, they're hard to get to know and are likely to remain lonely.

This brings up another link between Erikson's theory and work on adult attachment. There's evidence that people with avoidant attachments are less self-disclosing than other people (Mikulincer & Nachshon, 1991). People who don't self-disclose aren't liked as much as other people. As a result, avoidant people—many of whom are already lonely—are likely to remain lonely and isolated.

Adulthood

Young adulthood is followed by adulthood, the longest of the psychosocial stages, typically lasting into the mid-60s. The crisis of adulthood centers around being able to generate or nurture. For this reason the central conflict at this stage is termed *generativity versus stagnation.*

The desire for generativity is the desire to create things in the world that will outlive you (Kotre, 1984). One reflection of this desire is having children. By creating new lives tied to yours, you symbolically ensure your continuation into the future. Consistent with this, McAdams and de St. Aubin (1992) found that men who'd had children scored higher on a self-report measure of generativity than did childless men.

Although generativity is partly a matter of creating and guiding the growth of the next generation, the concept is broader than this. It includes creating ideas or physical objects, teaching young people who aren't your own children—anything that influences the future in a positive way (Table 11.4). Erikson believed that the desire for generativity reflects a shift in a person's concern from one close relationship (intimacy) to a broader concern with society as a whole. Consistent with this, autobiographical writings reveal that highly generative persons express high levels of commitment to assisting the next generation. They also reveal an integration between that commitment and the sense of agency within the self (Mansfield & McAdams, 1996; see also McAdams, Diamond, de St. Aubin, & Mansfield, 1997).

Adults who fail to develop this sense of generativity drift into stagnation, the opposite pole of this conflict. Stagnation is an inability or unwillingness to give of oneself to the future. People who are stagnating are preoccupied with their own needs. They

TABLE 11.4

Aspects of generativity (adapted from Kotre, 1984, p. 12).	
Aspect	**Description**
Biological	Creating, bearing, and nursing an infant
Parental	Raising, nurturing, shaping, and socializing children, providing them with family traditions
Technical	Teaching the skills that make up the "body" of a culture, training a new generation in techniques for doing things
Cultural	Creating, changing, and maintaining a symbol system that represents the "mind" of a culture, passing it on to the next generation

One way in which feelings of generativity are displayed is by helping the next generation learn about life.

have a self-centeredness or self-indulgence that keeps them from deeper involvement in the world around them. There's also evidence that an absence of generativity is related to poorer psychological well-being (Vandewater, Ostrove, & Stewart, 1997).

If there's a positive balance of generativity, the ego quality that emerges is *care*. Care is a widening concern for whatever you've generated in your life, be it children, something in your work, or something that emerged from your involvement with other people.

Old Age

The final psychosocial stage is maturity, or old age. This is the stage that marks the closing chapter of people's lives. It's a time when people look back and review the choices they made and reflect on their accomplishments (and failures) and on the turns their lives have taken (see also Box 11.3). The crisis here is termed *ego integrity versus despair*. If you come away from this review of the past feeling that your life has had order and meaning, with an acceptance of the choices you made and the things you did, the result is a sense of ego integrity. This is a feeling of satisfaction, a feeling that things went about the way you wanted them to, that you wouldn't change much.

The opposite pole of this conflict is despair. Despair is the feeling that your life was wasted. It's a sense of wishing you'd done things differently, but with the knowledge that it's too late. Instead of accepting the story that constitutes your life as a valuable gift, there's bitterness that things turned out as they did.

Emerging from this life review with a sense of integrity results in the ego quality of *wisdom*. Wisdom is a detached yet active concern with life, even as one confronts the impending reality of death (see also Baltes & Staudinger, 1993).

The Epigenetic Principle

There's one more conceptual issue to address in Erikson's theory: the idea that a given conflict also exists outside the stage in which it's focal. Erikson appealed to the

BOX 11.3

IS THERE A "MIDLIFE CRISIS"?

From Erikson's point of view, the last years of life are spent in review, examining choices that were made, values that were pursued, and passions that were abandoned. It's interesting that Erikson saw this review as coming late in life, after the opportunity to make changes has passed.

Others have also talked about a life review (Gould, 1980; Levinson, 1978; Sheehy, 1976; Vaillant, 1977), but one that occurs earlier, around age 40 or so. Given its timing, the phenomenon is popularly referred to as the "midlife crisis." It's a questioning of the decisions you've made over your adult years, the validity and worth of your goals, the adequacy of your life situation—nearly everything about your existence. It's a time of reevaluation, but it's also a chance to change the way things are before it's too late. If you don't like your life, change it. Make decisions over, rearrange your priorities, change careers, change your marriage (or perhaps leave it altogether).

The notion of a midlife crisis rests partly on the typical course of life's major events in Western cultures. It's common in the United States to finish college and take an adult job in one's early 20s, marry, and start raising a family in one's 20s and 30s. Depending on when the children are born, they're growing up and leaving home themselves when you're in your 40s or early 50s. Around this time it's also common to experience the death of one or both of your own parents. Many of the changes of midlife are profound ones. Is it any wonder that they seem to cry out for reevaluation of your life?

Another contributor to such a crisis is cultural assumptions about the timing of these events. As a result, people do a certain amount of checking to see whether their lives are "on schedule." If you're in your mid-30s, are you making as much money as you're supposed to be? Are you in line for the career advancement you planned on? If you're nearing 40 with no children, you can hear the biological clock ticking, telling you that you'll never have that experience if you don't hurry up. Comparing your life against these markers of "normal" life can produce a lot of soul-searching.

Is there a midlife crisis? As two people well on the far side of 40, we're inclined to feel there's truth to the idea. We know the feelings we've just written about (we also know why one of us just bought a Triumph motorcycle). Yet the evidence doesn't indicate that a midlife crisis is all that common. Two longitudinal studies have found little support for the idea in fairly large samples (Clausen, 1981; Haan, 1981). On the other hand, the subjects of those studies lived through some very difficult times—the Great Depression and World War II—and it's possible that having survived these experiences made them less likely to reevaluate their choices and goals at midlife. Perhaps the midlife crisis is actually a "baby boomer" phenomenon.

Alternatively, it may be that the midlife crisis isn't so much a matter of midlife as it is a manifestation of a more consistent tendency to be worried. This conclusion would fit with findings obtained by Costa and McCrae (1980) concerning life satisfaction over time. They found that satisfaction was relatively stable across a period of 10 years and that dissatisfaction was related to the broad disposition of neuroticism. Maybe, then, people who are inclined to worry do so throughout life, and it just happens to be more obvious at midlife.

concept of **epigenesis,** from the field of embryology. Epigenesis is the process by which an undifferentiated physical entity (a single cell) turns into a complex organism. For this process to occur requires some sort of "blueprint" at the beginning, with instructions for all the changes and their sequence.

As applied to Erikson's theory, the principle of epigenesis means that there's a readiness for each crisis at birth. Indeed, the issue that's focal at any given stage exists in some form at every other stage, both earlier and later. Each conflict is especially important during a particular stage, but it's there always.

The principle of epigenesis has several implications. It means your initial orientation to a particular crisis is influenced by the outcomes of all the earlier ones. It also means that in resolving the primary crisis of any particular stage, you're preparing solutions (in rudimentary form) for the ones that come later. As you deal in adolescence with the conflict between ego identity and role confusion, you're also moving toward handling the crisis of intimacy versus isolation. Finally, the epigenetic principle means that crises aren't resolved once and for all. Rather, your resolutions of previous conflicts are reshaped at each new stage of life (Whitbourne, Zuschlag, Elliot, & Waterman, 1992).

McAdams (1985) has suggested a metaphor for thinking about human life that conveys the epigenetic principle quite well. He suggests that the evolution of a person's identity through the life course forms a narrative, or story. As in any good book, the opening chapters begin setting the stage for things that happen much later on. Sometimes future events are foreshadowed, sometimes the things that happen early on simply create conditions that have to be responded to later. In later chapters, characters sometimes reinterpret events they experienced earlier, or understand them in different ways. All the pieces eventually come together into a full and integrated picture that's taken on qualities from everything that's happened throughout the story.

Comparing Erikson's Theory with Other Psychosocial Theories

Now that we've described the elements of Erikson's theory, let's refer briefly back to the other theories in this chapter, to make a final point. The theories discussed earlier surely represent contributions of their own. Yet, in a sense the fundamental theme of each is the same as that of the first crisis in Erikson's theory: basic trust versus basic mistrust. That's a big part of what security in attachment is about. It's at the heart of Horney's concept of basic anxiety. It seems implicit, as well, in the issues confronted in object relations theories. This issue is also the core of Erikson's own theory, providing the critical foundation on which the remainder of personality is built.

We humans seem to need to be able to trust in the relationships that sustain our lives. In the minds of many theorists, that trust is necessary for adequate functioning. People who are deeply mistrustful of relationships, or are constantly frightened about possibly losing relationships, have lives that are damaged and distorted. The damage may be slight or it may be significant. Avoiding such mistrust and doubt (or recognizing and overcoming it if it's already there) seems a central task in human existence.

Assessment

Let's turn now to assessment from the psychosocial viewpoint. In general, assessment here is similar to that of the ego psychologists. There are two aspects of assessment, however, that are specific to the psychosocial view.

Object Relations, Attachment, and the Focus of Assessment

One difference between assessment from psychosocial theories and assessment from other angles concerns what's being assessed. Specifically, the psychosocial approach places a greater emphasis than do other approaches on assessing the persons's view of relationships.

There are several ways in which a person's mental model of relationships might be assessed. Relevant measures range from some that are open-ended in nature (e.g., Blatt, Wein, Chevron, & Quinlan, 1979) to structured self-reports (e.g., Bell, Billington, & Becker, 1986). Some measures assess a range of issues pertaining to relationships (Bell et al., 1986). Others focus specifically on the attachments that you have to other people (e.g., Bartholomew & Horowitz, 1991; Carver, 1997a; Collins & Read, 1990; Griffin & Bartholomew, 1994; Simpson, 1990).

The object-relations measure of Bell et al. (1986) provides a good illustration of how the content assessed from this viewpoint differs from content assessed from other views. It has four scales. The *alienation* scale measures a lack of basic trust in relationships and an inability to be close. People who score high on this scale are suspicious, guarded, and isolated, convinced that others will fail them. This resembles the avoidant attachment pattern. A second scale measures *insecure attachment,* in a manner that resembles the ambivalent pattern. It reflects sensitivity to rejection and concern about being liked and accepted. People who score high on this scale enter relationships in a painful search for security, and are hypersensitive to signs of abandonment.

The third scale, *egocentricity,* reflects narcissism, a self-protective and exploitive attitude toward relationships. People who score high on this scale tend to view others only in relation to their own needs and aims. The final scale measures *social in-competence,* as reflected in shyness and uncertainty about how to engage in even simple social interactions. People who score high on this scale have trouble making friends and are interpersonally unresponsive and emotionally blunted.

In contrast to this multi-scale approach, the open-ended measure of Blatt et al. (1979) has a coding system that ranks people's perceptions of social relations in terms of developmental maturity. This measure asks you to describe your mother and father. If you're at a low level of developmental maturity you tend to focus on how parents acted to satisfy your own needs. Higher-level descriptions focus more on parents' values, thoughts, and feelings, apart from your needs. At a very high level, the description takes into account internal contradictions in the parent, and change over time. This measure reflects a person's level of separation and individuation from the parent.

Play in Assessment

Another aspect of the psychosocial view on assessment concerns the fact that this view emphasizes the experiences of childhood as determinants of adult personality. This view thus emphasizes assessment in children more than do other views. Further, the approach taken is quite different in some ways than the approaches suggested by other viewpoints.

In particular, assessment of children from this viewpoint tends to emphasize the use of play as an assessment tool. Several theorists have noted that children's play reveals their preoccupations (e.g., Axline, 1947, 1964; Erikson, 1963; M. Klein, 1935, 1955a, 1955b). Play lets them express their concerns in a way they can't do in words.

Erikson (1963) devised a standardized play situation, using a specific set of toys on a table. The child is to imagine that the table is a movie studio and the toys are actors and sets. The child is to create an interesting scene on the table and describe what's happening. Others use less structured play settings, but the elements almost always include a variety of doll characters (e.g., mother, father, older person, children, baby). This permits children to choose characters that are relevant to their own concerns or preoccupations.

The play situation is projective, because the child imposes a story on ambiguous stimuli. It has two objective characteristics, however. First, there is often a *behavioral record.* This includes what the child says about the scene and a description of the scene and the sequence of steps taken to create it. Second, the face value of the child's behavior receives more attention than is usual in projectives. It isn't automatically assumed that the child's behavior has deeply hidden meanings.

Children often reveal their
feelings through play.

Problems in Behavior, and Behavior Change

Given that psychosocial theorists focus on the nature of people's relationships, it's natural that they see problems as reflecting relationship difficulties. Here are three examples of how this approach applies to problems in behavior.

Narcissism as a Disorder of Personality

One psychosocial view focuses specifically on **narcissism** as a disorder. Indeed, this disorder was the starting point for Kohut's work on the self. Pathological narcissism involves a sense that everyone and everything is an extension of the self or exists to serve the self. There's a grandiose sense of self-importance and need for constant attention. Narcissists display a sense of *entitlement,* of deserving others' adulation. Not surprisingly, they exploit others.

Such individuals may seem agreeable at first, but longer exposure to them often results in more negative opinions about them (Paulhus, 1998). As one might expect, they are particularly likely to take credit for successes, but respond to failure with anger (Rhodewalt & Morf, 1998). Indeed, narcissists may erupt in extremes of rage when their desires are thwarted (Bushman & Baumeister, 1998), and they can be disruptive in the infantile demands they make on others.

Recall that Kohut said everyone begins life with a grandiose narcissism, which has to be tempered during development. Some people, however, never escape from it, and have a disorder of personality. To Kohut, the root of the problem is inadequate mirroring from parents during early childhood. This deeply frustrates the normal narcissistic needs and prevents the formation of an adequate self structure (Kohut, 1977). In a similar vein Kernberg (1976, 1980) said narcissism arises from parental rejection, as the child comes to believe that the only person who can be trusted (and therefore loved) is himself or herself.

A person in whom this narcissism isn't satisfied may distort reality in several ways to serve the narcissistic needs. For example, narcissistic people are more likely to inflate their judgments of their own performances in various arenas of life than are less narcissistic people (John & Robins, 1994). If threatened by being told that someone else has outperformed them, they're more likely to put the other person down (Morf & Rhodewalt, 1993).

Neurotic Needs

Another way of thinking about problems comes from Horney's ideas about basic anxiety. Horney believed that the strategies people use to combat basic anxiety can take on the appearance of needs if they're used too much. The strategies can thus become a fixed part of personality. Horney (1942) developed a list of 10 needs that can be acquired by attempts to deal with disturbed relationships (Table 11.5). She called them **neurotic needs** because they aren't effective solutions to the person's problem. Instead they often lead into vicious cycles.

Horney argued that neurotic needs give rise to three styles, depending on whether the need moves you *toward* others, *away* from others, or *against* others (Horney, 1945, 1950). Neurotic needs such as those for love and approval move you toward others, but in clingy dependency. Neurotic needs for independence and

TABLE 11.5

Horney's list of neurotic needs (and a brief description of each), which arise from overuse of various strategies of coping with anxiety (adapted from Horney, 1942, 1945).

Neurotic need for affection and approval. Indiscriminate wish to please others and live up to their expectations. Extreme sensitivity to any sign of rejection or unfriendliness

Neurotic need for a partner who will take over one's life. Feeling extremely afraid of being deserted and left alone

Neurotic need to restrict one's life within narrow borders. Being extremely undemanding, content with little, preferring to remain inconspicuous

Neurotic need for power. Craving power for its own sake, adoration of strength and contempt for weakness. May also be reflected in intellectual exploitation

Neurotic need to exploit others. Using others to your own advantage

Neurotic need for prestige. Basing your self-evaluation on public recognition

Neurotic need for personal admiration. Having an inflated picture of yourself and wishing to be admired for that, not for what you really are

Neurotic ambition for personal achievement. Wanting to be the very best, and driving yourself to greater and greater achievements as a result of basic insecurity

Neurotic need for self-sufficiency and independence. Setting yourself apart from others, becoming a "loner," refusing to be tied down to anyone or anything because of disappointment in attempts to find warm, satisfying relationships with people

Neurotic need for perfection and unassailability. Trying to make yourself impregnable and infallible. Constantly searching for flaws in yourself so that they can be covered up before becoming obvious to others

self-sufficiency move you away from others (as in the avoidant attachment pattern described earlier). Needs such as power and exploitation move you against others. Each need pattern may be thought of as a coping orientation.

Well-adapted people usually take one orientation at a time and shift from one to another flexibly as needed. Although a preference may develop for one style over the others, all three can be used. This flexibility is the hallmark of normal adaptation. True neurotics are more likely to rigidly adopt a single orientation, even in situations where one of the other styles is more useful.

Sometimes people take two or more orientations simultaneously. For example, they may move toward and against someone—as in the ambivalent attachment pattern described earlier. They may move toward and away from someone. Such patterns create inner conflict. Horney believed everyone does this a little. What separates the normal person from the neurotic in this respect is how *much* this happens. Neurotic people are more prone to take two or more orientations at once, causing inner conflict they aren't flexible enough to deal with.

Attachment and Depression

Another window on the nature and causes of problems comes from work on interpersonal issues and depression. It has been suggested by several theorists that an important cause of depression is interpersonal rejection (Blatt & Zuroff, 1992). This cause of depression resembles the presumed cause of the avoidant attachment pattern. That is, avoidance is believed to be a product of neglectful or rejecting parenting, which results in sadness, despair, and eventual emotional detachment (Hazan & Shaver, 1994; see also Carnelley, Pietromonaco, & Jaffe, 1994). The idea that interpersonal rejection can lead to depression has received a good deal of support (Blatt & Zuroff, 1992).

Further, it's been suggested that both the avoidant attachment pattern and depression to which it's linked can be transmitted from one generation to another. How can this happen? The pattern you acquire as a child is the working model you bring to bear when you have children of your own. If you're an avoidant adult because of parental rejection—and especially if you're a *depressed* avoidant adult—what kind of parent will you be? An emotionally distant one. You may be experienced as a rejecting parent—not because you dislike your child, but because you're so distant. Being emotionally unavailable, you may then create an avoidant child, just like you.

Thus, parents may transfer to the next generation precisely the attachment qualities that have made them unhappy themselves. There's evidence for this line of reasoning regarding rejection and depression (Whitbeck et al., 1992). There's also evidence of generational transmission of an erratic pattern of adult behavior that may be tied to the ambivalent attachment pattern (Elder, Caspi, & Downey, 1986).

Behavior Change

The process of therapeutic behavior change from the viewpoint of psychosocial theories reflects many of the same themes as we discussed for ego psychology. The therapeutic techniques tend to be focused on the here and now, and the person with the problem is viewed as a collaborator in the therapeutic process.

Nevertheless, a few additional techniques were developed by people working in the psychosocial tradition. For example, psychologists such as Erikson (1963), Virginia Axline (1947), and Melanie Klein (1955a, 1955b) developed **play therapy** techniques for use with children. These techniques give the child the opportunity to do as he or she wishes, without pressuring, intruding, prodding, or nagging from an adult. Under these conditions children can create distance from others (if they are worried about being smothered by a too ever-present parent) or can play out anger or the wish for closeness (if they're feeling rejected or unwanted). The playroom is the child's world. In it children have the opportunity to bring their feelings to the surface, deal with them, and potentially change their working models of relationships and of the self in positive ways (Landreth, 1991).

Because object relations and self theories emphasize the role of relationships in problems, they also emphasize relationships as part of the therapeutic process. The therapist tries to provide the kind of relationship the patient needs so the patient can reintegrate problematic parts of the self. Healing is brought about by providing a successful experience of narcissism or attachment (almost a kind of re-parenting), replacing the earlier emotional failure.

These therapy techniques can be seen as representing a way of restoring to the person's life a sense of connectedness to others. By modifying the representations of relationships that were built in the past, they permit the developing of more satisfying relationships in the future. The optimism that this approach holds about being able to undo problematic experiences from the past is reflected in the saying "It's never too late to have a happy childhood."

Psychosocial Theories: Problems and Prospects

As was true of ego psychology, the psychosocial neoanalytic approach is home to several theorists. Although they had very different starting points, there's a remarkable consistency in the themes behind their work. Each assumes that human relationships are the most important part of human life, and that how relationships are managed is a core issue in personality. Each tends to assume that people develop working models of relationships from early experience, which then are used to frame new relationships. Also implicit is the idea that growth requires a balance between being a separate, autonomous person and being closely connected to someone (see also Helgeson, 1994; Helgeson & Fritz, in press).

Psychosocial theories have the important strength of pointing us in directions that other theories don't. Thinking about personality in terms of attachment patterns, for example, suggests hypotheses that aren't readily derived from other viewpoints. Work based in attachment theory is leading to a better understanding of how personality qualities play out in social relations. This picture of the dynamics of this aspect of personality would very likely never have emerged without the attachment model as a starting point. Furthermore, extending the themes of attachment into models of greater complexity, such as Erikson's, creates a picture of change and evolution across the life span that would be nearly impossible to derive from other viewpoints. Without question, the psychosocial viewpoint adds something of great importance to our understanding of personality.

This is not to say that no unresolved issues remain for this approach. One important issue concerns a rather sharp clash between this view and the view of trait psychologists and behavior geneticists. As it happens, manifestations of adult attachment patterns correspond well to genetically influenced traits. Avoidants are essentially introverts, secures are extraverts, and anxious-ambivalents are high in neuroticism (Carver, 1997a; Shaver & Brennan, 1992). But do these patterns result from patterns of parenting (as held by psychosocial theorists), or are they genetically determined (as held by some behavior geneticists)? There are strong opinions on both sides of this question, and not so very much hard information. It's a question that will surely be examined more closely in the years ahead.

Indeed, in considering the prospects of this viewpoint for the future, we should note explicitly that research on these approaches is continuing to take place. Indeed, adult attachment remains one of the most active areas of research in personality psychology. The recent flood of research on this topic shows no sign of abating. Research on the implications of attachment patterns for the life of the child—and the adult—promises to yield interesting new insights into the human experience. The prospects of this area of work for the immediate future seem very bright, as do the prospects for the approach more generally.

SUMMARY

Psychosocial theories emphasize the idea that personality is intrinsically social and that the important issues concern how people relate to others. Several psychosocial theories focus on early life. Mahler's object relations theory proposes that infants begin life merged psychologically with their mothers and that they separate and individuate during the first 3 years of life. How this takes place influences later adjustment.

Another psychosocial theorist whose self psychology resembles object relations theory was Kohut. He held that humans have narcissistic needs that are satisfied by other people, represented as selfobjects. If the child receives enough mirroring (positive attention) from selfobjects (chiefly the mother), the sense of self develops appropriately. If there's too much mirroring, the child won't be able to deal with frustrations. If there's too little, the development of the self is stunted.

Many of the themes of object relations and self psychology were anticipated by Horney, who wrote that people suffer from basic anxiety, a feeling of being abandoned, isolated, and alone. People develop strategies to cope with this anxiety, some of which are similar to those observed by attachment theorists. If the strategies aren't successful in obtaining affection, they lead to a vicious cycle of increased anxiety.

Some of these ideas have also been echoed in the work of attachment theorists such as Bowlby and Ainsworth. Secure attachment provides a solid base for exploration. There are also patterns of insecure attachment (ambivalent and avoidant), which stem from inconsistent treatment, neglect, or rejection. These patterns appear stable until at least age 6. There's increasing interest in the idea that childhood attachment patterns persist and influence adult personality. There is now evidence that adult attachment styles influence many aspects of behavior, including how people relate to their romantic partners.

Another important theory of the psychosocial group is Erikson's theory of psychosocial development. Erikson postulated a series of crises from infancy to late adulthood, giving rise to ego strengths that influence one's ego identity—the consciously experienced sense of self. Erikson assumed that each crisis becomes focal at one stage but that each is present in a less obvious form throughout life.

The first crisis concerns the development of a sense of *basic trust*. The child then becomes concerned with control over its body and the sense of *autonomy* that goes along with that. The next issue is *initiative*, as the child seeks to exercise its power. As children enter the school years, they begin to realize that the social environment demands that they be *industrious*. With adolescence, the child enters a new stage of life and a crisis over *identity*. In young adulthood, identity issues give way to concern over *intimacy*. In adulthood, the person moves to a concern over *generativity*. Finally, in the last stage of life, people confront the *integrity* of their lives as a whole.

Assessment techniques from the psychosocial view are similar to those of ego psychology, but focus more on people's relationships. This approach also leads to use of play as an assessment method with children. The psychosocial view of problems focuses on the idea that problems are rooted in relationship issues. Kohut suggested that pathological narcissism stems from inadequate childhood mirroring. Horney suggested that people's strategies for dealing with basic anxiety involve moving toward, away from, or against other people. Adaptive functioning involves flexibly shifting from one strategy to another as needed. Poor adjustment comes from rigid reliance on one strategy. It has also been suggested that insecure attachment creates a risk for depression.

These theories approach therapy in ways similar to those of ego psychology, but there are additional variations. One of them is play therapy for children. Object relations and attachment theories also suggest that a relationship with a therapist is critical, in permitting reintegration of the sense of self or establishing a sense of secure attachment.

GLOSSARY

Attachment An emotional connection to someone else.

Basic anxiety A sense of insecurity, a feeling of being abandoned and isolated.

Ego identity The overall sense of self that emerges from transactions with social reality.

Ego quality (**ego strength** or **virtue**) The quality that joins one's personality through successful management of a crisis.

Epigenesis The idea (adopted from embryology) that an internal plan for development is present even at the beginning of life.

Identity crisis A time of intense exploration of alternative ways of viewing oneself.

Identity status The condition of whether an identity crisis has occurred and whether an identity has been attained.

Life-span development The idea that developmental processes continue throughout life.

Mirroring The giving of positive attention and supportiveness to someone.

Narcissism Grandiose self-importance and sense of entitlement

Neurotic needs Needs that emerge from overuse of strategies to combat anxiety

Object relations An individual's symbolized relations to other persons (such as parents).

Play therapy The use of play as a procedure for conducting therapy with children.

Psychosocial crisis (or **conflict**) A period when some interpersonal issue is being dealt with and growth potential and vulnerability are both high.

Selfobject The mental symbol of other person who serves functions for oneself.

Separation-individuation The process of acquiring a distinct identity; separating from fusion with mother.

Social interest The need to live in harmony with others.

Strange situation A procedure used to assess the attachment pattern of infant to mother.

Symbiosis A period in which an infant experiences fusion with mother.

Transference The viewing of other people through selfobject representations originally developed for parents.

Vicious cycle A cycle of needing affection, failing to obtain it, and thereby increasing the need.

PART six

The Learning Perspective

THE LEARNING PERSPECTIVE: Major Themes and Underlying Assumptions

The experiences of life change us, and they do so in ways that are lawful and predictable. This is the central assumption that underlies the learning perspective on personality. People have been interested in the processes of learning for a long time. At first, this interest was largely confined to those who studied lower animals. At first, this interest also focused primarily on small bits of behavior.

As knowledge grew, however, a tantalizing possibility began to take shape. The suspicion grew stronger that the principles of learning might constitute the basic building blocks of behavior. All behavior. Not just the actions of rats in laboratory cages, but also the more complex actions of human beings moving through the world. Personality, from this point of view, is an accumulated set of learned tendencies. It's all the tendencies that a person has learned over the course of a lifetime's experiences.

It's sometimes said that the basic metaphor of the learning perspective is the human being as a white rat. In a sense this is true, because many who take this perspective on behavior assume that learning processes are "universals," that is, that the processes are the same in virtually all animals. In that sense, a human being is nothing more than a very complex version of the rats and mice that occupy the attention (and the cages) of many scientists who study the learning process. This metaphor has been accepted by many of the learning theorists who've applied their findings to the understanding of personality. The principles that they've focused on are discussed in Chapter 12.

Although this metaphor proved useful as a starting place, many learning theorists ultimately came to believe that it's too simple. The processes of human learning began to appear more complex to some theorists than they'd been thought to be. The result was the need for a more elaborated metaphor, along with more elaborate theories of learning. In the new metaphor, the human being is still seen as learner, but now as a more self-directive learner and as a learner whose knowledge can accumulate in great leaps rather than just small increments. The learning is also seen as involving a set of cognitions, which play an important role themselves in behavior. The theories that draw on that expanded metaphor are discussed in Chapter 13.

The learning perspective on personality has also sparked something of a philosophical argument, which evolved and shifted as did the learning approach itself. In simple terms, the argument is about where behavior is "controlled." Is behavior controlled from within the person, or is it controlled by events and processes that are outside the person? The analysis of behavior offered by the earliest learning theorists took the view that behavior is shaped by external events, by stimuli and outcomes imposed from the environment. This assumption wasn't viewed with enthusiasm by everyone, perhaps partly because it doesn't represent a very flattering portrayal of human nature. More recently, many learning theorists have backed away from this assumption.

Nevertheless, one theme remains constant within the framework of the learning perspective across its two variants: Changes in behavior occur in predictable ways as a result of experience. By extrapolation, personality must also be susceptible to molding, grinding, and polishing by the events that form the person's unique and individual history.

chapter

12

Conditioning Theories

■ Lisa has a fondness for pastels. When asked why, she looks sort of blank and says she doesn't know, except that she's felt that way at least since her eighth birthday, when she had the most wonderful surprise party, decorated all in pale pink, green, and violet.

■ Nora works hard at her job at the library. She bustles from meeting to meeting, smoothing disagreements among the people she works with and making it easier for them to get their own projects accomplished. People express their appreciation to her in many ways—smiles, thank-you's, and last month a promotion to staff coordinator. The more signals she gets that she's doing a good job, the more enthusiasm she puts into each new morning.

Why are these people the way they are? Why do people have the preferences they do? What makes one person put so much effort into her work when someone else doesn't? One answer is that these aspects of behavior, which contribute so much to the individuality of personality, are acquired through learning.

The beginnings of what would become the learning perspective on personality go back a long way. The puzzle of just how learning takes place, what the elements of the process are, intrigued scientists from all over the world. The puzzle wasn't solved all at once, but a little at a time. Indeed, it isn't fully solved even yet. For example, there are still disagreements about whether learning is a single process with several manifestations or whether there are several distinct processes (e.g., Locurto, Terrace, & Gibbon, 1980; Rescorla, 1987; Staats, 1996).

From the learning perspective, personality consists of all the learned tendencies a person has acquired over the experiences of his or her life. If personality is the residue of learning, then it's obviously important to know how learning occurs. In this section of the chapter we focus on principles of learning that suggest how people's patterns of action and emotion develop (for broader discussion see, e.g., B. Schwartz, 1989).

For ease in presentation, we've adopted the view implicitly taken by most theorists: that there are distinct types of learning with their own distinct rules. This chapter focuses on two forms of learning termed *conditioning*—classical conditioning and instrumental conditioning. Much of the research on these processes used animals other than humans. Nonetheless, many theorists think these processes underlie the qualities we think of as personality.

Classical Conditioning

One of the earliest findings in the effort to understand learning was that responses could be acquired by associating one stimulus with another. This type of learning is called **classical conditioning.** It's also sometimes called Pavlovian conditioning, after the pioneering Russian scientist Ivan Pavlov, whose efforts opened the door to understanding it (e.g., Pavlov, 1927, 1955).

Basic Elements

At least two things are required for classical conditioning to occur. First, the organism must already respond to some class of stimuli in a reflexive manner. That is, the response must occur *reliably and automatically whenever the stimulus occurs*. A **reflex** thus is an existing connection between a stimulus and a response such that the one leads to the other.

Consider some examples of reflexes from day-to-day experience. When you put something dry, acidic, or sour in your mouth (think lemonade) your salivary glands start to work. When you see an object suddenly increase in size, as though it's approaching rapidly, you reflexively draw back. When areas of skin near sexual organs are gently rubbed, you feel sexual excitement. When you put your hand on a hot stove or touch a hot plate, you automatically yank your hand away. When someone smiles warmly at you, you automatically feel good. These reactions happen reflexively for most people. Some are innate, some are learned, but in each case a stimulus leads directly and reliably to a particular response.

The second condition required for classical conditioning is that the stimulus causing the reflexive response must be associated in time and place with another stimulus. This second stimulus is usually (though not always) "neutral" at first. That is, when it occurs by itself, it causes no particular response beyond being noticed. There aren't any special requirements for this stimulus. It can be pretty much anything—a color, a sound, an object, a person.

For clarity, people often describe the process of classical conditioning in terms of several stages (Figure 12.1). The first stage is the situation *before* conditioning occurs. At that point, only the reflex exists—one stimulus causing an automatic response. This stimulus is termed the **unconditioned** or **unconditional stimulus (US).** The response it touches off is called the **unconditioned** or **unconditional response (UR).** The word *unconditional* here means that there's no special condition required for the response to occur. It's automatic when the stimulus is presented (Figure 12.1, A).

The second stage is when conditioning takes place. This involves occurrence of the neutral stimulus along with, or slightly before, the US (Figure 12.1, B). The neutral stimulus now gets a technical name—**conditioned** or **conditional stimulus**

FIGURE 12.1

The various stages of a typical classical conditioning procedure (time runs left to right in each panel): (A) There is a preexisting reflexive connection between a stimulus (US) and a response (UR). (B) A neutral stimulus (CS) is then paired repeatedly in time and space with the US. (C) The result is the development of a new response, termed a conditioned response (CR). (D) Once conditioning has occurred, presenting the CS by itself will now lead to the CR.

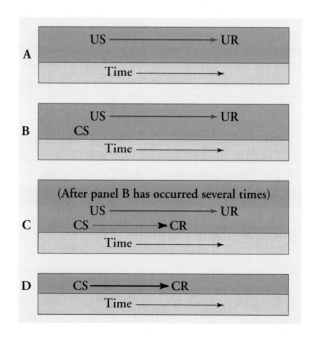

TABLE 12.1

Illustrations of the elements of classical conditioning in two common research procedures, in one common childhood experience, and in one common adult experience. (Note that the elements are arranged here in terms of stimulus and associated response, not in time sequence.)

	US	UR	CS	CR
(A)	Lemon juice in mouth	Salivation	Tone	Salivation
(B)	Shock to foot	Pain	Light	Fear
(C)	Ice cream in mouth	Smiles	Ice cream truck bell	Smiles
(D)	Romantically enticing partner	Sexual arousal	Mood music	Sexual arousal

(CS). Here are two easy ways to keep track of what that means. First, this is the stimulus that's becoming "conditioned." Second, a response occurs in the presence of this stimulus only under a special condition: that the CS be accompanied by the US. When the US comes, the UR occurs automatically, reflexively (and remember that this response occurs *whenever* the US is presented, whether something else is there or not).

When the US and the CS are paired frequently, something gradually begins to change (Figure 12.1, C). The CS starts to acquire the ability to produce a response *of its own*. This is termed the **conditioned response (CR).** The CR is often very similar to the UR. Indeed, in some cases they look identical (Table 12.1, row A), except that the CR is less intense than the UR. In other cases, the two can be distinguished (e.g., Hall, 1966). There is, however, an important similarity: Specifically, if the UR has an unpleasant quality, so will the CR (Table 12.1, row B). If the UR has a pleasant quality, so will the CR (Table 12.1, rows C and D).

How does any of this apply to your life? Let's go back to the examples used earlier to illustrate reflexes. Suppose you've taken to squandering your late evenings at a bar specializing in Italian wines and Sicilian folk music. Every time you take a sip of the extremely dry Chianti (US), your salivary glands pump like crazy (UR) in response to the acidity. Surrounding this reflexive experience are the strains of Sicilian folk songs (CS). Eventually you may come to develop a salivation response (CR) to the music itself.

As another example, suppose that while in that little bar you meet someone (US) who induces in you an astonishingly high degree of sexual arousal (UR). As you bask in candlelight, surrounded by green wine bottles, crimson wallpaper, and the soft strains of a Sicilian love song (all CSs), you may be acquiring a conditioned sexual response (CR) to those previously neutral features of the setting. Candlelight, for you, may never be the same again. The song you're hearing may gain a special place in your heart.

If you know that a US has occurred repeatedly for someone along with a neutral stimulus, how do you know whether conditioning has taken place? To find out, present the CS by itself—without the US (Figure 12.1, D). If the CS (alone) gets a reaction, conditioning must have taken place. If there's no reaction, there's been no conditioning. Generally speaking, the more frequently the CS is paired with the US, the more likely it is to lead to conditioning. If a US is very strong, however—if it causes a very intense UR—conditioning may occur with only one pairing. For example, cancer patients undergoing chemotherapy often experience extreme nausea from the medication and develop very strong CRs to surrounding stimuli.

Classical Conditioning as Anticipatory Learning

It has been suggested that CRs represent anticipatory reactions (Zener, 1937; see also Rescorla, 1972). That is, CRs, though involuntary, seem to reflect anticipation of, or preparation for, an impending US. Think back to earlier examples. If a tone sounds before lemon juice hits your mouth, the tone comes to serve as a signal that the lemon will be arriving shortly. The CR (salivation) prepares the surface of your mouth for the acidity of the lemon. As another example, if a child hears his father's steps coming up the stairs just before he gets a spanking, the steps signal the spanking and the reflexive pain. The CR (fear, and perhaps trembling) reflect anticipation of the pain.

Another clue that CRs may be anticipatory reactions is that they develop more easily in some situations than others. We said earlier that conditioning occurs through the more-or-less simultaneous presentation of the US and the CS. But classical conditioning is actually most effective if the CS slightly precedes the US (as in Figure 12.1). It's less effective if the two are simultaneous. It's even *less* so if the CS comes *after* the US (e.g., Schneiderman & Gormezano, 1964; Spetch, Wilkie, & Pinel, 1981; Spooner & Kellogg, 1947). This also makes it look as though an anticipatory reaction is being developed.

Don't necessarily assume that the anticipatory reaction is a *conscious* anticipation of the US. That is, in theory the tone needn't evoke the image of lemon juice. The sound of steps needn't lead to the inference that a spanking is coming. According to a strict conditioning analysis, the CR is connected *to the CS itself, not to an image of the US* that comes to mind when the CS occurs. The CS and the person's reaction to it are assumed to be bound together at this point, so the one reflexively produces the other (although see Box 12.1).

Once conditioning has taken place, the CS-CR combination can go on to function just as any other reflex. That is, once it's solidly established, this combination can serve as US and UR for another case of classical conditioning (Figure 12.2). For example, once soft candlelight leads to sexual arousal, the candlelight can be used to condition arousal to other things, such as particular *meals* that you eat by candlelight. This process is termed **higher-order conditioning.**

Given this extension to new cases, classical conditioning can be very pervasive. As conditioning takes place, more and more stimuli acquire the ability to produce reflexive reactions and thus to contribute to new conditioning. There are limita-

FIGURE 12.2

Once a link has been created between a stimulus and a response by classical conditioning, that new reflex can serve as a US–UR pair for additional conditioning, termed higher-order conditioning.

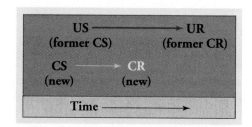

BOX 12.1

WHAT'S GOING ON IN CLASSICAL CONDITIONING?

Classical, or Pavlovian, conditioning has been a staple of psychology courses for decades. In most accounts, it's a process that was well mapped out early in the development of learning theory, and there's been little new to add since then. Not everyone agrees with this assessment, however, and there's been a new surge of interest in questions that lie just beneath the surface.

The usual view of Pavlovian conditioning portrays a low-level process in which control over a response gets transferred from one stimulus to another by their being together at the same time. Robert Rescorla (1988) says that's not the way it really is. He says that conditioning concerns *relations* among events in the world. In his view, organisms use the experiences that they have of relations between parts of the world to represent the structure of reality. Rescorla goes on to say that association in time and place isn't what makes conditioning take place. Rather, what's important is the information that one stimulus gives about the other. To Rescorla, learning is a process by which the organism's representation of the world is brought into line with the actual state of the world. Organisms learn only when they're "surprised" by something that happens to them.

One result is that two stimuli that are experienced together sometimes don't become associated with each other. For example (Kamin, 1968), consider two animals. One has had a series of trials in which a light (as a CS) has been paired with a shock (as a US). The other hasn't had this experience. Both then have a series of trials in which both the light and a tone (as *two* CSs) are paired with the shock. What's interesting is that the second animal acquires a CR to the tone, but the first one doesn't. Apparently the earlier experience with the light (alone) has made the tone redundant. That is, since the light already signals that the US is coming, there's no need to condition the tone.

In the same way, studies have found that cancer patients undergoing chemotherapy may be induced to form conditioned aversions to very specific foods, if an unusual food is given before the chemotherapy (Bernstein, 1985). Doing this can make that specific food a "scapegoat," and prevent the conditioning of aversions to other foods, which otherwise is likely to happen.

Rescorla also challenges other aspects of the traditional view. He argues against the assumption that classical conditioning is a slow process requiring many pairings of stimuli. He says, in fact, that learning in five to six trials is common. In summarizing his stance, Rescorla says "Pavlovian conditioning is not a stupid process by which the organism willy-nilly forms associations between any two stimuli that happen to co-occur. Rather, the organism is better seen as an information seeker using logical and perceptual relations among events, along with its own preconceptions, to form a sophisticated representation of the world" (1988, p. 154).

Rescorla is not alone in taking the view that internal events are more important in conditioning than previously realized. An analysis of classical conditioning with somewhat similar characteristics (but even more cognitive in certain respects) was proposed by Holyoak, Koh, and Nisbett (1989). Their model is based in part on ideas from cognitive psychology identified with the term *connectionism* (McClelland & Rumelhart, 1986). We can't present a complete account of this theory here, but its most important characteristic (for the issue we're raising here) is that it treats classical conditioning as *rule* learning.

The positions taken by Rescorla and by Holyoak et al. are clearly at odds with the point of view that's expressed in the body of this chapter. The views they express herald a broad issue that becomes more prominent in the next chapter: the role of cognition in the phenomena of learning.

tions, of course. The most potent USs are those that elicit very intense URs. The farther away you get from biological reflexes, the weaker the reflexes are, and the weaker is the conditioning that results.

Discrimination, Generalization, and Extinction in Classical Conditioning

Classical conditioning provides a mechanism for new responses to become attached to neutral stimuli. Yet the CS almost never recurs later on in precisely the same form as it did earlier. On the other hand, you run across many stimuli later on that are at least somewhat similar to the CS. What happens in those cases?

Learning theorists address this question with concepts called **discrimination** and **generalization.** Discrimination means telling things apart. More formally it means responding differently to different stimuli. For example, suppose your experiences in the Sicilian wine bar have led you to associate candlelight, muted crimson wallpaper, and wine bottles (as CSs) with sexual arousal (as CR). If you entered a room that resembled the bar (all other things being equal), you'd begin to feel a mellow glow (your CR). If you walked instead into a room with fluorescent lights and blue walls, the same glow would surely not emerge. You *discriminate,* in your conditioned reactions, between the two classes of stimuli.

Now a harder question: What would happen if you walked into a room with muted lamplight, walls painted burgundy, and green glass vases? These aren't quite the stimulus conditions that got linked to sexual arousal, but they're close. Here's where the process of generalization comes in. In all probability, you'd begin to feel the glow, although it might not be as strong as in the first room. As shown in Figure 12.3, generalization from conditioned stimuli definitely takes place. The intensity of the reaction falls off, though, as the stimulus gets farther and farther removed from the original CS (Hovland, 1937; Moore, 1972). To put it differently, generalization begins to give way to discrimination, as the stimuli become more different from the initial CS. Discrimination and generalization thus are complementary.

There's one more question about classical conditioning we need to answer to round out the picture. Do conditioned responses ever go away? Discussions of conditioning don't use terms such as *forgetting.* CRs do weaken, however, through a process called **extinction.** Extinction occurs when a CS comes repeatedly without the US (Pavlov, 1927). At first, the CS leads reliably to the CR (Figure 12.4). Gradually, over repeated presentations, the CR grows weaker. There's disagreement about whether the CR actually disappears or not. Even when a response stops in a given session, there's a "spontaneous recovery" the next day (e.g., Wagner, Siegel, Thomas, & El-

FIGURE 12.3

An illustration of generalization of a classically conditioned response to stimuli that are similar to the CS, and of discrimination regarding stimuli that are less similar to the CS. The CS is a tone of 1200 Hz. Tones that are similar to it (800, 1600 Hz) elicit CRs—generalization. Tones that are less similar (400, 2000 Hz) elicit fewer CRs—discrimination (data from Moore, 1972, combined across two groups).

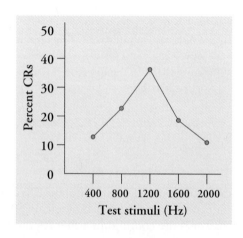

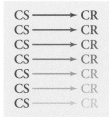

FIGURE 12.4

Extinction in classical conditioning. When a CS appears over and over without the US, the CR becomes progressively weaker and eventually disappears (or nearly does).

lison, 1964). Some believe that classical conditioning leaves a permanent record in the nervous system, the effects of which can be muted but never erased entirely (see Bouton, 1994).

Emotional Conditioning

As you may have realized already, much of the classical conditioning that takes place in humans involves responses with emotional qualities. That is, the stimuli that most clearly lead to reflexive reactions are stimuli that elicit good feelings (hope, delight, excitement) or bad feelings (fear, anger, pain). The term **emotional conditioning** is sometimes used to refer to classical conditioning in which the CRs are emotional reactions.

Conditioning of emotional responses is important in the learning view on personality for two reasons. First, it's argued that most of the likes and dislikes, the preferences and biases that define one's personality, develop through emotional conditioning. Conditioning theorists suggest that preferences develop through associations between neutral stimuli and events that reflexively produce good or bad feelings. Linking a neutral stimulus with a pleasant event creates a positive preference (Razran, 1940; Staats & Staats, 1958). Linking a stimulus with an upsetting event creates an aversion (Watson & Raynor, 1920; see also Cacioppo & Sandman, 1981; Riordan & Tedeschi, 1983; Staats, Staats, & Crawford, 1962). In fact, even hearing someone talk about a positive or negative trait in someone else can cause you to associate that trait with the person doing the talking (Skowronski, Carlston, Mae, & Crawford, 1998).

Different people experience different pieces of the world and thus experience different patterns of emotional arousal. Different people also experience even the same event from the perspective of their unique "histories." As we noted in Chapter 6, children from the same family experience the family environment differently (Daniels & Plomin, 1985). Given these variations, people can wind up with remarkably different patterns of likes and dislikes (Box 12.2). Thus emotional conditioning may play a major role in creating the uniqueness of personality (Staats & Burns, 1982).

Instrumental Conditioning

A second form of conditioning that underlies personality is called **instrumental conditioning.** (This phrase is often used interchangeably with *operant conditioning*, despite slight differences in meaning.) Instrumental conditioning differs in several

BOX 12.2

CLASSICAL CONDITIONING AND ATTITUDES

Where do people's attitudes come from? One answer to this question is that you develop attitudes through classical conditioning. This chapter describes how a neutral stimulus (CS) begins to produce an emotional reaction (CR) if it's paired with a stimulus (US) that already produces an emotional reaction. The conditioning approach to attitude formation holds that people come to have emotional responses to attitude objects (classes of things, people, ideas, or events) in exactly that way. If the attitude object is paired with an emotion-arousing stimulus, it comes to evoke the emotion itself. This emotional response, then, is the basis for an attitude.

One of the first experiments on classical conditioning of attitudes was conducted by Razran (1940). In an initial phase of the study, he presented several political slogans to subjects and had them indicate how much they approved of each. Later he presented the slogans again, under one of three conditions: while subjects were eating a free lunch, while they were inhaling noxious odors, or while they were sitting in a nondescript, neutral setting. Later on, subjects rated their approval of the slogans a second time.

Razran found that slogans paired with a free lunch were now rated more positively than before. Slogans paired with unpleasant odors were now rated more negatively than before. Slogans presented in the neutral room weren't rated differently than before. (Similar results were obtained by Nunnally, Duchnowski, & Parker, 1965). These findings are exactly what one would predict from the principle of classical conditioning.

This approach was later extended to conditioning of attitudes toward words (Staats, Staats, & Crawford, 1962). One group of words was presented with electric shocks. After several pairings, the words were presented without the shocks, and subjects rated how much they liked each. The ratings were more negative than ratings of words that hadn't been paired with shocks (for similar findings see Berkowitz & Knurek, 1969; Zanna, Kiesler, & Pilkonis, 1970). Even the *threat* of shock has been shown to produce conditioning—in this case, to another person who happened to be present (Riordan & Tedeschi, 1983).

These studies show that classical conditioning *can* be involved in development of attitudes, but they don't tell us whether attitudes *are* often acquired this way. How reasonable is this idea? Events that arouse emotions are common in day-to-day life, which provides opportunities for conditioning to take place. Consider, for instance, the traditional "business lunch," which is remarkably similar to Razran's experimental manipulation.

And don't forget the possibility of higher-order conditioning. It seems likely that words such as "good" and "bad" are tied in most people's experience to positive and negative events (Staats & Staats, 1957, 1958) and thus yield an emotional response. Think about how often parents use such words around their children, thereby providing opportunities for higher-order conditioning to take place. In sum, it seems not unreasonable that classical conditioning processes may underlie many of people's preferences for persons, events, things, places, and ideas. Inasmuch as these preferences are important aspects of personality, conditioning processes would appear to represent important contributors to the human experience.

ways from classical conditioning. For instance, classical conditioning is passive. When a reflex occurs, conditioning apparently doesn't require you to *do* anything—just be there and be aware of other stimuli. Instrumental conditioning, in contrast, is an active process (cf. Skinner, 1938). The events that define it begin with a behavior on your part (even if the "behavior" is the chosen act of remaining still).

One purpose of the business lunch is to associate your company and its products (as CSs) with the positive feelings produced by a good meal in a nice restaurant (as USs).

The Law of Effect

Instrumental conditioning is really a simple process, although its ramifications are widespread. The process goes like this: If a behavior is followed by a better or more satisfying state of affairs, the behavior is more likely to be done again later on in a similar situation (Figure 12.5, A). If a behavior is followed by a worse or less satisfying state of affairs, the behavior is less likely to be done again later (Figure 12.5, B).

This simple description—linking an action, an outcome, and a change in the likelihood of future action—is the "law of effect" deduced by Thorndike a century ago (Thorndike, 1898, 1905). The law of effect is simple but profound. It provides a way to account for regularities in behavior. That is, any situation permits many potential acts (Figure 12.5, C). Some of them come to occur with great regularity, oth-

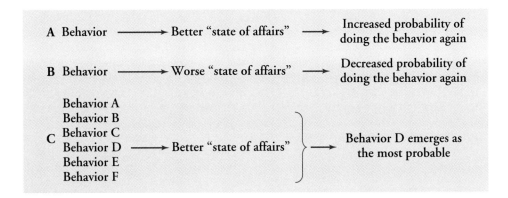

FIGURE 12.5

Instrumental conditioning: (A) Behavior that is followed by a more satisfying state of affairs is more likely to be done again. (B) Behavior that is followed by a less satisfying state of affairs is less likely to be done again. (C) This principle accounts for the fact that (over time and experiences) some behaviors emerge from the many possible behaviors as habitual responses that occur in specific situations.

ers happen once and disappear, never to return. Others turn up occasionally, but only occasionally. Why? Because some have been followed by satisfying outcomes, and others haven't.

Think of all the possible behaviors that a person might do in a given situation as forming a **habit hierarchy,** or a list of response potentials (Miller & Dollard, 1941). The list derives from prior conditioning. Some responses are very likely (because they've been followed by more satisfying states of affairs), others are less likely, and others even less so. For example, when you're in the cafeteria at noontime, getting and eating lunch are very likely behaviors, working on coursework is less likely (although maybe not too far down the list), and taking off all your clothes and reciting Shakespeare are very *un*likely. As another example, if you need to ask your parents for money, there are some tactics you use because they've worked in the past, and other tactics you've given up because they haven't worked. Habit hierarchies continually evolve, as the various actions you engage in are followed by either more or less satisfying states of affairs.

Reinforcement and Punishment

It wasn't too long before the term **reinforcer** replaced the cumbersome phrase "satisfying state of affairs." This term derives from the fact that reinforcers strengthen the tendency to do the action that came before them. A reinforcer is anything that strengthens a behavioral tendency. Reinforcers may satisfy biological needs (e.g., food or water) or may pertain to social desires (e.g., smiles and social acceptance). Some of them have acquired their reinforcing quality indirectly (e.g., money). There's even evidence that visual sensations (seeing something you like) can serve as reinforcers (Hayes, Rincover, & Volosin, 1980).

The exact nature of the reinforcer is immaterial to its reinforcing effect, but different kinds of reinforcers do have different names. A *primary reinforcer* is one that diminishes a biological need. A *secondary reinforcer* has gained reinforcing properties by association with a primary reinforcer (i.e., through classical conditioning) or by virtue of the fact that it can be used to *get* primary reinforcers (see Wolfe, 1936; Zimmerman, 1957).

Time out is an effective way of discouraging unwanted behavior in children.

The term **punisher** refers to unpleasant or aversive outcomes. Punishers reduce the tendency to do the behavior that came before them, although there's been some controversy over the years as to how effectively they change behavior (Rachman & Teasdale, 1969; Solomon, 1964; Thorndike, 1933). As with reinforcement, punishment can be either primary or secondary. That is, some events are intrinsically aversive (e.g., pain). Others are aversive because of associations with primary punishers.

There's another kind of distinction that's also important. When you think of reinforcement, things you find desirable probably come to mind—gifts, money, trips to fun places, CDs, and so on. When you think of punishment, you probably think first of pain—of being slapped or hit—or of being yelled at or frowned at. In reality, however, reinforcement and punishment are broader and more subtle concepts than that.

Reinforcement always implies moving the person's "state of affairs" in a positive direction. But this can happen in two ways. One way, of course, is receiving the good things that come easily to mind as reinforcers (gifts, money). These are more precisely termed **positive reinforcement.** "Positive" implies adding something good. When positive reinforcement occurs, the behavior that preceded it becomes more likely.

There's also a second category of reinforcement, though, called **negative reinforcement.** Negative reinforcement occurs when something aversive is taken away. For instance, when your otherwise pleasant roommate stops playing his annoying tape of "Polka Favorites" over and over, that's probably a negative reinforcer for you. Removing something unpleasant also moves the present state of affairs in a positive direction—from unpleasant to neutral. The event thus is reinforcing. Negative reinforcement can be fully as potent as positive reinforcement. Thus, whatever you did before the tape stopped will become more likely in the future.

Just as reinforcement comes in several forms, so does punishment. Most people think of punishment as adding pain, thereby moving the present state of affairs from neutral to negative. But sometimes punishment involves removing something good, changing from a positive to a neutral (thus less satisfying) state of affairs. This principle—punishing by withdrawing something desirable—underlies a tactic that's widely used to discourage unwanted behavior in children. It's called a **time out,** short for "time out from positive reinforcement" (Drabman & Spitalnik, 1973; Risley, 1968). A time out is removing the child from whatever activity is going on, to a place where there's nothing fun to do. Many who work with children find this practice appealing because it's more humane than painful punishments such as spanking. In principle, however, a time out creates a "less satisfying state of affairs" for the child and thus should have the same effect on behavior as any other punishment.

A final issue to be addressed concerning reinforcement is that it's hard to specify absolutely how "satisfying" an outcome is (and thus how reinforcing it is). An outcome's value is determined partly by your situation. If you're starving, being handed a box of stale Cheez puffs is a good outcome. If you've just had a sumptuous meal, the Cheez Puffs won't do as much for you. In the same way, a truly starving man may not be terribly impressed by sexual overtures from a beautiful woman, which in other circumstances would seem to him an *extremely* satisfying state of affairs.

This sort of thing has led many people (though not all) to think of instrumental conditioning as a process that occurs primarily when the person has a motivational state to which the reinforcer is relevant (see Box 12.3). Indeed, many people use the term *instrumental* more broadly, going beyond the conditioning process per se. This broader use of the word carries the connotation "goal directed," conveying the sense that the behavior is the instrument or tool by which a desired outcome is obtained.

BOX 12.3

THEORETICAL CONTROVERSY:
What Role Do Motives Play in Instrumental Conditioning?

As pointed out in the main text, you have to consider an organism's present state to know what's reinforcing to it. There are, however, several ways to think about this. Neal Miller and John Dollard (1941; Dollard & Miller, 1950), the first theorists to try to portray the full breadth of human personality in terms of learning, held that the nature of reinforcement is intimately related to motivation.

Their view of the nature of reinforcement relied on Clark Hull's (1943 theory of motivation. Hull said that when an organism is deprived of a needed substance (e.g., food or water), it experiences an increase in **drive.** When drive goes up, it increases the tendency to emit behaviors high in the habit hierarchy. Sooner or later, you get whatever you've been deprived of, which causes drive to go back down. According to Miller and Dollard, *drive reduction constitutes reinforcement.* In this view, to know what will be reinforcing to a person, you need to know the person's needs or motives.

Not all conditioning theorists have agreed that motivational concepts are helpful. An alternative point of view was posed by B. F. Skinner (e.g., 1953, 1974), who argued that the effort to explain behavior doesn't benefit from guessing about what's going on inside the organism. He was quite outspoken about his belief that concepts like motive, wish, desire—not to mention cognition—serve more to confuse the picture than to clarify it.

Skinner noted that use of terms such as *motive* or *wish* is often circular. That is, we often infer that

people are motivated to do something by whether they do it. The act is taken as evidence of an underlying motive. Skinner asked why we don't forget about the motive and simply analyze the acts. Indeed, Skinner felt that terms such as *drive* and *motive* are actually misleading, since they create the impression of an explanation while not really explaining anything.

Rather than talk about drives or needs, Skinner said, you should simply describe the stimulus conditions of *deprivation* versus *satiation*. Deprivation is a period of the absence of a consummatory behavior (for example, eating or drinking). Satiation is the end of a period of intense consummatory behavior. Both events are observable and can be measured. Along with knowledge of prior reinforcement contingencies, they provide all the information necessary to predict behavior. This theoretical position is often called **radical behaviorism** because it represents a strict (thus radical) application of the idea that one shouldn't invent imaginary mechanisms when behavior can be accounted for by observable events.

In sum, these two theoretical models agree in one respect and disagree in another. Both assume it's important to take the organism's "present condition" into account. But they take very different views on how to think about the organism's present condition.

Discrimination, Generalization, and Extinction in Instrumental Conditioning

Several ideas that were introduced in the context of classical conditioning apply to instrumental conditioning as well, with slight differences in connotation. For example, discrimination still means responding differently in the presence of different stimuli. But here the difference in response is caused by variations in prior reinforcement.

To understand how a difference develops, imagine that a stimulus is present whenever a behavior is followed by a reinforcer. Further, when the stimulus is absent, the behavior is *never* followed by a reinforcer. Gradually the presence or absence of the stimulus gains an influence over whether the behavior takes place. It becomes a

discriminative stimulus, a stimulus that turns the behavior on and off. The name comes from the fact that you use the stimulus to discriminate among situations, and thus among responses. Miller and Dollard (1941 called this a *cue* function. Behavior that's cued by discriminative stimuli is said to be *under stimulus control.*

Here's an illustration of discriminative stimuli that may fit with some of your own memories. Imagine a class of high school students whose regular teacher is stiff and formal and doesn't tolerate cutting up or wisecracks during class. The teacher sometimes misses class due to illness. The usual substitute is more relaxed and easygoing. If the truth were known, he'd rather have a good time with the class than stick to the lesson plan. On days when he's called in, cutting up in class is followed by more reinforcement than when the regular teacher's there. The highly predictable result is that quiet prevails for the regular teacher, but the class turns into a party when the substitute's there. Because this shift occurs as a function of the change in teacher (the discriminative stimuli), the students' behavior is under stimulus control.

Earlier in this section we mentioned the idea that people have a habit hierarchy (an ordering of the likelihood of doing various behaviors). We noted at that time that your hierarchy shifts constantly because of the ongoing flow of reinforcing (and nonreinforcing) events. It shifts constantly for another reason as well: Every change in situation means a change in cues (discriminative stimuli). Since the cues suggest what behaviors are reinforced in that situation, the shift in cues rearranges the list of behavior probabilities.

The concept of discriminative stimulus is important to reinforcement views of personality. It accounts for complexity in behavior. Very slight changes in the stimulus field dramatically alter the behaviors that occur. As traffic lights turn green, people drive forward; as the lights turn red, the same people stop. As the clock reads 12, people leave their desks and go to lunch; as the clock reads 1, the same people return and begin to work again. These differences in behavior are large in scope, but they're caused by extremely small changes in the surrounding array of stimuli.

The principle of generalization is also important here. It contributes a sense of continuity in behavior. As you enter new settings and see objects and people you've never seen before, you respond easily and automatically. The reason for this is similarities between the new settings and previous discriminative stimuli. You generalize behaviors from the one to the other, and action flows smoothly forward. You may never have seen a particular style of spoon before, but you probably won't hesitate to use it on the soup. You may never have driven a particular make of car before, but if that's what the rental agency gives you, you'll probably be able to handle it.

The principle of generalization gives conditioning theorists a way of talking about "traitlike" behavioral qualities. A person can be expected to behave consistently across time and circumstances when discriminative stimuli stay fairly similar across those times and circumstances. Because important stimulus qualities often *do* stay the same across settings (even if other qualities differ substantially), the person's action tendency also stays the same across those settings. The result is that, to an outside observer, the person appears to have a set of internal traits, or dispositions. From this view, however, consistency of behavior depends on similarities of environments (an idea that's not too different from the discussion of consistency in Chapter 4).

Extinction in instrumental conditioning occurs when a behavior that once led to a reinforcer does so no longer. As the behavior is done over and over—with no reinforcer—its probability drops. Eventually it dies out to the point where it's barely there at all (though just as in classical conditioning there's a tendency for spontaneous recovery, which is one reason some believe that it hasn't gone away; see Bouton, 1994; Rescorla, 1997, 1998). Thus extinction is a way in which behavioral tendencies fade.

Altering the Shape of Behavior

The concepts of reward and punishment provide a way of talking about how behaviors become more or less likely to occur. Thus far, however, we haven't dealt with how a behavior changes in its form. Still missing is the concept of **shaping.**

Let's look first at shaping in the laboratory. Many times it's not practical to wait for a desired act and then reinforce it. Instead, reinforcement is first given for a rough *approximation* of the behavior, which then begins to occur more often. Gradually you reinforce only closer and closer approximations of the desired act. This method is called **successive approximation.** Through it, the behavior of the organism comes to be very specific—that is, behavior is "shaped" in a particular direction. To characterize the process differently, the organism is learning a continually changing discrimination.

One might think of this principle as simply a convenient laboratory tactic, but much the same thing happens all the time outside the lab. Whether by chance or by design, general tendencies (e.g., going to school) are often reinforced at first. These general tendencies then are channeled into more specific tendencies (e.g., studying political science) by shifts in patterns of reinforcement. This shaping of behavior can ultimately result in specific and highly specialized tendencies (attending law school, becoming a state representative). Shaping, then, provides a way to understand the fact that behavior (indeed, personality) evolves continuously, along with changing reinforcement patterns.

Schedules of Reinforcement and the Issue of Persistence

The issue of whether behaviors stay likely or fall away and disappear is important in thinking about personality—especially growth and change in personality. Extinction is an important principle in understanding persistence, but it's not the only principle that matters. It turns out that the persistence of an action tendency is influenced by the *pattern* with which it's been reinforced in the past.

In reading about instrumental conditioning, people often assume that reinforcement occurs every time the behavior occurs. But common sense and your own experience should tell you life isn't really like that. Sometimes reinforcements are frequent, but sometimes they're fewer and farther between. These variations in frequency and pattern are called *schedules of reinforcement*. A simple distinction among schedules is between continuous and partial (or intermittent) reinforcement. In **continuous reinforcement** the behavior is followed by a reinforcer *every single time.* In **partial reinforcement,** the behavior is followed by a reinforcer less often than every time.

There are many patterns of partial reinforcement. The reinforcer can come after a certain *number of occurrences* of the behavior (your teacher smiles and says "good" every fifth time you contribute to class discussion). This pattern is called a ratio schedule. Or the reinforcer may depend on the passage of a period of time as well as the occurrence of the behavior (a week has to pass since he last smiled and said "good," but then he does it again the next time you contribute to class). This pattern is called an interval schedule. The numbers involved can be large (every tenth time) or small (every second time). The numbers can be fixed (every sixth time exactly) or variable (randomly varying, but every sixth time on the average).

Different schedules of reinforcement lead to different behavior tendencies across time. Figure 12.6 shows the action tendencies associated with each type of schedule (adapted from Reese, 1966; see also Lundin, 1961). The tendencies are described in

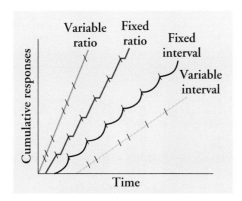

FIGURE 12.6

Behavioral tendencies created by four different types of reinforcement schedules, in which the total reinforcement across a long span of time is equivalent. Behavior is portrayed as "cumulative frequencies" of response—responses summed across time. Each small mark on the line represents the occurrence of a reinforcer. As you can see, some reinforcement schedules produce higher and more consistent rates of behavior than others (adapted from Reese, 1966).

this figure in terms of cumulative frequencies of response—responses added up across time. Each small mark on the line represents the occurrence of a reinforcer.

A *fixed ratio* schedule results in a high rate of responding, with a brief pause immediately after reinforcement. In human behavior, such a schedule is reflected in "piecework," in which a person is paid a certain amount per unit of work (object assembled, basket of vegetables picked, and so forth). A *variable ratio* schedule creates an even higher rate of responding, without the pauses after reinforcement. An example of a variable ratio schedule is gambling, which pays off occasionally but unpredictably.

The *fixed interval* schedule produces a pronounced and reliable "scalloping" of the curve, a complete absence of behavior immediately after reinforcement, followed by a gradual renewal, which accelerates until the next reinforcer occurs. A good illustration of this type of schedule is the study behavior of the student whose psychology course has tests at predictable intervals, and who studies most just before tests. This pattern also describes the behavior of the U.S. Congress, which passes most of its bills just before it adjourns (Weisberg & Waldrop, 1972).

The scalloping isn't apparent at all in the final schedule, the *variable interval* schedule. This one is characterized by consistent activity, as with the variable ratio schedule, but (in general) at a somewhat lower level of responding. An example of this schedule is the behavior of the student whose instructor gives pop quizzes unexpectedly, rather than tests at predictable intervals.

As you see, reinforcement patterns can get complicated. What's most important, though, is that infrequent and unpredictable reinforcement affects behavior differently than reinforcement that's frequent and predictable. There are two differences. The more intuitive difference is that you acquire a new behavior more quickly when reinforcement is frequent than when it's not. Eventually, even infrequent intermittent reinforcement results in relatively high levels of the behavior, but it may take a while.

The other effect is less intuitive but more important. It's often called the **partial reinforcement effect.** It shows up when reinforcement stops (Figure 12.7). Take away the reinforcer, and a behavior built in by continuous reinforcement goes away quickly. A behavior built in by partial (less frequent) reinforcement remains longer—it's more *resistant to extinction* (Amsel, 1967; Humphreys, 1939).

Apparently this effect isn't simply a matter of how easy or hard it is to tell when the extinction period is starting (Jenkins, 1962; Theios, 1962). Rather, there seems to be a subtle difference in what's conditioned in the first place (Amsel, 1967). In intermittent reinforcement, a nonreinforcement is actually becoming a discriminative stimulus that cues *persistence* (since, if you keep trying, you eventually get a reinforcement). Nonreinforcement continues to act as a discriminative stimulus for a

FIGURE 12.7

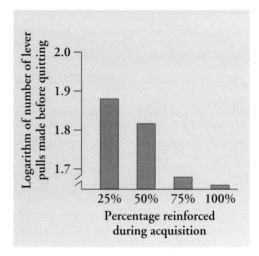

Effect of partial reinforcement and continuous reinforcement on persistence. Research participants were allowed to play a slot machine for as long as they liked, after first being rewarded on 25%, 50%, 75%, or 100% of the initial acquisition trials. As can be seen, partial reinforcement leads to greater resistance to extinction than does continuous reinforcement. That is, the groups initially rewarded less than 100% of the time persist longer when all reward is removed. Moreover, the lower the percentage of partial reinforcement initially given, the greater is the persistence shown (adapted from Lewis & Duncan, 1956).

long time, even when the reinforcer's gone for good. When you start with continuous reinforcement, though, the link between nonreinforcement and persistence never gets made. When the reinforcer goes away, nothing remains to keep the behavior going.

In the same vein, it has been argued that people learn to be industrious by receiving patterns of reinforcement that cause the sensation of effort to become a cue for persistence (Eisenberger, 1992). Thus, instead of finding the experience of effort aversive, these people find it desirable and rewarding. One can imagine a situation in which even a very aversive experience, such as fear, becomes a discriminative stimulus for persistence. Such a case would represent a kind of "conditioned courage."

The partial reinforcement effect carries a potentially important message. If you want a behavior to remain relatively persistent in someone, it's better not to reinforce it all the time. In fact, the lower the rate of reinforcement (provided it's enough to sustain the behavior), the stronger is the link between the cue of nonreinforcement and behavioral persistence. Ironically, although this view emphasizes the importance of reinforcement in producing behavior, it also emphasizes the importance of *non*reinforcement during conditioning in sustaining the behavior.

Learning "Irrational" Behavior

People who analyze behavior with conditioning principles often emphasize that the behavior need not really *cause* the reinforcer for conditioning to occur. The behavior needs only to be *followed by* the reinforcer. Whatever behavior preceded the reinforcer becomes strengthened by the reinforcer's occurrence.

This relationship can lead to some rather strange effects, which Skinner (1948) pointed out in a study of pigeons. Picture a pigeon in a cage, which gets a reinforcer (a bit of food) at a regular interval, regardless of what it's doing. Every occurrence of reinforcement strengthens the behavior that preceded it. At first, since the bird's behavior is somewhat random, several behaviors are strengthened. Eventually, though, some action is reinforced often enough that it starts to predominate. Because it's predominating, it's likely to be reinforced even more. The result is that the bird is now doing an entirely arbitrary behavior and is doing it regularly.

Because the pigeon acts as though these specific actions are causing the reinforcer, Skinner referred to the actions as *superstitious behavior.* He argued that when we see apparently irrational or senseless behavior in people, it probably developed in exactly the same way. Reinforcers occurred for reasons unrelated to the behavior, and they built the behavior in and shaped it into its present form. Skinner didn't assume, by the way, that the pigeon was thinking about the cause of the reinforcement, only that its behavior gave that outward appearance (see Box 12.4).

We should stress that there's no difference in principle between the process by which superstitious and irrational behaviors are acquired and the process by which any other behavior is acquired. To call a behavior irrational and senseless versus adaptive and functional is purely an observer's value judgment. To the conditioning theorist, all behaviors are acquired the same way (through reinforcement).

On the other hand, we should also note an important difference between the situation studied by Skinner and the situations people normally encounter. Skinner had complete control over the birds' environment. Thus he could easily ensure that reinforcers had a completely arbitrary pattern. In contrast, most environments

---

BOX 12.4

BEHAVIORISTS' VIEW OF THE ROLE OF THOUGHT IN CONDITIONING

Conditioning theorists hold that behavior tendencies are determined by reinforcement patterns. Most of them assume thought processes are irrelevant to this process (Rachlin, 1977). Although Skinner's pigeons may have acted *as though* they thought a particular action was producing the reinforcer, that appearance is illusory. Even if pigeons could think (which is questionable), their thoughts aren't behind the behavior. The reinforcement pattern is behind the behavior.

It's undeniable that people (unlike pigeons) talk and think. To conditioning theorists, however, these tendencies among humans simply reflect the fact that verbal behaviors (both overt speech and covert thought) become conditioned in particular ways (e.g., Miller & Dollard, 1941). That is, people have become conditioned to think in particular patterns and to talk in certain ways about their actions. Nevertheless, the real causes of all three phenomena—the behavior, the talk, and the thoughts—are the patterns of reinforcement.

Behaviorists try to avoid as much as possible using words such as *intention, thought, cognition,* and *consciousness* because they see them as unnecessary in explaining how people act (cf. Skinner, 1987)

and perhaps even misleading. Many behaviorists see the mental events that occur along with behavior and reinforcement as **epiphenomena**—phenomena with no causal role and perhaps no meaningful role at all. They just happen alongside the behavior, or may even be caused by the behavior itself as subjective offshoots (cf. Rachlin, 1977). Skinner (1989) pointed out, in this regard, that many words now used to describe mental states had their origins in descriptions of behavior. This history fits his contention that the behavior is what really matters.

This point of view has been more than a little controversial over the years. It hasn't been well received at all by people outside the behaviorist camp (see Catania & Harnad, 1988, for a wide-ranging discussion). Critics of the behaviorist position point out that a conditioning view has difficulty in accounting for a number of phenomena, including the emergence of language in children (Chomsky, 1959). This criticism has led some people to regard the conditioning view as incorrect. It led others more sympathetic to the learning perspective to modify the theories, a response that is taken up in the next chapter.

Many personal superstitions are learned through a schedule of random partial reinforcement.

where human behavior takes place aren't that way. For people, reinforcers more often result directly from some particular behavior. These contingencies shape most human behavior into orderly patterns that only more rarely appear to be superstitious or irrational.

Reinforcement of Dimensions of Behavior

There's one final point to be made about learning through instrumental conditioning: It's most intuitive to think that the occurrence of a reinforcer makes a particular *act* more likely to occur in the future. However, sometimes it seems that what becomes more likely isn't a concrete act, but rather some *quality* of action (Eisenberger & Selbst, 1994). For example, reinforcing *effort* in one setting can increase *effortfulness* in other settings (Mueller & Dweck, 1998). Reinforcing accuracy on one task increases accuracy on other tasks. Reinforcing speed on one task increases speed elsewhere. Reinforcing creativity produces more creativity elsewhere, whereas reinforcing focused thought produces more focused thinking in other contexts (Eisenberger, Armeli, & Pretz, 1998).

Thus, reinforcement can change not just particular behaviors, but whole dimensions of behavior. This idea broadens quite considerably the ways in which reinforcement principles can be thought of as acting on human beings. It suggests that reinforcers can act at many levels of abstraction. Indeed, perhaps many aspects of behavior at many different levels are reinforced *simultaneously* when a person experiences a more satisfying state of affairs. This possibility paints a far more complex picture of change through conditioning than you may have taken from earlier sections of the chapter.

Assessment

From the view of conditioning theories, personality is the accumulation of the person's conditioned tendencies or behavioral repertoire (Ciminero, Calhoun, &

Adams, 1977; Hersen & Bellack, 1976; Staats, 1996). By adulthood you have many conditioned emotional responses to various stimuli, which are experienced as attitudes and preferences. You also have conditioned tendencies to engage in various kinds of actions. These tendencies vary in probability, resistance to extinction, and the discriminative stimuli that cue them.

This view has at least three implications for the process of personality assessment. Most simply, this approach suggests that assessment should focus on behavioral qualities themselves, rather than on the cognitions that float around in people's heads, obscuring what's really important. The assessment procedures suggested by this approach examine observable aspects of people's emotional reactions, or their action tendencies per se, rather than trying to obtain a general sense of what the person is "like" (Kanfer & Saslow, 1965).

A second implication of this approach stems from the assumption that emotional responses are linked to specific CSs and that actions depend on discriminative stimuli (stimuli associated in the past with reinforcement of the actions). This assumption means that feelings and actions are tied to specific classes of situations or to cues within those situations. Thus, assessment should focus on specific classes of situations and specific responses rather than on sweeping generalizations about personality.

A final implication of this point of view is that there's no better form of assessment than direct observation. People can give self-reports of feelings and self-reports of act tendencies, but these may or may not be reliable or accurate. A better way of assessing people's responses is to observe. Put the person in the situation you're interested in and let the person do or feel what comes naturally. Then measure what happens, as directly as possible, with as little interpretation as possible.

Techniques

This view on personality is associated with two types of assessment techniques. One focuses on assessment of emotional responses, the other is broader in scope. One technique, sometimes called **physiological assessment,** makes use of the fact that emotional responses have several components. Besides subjective psychological qualities, emotions also have physiological aspects (Cacioppo & Petty, 1983; Greenfield & Sternbach, 1972). When you experience an emotion (especially if it's intense) many changes take place in your body: changes in muscle tension, heart rate, blood pressure, brain waves, sweat-gland activity, and more. The changes can be thought of as internal behaviors.

These responses can be measured by devices called physiographs. The reactions thus are an observable manifestation of emotional experiences. More specifically, the degree of response can be viewed as an index of the *intensity* of an emotional reaction. To illustrate more clearly, imagine yourself hooked up with electrodes to a physiograph, by which data are being collected about your body's responses. As you sit there, you are exposed to a series of stimuli that are sources of possible fear reactions—snakes, spiders, a view downward from a tall building, and so on. Measurement of your body's responses assesses the intensity of any fear you have. An observer could conclude, for example, that you're scared of heights but not bothered at all by snakes. All this can be assessed without a word from you. Your body's internal behavior is providing all the information. Some believe that these procedures are quite useful in assessment of problems such as post-traumatic stress disorder (Keane et al., 1998; Orr et al., 1998).

Physiological responses provide one index of the intensity of emotional reactions.

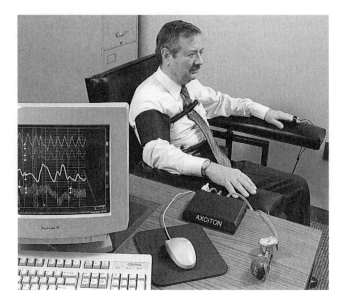

Physiological assessment is direct and objective. It's also elaborate and technical, and tends to be used more in research than in clinical applications. A second technique can also be applied to assessment of emotional responses, and this is a technique that can be applied more broadly. It's called **behavioral assessment** (Barlow, 1981; Staats, 1996), and it requires nothing more complicated than directly observing the person's behavior in situations of interest. Emotions such as fear can be assessed by behavioral indicators—trembling, paleness, staying distant, and so on. This technique can also be applied to assessing what kinds of activities people undertake, for how long, and in what patterns.

Behavioral assessment varies widely in how it's actually done. Sometimes the observer simply counts acts of specific types, checks possibilities from a prearranged list, or watches how far into a sequence of action a person goes before stopping (Lang & Lazovik, 1963; O'Leary & Becker, 1967; Paul, 1966). In other cases the procedure is more elaborate, using automated devices to record how long the person being assessed engages in various behaviors.

For example, behavioral assessment of children often uses recorders with separate channels to keep track of the frequency and duration of activities such as talking, running, and sitting alone (Lovaas, Freitag, Gold, & Kassorla, 1965). The observer in this research pushes a separate button that corresponds to each behavior category and continues holding for as long as that kind of behavior is being performed by the child whose behavior is being assessed.

These various techniques are useful but they do have their problems. Most obviously, they're elaborate and thus somewhat hard to use. Another problem is that different techniques don't always give the same results. The amount of behavioral avoidance displayed in a situation—an index one might expect to be highly correlated with fear—doesn't always correspond well with reports of the fear experienced (Bernstein, 1973). Physiograph records may not fit well with either of these measures. Given this kind of disagreement, it's hard to know which measure represents the "real" fear level.

Problems in Behavior, and Behavior Change

The approach discussed in this chapter holds that personality derives from classical and instrumental conditioning, and it says the same thing about less adaptive behavior. People sometimes learn things that interfere with their lives, and they sometimes fail to learn things that make life easier. This view suggests a basis for several categories of personality problems, deriving from the two types of conditioning we've been discussing. This point of view also suggests various ways of treating behavioral problems. As a group, the treatment techniques are termed **behavior modification** or **behavior therapy** (see Craighead, Kazdin, & Mahoney, 1981, for a broad review). These terms reflect the fact that this approach emphasizes changing the person's *behavior* (as opposed to changing an abstract quality such as a trait).

Classical Conditioning of Emotional Responses

One class of problems in people's lives is emotional reactions that interfere with effective functioning. For example, people sometimes experience intensely unpleasant anxiety when exposed to specific kinds of stimuli. The anxiety is also inappropriate, in that the same stimuli don't provoke comparable anxiety in other people.

Intense irrational fears of this type are called **phobias.** The phobic person experiences fear whenever a particular stimulus is present and often becomes anxious just by thinking of it. Although a phobic reaction can become associated with virtually any stimulus, some phobias are more common than others (see Table 12.2 for a list of some phobias). Common focal points for phobias are animals such as dogs, snakes, and spiders; closed-in spaces such as elevators; open or exposed spaces such as railings on high balconies; and germs and the possibility of infection.

The conditioning view assumes that these phobic reactions are classically conditioned (though see Box 12.5). At some point (in this view) the person must have experienced intense fear while in the presence of what's now the phobic stimulus (cf. Watson & Raynor, 1920). By classical conditioning, the previously neutral stimulus took on the ability to provoke the anxiety reaction. The same principle presumably applies no matter what the feared stimulus is, which confers a kind of generality that many psychologists find appealing.

TABLE 12.2

Names of some common and less common phobias and the stimulus that is the focus of each.

Name of Phobia	Feared Stimulus	Name of Phobia	Feared Stimulus
Acrophobia	Heights	Cynophobia	Dogs
Agoraphobia	Open spaces	Murophobia	Mice
Claustrophobia	Enclosed spaces	Trichophobia	Hair
Mysophobia	Dirt, germs, contamination	Anthophobia	Flowers
Xenophobia	Strangers	Astraphobia	Lightning
Arachnophobia	Spiders	Brontophobia	Thunder
Ophidiophobia	Snakes	Thanatophobia	Death

BOX 12.5

ANOTHER VIEW ON PHOBIAS AND RESPONSES TO ANXIETY

A somewhat different view on the development of phobic behavior was suggested by Miller and Dollard. Their view relies on *instrumental* conditioning, rather than solely on classical conditioning. Miller and Dollard assumed that people acquire new drives by classical conditioning from biologically built-in drives (Miller, 1948, 1951). Fear was seen as a learned drive that develops from the experience of pain. Once a fear drive is acquired, cues that arouse fear engage a drive to escape the fear. Remember that their theory equated drive reduction with reinforcement. If you avoid or escape from whatever has cued fear, the drive goes down. This reinforces the avoidance or escape behavior, making the same behavior more likely next time.

Consider an example: Imagine there are two ways to get to class in the morning. The shorter, faster route requires you to go over a high, scary bridge, an experience that's starting to make you anxious. As you approach the bridge, fear mounts—and so does the drive to escape the fear. One day you abruptly decide to go the long way and avoid the bridge. As you head away from the bridge, your drive level goes down and the avoid-ance behavior's reinforced. As a result, you're more likely to avoid the shorter route in the future. If this avoidance occurs often, you'll have a phobia concerning that bridge.

Some stimuli that cause anxiety can't be avoided through overt behavior because the stimuli are internal—your thoughts. How can you reduce the fear drive if your own thoughts are creating the fear? The answer is deceptively simple. Simply *don't think of whatever it is that's threatening you.* Successful "not-thinking" gets rid of the fear. It thereby causes a reduction in the drive, which reinforces the not-thinking tendency. In this way, Miller and Dollard created a way to account for the psychoanalytic phenomenon of repression in conditioning terms. Repression is not-thinking. It occurs because doing it reduces the fear drive. Eventually, the not-thinking response happens before the threatening thought even comes to mind. Thus, the thought never becomes conscious.

The fact that Miller and Dollard's theory was able to deal with this psychoanalytic phenomenon wasn't just a curious sidelight of their thinking. In fact, their theory was intended more generally to be an explicit attempt to address psychoanalytic concepts through the principles of learning. This analysis of phobic behavior and repression is just one example of their efforts in that direction (see also J. S. Brown, 1948, 1957; Miller, 1944). As suggested by this example, it proved to be possible to use the language of learning to understand events that Freud and others had viewed in very different terms.

As an example of the development of a phobia, consider the plight of Allison, who nearly drowned in a boating accident 3 years ago. The intense fear she experienced in that incident became tied to a wide range of stimuli that previously had been neutral (even positive) for her—stimuli such as her father's boat, the lake she was on, and other aspects of the surroundings. Since this experience, Allison has been unable to walk out on a dock or step onto a boat without trembling violently and turning ghostly pale. She can't even drive near the lake without becoming upset.

The conditioning view of how phobias develop also leads to suggestions about how to treat them (M. C. Jones, 1924). Two ideas are important here. The first is extinction. The anxiety reaction should become weaker if the CS (the phobic stimulus) is presented repeatedly without the US (whatever caused the fear during the conditioning). Interestingly enough, by actively avoiding the phobic stimulus in their day-to-day activities, people such as Allison are actually preventing extinction from taking place.

The second important idea is that a *different* emotion can become conditioned to the *same* stimulus. If the new emotion is incompatible with fear, it will gradually come to predominate over the fear (through a process termed **counterconditioning**). Although these two ideas—extinction and counterconditioning—differ slightly from each other, in practice they lead to the same general sorts of therapeutic procedures (e.g., Lang & Lazovik, 1963; Wolpe, 1961; see Davison & Wilson, 1973, for a review).

One important technique is **systematic desensitization.** Persons being treated are first taught how to relax themselves thoroughly. This relaxation response then becomes the incompatible "emotion" that's intended to take over from the anxiety. The therapist and the person with the phobia also construct an anxiety hierarchy— a list of situations involving the feared stimulus, ranked by the degree of anxiety they produce (Table 12.3). This hierarchy varies from person to person with respect to what situations create the greatest fear and also depends (presumably) on how the fear was acquired.

In the desensitization process you relax as completely as you can, then visualize a scene from the least-threatening end of the hierarchy. Any anxiety aroused by this image is allowed to dissipate. Then, while you continue to relax, you imagine the scene again. You imagine the lowest-threat scene repeatedly while you're in a state of relaxation, until the scene provokes no anxiety at all. Then you move to the next level. Gradually, you're able to imagine increasingly threatening scenes without anxiety. Eventually, the imagined scenes are replaced by the actual feared stimulus. As the anxiety is countered by the relaxation, you're able to interact more and more effectively with the stimulus that previously produced intense fear.

Systematic desensitization has proven very effective in reducing fear reactions, particularly when the fears focus on a specific stimulus (e.g., Brady, 1972; Davison & Wilson, 1973). It works far more quickly than do many other therapy techniques, and thus is less expensive. The technique has been of enormous benefit to persons with debilitating anxieties. How disruptive a phobia is, of course, depends on its focus. A

TABLE 12.3

An anxiety hierarchy such as might be used in systematic desensitization for one type of acrophobia (fear of heights). Each scene is carefully visualized while the person relaxes completely, working from the least threatening scene (at the bottom) to those that produce greater anxiety (toward the top).

Looking down from the top of the World Trade Center

Walking around the top floor of the World Trade Center

Looking out the window of a 12-story building

Looking over the balcony rail of a 4-story building

Looking out the window of a 4-story building

Looking up at a 30-story building from across a small park

Reading a story about the construction of a skyscraper

Reading a story that mentions a restaurant on top of the World Trade Center

Hearing a news story that mentions the tall buildings of a city

Seeing a TV news story in which tall buildings appear in the background

fear of elephants wouldn't have too great an impact on most people's lives, but anxiety over entering any store that's crowded with other people can cripple your very existence.

Procedures such as this also have secondary benefits. First, they've gone a long way to minimize the sense of shame that people feel when their emotions hamper their actions. The learning perspective teaches people that having fear is no reason for shame. Fear isn't a sign of a diseased personality. To the contrary, even irrational fears can result from ordinary events of life through the mechanism of classical conditioning.

Additional benefit can also come from learning a technique such as relaxation. These techniques are tools that people can apply more broadly, any time they feel anxious or upset (Goldfried, 1971; Goldfried & Merbaum, 1973). The techniques thus promote effective functioning far beyond the therapy setting in which they're first learned.

Although phobias provide a clear example of how the concepts of classical conditioning can be applied to problems, this isn't the only example. People often have other conditioned emotional responses that they don't want to have, such as anger. These undesired responses can be treated in the same way as fear: by extinguishing or counterconditioning the response.

It's hard to emphasize strongly enough how much the conditioning approach to dealing with phobias differs from approaches suggested by some of the other theoretical perspectives. For example, a psychoanalytic therapist (Chapter 9) wouldn't account for a phobia by looking for an instance of classical conditioning but would try instead to uncover deeply hidden conflicts from childhood. To the psychoanalyst, if it mattered at all what stimuli now elicit anxiety (and it might not even matter), it would only be to suggest in a symbolic way what the real problem might be. These two approaches are indeed quite different.

Classical Conditioning of Aversion

Classical conditioning in therapy is usually aimed at getting rid of conditioned responses. Sometimes, however, people want to *acquire* conditioned emotional responses. These are cases in which people now have positive emotional responses to stimuli they'd be better off disliking and avoiding. This would be a way of characterizing the situation of people who are trying to stop smoking or drinking (Cannon, Baker, Gino, & Nathan, 1986; Hackett & Horan, 1979) or who are trying to rid themselves of sexual practices they feel are inappropriate (Feldman & MacCulloch, 1971). The stimuli associated with those behaviors (liquor, cigarettes, and so on) are now associated with pleasant emotions. They would be easier to avoid if they provoked *un*pleasant emotions.

The application of conditioning concepts to this kind of situation is called **aversive conditioning** or **aversion therapy** (Rachman & Teasdale, 1969). The logic is much the same as the logic behind systematic desensitization, but with a slightly different goal. The goal now is to condition a *negative* emotional response (rather than a neutral one) to stimuli that now cause a positive response. Creating these associations requires presenting the stimulus as a CS along with a US that produces a reliable negative reaction. For example, nausea-inducing drugs are sometimes used as a US to be associated with the taste of liquor and settings tied to drinking (Cannon et al., 1986). As another example, electric shocks are sometimes used as a US to be associated with the touch of a cigarette (Powell & Azrin, 1968).

Aversive conditioning isn't as widely used as systematic desensitization. Partly this is because some find the procedures objectionable. Partly it's because questions have been raised about whether it is as effective as other procedures (Lichtenstein & Danaher, 1976; Powell & Azrin, 1968). Nevertheless, it does appear to be useful in some contexts (Cannon et al., 1986; Rachman & Teasdale, 1969).

Instrumental Conditioning and Maladaptive Behaviors

Another category of problems relates to the concepts of instrumental conditioning. The reasoning here stems from the idea that people's behavioral tendencies are built in through reinforcement. Furthermore, tendencies can be acquired in ways that make them resistant to extinction, even if they no longer lead to reinforcers.

How might this reasoning be applied to problems in behavior? Imagine that a certain behavior or class of behavior (e.g., throwing tantrums when your wishes aren't granted) was reinforced at one period of your life (when your parents gave in to such demands). The reinforcement strengthens the tendency to repeat this behavior. If reinforced often enough (and in the right pattern of partial reinforcement), the behavior becomes both frequent and persistent.

Later on (when you grow older), the behavior becomes less appropriate. It isn't reinforced as often now, although people do give in to it occasionally. (It's surprising how often people reinforce the very behaviors they wish would disappear.) Although the reinforcement is rare, the behavior continues (thanks to the partial reinforcement effect). The behavior may seem irrational to an observer, but from the conditioning perspective it's just showing resistance to extinction.

The principles of instrumental conditioning suggest that the way to change the undesired behavior is to change the patterns of reinforcement. More specifically, the best approach would be to increase the reinforcements after an alternative desired action while (if possible) further reducing the reinforcement of the undesired action. Such a procedure should shape behavior in the direction of greater adaptiveness, or suitability to the environment, as it now exists.

An example of this sort of strategy comes from the recent literature of health psychology. Childhood obesity is a risk factor for serious health problems later on. It stems in part from sedentary habits, such as watching TV instead of being active. Recent research has shown that reinforcing engagement in less sedentary activities causes both an increase in them and a decrease in the preference for sedentary activities (Epstein, Saelens, Myers, & Vito, 1997).

Instrumental Conditioning of Conflict

Another potential contributor to problems in personality is inconsistency in reinforcement. That is, a given act can be reinforced at some times and punished at other times. If the reinforcement and punishment occur in different stimulus settings, the person will learn a discrimination. But if the reinforcement and punishment occur in the same setting (or if the cues for discrimination are hard to tell apart), the person experiences a **conflict** (Dollard & Miller, 1950; Miller, 1944). That is, the reinforcement produces a tendency to do the behavior, the punishment produces a tendency to not do it.

Whichever tendency is stronger is presumably the one that will emerge overtly. The fact that the other tendency is there, however, means there will be discomfort as the behavior is being done (or not done). If the situation is conflicted enough, the person may even learn to treat punishment as a discriminative stimulus for continuing to do the behavior (if persistence is eventually followed by reinforcement). This person's behavior will appear especially irrational and can even be self-destructive, but it's a predictable result of inconsistent outcomes.

This issue is of special concern in child rearing, since parents can easily fall into the pattern of mixing reinforcement and punishment for the same behavior from the child. It's interesting that many of the transitions of childhood that can be difficult for these reasons are those noted by Freud many years ago—weaning, toilet training, establishing power relationships between parent and child. Freud saw these situations as creating conflicts (due to sexual pressures). The same situations seem analyzable in terms of the effects of inconsistent treatment by the parents.

Instrumental Conditioning and Token Economies

The principles of instrumental conditioning apply to the behavior of virtually anyone. The principles have even been used to shape the behavior of persons with serious mental disorders. The immediate goal of these efforts is to produce patterns of behavior that are more normal and thus more adaptive. The longer-range goal is to bring the person back into the normal flow of human events, reinstating the ordinary reinforcement contingencies that shape the behavior of most people, and reducing the person's dependency on caretakers for the necessities of life.

These projects are usually undertaken in institutions, where close control can be maintained over response-reinforcement relationships (although they're also used in other highly structured settings such as classrooms). In brief, the strategy involves creating a small-scale economy within the institution. Because it's usually based on tokens (rather than dollars), it's often called a **token economy** (e.g., Ayllon & Azrin, 1965, 1968; Kazdin, 1977; Krasner, 1970). The tokens act as secondary reinforcers, in much the same way as money does. That is, they're exchanged for special foods or special privileges (in some programs, they're needed even for ordinary foods and privileges).

The patients are given these tokens as reinforcers for socially desirable behaviors (such as making their beds or engaging in normal conversations with other patients or staff members). Consistent with the principles of instrumental conditioning, this reinforcement tends to increase desired behavioral qualities and decrease undesired qualities. Such programs have proven effective in shaping the behavior of hospitalized schizophrenics, whose behavior is extremely hard to change (e.g., Ayllon & Azrin, 1968; Krasner, 1970).

This technique isn't entirely free of problems. For example, behavior reinforced with tokens in the institutional setting is unlikely to be reinforced as often outside the institution. Thus the adaptive behavior may not persist outside the sheltered environment of the institution, unless steps are taken to make the transition a gradual one. Despite such limitations, token economies are an important weapon in the arsenal of therapeutic behavior change.

Instrumental Conditioning and Biofeedback

Another way in which instrumental conditioning concepts are used in therapy focuses on changing internal behaviors. The behaviors are usually small in scale—for example, variations in muscle tension that create headaches or influence blood pressure, muscle cramping that produces pain in one's neck or lower back, or small muscle movements in areas that are paralyzed. As implied by these examples, this therapy deals primarily with problems of pain or other conditions of ill health.

It was long thought that most internal behaviors of this type are outside voluntary control. Some years ago, however, it was discovered that people could learn to control the internal actions through procedures often regarded as instrumental conditioning. The procedures as a group are called **biofeedback** training.

A person undergoing biofeedback training has the task of engaging in an internal behavior that's specific in one sense but vague in another. For example, you might be asked to raise the temperature of your hand, reduce the muscle tension in your forehead, or lower your pulse rate. You aren't told *how* to do this, just to try to do it. While you try, you're attached to a machine that tells whether or not you've been successful. In fact, this machine continuously tells you whether you're successful, by a signal light or tone. The light or tone (the "biofeedback") serves as a reinforcer for whatever you did just before. The result is that people can learn to do very subtle internal behaviors through such training. Presumably once the behavior is well learned, it will continue to occur even without the biofeedback.

This technique has been proposed as a way to treat a variety of physical problems that seem to involve subtle muscle activity (Blanchard & Epstein, 1978). Many people, for example, can change their blood pressure during biofeedback, although the effect doesn't generalize well outside the training setting (Shapiro & Surwit, 1979). Biofeedback is also used as a treatment for many kinds of pain (Elmore & Tursky, 1981). It's even been suggested that biofeedback provides a way of retraining muscles after paralyzing events such as strokes (Fernando & Basmajian, 1978; Runck, 1980). Clearly this is an area of investigation in which a great deal of additional work is likely be done in the years to come.

Conditioning Theories: Problems and Prospects

The conditioning view on personality is influential among two groups of psychologists: some of the researchers who are actively involved in the experimental analysis of behavior in the laboratory, and clinicians who received their training during the heyday of the behavior therapies. The conditioning view is attractive to these two groups for two different reasons, which in turn represent two strengths of this view of personality.

First, the conditioning viewpoint emerged—as did no other perspective before it—from the crucible of experimental testing. The ideas that came to form this approach to behavior were intended to be subjected to close scrutiny, to be either upheld or disconfirmed through research. Many of the ideas have been tested thoroughly, and the evidence that supports them is substantial. This empirical base is important. Having a view on the nature of personality that can be verified by careful, objective observation is very satisfying to the researcher.

The second reason for the impact of conditioning ideas on people's thinking is the effectiveness of behavioral therapy techniques. Clinical psychologists found that many of people's problems in life can be treated effectively with fairly simple procedures. With this realization, the clinicians began to look carefully at the principles that appear to underlie the procedures. The learning perspective has taken on an aura of importance and credibility among this group of psychologists because of its relatively good fit with these effective techniques of behavior change.

Although many psychologists find this viewpoint congenial, it has its share of problems and criticisms. Some of the criticisms derive from a virtue we just named: the emphasis on research. More specifically, conditioning theorists have emphasized the utility of studying laboratory animals. They say that if the laws of learning are the same across different species, it makes no difference which animal they study. Many people, however, are wary of the assumption that underlies that strategy—that learning is the same across species. Indeed, skepticism on this point helped foster the development of a second generation of learning theories, discussed in Chapter 13.

A more subtle criticism concerns a tendency to simplify the situation under study. This simplification is particularly characteristic of work on conditioning. Emphasizing simplification ensures experimental control. Having control helps clarify the picture of cause and effect. But it sometimes results in experimental situations that seem to offer extremely few options for behavior. There's sometimes a nagging suspicion that the behavior observed occurred because there were so many pressures in its direction and so little chance for the subject to do anything *else*. What happens to behavior when the person leaves the laboratory? With more options available, will the regularities still hold up?

This question turns out to be a very important one for many species. Breland and Breland (1961), trying to apply operant procedures to train animals, were distressed to discover that reinforcers often were far less powerful than the animals' natural tendencies. For example, they tried to train a raccoon to pick up coins and put them into a "bank," but found he had a strong tendency to hold the coins and rub them together. He looked like a miser. He was only trying, though, to do what he would do with crayfish in his normal environment—rub them together to remove their shells. In the same way, pigs being trained to deposit wooden coins into a bank preferred to drop the coins, root them along the ground, and toss them into the air. The Brelands eventually questioned whether laboratory studies of instrumental conditioning really give an accurate picture of behavior in normal environments. Perhaps the picture being conveyed is actually quite a distorted one.

Another problem with this view is that it isn't really a complete theory of personality. Rather, it's a view of the determinants of behavior. Some people believe that this view is too simplistic to ever be adequate to an understanding of personality. The processes by which learning occurs presumably operate continuously, in a piecemeal and haphazard fashion. The human experience, on the other hand, seems highly complex and orderly. How do the haphazard learning processes yield such an orderly product?

To put it another way, conditioning theories tell us a lot about how a given behavior becomes more probable or less probable, but it doesn't tell us much about the person from whom the behavior is coming. The processes portrayed in the theories are cold and mechanistic. There seems to be little place in the learning perspective for the subjective sense of "personhood," little focus on the continuity and coherence that characterize the sense of self. In sum, to many people this analysis of personality simply doesn't convey the subjective experience of what it means to *have* a personality. Perhaps the greatest challenge to the conditioning approach, then, is to convince skeptics that it accounts for the elaborate subjective qualities that seem so important to personality.

SUMMARY

The conditioning approach to personality emphasizes two types of learning. In classical conditioning, a neutral stimulus (CS) is presented along with another stimulus (US) that already elicits a reflexive response (UR). After repeated pairings, the CS itself comes to elicit a response (CR) that's similar to the UR. The CR appears to be an anticipatory response that prepares for the US.

This basic phenomenon is modified by discrimination (with different stimuli leading to different responses) and extended by generalization (with different stimuli leading to similar responses). CRs decrease in intensity if the CS is presented repeatedly without the US, a process termed extinction. Classical conditioning is important to personality primarily when the responses being conditioned are emotional reactions (emotional conditioning). Classical conditioning thus provides a basis for understanding people's unique preferences and aversions, and it provides a way of analyzing certain psychological problems, such as phobias.

In instrumental conditioning (a more "active" process), a behavior is followed by an outcome that's either positively valued or aversive. If the outcome is positively valued, the tendency to perform the behavior is strengthened. Thus the outcome is called a reinforcer. If the outcome is aversive (a punisher), the tendency to perform the behavior is reduced. Discrimination in instrumental conditioning is responding in different ways to different situational cues, generalization is responding in a similar way to different cues, and extinction is the reduction of a behavioral tendency through nonreinforcement of the behavior. Behavior is shaped in new directions by reinforcing successively better approximations of the eventually occurring behavior. Reinforcers can occur in many patterns, termed schedules. The most important effect of variations in reinforcement schedules is that behavior learned by intermittent (partial) reinforcement is more persistent (under later conditions of nonreinforcement) than is a behavior learned by continuous reinforcement.

The conditioning approach holds that personality is the sum of the person's conditioned tendencies. Assessment, from this point of view, emphasizes the observation of various aspects of behavior tendencies, as they occur in specific situations. Assessment can focus on people's physiological responses, their overt behaviors, or their reports of emotional reactions in response to different kinds of stimuli.

The conditioning approach assumes that problems in behavior are the result of the same kinds of conditioning processes as result in normal behavior. Classical conditioning can produce intense and irrational fears, called phobias; instrumental conditioning can produce behavior tendencies that persist even when they are no longer adaptive. These various problems can be treated by means of conditioning procedures, which collectively are termed behavior therapy or behavior modification. Systematic desensitization counterconditions fear reactions with relaxation. Aversion therapy conditions negative reactions in the place of positive reactions. The principles of instrumental conditioning underlie a variety of therapy techniques. In a token economy (usually in an institutional setting), people receive secondary reinforcers (tokens) for engaging in desirable behaviors. In biofeedback training, people learn to engage in certain kinds of internal behavior for such goals as controlling pain.

GLOSSARY

Aversive conditioning (or **aversion therapy**) The conditioning of an aversive reaction to what's now a positive stimulus.

Behavior modification (or **behavior therapy**) The changing of behavior therapeutically through conditioning processes.

Behavioral assessment An assessment made by observing a person's overt behavior.

Biofeedback The technique of learning to control an internal behavior by instrumental conditioning.

Classical conditioning The pairing of a neutral stimulus with an unconditioned stimulus.

Conditioned stimulus (CS) A stimulus that's paired with a US to become conditioned.

Conditioned response (CR) A response to the CS that's acquired by classical conditioning.

Conflict The simultaneous arousal of two incompatible behavioral tendencies.

Continuous reinforcement A schedule in which reinforcement follows each instance of the behavior.

Counterconditioning The linking of an emotion to a stimulus that differs from the emotion the stimulus now causes.

Discrimination Responding in a different manner to different stimuli.

Discriminative stimulus A cue that controls the occurrence of behavior.

Drive A motivational state that increases behaviors which are high in the habit hierarchy.

Emotional conditioning Classical conditioning in which the CR is an emotional reaction.

Epiphenomena Phenomena that occur along with behavior but have no causal role in behavior.

Extinction In classical conditioning, the reduction of a CR by repeating the CS without the US; in instrumental conditioning, the reduction of a behavioral tendency by removing reinforcement.

Generalization Responding in a similar manner to somewhat different stimuli.

Habit hierarchy The ordering of a person's potential responses by their likelihood.

Higher-order conditioning Event in which a former CS now acts as a US in a new instance of conditioning.

Instrumental conditioning Conditioning in which a behavior becomes more likely because it is followed by a desirable event.

Negative reinforcement The removal of an aversive stimulus.

Partial reinforcement A schedule in which the behavior is reinforced less often than every time it occurs.

Partial reinforcement effect The fact that a behavior acquired through partial reinforcement is resistant to extinction.

Phobia An inappropriately intense fear of some specific class of stimuli.

Physiological assessment The measuring of physiological aspects of emotional reactions.

Positive reinforcement A reinforcement involving addition of a desired stimulus.

Punisher An undesired event which weakens the behavior that came before it.

Radical behaviorism The position that behavior should be explained solely on the basis of observable events.

Reflex An event in which a stimulus produces an automatic response.

Reinforcer An event that strengthens the behavior that came before it.

Shaping Changing the nature of ongoing behavior by reinforcing a specific aspect of the behavior.

Successive approximation Shaping by reinforcing closer approximations of the desired behavior.

Systematic desensitization A therapeutic procedure intended to extinguish fear.

Time out A disciplinary technique in which a child is temporarily removed from an enjoyable activity.

Token economy The shaping of behavior in institutions by using tokens as reinforcers.

Unconditioned response (UR) A reflexive response to an unconditioned stimulus.

Unconditioned stimulus (US) A stimulus that causes a reflexive (unconditioned) response.

Social-Cognitive Learning Theories

■   I was watching my 2-year-old the other day in the kitchen, when he reached in and popped open the childproof latch on one of the cabinet doors, just like that, and reached in for a pan. I was so surprised I thought my teeth were gonna fall out. Now, how do you suppose he figured out how to do that? Must've been from watching me, I guess.

■   My job has changed a lot since I hired on a year ago. The business has expanded really fast. In fact, the administrators haven't always had time to develop new procedures for everything we have to do. We've been having to make our own guesses about what would work best. It hasn't been too bad, though. We seem to be guessing right most of the time. Sometimes, of course, you don't know if a decision was right until a lot later on, but that just makes it more interesting.

As you saw in Chapter 12, the concepts of learning are powerful tools for analyzing behavior. The principles of conditioning described there seem to account well for two large categories of human experience. They explain emotional reactions that people develop and the attitudes and preferences that seem to derive from them. They also explain how action tendencies emerge and wane as a result of experiencing good and bad outcomes.

Powerful as those theories are, however, they haven't been completely accepted—not even by everyone who believes learning is the key to personality. Some became disenchanted with conditioning theories because they ignore certain aspects of behavior that seem obvious outside the lab. For example, people often learn by watching one another. People often decide whether or not to do something by thinking about what would happen if they did it.

How can conditioning theories account for a baby's suddenly doing something complex he'd never done before? How can they deal with the decision processes of a person trying to guess what to do in a particular situation at work? The conditioning theories don't seem wrong, exactly, but they seem incomplete. They explain some things well, but they don't cover everything.

From these dissatisfactions—and from the work to which they led—came what might be thought of as another generation of learning theories. They provide a learning viewpoint on personality, but they place more importance on mental events do than earlier theories. For this reason, they're often called *cognitive* learning theories. Because they also emphasize *social* aspects of learning more than was done before, they're often called *social* learning theories.

Elaborations on Conditioning Processes

The theorists of the newer learning approach didn't abandon conditioning principles. Instead, they began by suggesting elaborations on them—additional elements that embellish the picture. The easiest way to start a discussion of the newer views is with those embellishments.

Social Reinforcement

As social learning theory began to evolve, its theorists began to reconsider the usefulness of studying lower animals. Can human behavior be analyzed properly by studying laboratory rats, or is it wiser to focus on people? What variables matter most in *human* learning? Asking these questions led to a different view of reinforcement.

In particular, many came to believe that reinforcement in human experience (at least beyond infancy) has little or nothing to do with physical needs. Rather, most important to people are **social reinforcers**—acceptance, smiles, hugs, praise, approval, interest, and attention from others (Rotter, 1954, 1982; see also Bandura, 1978; Kanfer & Marston, 1963). The idea that most reinforcers for people are social is one of several senses in which these learning theories are social (for broader discussions of social reinforcement see Brokaw & McLemore, 1983; A. H. Buss, 1983; Stevenson, 1965; Turner, Foa, & Foa, 1971).

As an example of the power of social reinforcement, consider a study by Hall, Lund, and Jackson (1968). Participants were children who spent little of their school time studying. After assessing baselines, the researchers gave social reinforcement in the form of attention and bits of praise whenever a child engaged in studying. Figure 13.1 shows the impact of this procedure on one child. This child studied more than twice as much when social reinforcement was given than when it was not.

Emphasizing social reinforcement has a secondary theoretical implication. In particular, social learning theorists see little need to assume drives in order to discuss reinforcement (e.g., Bandura, 1977a; Rotter, 1954, 1982). They take this position partly because social reinforcers don't seem to act via physical need states. It isn't usually necessary, for example, that the person being reinforced be in a state of deprivation.

A description of social reinforcement should also mention the concept of **self-reinforcement.** This term actually has two meanings. The first is the idea that people may award themselves reinforcers after doing something they've set out to do (Bandura, 1976; Goldiamond, 1976; Heiby, 1982). For example, you might reward yourself with a pizza for studying 6 straight hours, or you may give yourself a new piece of stereo equipment after a semester of good grades.

The second meaning of self-reinforcement derives more directly from the concept of social reinforcement. It's the idea that you react to your own behavior with approval or disapproval, much as you react to someone else's behavior. In responding to your actions with implicit self-praise, you reinforce yourself. In responding with self-blame, you punish yourself. This sort of internal self-reinforcement and self-punishment plays an important role in social-cognitive learning theories of behavior and behavior change (Bandura 1977a, 1986; Kanfer, 1977; Kanfer & Hagerman, 1981; Mischel, 1973, 1979).

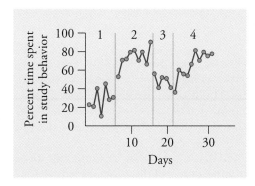

FIGURE 13.1

Results of a single-subject experiment on the effect of social reinforcement. A third-grade boy, whose baseline level of studying in class was quite low (period 1), was systematically given attention and approval for studying. This greatly increased his study behavior (period 2). To see whether the effect depended on social reinforcement, attention was removed, which caused a decrease in studying (period 3). Reinstituting the social reinforcement (period 4) caused a return to a high rate of studying (adapted from Hall et al., 1968).

Many of the important reinforcers affecting human behavior are social in nature.

Vicarious Emotional Arousal

Another elaboration on models of conditioning comes from the fact that people can experience events vicariously—that is, indirectly through someone else. Vicarious processes represent a second sense in which learning among humans is social. That is, vicarious processes involve two people, one to experience something directly, a second to experience it indirectly.

One type of vicarious experience is **vicarious emotional arousal,** or empathy. This occurs when you observe someone feeling an intense emotion and you start to experience the same emotion yourself (usually less intensely). Empathy isn't the same as sympathy, a feeling of concern and unhappiness when someone else is suffering (see Gruen & Mendelsohn, 1986; Wispé, 1986). In empathy, you feel the same feeling, good or bad, as the other person (Stotland, 1969a). Everyone can have this experience, but there are individual differences in its intensity (Eisenberg et al., 1994; Levenson & Ruef, 1992; Marangoni et al., 1995). There's also a suggestion that having had a similar experience in the past enhances empathy (Batson et al., 1996), but this occurred only among women.

Examples of empathy are easy to point to (see also Box 13.1). When something wonderful happens to a friend, putting her in ecstasy, you feel happiness yourself. Being around someone who's frightened makes most people feel jumpy. Laughter is often contagious, even when you don't know what the other person's laughing at. There's also evidence that being around someone who's embarrassed can make you feel embarrassed too (Miller, 1987).

Experiencing vicarious emotional arousal doesn't *constitute* learning. But it creates an opportunity for learning. Recall from Chapter 12 the category called emo-

BOX 13.1

EMPATHY AND ALTRUISM

The focus of this part of the chapter is the idea that vicarious processes influence learning. While we're talking about empathy, though, we'd like to point to another aspect of human behavior to which empathy is relevant: altruism, or helping. One general view on helping is that when you see someone else suffering, your empathic response causes you to take action to help. There are, however, different theories about *why* this happens.

A theory developed by Robert Cialdini and his colleagues (e.g., Cialdini, Schaller, et al., 1987) holds that empathy in such a situation causes you to become sad. One way to escape from the sadness is to do something to reduce the other person's suffering. Thus, empathy leads to helping as a way to reduce the bad feelings you're experiencing yourself, and the benefit to the other person is a side effect. A theory by Daniel Batson and his colleagues (Batson, 1990, 1991; Batson, Dyck, et al., 1988) holds that empathy creates a desire to relieve the suffering of the other person, plain and simple.

Which explanation is right? The answer may be both. There's now evidence that exposure to someone else's distress provokes a range of emotions rather than just one (Batson, Fultz, & Schoenrade, 1987; Fultz, Schaller, & Cialdini, 1988). The feelings include empathic distress, sadness, and sympathy (which is usually what's meant when the word empathy is used in this literature). These different feeling qualities may well lead to different motivations.

Research on these questions typically uses a procedure in which subjects are exposed to someone else's suffering while in a psychology experiment. Some studies manipulate empathy by telling one group of subjects (but not others) to focus on what the other person is feeling and experiencing. Sometimes individual differences in empathy are measured by self-report. The idea that empathy makes people feel distress that they wish to escape has been tested in several ways. Sometimes subjects have an easy way to escape from the situation (if you don't help, you'll never see the other person again), sometimes escape is hard (if you don't help, you'll continue to see the other person suffer). The prediction is that when empathy is low, having an easy way to escape from the suffering will reduce helping—and it does. When empathy is high, though, having an easy way out doesn't have an adverse impact on helping.

Despite some contradictory evidence (Batson, Bolen, Cross, & Neuringer-Benefiel, 1986; Smith, Keating, & Stotland, 1989), the data seem to suggest that empathic concern for someone else arouses a desire to ease that person's suffering, which is separate from a desire to reduce one's own distress (Batson, 1990). No matter which pathway predominates, though, it's clear that empathy plays an important role in bringing people to each other's aid.

---

tional conditioning. In emotional conditioning, feeling an emotion in the presence of a neutral stimulus causes that stimulus to become capable of evoking a similar emotion. It doesn't matter how the emotion is produced. It's only necessary that an emotion be *present*. The emotion can be caused by a stimulus you experience directly, but it can also arise vicariously. Thus, vicarious emotional arousal creates a possibility for classical conditioning. Such an event is **vicarious classical conditioning.**

Consider, for example, research in which participants watched another person while a tone sounded (a neutral stimulus), then that person received an electric shock and grimaced. After a series of pairings of tone and shock, the observers themselves began to react emotionally when the tone was sounded by itself (Berger, 1962; see also Bandura & Rosenthal, 1966; Craig & Weinstein, 1965; Vaughan & Lanzetta, 1980). This was true even though the observers never experienced pain directly. This change appears to represent vicarious classical conditioning.

FIGURE 13.2

Effect of vicarious reinforcement. Subjects are asked to say any word at random into a microphone whenever a signal is given. Subjects also hear someone they think is a co-subject say words periodically. In one condition, the experimenter reinforces the other voice by saying "good" every time it says a human noun. The measure of interest is how often the real subject says human nouns. As can be seen here, the reinforcement given to the other person causes a steady increase in the subject's tendency to do the same, despite the fact that the subjects were never reinforced themselves (adapted from Kanfer & Marston, 1963).

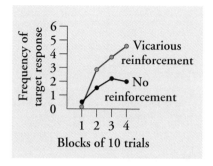

Vicarious Reinforcement

Another vicarious process may be even more important. This one, called **vicarious reinforcement,** is very simple: If you observe someone do something that's followed by reinforcement, you become more likely to do the same thing yourself (Kanfer & Marston, 1963; Liebert & Fernandez, 1970). If you see a person punished after doing something, you're less likely to do it. The reinforcer or punishment went to the other person, not to you. But your own behavior tendencies are affected as though you'd received it yourself (Figure 13.2).

This process is very important in human learning. It permits a lot of the trial and error of instrumental conditioning to take place secondhand. You don't have to "behave" all the time—just watch others behave and observe what follows. Learning this way lets you learn about a lot of situations that other people are in, including some you'd probably rather not experience firsthand. Taking advantage of this principle can save wear and tear on self-esteem, since you learn from other people's mistakes as well as from their successes. Sometimes vicarious reinforcement even produces better learning than does direct reinforcement. Apparently the vicarious situation

Empathy causes us to experience others' emotions. Others' grief elicits sadness from us, and happiness elicits joy. As you look at this picture, you are probably beginning to feel the same emotions that the people in the picture are experiencing.

lets you give "learning" the attention you'd normally have to devote to "behaving" (Berger, 1961; Hillix & Marx, 1960).

How do vicarious reinforcement and punishment influence people? Presumably seeing someone else reinforced after a behavior leads you to infer you'd get the same reinforcer if you acted the same way (Bandura, 1971). If someone else is punished, you conclude the same thing would happen to you if you acted that way (Bandura, 1973; Walters & Parke, 1964). Often the effects involve more elaborate inferences. You may, for example, limit your conclusion to situations resembling the one you observed. To put it differently, you may learn *discriminations* vicariously. For instance, you may learn from observing others that talking in class leads to a scolding, but only in certain classes.

Note that the effect of vicarious reinforcement appears to involve developing an implicit (or even explicit) expectancy—that is, a mental model of links between acts and reinforcers. This is one instance of a more general theme in the social-cognitive learning approach: the involvement of expectancies in learning. This theme will come up again later in the chapter.

Semantic Generalization

We said at the outset that the newer theories are more social and more cognitive than the earlier theories. So far we've considered some ways they're more social. Now let's look at some of the ways they're more cognitive.

Another elaboration on the basic principles of conditioning came from looking more closely at the phenomenon of generalization—responding in a similar way to stimuli that are similar to (but not the same as) those in which conditioning has already taken place. Most animals can generalize in response to varying lights or tones, but people can generalize in more interesting ways. They can do **semantic generalization,** generalization along a dimension of *meaning*. It's something people do often, and take completely for granted.

Semantic generalization, just as any other generalization, can occur in both classical conditioning and instrumental conditioning (Diven, 1936; Maltzman, 1968). As an illustration of how it happens in classical conditioning, imagine a person who's just been through a nasty divorce and who now has a negative emotional reaction (anger and anxiety) to the mere mention of the word *divorce*. This person might well generalize this emotional reaction to semantically related words such as *courtroom, settlement, alimony,* and *breakup.*

Semantic generalization is explained by assuming that conditioning doesn't take place to an environmental stimulus per se. Rather, it occurs toward cognitive elements representing aspects of the stimulus. Generalization occurs when mental links exist between the cognitive elements and *other* stimuli. Semantic generalization occurs when there are mental associations extending to other words with related meanings. The theories discussed in this chapter assume this kind of elaborate mental structure. This is one of several senses in which they are "cognitive" learning theories.

Rule-Based Learning

Another elaboration on conditioning is suggested by the idea that people use instrumental learning to learn *rules* rather than just to learn behaviors. Conditioning principles suggest that behavior tendencies build incrementally. Each reinforcer strengthens the tendency slightly. The longer the history of reinforcement, the stronger the tendency to behave in a certain way.

There are cases, though, that simply don't fit this picture. Perhaps the easiest illustration of how rules are used in human behavior comes from studies of language acquisition. Language uses an elaborate set of rules. For example, there are rules that specify how the parts of a sentence are ordered and rules concerning the formation of verb tenses and noun forms.

Early in life, children don't pay much attention to these rules. They're pretty well preoccupied with learning what specific words mean. As the children get older and what they say gets more complicated, they begin to use new word forms (e.g., new verb tenses), which they acquire word by word. At some point, though, children seem to realize that there are regularities to language, and they begin to use those regularities in their speech. The child may not be able to tell what the rule is, but the rule gets used when the child speaks. How do you know the child's learned a rule? Because at this stage the child sometimes *overregularizes,* that is, uses the rule even where it doesn't apply (Marcus, 1996).

Consider the English rule for specifying past tense, which is to add "ed" at the end (e.g., *cook* becomes *cooked*). There are many exceptions to this rule, verbs whose past tense is created a different way (*go* becomes *went, take* becomes *took, break* becomes *broke*). Children use these irregular verb forms perfectly well when they first learn them, apparently because they're memorizing the words (which may be happening by an incremental conditioning process). The words are used correctly right up to the point where the rule begins to be used. At that point, the child applies the rule to every verb, even the irregular ones. As a result, the child now begins to make errors. A child who said "I went into the back yard" only a few weeks ago now sometimes says "I goed into the back yard." This is evidence that the child is acquiring a rule.

Once rule-based learning begins to take place, it becomes a pervasive feature of human learning. Past early childhood, humans seem to respond to the outcomes they experience by learning implicit rules and conceptual principles. When you learn how to study for a psychology test, you're learning principles of preparation for tests in general. When you learn to drive, you're learning not just a set of movements, but rather a set of rules for creating forward motion, stopping, distancing from other cars, and so on. Whenever you've learned a rule, you can apply it to widely divergent new situations (e.g., preparing for an exam in a new course or driving in unfamiliar territory).

What, then, is the role of incremental conditioning in behavior? It may be that incremental learning influences how a rule or principle first emerges. That is, reinforcement processes may nudge you a little bit at a time in the right direction until you begin to identify the rule. When the rule comes into focus, concept learning takes over and the rate of learning increases.

Expectancies Concerning Outcomes

The learning theories we're discussing in this chapter include a facet that can be viewed in either of two ways. It can be seen as an elaboration on conditioning theories, or it can be seen as a step away from the domain of conditioning. This facet provides another sense in which these are cognitive learning theories. Specifically, the theories assume that people hold expectancies about whether a behavior will lead to desired outcomes (Rotter, 1954). This expectancy, then, is an important determinant of what the person does.

These expectancies are often discussed along with a view on motivation termed expectancy-incentive theory (we touched on this theory in Chapter 5). **Incentives** are the values that goals have for the person. Incentives don't necessarily depend on deprivation, which makes the concept different in important ways from the concept of drive. **Expectancies,** in this context, are implicit judgments about how likely a given behavior is to result in attainment of the goals. Predicting the person's behavior, from this view, requires that you take into account both incentives and expectancies (see Feather, 1982).

The idea that people hold expectancies and that expectancies influence action wasn't new when it was built into social learning theory (e.g., Brunswik, 1951; Lewin, 1951b; Postman, 1951; Tolman, 1932). But an emphasis on expectancies (in one form or other) has become a cornerstone of this approach to personality (Rotter, 1954; see also treatments by Bandura, 1977a, 1986; Kanfer, 1977; Mischel, 1973).

It's important to be explicit about how this view differs from the assumptions of the conditioning approach (see also Box 13.2). Conditioning theorists assume that reinforcement has a direct influence on the probability of the behavior. They *don't* assume that mental representations (expectancies) have a causal role. In the social-cognitive learning theories, in contrast, people are seen as thinking over the evidence that's available to them—past outcomes, the situation they now confront—and judging their chances of the desired outcomes. These expectancy judgments, then, have a causal influence on behavioral choices (e.g., Kirsch, 1985).

There are disagreements among theorists about exactly what kinds of expectancies matter. Major theories have been proposed concerning two specific types of expectancies. These ideas are described, in the order they were developed, in the next two sections.

Locus-of-Control Expectancies

The first idea was developed by Julian Rotter (1954, 1966) from his observations of people in therapy. Rotter's observations led him to a simple conclusion: Different people, given virtually identical conditions for learning, learn different things. More specifically, some people react to reinforcement just as you'd expect from the principle of instrumental conditioning. Others act as though they haven't learned anything at all.

As an illustration, imagine two freshmen, Bert and Ernie, who are shy and have trouble making conversation with women. Each goes to the university guidance center for help, and the therapist provides suggestions concerning topics of conversation, ways to make the conversation move along, and so on. After some practice, the therapist asks each young man to go out and have a conversation with an attractive young woman who works in the next office.

In each case, the woman's response is pleasant and positive. Bert returns to the therapist and says, "I did things you suggested and she seemed to like me. I'm going to remember those suggestions from now on, because they really seem useful." Ernie returns and says, "I did things you suggested and she acted friendly, but I don't know why. It couldn't have been anything to do with me." Bert's response looks like instrumental learning—if something works well enough to be reinforced, it tends to be done again. But what sense does Ernie's response make?

Rotter became convinced that people differ from each other in the extent to which they think there's a cause-and-effect link between their behaviors and the reinforcers that follow. Rotter assumed, as do most social learning theorists, that believing in the connection is necessary for instrumental learning to occur. Because some people (like Bert) see a link between behavior and reinforcer, their behavior is affected by the reinforcers. People who don't see a link (like Ernie) react more haphazardly to reinforcers. Instrumental conditioning, for these people, isn't straightforward at all.

The phrase used in discussing this idea is **locus of control** (Rotter, Seeman, & Liverant, 1962; Rotter, 1966, 1990). *Locus* means place. People termed *internals*

BOX 13.2

THEORETICAL CONTROVERSY:
How Does Learning Take Place?

Thus far we've treated the principles of the social-cognitive learning theories as elaborations on earlier conditioning theories. Our aim has been to show how the various changes can be inserted into the picture of the learning process that was drawn in Chapter 12. Some of the modifications, however, raise serious questions about the conditioning concepts that they seem at first to embellish. This box briefly explores two aspects of this question (see also Brewer, 1974).

The Role of Awareness

The first issue concerns the role of awareness in conditioning. It's long been assumed that conditioning—particularly classical conditioning—occurs automatically (cf. Skinner, 1953). There's reason, though, to suspect that the effects actually involve cognition. For example, several studies seem to indicate that people show little or no classical conditioning from repeated pairings of stimuli unless they realize the stimuli are correlated (e.g., Chatterjee & Eriksen, 1962; Dawson & Furedy, 1976; Grings, 1973). On the other side of the coin, sometimes merely expecting an aversive event (as a US) can produce conditioned responses to other stimuli (Bridger & Mandel, 1964; Spacapan & Cohen, 1983). There's also evidence that people change their behavior in response to reinforcers only when they've become aware of what's being reinforced (Dulany, 1968; Spielberger & DeNike, 1966).

Extinction may also involve cognitive mediation. After classical conditioning of a fear response, a statement that the painful US will no longer be given sometimes eliminates fear of the CS (Bandura, 1969; Grings, 1973). Classical conditioning was supposed to be automatic and independent of thought. It was supposed to link stimuli directly with responses. But effects such as these suggest that expectations may play an even more central role than do external stimuli (Bandura, 1986).

The Concept of Reinforcement

The second issue concerns the concept of reinforcement—and, by implication, the very nature of instrumental conditioning. According to conditioning theorists, reinforcers are events that strengthen the tendency to do the behavior that preceded them. Yet Bandura (1976, 1977a), a prominent social learning theorist, explicitly rejected this sense of the reinforcement concept, while continuing to use the term *reinforcement* (see also Bolles, 1972; Brewer, 1974; Rotter, 1954).

If reinforcers aren't strengthening action tendencies, what are they doing? Bandura's answer is that they do two things: By providing information about outcomes, they lead to hypotheses (expectancies) about what actions are useful in what settings. They also provide the potential for future motivational states through mental anticipation of the reinforcer in the future. Many people would agree with Bandura that these functions are important. But do the functions really constitute "reinforcement" in any meaningful sense? If not, do they actually belong in the process of instrumental conditioning?

The two issues addressed here—the nature of reinforcement and the role of awareness in conditioning—raise a far broader question: If reinforcement doesn't strengthen response tendencies, and if conditioning isn't really conditioning, then just how strong a conceptual connection remains between the social-cognitive learning theories and the conditioning theories from which they grew?

(internal locus of control) see reinforcers as controlled from within, by their own actions. Those termed *externals* (external locus of control) see reinforcers as controlled by something outside themselves, something other than their own actions. Although locus of control is a continuous dimension, it's often described in terms of its endpoints. Because the terms *internal* and *external* are so commonly used to refer to the two orientations, the concept is referred to with the letters *I-E*.

This dimension has been studied both in experiments and in individual-difference research. In experiments, temporary variations in locus of control are created by telling some people that task outcomes are caused by skill (internal) and telling others they're caused by chance (external). In one such study, Phares (1957) found that subjects with skill instructions used their outcomes as a guide to likely future outcomes. This is just what should occur from instrumental conditioning. It didn't occur, though, among those told their outcomes were based on luck (see also Holden & Rotter, 1962; Rotter, Liverant, & Crowne, 1961; Walls & Cox, 1971).

A large body of evidence has also accumulated (hundreds of studies) concerning individual differences in locus of control (for reviews see Lefcourt, 1976; Phares, 1976). People who report an internal locus of control adjust their expectancies upward after experiencing success and downward after failure. Externals, in contrast, often shift their expectancies in the direction *opposite* to the prior outcome (which also occurs in chance situations, see Battle & Rotter, 1963; Feather, 1968; Lefcourt & Ludwig, 1965). These differences in how people learn have important implications for other, more elaborate behaviors, including such areas as academic achievement (reviewed by Findley & Cooper, 1983).

Most research in this area has used Rotter's measure (1966) of locus of control, but this scale has been criticized on several grounds: For one, it measures only generalized expectancies rather than specific ones. It also mixes perceptions of control over personal outcomes with perceptions of control over entities such as governments (cf. Gurin, Gurin, Lao, & Beattie, 1969; Mirels, 1970). Finally, there is more diversity among externals than internals, because there are many different ways to have an external control orientation (Hersch & Scheibe, 1967).

These criticisms led to new measures (Lefcourt, 1981). Several groups, for example, created measures that focus selectively on one domain of behavior at a time (Lefcourt, Martin, Fick, & Saleh, 1985; Lefcourt, Von Baeyer, Ware, & Cox, 1979; Paulhus, 1983; Paulhus & Christie, 1981; Wallston & Wallston, 1978, 1981). Another effort has been to separate causal influences from one another. For example, Levenson's (1973, 1981) scale distinguishes between chance factors and powerful others as external causes of outcomes.

Although the locus-of-control concept has been very influential, a theoretical question has been raised about it. Recall the underlying rationale—instrumental learning requires seeing a link between action and outcome. Rotter (1966) assumed that this link depends on having a sense of internal locus of control. Others, however (e.g., Weiner, Heckhausen, Meyer, & Cook, 1972), have challenged that view, noting that much of the relevant evidence confounds two qualities.

Consider the experiments described earlier in which task outcomes were said to be based on either luck or skill. These two descriptions differ in the locus of the causes of outcomes, but they also differ in other ways. For example, skill is a *stable* causal force, whereas chance is more *variable*. Which dimension influences changes in expectancy, locus or stability? Research tends to favor stability (e.g., Diener & Dweck, 1978; McMahan, 1973; Meyer, 1980; Weiner et al., 1972; Weiner, Nierenberg, & Goldstein, 1976).

This raises broader questions about the meaning of the locus-of-control literature more generally. For example, does the I-E personality scale similarly confound locus with stability? This question hasn't been answered. More recently, it's been suggested that the I-E scale confounds locus with confidence about outcomes, with internals being more confident than externals (Carver, 1997b). This would suggest the possibility that expectancies about good outcomes in the future may be what matters.

Efficacy Expectancies

A second variation on the broad theme of expectancies also derives partly from clinical experience. Albert Bandura (1977b) argued that people with problems generally know exactly what actions are needed to reach the outcomes they want. Just knowing what to do, however, isn't enough. You must also be confident of your ability to *do* the behavior. This perceived ability to carry out a desired action is what Bandura terms **efficacy expectancy,** or self-efficacy. To Bandura, when therapy works, it's because the therapy has restored the person's sense of efficacy, or confidence in the ability to carry out actions that earlier were troublesome.

The concept of efficacy expectancy draws conceptually upon a variety of earlier sources, including White's discussion (1959) of competence motivation (outlined in Chapter 10). White held that the competence motive is central to human behavior. Bandura argues more specifically that a sense of personal efficacy is needed for people to strive consistently (see also Box 13.3).

Efficacy expectancy isn't the same as internal locus of control, despite superficial similarities. In principle, people with internal locus of control are people who see both good and bad outcomes as following from their own actions. But they don't necessarily feel they have the competence to act in effective ways. In theory, they're just as likely to view bad outcomes as indicating that they're bad at what they're trying to do. For example, Joe has an internal locus of control. This is reflected in his belief that getting good grades is directly related to preparing for exams. He also believes he doesn't know how to prepare for exams. Thus, it's possible for people with an internal locus of control to have low expectancies of personal efficacy.

What of the person with an external locus of control? This question's a little trickier. In a sense, the concept of self-efficacy seems less relevant to these people at all. If their outcomes are dependent on the whims of fate or on powerful people around them, efficacy isn't much of an issue. One might argue that the absence of a sense of personal control implies a low sense of personal efficacy. On the other hand, Bandura sometimes treats a belief in the efficacy of external agents (e.g., medications) as equivalent to the belief in one's own personal efficacy. This suggests that even externals can have high efficacy expectancies if they see themselves as lucky or as well connected.

Research on Bandura's concept began by focusing on behavioral and cognitive changes associated with the experience of therapy. The work expanded to examine a wide range of other topics (reviewed by Bandura, 1986, 1997). For example, Brown and Inouye (1978) found that people with perceptions of high self-efficacy are more persistent on problems than people with lower efficacy perceptions. Wood and Bandura (1989) found that efficacy beliefs influenced the performances of business students in a simulation of a management task. Manning and Wright (1983) found that efficacy perceptions predicted the ability to control pain during childbirth (see also Litt, 1988), and Cozzarelli (1993) found that efficacy perceptions predicted adjustment to the experience of abortion. There's even evidence that acquiring a sense of efficacy can have a positive influence on immune function (Wiedenfeld et al., 1990).

Beyond these associations, perceptions of efficacy seem to be embedded in the positive effects of other variables. For example, there's evidence that efficacy perceptions are a path by which social support causes people to have a sense of well-being (Major et al., 1990). There's also evidence that self-esteem and optimism operate via perceptions of efficacy (Major, Richards, Cooper, Cozzarelli, & Zubek, 1998).

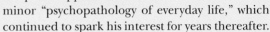

BOX 13.3

THE THEORIST AND THE THEORY: Bandura Stresses Personal Agency, But Also Appreciates the Role of Chance

Albert Bandura has made many contributions to the learning perspective on personality, having done pioneering work on observational learning and the effects of social reward. More recently he has argued forcefully for the importance of feelings of personal efficacy. Yet this theorist who places such emphasis on personal agency has also been outspoken in pointing to the role that chance encounters play in determining the course of people's lives, including his own.

Bandura was born in 1925 in a small town in northern Alberta, Canada, the son of wheat farmers of Polish descent. His town's school had only two teachers and a handful of students, but it was good enough to send him on to college at the University of British Columbia. There, sharing a ride to class with several other students, he had a chance encounter that would change his life. His friends, mostly premed and engineering students, had very early classes. Lacking anything better to do at that early hour, Bandura decided to kill time by taking a psychology course. He liked it so much he decided to make psychology his career (Evans, 1989).

A similar chance encounter helped Bandura find a special interest in *clinical* psychology. During a summer spent as a laborer, filling potholes in the Alaskan highway in the Yukon, he found himself in the company of an odd assortment of char-

acters, people who had fled to the remote North for a variety of unsavory reasons. This chance exposure to a range of bizarre individuals caused Bandura to develop an appreciation for the minor "psychopathology of everyday life," which continued to spark his interest for years thereafter.

A third chance encounter is also notable, in part because Bandura himself marked its importance in the course of his life (Bandura, 1982b). While a graduate student he went one day for a round of golf with a friend. By chance they found themselves playing behind two attractive young women. The two twosomes became a foursome for the remainder of the round, and one of the women later became Bandura's wife. As Bandura (1982b) wrote, without this chance encounter "it is exceedingly unlikely" the two of them would ever have met.

Surely this story isn't unique. Many lifelong relationships begin with improbable and unforeseen encounters. Indeed, Bandura's point was how often life is influenced in dramatic and critical ways by chance events. It's somewhat ironic, though, that chance encounters played such an important role in determining the life goals of this theorist whose belief in human self-agency came to be so strong.

Observational Learning

As we said earlier, many aspects of social learning theory can be viewed as elaborations on the concepts of classical and instrumental conditioning. There is, however, at least one part of social learning theory that leaves the conditioning concepts behind, suggesting a completely different basis for learning. This part is called **observational learning.** Two people play roles in this process, providing yet another basis for the term *social learning theory.*

Observational learning takes place when one person performs an action, another person observes, and the observer thereby acquires the ability to repeat the act (Bandura, 1986; Flanders, 1968). For such an event to represent observational learning unambiguously, the behavior should be one the observer doesn't already know. At a minimum, the behavior should be one the observer hadn't previously tied to the context in which it's now occurring.

TABLE 13.1

Four categories of variables (and specific examples of each) that influence observational learning and performance (adapted from Bandura, 1977a, 1986).
Attention for Encoding

Characteristics of model:
    Is the model attractive, powerful, or an expert?
Characteristics of behavior:
    Is the behavior distinctive, clear, and simple?
Characteristics of the observer:
    Is the observer motivated to attend and capable of attending?

Retention
Use of imagery as an encoding strategy Use of language as an encoding strategy Use of mental rehearsal to keep in memory
Production
Observer's capacity to produce necessary responses Observer's prior experience with overall behavior Observer's prior experience with components of behavior
Performance

Consequences to model:
    Is the model rewarded or punished, or are there no consequences?
Consequences to observer:
    Is the observer rewarded or punished, or are there no consequences?

Observational learning allows people to pack huge amounts of information into their memories quickly. It thus is very important. Observational learning takes place as early as the first year of life (Meltzoff, 1985). What's most remarkable about it is how simple it is. It seems to require little more than that the observer notice and understand what's going on.

This last statement requires several qualifications, which in turn help to give a better sense of what observational learning is (Table 13.1). First, observational learning requires the observer to pay *attention* to the model (the person being observed). If attention isn't devoted to the right aspect of the model's behavior, the behavior won't be encoded well enough to be remembered.

This principle has a number of implications. For example, it means that observational learning will be better with some models than others. Models that command attention for some reason—such as their power or attractiveness—are most likely to be effective. The attention principle also means that some *acts* are more likely to be encoded than others. Acts that are especially salient or prominent have a greater impact than acts that aren't (cf. McArthur, 1981; Taylor & Fiske, 1978). Other variables that matter at this stage are the observer's capabilities, intent, and concentration. For instance, if an observer is distracted by music while viewing a model, he may miss entirely what she's doing.

Having readily available summary labels for action sequences greatly simplifies the task of storing things in memory. Reprinted by permission: Tribune Media Services.

A second important set of processes in observational learning concern *retention* of what's observed (Zimmerman & Rosenthal, 1974). In some way or other, what's been observed must be represented in memory (which makes this a cognitive as well as a social sort of learning).

Two strategies of encoding predominate. One is called *imaginal coding*, the other is called *verbal coding*. Imaginal coding means creating images—mental pictures of what you're seeing. Verbal coding means creating a description to yourself of what you're seeing. Either strategy can produce a memory that can later be used to repeat the behavior (Bandura & Jeffery, 1973; Bandura, Jeffery, & Bachicha, 1974; Gerst, 1971). Mental rehearsal is also an aid to memory and thus to observational learning (Jeffery, 1976).

Once an action's been put in memory, there's one more requirement for the act to actually occur. Specifically, what was seen must be translated into a form you can *produce* in your own actions. How successfully that's done will depend partly on whether you already know some of the components of the act. It's easier to reproduce a behavior if you have skills that underlie it or know component movements involved in it. That's why it's often so easy for experienced athletes to pick up a new sport. They typically already know movements similar to those the new sport requires.

The importance of having components available also applies to the encoding process (see Johnson & Kieras, 1983). For example, if you already know names (or have good images) for components of the modeled activity, you have to put less into memory. If you have to remember every little thing, it gets more complicated and harder to keep straight. Think of the difference in complexity between the label "sauté one onion" (or the label "remove the brake pad assembly") and the set of physical acts to which the label refers. Now think about how much easier it is to remember the label than the sequence of actions. Using the label as a form of mental shorthand simplifies the task for memory. But you can use this strategy only if you know what the label refers to (see cartoon above).

Acquisition versus Performance

Observational learning permits fast learning of complicated behaviors. Given the processes just discussed, it also seems to be a case of "the more you already know, the easier it is to learn." There's an important distinction to be made, however, between *acquisition* of a behavioral potential and the *performance* of the behavior. People don't always repeat the actions they see others display. A great deal is learned that's never done.

Many complex behaviors are acquired by children through observational learning.

To know whether observational learning will result in behavior, we need to know something else. We need to know the person's incentives (Bandura, 1977a, 1986)—what reinforcement or punishment the person expects the behavior to lead to. A good illustration of the distinction between acquisition and performance comes from a study of children done by Bandura (1965). Subjects saw a 5-minute film in which an adult model performed a series of distinctive aggressive acts toward an inflated doll. The model accompanied each act with statements to himself, each associated with one aggressive behavior. For example, as he pounded the doll on the head with a mallet, he said, "Sockeroo—stay down."

At this point three experimental conditions were created, using three versions of the film. In one condition, another adult entered the picture and praised the model as a "strong champion" and said his excellent performance deserved a special treat. He then gave the model a soft drink and candy, making it clear that these rewards and the social approval were both consequences of the aggressive acts.

In a second condition (the no-consequence control group), this final scene was simply omitted. In a third condition, this scene was replaced by one in which the second adult came in and punished the model for the aggressive actions. In this condition the model was called a "big bully" and was spanked by the other person, who made it clear that the punishment resulted from the aggressive acts.

After seeing one of these three films, the child who was the subject was taken to an observation room that held a wide range of toys. Among the toys was a blown-up doll identical to the one in the film. The child was left alone for ten minutes on a pretext, and observers noted how many of the previously modeled aggressive acts the child repeated. The number of acts the child did was the measure of spontaneous *performance*.

Ten minutes later, the experimenter returned to the room. At this point the child was offered an incentive (fruit juice and picture stickers) to show the experimenter as many of the previously viewed aggressive acts as the child could remember. The number of behaviors that could be correctly shown was the measure of *acquisition*.

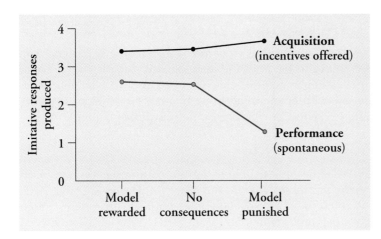

Acquisition and performance. Subjects observed a model display a series of aggressive acts that led to either reward, no consequences, or punishment. Subjects then had an opportunity to imitate the model spontaneously (performance). Finally, they were asked to demonstrate what they could remember of the model's behavior (acquisition). The study shows that reinforcement of the model plays no role in acquisition but does influence spontaneous performance (adapted from Bandura & Walters, 1963).

The results of this study are very instructive. The top line in Figure 13.3 shows the numbers of acts children reproduced correctly in the three experimental conditions, given an incentive for doing so (the measure of acquisition). It's obvious there isn't a trace of difference in acquisition. Reinforcement or punishment for the model had no impact on this measure.

Spontaneous performance, though, shows a different picture. The model's outcomes had an effect on what behaviors the observers did on their own. The effect of punishment was greater than that of reward, as in many studies (Thelen & Rennie, 1972), although there's other evidence that both reward and punishment can be effective in this sort of situation (e.g., Kanfer & Marston, 1963; Liebert & Fernandez, 1970; Rosekrans, 1967).

In conclusion, vicarious reinforcement influences whether people spontaneously do behaviors that have been acquired through observation. This effect is the same as any other instance of vicarious reinforcement and thus reflects vicarious instrumental learning. In contrast, reinforcement of the model has no influence on the acquisition of the behavioral potential. Thus observational learning and instrumental learning are distinct processes.

Although reinforcement doesn't influence observational learning directly, it can have an indirect effect. Recall that encoding requires attention to the act being modeled. Don't forget that paying attention is itself a behavior, similar in principle to other behavior. Its frequency or probability can be influenced by reinforcement. If you think that paying careful attention to something will be reinforced (for instance, if you were offered $50 to remember what a model is doing), then you'll pay careful attention. Thus reinforcement can influence a function on which acquisition depends.

Observational learning is a powerful process in human learning (and, some say, in the learning of other animals, Zentall, Sutton, & Sherbourne, 1996). Its power and its value to personality development lie in the fact that it allows huge amounts of information to be added to a person's behavioral repertoire quickly. It's much faster than shaping through instrumental conditioning or even vicarious instrumental conditioning. On the other hand, this process doesn't seem to determine which acts occur in which situations (motivational and reinforcement variables seem to do that). Rather, it's a way for diverse behavior potentials to be acquired for use. To paraphrase Bandura (1977a), once the ability to engage in observational learning is acquired (in infancy), it's virtually impossible to prevent people from learning what they see.

Manifestations of Cognitive and Social Learning

The processes described thus far provide a set of tools for analyzing behavior. To indicate how broadly the ideas can be used, the next sections describe two areas of study in which these processes play central roles (see also Box 13.4). The processes tend to become tangled up with one another in each area. Nevertheless, the components can be distinguished conceptually, and we'll do so as we go along.

Modeling and Sex Role Acquisition

Sex roles are behavioral qualities that people in a given culture see as more desirable, or more appropriate, in one sex than in the other (cf. Deaux & Lewis, 1984; Eagly, 1987). As with all roles, they are expectations, or implicit rule systems, about how to act. A variety of sources indicate that American society has a fairly stereotyped set of sex roles (although they are always in evolution) and that knowledge of them is acquired early in life.

BOX 13.4

MODELING AND DELAY OF GRATIFICATION

Social-cognitive learning theories emphasize that people's acts are determined by cognitions about potential outcomes of their behavior (Kirsch, 1985). This emphasis fits with the concept of **self-control,** the idea that people can regulate and restrain their own actions.

Self-control is an idea we considered at length in Chapter 10. As noted there, people often face the choice of getting a desired outcome immediately or getting a better outcome later on. The latter choice—delay of gratification—isn't all that easy to make. Imagine that after saving for 4 months, you have enough money to go to an oceanside resort for two weeks. You know that if you saved for another 10 months, you could take the trip to Europe you've always wanted. One event is closer in time. The other is better, but getting it requires more self-control. Ten more months with no vacation is a long time.

As we noted earlier, many variables influence people's ability to delay. Of interest at present is the role played by modeling (Mischel, 1974). As an illustration, consider a study by Bandura and Mischel (1965) on fourth and fifth graders who (by a pretest) preferred either immediate or delayed reward. Children of each preference were put into one of three conditions. In one, the child saw an adult model make a series of choices between desirable items that had to be delayed and less desirable ones that could be had immediately. The model consistently chose the opposite of the child's preference. Children in the second condition read about the model's choices. In the third condition (a control group), there was no modeling.

All the children were given a series of delay-of-gratification choices just afterward and another series a month later. Exposure to a model who chose immediate rewards increased the tendency of delay-preferring children to choose immediate reward too. In the same manner, exposure to a model who chose delayed rewards increased the tendency of immediate-preferring children to delay. These tendencies were maintained a month later. Similar effects were shown among 18- to 20-year-old prison inmates who'd had only weak tendencies to delay gratification before being exposed to models showing strong preference for delay (Stumphauzer, 1972).

How do models exert this influence on self-control? Presumably through vicarious reinforcement. In the Bandura and Mischel study (1965), for example, the model vocalized reasons for preferring one choice over the other. The statements imply that the model felt reinforced by his choices (see also Bandura, Grusec & Menlove, 1967; Mischel & Liebert, 1966; Parke, 1969). Thus, people obtain information from seeing how others react to experiences and use that information to guide their own actions.

How is this knowledge acquired? It seems to involve several processes discussed in this chapter. It may involve learning explicitly stated rules ("Little girls don't play tackle football" or "Little boys don't wear dresses"). Observational learning also plays a role (Sears, Rau, & Alpert, 1965). Sons who watch their fathers shaving and working with wrenches encode aspects of the activities. Daughters who watch their mothers do housework and cook encode aspects of those activities.

But wait a minute. Don't children watch both parents? Shouldn't children of both sexes learn the same things by observational learning? Yes and no. Certainly both boys and girls do encode a lot of information about the activities of both genders. But there's some evidence that a discrimination is made even in encoding. A study by Maccoby and Wilson (1957) suggests that children encode more from same-sex models than they do from opposite-sex models (although other research has found no such difference—Bussey & Bandura, 1984).

Why would there be a difference in encoding? Subjects in the Maccoby and Wilson study reported liking and identifying with same-sex characters more than opposite-sex characters. Other research shows that children prefer same-sex adults (Stevenson, Hale, Hill, & Moely, 1967; see also Mischel, 1970). People presumably attend more to models they like than to models they don't like, which causes greater encoding.

A far greater contributor to gender-role behavior is the subtle web of social reinforcement, both direct and vicarious. Children are rewarded in subtle and not-so-subtle ways for attending to and acting like adults and children of their own sex. Little Tommy gets more smiles and affection for watching Daddy change the oil in the car than for watching Mommy put on her makeup. Little Suzy is treated the opposite way. Given these patterns of reinforcement, Tommy and Suzy spend more of their time watching the activities of one adult than the other. They also probably see these activities differently in terms of relevance to themselves.

Despite having a preference for models of their own sex, children undoubtedly learn a great deal of opposite-sex-role behavior. That they don't *do* the behaviors reflects the distinction between acquisition and performance. At an early age, children note which actions are gender-appropriate and tend to perform (spontaneously) only gender-appropriate ones (Bussey & Bandura, 1984). Why? Because of the reward and punishment contingencies they've been led to anticipate (Fagot, 1977; Raskin & Israel, 1981). Suzy may be praised and cuddled after putting on makeup, but Tommy won't get the same response for the same behavior (nor will the message be lost on Mikey, if he happens to be watching).

Although live models (other children and adults) are important in the acquisition of sex roles and other behavior, **symbolic models** are also important. Indeed, only recently have psychologists come to realize how pervasive an influence such models exert. Symbolic models are figures on TV, in movies, magazines, books, and so on. The actions they portray and the patterns of reinforcement surrounding those actions can have a big impact on both acquisition and performance tendencies of observers. If TV portrays women as weak and powerless, observers learn that weakness is part of feminine behavior. If TV portrays men as hiding their emotions, observers learn that masculinity means not showing feelings.

Concern over the power of media to shape our conceptions of sex roles is one facet of a broader interest in the nature of sex roles themselves. It's implicit in the social learning view that there's nothing magic about the behavioral contents of these or any other role definitions. Indeed, from this point of view, role definitions are all a little arbitrary. Given that there's something of value in each sex role, many wonder whether there might not be virtue in encouraging people to develop the positive qualities of both roles.

Having both "masculine" qualities (e.g., assertiveness, competitiveness) and "feminine" qualities (e.g., gentleness, sympathy) has been termed **androgyny** (S. L. Bem, 1974, 1975; Kaplan & Bean, 1976; Kaplan & Sedney, 1980). It's been suggested that such diversity makes people more adaptable and flexible. Thus, androgynous persons should be happier and better adjusted (see Spence, Helmreich, & Stapp, 1975), although research hasn't always supported this assertion (see, e.g., Locksley & Colten, 1979). The concept of androgyny has met with a good deal of interest (for a review, see Taylor & Hall, 1982), and the question of whether it confers adaptiveness is likely to receive further attention, given the implications it has for sex roles in new generations of children.

Modeling of Aggression and the Issue of Media Violence

Another topic to which social-cognitive learning theories have been applied is the role of symbolic models in aggression. This topic is particularly sensitive, given the high rate of violence in TV programs and movies (a 1992 estimate held that by the time average children reach age 18 they've watched 40,000 murders on TV, and the number is steadily increasing). All the processes by which models influence observers are implicated here, to one degree or another. At least three processes are proposed, and there is substantial support for all of them (though see Freedman, 1986, for a cautionary note).

First, people who observe innovative aggressive techniques (live or on film) can and do acquire the techniques as behavior potentials by observational learning. That is, observational learning *does* occur wherever it *can* occur. This is well documented (Geen, 1998; Heller & Polsky, 1975). This principle looms large as producers strive to make movies "new and different" every year. Among the sources of novelty inevitably are new methods for inflicting pain.

Second, observing violence that is permitted, condoned, or even rewarded by other people helps promote the belief that aggression is an appropriate way to deal with conflicts or disagreements. Vicarious reinforcement thus increases the likelihood that viewers will use such tactics in their own actions. (By implication, at least, this is also the reason why some people worry about there being too much sex on TV and in movies.)

When it's suggested that violence is reinforced in the media, a common reply is that "bad guys" in TV and movie stories are punished for their misdeeds. It's important to note two things, though. First, punishment usually comes late in the story, after aggression has already yielded a lot of short-term reinforcement. Thus, aggression is linked more closely to reinforcement than to punishment. Second, the actions of the heroes usually are just as aggressive as those of the bad guys, and these actions are highly reinforced. Thus, apart from whether the bad guy is punished, the portrayal gives a clear message that aggression is a good way to deal with problems.

Does viewing "acceptable" aggression make people more likely to use aggression in their own lives when they're annoyed? The overwhelming majority of the evidence says yes. Whether the model is live (e.g., Baron & Kempner, 1970) or symbolic (e.g., Bandura, 1965; Liebert & Baron, 1972), exposure to aggressive models increases the aggression of observers.

The final point to be made here is more diffuse than the first two. It's that repeated exposure to violence *desensitizes* observers to the implications of human suffering. The shock and upset that most people would otherwise associate with acts of extreme violence become extinguished by repeated presentations of violent stimuli. Washington D.C.'s police chief was quoted in 1991 by columnist Sandy Grady as say-

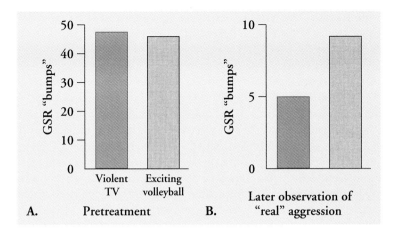

FIGURE 13.4

Habituation to aggression by viewing aggression. (A) Subjects watched a videotape of either an exciting volleyball championship or a violent TV program, which were equally arousing (as measured by GSR bumps). (B) When seeing an apparently real confrontation that resulted in physical violence, subjects who had watched the violent TV reacted less to this aggression than did the other group. Presumably watching the TV violence made them less sensitive to later "real life" violence (adapted from Thomas et al., 1977, Experiment 1).

ing "When I talk to young people involved with violence, there's no remorse, . . . no sense that this is morally wrong."

Evidence that desensitization can occur comes from several sources (e.g., Cline, Croft, & Courrier, 1973; Geen, 1981; Thomas, Horton, Lippincott, & Drabman, 1977). Results of one study (Thomas et al., 1977, Experiment 1) are shown in Figure 13.4. Subjects were attached to a machine that measured their emotional reactions, as "bumps" of arousal in their galvanic skin responses. They first watched a videotape of either an exciting volleyball championship or a violent program. As can be seen in Figure 13.4, A, the tapes were (overall) equally arousing. Later, subjects briefly viewed what they thought was a real confrontation resulting in physical violence and property damage. As Figure 13.4, B indicates, those who'd seen the violent TV show reacted less to this than did the other group. Watching the TV violence presumably made them less sensitive to "real life" violence.

This process has potential long-term consequences that are profoundly worrisome. As people's emotional reactions to violence are extinguished, being victimized (and also victimizing others) is coming to be seen as an ordinary part of life. It's hard to study the effects of this process in their full breadth. Such effects are pervasive enough, however, that they represent a real threat to society.

Assessment

Let's turn now to the process of personality assessment in the social-cognitive learning approach to personality. This section addresses the social-cognitive learning view on assessment in general terms and makes explicit some of the logical threads that underlie it.

Three issues are important. The first concerns widespread use of self-report devices in assessing personality, as opposed to behavioral observation. Recall that the cognitive view of learning emphasizes the role of thoughts in behavior. From this point of view it's only natural that people's reports of their tendencies to act and to experience various kinds of cognitions and feelings should be taken as appropriate and useful sources of information.

The second issue concerns the kinds of variables measured. Again fitting with the assumption that cognitive processes are determinants of behavior, assessment from this view tends to focus on *experiential* variables. That is, rather than charting behavior, the assessment devices frequently ask people how they feel in certain situations or what kinds of thoughts go through their minds in those situations (see Table 13.2 for an illustration). Particularly important in at least some of these measures are people's expectancies—expectancies of control, expectancies of coping, and expectancies of personal efficacy. This emphasis is no surprise, of course, since expectations are regarded as so important in this orientation to behavior.

A third and final issue is also implicit in the foregoing. In particular, assessment in the social-cognitive learning view tends to emphasize responses to specific categories of situations. This emphasis characterizes assessment throughout the learning perspective on personality. It acknowledges the fact that behavior can vary drastically from one situation to another. The social-cognitive learning view differs from the conditioning view, however, in its increasing emphasis on *personal* perceptions of situations rather than *objective* definitions of situations (e.g., Mischel, 1973). For example, one person may view a philosophy class as an opportunity to learn something new; another person may view the same class as a threat to his grade point average. In the view of this approach, it's the person's cognitive representation that deter-

TABLE 13.2

Assessing people's psychological experiences in difficult exam situations.
The first set of items (answered on 5-point scales) examines emotional reactions to the exam, the second set examines cognitions that can interfere with test performance.

Emotionality

I feel my heart beating fast.

I am so tense that my stomach is upset.

I have an uneasy, upset feeling.

I am nervous.

I feel panicky.

Worry

I feel regretful.

I am afraid that I should have studied more for this test.

I feel that others will be disappointed in me.

I feel I may not do as well on this test as I could.

I do not feel very confident about my performance on this test.

Items from Morris, Davis, & Hutchings, 1981.

mines how the person acts. Thus the cognitive representation must be taken into account in assessment.

Problems in Behavior, and Behavior Change

We now turn to two final issues: how problems in behavior are conceptualized within the social-cognitive learning view and what sorts of treatment procedures have been derived from this view. Again, the discussion combines concepts from conditioning theories with concepts that are more cognitive in nature.

Conceptualizing Behavioral Problems

The principles of conditioning suggest that inappropriate emotions such as fear result from classical conditioning. Similarly, inappropriate behavioral tendencies can result from prior reinforcement patterns. The social-cognitive learning approach goes on to suggest additional contributors, employing three key principles: vicarious conditioning, expectancies, and observational learning.

Thinking about the role of vicarious processes suggests two changes to earlier analyses. First, developing an emotional response (such as fear) toward a stimulus need not involve direct experience with it. You can acquire emotional responses vicariously. Second, your patterns of overt action can be influenced by watching outcomes that other people experience. Vicarious reinforcement can build in behavior, even if the behavior isn't desirable. Vicarious punishment can reduce your tendency to do a behavior, even if it's something that's actually adaptive.

All these effects may be viewed as mediated in part by expectancies (see Bandura, 1986). If you *expect* to experience strong fear in high places (even if the expectation is unfounded), you'll avoid high places. If you *expect* to get social approval for bullying someone else, you may do it. If you *expect* to be rejected by an attractive person, or to do badly on an exam, or even to do badly at "life" (Scheier & Carver, 1992), you may not try. These expectations can develop from direct experience, from vicarious experience, from things that other people tell you, or from putting two and two together in your own head.

However expectations are acquired, they can have powerful effects on your actions and feelings. Unfavorable expectations can cause you to stop putting forth effort at what you're doubtful about, thereby preventing the possibility of success. The conviction that you won't succeed leads to a pattern of low motivation and reduced effort that's sometimes called **learned helplessness** (see also Box 13.5).

A final source of problems in behavior from the viewpoint of the social learning approach is somewhat more specific. Problems sometimes reflect **skill deficits.** A person with a skill deficit has a problem because of an inability to do something that's necessary or desirable. One principle underlying skill deficits is a deficiency of observational learning. That is, when people have inadequacies in certain areas of behavior, it's often because they never had good models to learn from. Without being able to learn how to do important things in life (such as cooking, taking notes in class, dancing, and many others), there can be gaps in the ability to function.

Note that having a skill deficit can influence the development of expectations. People who know they lack particular skills come to anticipate bad outcomes in activities where the skills are needed. (For example, people who see themselves as lacking social skills come to expect the worst in new social situations.) People who do have skills may come to view the situations as being under their personal control (Lefcourt et al., 1985).

BOX 13.5

HELPLESSNESS: CASE STUDY OF A THEORY

The concept of learned helplessness originated in the finding that exposure to painful and unavoidable shocks made it harder for dogs to learn an avoidance or escape response when doing so became possible (Overmier & Seligman, 1967; Seligman & Maier, 1967). This finding led to a flood of studies of humans. The typical procedure in human research looks at effects of prolonged failure on later performances. Extensive failure often has an adverse—sometimes devastating—impact on later performance (e.g., Hiroto & Seligman, 1975; Miller & Norman, 1979; Roth, 1980). This has particular implications for analyzing problems such as depression (Abramson, Metalsky, & Alloy, 1989; Abramson, Seligman, & Teasdale, 1978).

The evolution of theories of helplessness makes an interesting case study. It's particularly interesting when viewed in combination with the issue discussed in Box 13.2—the relationship between conditioning theories and social-cognitive learning theories. The first explanation for the helplessness effect was based, somewhat loosely, on conditioning principles. Exposure to unavoidable shock results in learning that an outcome (removal of pain) isn't contingent on behavior (avoidance attempts). The result is reduction in effort, to the point where the animal no longer tries at all. Indeed, the term *learned helplessness* was coined because the animal looked as though it had learned it was helpless to avoid the shocks. In conditioning terms, the pretreatment extinguished the attempt to escape. Thus the animal simply doesn't do any escape behavior when it actually would work.

As analogous research was done on people, however, the theory became progressively more cognitive in nature. Explanations of helplessness in humans typically rely on expectations of future noncontingency (Abramson et al., 1978) or expectations of being unable to control outcomes (Wortman & Brehm, 1975). In simple terms, the person develops (temporarily) the idea that good outcomes can't be obtained because they're not related to his or her actions.

More-recent analyses of helplessness have included additional cognitive processes. Several analyses emphasize attributional variables, as a way of discussing how the expectation of bad outcomes develops (Abramson et al., 1978; Miller & Norman, 1979; Roth, 1980). Vicarious and verbal-symbolic processes also appear to play an important role here. For example, watching someone else experience noncontingency (particularly someone you think has the same ability level as you) can produce behavioral impairments in you (Brown & Inouye, 1978; DeVellis, DeVellis, & McCauley, 1978). These various effects appear to indicate that the *cognition* of uncontrollability is critical to helplessness, rather than actual uncontrollability.

As if these weren't cognitive enough, another approach adds yet another layer of thought processes. This approach (Frankel & Snyder, 1978; Snyder, Stephan, & Rosenfield, 1978) holds that people do poorly after prolonged failure because the failure threatens self-esteem. Rather than risk looking foolish on a later task, they stop trying. This withdrawal of effort creates a face-saving attribution while at the same time (ironically) causing the poor outcome they'd been afraid of in the first place (Frankel & Snyder, 1978).

Thus a phenomenon identified in the animal conditioning lab was extended to human behavior. In doing this, however, theorists who pursued the phenomenon have increasingly invoked cognitive processes as a way of accounting for it. Doing so raises questions. Do the same processes apply to human helplessness as apply to helplessness in other species? One probably wouldn't want to argue that dogs stop trying to escape because they're concerned about their self-esteem. But what about the other processes—expectancies and attributions? At the moment, there's no clear answer to this question.

Modeling-Based Therapy for Skill Deficits

It will be no surprise to discover that modeling plays an important role in the therapy techniques identified with the social-cognitive learning viewpoint. Techniques involving modeling have been used in two areas: skill deficits and emotion-based problems.

When people lack specific types of adaptive behaviors or skills, the skills can often be added through models. The model is put in the situation for which the skill is lacking and makes an appropriate action or response to the situation. The observer (the person in therapy) is then encouraged to repeat the action. This repetition can be overt (action), or it can be covert (mentally practicing the action). Indeed, the modeling can also be covert, with the subject told to imagine someone else doing a particular behavior within a particular scenario (Kazdin, 1975).

In principle, modeling can be used to supply missing skills any place there are deficits. Research on this subject, however, commonly focuses on such behaviors as basic social skills (e.g., La Greca & Santogrossi, 1980; La Greca, Stone, & Bell, 1983; Ross, Ross, & Evans, 1971) and assertiveness (Goldfried & Davison, 1976; Kazdin, 1974, 1975; McFall & Twentyman, 1973; Rosenthal & Reese, 1976). Assertiveness is acting to make sure that one's rights aren't violated, while at the same time not violating someone else's rights. It can be difficult to know just how to respond to hard situations in a manner that's properly assertive. But models who provide specific illustrations of appropriate responses (combined with a little practice to make sure you can do the same thing) can make a big difference.

In therapies dealing with skill deficits, the role of observational learning is often intermingled with that of vicarious reinforcement. There are cases, though, in which one or the other seems to predominate. In some instances, people literally don't know what response to make in a given category of situations. Observational learning is most relevant here, because it provides new responses. In other cases, it's not so much that people don't know what to do, but rather that they have doubts about whether doing it will work. In these cases vicarious reinforcement would seem to play a larger role.

Modeling and Responses to Fear

In discussing modeling and fear-related behavior problems, a distinction is made between two kinds of models: those who exhibit mastery and those who exhibit coping (e.g., Meichenbaum, 1971). A **mastery model** is one who seems to be completely without fear in dealing with what the person in therapy fears. This sort of model presumably works through vicarious extinction of the conditioned fear response, as the observer sees that the model experiences no distress (M. C. Jones, 1924; see also Denney, 1974).

In contrast, a **coping model** is one that initially is fearful but overcomes the fear and eventually handles the situation. The effect of this model presumably depends on the fact that the model is in the *same situation* as the observer but is (noticeably) able to overcome the fear by active coping effort. This effect seems more cognitive than that of the mastery model. Although the evidence isn't entirely consistent, coping models seem more effective than mastery models in therapy for fears (Kornhaber & Schroeder, 1975; Meichenbaum, 1971). This effectiveness attests to the powerful role that cognitive processes can play in coping with fear.

Another distinction to be made here is between modeling in which the observer just observes and **participant modeling,** in which the model (often the therapist) performs the behavior in front of the other person, who then repeats it. Participant modeling usually involves a lot of verbalization, instruction, and personalized assurance from the model. It takes more of the therapist's time, but it's more powerful as a behavior-change technique (e.g., Bandura, 1982a; Bandura, Adams, & Beyer, 1977).

In a typical modeling therapy for a specific fear, a model approaches, engages, and deals effectively with the feared stimulus. While doing so, the model describes the feelings that develop and the sorts of mental strategies that are being used to cope. Then the observer tries to do the same thing, first with the therapist's help, then alone. This procedure has been effective at reducing fear and increasing coping effort in a variety of domains. These include fears aroused by animals such as dogs and snakes (Bandura, Adams, & Beyer, 1977; Bandura, Grusec, & Menlove, 1967; Bandura & Menlove, 1968), by surgery, injections, and dental work (Melamed & Siegel, 1975; Melamed, Weinstein, Hawes, & Katin-Borland, 1975; D. T. A. Vernon, 1974), and by test taking (Cooley & Spiegler, 1980; Malec, Park, & Watkins, 1976; Sarason, 1975).

Therapeutic Changes in Efficacy Expectancy

The research just outlined indicates that models who display an ability to cope with difficulties can help people to overcome their own fears. But how does it happen? Bandura (1977b) says these effects illustrate a broader principle behind behavior change. He says that when therapy is effective (through whatever technique), it's effective by increasing the person's sense of efficacy for dealing with a given class of situations. In his view, when a model shows an ability to overcome fear, it helps give observers a sense that they can also overcome their fear. This enhanced perception of personal efficacy, then, results in greater effort and persistence.

These ideas, which were introduced earlier in the chapter, have been tested in several studies of the therapy process (e.g., Avia & Kanfer, 1980; Bandura et al., 1977; Bandura, Adams, Hardy, & Howells, 1980; Bandura & Schunk, 1981; DiClemente, 1981; Gauthier & Ladouceur, 1981). As an illustration, consider an experiment by Bandura et al. (1977) in which subjects with intense fear of snakes were given one of three treatments. In a participant-modeling condition, subjects watched a thera-

Seeing someone else cope successfully with something that you fear can help you develop the ability to cope successfully yourself.

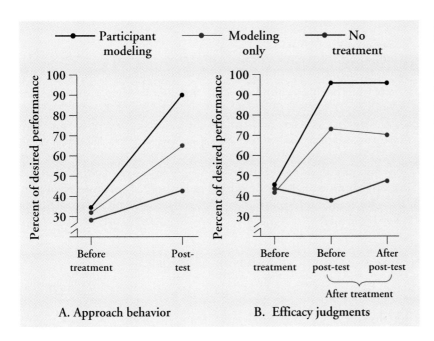

A. Approach behavior   B. Efficacy judgments

FIGURE 13.5

(A) Level of approach toward a feared stimulus and (B) self-efficacy judgments. Both behavior and efficacy perceptions were assessed before therapy (left side of each panel) and afterward (right side of each panel). Efficacy perceptions were assessed both before and immediately after the behavioral post-test (adapted from Bandura, Adams, & Beyer, 1977).

pist perform a series of increasingly threatening actions with a live snake. Then, with the therapist's assistance, the subject attempted many of the same actions. In a modeling-only condition, subjects were exposed to a model but didn't practice the activities themselves. Subjects in a control condition had no therapy at all.

Subjects were tested both before and after therapy on a behavioral avoidance test. This test required them to try a variety of actions with the snake (which were increasingly anxiety arousing) without assistance. Subjects also rated their expectations for being able to perform each of the acts that made up the avoidance test. They made these ratings at three times—after the behavioral pretest and both before and after the behavioral post-test. This self-report constituted the measure of perceived self-efficacy.

Figure 13.5, A shows that participant modeling had a more positive impact on behavioral approach than did modeling without practice, which had a more positive impact than no treatment. These differences in behavior were paralleled by differences in efficacy statements (Figure 13.5, B). Moreover, both approach behavior and efficacy judgments generalized (particularly for the participant-modeling group) to a snake that looked distinctly different from the snake used during the treatment procedures.

In Bandura's view, results such as these make several points (see Bandura, 1986, 1997). The broadest is that change in efficacy expectancy can mediate behavior change. That is, the behavior changes *because* there's been a change in the expectancy. Two other points concern factors that determine efficacy perceptions. Notice that expectancy ratings in this study changed most after therapy among people who had an opportunity to show themselves that they could cope (the participant modeling group). This fits with Bandura's belief that *performance accomplishments* are the strongest influence on efficacy perceptions.

The study also demonstrates a second influence on efficacy perceptions, however: *vicarious experiences.* That is, the modeling-only group was able to outperform the control group and also reported a stronger sense of efficacy. Vicarious consequences don't have as strong an influence as do personal outcomes, but they definitely seem to play a role. Bandura (1977b) also holds that *verbal persuasion* and *emotional arousal* can influence efficacy perceptions, although neither was examined in this study.

Bandura's theory has been very influential, though it's also had some criticism (commentaries, both pro and con, can be found in Rachman, 1978). Most of the discussion bears on whether efficacy perceptions are causes of behavior or consequences, but there are also other issues. For example, focusing on efficacy perceptions proves not to be useful for all persons—some people prefer that the responsibility for changing their behavior lie elsewhere (Burger, 1989; Chambliss & Murray, 1979). This finding leads to the question of whether perceptions of personal efficacy are critical, or simply expectations that desired outcomes will occur (Carver & Scheier, 1986, 1998).

Self-Instructions and Cognitive Behavior Modification

A final approach to therapy we'll note here is called **cognitive behavioral modification** (Meichenbaum, 1971, 1972, 1977; Meichenbaum & Goodman, 1971). This approach rests on the idea that problems stem from ineffective and disruptive cognitions that slip into people's minds unnoticed. More specifically, people often tell themselves that problems are bigger or less resolvable than they really are—even tell themselves they can't cope. The expectation of a bad outcome causes them not to try. The goal of the cognitive behavioral therapies is to get the person to recognize instances of maladaptive thinking and to make suitable adjustments.

This process involves teaching the person to identify stimuli that bring out negative or interfering cognitions. Then the therapist and client develop a set of substitute cognitions designed to be adaptive and functional (Table 13.3). These cognitions usually emphasize the following strategy: (1) breaking the situation you're confronting into concrete components, each of which can be mastered by itself; (2) acknowledging that problem emotions such as anxiety, anger, or pain may exist, but focusing on a determination not to be overwhelmed by them; and (3) redirecting yourself to the instrumental actions that have to be done to manage the situation effectively, instead of worrying about how well you'll do.

One more category of self-statements is used after the coping attempt is finished. These statements emphasize that progress in developing coping skills is incremental—if you didn't do as well as you hoped this time, you'll do better next time. This sort of self-statement helps prevent people from becoming discouraged (i.e., from developing unfavorable expectations). Once these mental statements have been laid out and learned, the person practices using them whenever confronting the category of problem that's being dealt with.

Cognitive-behavioral therapies often focus on specific problems such as test anxiety (Meichenbaum, 1972), anger (Novaco, 1978), physical pain (Turk, 1978), and children's impulsiveness (Meichenbaum & Goodman, 1971). It should be obvious from the nature of what's involved, though, that generalization to other kinds of stressful experiences is easy. For example, one study found that teaching coping skills to handle test anxiety resulted in lowered anxiety, improved academic performance, and higher levels of a generalized sense of self-efficacy (Smith, 1989). The term **stress inoculation** is sometimes used to refer to the process of training people to use these techniques not just for one problem but for a broad range of stressful events (Meichenbaum, 1985).

TABLE 13.3

Examples of coping statements used in cognitive therapy.
The purpose of the therapy is to train people to engage in effective self-instructions such as these rather than fill their minds with negative thoughts when engaged in a stressful or fear-inducing activity (from Meichenbaum, 1974).

Preparing for the Stressor

What exactly do you have to do?

You can develop a plan to deal with it.

Don't worry—worry won't help anything.

No negative self-statements—just think rationally.

Confronting and Coping with the Stressor

One step at a time—you can handle the situation.

This anxiety is what the doctor said you would feel. It's a reminder to use your coping exercises.

Don't try to eliminate fear totally—just keep it manageable.

When fear comes, just pause.

Keep the focus on the present—what is it you have to do?

After the Coping Attempt

It's getting better each time you use the procedures.

You can be pleased with the progress you're making.

Social-Cognitive Learning Theories: Problems and Prospects

The social-cognitive learning view on personality has been influential in personality psychology over a period of several decades. Some reasons for its influence are the same as those noted earlier for the conditioning view. That is, the concepts of this approach have been tested extensively in research settings and have generally been supported. Similarly, cognitive-behavioral therapy techniques have been shown to be very effective for many kinds of problems.

The social-cognitive learning approach also benefits further from having addressed problems confronted by the conditioning approach. A criticism of the conditioning approach mentioned in Chapter 12 was that research on conditioning usually involves drastically simplified laboratory situations. This criticism is far less applicable to the social-cognitive learning approach. People conducting research within its framework have examined human behavior in very diverse settings and contexts. People have studied locus of control and efficacy perceptions in situations as varied as have been studied by any group of personality psychologists.

Another criticism of the conditioning view was that it seemed to have little place for the sense of "personhood," the continuity and coherence that characterize the sense of self. This criticism is also less applicable to the social-cognitive learning theories. Concepts such as the sense of personal efficacy have a great deal to do with that sense of personhood, even if the focus is on only a limited part of the person at any given time. The idea of evaluating oneself with respect to the attainment of desired incentives also evokes the sense of personhood.

A problem remaining for both learning viewpoints concerns the relationship between the two. The two approaches to learning that are described in Chapters 12 and 13 are split by a disagreement so fundamental that it's hard to know how a single perspective can be welded from the two pieces. We minimized this issue somewhat while presenting the theoretical principles, but it deserves reexamination.

The problem is this: In explaining behavior, the conditioning approach restricts itself to events that are observable. Behavioral tendencies are explained from patterns of prior experiences and present cues. Nothing else is needed. If cognitions exist, they are irrelevant—foam on the stream of behavior, shaped by the same forces as shape behavior, but not really important in understanding behavior. The social-cognitive learning approach stands in direct opposition to this view. Expectations cause behavior. Actions follow from thinking, rather than occurring in parallel with thinking.

This latter characterization fits more with the introspections that most people have about their own lives. As noted earlier, however, treating cognitions as causes of behavior may mean rejecting some of the most fundamental tenets of the conditioning approach. In the more cognitive view, classical and instrumental conditioning aren't incremental processes occurring outside awareness; rather, they depend on expectancies and mental models. Reinforcement is seen as providing information about future incentives, instead of acting directly to strengthen behavioral tendencies.

Nor is the emphasis on expectancies and other cognitions the only area of conflict between the approaches. Social-cognitive learning theorists agree with conditioning theorists that reinforcement is necessary to maintain behavior (despite holding a view of the reinforcement process that differs drastically from that of conditioning theorists). But sometimes a behavior is maintained with no obvious external reinforcer. In such a case, the theorists assert that the behavior is being supported by self-reinforcement. The appeal to self-reinforcement is far from satisfying, both to conditioning theorists and to people who stand outside the learning perspective. If self-reinforcement accounts for behavior *sometimes,* why isn't it adequate *all the time?* Why is external reinforcement *ever* necessary? How do you decide when it's needed and when it isn't?

One challenge for the evolution of the thinking of the social-cognitive learning theorists is to determine how—or whether—their ideas can be reconciled with the principles of conditioning. Are the newer theories extrapolations from the previous theories, or are they fundamentally different? Can they be merged, or are they competitors for the same theoretical niche? That is, some people would say that the newer version of the learning perspective should simply *replace* the conditioning version—that the conditioning view was wrong, that human learning simply doesn't occur that way.

Some people have abandoned the attempt at integration, and also abandoned the competition for the niche. They have simply stepped away from the issue altogether. For example, in recent years Bandura has dropped the word *learning* from the phrase he uses to characterize his theory. He now calls it social-cognitive theory (Bandura, 1986). This raises the question of whether his current ideas should be seen as belonging to the learning perspective on personality at all.

Bandura's change of label reflects a more general trend among people who started out within the social learning framework. Many of these theorists and researchers have been influenced over the past 20 years by cognitive psychology and the ideas that have arisen there. Many people who used to label their orientation as a social learning view now would hedge. Some of these people would give their orientation a different label today, which would be more likely to include terms such as *cognitive* and *self-regulation*. Indeed, there has been a gradual fraying of the fringe of the social learning approach, which meshes with the newer cognitive self-regulation theories. This overlap will become more apparent to you in later chapters.

This blurring and shifting between bodies of thought raises a final question for the social-cognitive learning approach. Will this approach retain its identity as an active area of work in the years to come, or will it disperse, its themes absorbed by other viewpoints?

SUMMARY

Dissatisfactions with the conditioning approach led to development of another generation of learning theories. They're called cognitive because they emphasize the role of thought processes in behavior, and social because they emphasize the idea that people often learn from one another. Several aspects of these theories can be thought of as elaborations on conditioning principles, although close examination of the elaborations raises questions about the validity of those conditioning principles.

These elaborations include an emphasis on the role of social reinforcement (rather than other sorts of reinforcement) in shaping behavior. Social reinforcers such as acceptance and approval can also be applied to oneself. Because humans have the capability for empathy (vicariously aroused emotions), we can experience classical conditioning vicariously. We also experience reinforcement and punishment vicariously, causing shifts in action tendencies on the basis of someone else's outcomes. Functions such as discrimination and generalization are broadened in these theories to include such phenomena as semantic generalization. This view also holds that human learning is not always incremental. That is, we often learn rules and then apply them to new situations.

A fundamental principle that seems to underlie many aspects of human learning is that expectancies concerning upcoming events and outcomes play an important part in determining our responses. Specific theorists have also focused on two additional kinds of expectancy. Rotter holds that people who expect their outcomes to be determined by their actions (internals) learn from reinforcers, but that people who expect their outcomes to be unrelated to their actions (externals) do not. Bandura holds that perceptions of personal efficacy or competence determine whether a person will persist when in stressful circumstances.

One portion of this approach to personality stands as completely distinct from conditioning principles: the process of acquiring behavior potentials through observational learning. This process requires only that an observer attend to a model (who is displaying a behavior), retain some memory of what was done (usually a visual or verbal memory), and have the component skills to be able to reproduce what was modeled. This process of acquisition is not directly influenced by reinforcement contingencies, although reinforcement can have an indirect effect by influencing how much attention is paid to the model. On the other hand, spontaneous performance of the acquired behavior is very much influenced by perceptions of reinforcement contingencies.

It's easy to see the importance of the various processes of social-cognitive learning in many domains, including the acquisition of sex role behavior, the tendency to be aggressive, and strategies that are used to delay gratification.

Personality assessment within this framework emphasizes the use of self-report devices. Many of these instruments are designed to measure subjective qualities such as feelings, cognitions, and expectancies (consistent with the emphasis placed on these qualities as determinants of behavior). There is also a growing emphasis on assessment within the context of the person's own definitions of situations.

Problems in behavior can develop through both vicarious and direct learning. Problems also result when people haven't had the opportunity to learn needed behaviors from models. Therapy techniques based on the social-cognitive learning approach often involve modeling procedures, whether as an attempt to remedy skill deficits through observational learning or as an attempt to show the utility of coping skills through vicarious reinforcement. Such techniques seem most effective when subjects overtly engage in the behaviors under the therapist's guidance, which led Bandura to suggest that improvement is mediated by a growing sense of efficacy. Other therapies emphasize the idea that people often hurt themselves by saying things to themselves that are negativistic. These therapies teach people to stop these negative self-statements and substitute self-statements that emphasize active, effective coping.

GLOSSARY

Androgyny The condition of having both masculine and feminine qualities.

Cognitive behavior modification A therapeutic technique that attempts to change behaviors by changing thought patterns.

Coping model A model that displays fear but ultimately handles it.

Efficacy expectancy Confidence of being able to do something successfully.

Expectancy Judgment about how likely a specific behavior is to attain a goal.

Incentive The desirability of an outcome.

Learned helplessness A state of low motivation and effort following extensive exposure to lack of control.

Locus of control A dimension of believing that your outcomes are caused by yourself or by external forces.

Mastery model A model that displays no fear.

Observational learning The acquisition of the ability to do a new behavior by watching someone else do it

Participant modeling The act of practicing a behavior that's hard for oneself while using the therapist as model.

Self-control The regulation and sometimes restraint of one's own activities.

Self-reinforcement The approval one gives to oneself for one's own behavior.

Semantic generalization Generalization along a dimension of meaning.

Sex role The behaviors associated more with members of one sex than the other.

Skill deficit The absence or insufficiency of a needed behavior or skill.

Social reinforcement Praise, liking, acceptance, or approval received from someone else.

Stress inoculation A therapy to develop the ability to cope with broad range of stressors.

Symbolic models Models in print, movies, TV, and so on.

Vicarious classical conditioning Conditioning in which the UCR occurs via empathy.

Vicarious emotional arousal The tendency to feel someone else's feelings along with them; also called *empathy*.

Vicarious reinforcement Event in which a reinforcement experienced by someone else has a reinforcing effect on one's own behavior.

The Phenomenological Perspective

PART *seven*

THE PHENOMENOLOGICAL PERSPECTIVE:
Major Themes and Underlying Assumptions

Every person who ever lived has been unique. No two people have ever shared quite the same orientation to life. In fact, no two people ever experience any event in precisely the same way. This is true whether the event is perceptual (seeing or hearing something), or cognitive (thinking about something or coming to a conclusion), or behavioral (acting in one way or another). Each of us has a slightly different physical perspective on every event we witness. Each of us also has a unique psychological view on life, causing us to interpret in slightly personalized ways all the information we take in from the world.

The phenomenological perspective on personality has its roots in the uniqueness of each person's frame of reference. One major theme underlying this perspective is that the subjective experience of reality is extremely important. The personal frame of reference that makes each of us different from everyone else exerts a very powerful influence on every bit of our lives. Indeed, the word *phenomenology* literally means "the subjective experiences of an individual." Pressed to its logical

extreme, this emphasis on the subjective and personal implies that "objective" reality is unimportant. All that really matters is the subjective frame of reference that the individual takes toward the *experience* of reality.

Another theme that characterizes the phenomenological perspective is the idea that people can determine for themselves (indeed, *must* determine for themselves) what their lives are to be like. Self-determination—free will—is part of human nature, to be exercised by each person who chooses to do so. Unfortunately, some people allow themselves to slip into thinking they don't have this capacity. Some people allow regrets over the past or worries about the future to blind them to opportunities of the present. In the phenomenological view, this happens only when people lose sight of the freedom of self-determination that's actually theirs.

A final assumption that underlies much of this perspective on personality is that human beings are intrinsically good and self-perfecting. According to this view, it's human nature to be drawn consistently in the direction of greater health, self-sufficiency, and maturity, unless there are strong pressures to the contrary. The theories that make up this perspective thus are optimistic theories—focused on possibilities and potentials rather than on constraints and limitations. If there's a metaphor that characterizes the phenomenological perspective, it may be the human being as an opening flower or growing tree, evolving naturally toward greater beauty and completeness.

The phenomenological perspective on personality is represented by theories of two types. The theories are treated separately from each other, based on which of these themes they emphasize. Some of the contributors to the phenomenological perspective place greatest emphasis on self-determination and the intrinsically positive nature of the human being. This aspect of the approach is discussed in Chapter 14. Another theorist who's contributed to this perspective emphasized more strongly the subjective nature of people's perceptions and cognitions. He suggested that we literally create for ourselves a unique and personal world of experience. This aspect of the phenomenological perspective is discussed in Chapter 15.

Humanistic Psychology: Self-Actualization and Self-Determination

■ Julia spends most of her waking hours doing things for others. She talks often with her mother, whose life never goes smoothly and who always seems to want more from Julia than Julia has to give. When dealing with her mother Julia sometimes feels as though she's being drawn into quicksand, but she never complains. Then there's Eric, a guy she used to date. Eric's life is a mess, and he often calls Julia late at night for comfort and advice. Although she needs her sleep, she never refuses him a sympathetic ear. In her actions, Julia seems to be setting her own life aside for the benefit of others. It's as though she thinks she's unworthy as a person unless she does so. Deep inside, a small voice says she's wrong about that (although she's usually too busy to hear). And sometimes, just sometimes, she has the feeling that a different destiny awaits her, if she could only free herself to find it.

The experience of being human is mysterious, exciting, and challenging. You are living out a pattern of events, feelings, thoughts, and choices different from those experienced by any other person who's ever lived or will ever live in the future. You are continuously "becoming," evolving from a simpler version of yourself into a more complex version of that same self. It's sometimes mystifying, because you don't always understand why you're feeling what you're feeling. But the fact that the life you're living is your own—a set of sensations that belongs to you and nobody else—makes the experience also vivid and compelling.

How does your self know *how* to "become"? As you become more complex over your lifetime, how do you still remain yourself? Why do you sometimes feel as though part of you wants to grow in one direction and another part wants to grow in another direction? Why is it that even when things are pulling in different ways inside you, you still have the sense of being a single integrated person? What are the qualities that make this experience of being human so different and so special? These are among the questions asked by theorists whose ideas form the phenomenological perspective on personality. In this chapter, we examine some of the answers those theorists have provided.

The subject of this chapter is sometimes referred to with the phrase **humanistic psychology,** or the *human potential movement.* These terms reflect the assumption that everyone in the world has the potential for growth and development. No one—absolutely no one—is inherently bad, incapable, or unworthy. A goal of humanistic psychology is to help people realize this about themselves. In that way, people who've let themselves fail to reach their true potential will have the chance to grow. The ideas of the human potential movement developed largely in the context of therapy. This approach thus emphasizes that there's a continuity between being "normal" and having problems in living.

Self-Actualization

An important figure in humanistic psychology was Carl Rogers. His ideas provide a way to talk about the nature of personality, how potential is realized, and what can keep that from happening. In Rogers's view the potential for positive, healthy growth will naturally express itself in every person's behavior, if there are no strong opposing influences. This tendency toward growth is termed **actualization.** Actualization is a tendency to develop capabilities in ways that *maintain or enhance the organism* (Rogers, 1959). It's presumed to exist within every living creature.

The actualizing tendency is reflected partly in physical functioning. For example, your body actualizes as your immune system works to remove disease organisms. Your body actualizes when it grows bigger and stronger. The actualizing tendency also applies to personality (cf. Ford, 1991b). When actualization promotes maintenance or enhancement of the self, it's called **self-actualization.** Self-actualization moves you toward greater autonomy and self-sufficiency. It expands or enriches your life experiences, and it enhances creativity. It promotes *wholeness,* **congruence,** or *integration* within the person, and minimizes disorganization or incongruence.

Rogers assumed that the actualizing tendency is part of human nature. This is also reflected in another term he used: the **organismic valuing process.** This phrase refers to the idea that the organism automatically evaluates its experiences and actions to tell whether they're actualizing. If they aren't, the organismic valuing process creates a nagging sense that something isn't right.

Rogers used the term **fully functioning person** to describe someone who is self-actualizing. Such people are open to experiencing their feelings, aren't threatened by them, no matter what the feelings are. They trust the feelings, rather than questioning them. Fully functioning people are also open to experiencing the world. Rather than hide from it, they immerse themselves in it. The result of these tendencies is that the fully functioning person lives a life filled with meaning, challenge, and personal excitement, although living this way also involves a willingness to risk pain. The fully functioning person isn't a particular *kind of person*. Rather, it represents a *way of functioning* that can be adopted by anyone willing to live that way (see also Box 14.1).

The Need for Positive Regard

As important as self-actualization is, it isn't the only important influence on human behavior. People also have a strong motive to be accepted and to have the love, friendship, and affection of others—particularly others who matter to them (often termed *significant others*). Rogers used the term **positive regard** to refer to this acceptance (see Baumeister & Leary, 1995).

Positive regard can come in two different ways, and the difference is important. Affection given without special conditions—with no "strings" attached—is termed **unconditional positive regard.** Sometimes, though, affection is given only if certain conditions are satisfied. The conditions vary from case to case, but the principle is the same: I'll like you and accept you, but only *if* you act in a particular way. This is called **conditional positive regard.** Much of the affection that people get in their day-to-day lives is conditional.

Another phrase used in discussing conditional regard is **conditions of worth.** Conditions of worth are the conditions under which the person is judged to be worthy of positive regard. When people change their actions to conform to a condition of worth, they're doing so not because the act is *intrinsically* desirable, but to get positive regard from other people (see cartoon at right).

Rogers argued that after years of having conditions of worth applied to us by the people around us, we start to apply them to *ourselves*. We give ourselves affection and acceptance only when we act in ways that satisfy those conditions. This pattern of self-acceptance (and self-rejection) is termed **conditional self-regard.** Conditional self-regard makes you shift your behavior to fit the conditions of worth you're applying to yourself.

BOX 14.1

THE THEORIST AND THE THEORY:
Carl Rogers as a Fully Functioning Person

Although Carl Rogers apparently didn't consciously draw on his own life in developing his theory, his life certainly embodied all the theory's principles. Rogers lived a life characterized by a willingness to change and openness to experience. Several times he left the security of the familiar and moved in new directions, using only his intuitions and emotions as guides. Rogers was very much the fully functioning, self-actualizing person his theory describes.

Rogers was born in Oak Park, Illinois, in 1902, the middle child in a large family. His parents were conservative and devoutly Christian—world views they tried to instill in their children. During college he decided to pursue a life in the ministry. At the same time he also participated in a 6-month-long religious conference in China. This trip had a profound effect on him. The exposure to religious leaders from different cultures changed his own thinking about religious issues. He began to entertain the possibility that all he had believed might be wrong—that Jesus may have been only a man, rather than divine. At this point, Rogers wrote to his parents announcing his independence from their religious views, fully realizing the emotional cost that such an act would incur.

Rogers took his degree in history, then continued to pursue his remaining interest in religion, while also taking courses in psychology. After a pe-riod of dividing his efforts this way, he abandoned the path of religion forever and began to study psychology full-time. Having received his doctorate, Rogers took his first job in Rochester, New York. Here two experiences greatly influenced his thinking. First, his clinical experience made it apparent to him that psychoanalytic therapy was often ineffective, although its use dominated the group in which he worked. Second, he realized that there were vast disagreements among his senior colleagues about how to deal with specific cases. In short, conventional wisdom didn't seem to be working, and the authorities couldn't seem to agree among themselves about what to do. To Rogers, it was time to go it alone and develop his own way of treating problems in therapy.

In 1939, Rogers published the first of his books on the therapy technique he'd developed. This led to a series of academic appointments at several universities. In his later years, he left the familiar confines of academia and set out once again to make a change. The latter part of his career took place at the Western Behavioral Sciences Institute in California—where he pursued his developing interest in group therapies of various kinds—and at the Center for Studies of the Person.

SHOE by Jeff MacNelly

People sometimes attempt to impose conditions of worth on other people.
Reprinted by permission: Tribune Media Services.

We all have a strong need to experience positive regard from others, to feel wanted, appreciated, and respected.

Conditions of worth and conditional regard have an important impact. *Altering your behavior, values, or goals to obtain acceptance can interfere or conflict with self-actualization.* Because self-actualizing is more important than fulfilling conditions of worth, self-actualization should get first priority. Because the need for positive regard is so salient, however, its influence is often felt more keenly.

Let's consider a couple of examples to see how these two motives can conflict with each other. Joel is a young man who's decided to give up a possible career in music because his father needs help in the family business. In making this decision, Joel is responding to what he senses as conditions of worth imposed by his family. Bowing to that condition of worth, however, may mean denying something that's important inside him, something that's truly a part of who he is.

The same kind of conflict is experienced to some degree by Julia, the woman described in the chapter opening. Recall that Julia spends much of her time and energy giving of herself to others. Her actions, however, seem driven by a need to prove herself worthy as a human being. She seems to be applying conditions of worth to herself. By trying to live up to those demands, Julia prevents herself from hearing the voice of self-actualization and from growing in her own way.

Finally there's Jayne, who feels a strong desire for a career, but whose parents want her to marry soon and raise a family. If her parents won't fully accept her unless she bends to their wishes, they're creating a condition of worth for her. Accepting this condition may interfere with her self-actualization. Remember, though, that conditions of worth aren't always imposed from outside. It's entirely possible that Jayne's desire for a career may itself be a condition of worth, a self-imposed condition (just as may be Julia's need to prove her worthiness by giving to others). Jayne may have decided she won't accept herself as a complete person unless she has a career.

What defines a condition of worth is that it's a *precondition for acceptance,* whether self-acceptance or acceptance from others. A condition of worth is always coercive—it pushes you into doing whatever it requires of you. Whenever such conditions are involved, they can prevent self-actualization from taking place.

Self-Determination

The ideas of Rogers are echoed in a more recent theory of **self-determination** proposed by Ed Deci (Deci, 1975) and expanded upon by Deci and Richard Ryan (1980, 1985, 1987, 1991, 1995; Ryan, 1993). The central idea is that people's behavior can reflect several different underlying dynamics. Some actions are *self-determined*—done because the actions have intrinsic interest or value to the person. Other actions are *controlled*—done to gain payment or to satisfy someone's pressures or demands. A behavior can be controlled even if the control occurs entirely inside your own mind. If you do something because you know you'd feel guilty if you didn't do it, you're engaging in controlled behavior.

Whether behavior is controlled or self-determined can have a variety of consequences. One of them is how long you'll stay interested in the activity. People stay interested longer when their actions are self-determined than when they're controlled. There's a great deal of evidence that promising rewards for working on activities can undermine people's interest in them (Deci & Ryan, 1980). The effect has been found in children as well as adults. In children it has been characterized as "turning play into work" (Lepper & Greene, 1975, 1978).

It's apparently not the reward itself that creates the effect. What matters is whether the people see their actions as self-determined. Telling people they're going to be paid for working on the task generally seems to make them infer that their behavior isn't self-determined. As a result, they lose interest.

Sometimes, though, the presence of reward increases motivation instead of undermining it (Deci, 1971; Elliot & Harackiewicz, 1994; Harackiewicz, 1979). Why? Deci (1975) argued that reward has two aspects. It has a *controlling* aspect—implying that your actions aren't self-determined. But it can also have an *informational* aspect—telling you something about your skills (Rosenfield, Folger, & Adelman, 1980). If a reward says you are competent, it increases motivation (Koestner, Zuckerman, & Koestner, 1987). If the reward implies a condition of worth, however, or if it implies you're engaged in the activity only for the reward, its controlling aspect is more salient and motivation falls off.

Findings such as these support the idea that people are motivated by a desire for self-determination and autonomy. Such effects led Deci and Ryan to propose more broadly that people need to feel they're deciding things for themselves. In this view, accomplishments—such as doing well in your courses—are satisfying only if you feel a sense of self-determination about them. If you feel you've been forced to accomplish those things, or pressured to do so by others, you'll have less satisfaction and less motivation (Flink, Boggiano, & Barrett, 1990; Grolnick & Ryan, 1989). Indeed, there's evidence that pressuring *yourself* to do well can reduce intrinsic motivation (Ryan, 1982). This finding fits the idea that people can impose conditions of worth on themselves.

Deci and Ryan (1991) and their colleagues have examined several consequences of the distinction between self-determined and controlled behavior. In discussing these classes of behavior, two further phrases are important. *Introjected regulation* is what happens when a person incorporates a value pertaining to behavior, but treats the value as a "should" or an "ought." That is, the behavior is done to avoid guilt or anxiety, or to obtain approval or self-approval. If you try to do well in a course so you won't feel guilty about wasting your parents' money, that's introjected behavior. Introjected behavior is controlled. In contrast, in *identified regulation* the person accepts the behavior as personally meaningful and valuable. If you try to do well in a course because you believe the information it contains is important, that's identified regulation. Identified regulation is self-determined.

People who function in an introjected (controlled) way are different in many ways from people who function in an identified (self-determined) way. For example, one study found that religious behaviors used in an identified way relate to good mental health, but if they're used in an introjected way they relate to poor mental health (Ryan, Rigby, & King, 1993). Another project found that aspiring to financial success (which presumably reflects controlled behavior) also relates to poorer mental health, whereas aspiring to community involvement relates to better mental health (Kasser & Ryan, 1993).

A recent follow-up to the latter project determined that *why* a person has either of those aspirations is more important than just having the aspiration. That is, wanting either financial success or community involvement for controlling reasons (e.g., because it will make people like you) is bad; wanting either financial success or community involvement for self-determined reasons (e.g., because the process is intrinsically enjoyable) is good (Carver & Baird, 1998).

The pressures that lead to introjected regulation seem to stem from the desire to be accepted by others or to avoid a sense of guilt over doing things you think other people won't like. This fits with Rogers's belief that failure to self-actualize has its roots in the desire for positive regard from others. Still, a lot may depend on the extent to which significant others place conditions of worth on you and how willing you are to bend to conditions of worth. Recent research indicates that the need for relatedness doesn't have to lead to introjected regulation. In this research, a measure of autonomy in behavior related to more open and positive communication with significant others. People who interacted defensively were those who reported regulating their lives in a controlled fashion (Hodgins, Koestner, & Duncan, 1996).

Having a sense of autonomy also seems to foster further autonomy. In one research project, medical students who thought their professors were supportive of their own autonomy became even more autonomous in their learning over time (Williams & Deci, 1996). They also felt more competent in the skills they were learning. And finally, they acted toward others in ways that were supportive of *their* autonomy.

Free Will and Reactance

Humanistic psychologists emphasize the idea that people have freedom to decide for themselves how to act, what to become. For example, Rogers believed that people are free to choose whether to act in self-actualizing ways or to bend to conditions of worth. Deci and Ryan believe that people are exerting their will when they choose to act in self-determined ways.

The concept of free will is interesting as well as controversial. It's nearly impossible to know for sure whether people have free will, but people certainly act as though they *think* they do. This is reflected in a phenomenon called **reactance** (Brehm, 1966; Brehm & Brehm, 1981). Reactance occurs when a person expects to have a freedom of some sort and sees the freedom as being threatened. The result is an attempt to regain or reassert that particular freedom.

A good deal of "contrary" behavior seems to reflect this process. Watch a young child who's been told she can't do something. She now wants to do it all the more. In the same way, "playing hard to get" can create more attraction. It's as though there's an extra challenge in the idea that a person is unobtainable. The best illustration of reactance, however, may be the response that's commonly heard when one person is pressuring another: "Don't tell me what to do!"

When we are prevented from doing something that we want to do, our desire to do that activity increases even more.

Although external threats to freedom can produce reactance, you can also threaten your freedom yourself. Odd as it may sound, even having an initial preference for something can be a threat to freedom. Imagine you're going to dinner at a nice restaurant. Everything on the menu looks good. You've been thinking about shrimp all afternoon, so you have an initial preference. *Having this preference implicitly interferes with your freedom to choose something else.* The result is indecision. People in this situation tend to step back from their initial preference and get more interested in alternatives (e.g., Linder & Crane, 1970; Linder, Wortman, & Brehm, 1971). The closer to the decision, the more the indecisiveness, because once the decision is made you can't go back (see Figure 14.1).

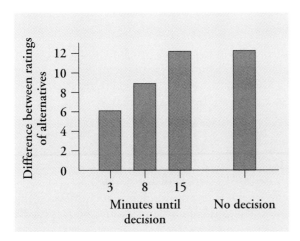

FIGURE 14.1

Subjects in this research were going to have to choose between two people, one of whom would interview them about a series of sensitive topics (except for a control group who didn't expect to make a decision). Each subject was given written descriptions of the two people and then was asked for an initial opinion about each. If the subjects thought the decision was later (15 minutes), they reported opinions of the two that differed considerably, suggesting an initial preference. If they thought the decision would have to be made soon (3 minutes), the ratings became similar to each other. Thus, as people come closer to decisions, they display increasing indecision (adapted from Linder & Crane, 1970).

The Self and Processes of Defense

The concept of self is very important to the approach taken by Rogers. For this reason Rogers is sometimes called a *self theorist*. Like many theorists, he assumed that the self doesn't exist at birth but that infants gradually differentiate self from nonself. As the person grows, the self becomes more elaborate and complex. It never reaches an end state but continues to evolve over the years.

Rogers used the term *self* in several ways. Sometimes he used it to refer to the subjective awareness of being (Rogers, 1965). At other times he used it interchangeably with *self-concept*. The self-concept is the set of qualities a person views as being part of himself or herself (much like Erikson's concept of ego identity, Chapter 11). Many distinctions can be made among the elements that form the self-concept. One of them is between the actual (or real, or experienced) self and the ideal self. The **ideal self** is an image of the kind of person you want to be. The **actual self** is what you think you're really like as a person right now.

Recall that self-actualizing is supposed to promote greater congruence. One aspect of this congruence relates directly to this distinction between actual and ideal selves. In particular, as self-actualization takes place, it creates a closer fit between the actual and the ideal. It leads you to become more like the self you want to be.

There's a second kind of congruence that's also important—between the actual self and experience. That is, the experiences you have in life should fit with the kind of person you think you are. For example, if you think you're a kind person and you find yourself acting in a way that's insensitive and unkind, there's an incongruity between self and experience. If you think you're a smart person but find yourself doing poorly in a course, there's an incongruity between self and experience. Self-actualization should tend to promote a closer congruence here, as well.

Incongruity, Disorganization, and Defense

Incongruence is disorganization, a breakdown in the unitary sense of self. You don't always sense this consciously, but the organismic valuing process notes it automatically. Incongruence (whether it's a gap between real and ideal or whether it's experiencing something that doesn't fit your self-image) leads to anxiety.

It isn't always possible to have complete congruence. Rogers assumed, though, that people defend themselves against even the *perception* of disorganization, to avoid the anxiety it creates. Defenses against perceptions of incongruity form two categories, which aren't so different from some of the defenses addressed by psychoanalytic theory (Chapter 9).

One category of defense involves *distortion of experience*. An example is rationalization—creating a plausible but untrue reason to explain why something is the way it is. Another distortion of experience occurs when you perceive an event as being different from the way it actually is. For instance, if you say something that makes someone else feel bad, you may protect yourself by assuming that the other person wasn't really bothered.

The second category of defense involves *preventing threatening experiences from reaching awareness at all*. Denial—refusal to admit to yourself that a situation exists or an experience took place—serves this function. A woman who ignores overwhelming evidence that her boyfriend is unfaithful to her is engaged in denial.

You can also prevent an experience from reaching awareness more indirectly, by not letting yourself get into a situation where the experience would be *possible*. By taking steps to prevent it from occurring, you deny the experience access to consciousness. This is a subtle defense. For example, a person whose self-image is threatened by sexual feelings among strangers may avoid going to the beach or to nightclubs, thereby preventing the experience from occurring.

Self-Esteem Maintenance and Enhancement

Defenses act to maintain and enhance the congruity or integrity of the self. Another way to put it is that defenses protect and enhance self-esteem (though see Box 14.2). The idea that people go out of their way to protect their self-esteem has been around

---

BOX 14.2

HOW CAN YOU MANAGE TWO KINDS OF CONGRUENCE SIMULTANEOUSLY?

This section of the chapter discusses how people protect or enhance their self-images, to defend against perceptions of incongruence between the actual self and the ideal self. Don't forget, though, that another kind of incongruence—between the self and experience—is also distressing. Interestingly enough, there are circumstances where the desire to avoid one kind of incongruity can plunge you right into the other.

What kind of circumstance would do that? An example is suggested by the work of William Swann and his colleagues on what they call self-verification (e.g., Swann, 1987, 1990). The principle behind this research is that once people have an idea of what they're like, they want to have that self-concept confirmed by other people's reactions to them. This resembles the idea that people want their experience to be congruent with their self-concept. For example, if you think you're a good athlete, you want others to think so too. If you think you're shy, you want others to realize it. It may seem odd, but the desire to verify beliefs about yourself extends even to beliefs that are unflattering (Swann, Wenzlaff, & Tafarodi, 1992). If you think you're not good looking, you'd rather have someone else agree than say the opposite.

But there's a problem. For a person who holds a negative self-view, there's a built-in conflict between self-verification and self-enhancement. Self-verification is trying not to have incongruity between one's self and one's experience. Self-enhancement is trying not to be aware of incongruity between a desired self and one's actual self. Unfortunately, attempts to diminish the two incongruities can pull a person in opposite directions.

Swann and his colleagues argue that both of these forces operate in everyone. Which one dominates at a given moment depends on your options. Keep in mind that most people's self-concepts contain both positive and negative qualities (Swann, Pelham, & Krull, 1989). Suppose, then, you had the chance to obtain information about yourself (from another person, or from a personality test). Would you prefer to get information about what you view as your best quality, or about what you view as your worst? Given this option, most people prefer to learn about something they view as desirable. This fits the self-enhancement tendency.

But suppose you know that the quality you can get information on is one you think is bad. Would you rather get information about how you're good in that quality, or information about how you're bad? The answer obtained by Swann et al. (1989) is that people tend to seek the unfavorable information if the information is about a quality they think is bad.

In sum, the self-enhancement tendency seems to influence where you look (and where you don't look) when you consider the relation between your actual and desired selves. You prefer to look at favorable self-aspects. Once you're looking at some self-aspect in particular, though, the self-verification tendency influences the kind of information you focus on. You focus on information that confirms your view of who you are—that it, fits your experienced self to your actual self. In each case, the effect is to enhance perceptions of congruence, consistent with the ideas proposed by Rogers.

(in various forms) for a long time. It's been an active area of research under several labels, including self-esteem or self-evaluation maintenance, self-affirmation, ego-defensiveness, and egotism (e.g., Darley & Goethals, 1980; M. L. Snyder, Stephan, & Rosenfield, 1976, 1978; Steele, 1988; Tesser, 1986, 1988; Tesser & Campbell, 1983).

It is often argued that two conditions are required for you to become concerned about maintaining (or enhancing) self-esteem (e.g., Snyder et al., 1978). First, an event must take place that's attributable to you (if events occur for reasons outside your control, they have no personal relevance). Second, the event must be good or bad, thereby having connotations for self-esteem.

What happens when there's a threat to self-esteem? Just as Rogers anticipated, people either distort perceptions or keep them from awareness. To put it differently, if self-esteem is threatened, people minimize the negativeness of the event (or maximize its positiveness), thereby distorting their perceptions. Alternatively, they try to prevent the event from being attributed to permanent qualities of the self, thereby denying its relevance.

Let's consider a couple of examples. A familiar threat to self-esteem is failure: doing badly at something or looking foolish in front of someone. Failure—whether academic, social, or whatever—can make most of us feel inadequate as human beings. What do people do when they fail at something? They make excuses (C. R. Snyder & Higgins, 1988). They try to avoid responsibility for the failure—blame it on things beyond their control. There's ample evidence that people attribute failures to task difficulty, to chance factors, to other people, or (in a bind) to a lack of effort (e.g., Bradley, 1978; Snyder et al., 1976, 1978). This occurs whether the failure is as simple as failure on a laboratory task, or as profound as the experience of divorce (Gray & Silver, 1990). Blaming something else creates distance between the threatening event and permanent aspects of yourself. Given the distance, the failure doesn't threaten self-esteem.

When you experience success, on the other hand, you have the chance to *enhance* self-esteem. You can do this by attributing the success to your abilities rather than to other causes (Agostinelli, Sherman, Presson, & Chassin, 1992; Bradley, 1978; Snyder et al., 1976, 1978; Taylor & Brown, 1988). Indeed, there's evidence that people think that their positive qualities are under their own control, allowing them to claim credit for being the way they are (Alicke, 1985).

So far, we've focused on distorted explanations for events. A person can also protect self-esteem by distorting perceptions another way. As said earlier, an event is relevant to self-esteem only if it has an impact that's either good or bad. Another way to be self-protective, then, is to distort your perceptions of the impact. An academic failure isn't a failure if the course doesn't matter to you. Making a bad impression on someone isn't a problem if that person isn't worth bothering with.

This sort of distortion also seems to occur. Consider, for example, a study in which subjects were told they'd done well or done poorly on a test (Greenberg, Pyszczynski, & Solomon, 1982). They then were asked to indicate how valid they thought the test was and how important it had been for them to do well on it. Those who believed they'd done well saw the test as more valid and more important than did those who believed they'd done poorly.

Self-Handicapping

Distorting perceptions is one way to protect self-esteem when bad outcomes occur. But there's also a second way—denial to awareness. Consider effects known as **self-handicapping** (e.g., Arkin & Baumgardner, 1985; Berglas & Jones, 1978; Higgins,

Snyder, & Berglas, 1990; Jones & Berglas, 1978; Jones & Pittman, 1982). Self-handicapping is acting to create the very conditions that tend to produce a failure. For example, if you have a test tomorrow, it's self-handicapping to stay up partying all night instead of studying. If you want to make a good impression on someone, it's self-handicapping to show up drunk or drenched in sweat.

Why would you want to do this to yourself? If you want to reach a goal, why create conditions that make it harder? The theory is that a hard goal can create a threat to self-esteem. If the goal is challenging, there's a substantial risk of failure. You can't fail, though, if success is prevented by circumstances beyond your control. If those conditions exist, the stigma of failing is removed. If you fail the test or make a poor impression, well, *no one* could do well under those conditions. So it wasn't really a failure at all. Thus you've denied to yourself the awareness of having failed. Note that if a self-handicapping strategy is going to be successful, you need to be *unaware of using it*. If you realize you're setting up barriers for yourself, the barriers won't have the same psychological meaning.

Self-handicapping may be much more common than most people realize (for a broad treatment see Higgins et al., 1990). The idea has even been extended to phenomena that are usually viewed differently—for example, test anxiety. Everyone knows people who say they freeze up during tests, even though they know the material. Claiming to be test anxious may have a self-handicapping function, helping protect self-esteem (Greenberg, Pyszczynski, & Paisley, 1984; Smith, Snyder, & Handelsman, 1982). That is, being test anxious provides an explanation for a potential failure that doesn't reflect on your ability.

The idea that people act in self-handicapping ways can be applied widely. It's been applied to such phenomena as the experience of physical symptoms (Smith, Snyder, & Perkins, 1983) and self-reports of shyness or depression (Arkin, Lake, & Baumgardner, 1986; Bernstein, Stephenson, Snyder, & Wicklund, 1983; Schouten & Handelsman, 1987; C. R. Snyder, Smith, Augelli, & Ingram, 1985). There undoubtedly can be other applications of the idea as well, as people think more about the meanings that may underlie various kinds of behavior.

Although self-handicapping may be common, it's not a good thing to do. People who tend to self-handicap are poorer copers than other people, coping by withdrawing and focusing on their distress (Zuckerman, Kieffer, & Knee, 1998). It's also worth repeating that self-handicapping often results in the very failure that prompted it (Zuckerman et al., 1998).

Self-Actualization and Maslow's Hierarchy of Motives

Rogers wasn't the only theorist to emphasize the importance of self-actualization. Another who did so was Abraham Maslow (1962, 1970). Maslow was interested in the qualities of people who seem to get the most out of life—the most fully functioning of persons, the healthiest, and the best adjusted. He spent most of his career trying to understand how these persons were able to be so complete and so well adapted (see Box 14.3).

As part of this effort, Maslow looked closely at how people deal with the world. He eventually came to examine the concept of motivation and how motives are organized. Although Maslow thus was a motivational theorist, his view of motivation was very different from the view discussed in Chapter 5.

Maslow came to view the various human needs (which he termed *instinctoid*, or instinctlike) as forming a hierarchy (Maslow, 1970). This hierarchy is often portrayed

THE THEORIST AND THE THEORY:
Maslow's Focus on the Positive

Abraham Maslow focused his work almost exclusively on the positive side of human experience. He was interested in what caused some people to achieve greatness in their lives and to succeed where others failed. He cared about issues of growth and the realization of human potential. It's clear that these interests were influenced by events in his own life.

Maslow was born in 1908 in Brooklyn, the oldest of seven children of Russian-Jewish immigrants. His home life was definitely not one that fostered personal growth. His father thought little of him and even publicly ridiculed his appearance. This experience led young Maslow to seek out empty cars whenever he rode the subway, to spare others the sight of him. If Maslow's father treated him badly, his mother's treatment was worse. Because the family was poor, she kept a lock on the refrigerator to keep the children out, feeding them only when she saw fit. Maslow once characterized her as a "cruel, ignorant, and hostile figure, one so unloving as to nearly induce madness in her children" (Hoffman, 1988, p. 7).

Maslow was later to say that his focus on the positive side of personality was a direct consequence of his mother's treatment of him. It was a "reaction formation" to the things his mother did and the qualities she represented (Maslow, 1979, p. 958). Thus, from a life begun in hardship came a determination to understand the highest and best in human experience.

Maslow entered college intending a career in law, but he quickly became disenchanted because law focuses so much on evil and so little on what's good in people. He turned then to psychology. According to Maslow, that was when his life really started. His doctoral work, done under the direction of well-known primate researcher Harry Harlow, focused on how dominance is established among monkeys. Thus, even while conducting animal research, Maslow was interested in what sets exceptional individuals off from others who are less special.

Maslow shifted this research interest to humans during the period surrounding World War II. New York in the 1930s and 40s was a gathering place for some of the greatest intellectuals of Europe, who were escaping from Nazi Germany. Maslow was quite taken with several of these people and found himself trying to find out everything he could about them. In this search to understand how these individuals came to be the way they were, Maslow was sowing the seeds of more formal work to come later. This formal research was prompted in part by the eruption of war. That is, Maslow was deeply moved by the suffering and anguish that the war caused, and he vowed to devote his life to proving that humans were capable of something grander than war, prejudice, and hatred. He proceeded to do just that, by studying the process of self-actualization.

---

graphically as a pyramid (Figure 14.2). Maslow pointed out that needs vary in their immediacy and power. Some needs are extremely primitive, basic, and demanding. Because they're so fundamental, they form the base of the pyramid. These needs are *physiological*—pertaining to air, water, food, and so on—things obviously necessary for survival. The qualities at the next higher level of the hierarchy are also necessary for survival, but they're less demanding. These are *safety and (physical) security needs*— shelter from the weather, protection against predators, and so on.

Maslow considered this second class of needs to be less basic than the first class because safety needs require satisfaction less frequently than do physiological needs, and when satisfied, they usually remain so for longer periods. You need to get oxygen every few seconds, water every few hours, food once or twice a day. But once

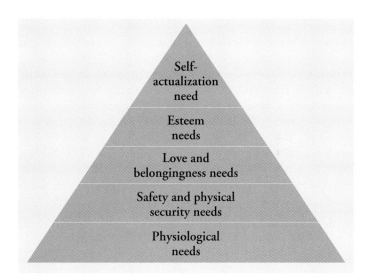

FIGURE 14.2

Maslow's theoretical hierarchy of needs. Needs lower on the hierarchy are more demanding and animalistic. Needs higher on the hierarchy are more subtle, but more distinctly human.

you've found a house or apartment, you have physical shelter for quite a while (as long as you pay the rent). If both your apartment and your air supply became inaccessible, you'd surely try to regain the air first and worry about the apartment later.

At the next level of Maslow's hierarchy, the needs begin to have more *social* qualities. The level immediately above safety needs is the category of *love and belongingness.* Here the needs are for companionship, affection, and acceptance from others (much like the need for positive regard posited by Rogers). Needs of this type are satisfied through interaction with other people.

Higher yet on the pyramid are *esteem needs*—needs that bear on evaluation (and self-evaluation). Esteem needs include the need for a sense of mastery and power and a sense of appreciation from others. Notice that this last need differs from the acceptance and affection mentioned in the last paragraph. *Acceptance* may not be evaluative, but *appreciation* is. You're appreciated and esteemed for some quality or qualities that you possess. The need for appreciation thus is more elaborate than the need for acceptance.

At the top of this hierarchy stands *self-actualization.* Maslow used this term much as Rogers did, to mean the tendency to become whatever you're capable of becoming—to extend yourself to the limits of your capacities. Self-actualization, to Maslow, is the highest of human motives.

This hierarchical organization of motives has several implications. The pyramid provides a visual analogue for Maslow's core assumption. The assumption is that low-level needs are more primitive—and more demanding—than needs higher on the hierarchy. As we said earlier, the need for air is more demanding than the need for shelter. Maslow's assumption was broader than that, however. He also assumed that the need for physical shelter is more demanding than the need to have a sense of being accepted, and that the need for a sense of belonging is more demanding than the need to be appreciated or powerful. Maslow thus held that the intensity of the motive force weakens as you move step by step up the pyramid.

On the other hand, as you move up through the hierarchy, the needs are also more distinctly human and less animalistic. Thus, to Maslow there's a trade-off between the constraints of biology and the uniqueness of being human. We have needs that make us different from other creatures, with self-actualization being the highest and most important. But we can't escape the motives that we share with other creatures. Those needs are more powerful when they're unsatisfied than are the needs that make us special.

In general, then, people must deal with the needs they have at lower levels of the pyramid before they can attend to needs that are higher. There are two further implications of this. The first is that if a need begins to develop at a lower level while you're trying to satisfy a higher one, *the developing lower-level need can cause you to be pulled away from the higher-level one.* Your attention, in effect, is pulled downward, and you're forced to do something about the more basic need (see Wicker, Brown, Wiehe, Hagen, & Reed, 1993).

The second implication concerns the process by which people move up through this set of needs. It may be precisely the freeing of your mind from the demands of low-level needs that lets you become attuned to the quiet voice of the self-actualization tendency. Remember, the farther up the pyramid you go, the weaker and more subtle is the motive. Self-actualization, the highest motive, is also the most subtle and thus the hardest to notice. Only when the other needs are quieted can this one be attended to.

The steps on the hierarchy also differ from each other in one more way. Maslow said that motives low on the pyramid are **deficiency-based motives,** whereas the high levels (particularly self-actualization) are **growth-based motives** (Maslow, 1955). That is, lower needs arise from deprivation. Satisfying such needs means escaping unpleasant conditions. Self-actualization, in contrast, is more like the distant call of your still-unrealized potential as a person. Satisfying this need isn't a matter of avoiding an unpleasant state. Rather, it's the seeking of growth (see also Markus & Nurius, 1986).

Finally, we should make a point about the relation between Maslow's ideas and those of Rogers. Rogers emphasized two motives. The first was the self-actualizing tendency, which he saw as critical. The second was the need for positive regard—affection and acceptance. This need is also important—and very powerful. Indeed, Rogers regarded it as so powerful that it often leads people to ignore the actualizing tendency.

It's possible to see a commonality between these ideas of Rogers and the more elaborate structure laid out by Maslow (Figure 14.2). The bottom two levels of Maslow's pyramid refer to needs that Rogers ignored. Rogers focused on social needs, which for Maslow begin at the third level. Maslow assumed, as did Rogers, that the need for acceptance could be more demanding than the need for self-actualization. The structure of this hierarchy clearly implies that people can be distracted from self-actualization by the need for positive regard.

The intermediate level of Maslow's pyramid—esteem needs—can be viewed as an elaboration on the need for positive regard. Esteem needs seem similar in many ways to Rogers's conditions of worth. The two theorists differ somewhat in how they viewed this motive. To Rogers, bowing to conditions of worth is bad. To Maslow, esteem needs are part of being human, although more primitive than the need to self-actualize. The two agreed, however, that this need can get in the way of self-actualization. In sum, despite the fact that these two theorists each had unique ideas about personality, their theoretical views also have much in common.

Characteristics of Frequent Self-Actualizers

The concept of self-actualization is in many ways the most engaging and intriguing of all the ideas generated by these theorists. Although Maslow developed a broad picture of human motives, it was self-actualization that most fully absorbed his interest and imagination. As noted earlier, he devoted much of his career to studying it.

According to Maslow, everyone has the potential to self-actualize, and everyone has an intrinsic desire to become more and more the person that he or she is capable of being. Because self-actualization is so diffuse a quality, it can appear in virtually any kind of behavior. It isn't just the painter, musician, writer, or actor who can be self-actualizing—it's any person who's in the process of becoming more congruent, more integrated, more complete as a person.

Despite the belief that every person has this potential, Maslow also recognized that some people self-actualize more often than others. To better understand self-actualizing, he sought out people who displayed self-actualizing properties often. He worked hard to describe these people, in part because self-actualization is such a hard concept to grasp. By describing them he hoped to help others recognize self-actualizing experiences in their own lives.

Maslow came to believe that frequent self-actualizers share several characteristics (Maslow, 1963, 1968). Here are a few of them (for a more complete list, see Table 14.1):

Self-actualizers are *efficient* in their perception of reality. That is, their experience is in extra-sharp focus. Self-actualizers can spot the confused perceptions that others have and cut through the resulting tangles. People who frequently engage in self-actualization are also *accepting*. They accept both themselves and others. This self-acceptance isn't smug self-assurance. Self-actualizers realize they're far from perfect. They accept themselves *as they are*, imperfections and all. The same is true of their reactions to people around them. The frailties of others are accepted as a part of who they are. (Note the similarity here to the mature acceptance of inner conflict that's a goal of psychoanalytic therapy.)

TABLE 14.1

Characteristics of self-actualizers (based on Maslow, 1968).
Self-actualizing people . . .
are *efficient* and accurate *in perceiving* reality
are *accepting* of themselves, of other people, and of nature
are *spontaneous* in thought and emotion, natural rather than artificial
are *problem-centered*, concerned with eternal philosophical questions
are *independent* and *autonomous* when it comes to satisfactions
have a continued *freshness of appreciation* of ordinary events
often experience "*oceanic feelings*," a sense of oneness with nature that transcends time and space
identify with all of *humanity*—are democratic and respectful of others
form *deep ties*, but *with only a few persons*
appreciate, for its own sake, the *process* of doing things
have a *philosophical*, thoughtful, nonhostile *sense of humor*
have a childlike and fresh *creativity and inventiveness*
maintain an inner *detachment from* the *culture* in which they live
are sufficiently *strong*, independent, and guided by their own inner visions that they sometimes appear *temperamental* and even *ruthless*

Another characteristic of the self-actualizer is a mental *spontaneity.* This is reflected in an ongoing creativity without artificiality. This is often linked to a *freshness of appreciation* of the experiences of life, an excitement in the process of living. The idea that creativity is associated with self-actualization rather than with other motives has received support (Amabile, 1985). In this research, writers were led to think about the act of creation either from the view of extrinsic incentives (thus motives lower on Maslow's hierarchy) or from the view of qualities intrinsic to the act itself (by implication, self-actualization). They then wrote a poem. Judges later rated the creativity of the poems. Those written after thinking about external incentives were seen as lower in creativity than those written from the self-actualizing orientation.

The self-actualizing person is often said to be *problem-centered,* but this phrase is a little misleading. The word *problem* here refers to enduring questions of philosophy or ethics. Self-actualizers take a wide view, concerning themselves with universal issues. Along with this concern for universals goes an independence from their own culture and immediate environment. The self-actualizer lives in the universe, and only incidentally in this apartment, city, or country. Frequent self-actualizers (who have generally satisfied their relationship needs) know that relationships require effort. They have deep ties, because relationships matter to them, but the ties are often limited to a very few others.

Toward the end of his life, Maslow made a distinction between two kinds of self-actualizers (Maslow, 1971). One of them we've already described. Maslow called the others **transcendent self-actualizers.** These people are so invested in experiences of self-actualization that it becomes the most precious aspect of their life. They are more consciously motivated by universal values or goals outside themselves (such as beauty, truth, and unity) than are other self-actualizers. They're more holistic about the world, seeing the integration of all its elements. There's a greater transcendence of the self, so that self-actualization almost becomes "universe-actualization." All of experience seems sacred to them. They view themselves as instruments by which their capabilities are expressed, rather than the owners of those capabilities. From this characterization comes the term *transpersonal* (beyond the person), which is sometimes used to refer to this way of viewing human potential (see also Box 14.4).

The Peak Experience

In trying to describe the process of self-actualization, Maslow also focused on moments in which self-actualization was most clearly occurring. Remember that not every act involves self-actualization, even for a person who self-actualizes a great deal. Maslow used the term **peak experiences** to refer to moments of intense self-actualization.

In peak experiences, people have a sense of being connected with the elements of their surroundings. Colors and sounds seem crisper—there's a sharper clarity in perceptions (see Privette & Landsman, 1983). There's also a loss of the sense of time as the experience flows by. The feelings associated with the peak experience are often those of awe, wonder, or even ecstasy. The peak experience is something that tends to take you outside yourself. You aren't thinking about yourself but rather are experiencing whatever you're experiencing as fully as possible.

Peak experiences *can* occur in a passive way (for instance, in examining a great work of art). Usually, though, they occur when people are engaged in action of some kind (Csikszentmihalyi, 1975; Privette & Landsman, 1983). The person having a peak

BOX 14.4

SELF-ACTUALIZATION AND *YOUR* LIFE

By now you've read a lot about the concept of self-actualization, and it may all sound pretty abstract. To get a more concrete feel for the idea, try spending a few minutes thinking about how it applies to your own life.

For example, think about how Maslow's hierarchy of needs pertains to your current existence. Which level of the hierarchy dominates your day-to-day experiences? Are you mostly concerned with having or maintaining a sense of belonging to some social group (or perhaps feeling a sense of acceptance and closeness with a particular person)? Is the need to feel valued and respected for your positive qualities what you're currently focused on? Or are you engaged in trying to grow as close as possible to the blueprint hidden inside you holding the secret of your possibilities?

Now think back to your junior year of high school and what your life was like back then. What were your needs and concerns during that period? Since then have you moved upward on the hierarchy, or downward, or are you focused at about the same level?

Here's another question: Think about your current "mission" in life, the goal that gives your life focus and provides it meaning. Where did this goal come from? Did it get passed down to you by your parents (or by someone else)? Or does it come from deeper inside you? How *sure* are you that your goal is your own and not someone else's assignment for you to do as a condition of worth? How sure are you that it isn't an assignment you've given *yourself*? What would it feel like to spend the rest of your life doing assignments? What would it mean to you to have your life play out that way?

Another question: You can't always do what you want, everyone knows that. Sometimes you have to do things you *have* to do. But how much of the time? How much of your time—how much of your *self*—should be used up doing your duty, being obedient to conditions of worth, before you turn to your other needs? How dangerous is it to say to yourself that you'll do these assignments—these duties—for a while, just for a while, and that after a few weeks or months or years you'll turn to the things you really want? How sure are you that you won't get in a rut and come to see the assignments as the only reality of life? How sure are you that you'll be able to make the decision to turn to your own self-actualization, years down the road, when it's become such a habit to live up to conditions of worth?

Not every experience in life is self-actualizing. Even people who self-actualize extensively sometimes get stalled and have trouble with it. When *you* find yourself unable to move in a self-actualizing direction, what's preventing it? What are the barriers to growth that you confront from time to time? Are they the demands of other needs? Do they stem from your relationships with your parents and family? With your friends? Are they barriers that you place in front of yourself?

Obviously, these questions aren't easy to answer. You can't expect to answer them fully in just a few minutes. People spend lifetimes trying to answer them. But these questions are important, and thinking about them for a little while should give you a more vivid sense of the issues that the phenomenological approach raises.

experience is typically so immersed in an activity that the activity seems to "become" the person. Csikszentmihalyi has given the term **flow** to such optimal experiences (see Csikszentmihalyi & Csikszentmihalyi, 1988; Csikszentmihalyi, 1990).

We should reemphasize that it's not necessary that the activity involve artistic creation or any such thing. What's important isn't *what*'s being done, but rather how it takes place. If you're completely immersed in it, if it's stretching you as a human being, it can be a peak experience.

Peak experiences occur when a person is deeply engaged in a demanding activity and fully caught up in the moment. Imagine how this football player feels while scoring this touchdown.

Existential Psychology

Thus far we've focused on several themes of the humanistic perspective. These include the idea that people have a natural tendency toward growth, that people can exert free will to change the course of their lives, that people defend against perceptions of incongruence and try to prevent them from arising, and that the motive to grow stands at the summit of a hierarchy of motives.

However, there's another side to talk of growth and human potential: The possibilities for self-actualization bring with them responsibilities. They have a cost. This is one message of another group of phenomenologically oriented psychologists called **existential psychologists.** The term *existential* is related to the word *existence*. It's identified with a philosophical view that stresses the idea that existence is all anyone has. Each human being is alone in an unfathomable universe. This philosophical view also stresses the idea that each person must take responsibility for his or her choices in life. In emphasizing the importance of the individual's personal experience of reality, this view fits the phenomenological orientation.

The Existential Dilemma

A concept that's come to be seen as central to the existentialist point of view is **dasein.** This German word is generally translated as "being-in-the-world." This phrase is used to imply the totality of a person's experience of the self as an autonomous, separate, and evolving entity (Binswanger, 1963; Boss, 1963; May, 1958). The term *dasein* also emphasizes that humans have no existence apart from the world and that the world has no meaning apart from the people in it.

To the existentialists, the basic issue in life is that life inevitably ends in death, which can come at any time. Death is the one absolute that no one escapes, no matter how actualizing your experiences are. Awareness of the inevitability of death provokes anxiety (more properly termed *angst*), or dread, or anguish far deeper than the anxiety experienced over incongruity. This distress arises because death is a threat to *dasein*. There exist only being and not-being, and we constantly face the polarity between them.

How should you respond to this realization? To the existentialists, this is the key question in life. The human choice is to retreat into nothingness or have the courage to *be*. In its most extreme form, the choice is whether to commit suicide, thereby avoiding the absurdity of a life that will end in death anyway. But the choice of nothingness can also occur in less extreme ways. People can choose not to act authentically, not to commit themselves to the responsibilities and goals that are part of who they are. They can simply drift, go along with one or another crowd. When people fail to take responsibility for their lives, they're choosing nothingness.

What's involved in taking the other choice, the choice to be? To the existentialists, life has no meaning unless you create it. Each person with the courage to do so must assign meaning to his or her existence, thereby resolving the existential dilemma. You assign meaning to your life by acting authentically, by being who you are. Indeed, the very recognition of the existential dilemma is an important step to doing this. As May (1958, p. 47) put it, "To grasp what it means to exist, one needs to grasp the fact that he might not exist."

It should be understood that exercising this freedom isn't easy. It can be hard to find the way to knowing who you are, and it can be hard to stare death in the face. It's often easier to let other people decide what's right and proper, and just go along. Existential psychologists believe, though, that all persons have the responsibility for making the most of every moment of their existence and fulfilling that existence to the best of their ability (Boss, 1963; see also Frankl, 1969; May, 1969). This responsibility is inescapable, and it's not to be taken lightly.

Although people are responsible for their choices, even honest choices won't always be good ones. You won't always feel right about the experiences of your life. You sometimes won't deal perfectly with people you care about. You'll sometimes lose track of your connection to nature. Even if your choices are wise ones, you'll still have **existential guilt,** guilt over failing to fulfill all your possibilities in life. This guilt is strongest when a person who's free to choose fails to do so. But a person who's aware is never completely free of existential guilt, because it's impossible to fulfill every possibility in life. In realizing certain of your capabilities, you prevent other ones from being expressed. Thus existential guilt is inescapable. It's part of the cost of being.

Emptiness and Loneliness

The existentialists also focus on the problem of emptiness and loneliness in life. They are concerned that people have lost faith in values (May, 1953). Many no longer have a sense of worth and dignity, partly because they've found themselves powerless to influence unresponsive forces such as government and big business. The planet warms and we're all powerless to do anything. The financial institutions of our world require multibillion dollar bail-outs, and we're all stuck with the bill. The leaders of our country commit us to wars without declaring them as wars, and the consequences are ours to bear.

Existentialists point out that when people lose their commitment to a set of values, they experience a sense of emptiness and meaninglessness. When people feel this way, they turn to others for answers. The answers aren't there, however, because the problem is really within the person. This illustrates once again the existentialist theme that you must be responsible for your own actions and that truth can come only from within and from your actions.

Assessment

In thinking about personality assessment, one issue is how to go about it. Other chapters have described approaches ranging from projective techniques to physiological assessment. The phenomenological viewpoint suggests yet another approach.

Interviews in Assessment

Phenomenological psychologists are less tied than other psychologists to the structure of specific measuring instruments. To the phenomenologist, assessment isn't a process of having a person complete a questionnaire or respond to a standard set of stimuli. It's a process of finding out *what the person is like*—by any means available.

Given this orientation, these psychologists are very much at home with the interview as an assessment technique. The interview offers maximum flexibility. It allows the person being assessed to say whatever comes up. It allows the interviewer to follow stray thoughts and ask questions that might not occur at another time. It allows the interviewer to get a subjective sense, from the process of *interacting* with the other person, of what that person is like.

Finding out what a person is like in this way requires a good sense of empathy. After all, the interviewer is trying to enter the other person's private world, to see him or her from the inside. Rogers (1980) held that empathy isn't automatic. Good empathy requires sensitivity to small changes. You must repeatedly check the accuracy of your sensing, to make sure you haven't taken a wrong turn. (Empathy isn't useful only in interviewing, by the way. In Rogers's view it's an important contributor to the process of doing therapy, and it's an important part of being a fully functioning person.)

An extensive interview produces a good deal of information, which sometimes is subjected to **content analysis** (e.g., Marsden, 1971). In a content analysis, statements made by a client are grouped in some theoretically meaningful way. The psychologist then sees how many statements fall into each category. For example, during an interview, Susan made 2 statements about herself expressing self-approval or acceptance, 18 expressing self-disapproval, and 15 that were ambivalent. One might infer from this that Susan isn't very satisfied with herself.

Content analysis of interviews can also be used to assess a person's progress in therapy. For example, in another interview after 3 months of therapy, Susan made 5 statements that expressed approval of herself, 5 that expressed disapproval, and 8 that were ambivalent. One implication of this might be that Susan is now less negative about herself than before therapy. Another implication may be that she is less focused on herself in general than she was earlier.

Although interviews can be useful, the flexibility that makes them useful also limits them. Unless an interview is highly structured (and a phenomenologically oriented psychologist wouldn't tend to use such an interview), it can be hard to compare one with another. If Jane makes more negative self-references than does Sally, is it because Jane dislikes herself more than Sally? Or did the interviewer just happen to follow up a particularly bothersome aspect of Jane's self-image and miss Sally's areas of bad feelings about herself? If Susan makes more negative self-references before starting therapy than later, is it because she's more satisfied with herself later, or because the interviewer failed to get into self-critical areas in the later interview?

In addition to this sort of problem, it's clear that what a person says in an interview can differ widely as a function of other variables. For example, the client is likely to be much more self-disclosing if the client and the interviewer have good rapport than if they don't (Jourard, 1974). In fact, even small differences in an interviewer's verbal behavior can produce large differences in what people say (Matarazzo & Wiens, 1972). Thus many people view the interview as primarily a tool for obtaining informal impressions rather than for comprehensive assessment.

The Q-Sort and Measurement of the Self-Concept

Another issue in assessment concerns what qualities to assess. Two answers are suggested by the theorists whose views have been discussed in this chapter. The first answer is that the self-concept is an important aspect of personality. Accordingly, one focus for assessment is the way in which people view themselves.

A technique that Rogers preferred for assessing the self-concept is called the **Q-sort** (e.g., Block, 1961; Rogers & Dymond, 1954; Stephenson, 1953). There are many variations on this procedure, but the basic process is the same. Q-sorts always involve giving the person a large set of items, printed on separate cards. The items often are self-evaluative statements such as those in Table 14.2, although they can also be phrases, words, or other things. The person doing the Q-sort is asked to sort the cards into piles (see Figure 14.3). One pile contains statements that are *most like you,* another pile contains statements that are *least like you,* and other piles represent gradations between the two extremes.

There are also rules about how many statements are permitted to go into a given pile (Figure 14.3). Usually people start by sorting in general terms (like me, not like me, and neither) and then sorting further to make more subtle differentiations. By the time you get done sorting, you've had to look hard at the statements and decide which one or two are *really* like you, and which ones are less so. The technique thus forces you to decide what you're like by comparing qualities to each other. The Q-sort differs in this respect from rating scales in which each response is separate and unrelated to the others. The latter scales allow you to say that all the descriptors apply equally well (or poorly). This can't possibly happen in a Q-sort.

A simple Q-sort involves sorting the statements according to how you think you *actually are.* That's the most basic information a Q-sort can give: descriptions of how people see themselves. Q-sorts can also be used, though, to derive more complex and

TABLE 14.2

Statements commonly used in Q-sort procedures.

I am intelligent.	I am ambitious.
I often feel guilty.	I am an impulsive person.
I am optimistic.	I get anxious easily.
I express my emotions freely.	I make strong demands on myself.
I understand myself.	I get along easily with others.
I am lazy.	I often feel driven.
I am generally happy.	I am self-reliant.
I am moody.	I am responsible for my troubles.

FIGURE 14.3

In the Q-sort procedure, you sort a set of items (printed on cards) into a row of piles. At one end of the row is the single item that's most like you; at the other end is the single item that's least like you. The other piles represent gradations between these two points. As you can see from the numbers in parentheses, the piles toward the middle are permitted to have more cards in them than the piles closer to the end points. Thus, you're forced to decide which items really are very much like and unlike yourself.

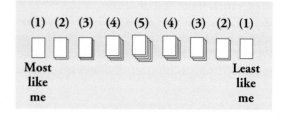

interesting kinds of information. Sometimes people sort the statements again according to what they were like earlier in their lives. It's then possible to look at how well the two match up. That is, are statements rated *very much like me* during the previous time the same ones rated *very much like me* now? If not, where do the "now" statements fall in the "4 years ago" sort? Differences between the two reflect changes in the self-concept over time.

It's also possible to sort for the ideal self (the kind of person you think you want to be). Then you can look to see how much difference or similarity there is between the sort for the ideal and the sort for the actual self. Similarity in this case reflects *congruence,* the degree of closeness between your ideal self and your perceived self.

Q-sorts can be used for a variety of other purposes as well. For example, the items don't have to be self-evaluative statements. They can also be such things as objects or activities, to be rated from most preferred to least preferred. Given this flexibility in use, the Q-sort represents a very general tool for personality assessment.

Measurement of Self-Actualization

A second content for personality assessment is suggested by the emphasis placed on the tendency toward self-actualization. Given this emphasis, it would seem desirable to measure the degree to which people have the characteristics linked to frequent self-actualization.

One instrument used for this purpose is the Personal Orientation Inventory (POI), developed by Shostrom (1964, 1974; see also Knapp, 1976). The POI consists of paired statements. People choose the one from each pair they agree with most. The POI has two major scales. One of them is called *time competence.* It reflects, in part, the degree to which the person lives in the present, as opposed to being distracted by the past and the future. As the word *competence* hints, though, this scale also has a more complex meaning. Time-competent people are believed to be able to tie the past and the future with the present in an effective and realistic way. They sense a continuity among these three aspects of time. Time-*in*competent people, in contrast, have split the present off from the past and the future. They live primarily with regrets and resentments from the past or with idealized goals or fears for the future. They aren't just focused on a period other than the present, however. They're also ineffective in linking the time frames with each other.

The second major scale assesses a tendency to be *inner-directed* in the search for values and meaning in life. Obviously, no one could function in a society with no sense of other-directedness. Self-actualizers, though, are believed to have a stronger tendency toward inner direction than people who are less self-actualizing.

The POI has been used in a variety of studies, but there remains some question concerning its validity as a measure of self-actualization. Most of the validating research on the POI focuses on its ability to distinguish between people who do and do not have indications of pathology (e.g., Fox, Knapp, & Michael, 1968; Shostrom & Knapp, 1966). Somewhat more promising is the finding that people's scores improve after a series of group therapy sessions (Dosamantes-Alperson & Merrill, 1980).

In part because of such questions about the POI's validity (and in part because it's very long), Jones and Crandall (1986) developed a 15-item scale to measure self-actualization. Their scale has four factors, reflecting self-direction, self-acceptance, acceptance of emotions, and trust and responsibility in interpersonal relations. As with the POI, there's evidence that scores on this scale change as a function of group therapy (Crandall, McCown, & Robb, 1988).

Problems in Behavior, and Behavior Change

How are problems in living and the process of behavior change conceptualized in this view of personality? Recall that for humanists the fully functioning person is attuned to the actualizing tendency, and is experiencing a sense of coherence and consistency within the self and between the self and present experiences. These people aren't trying to live up to conditions of worth—they're being who they are. To Rogers and others, an absence of congruity within the self results in psychological problems (for supporting evidence of various kinds see Deci & Ryan, 1991; Ford, 1991a; Higgins, 1987, 1990; Ryan, Sheldon, Kasser, & Deci, 1996).

To Rogers, incongruity (between experience and self-concept, or within the self-concept) is experienced as anxiety (though see Box 14.5 for a different view). Anxiety thus is a signal from the organismic valuing process that the holistic self is in danger of disorganization. Despite the fact that we have ways of protecting the self from such threats (discussed earlier in the chapter), anxiety sometimes intrudes. This is especially likely to occur if the person focuses too much on conditions of worth and engages in actions that interfere with self-actualization. If incongruities become extreme or frequent, the person is likely to show characteristics that are labeled *neurotic*. If the disorganization is extreme enough, the person may be labeled *psychotic*.

The process of therapy, to Rogers, is essentially the process of reintegrating a partially disorganized self. In part, this involves reversing the processes of defense to confront the discrepancies between the elements of the person's experience. Doing so isn't easy, however. Rogers believed that an important condition must be met before such changes can occur.

Specifically, the conditions of worth that distorted the person's behavior in the past must be stripped away. The person still needs positive regard. But it must be *unconditional*. Only then will the person feel able to confront the discrepancies in his or her self. Removing the conditions of worth will allow the person to focus more fully on the organismic valuing process, the quiet inner voice that knows what's good and what's bad for you. This in turn allows a reintegration of the self.

Unconditional positive regard, then, is a key to therapy. But it's a complex key. For unconditional regard to be effective, it must be positive regard that's given *from the person's own frame of reference*. That is, acceptance from someone who knows nothing about you or your feelings is hardly acceptance at all.

> **BOX 14.5**

SELF DISCREPANCIES AND EMOTIONS

Rogers believed that incongruity of any sort results in anxiety. This belief is challenged by work conducted by Tory Higgins (1987) and his colleagues, who argue that the situation is more complicated. Higgins says that three self-aspects need to be taken into account, rather than two: the *actual,* the *ideal,* and the *ought* self. To Higgins, the ideal self is what you wish for yourself, the self to which you aspire. The ought self is defined by duty or obligation. An ought is someone you feel compelled to be rather than desire to be. An ought self sounds very much like a condition of worth. Higgins refers to the ideal and the ought as **self guides,** because they serve as comparison points for the actual self and as guides for behavior.

Higgins assumes, as did Rogers, that incongruities between these self guides and the actual self produce negative feelings. Unlike Rogers, however, Higgins makes a distinction between two emotions, which come from two different kinds of incongruities. Specifically, Higgins holds that discrepancies between actual and *ideal* self cause feelings of depression and dejection. Discrepancies between actual and *ought* self cause feelings of anxiety.

Higgins and his colleagues have done several studies to investigate predictions made by this theory, and the studies have consistently supported the reasoning (e.g., Higgins, Bond, Klein, & Strauman, 1986; Strauman, 1989; Strauman & Higgins, 1987). In most studies, self-concepts are assessed by having people first list 10 attributes they think contribute to their actual selves, then

10 attributes they think contribute to their ideal selves, and finally 10 attributes they think contribute to their ought selves. The extent of discrepancy between actual and ideal is computed by seeing how many matches there are on the two lists and how many mismatches (opposites) there are. A similar procedure is used to assess discrepancy between actual and ought. Either in the same session or at another time, subjects also report their moods, including feelings of depression and feelings of anxiety.

The usual finding from this research is that the extent of actual-ideal discrepancy is uniquely related to depression but not anxiety. Extent of actual-ought discrepancy is uniquely related to anxiety but not depression. These results are especially impressive in light of the fact that depression and anxiety tend to occur together. In fact, many psychologists have viewed these feelings as different facets of the same phenomenon. Being able to point out a way of distinguishing between them is no small feat.

It's also of interest that the ought self seems to be closely linked conceptually to the notion of conditions of worth. That is, an ought is an obligation, a duty. The ideal self, in contrast, isn't tied to conditions of worth. This body of research, then, suggests a modification of the position taken by Rogers. Incongruities that derive from failures to meet *conditions of worth* seem to be reflected in anxiety. Incongruities that derive from a failure to self-actualize are reflected in dejection.

This provides a second reason why it's important for a therapist to have a strong sense of empathy. The first was that empathy is necessary to get an adequate sense of what the client is like in interviews. The second is that it's necessary if the therapist is to show unconditional positive regard for the client in a way that will facilitate reintegration of the client's personality.

There's one more potential problem here. Sometimes people undertake therapy to *satisfy* someone's conditions of worth for them. It stands to reason that people who are trying to make changes for autonomous reasons will do better than people trying to make similar changes to satisfy conditions of worth. In at least one domain of change—weight loss—there's evidence that this is so. Those who were losing weight for autonomous reasons lost more and kept it off longer than those who were doing it for less autonomous reasons (Williams, Grow, Freedman, Ryan, & Deci, 1996).

Client-Centered Therapy

The technique that Rogers developed to assist people in reintegrating themselves and regaining congruity between themselves and their experience is called **client-centered therapy,** or person-centered therapy (Rogers, 1951, 1961; Rogers & Stevens, 1967). As the phrase implies, the client in this therapy has responsibility for his or her own improvement. Recall that Rogers assumed people have an intrinsic tendency toward actualizing. He reasoned that if people with problems can be put in a situation in which distractions and demands (conditions of worth) are removed, they should be able to reintegrate themselves with the guidance of this natural tendency. This is much like the rationale for putting a bandage on a wound. The bandage doesn't heal you. But by maintaining a sterile environment, it permits the natural healing process to take place more easily.

In person-centered therapy, the therapist displays empathy and unconditional positive regard. This allows the client to escape (temporarily) from salient conditions of worth and to begin exploring aspects of experience that are incongruent with the self-concept. Throughout this exploration, the therapist remains nondirective and nonevaluative, showing no emotion and giving no advice. The therapist's role is to *remove* the pressure of conditions of worth. By avoiding evaluative comments (saying that something is good or bad), the effective therapist avoids imposing additional conditions of worth.

Rather than being evaluative, the therapist tries to help clients gain a clear perspective on their own feelings and experiences. In general, this means reflecting back to the client, in slightly different ways, things the client is saying, so the client can reexamine them from a different angle. There are two variations on this procedure, which have two different labels.

The first label is **clarification of feelings.** Part of what the client will be doing in the therapy session is emotional—expressing feelings about things, either directly in words or indirectly through other means. As feelings are expressed, the therapist repeats those expressions in different words. The purpose here is to make clients more aware of what their true feelings are. Simply being reminded of the feelings can help this to happen.

The usefulness of this technique should come as no surprise. Feelings are often fleeting. When people express feelings in their words or actions, they often fail to notice them. Moments later they may be totally unaware of having had them. If the feelings are threatening, people actively defend against recognizing them by denying them access to awareness. The process of reflecting feelings back to the client allows the nature and the intensity of the feelings to become more obvious to the client. This puts the client into closer touch with the experience.

The second kind of reflection in person-centered therapy is more intellectual and less emotional. It's called **restatement of content.** This procedure is equivalent to what we just described, but it operates in terms of the *ideas* contained in the client's statements, the cognitive content of what the client says.

Is client-centered therapy effective? The answer seems to be that it's about as good as other therapies (Smith & Glass, 1977). Studies of this technique focus primarily on changes in self-image, and there's evidence that people do change their pictures of themselves after client-centered therapy, so that their perceived self becomes more congruent with their ideals (e.g., Butler & Haigh, 1954: Truax & Mitchell, 1971).

An illustration of the potential of client-centered therapy is the extensive account Rogers (1954) wrote about the changes experienced by one woman. She entered therapy as a passive rejected person and changed dramatically over the course of therapy. In her initial Q-sorts of her actual self, she said she most resembled statements such as "I usually feel driven" and "I am responsible for my troubles." Statements such as "I make strong demands on myself" and "I am optimistic" were least like her. After therapy, her Q-sort actual self included "I feel emotionally mature" and "I am self-reliant" as being most like her. Least like her were such things as "I feel helpless" and "I often feel guilty" (Rogers, 1954, p. 275).

Encounter Groups

Another strategy aimed at helping people attain better personal integration involves sharing growth experiences in a group (e.g., Perls, 1969; Rogers, 1970; Schutz, 1967). These groups aren't really therapy groups, but are aimed at benefiting anyone who wants to undertake them. The groups have had several names, each connoting an aspect of the experiences they're intended to promote. One name is **encounter group,** because the group is to help people to encounter the reality of their own experiences more directly. Another name is **sensitivity group,** because the group's goal is to make people more sensitive to their experiences.

Groups vary in several ways but typically share certain features. Most incorporate exercises to get people into closer touch with their sensory experiences and their emotions. It's also common to encourage people to act out fantasies, impulses, and feelings in the group in an atmosphere of mutual trust and unconditional regard (Rogers, 1970).

Many people who have these group experiences are enthusiastic about them (although see Box 14.6). People are more empathic after the group experience (Dun-

Encounter groups grew out of the phenomenological perspective as a way of getting people into closer touch with their feelings. A modern-day counterpart is the support group.

BOX 14.6

DEINDIVIDUATION: A Different View of Encounter Groups

Most phenomenological psychologists feel that encounter group experiences have positive effects on people's lives. There is, however, a body of research suggesting that there may be a dark side to such group experiences. The label given to this research is **deindividuation.** The purpose of the research is to better understand the causes and consequences of becoming psychologically absorbed in a cohesive group.

Interest in such effects goes back many years (e.g., LeBon, 1896; Tarde, 1903). Only later, however, did research begin to indicate how this state occurs and what its effects are (e.g., Diener, 1977, 1979, 1980; Festinger, Pepitone, & Newcomb, 1952; Zimbardo, 1969). Studies typically have at least two groups. One group is designed to promote feelings of individuality. The second group is designed to enhance feelings of absorption in the group and lessened individuality—the hallmarks of deindividuation.

These two psychological states have been produced in a variety of ways. For example, Diener (1979), enhanced individuality by having subjects write essays about what made them unique. He also had subjects listen to music and describe how it matched the persons they thought themselves to be. Subjects in the deindividuation condition sang songs together, "elevated" a person by lifting him or her into the air, bodily prevented an assistant from breaking into a circle they'd formed, and danced around the room. Interestingly enough, these activities are similar to exercises used in some encounter group sessions.

Findings from deindividuation studies have been straightforward and consistent. Put simply, deindividuated subjects are more likely to engage in antinormative behavior than those who haven't been deindividuated. They're more likely to use obscenities (Festinger et al., 1952), to be aggressive (Prentice-Dunn & Rogers, 1980, 1982; Rogers & Prentice-Dunn, 1981; Zimbardo, 1969), and to engage in age-inappropriate activities such as sucking on baby bottles and playing in mud (Diener, 1979).

Group encounters, then, produce a wide range of consequences. They do seem to alter how people express themselves and experience emotional states. This change can lead people into closer contact with their feelings and impulses, as Rogers, Maslow, Perls, and others have argued. On the other hand, this contact may have its costs, in the form of a shedding of the social norms that serve to contain undesirable and antisocial behavior.

Although the negative consequences of such experiences are unfortunate, why they occur is easy to explain—even from the humanistic perspective itself. As noted earlier in the chapter, Rogers said you can't attend to the organismic valuing function without ignoring conditions of worth. The rules that fall by the wayside during deindividuation are standards of conduct that often constitute conditions of worth. Thus the shedding of even useful standards may be necessary for people to become fully functioning persons.

Ultimately, then, an overall evaluation of encounter group activities must depend on the frame of reference used to judge them. From the perspective of the individual, the experience is generally positive because it puts people into closer contact with their feelings. From the perspective of society, however, the experience may sometimes be negative because the rules of conduct that make group living possible seem to be at least partially discarded along the way.

nette, 1969) and feel a greater sense of being under their own control (Diamond & Shapiro, 1973). On the other hand, one study found that the label *encounter group* led to benefits even when the participants were engaging in ordinary recreational activities (McCardel & Murray, 1974). This finding raises questions about the means by which groups actually exert beneficial influences.

Beyond Therapy, to Personal Growth

As is suggested by the previous section, to humanistic psychologists therapy isn't a special process of fixing something that's wrong and then forgetting about it. Rather, it's on a continuum with other life experiences. In this view, a person who's living life to the fullest should always be engaged in more or less the same processes as occur in therapy. The encounter group isn't aimed at repairing disintegrations in personality. Rather, it's a way for people who have average lives—or even very good lives—to enrich their experiences and self-actualize even more completely.

Rogers's view of the ideal way of life is captured in the phrase *fully functioning person*. He believed that personal growth throughout life should be a goal for everyone. The conditions needed for growth are the same as those needed for effective therapy. Growth requires that people with whom you interact be genuine and open, with no holding back and no false fronts. It requires empathic understanding by those persons, together with unconditional positive regard. This view on growth is similar to Maslow's view on self-actualization: Growth isn't a goal that's reached once and cast aside. It's a way of living to be pursued throughout your lifetime.

Humanistic Theories: Problems and Prospects

The humanistic viewpoint is regarded by many people as the most intuitively "accessible" of the various approaches to personality. The intuitive appeal of this view derives partly from its emphasis on the uniqueness and validity of each person's experience. Indeed, this view treats each person's subjective experience as being of primary importance. This emphasis on personal experience fits well with what many people bring to mind when they think of the word *personality*, especially when they think of their *own* personality. For this reason this viewpoint feels comfortable and seems commonsensical to many people.

This viewpoint also has at least two other virtues. First, it takes a generally optimistic and positive view of human nature. Humanistic psychologists such as Rogers, Maslow, Deci, and Ryan have argued strenuously that people are intrinsically good—are naturally motivated to be the best they can be. According to this view, that motive will be expressed in everyone, as long as other circumstances don't interfere too much.

This optimistic outlook on humanity is also reflected in a "practical" virtue of the humanistic view. It has emphasized the importance of fully experiencing and appreciating your own reality and of maintaining close contact with your feelings. This emphasis provides a strategy for living that many people have used as a tool to enrich their lives. The benefits sometimes have come through formal therapy experiences. But remember that many phenomenologists assume there's no real distinction between therapy and the more ordinary "course corrections" that are part of normal living. Thus the move toward personal enrichment has come for many people in informal ways. It's been sort of a self-guided exploration of how to make one's life better.

Although humanistic psychology certainly has virtues, it has problems as well. One problem historically has been a lack of precision. It's sometimes been hard to generate easily tested research hypotheses from the theories. For example, consider self-actualization. To study self-actualization, you need to know the areas of life to which the actualizing tendency is relevant for each person you're studying. Remember that actualization occurs in different ways within different people. In theory, it might be necessary to study as many types of behavior as there are people being studied. This makes it hard to evaluate any observations you make.

This difficulty is a serious one, and it should not be minimized or taken lightly. On the other hand, more recent psychologists have taken many steps to overcome it. Deci and Ryan and their coworkers, who share many orienting assumptions with earlier humanists, have devised hypotheses that can be tested, apparently because they have a somewhat narrower focus than did people such as Rogers and Maslow. Findings from research on topics such as self-determination provide support for many assumptions of the humanistic viewpoint.

A second set of criticisms of humanistic psychology concerns a quality we just described as a virtue: its optimistic, positive view of human nature. This view is sometimes criticized as being arbitrary. It seems to have no basis other than the theorists' conviction that people are inherently good. The assumption that there's a self-actualizing tendency is also criticized as arbitrary. Both of these assumptions are generally taken as matters about which there's no point in arguing. Though the assumptions feel good and reassuring, some people don't believe they're viable.

Beyond the criticism that these assumptions are arbitrary, they're even criticized by some as being naive, sentimental, and romantic. Critics say that if the assumptions were carried to their extreme, it would require that each person be permitted—indeed be encouraged—to live life to the fullest, regardless of the consequences for anyone else. The result of such unrestrained self-expression would be chaos. Such a way of life would create serious interpersonal conflict whenever one person's self-actualization somehow interfered with someone else's self-actualization.

It's also worth noting that the optimistic overtones that permeate so much of humanistic psychology are largely missing from the writings of the existentialists. Whereas humanists such as Rogers and Maslow emphasized the fulfilling quality that can come from making your own way in the world, the existentialists emphasize that doing this is hard and can be very painful. Living honestly means confronting harsh realities and absurdities and rising above them. This picture is very different from the one painted by Rogers and Maslow. It can be difficult to reconcile the warm and glowing optimism of the one view with the angst of the other.

Another point of contention about this view on personality concerns the concept of free will. Humanists tend to assume that people can decide for themselves what to do at any point in their lives. Others regard this conception of free will as a convenient fiction, an illusion that at best is misleading. Surely people act as though they *think* they have free will. But how to demonstrate the *existence* of free will has never been an easy question to answer.

What, then, are the prospects for this approach to personality? Although many questions remain to be answered, the future of this way of thinking seems substantially brighter than it did two decades ago. Several areas of vigorous and enthusiastic research activity have opened up seams of knowledge bearing on assumptions made years earlier by pioneers of humanism. Work on topics such as self-determination continues to be very active, as does work on various self-discrepancies and emotional reactions. The development and exploration of these sorts of ideas is a source of considerable encouragement for the future prospects of this approach.

SUMMARY

The theorists of this chapter emphasize that people have an intrinsic tendency toward self-actualization. Self-actualization is the tendency to develop your capabilities in ways that maintain or enhance the self. This tendency promotes a sense of congruence, or integration within the person. Its effectiveness is monitored by the organismic valuing function.

People also have a need for positive regard—acceptance and affection from others. Positive regard may be unconditional, or it may be conditional on your acting in certain ways. These conditions of worth mean that the person is held "worthy" only if he or she is acting in the desired manner. Conditions of worth, which can be self-imposed as well as imposed by others, can cause you to act in ways that oppose self-actualization.

Contemporary work on these themes focuses on the difference between behavior that's self-determined and behavior that's controlled in some fashion. Studies of self-determination show that people enjoy activities more if they feel they're doing them from intrinsic interest instead of for extrinsic reward. People whose lives are dominated by activities in which they are controlled are less healthy.

Many theorists of this group assume that people have free will. This is a very hard idea to test, but people certainly act as though they have free will. Studies of reactance show that people resist threats to freedoms they expect to have, even if the threat to freedom is self-imposed.

Behavior that opposes the actualizing tendency creates disorganization in the sense of self. Disorganization can be reduced by two kinds of defenses. You can distort perceptions of reality to reduce the threat, or you can act in ways that prevent threatening experiences from reaching awareness—for example, by ignoring them. Use of these defenses is seen in the fact that people blame failures on factors outside themselves while taking credit for successes. People also engage in self-handicapping strategies, creating esteem-protective explanations for the possibility of failure before it even happens.

Maslow elaborated on the idea of self-actualization by proposing a hierarchy of motives, ranging from physical needs (most basic) to self-actualization (at the top). Basic needs are more demanding than higher needs, which (being more subtle) can affect you only when the lower needs are relatively satisfied. Maslow's intermediate levels appear to relate to the need for positive regard, suggesting why it can be hard to ignore the desire for acceptance from others.

Existential psychologists point out that with freedom comes the responsibility to choose for yourself what meaning your life has. The basic choice is to invest your life with meaning or to retreat into nothingness. Even if you choose the former, you can't escape existential guilt entirely: No life can ever reflect all the possibilities that it holds, because each choice interferes with other possibilities.

This view on personality uses many assessment techniques, including both interviews and self-reports. It emphasizes two kinds of content: the self-concept and level of self-actualization. The self-concept can be assessed by the Q-sort, in which a set of items is sorted into piles according to how much they apply to oneself. Different "sorts," focusing on the present self, the prior self, the ideal self, and so on, can be compared with each other to gain additional information.

From this perspective, problems derive from incongruity. Large incongruity is reflected as neurosis; when even more extreme, the result is psychosis. Therapy is a process of reintegrating a partly disorganized self. For reintegration to occur, the client must feel a sense of unconditional positive regard. In client-centered therapy, people are led to refocus on their feelings about their problems. The (nonevaluative) therapist simply helps clients to clarify their feelings. Encounter groups are an extension of the logic of this therapy into ordinary living, with the aim of helping people to experience continued personal growth.

GLOSSARY

Actual self One's self as one presently views it.

Actualization The tendency to grow in ways that maintain or enhance the organism.

Clarification of feelings The procedure in which a therapist restates a client's expressed feelings.

Client-centered therapy A therapy that removes conditions of worth and has clients examine their feelings.

Conditional positive regard Affection that's given only under certain conditions.

Conditional self-regard Self-acceptance that's given only under certain conditions.

Conditions of worth Contingencies placed on positive regard.

Congruence An integration within the self, and a coherence between the self and one's experiences.

Content analysis The grouping and counting of various categories of statements in an interview.

Dasein "Being-in-the-world," the totality of one's autonomous personal existence.

Deficiency-based motive Motive reflecting a lack within the person that needs to be filled.

Deindividuation Immersion in a group, which can produce antinormative behavior.

Encounter group A quasi-therapy procedure aimed at personal growth.

Existential guilt A sense of guilt over failing to fulfill all of one's possibilities.

Existential psychology The view that people are responsible for investing their lives with meaning.

Flow Experience of being immersed completely in an activity.

Fully functioning person A person who's open to the experiences of life and who's self-actualizing.

Growth-based motives Motives reflecting desires to extend and elaborate yourself.

Humanistic psychology A branch of psychology emphasizing universal capacity for personal growth.

Ideal self The personal values to which one aspires.

Organismic valuing process The internal signal that tells whether self-actualization is occurring.

Peak experience A subjective experience of intense self-actualization.

Positive regard Acceptance and affection.

Q-sort An assessment technique in which descriptors are sorted as applying to oneself or not.

Reactance A motive to regain or reassert a freedom that's been threatened.

Restatement of content A procedure in which a therapist rephrases the ideas expressed by a client.

Self-actualization A process of growing in ways that maintain or enhance the self.

Self-determination Deciding for oneself what to do.

Self guides Qualities of the self one desires to be (ideal) or feels compelled to be (ought).

Self-handicapping The creating of situations that make it hard to succeed, thus enabling avoidance of self-blame for failure.

Sensitivity group Another name for encounter group.

Transcendent self-actualizers People whose actualization goes beyond the self to become more universal.

Unconditional positive regard Acceptance and affection with "no strings attached."

■ Rachel and Jerry are sitting in the lounge taking a break from studying. They're talking about a new movie they'd both seen in the last couple of days, and they're disagreeing loudly about how good it was (or wasn't). Rachel thinks the plot was subtly intricate and that there was a delicate tension throughout the film. Jerry thinks there wasn't any plot at all and that the film could not possibly have moved more slowly. At this point Susan joins them and chimes in with her opinion. She didn't see the nuances of plot that Rachel saw, but she points out that the film had a lot of symbolism. Jerry just shakes his head in wonder.

The world that surrounds us is the same for everyone. An oak tree growing across the street is the same physical object when *you* look at it as when anyone else looks at it. A building stands there—brick and mortar—and no matter who's inside, or in front of it, or driving by it, its nature doesn't change. Physical reality is, after all, physical reality.

But people's experience of the world isn't based entirely on physical reality. Rachel, Jerry, and Susan saw the same film. But the experience wasn't even remotely the same. The same is potentially true of all of life's experiences. For example, consider again that oak tree across the street. *You* might look at it and sense a graceful product of nature's mysteries. Someone else may glance at the same tree and see a source of shade on a hot day. Another person sees a nuisance—a tall thing covered with leaves that soon will have to be raked. A fourth person may see a source of hardwood for making furniture. The physical reality is the same for all, but the *experience* of it varies widely from person to person.

This is true in experiencing ourselves, the people around us, the actions we engage in, and the events that make up our lives. Consider John, a college student who works extra-hard at his studies, spending weekends in the library instead of partying. John sees his actions as an attempt to learn as much as he can, about as many things as he can, while he has the chance. John's father sees his son's actions as an effort to establish a good academic record, thereby getting a good start toward a high-paying job. To one of John's professors, the pattern is a clear effort to overcompensate for feelings of inferiority. Dan, a casual friend, sees in John a sort of mindless compulsiveness. Susan, an even more casual friend, thinks it's silly to study so much, and she sees John as an incredibly dull person.

How is it that people have such different experiences when exposed to the same realities? Where do these differences in interpretation come from? Some personality psychologists answer these questions by saying that physical reality isn't the essence of human experience. It's merely the raw material. No one can examine all the raw material available—no one has the time. No one can deal with *just* raw material, either—you have to impose some sort of organization on it, create order from the chaos. So each person *samples* the raw material and constructs a personal vision of how reality is organized. These mental representations then provide the basis for future perceptions, interpretations, and actions (Jussim, 1991).

It can be argued that personality consists of the organization of mental structures through which the person views reality (or which the person imposes on reality). This is essentially the position that was taken by George Kelly, whose ideas are the subject of this chapter (Kelly, 1955; for reviews, see Adams-Webber, 1979; Bannister, 1970, 1985; Bonarius, Holland, & Rosenberg, 1980; Mancuso & Adams-Webber, 1982).

Kelly is discussed in the context of the phenomenological perspective, because he emphasized the uniqueness of each person's subjective world view. Accordingly, as you read about his ideas you'll see some similarity to themes of Chapter 14, such as the idea that people choose for themselves how to think and act. But in many ways Kelly's ideas also foreshadow a cognitive viewpoint that began to form nearly two decades later (discussed in Chapter 16). It may be useful to think of Kelly's theory as creating a bridge between the phenomenological perspective and a newer perspective that hadn't yet come into being.

Personal Constructs and Personality

Kelly argued that the best way to understand personality is to think of people as scientists. This is a view that was also being promoted about the same time by Fritz Heider (1958), one of the earliest cognitive theorists in social psychology. Just as do scientists, all of us have a need to predict events with some regularity and to understand the things that take place around us. Just as do scientists, all of us develop theories about reality.

The need for prediction is basic to life. It shows up in every aspect of behavior. You may not realize it until you think about it, but you're making an implicit prediction about the nature of the world every time you turn on a faucet and expect to see water come out. You test the predictability of reality whenever you do something as simple as turning a doorknob (expecting the door to open) or eating (expecting not to get sick). In truth, it's hard to think of any action that doesn't involve making implicit predictions about how reality is organized. Often these predictions are made automatically and unconsciously, but they're predictions nonetheless.

Because so much of human life is social, the desire for predictability and the attempt to predict successfully are especially important in interpersonal events. Every time you look at someone's expression and use it as a guide to his or her feelings, you're trying to predict social reality. Virtually all social encounters—even those as simple as buying something at a store—involve many implicit assumptions and predictions. In order to choose our own actions we need to understand or interpret other people's actions.

Each person responds to this need to predict by constructing a personal view of the world and how it works. This view, or theory, serves as a guide to predicting and interpreting future events. To use Kelly's term, people generate a set of **personal constructs** and then impose those constructs on external reality. In his view, people don't experience the world directly. Rather, they know the world through the lens of their constructs. This is the essence of what Kelly called his "fundamental postulate" of human behavior: that *people's behavior, thoughts, and feelings are determined by the constructs they use to anticipate or predict events.*

Kelly saw constructs as important because he believed that all events in life are open to multiple interpretations (see also Box 15.1). Kelly used the term **constructive alternativism** as a label for this idea and for the further assumption that people decide for themselves what constructs to use in interpreting events. Kelly held that people can always alter their experiences, even looking back on them, by construing them in different ways.

We should perhaps say something about the meaning of the word *event* before going on. Kelly used this word to refer broadly to virtually anything in a person's experience. We'll use it the same way here. *Event* can refer to objects, people, feelings, experiences, or physical events. We should perhaps also say something about the

BOX 15.1

APPRAISAL AND STRESS

Kelly's assertion that personal constructs determine how people see the world is echoed in a number of other theories. An example is a theory of psychological stress developed by Richard Lazarus and his colleagues (e.g., Lazarus, 1966; Lazarus & Folkman, 1984). You doubtlessly have an intuitive understanding of what the term *stress* means. However, the nature of stress has been hard for psychologists to agree on. Lazarus has taken a very "cognitive" view of the concept, which fits nicely with many of the ideas under discussion in this chapter.

Lazarus argues that the experience of stress involves three interdependent processes. The first, **primary appraisal,** is the process of perceiving an impending threat. The next, **secondary appraisal,** is the process of determining what should be done (of the many things that might be done) to deal with the threat. The third element, **coping,** is the effort to do whatever's been chosen as the best way to handle the threat. It should be obvious that this analysis of stress relies extensively on the concept of appraisal. Appraisal is weighing and evaluating the meaning of the raw material of one's perceptions. The word *appraisal*, in fact, is similar in meaning to the word *construal*.

Lazarus emphasizes that the two appraisal processes in his theory rely heavily on the person's internal representation of reality. As a result, many kinds of "stress" can easily be said to be in the mind of the beholder rather than in the outside world.

That is, perceiving a threat (versus no threat) is largely a matter of how people construe the situations they're in. A bustling city street may seem absolutely harmless to one person, enticing to another—but the same street may appear fraught with peril to someone else.

Similarly, how people choose to respond to a threat will depend partly on how they construe various actions. For one person, walking away from a threat means losing face or looking foolish, whereas for another person, the same response means being efficient and not wasting energy. In both cases personal interpretations are crucial determinants of what the person experiences and how the person acts in response to a given event.

Lazarus also assumes that people often *reinterpret* the meanings of events, either while they are taking place or afterward. These reappraisals may be induced by changes in the situation or by changes in the constructs that the person brings to bear on the situation (e.g., Holmes & Houston, 1974). In some cases, called **defensive reappraisal,** the act of reappraising seems calculated to produce the best possible construal, even if it's unrealistic. In other cases, however, the reappraisal seems to be more a matter of finding an interpretation that fits the event well. This emphasis on people's ability to reorganize their interpretations of stressors is similar to the philosophical orientation that Kelly called *constructive alternativism*.

word *construe*. This word refers to mental processes that range from perception to understanding and interpretation. It's a broader word than any of these, in that it encompasses all these processes. It's also a more specific word, in the sense that it more strongly implies actively taking a point of view.

Using Constructs

Applying a construct to an event is slightly more complex than it might seem at first. The process is similar to the way a scientist uses a theory. That is, when you apply a construct, you hypothesize (implicitly) that the construct will fit an event. Then you *test* the hypothesis by applying the construct and predicting a consequence. If your prediction is confirmed, you know the construct applies and you retain it as useful. If your prediction is *dis*confirmed, you may reconsider when to apply the construct, you may revise the construct, or you may even abandon it. Constructs that successfully predict events most of the time have a high degree of **predictive efficiency.**

To illustrate, consider Ann's view that some men see women as unique individuals with their own distinct patterns of qualities, whereas other men see women as stereotypes. When meeting and first talking with Jim, she regards him as a man who views women as individuals. She's about to test this hypothesis by making the implicit prediction that he'll be interested in her weekend activity, racing sports cars. If Jim is interested or impressed, her prediction is confirmed. If he recoils in horror, the prediction is disconfirmed, and something about how Ann applies the construct, or something about the construct itself, may require revision.

Kelly's starting point was that people use their constructs to predict and anticipate events. He expanded on this basic idea by making a set of more focused statements, called *corollaries,* about constructs and how they're used. Let's consider in more detail what constructs are like, as reflected in some of these corollaries.

Constructs Are Bipolar

Kelly assumed that personal constructs are bipolar. That is, a construct consists of a pair of opposing characteristics. Examples are "friendly versus unfriendly" and "stable versus changeable." The pole that you're applying to the event you're construing is called the **emergent pole** of the construct. If you think of a person as friendly, you're applying your friendliness construct, with "friendly" as the emergent pole.

The end of the construct that's *not* being actively applied to the event being construed is the **implicit pole.** The implicit pole is just as important as the emergent pole in defining the nature of the construct. It's completely meaningless to think of someone as friendly unless you have an implicit recognition that it's possible for people to be *un*friendly. Thus both ends of the dimension are involved in the mere existence of the construct, even though it's easy to lose track of that when you're using the construct.

Kelly believed that constructs are dichotomous as well as bipolar. That is, he believed that people use constructs in a yes-or-no manner, rather than as varying along a continuum. Kelly acknowledged that people see lots of gradations along dimensions, but he had a way to deal with that (Kelly, 1955). He assumed that gradations arise from an organization of interrelated dichotomous constructs. The organization makes finer and finer distinctions, as one dichotomous decision leads to another one at a lower level (Figure 15.1).

FIGURE 15.1

A dichotomous decision, repeated several times across ever-finer units, creates a set of possibilities that duplicates the range of variation along a continuum. The simple set of decisions illustrated here yields 16 gradations. Given a few more decisions, the result would be indistinguishable from a continuously varying scale.

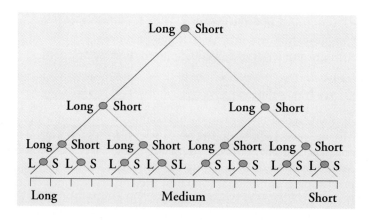

People have a need to understand and predict events around them. People differ greatly from each other, however, in how they interpret any given event.

For example, consider the construct long versus short. You can use it as a dichotomy, then repeat the process over and over again. It's as though you decide how long something is in a quick series of steps. First you decide if it's basically long or short. Assume for the moment you decided it's long (long thus is the emergent pole). That throws out half the scale (the right half of Figure 15.1). Then you decide whether it's long or not within the domain of the generally long. That decision further reduces the range by half, and you can make another decision within whatever part is left. If you do this often enough, the decisions become so fine-grained that for all practical purposes the result is equivalent to a continuum.

Consistent with Kelly's general view, there's considerable evidence that people tend to polarize their perceptions, particularly social perceptions, seeing the world in black and white terms. For example, when people are in different social groups, they tend to think of the two groups in terms of "us versus them" (Tajfel & Turner, 1986). When people are very committed to partners in close relationships, they tend to devalue the attractiveness of potential alternative partners (Johnson & Rusbult, 1989). This sort of finding seems to provide indirect support for Kelly's argument that people construe the world in terms of dichotomies.

The Role of Recurrences

An important aspect of constructs is that they reflect qualities that *recur* in the person's experience, that show up repeatedly. It's rare for a construct to emerge on the basis of a single event. Constructs evolve over time and across repeated experiences. The process of developing a construct from a series of events is complicated by the fact that no two events are exactly alike, even if they're from the same general "family" of events. Think, for instance, of filling your car at a gas station. The experience is somewhat the same each time, but it's not completely identical from one time to another.

The fact that constructs are based on recurring elements makes good sense from the viewpoint we began with—that is, that people try to anticipate events according to a personal theory. The kind of theory that's most sensible to invent and apply would be one that's been useful in construing *many* events, not just a few. It follows, then, that personal constructs should be based on *recurring* themes or qualities.

Range and Focus of Convenience

Although recurrences are important, it's also important to recognize that most constructs won't be useful *everywhere* in your experience. A few constructs can be used widely—for example, "good versus bad." But most are much more limited in scope, and some apply only narrowly. For example, the construct "friendly versus unfriendly" can be applied to fewer events than "good versus bad," "supportive versus not supportive" can be applied to even fewer events, and "willing to lend class notes versus unwilling to lend class notes" can be applied to even fewer. The set of events for which a construct is useful is termed its **range of convenience.** The range of convenience is wide for some constructs, more restricted for others.

When people try to apply a construct to events outside its range of convenience, there's usually a loss of predictive efficiency. For example, the range of convenience of the construct "happy versus sad" includes people, some animals, songs, many social events, and possibly such things as skies and flowers. It would be harder to apply the same construct to events such as stones or spaghetti. The result of *trying* to make such an application is likely to be a loss of predictive efficiency. In general, it's not too often that people try to apply a construct to events that fall outside its range of convenience.

The range of convenience of a construct isn't permanently fixed, however, because sometimes you *do* apply it outside its range of convenience and do so successfully. The **permeability** of a construct is the degree to which its range of convenience can be altered to include new events. A construct that's permeable allows new types of events to be added into its range of convenience fairly easily. A construct that's impermeable is more rigidly defined and is less likely to allow new events to be added to its range of convenience.

Another aspect of a construct's applicability is its **focus of convenience:** the set of events for which the construct is *most* predictive. Focus and range of convenience, although related to each other, aren't the same. A construct's focus of convenience is some *portion* of its range of convenience.

To illustrate the difference, consider the constructs "sociable versus unsociable" and "polite versus impolite," and situations to which you might apply them. If you wanted to guess how many people Jane will talk to at a party, you'd probably be better off using the construct of sociability than politeness. This event falls within the range of convenience of both constructs, but talking to people at a social event is almost the essence of sociability, and clearly falls within its focus of convenience. If you wanted to predict how Jane would reply to a surly store clerk, the sociability construct might work. But you'd probably be better off predicting from politeness. Its focus of convenience is events that involve role-based behavior and the use of specific social conventions.

Both the party and the interaction with the store clerk are within the *range* of convenience of each construct. But differences in *focus* of convenience make one construct more useful than the other for each type of event.

Elaboration and Change in Construct Systems

As indicated previously, people's constructs evolve across time and experience. Change can come in several ways. If a construct continues to predict events well, it becomes more refined. If it predicts in new and interesting ways, it grows and elaborates.

Kelly gave names to these two kinds of changes in a construct system. **Definition** occurs during ordinary use of a construct. It involves applying the construct in a familiar way to an event it's very likely to fit. Applying it this way allows the construct to become more explicit or possibly more refined and precise. For example, people often squeeze avocados to tell whether they're ripe. The construal "ripe" implies a prediction of what you'll find when you cut the avocado open. Repeated application of this technique allows you to refine your sense of how much softness in the avocado implies the perfect level of ripeness.

The other kind of elaboration, called **extension,** involves using the construct to predict or construe an event for which it hasn't been used before. This use has a greater potential for predictive error, given your unfamiliarity. But it also provides a greater potential for elaboration. That is, if the construct predicts well in unfamiliar territory, it thereby proves to be more broadly useful than had been obvious before. This outcome thus adds more information than does definition. As an example, a person who's familiar with avocados, but not cantaloupes, may apply the squeeze technique to determine whether a cantaloupe is ripe. If the prediction made in this manner proves accurate, the ripeness construct has been extended.

The principle of extension is related to the concept of permeability, which we just discussed. Constructs that are relatively permeable are applied to new events more easily than are those that are less permeable. Thus they're more capable of being modified by the process of extension.

Both extension and definition are important in the elaboration and evolution of a construct system. Indeed, both are necessary. They differ in important ways, however. To characterize the differences in general terms, definition is the "safer" of the two, whereas extension is potentially the more "informative."

Which process is more likely to occur depends on several factors. Some people are chronically more likely than others to go out on a limb and try to look at things in new ways, as extension requires. Indeed, some people make a habit of seeking out opportunities to engage in extension (see also Box 15.2). On the other hand, it's rare for people to do this throughout their construct systems at once. That is, people usually engage in definition in one domain as a way of creating a sense of security. They're then able to feel more at ease while trying extension (which is psychologically more risky) in other domains.

Temporary situational factors probably also influence whether definition or extension occurs. For instance, being upset or anxious (maybe because of a previous inaccurate prediction) may inhibit extension and lead to definition. In contrast, boredom may lead to a desire for extension (Sechrest, 1977). Knowing which will occur at any given time may ultimately require knowing whether the person is then motivated toward security or adventure.

Evolution of a construct system through definition and extension represents growth. By implication at least, both are produced by people's choices concerning how to apply their constructs. Sometimes, though, circumstances *force* changes on people, and these changes can be disruptive. For example, when people experience a very unusual event, they sometimes don't have constructs for interpreting it. If an existing construct is used and fails badly, or if the person feels the absence of *any* construct to apply, the result can be a major change in the construct system. We'll consider the question of forced change later in the chapter, when we take up the question of how to think about problems in adjustment.

BOX 15.2

THE THEORIST AND THE THEORY: George Kelly, Conceptual Pioneer

Just as individuals must elaborate and extend their construct systems, so must theorists. George Kelly was a theorist who was always willing to shift his construct system in directions that felt right to him, no matter what anyone else thought. His ideas moved along paths not yet traveled by personality theorists of his age. He displayed a true pioneering spirit in his work, a pioneering spirit that also had a counterpart in his personal history.

Kelly was born in 1905 on a farm in Kansas. When he was four, his parents uprooted the family to move to Colorado to homestead a parcel of land (Thompson, 1968). Homesteading was a risky and adventurous life under the best of circumstances, and the circumstances the Kellys encountered weren't exactly the best—the land they'd claimed had no water. As a result, they soon moved back to Kansas. Still, their westward migration reflected considerable independence of spirit. This spirit is also reflected in Kelly's theoretical independence.

Two other experiences in Kelly's life also appear to be reflected directly in the theory he developed. The first occurred while he was teaching at a junior college in Iowa. Among his duties there was serving as drama coach. The fact that Kelly held this post is interesting for two reasons. First, it may well have helped sensitize him to the elusive nature of objective reality and the importance of the person's private understanding of events in creating a personal reality. This theme permeates his theory. Second, Kelly later developed a novel form of therapy, in which the client is asked to perform a role as if in a play. It seems likely that the idea for this technique, which is described later in the chapter, derived in part from Kelly's experiences with acting.

The other noteworthy experience occurred when Kelly was on the faculty at Fort Hays State College in Kansas. While there he developed a traveling clinic program to serve public schools by helping teachers deal with problem children. Kelly made two observations during this period that influenced his later thinking. First, he discovered that inventing an unusual explanation for a client's problem often caused improvement. It didn't seem to matter what the explanation was, as long as it had two qualities. It had to account for the facts as the client understood them, and it had to suggest the possible usefulness of looking at the situation in a different way. If people could be made to look at their situation differently, they seemed to improve. Second, Kelly discovered that the problems teachers were reporting often said more about the teachers than about the students. That is, it was the way the teacher was construing the child's behavior that defined the problem, not the child's behavior itself. Both observations were strongly reflected in Kelly's theory.

Finally, by all evidence Kelly was a practical man (he'd originally planned to be an engineer). If something worked for him either as a clinician or as a theorist, he kept it. If it didn't, he got rid of it. To a practical man, this is just common sense. That simple idea went on to become an important element in his vision of human mental life: If a construct works—if it predicts events—it stays. If it doesn't, it goes.

Organization among Constructs

The personal construct is the basic unit of analysis in this theory, but constructs don't rattle around loose in people's minds, to be applied piecemeal. Kelly assumed that a person's constructs are interrelated in an organized and coherent fashion. Specifically, he argued that constructs are organized in a hierarchy, with some constructs at low (subordinate) levels of abstraction, and others at higher (superordinate) levels, subsuming or taking in the more basic ones (see also Epstein, 1983). For example, "good versus bad" may subsume "generous versus stingy," "friendly versus unfriendly," and "broken versus unbroken." Good versus bad thus is superordinate to all of the others.

Earlier in the chapter we talked about how a hierarchy of constructs could create a sense of continuous variability along a dimension. In the example we used to illustrate that idea (construal of length), the same fundamental quality was dichotomized at each decision point. The case we're talking about now is a little bit different. The qualities at the different levels are related to one another, but they aren't the same as each other.

The hierarchical arrangements that people have among their constructs aren't assumed to be permanently fixed. The organization is retained only if it has predictive efficiency—just as is true of the constructs themselves. One kind of change that can occur in the hierarchy is for a superordinate construct to change in what particular subordinate constructs it includes. For example, Alice's "friendly versus unfriendly" construct used to subsume "polite versus impolite." She eventually grew to see these two as not related. In her new organization, politeness is related instead to constructs such as "manipulative versus not manipulative."

Novel situations challenge our construct systems because they present us with events that we cannot readily understand or interpret.

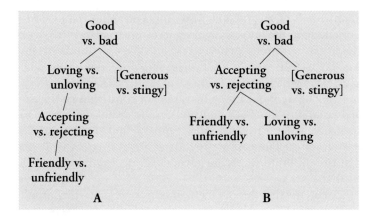

FIGURE 15.2

Two potential hierarchies of constructs held by two different people (or by one person at two different times) incorporating the same constructs but organized differently. In organization A, loving versus unloving subsumes accepting versus rejecting, which in turn subsumes friendly versus unfriendly. In B, accepting versus rejecting subsumes both friendly versus unfriendly and loving versus unloving. Someone with organization B would hold acceptance as fundamental and as implicit both in friendliness and in loving, which are distinct from each other. Someone with organization A would treat loving as fundamental and as implicit in acceptance, which in turn is implicit in friendliness.

Indeed, organizations among constructs can be even more fluid than this. It's possible in principle for two constructs to *reverse* their places in the hierarchy, so that the formerly subordinate one becomes superordinate and vice versa. For instance, Judy's "loving versus not loving" construct used to be a broad characteristic that encompassed a number of others such as "accepting versus rejecting," which was more specific. Over time and experience, though, she came to see the sense of "acceptance" as broader and more fundamental. Her viewpoint shifted so that "loving" was encompassed by "acceptance." She now has a different organization, in which the relationship between constructs has reversed (see Figure 15.2).

Organization among constructs also plays a role in creating individual differences in personality. Assume for a moment that two people have similar sets of constructs but different *organizations* among them (Figure 15.2). These two people would be quite different from each other in how they construe the world.

There's one last point to be made about these hierarchies of constructs. Although the organization of your hierarchy can change over time, at any given moment the organization places constraints on your construals and actions. In particular, using a superordinate construct dictates which subordinate constructs you're most likely to use while engaging in more fine-grained construals of the same event. That is, any superordinate construct subsumes some lower-level constructs but not others. Using a superordinate construct will channel you toward using subordinate constructs that fall under it, and away from constructs that don't. This, in turn, will greatly influence the character of your subsequent impressions.

For example, Julie walks up to David after class, converses for a few minutes, and then asks him whether he wants to study with her for their upcoming test. If David initially construes Julie as a "good" person, he's likely to apply constructs that fall under "good" in his hierarchy as he further construes her behavior. He may interpret her conversation as enjoyable, the offer to study together as sincere, and the proposed study session as possibly fun as well as helpful. If David initially construes Julie as a "bad" person, he'll apply different constructs to the same aspects of her behavior. He may see her conversation as manipulative, the offer to study together as an insincere attempt to use him for her own purposes, and the proposed study session as an annoying waste of time.

Individuality of Constructs

Thus far our discussion of the nature of constructs and their organization has largely disregarded the word *personal*. The word *personal*, however, was every bit as important to Kelly as the word *construct*. Kelly emphasized that each person creates an understanding of reality that's separate from everyone else's. Each person's construct system is unique.

It's easy to be misled on this point by the fact that people typically have no difficulty using words to refer to many constructs. However, words don't always mean exactly the same to one person as they do to another. Perhaps the easiest illustration of this point is the deceptively simple statement "I love you." This sentence can have a vast number of meanings, depending on who's saying it to whom and the psychological context in which it's being said.

Indeed, even when two people think they agree about the meaning of a single word, it's impossible to be sure they do. For example, you say that something is red, and I agree with you: It's red. But is your experience of the event, your construal of it, exactly the same as mine, or even close to being the same as mine? Who can know? In principle, the same problem occurs throughout all experience. And that is precisely Kelly's point concerning people's constructs. Even if the words are the same, the constructs are probably not. Indeed, Kelly emphasized that constructs are "preverbal" and that people can have a hard time representing their constructs even to themselves, except as raw experience (Kelly, 1969; see also Riedel, 1970).

If everyone's constructs are potentially so different from those of other people, how do we ever communicate? How do we ever get along with one another? The answer in part is that your constructs aren't *totally* divergent from those of other people. Remember, constructs are kept only if they have predictive efficiency. If they fail to predict events adequately, you modify or discard them and create new ones. By the time you get to be an adult, you've tested your constructs quite a bit, and everyone else has also gone through the same process. There has to be *some* degree of similarity between your construct system and those of other people, or the systems wouldn't have been maintained for so long.

Nevertheless, construct systems do differ enough that there's a lot of potential for disagreement. How then do people find a sense of harmony with each other? How do they even get to know each other? In Kelly's view the process of getting to know other people is partly (perhaps largely) a matter of testing your constructs against theirs. If you find that you agree about what constructs apply to various events, you feel comfortable with each other. To put it another way, two people with similar construct systems see the same things when they look at the world. That similarity of views is reassuring and forms the basis of a friendship. From this view, you feel your way toward relationships with other people by jointly assessing similarities in construct systems (see Duck, 1973, 1977; Duck & Allison, 1978; Klion & Leitner, 1991; Tesser, 1971).

Both the use of constructs in forming impressions of other people and the fact that different people use different constructs are nicely illustrated in research conducted by Higgins, King, and Mavin (1982). Subjects in this research were asked to write down the traits of several specific friends (Study 1) or the traits of several specific types of people (Study 2). The traits that a given subject wrote down frequently (Study 1) or wrote down first (Study 2) were taken by the researchers as representing important constructs for that person, because they were so "accessible" in memory.

Several days later, in what was portrayed as a separate study, subjects read a description of a target person that was written specially for each subject. The description incorporated several of the subject's important (accessible) constructs and several unimportant (less accessible) constructs. After doing another task (to interfere with memory), subjects wrote their impressions of the target person and then tried to recall the descriptions they'd read. As expected, subjects were influenced by the presence of constructs that were important to them personally, and they tended to disregard less important ones (Figure 15.3). Indeed, subjects had a harder time even recalling the unimportant constructs. Apparently, then, different people do rely on different mental dimensions in construing others.

Similarities and Differences between People

In Kelly's view, people are psychologically similar to one another if their systems of constructs are similar. Two people need not have experienced the same set of events to have similar constructs. Nor will two people who do experience the same set of

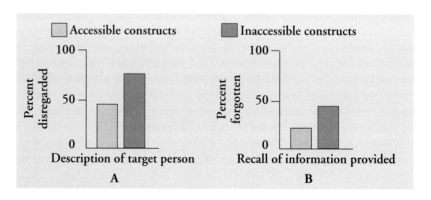

FIGURE 15.3

Subjects received a description of a person that was made up of several accessible constructs (ones that the subjects used spontaneously) and several inaccessible constructs (ones they didn't use spontaneously). (A) In writing their impressions of this person later on, subjects gave a lot of weight to the accessible constructs that had been mentioned and tended to disregard the others. (B) Indeed, they were even less able to remember the inaccessible constructs when asked to recall the initial description of the target person (adapted from Higgins, King, & Mavin, 1982, Experiment 1).

events necessarily develop similar constructs. A given construct can emerge from a thousand different events, and any event can be construed in many different ways. What makes people similar to each other is similarity in their *patterns of construals*—however the patterns arise—not similarity in their "learning histories" (see also Gilovich, 1990).

To Kelly, this principle applies to differences and similarities between individuals and also to differences and similarities between cultures. People from a given culture typically share a physical environment and manner of upbringing, but to Kelly this is of secondary importance. To him the essence of a culture is a similarity in how people construe their experiences (Kelly, 1962).

Recent research appears to support the idea that cultural differences do relate to variations in people's constructs (Triandis et al., 1984). Each subject in this research made judgments about what kinds of behavioral elements occur in different kinds of social interactions. Analysis of judgments made by each subject revealed something of the constructs applied by that person to social situations. Comparisons from one person to another indicated that people from the same culture shared elements of their construct systems. These similarities were *not,* however, shared as widely across the different cultures.

Role Taking

According to this theory a true social interaction requires an elaborate set of cognitive processes. It involves an attempt by each person to construe some part of the construct system held by the other. In other words, to interact meaningfully with someone else requires you to try to understand and anticipate how that person is understanding and anticipating reality. This is what Kelly meant by **role taking** with respect to another person.

When in a role, you're especially interested in understanding how the other person views *your* role. What does the person expect of you? What constructs is the person using to predict your behavior? If you can create a sense of the answers to these questions in your own mind, you can then act in ways that will be interpretable to the other person within his or her construct system (see Box 15.3 for a view that complements this analysis in some ways but sharply challenges Kelly in other ways).

Is it possible to take roles effectively if your construct system isn't the same as those of the other people involved? The answer is yes and no. Role taking is more complete and effective if you construe the other person's construct system in more or less the way that it actually exists. But it's not the entire construct system that matters. How effective your role playing is depends mainly on how accurately you construe the other person's construction of *your* role.

Evidence that people work to get clearer pictures of each other's roles when interacting comes from research on people's attempts to establish a mutually understood common ground in a conversation. As an example, when an expert talks with a novice, the expert has to use different terms than when talking with another expert, and must also decide how much detail to convey. But this decision isn't made just once. The expert has to continue to gauge whether the novice is following the conversation, and adjust further if necessary. Research indicates that this sort of continued adjustment does take place in people's conversations (Isaacs & Clark, 1987). Furthermore, it's an interactive process between the conversation partners. People who overhear the conversation don't grasp the common ground as clearly as do the people conversing (Schober & Clark, 1989).

BOX 15.3

DOES THE SELF CREATE REALITY, OR DOES SOCIETY CREATE THE SELF?

The major theme of Kelly's orientation to personality is that people develop personalized systems of constructs. They then impose these internally generated constructs on events to interpret them. From this point of view, the self is the architect of its own experience. All understanding ultimately comes from within.

How accurate is this view? Where do people's constructs really come from? There's another viewpoint that suggests a different origin for people's understanding of reality. This viewpoint, called **symbolic interactionism,** holds that the self isn't an intrinsic part of the person but instead develops from repeated social interactions. From this point of view, people don't impose self-generated construals on social reality. Rather, people's construals are created *for* them by their social relations. The major theorists of this viewpoint (Baldwin, 1902; Blumer, 1969; Cooley, 1902; Mead, 1934; Shibutani, 1961) were sociologists and social psychologists rather than personality psychologists. Nevertheless, their ideas have intriguing implications for personality (see Lauer & Handel, 1983, for a review).

Symbolic interactionists point out that human life is communal rather than solitary and that communication (through symbols) plays a central role in interactions (thus the term *symbolic interactionism*). Symbolic interactionists assume that a self emerges through social interaction in the following way. You can't communicate effectively with someone else (or understand someone else's communication to you) without taking on the other person's perspective or role. It's particularly important in many kinds of communication to understand the other person's perspective on *yourself*. This part of the symbolic interactionist position sounds a lot like Kelly's assumptions about the nature of role taking.

The symbolic interactionists proposed, however, that early in life you don't have the ability to take another person's perspective on you. Nor does this ability appear automatically as you get older. Rather, it's acquired only *through the process of interacting with other people*. Only when you try to interact with others do you confront the fact that they have their own perspectives. As you begin to realize this, you try to take those perspectives. Through perspective taking, the self comes to exist. According to Mead (1934), repeatedly trying to adopt the perspective that other people hold on you causes you to develop a mental representation of their view. This view is called the **perspective of the generalized other** because it derives from many other people's vantage points on you, rather than just one. According to the symbolic interactionists, it's only when you've acquired the perspective of the generalized other that a self can be said to genuinely exist.

The perspective of the generalized other is important in the symbolic interactionist view of human social behavior. Once you're capable of taking the perspective of the generalized other, you're capable of regulating your behavior as part of a social unit. When you consider possible actions, you consider this internalized sense of the social matrix and evaluate the actions from that viewpoint. You use that viewpoint to decide how to act, which in turn can influence how you see yourself in the future (Schlenker, Dlugolecki, & Doherty, 1994).

Thus, to the symbolic interactionists the self evolves from society rather than vice versa. At present this idea is interesting because it suggests a different origin for people's constructs than is implicit in Kelly's theory. In particular, this view suggests that many (perhaps all) of the constructs we apply to ourselves, and perhaps many of the constructs we apply to other entities, are acquired from *other people* rather than being generated from our own points of view.

We play many roles in the course of our lives, not all of which are very important or have more than superficial impact. The "store customer" role, for instance, matters little to most of us most of the time. Other roles, however, are extremely important—even central to our lives. These roles, which Kelly termed **core roles,** are major determinants of our sense of identity. Examples of such roles are occupational and professional roles, the roles of parent and child, close friend, lover, and so on. Whether any of these actually is a core role will depend on the individual, of course.

Because core roles are important, failing to perform them adequately can have adverse consequences. Kelly said that failing to enact a core role in the way that the role is construed by another person produces guilt. **Guilt** thus is an awareness of a disparity between your actions and the actions you see as fitting the other's expectations for your role. This definition of guilt is similar in some respects to Rogers's discussion of "conditions of worth" (Chapter 14), in which people feel uncomfortable when they fail to live up to others' expectations for them.

Personal Constructs and Behavioral Consistency

Back in Chapter 4 we addressed in some detail the issue of behavioral consistency. We noted there a variety of evidence that people are less consistent in their actions than would seem to be implied by early trait or type orientations to personality. This evidence led to the emergence of an "interactionist" point of view, in which personality and situational forces are seen as joint determinants of behavior.

The personal construct viewpoint allows us to address this issue in a manner that differs slightly from the way it was presented in Chapter 4 but resembles somewhat the social learning approach (Chapter 13). In particular, it suggests that to predict a person's behavior in any given situation we need to know how the person *construes* the situation. An individual will act in a consistent way across situations *to the degree that the situations are construed in similar ways*. It doesn't matter whether the situations look the same or different to an outside "objective" observer. What matters is whether the person whose behavior you're interested in perceives the situations as similar. Similar construals of situations should yield cross-situational consistency, whereas divergent construals should yield less consistency. Such an outcome is directly implied by Kelly's theory.

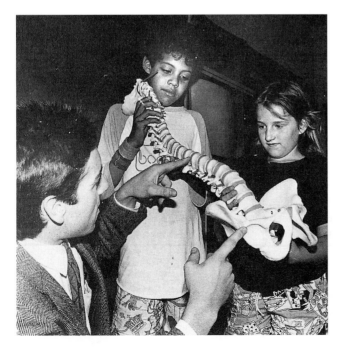

An effective communicator presents ideas at a level his listeners can understand.

FIGURE 15.4

When people construe several situations as involving similar qualities of behavior, their behavior tends to be consistent across those situations. When people construe situations as involving qualities that differ across the situations, their behavior tends to diverge across those situations.

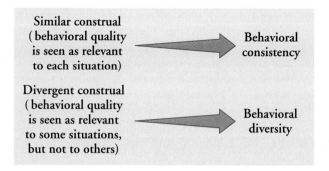

Research by Lord (1982) supports this idea. Subjects in this study described six common situations (e.g., keeping good lecture notes, keeping an orderly closet), in terms of what characteristics would go into being "conscientious" in that situation. The descriptions were done using a variation on the Q-sort method described in Chapter 14. These Q-sorts produced profiles indicating how the subject viewed the characteristics of each situation. These profiles then could be compared with one another (for each subject) to assess their similarity.

Subjects' actual conscientiousness then was rated by an observer who appeared at unannounced times in six situations corresponding closely to those the subjects had rated. Comparisons revealed that subjects' level of conscientiousness was most consistent across the situations that they'd construed in similar terms (see also Figure 15.4). Behavior was less consistent across situations that they'd construed in divergent terms.

Assessment

We've focused in this chapter on the idea that personality is defined by the constructs that a person uses in dealing with the environment. Personality assessment from this viewpoint likewise emphasizes assessment of the constructs the person uses.

Kelly's Role Construct Repertory Test

In considering how to gain an accurate view of another person's system of constructs, Kelly confronted a dilemma. It's useless to engage in behavioral observation, because a given behavior might stem from the use of any of several constructs. On the other hand, asking people to describe their constructs isn't satisfactory either, for several reasons.

First, although we've been giving names to constructs throughout the chapter, constructs aren't always easy to label. Many are intuitive or preverbal, existing in a kind of private experiential language that can't be expressed. Second, since people aren't used to describing their constructs, they may not do a good job at communicating what they mean, even if they can put it into words. Finally, the words that people choose to describe constructs are often so general that it's hard to get much specific meaning from what's being said.

Faced with these problems, Kelly tried to devise a strategy for getting at people's constructs. Rather than have them verbalize the constructs, he had people actively engage in construals. Across repeated construals, the nature of the construct system should begin to reveal itself. Kelly called his procedure the *Role Construct Repertory Test,* a name that's usually shortened to **Rep Test.** As is implied by the longer title, this test often (although not always) focuses on constructs used to perceive aspects of people and their roles.

The Rep Test involves the use of a grid printed on paper (see Figure 15.5). In this grid, significant persons in one's life (who have different roles) are listed at the heads of columns, and the rows are used to specify a set of comparisons and construals to be made. You begin the test by reading a definition for each role that's being used and deciding *who in your life* best fits that definition. Then you write that person's name on the grid next to the role label, not using any person's name twice.

Then you start with the construals. For each row, you're asked to think about the people listed in three specific columns (marked by circles in the figure). More precisely, you're to think of an important characteristic that makes two of those three people similar to each other and different from the third person. Once you've decided, you mark the two that are similar and write a word or phrase in the column headed "emergent pole" to indicate how the two are alike. In the column headed "implicit pole," you indicate how the third person is different. Then you look at the people (roles) in the other columns, decide whether they fit the emergent pole of the construct or the implicit pole, and mark each accordingly.

You then repeat the whole process row by row. As you go through the rows, starting with different groupings of three people each time, you're generating a list of constructs. These aren't the only constructs that you have, but since the people listed across the top are people who play important roles in your life, the constructs that emerge are probably fairly important in your construals of people. Several of the comparisons made in the Rep Test are of interest in their own right. Consider line 3 in Figure 15.5, where you're asked to think about yourself, an attractive person, and a pitied person. Which of these two will you see as more like yourself, and why? The result of this comparison reveals something about your feelings toward yourself and also what aspect of yourself comes easily to mind.

FIGURE 15.5

Example of the sort of grid used in the Rep Test. You begin by placing the names of the people who play various roles in your life in the slanted sections at the top. Then you conduct a series of comparisons among sets of three people at a time, deciding how two of them are similar to each other in a way that makes them different from the third (see text for more complete description). From Kelly, 1955. Reproduced with permission of Gladys Kelly.

Sort no.	Yourself 1	Mother 2	Father 3	Spouse 4	Pal 5	Rejecting person 6	Pitied person 7	Attractive person 8	Emergent pole	Implicit pole
1						○	○	○		
2	○			○	○					
3	○						○	○		
4				○	○			○		
5	○	○	○							
6		○	○			○				
...										
n		○		○		○				

The roles listed in Figure 15.5 represent only a few of the roles included in the full Rep Test. Furthermore, people completing this test also usually do many construals, thus providing a much larger base of information. This procedure has also been adapted to assess construals of other sorts of events: for instance, social issues (Epting, 1972), occupations (Shubsachs, 1975), and situations (Krieger, Epting, & Leitner, 1974; Neimeyer & Neimeyer, 1981).

Though the Rep Test is useful and interesting, it has important limitations. As noted earlier, people's constructs can't always be verbalized. The Rep Test attempts to get around this problem by asking people to actively construe other people and to use whatever construct naturally comes to mind to determine what makes people similar or different. This strategy only partly handles the problem, though, because the person still has to provide a label for the construct that was used.

This requirement of the test creates two potential problems. The first is the ordinary problem of knowing whether the word used to identify the construct means the same thing to one person as to another. The second problem stems from the fact that being asked repeatedly to label your constructs may create a bias concerning what constructs you use while doing the test. Specifically, you may be inclined to report *only constructs that are easily verbalized,* even if those aren't the most important constructs in your mind (cf. Shubsachs, 1975). Thus even the Rep Test may be susceptible to the problems that are inherent in just asking people to describe their construct systems.

Problems in Behavior, and Behavior Change

The focus on the importance of personal constructs in personality is also maintained in considering the nature of psychological problems and what's involved in the process of therapy (see also Neimeyer, 1985).

Personal Constructs and Psychological Distress

Recall that in Kelly's view normal human functioning involves the successful anticipation and interpretation of events through a system of personal constructs. A direct extension of this view is to suggest that problems in behavior involve problems in interpreting or predicting events.

Such difficulties can arise for several distinct reasons. One possibility is that you may confront events that differ drastically from any previously experienced. Because of this lack of experience, you may not have constructs that seem relevant to the event. The event, in effect, is beyond your ability to understand. Alternatively, you may be trying to construe the event with a construct whose predictive efficiency has fallen off. Kelly argued that when people don't have adequate constructs, they feel uncertain and helpless—an experience he labeled **anxiety.** If the event is outside the available construct system, people in such a situation sometimes even have trouble grasping why they're experiencing anxiety.

How often do people experience events that differ greatly from their previous experiences? Perhaps more often than you might imagine. Think back to your first week at college, for example. That period was probably filled with new experiences, experiences that differed enough from what you'd known before to make you wonder what was going on. Perhaps you even felt concern or apprehension. The same feelings can occur for someone entering a new job (Van Maanen, 1973, 1975), being hospitalized for an illness, or having her first child (Deutsch et al., 1988). In fact, anytime you do *anything* for the very first time, it can be unsettling, just because it's the first time and you don't know just what to expect.

As more extreme cases, consider the experiences of people involved in disasters such as terrible storms, fires, or earthquakes. It's often suggested that such experiences are traumatic precisely because they are so unlike anything most people have ever gone through before. Consequently, the person has no constructs for interpreting the event or anticipating its consequences. Consider, as well, people in the midst of a divorce, victims of crime, or those who unexpectedly win huge sums of money. These people are suddenly experiencing things that prior events in their lives haven't prepared them for. Part of the difficulty involved in living through these events is the very lack of constructs available for use in understanding and anticipating their consequences and implications.

It's unpleasant to discover that your constructs are inadequate to deal with events. Even worse, however, are events which suggest that important aspects of your present construct system may be completely wrong, and that major changes may be necessary (cf. Leitner & Cado, 1982). The more central the construct that's challenged, the more extensive is the change that's necessary, and the greater is the problem. The awareness of an imminent comprehensive change in one's fundamental construct system is termed **threat.** The experience of threat is much the same as the experience of anxiety, but more extreme. Both arise from poor prediction from the construct system. In the case of threat, however, the failure is more massive and fundamental than in cases of anxiety.

Dealing with Anxiety and Threat

It's logically straightforward to alleviate anxiety (or even threat) resulting from inadequate constructs, although it can be more difficult to do so in practice. One way is to generate a new construct. This response to poor prediction is probably a major source of new constructs across a person's lifetime (see also Box 15.4). The other way is to modify an existing construct so the experience can be successfully construed through it. If the event can now be construed with predictive efficiency, the anxiety or threat should evaporate.

As indicated earlier in the chapter, sometimes you can modify a construct by extending its range of convenience. Doing this means saying, in effect, that the new experience really isn't completely new. It has similarities to other experiences you've had in the past; you just didn't notice it before. Sometimes this doesn't work, though, and you have to change the construct. One change may even require further changes. To see why, recall the idea that your construct system forms a hierarchy in which subordinate constructs contribute to and help define high-level constructs. When you change your sense of what the construct means to you, you're rearranging some of the connections in your hierarchy—maybe even a lot of connections.

Sometimes the problem isn't that you don't have a construct to apply but that you're continuing to use a construct that's outlived its usefulness. Sometimes you're treating a construct as though it has a broader range of convenience than it actually has. The result in each case is unsuccessful anticipation of new events. Again, the solution is to reorganize your construct system. In this case, however, the reorganization just means making the range of convenience of the construct more restricted than it had been.

From the personal construct view on personality, the dissatisfaction that goes with poor prediction or anticipation of events is the primary symptom of problems

RECONSTRUING YOUR WORLD AFTER A TRAUMATIC EVENT

Minor adversity strikes almost everyone occasionally—getting a test score that falls a point short of the desired grade, finding a ticket on your car window after shopping just a little too long, or coming down with the flu just before spring break. Most people's constructs allow them to interpret and understand such minor inconveniences (e.g., "stuff happens"). But what about traumatic events—being diagnosed with a life-threatening illness, hearing that members of your family were just killed in a car accident, being raped or beaten?

Common sense suggests that truly traumatic events are harder to integrate into one's world view than minor events. There are many reasons for this. For one thing, traumatic events often are sudden and unexpected. Traumatic events often create irreversible, long-lasting problems for the future. By their very nature, traumatic events suggest a world that's unpredictable, uncontrollable, and unsettling (Tedeschi & Calhoun, 1995). They can even undermine the most basic assumptions people hold about themselves and their world (e.g., Horowitz, 1986; Janoff-Bulman, 1992).

Kelly's theory suggests that people in this situation will struggle to create new constructs for interpreting the traumatic event. That's also what more recent theorists suggest. Tedeschi and Calhoun (1995) argue that a traumatic event partly destroys the person's worldview. They also argue that the event thereby initiates the potential for growth. The shattering of one worldview prompts an effort to construct a new, more meaningful one. Others have made similar arguments (e.g., Taylor, 1983; Thompson & Janigian, 1988).

Research has even begun to document that making sense of traumatic events helps people adjust and move forward. For example, Thompson (1985) studied people whose homes were severely damaged by fire. Those who found a positive meaning in the event coped best with it. She found similar effects among people who had suffered strokes (Thompson, 1991). Mendola, Tennen, Affleck, McCann, and Fitzgerald (1990) examined women diagnosed with infertility. Those who better adapted cognitively to this news also showed more psychological well-being.

These and other studies have helped establish a link between psychological well-being and the capacity to understand and find meaning in traumatic events. Finding meaning seems to promote physical health as well. For example, Bower, Kemeny, Taylor, and Fahey (1998) examined immune functioning and mortality among HIV-positive gay men who had recently experienced an AIDS-related death of a partner or close friend. Men who found meaning in the death showed better immune functioning during the months afterward, compared those less able to find meaning. Those who found meaning also had a lower rate of AIDS-related mortality during that period. Thus, finding meaning may not only enhance well-being after a traumatic event, it may also help keep people alive.

in self-management. This dissatisfaction is what leads a person to seek help. Keep in mind that the construct system is the essence of personality, from this point of view. The process of therapy is one of assisting people in elaborating or altering their construct system to improve its predictive efficiency (see Epting, 1980; Fransella, 1972). Better prediction will result in reduced anxiety, distress, and dissatisfaction.

Fixed Role Therapy

What kinds of therapeutic procedures help to attain this goal? It's important to keep in mind that Kelly didn't assume that there was some "perfect" construct system that people should adopt to be better adjusted to reality. Everyone has a personal view of the world. Each person must evolve an arrangement of constructs that will be functional from that personal viewpoint. The goal of the therapy procedure is to facilitate the evolution of the construct system in its own way.

Kelly believed the best way to facilitate evolution of the construct system is to induce the person to change overt behavior. This change in turn will force the person to generate unusual construals of the events that result. The procedure that Kelly developed for doing this is called **fixed role therapy.** In this procedure the client enacts the role of a hypothetical person, one carefully structured to have certain characteristics that the client wants. This fixed role character is even given a name, to provide a sense of identity to the role.

The therapeutic process begins with an assessment in which the client completes a variety of instruments, including a self-characterization sketch or a self-description. On the basis of this, the therapist develops a role for the client to enact. The role is a composite of some of the client's positive characteristics and of characteristics that the client feels unable to display. These are characteristics for which constructs presumably are lacking.

The use of a composite role has several benefits. Including familiar characteristics helps to make the role easier to adopt because it keeps the role from being entirely alien. Similarly, the fact that preexisting *positive* qualities are built into it helps to create a sense of confidence in your ability to enact the role and strengthens the use of constructs that contribute to those positive qualities.

When the fixed role has been established, you're asked to try to enact the role for a while. The idea is not to adopt the role as a permanent part of your personality but just to enact it for some period. This instruction makes it clear that there's little risk involved, which takes some of the pressure off. If you aren't happy with how something has gone, the experience can be viewed as just a bit of acting that needs more polishing, not a drastic failure. It often happens, however, that after a while clients stop thinking of the role as a role and start to think of it as a natural part of themselves.

Enacting this fixed role forces the client to construe events in ways that differ from those used previously. For example, consider Luke—a man who sees himself as shy and passive and interpersonally inadequate. Luke might be asked to take on the fixed role of a person who's quiet but "deep"—a person others find interesting and stimulating, but who doesn't always show those characteristics openly because he's often more interested in learning something from others than in displaying his own knowledge; a person who has a pronounced but subtle influence on others, so that people don't always realize they're being influenced until later on.

Notice that this role (which is adapted from Kelly, 1955, p. 121) is a composite of Luke's self-image and the characteristics that he sees himself as lacking. The role incorporates quietness (which Luke does display) but recasts it within the framework of a general effectiveness in interpersonal interaction. In order to enact this role, Luke must see his behavior in ways that differ from his previous view of himself. In construing his quietness as a positive act of benefiting from others rather than as a sign of passivity and inadequacy, he's rearranging his system of constructs. As he enacts this fixed role over time, he should gradually reorganize his construct system, modifying constructs at some points and perhaps developing new constructs at other points. The result should be a system with a high degree of predictive efficiency that permits the person to live a more satisfying life than was true before.

Personal Construct Theory: Problems and Prospects

Personal construct theory shares a couple of strengths with the humanistic theories described in Chapter 14. Its emphasis on the uniqueness and validity of each person's experience fits with the emphasis in those theories on the importance of subjective experiences. Similarly, the principle of constructive alternativism suggests a basis for believing that people tend toward being better over time. That is, people can always reconstrue events in more and more functional ways.

The personal construct view places less of an emphasis on will than did the theorists of the humanistic orientation. Although in principle you're free to determine for yourself how to construe the present, past experiences have a big influence on present construals. When people make drastic reorganizations of how they view the world, they probably don't do so easily or without strain. It remains an open question, then, how free people actually are from their past.

Perhaps the greatest strength of this view on personality is one that was wholly unanticipated by its author. As you will see in the next chapter, Kelly's intuitions foreshadowed several themes that would emerge again later from very different sources. The reemergence of these ideas came from a segment of psychology other than personality. They returned to personality only through a circuitous path. Kelly's view, however, was much more idiographic than the newer view (recall the emphasis on the idea that constructs are personal). This idiographic emphasis "humanizes" the ideas in a way that the newer views don't.

One problem that personal construct psychology has had historically is that it hasn't been terribly conducive to research. There is a cadre of personality psychologists who are devoted to personal construct psychology, but the group is relatively small in number.

What are the prospects for this view on personality? We've continued to include it here largely because of its status as a forerunner of cognitive theories. It's hard to overstate the extent to which this characterization is true. Certain of Kelly's principles are strikingly similar to those emerging from this new literature. In some respects, it is this convergence of lines of thought that provides a basis for contemporary interest in personal construct psychology. Lacking an active research literature of its own, however, personal construct psychology is beginning to acquire the aura of ideas that are primarily of historical interest. It may be on its way to fading from the scene, perhaps becoming a footnote to the newer cognitive models.

SUMMARY

Kelly believed that people have a fundamental need to predict the events that they experience. They do so by developing a system of personal constructs, which they use to interpret or construe new events. Constructs are derived from recurring elements in one's experience, but because they're developed separately by each person, each person's system of constructs is unique. Constructive alternativism is the idea that any event for any person is open to multiple interpretations and that people decide for themselves how to construe each event.

People implicitly evaluate their constructs over time in terms of predictive efficiency, or the degree to which the constructs allow the person to interact successfully with the world. Kelly treated constructs as bipolar and dichotomous. Each construct under use has an emergent pole—the end of the conceptual dimension that is being applied to the event being construed. The implicit pole of the construct is the end not being applied. A construct's range of convenience is the range of events to which it can be applied meaningfully. Its focus of convenience is the range of events for which it is optimally predictive.

Constructs can be refined by actively using them in familiar ways (a process called definition) and can be elaborated by using them in unfamiliar ways (a process called extension). Changes in one's construct system can also be induced by situations in which one finds oneself without adequate constructs to interpret an event. Constructs are organized in a hierarchical system of inclusiveness. This organization is not permanent, however, just as the constructs themselves are not permanent. How long any aspect of the construct system remains stable depends on its predictive efficiency.

Kelly held that constructs are unique to each person, despite the fact that they're often illustrated by examples labeled with familiar words. The fact that each person's constructs are potentially different from those of other persons raises questions about how people can interact effectively. In Kelly's view, getting to know other people means testing one's own constructs against theirs. People are similar to the extent their construct systems are similar. Interpersonal interaction in this viewpoint involves the taking of a role with respect to some other person. Role taking entails construing how the other person is construing yourself in your role. Core roles are those roles that are particularly important to one's sense of identity.

Assessment from Kelly's viewpoint is done by the Rep Test, which assesses the constructs that people use in construing their role relations and other aspects of their experience. Kelly's viewpoint on problems in self-management was that people experience anxiety when events fall outside the range of convenience of their construct systems, and they experience threat when they anticipate a major reorganization of important aspects of their construct systems because of poor predictive efficiency. Kelly developed fixed role therapy as a way of getting people to engage in behaviors that they would not ordinarily engage in, for the purpose of developing different ways of construing events in their lives.

GLOSSARY

Anxiety The response to inability to impose a construct adequately on an event you're experiencing.

Constructive alternativism The idea that any event can be construed in many ways.

Coping The effort to handle a threat by executing whatever response has been chosen.

Core roles The roles that are central to one's life, contributing to one's identity.

Defensive reappraisal The process of defining a threat out of existence.

Definition The applying of a construct in a familiar way, causing refinement of the construct.

Emergent pole The end of a construct that's being applied to the event being construed.

Extension The applying of a construct to an unfamiliar event in an attempt to increase its range of convenience.

Fixed role therapy A therapy in which clients enact roles that differ somewhat from their current self-perceptions.

Focus of convenience The range of applicable events for which a construct has the best prediction.

Guilt The sensing of a discrepancy between one's acts and another's role expectations for oneself.

Implicit pole The end of the construct that isn't being applied to the event being construed.

Permeability The degree to which a construct extends to events it hasn't been applied to yet.

Personal construct A mental representation used to interpret events.

Perspective of the generalized other An integrated sense of others' views of you.

Predictive efficiency The degree to which a construct can be applied successfully to events.

Primary appraisal The process of perceiving a threat in the environment.

Range of convenience The range of events for which a construct is useful.

Rep Test A test used to identify a person's major constructs.

Role taking The process of construing how another person construes you.

Secondary appraisal The process of determining how to respond to an environmental threat.

Symbolic interactionism A theory in which the self arises from the process of social interaction.

Threat The perception of an impending reorganization of one's construct system.

PART eight

The Cognitive Self-Regulation Perspective

THE COGNITIVE SELF-REGULATION PERSPECTIVE:
Major Themes and Underlying Assumptions

The human nervous system is a vast and elaborate network of tiny cells that communicate continuously with each other. They relay information from one place to another throughout your life, whether you're awake or asleep. This network has been compared to many other systems over the decades, including an organization of hydraulic tubes, a network of telephone lines, and a paper-shuffling bureaucracy. The last 25 years or so, however, have seen the emergence of another comparison: the nervous system as a computer.

This metaphor appeals to many cognitive psychologists, because of a similarity between certain mental processes—organizing perceptual experiences and storing them in patterns—and certain computer functions. The metaphor also appeals to people who study motor control, because computer-driven robots can mimic many aspects of human motion. Indeed, it's been suggested that the *robot* metaphor is actually better, because human life is filled with actions aimed at attaining goals (Batson, 1990). To some theorists, then, it doesn't seem outlandish to ask whether human beings, ex-

ploring the world in pursuit of their goals in life, are not perhaps the ultimate "guided missiles."

Given the brief history of these metaphors, it will be no surprise that theories relating them to personality aren't as fully developed as theories with longer histories. Nevertheless, this way of thinking does seem to have implications for personality, which are described in Chapters 16 and 17.

The ideas presented there incorporate at least three underlying assumptions. The first and broadest is that understanding human behavior means understanding how people deal with the information that surrounds them. *Information* is a pretty vague term, but it's easy to get a sense of what it means. Look away from this page for a moment and around the room you're in. You're surrounded by visual stimulation, probably auditory stimulation as well (especially if you study with the stereo on), and maybe there are other people around, doing various things. Each of these is a source of information. The information comes to you in tiny bits, but you don't experience it that way. You see a wall, not unrelated blotches of color.

You hear a song, not unconnected bits of noise. You have an impression of a person, not an assortment of facts. To have these experiences, you must integrate and organize the bits of information the world provides you. From this function comes the term *information processing.*

A second assumption behind this view is that the flow of life consists of an elaborate web of decisions. Some of the decisions are made consciously, but far more are made implicitly, outside awareness. Your personality is represented partly by how the decision making flows in your mind, what biases are created by the mental organization you have and how you use it.

The idea that life is a continuing flow of decisions also relates to the computer metaphor. Digital computers are decision-making devices. The smallest elements of computers are electronic switches that continuously embody one of two possible qualities (yes or no, on or off, open or shut). Each of these elements thus is continuously manifesting a decision. Many theorists assume that human thought is a similar stream of implicit decisions.

These two assumptions underlie ideas presented in Chapter 16. Chapter 16 describes cognitive theories about how the mind is organized and how personality thus is structured. The ideas outlined there concern how events are represented in memory and how the memories guide your later experience of the world. People have representations of several types, which are interwoven. How all this complexity is organized is an important issue, from the cognitive vantage point.

A third assumption behind this perspective on personality is that human behavior is inherently goal directed. The idea that behavior is goal directed represents an approach to motivation, but one that differs somewhat from the view we considered in Chapter 5. The idea that goals underlie behavior may not sound like it belongs in the computer metaphor, but it's important in robotics. A robot has a purpose (or several) that it's trying to fulfill. It has a representation of its goal, and it tries to move toward that representation.

This view on personality assumes that people act in much the same way—taking up (or creating) goals and trying to move toward them. To ensure that they're moving in the right direction, people monitor their progress. From this characterization comes the term *self-regulation.* In this view, human action is continued striving to attain some goal or other. Life is a never-ending stream of sensing, checking, and adjusting—an ever-continuing process of moving toward a network of self-defined goals. This idea is the basis of Chapter 17.

These two chapters are more interconnected than were the pairs of chapters on any other perspective other than psychoanalysis. The ideas described in Chapter 16 provide a background to some of the ideas in Chapter 17. The ideas in these two chapters aren't so much alternative views as interrelated views. The two sets of concepts use similar metaphors, and one set of ideas flows into the other. Chapter 16 focuses on the individual's mental world (as viewed in today's cognitive framework); Chapter 17 focuses on how this mental world is reflected in actions. In this way, then, the chapters are interdependent.

Contemporary Cognitive Views

■ Joe is a music major, and Suzanne is flirting with the idea of majoring in art. Their friend Chris has had trouble picking a major, being more or less obsessed by how many interesting women he's met at the university. The three friends attended a reception last night at the home of the Dean of Students, and today they're comparing impressions. "Did you notice the paintings on the walls in the living room and den?" Suzanne gushes, "They were terrific." "What paintings?" asks Joe. "I was looking at his CDs and trying to figure out why anyone who owned so much Pat Metheny would bother with some of the trash this guy listens to." Chris looks incredulous. "Paintings? CDs? Pat Metheny? Were we at the same reception? How could you have wasted your time on things like that when Sandy Faller was there? She's just fascinating. There wasn't anything else in that place worth noticing."

These three people were at the same event, but they paid attention to three entirely different aspects of what was around them. Their memories of the setting and of the event itself were quite different from each other. It's as though something caused each to focus on a particular aspect of what was going on and ignore the rest. Why would this happen?

Some would say this is a straightforward reflection of normal cognitive processes, which (despite leading to different outcomes) worked exactly the same in all three people. The processes led them to notice and remember different things because of differences in what was already in their minds. They all had frameworks in mind for interpreting the experience, and they used the frameworks in the same way. It's just that the frameworks they used were different.

How people structure and represent their experience of life is one of the focuses of cognitive psychology. The past two and a half decades have seen an explosion of interest in cognitive processes, among personality psychologists as well (e.g., Cantor & Kihlstrom, 1981, 1987; Fiske & Taylor, 1984; Wyer & Srull, 1984, 1986). Hundreds of studies have investigated how people organize things in memory. A picture of these processes has begun to emerge and to influence how some people think about the nature of personality.

Part of the picture is startlingly similar to ideas put forward much earlier by George Kelly, whose theory was described in Chapter 15. Oddly enough, though, Kelly never saw himself as a cognitive theorist. In fact, he actively tried to dissociate himself from that idea (Neimeyer & Neimeyer, 1981). The newer work on cognitive processes grew from other lines of thought (e.g., Bruner, 1957; Heider, 1958; Koffka, 1935; Köhler, 1947; Lewin, 1951a). In what eventually was termed the "cognitive revolution," Kelly was pretty thoroughly ignored.

Yet many assumptions behind the current view of cognition in personality resemble his. For example, today's cognitive theorists view people as implicit scientists who want to predict the world. On the other hand, today's view takes a slightly different slant on *why* this is so. Today's view is that you're surrounded by more information than you can use. You can't check every bit, so you don't try (Gigerenzer & Goldstein, 1996). Instead, you impose organization, use a few bits to make inferences about the rest (Anderson, 1991; Nisbett & Ross, 1980). This saves mental resources (Macrae, Milne, & Bodenhausen, 1994). This is good, because you usually have several things on your mind at once, and you *need* those resources. You can conserve in this way, however, only if you can predict events well.

Representing Your Experience of the World

Cognitive theorists are interested in how people organize, process, store, and retrieve memories of their experiences—how they "process information" (see also Box 16.1). How *do* people organize and store information in memory?

Schemas and Their Development

Theorists generally agree that people impose order on experiences from recurrences of similar qualities across repeated events. This "order" takes the form of **schemas,**

BOX 16.1

INFORMATION AND INFORMATION PROCESSING

Talking about "processing information" begs a question. What's **information**? Information is technically defined as anything that reduces uncertainty (Brody, 1970). It's easier to get a handle on the idea, however, by talking about examples instead of defining it.

A common example is that information is conveyed by the state of an electronic relay in a computer—it's either open or closed. Its state is saying either yes or no. As a second example, when a stimulus stimulates a receptor cell (a light beam hits your retina or a sound wave reaches your ear), information is conveyed (i.e., that the stimulus has arrived). The receptor's activity is also saying yes or no. Either the stimulus is there or it isn't.

The information in a sensory event is delivered to you in a huge collection of little bits. Your retina has many receptors, each of which reacts to little bits of light. What you perceive, though, isn't an assortment of little bits. As the message moves toward consciousness, it gets "processed," changed in several ways. For example, sometimes a nerve cell sends a message onward if it's stimulated by one receptor, sometimes it does so only if it's stimulated by *several* receptors simultaneously. The information conveyed in the latter case is special. It tells something about the *size* of the stimulus. The first case doesn't.

With many steps between the receptor cell and the eventual destination, the potential for processing becomes great, and the information sent onward can become increasingly abstract. On the other hand, simple information that was there at the start can also be sent on separately. As you think about information processing and human experience, though, you'll have to keep in mind

that information comes in widely varying levels of abstractness.

Let's look at two more examples. The first shows how information at different levels can come from a single event. Imagine that light is creating a moving pattern of responses across your retina. The pattern tells you you're seeing an object and that it's round and pale green. Other information integrated from both eyes indicates that the object is about 30 feet away, that it's a tennis ball, and that it's a pretty "dead" tennis ball, since the players have to wallop it hard to get it to move. One player, you notice, has better form than the other. Note how *much* information there is in this perception and how it varies in abstractness, from "color" to the subtle nuances of movement that convey a sense of "form."

A second example shows how an event of the same form can convey vastly different amounts of information in different contexts: Imagine that an airline has been losing money. With contracts about to expire, management is trying to get the union to accept pay cuts. Each union member has to vote to accept the contract (yes) or reject it (no). Each vote thus is a bit of information. After the vote, the union head will go to the airline management and say yes or no. *His* statement (of the same form) conveys far more information, with far more implications.

When information is processed, part of what's happening is that you're sorting out various attributes of the experience. These attributes (at various levels of abstractness) contribute to the interpretation or become part of the memory. This is part of what's conveyed by the term *information processing*.

mental organizations of information (also referred to as *knowledge structures*). Once developed, these structures are used to recognize and understand new events.

Schemas are usually assumed to include information about specific cases (**exemplars** of the category) and also information about the more generic sense of what the category is. That is, for any given category (e.g., college football players), you can bring to mind specific examples; you can also bring to mind a general sense of the nature of the category as a whole (a "typical" football player).

There are several theories about the form of these schemas (Anderson, 1985; Newell, 1990; Suppes, Pavel, & Falmagne, 1994). Some believe they form around the "best member" of the category, called its **prototype.** In some theories this is the best *actual* member you've found so far. In other theories it's an *idealized* member, an average of the members you've found so far. Other people think no prototype is actually stored at all. Instead, the category is a collection of attributes—elements that help define what the category is. Attributes that often occur in the category tend to seem "prototypic" because they're there so often.

It's also been suggested that many categories don't have explicit definitions. The features of the category all contribute to its nature, but aren't *necessary* for category membership. For example, your schema for birds probably includes the idea that birds fly. There are birds that don't fly, though (e.g., chickens, penguins). This means that flying can't be a *defining* feature of birds. On the other hand, knowing that an animal flies does make it more likely that it'll fit the bird schema. So flying certainly does count for something.

The term **fuzzy set** has been used to describe this latter arrangement (Zadeh, 1965; see also Lakoff, 1987; Medin, 1989). That is, the schema is defined in a fuzzy way by a set of criteria that are important but not necessary. If exemplars have more of the attributes that contribute to the category's implicit definition, they're more likely to be taken as category members. But if there's no *defining* criterion, members can differ a lot from one another in the attributes they do and don't have.

These theories differ, but the effects of a schema are much the same in all of them. Any event is a collection of small elements, people, movements, objects in use, and so on. But unless you have a sense of what the event's *about,* the elements might just as well be random. They're there, but they have no integrated meaning. In the same way, the attributes of an object are just a collection of bits, unless you have an overriding sense of what the object *is.* The schema, in effect, is the glue that holds the bits of information together.

Once schemas are developed, they're used to recognize new experiences. That is, new events are identified by comparing them to schemas (Anderson, 1976, 1985; Medin, 1989; Rosch & Mervis, 1975; Smith, Shoben, & Rips, 1974). If the features of the new stimulus resemble a schema, the new stimulus can be identified. This seems to be how we recognize objects and events in the world and understand what people say to us. Each new perception is based partly on incoming information and partly on what's in memory (Jussim, 1991).

Manifestations of Schemas

How do we know schemas exist? Schemas have several effects. For one, they make it easier to code new information in memory. It's as though the schema were made of Velcro, with hooks on which new information is easily snagged.

Let's illustrate. Read this passage: "First, you arrange things into different groups. Of course, one pile may be sufficient, depending on how much there is to do . . . it is better to do too few things at once than too many. In the short run this may not seem important, but complications can easily arise. A mistake can be expensive, as well."

Was that passage confusing? Would it be easy to remember it? If you knew ahead of time that it was about washing clothes, it would have made more sense and would have been easier to remember (Bransford & Johnson, 1972; Smith, Adams, & Schorr, 1978). The label "washing clothes" evokes a schema. Instead of trying to remember words, you'd fit the information into the organized structure. The structure helps the bits make coherent sense and makes them easier to remember. One effect of schemas, then, is easier coding of new material.

Another effect of schemas comes from the fact that many events don't contain complete information about what's going on. If there's enough information to bring up a schema, though, you get additional information *from memory*. You assume that most information in the schema is true of the new event, because it's been true so often in the past. For example, if you hear a story about someone doing laundry, you're likely to assume the person put soap in the washer, even if that isn't mentioned. Indeed, later on you may even believe you'd been told about the soap, when you hadn't (Bransford & Franks, 1971; Cantor & Mischel, 1977). Information you assume to be true unless you're told otherwise is called **default** information.

One obvious use of default information is in stereotypes. When one aspect of a stereotype is brought to mind, you tend to assume other aspects as well (e.g., Brewer, Dull, & Lui, 1981; Deaux & Lewis, 1984; D. L. Hamilton, 1979). If you hear that a person is a "kindly grandmother" type, you're likely to assume she's helpful, optimistic, and old-fashioned. People automatically assume schema-consistent information, even when they aren't told it. A second effect of schemas, then, is to bring default information from memory to fill gaps.

A third effect of schemas concerns the fact that memory is selective. You don't remember everything you experience, but you don't remember random bits either. What you remember is influenced by what schema you use to view an event. The schema suggests where to look for information: specifically, you look for information that's relevant to the schema. If you change schemas, you change guidelines about what to look for. As a result, you notice and encode different things.

Here's an example. If you looked at a house from the viewpoint of a potential burglar, you'd notice and remember jewelry, TVs, and stereos. If you looked as a potential buyer, you'd remember other things (Anderson & Pichert, 1978). Think back to the opening of this chapter. Suzanne's "living room" schema is tied to her interest in art. It led her to notice paintings. Joe, whose major interest in life is music, noticed things relevant to music. Chris's attention was somewhere else, and he hardly noticed the paintings or the stereo at all.

These coding biases can be self-perpetuating. That is, schemas don't just tell you where to look for information. They also suggest what you're going to find. As a result, you're more likely to remember information that *confirms* your expectation than information that doesn't. This, in turn, can make the schema more solid in the future, and thus even more resistant to disconfirmation or change (Hill, Lewicki, Czyzewska, & Boss, 1989).

Socially Relevant Schemas

When cognitive psychologists began to study how categories form and are used, personality psychologists were close behind. They found that people naturally form categories of socially meaningful stimuli. The term **social cognition** is often used to refer to such processes (e.g., Fiske & Taylor, 1984; Higgins & Bargh, 1987; Schneider, 1991; Taylor & Crocker, 1981; Wyer & Srull, 1984, 1986).

Work on social cognition has shown that people have schemas for lots of things. Examples are stereotypic categories of people (e.g., Brewer, Dull, & Lui, 1981; Dodge, 1986; Cantor & Mischel, 1977; D. L. Hamilton, 1979), individuals (Andersen & Cole, 1990), and gender roles (Bem, 1981; Deaux & Major, 1987; Lobel, 1994). People have schemas for environments (e.g., Brewer & Treyens, 1981; Tversky & Hemenway, 1983), stereotypic social situations (e.g., Cantor, Mischel, & Schwartz, 1982; Schutte, Kenrick, & Sadalla, 1985), and categories of social relationships (Baldwin, 1992; Baldwin, Carrell, & Lopez, 1990; A. P. Fiske, 1992; Haslam, 1994). People even have schemas for the structure of music (Chew, Larkey, Soli, Blount, & Jenkins, 1982) and the experience of emotions (Roseman, 1991; Shaver, Schwartz, Kirson, & O'Connor, 1987). Schemas vary in complexity and richness (see also Box 16.2), and people differ in how readily they develop them (Moskowitz, 1993; Neuberg & Newsom, 1993). Yet the knowledge that people acquire in these various domains seems to be organized.

Many of the schemas used in social perception seem to have an additional complicating feature. Wright and Mischel (1988) argued that trait terms (which are incorporated in many social schemas) have a kind of "if–then," property, a conditional quality. Saying someone is aggressive doesn't mean you think the person is aggressive every moment. It means you think he's more likely than most people to react aggressively to a certain class of situations.

Evidence from several sources supports this view. In spontaneously describing others, people often use "hedges," statements of conditions under which the person acts a particular way (Wright & Mischel, 1988). This suggests that people normally think in conditional terms.

Other research (which we brought up in Chapter 4) looked at the behavior of children in terms of its if–then properties (Shoda, Mischel, & Wright, 1994). This study found that a given child's profile of behavioral responses to classes of situations was very stable. People don't have the *same* profile—situations that make you hostile may not be the situations that make someone else hostile. But the profile tends to remain stable for each person. Thus the unique profile of if–then relations seems to represent a kind of "behavioral signature" for each person's personality (Shoda et al., 1994). Indeed, Mischel and Shoda (1995) suggested that these profiles of if–then relations may in some sense *define* personality.

The findings of this area of work suggests that schemas are deeply interconnected to one another. That is, schemas about what people are like seem to relate closely to schemas about the nature of situations. Both of these seem to be connected to schemas for acting. Although you may be focusing on one of these at a time, the use of one implicitly involves the use of the others as well (Shoda, Mischel, & Wright, 1989).

Self-Schemas

A particularly important schema is the one you form about yourself (Greenwald & Pratkanis, 1984; Markus, 1977; Markus & Wurf, 1987; T. B. Rogers, 1981), the **self-schema.** The meaning of this term is a little like that of *self-concept,* but it's also a little different. The self-schema acts just like any other schema. It makes it easier to remember things that fit into it. It provides you with lots of default information about yourself, which you assume is true unless something says otherwise. Your self-schema also tells you where to look for new information in events you experience. Your current self-schema can even create a bias in recalling your past, twisting your recollections to fit closer with how you see yourself now (Ross, 1989).

BOX 16.2

EXPERIENCE, SCHEMAS, AND EXPECTATIONS

Schemas differ from person to person, partly because people have different amounts of experience in any given domain. Some, for example, have elaborate mental representations of the diversity of wines produced in the world; other people know only that some wine is red and some is white. College seniors have an extensive grasp of the slang terms used to label different types of students; freshmen don't know as many connotations of the terms (Friendly & Glucksberg, 1970).

Another illustration of this point comes from studies by Lurigio and Carroll (1985). This research describes how experienced probation officers differ from other people—including less experienced probation officers—in their schemas about various offenders. The experienced officers had distinct and detailed schemas, the others didn't.

This difference between groups also had implications for how they expected the offenders to act in the future. Participants in one study read case files that portrayed either schematic cases (burglar, drug addict, female welfare fraud, and white-collar criminal) or cases of mixed content.

The participants themselves were either experienced probation officers or clerical staff. All made judgments about each case, including how cooperative the offenders would be during contact with probation officers, how regularly they'd report when they were supposed to, and how likely they were to make it through probation successfully.

The findings illustrate the impact of schematically organized knowledge on expectations. When the cases didn't fit any schema well, differences between probation officers and clerical workers were minimal. When the cases fit a schema, though, differences emerged. Probation officers made sharp discriminations among the schematic cases on expectations for cooperation, regularity of reporting, and (as shown in the figure) likelihood of completing probation. Clerical workers, on the other hand, didn't discriminate at all among the cases. These findings indicate that experience leads people to develop rather specific expectations about which behaviors to anticipate from a given category of persons with whom they interact.

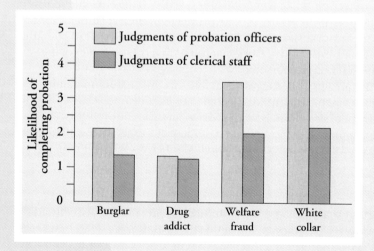

As with any schema, the default information in a self-schema can influence many aspects of experience. For example, suppose your self-schema includes the idea that you're extremely attractive to the opposite sex, and the idea that you're not a very good student. Someone comes up to you after class and starts asking you about things that'll be on an upcoming exam. How do you interpret this? Given this self-schema, you're likely to assume this person is looking for an excuse to talk to you rather than being interested in the exam. If the person really *does* want to know about the exam, it'll probably take you longer to realize it than it would take someone whose self-schema included being a good student.

How does the self-schema differ from other schemas? For one thing, it seems to be larger and more complex (Rogers, Kuiper, & Kirker, 1977). This makes sense, since you've probably spent more time noticing things about yourself than about anything else in the world. The self-schema is also used more often in day-to-day events than other schemas, and it tends to include more emotional elements (Markus & Sentis, 1982). It also seems to link to the trait labels that people use to describe themselves (Fekken & Holden, 1992).

Although there are many apparent differences between the self-schema and other schemas, there remain questions about whether the self-schema truly is special. Properties that seem prominent in the self-schema turn out to also be present in other schemas that are very well-developed (Greenwald & Banaji, 1989; Karylowski, 1990). Perhaps this is why the self-schema seems special—because it's so well developed.

Although the self-schema seems to be more complex than other schemas, there are individual differences in how complex it is (Linville, 1987). Some people have many different self-aspects, which they keep distinct from each other. Each role these people play in life, each goal they have, each activity they engage in, has its own separate existence in their self-image. These people are high in **self-complexity.** Other people's self-aspects are less distinct from each other. These people are lower in self-complexity.

This difference has interesting implications. For people who are low in self-complexity, feelings relating to a bad event in one aspect of life tend to spill over into other aspects of the sense of self (Linville, 1987). For example, having trouble with a course may make you more likely to also feel bad about how things are going in your social life. This spillover doesn't happen as much for people high in self-complexity. Apparently the separations and boundaries they've developed between self-aspects prevents it (see also, Niedenthal, Setterlund, & Wherry, 1992; Showers & Ryff, 1996).

A given set of information about the self can also be organized in many ways. For example, think about yourself as a student. You might organize that information so that your positive qualities (curious, motivated, creative, analytical) are in one schema (you as "Renaissance scholar") and your negative ones (tense, insecure, competitive, moody) are in a separate schema (you as "test-taker"). Alternatively, you might organize the same information in an emotionally mixed fashion—you as "humanities student" (creative, insecure, motivated, moody) and you as "science student" (analytical, competitive, curious, tense).

The first arrangement is great if the negative category comes up only rarely. It's bad, though, if the negative one is an important one and comes up a lot (Showers, 1992a, 1992b). The second arrangement, which has goods and bads mixed together, is less likely to cause you to experience either extreme highs or extreme lows.

How do people acquire (or fail to acquire) complexity in the self-schema? It may be partly a matter of how much you think about yourself. Nasby (1985) found that people who report spending a lot of time thinking about themselves have self-schemas of greater complexity and detail than people who think about themselves less. Apparently the very process of thinking about yourself causes a continued growth and articulation of the self-schema.

Another way of thinking about self-complexity is that it involves a family of self-schemas, rather than a single one (e.g., Cantor & Kihlstrom, 1987; Markus & Nurius, 1986). In a sense, you're a different person when you're in different contexts. You make different assumptions about yourself, and you attend to different aspects of what's going on. When you move from one set of friends in a study group to another set of friends for a party, for example, it's as though you're putting aside one schema about yourself and taking up a new one.

Not only may people have distinct self-schemas in different contexts, but self-schemas may vary in another way. Markus and her colleagues (e.g., Markus & Nurius, 1986), suggest that people develop images of selves they'd like to become (Hewitt & Genest, 1990), selves they're afraid of becoming (Carver, Lawrence, & Scheier, in press), and selves they expect to become. Other selves that have been suggested include the disliked self (Ogilvie, 1987) and selves you think you ought to be (Higgins, 1987, 1990). These various **possible selves** can be brought to bear as motivators, because they provide goals to approach or to avoid.

Entity and Incremental Schemas

Another difference in self-schemas is a difference in how people conceptualize the qualities that make up the self. The clearest example is thinking about abilities (Dweck & Leggett, 1988; see also Nicholls, 1984). To some people, ability is a fixed *entity*—something you have more of or less of, but which doesn't change. To other people, ability is something you can *increment*—increase through experience.

Both views can reflect clear and complex schemas about whatever the ability is. However, the two views lead people to react differently to difficulty. People with an entity view tend to see task performance as having the goal of *proving* their ability. If they don't do well, they're distressed and want to quit. People with an incremental view tend to see their actions as having the goal of *extending* their ability. If they don't do well, they're challenged to figure out why.

Most of the research discussed by Dweck and Leggett examined children, and examined naturally occurring differences in schemas. However, Wood and Bandura (1989) created the same difference experimentally among adults, with much the same result. Participants in this study performed a challenging managerial task, after being led to hold either an entity or an incremental view of decision-making skills. Using the entity view caused a loss of confidence as the task proceeded, a loss of efficiency in strategies used, and poorer performance.

People who hold an incremental view of ability treat setbacks as challenges for future improvements.

Semantic Memory, Episodic Memory, and Scripts

We've been discussing schemas in general terms, but it's now time to point to a distinction among them. Memories about the world are organized in at least two ways (Tulving, 1972).

The first, **semantic memory,** is memory organized according to meaning. To put it another way, semantic memory is a set of categories of objects and concepts. The categories can hold perceptual information, linguistic information, and feelings (Schwarz, 1990). As an example, most people have a schema for "boats," with a set of images of what boats look like and words that describe the nature of boats. This schema often has affective qualities as well, if the person thinks of boats as a source of either fun or danger.

Stereotypes of people are also part of semantic memory. Stereotypes incorporate visual impressions, descriptive words, and affect (liking or disliking for the people of this category). As with all schemas, semantic memory holds specific exemplars, along with a way of portraying the generic case that the category represents.

A second type of organization, **episodic memory,** is memory for events, or "episodes." It's memory for your subjective experiences in space and time (Tulving, 1993). In episodic memory, the elements of an event you experienced are strung together as they happened (see Box 16.3, for a discussion of how people code events). Some episodes are long and elaborate—for example, going to high school. Others are brief—for example, a screech of tires on pavement, followed by crashing metal and tinkling glass. A brief event can be stored both by itself and as a part of a longer event (e.g., a car crash may have been a vivid episode in your experience of high school).

When enough episodes of a given type have been experienced, a schema begins to form that's important enough to have a special name: a **script** (Schank & Abelson,

Events with agreat emotional impact often become stored in episodic memory. Many people remember, for example, hearing about the start of the Gulf War.

BOX 16.3

BREAKING UP THE FLOW OF EVENTS:
How Do People Analyze and Remember Movements?

We obviously can understand and interpret the actions of other people. But how exactly do we go about breaking a continual flow into pieces to code into memory? Research by Darren Newtson and his colleagues (e.g., Newtson & Engquist, 1976; Newtson, Engquist, & Bois, 1977; Newtson, Rindner, Miller, & LaCross, 1978) gives intriguing insight into this question.

Newtson found a way to study how people break up acts they see. More specifically, he found a way to find out where people see *boundaries* between action bits. The technique is simple: Subjects watch films of everyday behaviors and press a button (which creates a record, coordinated with the film) each time they feel that one meaningful act ends and another begins. The boundaries that they indicate are termed *breakpoints*.

Something important seems to be happening at breakpoints. For example, if previously determined breakpoints are removed from a film, new subjects readily notice the skips. They're much less likely to notice the removal of film that isn't at a breakpoint. Apparently breakpoints are places where people are doing the most visual encoding. This makes people notice anything unexpected there, such as a skip.

Why is so much encoding going on at these points? The answer seems to be that a breakpoint between act segments constitutes *the occurrence of a distinctive change* from one recognizable state to another state (Newtson et al., 1977). This change is where uncertainty is eliminated about what an action is "becoming." Thus a lot of information is conveyed at these points, leading to more intense encoding. (Note that this argument is consistent with the definition of information given in Box 16.1—reduction in uncertainty.)

As one illustration of this principle, Newtson et al. (1977) point to the fact that setting a cup down onto a flat surface is exactly the same action as *tapping* the cup on the surface—right up to the point where either the handle is released or the cup is lifted back up. The act can't be perceived and coded as "setting down" until the point of release, and it can't be coded as "tapping" until the cup starts upward again. The release or the lifting—whichever happens—removes the ambiguity. Not surprisingly, then, this point turns out to be a breakpoint.

Another finding from this research is that as people become more familiar with an activity, they mark fewer breakpoints (Newtson et al., 1978). This suggests that after a while people stop noting every single change and attend only to breakpoints that define a change *at a higher level of abstraction*. To put it a different way, experienced observers take more of the action for granted than do less experienced observers. This fits Schank and Abelson's argument (1977) that when people develop schemas for understanding familiar events (scripts), the schemas include many default assumptions.

If experienced observers are ignoring more of the concrete aspects of what they're seeing, what are they doing instead? Presumably, freedom from having to monitor the low-level information allows people to devote greater attention to the more abstract information available in the event (cf. Markus, Smith, & Moreland, 1985). Presumably they're thereby able to further refine their understanding of what they're seeing at the higher level of abstraction.

1977). Scripts are prototypes of event categories. They're used, in part, to perceive and interpret common events such as going to the hardware store, mowing the lawn, dining out, and so on. Scripts provide perception with a sense of duration and—perhaps even more importantly—a sense of flow and change through the event.

An example is the script for "dining out" (Schank & Abelson, 1977). Dining out is familiar enough that you take lots of details for granted when you hear someone talk about it. You probably won't have much trouble understanding this description:

Scripts refer to well-defined sequences of behavior that tell us what to expect and what to do in certain situations, such as eating at a restaurant.

"John went to a new Thai restaurant last night. He had chicken curry, very spicy. After paying his bill, he went home."

As with all schemas, scripts include default information. You understood the description, but you probably added many details to what you read. You probably assumed that John drove to the restaurant (although you may have assumed that he walked). You probably assumed that John ordered the chicken before he ate it, rather than snatching it off someone else's table. And you probably assumed that the bill he paid was for his dinner, rather than for broken dishes or furniture. In all these cases, you supplied information to fill in gaps in the story.

A final point about this script: It has room for lots of diversity. John could have arrived at the restaurant in many ways, he could have gone to any of many different restaurants, chosen to order and eat any of a wide array of dishes, accompanied the meal with beverages or not, had conversations or not, and paid in any of several ways. Despite this range of options, the basic structure remains the same. Thus, when you encounter a new variation on it, you easily understand it as "dining out." The same is true of scripts for other common events.

Though it's possible to distinguish between semantic and episodic memory, a lot of experience is coded both ways simultaneously. For example, a friend once told one of us (an event, now stored in episodic memory) about the nature of impressionist art (information now in semantic memory). Similarly, conceptual categories (semantic) often develop through repeated exposures to regularities in experiences (episodic). For example, if a young child tries to play with several animals and has varying degrees of success, it may help lead the child to discover that dogs and cats are two different categories of animals.

Attribution

An important aspect of perceiving and interpreting events is judging their causes. Judging the cause of an event tells you what kind of event it was (e.g., intentional vs. accidental). It also tells you something about how likely it is to occur again. The process of judging the cause of an event is called **attribution** (Heider, 1944, 1958).

Attribution has been studied extensively. This has revealed several principles that lie behind people's judgments about the causes of events they experience and witness (Anderson & Weiner, 1992).

For one, people tend to interpret events they personally experience (as actors) differently than events they witness or hear about (as observers). Observers tend to see other people's behavior as being intentional and as reflecting their personality (Jones & Nisbett, 1971). The actors themselves, however, tend to see their behavior (the very same acts) as reflecting causal forces in the situation.

Thus the same action can be regarded in very different ways depending on your viewpoint. For example, if *you* get up in a disorganized meeting and take charge, *I* may think it's because you're pushy. If *I* do the same thing, I'd think it happened because the situation begged for someone—anyone—to take charge if the meeting was ever to end. This attributional difference is a clear illustration of Kelly's principle of constructive alternativism (discussed in Chapter 15)—that the same action can be construed in multiple ways. It also shows that people have natural biases in understanding reality, depending on which role they're in.

The process of making attributions doesn't occur in a vacuum. It relies on people's extensive knowledge of the nature of social situations (Read, 1987). Once again, default values provided by your schemas give you cues to make inferences beyond the information that's present (Carlston & Skowronski, 1994). And once again, using different schemas (different mental orientations to the event) causes you to make different inferences. In this case, though, the inference is about the cause behind the event.

Another important aspect of attribution is the causal interpretations that people make for good and bad outcomes—successes and failures. Success and failure can have many causes, but special attention has been given to four particular causes: ability, effort, degree of task difficulty, and luck or chance factors.

The best-known analysis of how people use these causal categories is that of Bernard Weiner (1979, 1986, 1990). Weiner points out that these causes tend to represent opposite ends of a dimension of *locus of causality:* Either the cause is internal, a part of yourself (ability, effort), or it's external, outside yourself (chance factors, task difficulty). Causes also vary in *stability*. Some causes seem fairly stable (ability), whereas others vary from one time to another (effort). In general, people tend to see success as having an internal stable cause—specifically, their ability. (Perhaps this is because this explanation enhances their self-esteem, as suggested in Chapter 14.) People tend to see their failures as having been caused by relatively *un*stable influences—bad luck or too little effort.

Although these general tendencies exist, people also vary in their attributional tendencies. These differences have important implications. Consider failure. If you see a failure as caused by unstable factors, there's little need to worry for the future. That is, if the cause is unstable, chances are you'll face a different set of circumstances next time. If the cause is stable, on the other hand, it creates a very different picture. If you failed because you don't have the ability, or because the world is permanently against you, then you're going to have to face that same situation the next time and every time.

In the latter case, your anticipations about the future will be for continued failure. Your behavior, thoughts, and feelings can be deeply affected by that expectation. Several theorists have argued that perceiving stable and permanent reasons for bad outcomes in life leads to depression (e.g., Abramson, Alloy, & Metalsky, 1995; Abramson, Metalsky, & Alloy, 1989; Abramson, Seligman, & Teasdale, 1978; Weiner

& Litman-Adizes, 1980) and perhaps even sickness and death (e.g., Buchanan, 1995; Peterson, 1995).

Activation and Use of Memories

We've devoted a lot of attention to various aspects of people's knowledge structures. How do psychologists think about the connections among these various elements in memory? One view is that memories form an elaborate network (Figure 16.1). The links between memories reflect communication between areas of mental storage, termed **nodes.** Some links are semantic, linking attributes that contribute to the category (Figure 16.1, A). Others are episodic, linking events that made up the event (Figure 16.1, B). In this view of memory, your knowledge is an elaborate web of associations of different strengths among an enormous number of nodes of information.

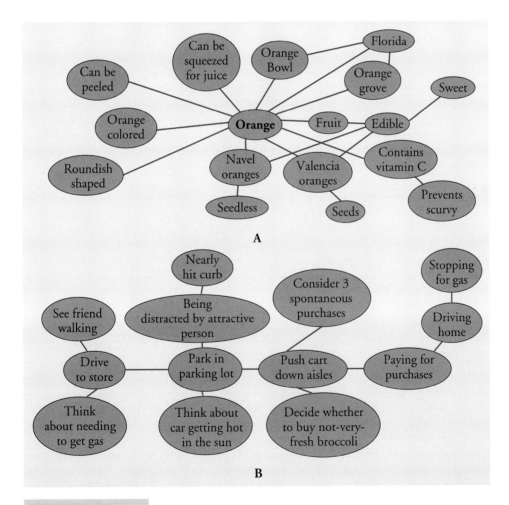

A

B

FIGURE 16.1

(A) Part of the network of semantic associations surrounding the concept "orange."
(B) Part of the network of episodic memories surrounding the event "going to the grocery store for broccoli, strawberries, and beer."

When a memory node is activated, the information in it appears in conscious awareness. Nodes can be activated by an intentional search through memories, but they can also become activated in other ways. As a node becomes active, a *partial* activation spreads to nodes related to that one. The closer and stronger the relation, the more the spread. Partial activation makes it easier for the related area to come all the way to consciousness. That is, since it's already partly activated, it takes less of a boost to make it fully active.

To return to the examples in Figure 16.1, thinking of an orange partially activates all the semantic nodes closely related to the orange. Thinking of an orange tends to remind you of navel oranges and the fact that they're seedless, the color and flavor of oranges, orange trees, and maybe the Orange Bowl. Since both orange groves and the Orange Bowl are in Florida, you may be slightly reminded of Florida, as well. In the same way, thinking about part of an episode partially activates nodes related to it. Thinking about being in the store parking lot tends to remind you vaguely of the woman (or man) you saw there, which in turn may remind you of the fact that you almost lost control over your driving and ran up over the curb.

The examples in the previous paragraph involve *partial* activation. The memory may not make it all the way to consciousness without another boost from somewhere. But it's *more likely* to make it to consciousness than it was before. An extra boost sometimes comes from another source (for example, seeing someone who looks a little like the person in the parking lot or hearing the song that was on the radio while you were parking). Given that extra boost, the node becomes active enough for its content (in this case, the image of the person) to pop into awareness. If the node hadn't already been partially activated, the boost given by the other stimulus wouldn't have been enough.

The idea that spreading activation causes easier access to related memories has been tested by a technique called **priming.** Priming is activating some node of information in an initial task. Priming procedures typically are used to investigate two questions. One is whether *related* information thereby becomes more accessible. The other is whether priming makes the *same* node more accessible later on. That is, once priming has taken place, it must take a while for the activation to fade. This would leave the node more accessible than it would be otherwise, until the activation was gone.

A number of studies suggest that priming a semantic category makes both it and closely related categories more likely to be used later, provided the use is plausible. For example, Higgins, Rholes, and Jones (1977) had people do a task requiring them to remember a set of trait terms. Later they were asked to describe a person who'd been portrayed ambiguously. The descriptions tended to be colored by the words that they'd had to remember earlier.

In another priming procedure, Srull and Wyer (1979) had people do a task that required them to read hostility-related words. Later, in what was presented as a different experiment, they were more likely to see the behavior of an ambiguously portrayed person as being hostile (Figure 16.2). They also rated him more negatively on other evaluative terms, suggesting a spread of activation to related areas of memory. Other studies indicate that effects such as these occur only when the primed information can plausibly be applied to the later stimuli (Herr, Sherman, & Fazio, 1983; Higgins & Brendl, 1995).

There's also evidence that people differ in what categories they have readily accessible to them (Bargh, Lombardi, & Higgins, 1988; Higgins, King, & Mavin, 1982; Lau, 1989). The categories that are most accessible to people are the ones they *use*

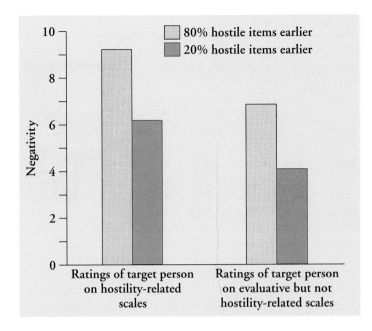

FIGURE 16.2

Participants read a set of items, 80% of which (or 20% of which) contained words related to hostility. Later, in what they thought was a different experiment, they read an ambiguous portrayal of a target person and rated him on two sets of scales, some pertaining to hostility and others evaluative but not directly related to hostility. Reading a larger number of hostile words caused the target person to be seen as more hostile and as less pleasant (adapted from Srull and Wyer, 1979, Experiment 1, immediate condition).

the most. Thus, differences in chronic accessibility reflect people's readiness to use particular schemas in seeing the world (Bargh & Pratto, 1986).

Broader Statements on Cognition and Personality

Much of the work making up the cognitive view of personality examines specific mental processes behind personality. This work is somewhat restricted in scope. Several theorists, however, have made broader statements about cognition and personality. These statements are intended to indicate what kinds of variables have to be considered in a cognitive view, if it's to grow into a viable perspective on personality.

Cognitive Person Variables

One of these theoretical statements was written some time ago by Walter Mischel (1973), a theorist who's had a major influence on the development of today's cognitive viewpoint (see also Box 16.4). As is true of many theorists who now hold a cognitive view on personality, Mischel was identified earlier with the *cognitive-social learning* view. His 1973 theoretical statement represents something of a transition between Mischel the learning theorist and Mischel the cognitive theorist.

Mischel proposed that an adequate theory of personality has to take into account five classes of cognitive variables in the person. These variables are all influenced by life's experiences (and thus by learning). With all these various criteria in mind, Mischel called them "cognitive social learning person variables." He intended them to take the place of traits in analyzing human behavior (see also Mischel, 1990).

One class of variables is the person's *competencies*. These are the skills that people develop over their life's experiences. Just as people develop skills for manipulating the physical world, they develop social skills and problem-solving strategies, tools for analyzing the social world. Competencies aren't static knowledge about things. They

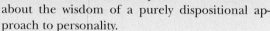

BOX 16.4

THE THEORIST AND THE THEORY:
Mischel and His Mentors

Professional mentors influence their students in many ways. Most commonly they impart a set of general skills and a way of looking at the world, which the students go on to apply to research domains of their own choosing. It's also common for students to adopt the theoretical views of their mentors temporarily, but it's equally common for them to change views after a few years, as other ideas come along. Occasionally, however, an imprint is made on the mind of a student that reverberates for a long time in the student's work. This seems to be the case in the career of Walter Mischel.

Mischel was born in Vienna in 1930 and lived within walking distance of Sigmund Freud's house. When Mischel was nine, his family fled to New York to escape Nazism. He grew up in New York and became a social worker, initially using Freud's theory of personality. His enthusiasm for psychoanalysis waned considerably, however, when he tried to apply its ideas to dealing with juvenile offenders in New York's Lower East Side.

After a stint as a social worker, Mischel set off to continue his education. At Ohio State University he came under the influence of two psychologists who were already making a mark on personality psychology, George Kelly and Julian Rotter. Kelly's ideas (described in Chapter 15) emphasized the importance of personal constructs in people's handling of their social and physical worlds. Rotter's ideas (described in Chapter 13) concerned the important role played by people's expectations in determining their behavior. Both Kelly and Rotter were also skeptical about the wisdom of a purely dispositional approach to personality.

Mischel's work has incorporated all three of these themes, although Mischel has also taken each theme in directions of his own. For example, as discussed in Chapter 4, Mischel (1968) sparked a huge controversy in personality psychology over the question of whether behavior has enough cross-situational consistency to warrant believing in dispositions. He spent much of his career focusing on issues in the cognitive-social learning perspective, including the role played by various kinds of expectancies. In the past two decades his views have become increasingly cognitive, leading to what some see as a resolution of the controversy he sparked in 1968. As we noted at the start of this chapter, the emergence of today's cognitive view on personality has roots in several places other than Kelly's ideas. Surely, however, one reason for the emergence of this cognitive view is the impact that Kelly the mentor had on the young Walter Mischel.

are active processes that people can bring to bear on situations they confront. Different people have different patterns of competencies, of course, and people differ in how competent they are in any given area. Some people have the ability to empathize with others, some people have the skill to fix brakes, and some have the ability to make people laugh. Situations also vary in what competencies they call for (Shoda, Mischel, & Wright, 1993). Thus different situations favor different persons.

Mischel termed the second class of variables *encoding strategies and personal constructs*. This class includes what Kelly had in mind when he wrote about the unique world view that each person develops. It also includes the effects of schemas. You approach, notice, interpret, and categorize events and people differently, depending on the schema you're using. (You look at the house one way if you're a potential buyer, another way if you're a potential burglar.) It's not the objective situation that determines how you react, but how you interpret it. Two people react to a situation differently because they literally experience it differently (see also Box 16.5). Much of the work that's been done in the cognitive view on personality over the past 25 years pertains to this class of variables.

Competencies and encoding strategies describe people's capabilities and their ways of viewing the world. But to know what a person is going to *do* in that world, you need to know a couple more things. For one thing, you need to know the person's *expectancies* (the third class of variables Mischel discussed). Mischel pointed to two kinds of expectancies. One of them is the anticipation that one event typically is followed by another. For example, hearing a siren is often followed by seeing an emergency vehicle. Seeing black clouds and hearing thunder are often followed by rain. Smelling or seeing smoke often is followed by seeing fire. This sort of expectancy about what's connected to what provides continuity in experience. These expectancies play a large role in scripts.

The second expectancy of interest to Mischel is what he called *behavior-outcome expectancy*. This is the knowledge that particular acts typically lead to particular outcomes. These are much like the outcome expectancies in Bandura's social cognitive learning theory (discussed in Chapter 13). Entering a restaurant (behavior) is

---

BOX 16.5

DELAY OF GRATIFICATION: The Role of Cognitive Strategies

Several previous chapters have discussed people's ability to delay gratification, to wait for something good until a later time. From a psychoanalytic view (Chapter 8), doing this is a matter of ego processes holding the id in check until the time is right for fulfilling its desires. From the view of ego psychology (Chapter 10), ego control and resiliency are the variables that determine this self-restraint. From the point of view of the learning perspective (Chapter 13), whether a person delays or not depends on such variables as the reward structure of the situation and the behavior of salient models.

The cognitive point of view suggests yet another angle on the process of delaying gratification. It turns out that an important influence on delay of gratification is the mental strategies that people use (Kanfer, Karoly, & Newman, 1975; Mischel, 1974, 1979). What people think about—and *how* they think about it—can make delays easier or harder to tolerate.

Early research established that preschoolers will wait 10 times longer for a desired food if it isn't visible than if it is (Mischel & Ebbesen, 1970). On the other hand, subjects found delays easier to tolerate if pictures of the rewards were present (Mischel & Moore, 1973). Later research showed

that these effects can be changed and even reversed, by varying how the children *think* about the desired object. In particular, thinking about consummatory aspects of a food reward, such as its taste, makes it nearly impossible for children to delay at all (Mischel & Baker, 1975). On the other hand, attending to qualities of the reward that aren't associated with eating makes it possible for children to tolerate delay quite easily (see also Kanfer et al., 1975; Moore, Mischel, & Zeiss, 1976; Toner & Smith, 1977).

Research on how these self-control strategies evolve shows that there's a natural progression over time (Mischel, 1979). At first, children attend to aspects of the reward that are most appealing (such as taste), which is ineffective (Yates & Mischel, 1979). Eventually they begin to generate cognitive strategies to keep these thoughts from their awareness. The result is increased self-restraint. As Mischel (1990) points out, it's not what's in front of the children that's important but what's going on in their heads. This research thus reinforces one of Mischel's major theoretical points, and a theme that runs throughout this chapter—the importance of people's mental strategies in determining their behavior.

usually followed by being greeted and seated by a host or waiter (outcomes). Being friendly to other people (behavior) is usually followed by friendly responses in return (outcomes). Entering the right pattern of codes into an automated teller machine (behavior) usually leads to receiving money (outcome). If the rules you know match up to reality, your actions will be effective. If you've learned a set of behavior-outcome expectancies that don't fit the world, though, you'll be less effective.

Expectancies about links between actions and outcomes begin to specify how a person will act. That is, people don't act randomly; they do things they think will produce outcomes. But what outcomes? The outcomes they *want*. The fourth piece of the puzzle, then, is knowing what outcomes the person wants—the person's *subjective values*. These are the incentives that stir people into movement, motivate them to make use of their expectancies about links between behavior and outcome. If the outcome that's available isn't one the person cares about, all that knowledge will sit there unused.

The fifth and final set of cognitive variables that Mischel discussed is what he called *self-regulatory systems and plans*. People have to set goals, make plans, and do the various things that need to be done to see that the plans are realized in action. This category covers a lot of ground. Since the time Mischel proposed his five categories of cognitive person variables, this category has taken on something of a life of its own. In part for this reason, we'll talk about self-regulatory systems separately, in Chapter 17.

Social Intelligence

Another theoretical statement from a cognitive point of view was made by Nancy Cantor and John Kihlstrom (1987; see also Cantor, 1990). Their statement focuses mostly on the first three classes of Mischel's variables. Cantor and Kihlstrom used the term **social intelligence** to refer to the skills, knowledge, and abilities that people apply to social experiences. As did Mischel, they emphasized that people bring unique patterns of competencies and constructs to the situations they encounter.

Cantor and Kihlstrom also argued that much of human experience can be viewed as problem solving. People have to interpret the situations they're in, and they have to come up with strategies for dealing with those situations, solving the problems they contain. For example, suppose you get a poor grade on your first exam in a course. What's the meaning of that grade? Does it mean you're stupid, you were poorly prepared, or the instructor was out to get you? Is it a threatening experience, an annoying one, or simply a challenge? What will you do now? Study harder? Study in a different way? Get extra help from the teaching assistant? Get help from someone you know in class? Drop the course?

According to Cantor and Kihlstrom you'll use your own individualized social intelligence to work your way through the various phases of the problem and its solution. Everyone has a slightly different knowledge base to use in interpreting his or her experience, and everyone has a slightly different base for responding. Thus, behavior differs from person to person, sometimes radically, because people use their social knowledge to interpret the situations differently.

Assessment

Personality assessment, from the cognitive viewpoint, emphasizes assessment of people's mental structures. More concretely, assessment from this orientation is a pro-

Cognitive assessment is sometimes facilitated by having the person view a videotape of his or her previous behavior.

cess of finding out how people conceptualize themselves and their experiences in life, how that knowledge is organized, and how it's used.

For some time now, there have been many ways to assess people's mental pictures of reality (see, e.g., Merluzzi, Glass, & Genest, 1981). Called **cognitive assessment** techniques, they range from interviews and self-report scales to think-aloud protocols, in which people say what comes into their minds while doing an activity. One variation on this is thought sampling (which is less continuous but gives similar kinds of data). Another is retrospective thought listing (which also gives similar data but requires you to think back to the event, rather than report while it's occurring). Sometimes when people reconstruct thoughts they do so strictly from memory. Sometimes they're assisted by aids such as tapes of their previous behavior.

These techniques have been applied to widely varying kinds of experiences. Cognitive assessment procedures are used to examine the experience of anxiety and depression, along with cognitive processes in anger control and pain control. They've also been used to assess action tendencies such as binge eating, smoking, sexual deviations, and even the performances of elite athletes (Merluzzi et al., 1981).

Think-Aloud and Thought Sampling

Which technique is used at any given time is often determined by the type of cognitive event being assessed. For example, think-aloud approaches are typically used to examine cognition during problem solving or other events involving the use of strategies. They're aimed at finding out what thoughts occur at various stages of problem solving, with an eye toward understanding which strategies are effective and which aren't.

Thought sampling typically has somewhat different purposes. In this technique, subjects are randomly paged to report what they've just been thinking and doing (e.g., Csikszentmihalyi, 1978, 1982, 1990; Hormuth 1990; Hurlburt, 1979; Klinger, 1977). Rather than looking at one specific task, this procedure lets you sample across a wide range of naturally occurring events. That way you can find out what cognitions and emotions go along with the various events. The result is a clearer picture of what events feel like to the people who are part of them.

Csikszentmihalyi and his colleagues have examined several aspects of cognition across a wide range of experiences in this way (Csikszentmihalyi & Csikszentmihalyi, 1988). Subjects are paged at irregular intervals, and they record information about their activities, thoughts, and feelings. As we noted in Chapter 14, one of the particular focuses of this work has been on the circumstances surrounding optimal experience, or flow.

This research has produced a number of interesting findings: For one, positive feelings are generally tied to voluntary activities, as opposed to activities that people *have* to do. Positive feelings of satisfaction, freedom, alertness, and creativity also relate to activities in which people's attention is tightly focused on what they're doing, rather than focused elsewhere or divided among several things (Csikszentmihalyi, 1978). Interestingly, positive feelings of immersion in activities don't come just in recreation—they're also likely to arise during work (see Table 16.1).

Self-Monitoring

Another assessment technique, termed event recording or self-monitoring, involves identifying and recording *instances of specific event types,* rather than recording whatever's taking place at a given moment (Ewart, 1978; Mahoney, 1977; Nelson, 1977). Self-monitoring involves noting instances of a particular behavior or emotion, and recording other information about what was going on at the time (for example, the time of day, whether you were with others or alone, what the situation was, what your thoughts were, what your feelings were). Doing this lets you see regularities in the

TABLE 16.1

Positive feelings of being deeply and pleasantly involved in one's activities are tied to a wide range of activities. Subjects were given descriptions that expressed such feelings and were asked to indicate one context in which they themselves had had similar experiences in their own lives (adapted from Csikszentmihalyi, 1982).

Activity named	Percent of subjects naming it
Work activities (working, being involved in challenging problems at work)	31
Hobbies and home activities (cooking, singing, photography, sewing, etc.)	22
Sports and outdoor activities (golf, dancing, swimming, etc.)	18
Social activities (spending time with spouse or children, parties, vacationing)	16
Passive attending activities (listening to music, reading, watching TV)	13

contexts that surround problem behaviors and emotions. You get a better understanding of what schemas you're automatically using.

This technique is often used to help people identify situations in which they feel such emotions as anxiety, depression, or anger. It's also used to help people realize when and where they do behaviors that are problems for them—such as overeating, smoking, or drinking (e.g., Marlatt & Gordon, 1979). It's believed that these problematic actions and emotions are often cued automatically by situational elements the person pays little attention to. If a systematic record is kept, the person can identify the cues. Further, it should become easier to identify the cues *as they recur in the future*. This, in turn, should make it easier to prevent the automatic occurrence of the problem behavior or problem emotion. That is, once you know you're doing something, it's easier to stop yourself from doing it.

As a group, cognitive assessment techniques are useful ways to find out what's happening in people's minds in various situations. One of the strengths of this approach also limits its usefulness, though. In particular, the reports always represent the person's unique point of view. Sometimes (for a variety of reasons) people report only part of what they were thinking, and what's reported may or may not be the crucial part. On the other hand, the reports can suggest links among variables that aren't even mentioned. For instance, a person may be using a particular strategy (e.g., avoidance) to deal with a class of events (interpersonal disagreement) without being fully aware of it. The reports may point to the use of that strategy, even if it's not noted directly.

Diagnostic Categories as Prototypes

The cognitive approach has a final implication for assessment, which differs considerably from what we've said thus far. This point isn't so much about assessment tactics as it is about an end result of assessment. In particular, it concerns how clinicians organize their own knowledge about the nature of people's problems.

People with psychological problems aren't just one big group. Rather, they can be fit to several diagnostic categories on the basis of symptoms. Mental health professionals have tried for decades to distinguish categories from one another. Categories used to be specified in terms of defining characteristics. If a person had all of a specific set of qualities, he was defined as being in that category. If he didn't, he wasn't. More recently, it's been argued that this strategy is misleading and that another one is better.

The alternative is suggested by a view of the nature of categories that we discussed earlier, in which categories don't have explicit definitions. Rather, the category is a fuzzy set, made up of a set of features that category members often have but sometimes don't. In the same way, a diagnostic category may be a collection of features that are *often* present in members of that category, *but not always* (Cantor, Smith, French, & Mezzich, 1980).

This view has an important implication for making diagnoses. Using the old strategy, if a person generally fits a diagnostic category but lacks a specific feature, the psychologist would hesitate to place the person in that category. Using the newer strategy, the psychologist may be more willing to do so. The degree to which a person fits a diagnostic class, under the newer strategy, is determined by the *proportion* of features that fit that category, perhaps weighted by how common a feature is to that class. This approach emphasizes the idea that diagnosis is probabilistic rather than exact (Cantor et al., 1980).

Problems in Behavior, and Behavior Change

The focus on cognitive structure that's been so apparent throughout this chapter is also involved in how this view conceptualizes psychological problems and therapeutic behavioral change.

Information Processing Deficits

One implication of the cognitive view is that some problems reflect deficits in basic cognitive or memory functions: attending, extracting information, and so on. For example, people with schizophrenia require more time than other people to recognize stimuli such as letters (Miller, Saccuzzo, & Braff, 1979; Steronko & Woods, 1978). It isn't clear whether this implies a deeper problem, or whether it bears only on perceiving. Just by itself, however, this problem would account for some of the difficulty a schizophrenic person experiences in life.

Another simple idea in cognitively oriented discussions of problems is that there's a limit on people's attentional capacity. If you waste too much attention on things that are irrelevant to what you're trying to do, you get less efficient at what you're trying to do. This limitation can also make it hard to learn. For example, being anxious can impair your ability to process other information because the anxiety itself takes up so much of your attention (Newman et al., 1993; Sorg & Whitney, 1992). For this reason, people with test anxiety or social anxiety become less efficient when the anxiety is aroused. A related argument about overloads in attention has been used to explore the deficits associated with depression (Conway & Giannopoulos, 1993; Kuhl & Helle, 1986).

An idea related to this one is that people sometimes don't *deploy* their attention effectively. For example, Wine (1982) suggested that test-anxious people focus on irrelevant aspects of the situation instead of on the task itself. Because they attend to the wrong aspect of the situation, they perform poorly.

It has also been suggested that there are broader styles of processing social information that create problems in adjustment (Crick & Dodge, 1994). For example, children who are overly aggressive appear to pay less attention than other children to information about the other child's intentions (Dodge, 1986; Dodge & Crick, 1990). Ignoring that information, they misjudge the other's intent and often respond aggressively. This may also be true of violent adults (Holtzworth-Munroe, 1992).

Why do people deploy their attention in ineffective ways? Perhaps because their schemas lead them to do so. Recall that one effect of schemas is to tell you where to look for information in a new event: You look for information that fits the schema. Thus a biased or faulty schema can bias information search, which can lead to misinferences and inappropriate actions.

Depressive Self-Schemas

This line of thought also suggests a broader way to apply the cognitive view on personality to problems. That is, it may be that many problems stem from the development of schemas that in one way or another interfere with effective functioning.

This sort of reasoning has been applied to several kinds of problems, the most notable being depression. Several theorists have suggested that people sometimes develop ideas or assumptions about the world that are inaccurate or distorted. These ideas then have negative effects on the person who holds them (e.g., Beck, 1972,

1976; Ellis, 1962, 1987; Meichenbaum, 1977; Young & Klosko, 1993). Aaron Beck (1972, 1976; Beck, Rush, Shaw, & Emery, 1979) is one theorist who suggests that depression and other problems arise from such distortions. In effect, people with such problems are using faulty schemas to interpret events. They rely on negative preconceptions of one kind or another (their schemas) and ignore other information that's available in the environment (though see Box 16.6).

In Beck's view, the distorted schemas are used quickly and without intent. They produce a stream of what he calls **automatic thoughts.** These automatic thoughts (e.g., "I can't do this"; "What's the point of trying?"; "Everything's going to turn out wrong") influence feelings and behaviors. This pattern also has a "run-on" quality, because the negative feelings lead to more use of negative schemas (perhaps by spreading activation). This in turn leads to more negative affect (cf. Nolen-Hoeksema et al., 1993; Wenzlaff, Wegner, & Roper, 1988). Indeed, there's evidence that expecting distress makes distress more likely (Kirsch, 1990; Kirsch, Mearns, & Catanzaro, 1990).

BOX 16.6

THEORETICAL CONTROVERSY:
Whose Perceptions Are Distorted, Anyway?

Beck's theory of depression is based on the assumption that people who get depressed make a variety of cognitive distortions. He sees these distortions as leading to depressed feelings and to other symptoms of depression, such as reduced activity. However, research has raised questions about who's doing more distorting—people who are depressed or people who aren't.

In one research program bearing on this question (reviewed by Alloy & Abramson, 1988), subjects were presented a series of problems. For some subjects, there was a connection between their responses and the outcome of the problem. For others, there was little or no relation between response and outcome. The measure of interest was subjects' estimates of the degree to which their responses had controlled the outcomes.

The results were surprising. The researchers found that depressed persons were in fact fairly *accurate* in their judgments. People who weren't depressed, on the other hand, were less accurate. They tended to overestimate the control they'd had over desirable outcomes—in reality the outcomes were random. No one was surprised that the depressed and nondepressed groups differed from each other. What was surprising was the fact that it was the *depressed* persons who apparently had the better grip on reality.

Another study that made a similar case (Lewinsohn, Mischel, Chaplin, & Barton, 1980) looked at people's perceptions of their own social competencies, compared with judgments made of them by other people. Subjects were observed in social interaction and were rated on several dimensions by observers. Subjects also rated themselves. The results revealed that people who weren't depressed saw themselves in a better light than the observers did. People who were depressed saw themselves pretty much as the observers saw them. Again, the depressed subjects appeared to have a better grasp on reality than did the nondepressed.

What are the implications of these findings for Beck's theory of depression? In answering this question, it's important to keep in mind that depressed people *did* differ from nondepressed people, in the expected direction, in each case. Thus Beck's argument that depression involves distortion—*in comparison with other people*—still holds. What was startling was that this distortion resulted in greater rather than less accuracy. Thus if Beck's theory about depression is correct, it seems to need one additional assumption: that the perceptions of nondepressed people incorporate a rosy and unrealistic glow of optimism. A number of people have, in fact, reached precisely this conclusion (Taylor & Brown, 1988; Weinstein, 1989).

People who are prone to depression or anxiety seem to over-rely on information stored in memory and to under-rely on the reality of the present situation. The problem with this is that the self-schemas of these people also tend to be especially negative (Kuiper & Derry, 1981; Segal, 1988). When people with problems use these schemas, they naturally expect bad outcomes. They don't look at the situation with an open mind but instead attend to and encode the worst side of what's happening (Gotlib, 1983).

Beck uses the term **cognitive triad** to refer to negative thinking about three important aspects of life: the self, the world, and the future. He also believes that depressed people use other distortions. For example, they *overgeneralize* in a negative way from a single bad outcome to their overall sense of self-worth (Carver, 1998; Carver & Ganellen, 1983; Carver, La Voie, Kuhl, & Ganellen 1988). They also make *arbitrary inferences,* jumping to negative conclusions when there isn't evidence to support them (Cook & Peterson, 1986). Depressed and anxious people are susceptible to *catastrophizing,* anticipating that every problem will have the worst possible outcome. They also interpret bad outcomes as permanent (Abramson et al., 1978; Abramson, Metalsky, & Alloy, 1989). The result of all this is a sense of low self-worth and hopelessness for the future (Haaga, Dyck, & Ernst, 1991; Roberts, Gotlib, & Kassel, 1996; Roberts & Monroe, 1994).

Cognitive Therapy

In Beck's view, the point of therapy is getting the person to put faulty schemas aside and build new ones. People must learn to recognize automatic self-defeating thoughts and substitute other self-talk for them, a process that's termed **cognitive restructuring** or **reframing.** They should also try to focus on the information in the present situation and rely less on preconceptions. To put it differently, the person should become more *controlled* in processing what's going on, and less *automatic* (cf. Barber & DeRubeis, 1989; Kanfer & Busemeyer, 1982).

The procedures used for changing faulty schemas and their consequences are known broadly as **cognitive therapy** (Beck, 1976, 1991; Beck et al., 1979). There are several different techniques. One surprising one is getting people to go ahead and do things that they expect (unrealistically) to have bad consequences. If the bad outcome doesn't happen, the people are thereby led to reexamine—and perhaps change—their expectations.

More generally, people are encouraged to view their thought patterns as hypotheses to be tested, instead of as certainties. They're also encouraged to test the hypotheses. For example, if you're a person who thinks a single failure means you can't do anything right, you might be told to examine your skills in other domains immediately after a failure. If you're a person who thinks everyone will despise you if you do anything wrong, you might be told to test this assumption by being with friends the next time you do something wrong.

There's evidence that even a small amount of this sort of "reality testing" can have a large impact on how people view themselves. In one study (Haemmerlie & Montgomery, 1984), college students with strong social anxiety were given a simple treatment for it. The treatment was a conversation with a member of the opposite sex, who'd been told to initiate conversation topics, to use the pronoun *you* fairly often, and to avoid being negative. These "biased interactions" were held twice, separated by a week, for about an hour each time. The result was a large reduction in signs of anxiety (Figure 16.3).

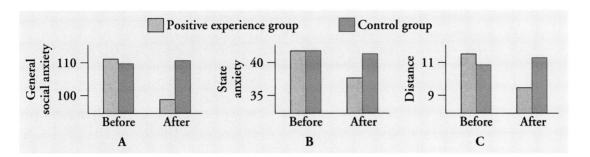

FIGURE 16.3

Scores before and after on three measures among socially anxious men who engaged in unpressured positive conversations with a woman on two different occasions, compared with scores of subjects who did not do so. The measures are (A) self-rated general social anxiety, (B) self-rated state anxiety (taken while in the presence of an attractive woman), and (C) distance from the woman while engaged in a cooperative task. The pleasant experiences improved subjects' scores on all these variables (adapted from Haemmerlie & Montgomery, 1984).

Cognitive therapy techniques are sometimes used by themselves, and sometimes they're combined with other techniques (discussed in Chapter 13 under the label cognitive-behavioral therapy). Cognitive techniques aren't limited to treatment of depression and anxiety—they've also been applied to problems such as anger control (e.g., Deffenbacher et al., 1988). These techniques appear to represent important tools in the attempt to help people move toward more effective self-management.

Contemporary Cognitive Theories: Problems and Prospects

Some psychologists find the cognitive view on personality intriguing, others find it less so. Those who are optimistic about it acknowledge that its relatively recent origin leaves some loose ends dangling and questions unanswered. Critics of this view, on the other hand, believe this approach is just a passing fad.

One criticism of the cognitive view is that some who employ it take the computer metaphor too literally. It's important to keep in mind that knowing how a computer accomplishes something doesn't necessarily tell us anything at all about how people do the same thing. There may be dozens of ways to get a computer to do something, but there's no assurance that any of these ways is even remotely the same as the way a person does it.

A common response to this criticism is that the computer metaphor provides useful conceptual tools, even if it's hard to be sure how far to press the analogy. When the metaphor is taken in its general form, rather than as a precise blueprint for personality, it yields interesting suggestions about the nature of human thought. These suggestions have often been supported in subsequent research.

Another criticism of the cognitive view is that it is nothing more than a transplantation of cognitive psychology into the subject matter of personality. What's gained by knowing that a person's knowledge about the world (including the self) is schematically organized? What does it tell you about personality to know these knowledge structures can be pulled into use by priming them in the course of a prior event?

One reasonable answer to this criticism is that these aspects of the mind's functioning do seem to have clear and important implications for day-to-day behaviors that we usually think of in terms of personality. People absorb new experiences in terms of their current understanding of the world, and it's useful to know what biases are created by that current understanding (i.e., schema). How people interpret their experiences is also influenced by the goals they have in mind. Because different people have different goals, they experience events in very different ways. The fact that people's construals can be influenced by priming is of special interest, because it relates to an idea of Freud's but puts a very different spin on it. The idea is that people do things for reasons they're unaware of. The priming effect shows that this does happen, but the reason need not reside in the unconscious. The process may be far more superficial (and for that reason less ominous).

The broadest answer to criticisms of the cognitive view, however, may be this: The cognitive viewpoint on personality is part of a broad attempt to understand the operating characteristics of the mind. A better understanding of those characteristics can't help but illuminate important aspects of human life, including those of personality. From this view, personality is a reflection of the complexities of the mind and its workings. We can't understand the former fully without understanding the latter.

SUMMARY

The cognitive orientation to personality is related to Kelly's theory of personal constructs, to the social learning view on personality, and to cognitive psychology. This view focuses on how people attend to, process, organize, encode, store, and retrieve information. Schemas are mental organizations of information that develop over experience and are used to categorize events. Some see schemas as organized around prototypes (best members), some emphasize the idea that schemas have fuzzy, or inexact, definitions. Schemas facilitate coding of new events; they provide information to fill in the gaps of events; they also orient you to new experiences, suggesting where to look for more information.

Social cognition refers to the cognitive processes that bear on stimuli relevant to social behavior. People develop schematic representations of other people, and environmental and social settings. People also develop self-schemas—representations of themselves. The self-schema is more elaborate than other schemas, but it seems to follow the same principles.

Schemas can represent both concepts (in semantic memory) and events (in episodic memory). Each aspect of memory holds both specific cases and generalities. Stereotypic event categories are called scripts. Many psychologists view memory as a vast set of nodes, linked to each other by various kinds of associations. Activating one node in memory causes partial activation of related nodes, causing that information to become more accessible.

Comprehensive statements on how a cognitive view of personality can be developed emphasize the importance of people's schemas, their encoding strategies, their personal competencies, their expectancies about how things are interrelated in the world, their values or incentives, and their self-regulatory systems. Also emphasized is the idea that social life is a continual process of problem solving, to which people bring the intelligence (skills and knowledge) they've acquired over their lives.

Assessment from this viewpoint is the process of determining the person's cognitive tendencies and contents of consciousness. Cognitive assessment techniques include think-aloud procedures, thought sampling, and monitoring of the occurrence of particular categories of events. These procedures give a clearer idea of what sorts of thoughts are coming to mind in various kinds of situations, typically situations that are problematic.

Problems in behavior can come from information processing deficits (e.g., difficulty encoding, ineffective allocation of attention). Problems can also arise from development of negative self-schemas. In this view, depression results from various kinds of cognitive distortions, all of which cause events to seem more unpleasant or as having more negative implications than is actually true. Cognitive therapy involves, in part, attempting to get people to stop engaging in these cognitive distortions and develop more adaptive views of the events that they experience.

GLOSSARY

Attribution The process of making a judgment about the cause or causes of an event.

Automatic thoughts Self-related internal dialogue that often interferes with behavior.

Cognitive assessment Procedures used to assess cognitive processes and contents of consciousness.

Cognitive restructuring or **reframing** The process of taking a different and more positive view on one's experience.

Cognitive therapy Procedures aimed at reducing cognitive distortions and resulting distress.

Cognitive triad Negative patterns of thinking about the self, the world, and the future.

Default Something assumed to be true until you learn otherwise.

Episodic memory Memory organized according to sequences of events.

Exemplar A specific example of a category member.

Fuzzy set A category defined by a set of attributes that aren't absolutely necessary for membership.

Information Anything that reduces uncertainty.

Node An area of memory storing some element of information.

Possible self An image of oneself in the future (expected, desired, feared, etc.).

Priming The process of activating an element in memory by using the information that's contained in it.

Prototype The representation of a category in terms of a "best" member of the category.

Schema An organization of knowledge in memory.

Script A memory structure used to represent a highly stereotyped category of events.

Self-complexity The degree to which one's self-schema is differentiated and compartmentalized.

Self-schema The schematic representation of the self.

Semantic memory Memory organized according to meaning.

Social cognition Cognitive processes focusing on socially meaningful stimuli.

Social intelligence The skills and knowledge people bring to bear on problems in social life.

chapter

17

Self-Regulation

■ As Carolyn awakes, thoughts come to mind about the presentation she's to give this morning. While dressing, she rehearses the points she intends to make. She catches herself skipping too quickly from one to another, and makes a mental note to slow down in the middle section so she doesn't leave anything out. For the twentieth time she retraces her logic, looking for flaws. She wants this to be perfect, to nail down the recommendation for law school she's going to ask her professor for next week. She has planned what to wear to make the impression she wants to make, and just before leaving she checks her appearance in the hall mirror. A little poking and rearranging of her hair, and she turns to go. As she opens the door she runs a mental checklist of what she needs to have with her—notes for her presentation, money, purse, keys, and—oh, yeah—the photos she said she'd show Susan. Grab the photos. Check to see that the door's locked. Check to be sure there's enough gas in the car. Check to see if there's enough time to take the scenic route to campus. And she's off. Good, Carolyn thinks, things are going just the way I want them to. Everything's right on track.

Something that's obvious about human behavior is that people shift from one task to another as the day proceeds, yet there's usually continuity as well. Your day is usually planful (despite occasional disruptions) and it includes many activities. How do you move so easily from one thing to another, do what you set out to do, and keep it all organized? These are some of the questions behind this chapter.

The approach to personality discussed in Chapter 16 made use of a metaphor in which human beings represent a kind of living computer. Here we extend that metaphor to a related field called *robotics*. Robots combine computer functions with other functions. Rather than just process and store information, they engage in actions.

Although robotics is still a young field, impressive strides have been made (Beer, 1995; Maes, 1990, 1994). Industrial robots now do the welding on car bodies. Robotic arms handle dangerous chemicals. Robots explore the far reaches of outer space and the inner slopes of volcanoes. The growth of robotics has also begun to change the way some people think about human nature. As more is learned about how to get machines to do complex things, a suspicion has begun to develop that the ideas behind these engineering marvels may promote a better understanding of how human beings function.

Do humans resemble robots? The idea may not seem too odd when you think about controlling arm and leg movements. It's probably harder, though, to see how the analogy could make sense for higher aspects of life. How can the aspirations, desires, and dreams of living, breathing people relate to machines of silicon and wire? Where does a robot have room for *emotions*—hopes and fears, joys and sorrows?

Though it may seem far-fetched, several theorists over the past 30 years or so have suggested that this analogy has considerable merit (e.g., D. H. Ford, 1987; MacKay, 1963, 1966; Miller, Galanter, & Pribram, 1960; Powers, 1973; Newell & Simon, 1972; Simon, 1967). In this chapter we discuss some of the ideas embedded in this analogy and how they might be used in viewing human behavior.

Perhaps the easiest way to start with these ideas is to think of them as a view of motivation. In particular, much of this chapter focuses on how people adopt and attain goals, how they prioritize them, and so on. In some ways these functions resemble those discussed in Chapter 5, under the need and motive view of personality.

The approach here is different enough from that one, however, that we think they're best treated separately.

From Cognition to Behavior

The cognitive view of personality, discussed in Chapter 16, assumes a vast organized network of memories. As we continue, we'll be taking the same general view, with schemas organizing knowledge. Now, though, the focus is on how the cognitions result in behavior.

Schemas for Action

How does behavior emerge from people? One answer to this question derives from ideas introduced in Chapter 16. We noted there that the schemas people use to understand events include information about behavior. For example, you have to analyze information about behavior to recognize what people are doing.

You also need behavioral information of another kind. You need information to tell you how to *produce behavior.* Just as people have schemas for recognizing, they have schemas for moving. These are called **motor schemas** (Adams, 1976; Kelso, 1982; Rosenbaum, 1987, 1990; Salmoni, Schmidt, & Walter, 1984; Schmidt, 1976, 1988).

Motor schemas are important, but they're not the only schemas used in acting. You also have schemas that help you *decide what to do* in a given situation (Burroughs & Drews, 1991; Dodge, 1986). They're not quite motor schemas, because they don't

A basic assumption of the cognitive self-regulation perspective is that robots and people operate according to similiar principles.

specify movements. Instead, they specify a plan of action (e.g., "go to the grocery store for some sugar and coffee"). By specifying actions this way, they *invoke* motor schemas ("stand," "walk," "unlock car," etc.). Thus, they're a starting point for behavior. For this reason, this information can also be thought of as "behavior-specifying" information.

What's the relation between the information used to recognize acts and the information used to do acts? Schank and Abelson (1977) said scripts are used for both purposes. The dining out script lets you understand someone else's evening, and it also reminds you what actions *you* need to take—order before you're served, and pay the bill before you leave. It isn't clear, though, whether one script serves both purposes or whether there are two parallel forms, one for understanding and one for doing (Petri & Mishkin, 1994).

It *is* clear, though, that the information that specifies "doing" is at least closely linked to information used for "understanding." Several studies have used priming techniques to activate schemas for understanding, and found that this information influenced people's later behavior.

In one study (Carver, Ganellen, Froming, & Chambers, 1983), participants were asked to form sentences from scrambled sets of words. Some of them had word sets with a great deal of hostile content, others had word sets with no hostile content. Shortly afterward, all did a task in which they gave punishment to someone in a learning task. Those who'd been exposed to the material with hostile content gave stronger punishment than those exposed to less hostile content (Figure 17.1, A).

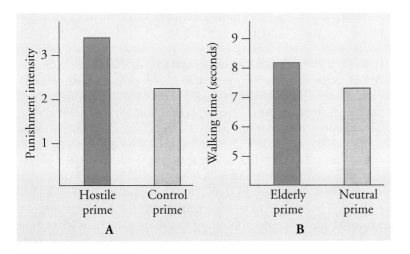

FIGURE 17.1

Effects of priming an *interpretive* schema on *behavior* that's related to that schema. (A) People who had been exposed to hostile content in a sentence-formation task gave punishments of greater intensity in a later task than people who had been exposed to less hostile content. (B) People who'd been exposed to elements of the elderly stereotype in a sentence-formation task took longer to walk to the elevator when leaving the experiment than people exposed to neutral words. (Panel A is based on data from Carver et al., 1983, Study 2; Panel B is based on data from Bargh et al., 1996, Experiment 2.)

Another study used a scrambled-word task to prime the stereotype of the elderly (Bargh, Chen, & Burrows, 1996). Subjects in one condition had many words pertaining to that stereotype, those in another condition did not. Each participant then received credit and left. The dependent measure, measured unobtrusively, was how long it took participants to walk down the corridor on their way out. Those exposed to the stereotype of the elderly walked more slowly than did the others (Figure 17.1, B).

The interpretation for these effects goes like this: To form sentences from the words, you have to understand the words. Understanding the words requires activating nodes of meaning in memory. This activation spreads to nodes bearing on related qualities of *behavior*. This quality then emerges in the person's own behavior (Bargh, 1997; D. A. Norman, 1981).

The idea that behavioral schemas are linked in memory to schemas for understanding thus provides a simple way for behavioral qualities to become active. As you perceive (or think about) situations you're in, people you're with, and so on, you're using certain memory nodes. Behavioral qualities linked to those nodes become partially activated (Dodge, 1986; Huesmann, 1988). The behaviors thus become more likely to occur. The activation is automatic, and the behavioral quality emerges with little or no thought (Bargh, 1997).

Behavioral Intentions

What we just described is an automatic and mindless way for qualities to emerge in behavior. Sometimes behavior is that automatic, but not always. Sometimes it stems from intentions. Icek Ajzen and Martin Fishbein (Ajzen, 1985, 1988; Ajzen & Fishbein, 1980), who have analyzed the process of forming intentions, say it involves a kind of mental algebra, leading to a probability of going forward. If the probability is high enough, an intention is formed to do the act. Forming an intention isn't the same as doing the action (Gollwitzer, 1990), but it's an important step in that direction.

Ajzen and Fishbein suggested that when people are deciding whether to do something, they weigh several kinds of information (Figure 17.2). They think about the action's likely outcome, and how much they want that outcome. As an example, you might think that spending your savings on a Caribbean trip over spring break will result in a lot of fun, and you really want that fun. The outcome and its desirability merge to form an **attitude** about the behavior. Because they stem from your own wants, attitudes are *personal* orientations to the act.

Two other kinds of information pertain to the act's *social* meaning to you. One of them is whether people who matter to you want you to do the act. For example, you might think about your parents, who don't want you to take the trip—they want you to come home for spring break. (Alternatively, you might think about your friends, who think the trip is a great idea.) The other element is how much you want to please the people you're thinking about—because you care about them, or because you want to make a good impression on them. How much do you want to please your parents, or at least stay on their good side? (Or how much do you want to go along with your friends' wishes?) What the other people you're thinking about want you to do and how much that matters to you merge to form a **subjective norm** about the action.

The next step is forming the intention. This involves combining the (personal) attitude and the (social) subjective norm. If the attitude and subjective norm both favor the behavior (e.g., if you're thinking about your friends and what they want), you'll form a strong intention to do it. If attitude and subjective norm oppose the behavior, you'll form a strong intention *not* to do it.

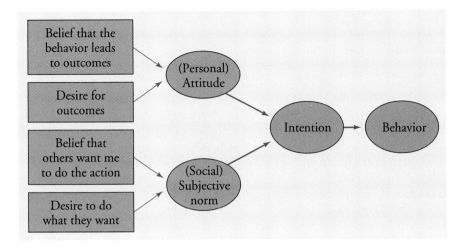

FIGURE 17.2

Foundations of intentions. The belief that an act will produce a particular outcome and the personal desirability of the outcome merge to form an attitude (a personal orientation to the act) The belief that other people want you to do the act and the desire to go along with their wishes merge to form a subjective norm (a social orientation to the act). The attitude and the subjective norm are weighted in forming the intention. The intention then influences the behavior (adapted from Ajzen, 1988).

The process is more complex—and more interesting—when attitude and subjective norm conflict. Sometimes you want the outcome a behavior will lead to, but you know your parents (or your friends) don't want you to do it. In this case, what intention you form depends on which matters more to you—satisfying yourself or satisfying your parents (or friends).

Goals

Whether or not it's been apparent, the ideas discussed thus far all imply that behavior is directed toward attaining goals. That is, motor schemas have the goal of creating particular body movements. And forming an intention means setting up a goal for action.

The idea that human experience is organized around goals has been discussed a lot in the last 18 years or so (e.g., Austin & Vancouver, 1996; Elliott & Dweck, 1988; Pervin, 1983, 1989). Different theorists use different terms, including *life tasks* (Cantor & Kihlstrom, 1987), *personal strivings* (Emmons, 1986), *current concerns* (Klinger, 1975, 1987), and *personal projects* (Little, 1983, 1989). Though labels differ, the core theme is largely the same. In each case, the point is that people's goals energize their activities, direct their movements, and even provide meaning for their lives (Baumeister, 1989). In this view, the self is made up partly of the person's goals and the organization among them. Indeed, traits seem to derive their meaning from the nature of the goals that lie behind them (Read, Jones, & Miller, 1990).

All these constructs assume overall goals and subgoals. A person's life tasks can usually be achieved in many ways. The way you choose depends on other aspects of your life. Each person devises strategies for pursuing his or her life tasks, which may differ a lot from one person to another (Langston & Cantor, 1989). For example, someone who's relatively shy will have different strategies for making friends than will a person who's more outgoing.

Goal Setting

Many goals are nonevaluative. That is, although they represent intended and desired actions, they don't imply a standard of achievement or excellence. The goal of going water skiing on a Saturday afternoon doesn't necessarily imply a goal of excellence (though it might). Forming an intention to go to the grocery store before relaxing for the night creates a guide for behavior, but it doesn't make much sense to think about it as challenging.

On the other hand, performance level is clearly an issue in some areas of life. In many activities, the goal isn't just to perform, it's to perform *well*. An example is a college course. The goal isn't just completing the course, it's getting a good grade. Another example is business performance. The goal isn't just to survive, but to excel. A question that arises in such contexts is this: Does setting a particular level of goal have an impact on how well you do?

There's considerable evidence that it does (Locke & Latham, 1990). Setting higher goals leads to higher performance. This is true when high goals are compared to easy goals, and it's also true when they're compared to a goal of "do your best." It seems that "do your best" isn't taken literally. It's taken as an instruction to try to do reasonably well. Thus, it leads to poorer performance than does a specific challenging goal.

Why do higher goals lead to better performance? There are three interrelated reasons. First, a higher goal causes you to *try* harder. For example, you know you won't solve 50 problems in 10 minutes unless you push yourself. So you start out pushing yourself. Second, you're more *persistent*. You realize that a brief spurt of effort won't do—you'll have to push yourself the entire time. Third, high goals make you *concentrate* more, making you less susceptible to distractions. In all these respects, a lower goal causes people to ease back a little.

The positive effect of setting high goals is well documented. It does, however, have an important limitation. In particular, if you're given a goal that's totally unrealistic, you won't adopt it. You won't really try for it. If you don't adopt the goal, it's as if the goal doesn't exist. The key, then, is taking up a goal that's high enough to sustain maximum effort, but not so high that it's rejected instead of adopted.

Self-Regulation and Feedback Control

So far we've discussed behavioral schemas, the development of intentions, the use of goals, and the impact of setting high goals. Now we turn to a different question. Once a goal's been set, an intention formed, or a motor schema activated, what makes sure the behavior you actually *do* is the one you *set out* to do? This question brings us to the concept of feedback control (Carver & Scheier, 1981, 1998; MacKay, 1963, 1966; Miller et al., 1960; Powers, 1973; Scheier & Carver, 1988; Wiener, 1948).

Feedback Control

A **feedback loop** is a self-regulating system with four parts (Figure 17.3). First is a value to self-regulate toward—a *goal* or *standard of comparison*, or *reference value* for

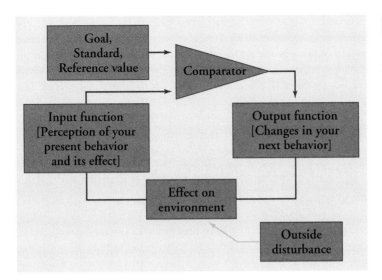

FIGURE 17.3

Schematic diagram of a discrepancy-reducing feedback loop, which shows the basic processes presumed to underlie (self-corrective) behavioral self-regulation in both artificial and living systems.

your behavior (all these terms mean the same thing here). These values can come from many places. Intentions can be goals. So can motor schemas. So can "possible selves" you envision for yourself in the future (Markus & Nurius, 1986).

The second element is a perception of your present behavior and its effects. This simply means noting what you're doing and what effect it's having. Sometimes this is just a flicker of awareness. Sometimes it means thinking carefully about what you've been doing over a longer period. Sometimes people *literally* watch what they're doing (e.g., at exercise clubs or dance studios). Usually, though, perceiving your behavior just means sensing in a vague way what you're doing.

In order for feedback control to occur, people need to monitor what they are currently doing.

In a self-regulating system these perceptions are periodically *compared with the goal* (by a component termed a **comparator**). If you're doing what you intend, the comparison shows no discrepancy between the two values, and you continue as before. If your behavior *differs* from your intention, though, a final process kicks in (Figure 17.3). This process changes the behavior, adjusts it to bring it more in line with your intention.

The word *feedback* is applied to such a system because when you adjust the action, the result is "fed back" in the form of a new perception, which then is checked against the reference value. The feedback loop is also called a *control system,* partly because its overall effect is to nudge new perceptions in the direction of the desired goal. The term *control* also reflects the fact that each event in the feedback loop depends on the outcome of a previous process. Thus each prior process "controls" what happens next.

This view has many implications. For one, it assumes that behavior is purposeful (in line with the goal concepts discussed earlier). In this view, virtually all behavior involves trying to conform to some reference value. Life is a process of establishing goals and intentions (both short-term and long-term), and adjusting behavior to match them more closely, using feedback perceptions as a guide to whether you're doing as you intended.

Another implication of the logic of feedback loops is that self-regulation is continuous and never-ending. Every change in the output function changes the present condition. The new condition must be checked against the reference value. Moreover, behavioral reference values themselves are often dynamic—evolving over time. Consider, for example, the goal of making a good impression on someone (and maintaining it), or of doing well in school, or of taking a vacation trip. You "do well in school" not by reaching a particular end point, but by doing well at many tasks repeatedly over time. You "take a vacation trip" not by leaving and returning home, but by doing a series of activities that constitute "vacationing" Thus there's a continuous interplay between adjusting your action and moving forward to the next phase of a continually evolving goal.

Again, referring to something as a standard in this context means it's the value being used as a guide for behavior. It doesn't *necessarily* imply it's a high standard of excellence (though it can be). Think of the student who's regulating his or her study behavior around the goal of making a C in a course, by being sure to look over class notes the night before the exam but not doing much more. The *structure* of this behavior (setting a goal, checking, and adjusting as needed) is exactly the same as that of a student who's trying to make an A. They're just using two different comparison values. (For a theoretical controversy about the meaning of these processes see Box 17.1.)

Self-Directed Attention and the Action of the Comparator

Does human behavior follow the pattern of feedback control? Evidence comes from work on the effects of self-directed attention. We've suggested that when you have a goal or intention, directing your attention toward yourself engages the comparator of the loop that's managing your behavior (Carver & Scheier, 1981, 1998).

Studies of self-directed attention use two methods. In some research, participants are exposed to manipulations that remind them of themselves (e.g., an audience, a TV camera, or a mirror that shows their reflected image). In other studies, researchers measure the strength of people's dispositional tendency to be self-reflective, using the Self-Consciousness Scale (Fenigstein, Scheier, & Buss, 1975).

BOX 17. 1

THEORETICAL CONTROVERSY:
Feedback versus Reinforcement

In discussing feedback processes, we should point to a disagreement among theorists. It's long been known that people engaged in task-directed action benefit from knowledge of the results of their prior efforts (Locke & Latham, 1990; Schmidt, 1988). Research on knowledge of results has been interpreted in different ways by different people. In the main text we're emphasizing the idea that knowledge of results is informational feedback, which people can use to adjust their behavior. It's sometimes argued, though, that informational feedback is a *reinforcer* (see Kulhavy & Stock, 1989). That is, telling people they performed well is reinforcing and telling them they performed poorly is punishing. That's a rather different view of what's going on.

Raising this question about the effects of knowledge of results raises a much broader question about self-regulation. Are the concepts of reward and punishment necessary to account for shifts in behavior? Or are they perhaps superfluous?

People whose work is discussed in this chapter don't all agree on how to answer these questions. Some theorists identified with the term *self-regulation* appeal to the concept of self-reward as important to self-regulation. For example, Bandura (1986) holds that a crucial aspect of self-regulatory activity is the self-reward or self-praise that a person engages in after attaining a desired goal, and the self-punishment or self-blame that occurs after failing to reach it. A similar position has been taken by several others (Kanfer, 1977; Pervin, 1983).

We, on the other hand, have taken the position that this concept isn't needed (Carver & Scheier, 1981, 1990). In our view, it doesn't add anything to say that the person engages in self-praise after goal attainment. Although self-praise may occur, self-praise is a reaction to an event that *itself* matters more. The crucial events, in this view, are the goal attainment itself and the person's realization of how it was that the goal was reached.

In thinking about this question, it's of interest that learning theorists themselves have argued for a long time about the role played by reinforcement in learning. Tolman (1932) believed that reward—even to a laboratory rat—doesn't stamp anything in, but just provides information that the animal can learn from. In particular, the animal learns what leads to what in the world, by experiencing the events in association with one another. Tolman said rewards and punishments aren't necessary for learning, but they do sometimes draw attention to aspects of the learning situation that are particularly relevant.

It's also been found that a simple social reinforcer such as saying "good" has more impact if you've been led to believe that the person saying "good" does so only rarely (Babad, 1973). Presumably this is because events that are rare provide more information than events that are common. This finding joins with Tolman in suggesting that it may be the *informational value* of the reinforcer that matters, rather than the reinforcer itself.

The idea that self-directed attention engages the comparator of a feedback loop leads to two kinds of predictions. First, self-focus should increase people's tendency to compare their goals with their current behavior. It's hard to study this directly, but here's an indirect way. Create a situation where people can't make the mental comparison between their goal and the current behavior without taking steps to get some concrete information. Put people in that situation, then measure how strongly they go after the information. Presumably seeking the information means that more comparisons are taking place. In studies based on this reasoning, self-focused subjects sought this kind of comparison-relevant information more than those who were less self-focused (Scheier & Carver, 1983).

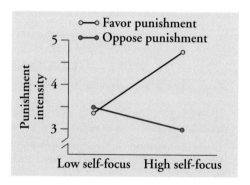

FIGURE 17.4

Level of punishment given to another person, as a function of self-directed attention and subjects' attitudes toward the use of punishment. Subjects who favored punishment used more of it than those who opposed punishment, but only if self-focus was high (adapted from Carver, 1975, Experiment 1).

If self-directed attention engages a comparator, a second consequence should also emerge: Behavior should shift to become more closely regulated to the goal. This also happens. As an illustration, people in one study said they either opposed or favored the use of punishment as a teaching tool (Carver, 1975, Experiment 1). Later, all of them had to punish someone for errors in learning. All were told to use their own judgment about how much punishment to use. Only those who were self-aware actually matched their choices to their opinions (Figure 17.4).

Many other studies also show that self-focus leads to goal matching. Various types of behavior have been studied, including aggression (Carver, 1975; Scheier, Fenigstein, & Buss, 1974), clerical tasks (Carver & Scheier, 1981; Wicklund & Duval, 1971), and use of the equity norm (Greenberg, 1980; Kernis & Reis, 1984). The values conformed to ranged from personal attitudes (Carver, 1975; Gibbons, 1978) to social norms (Diener & Wallbom, 1976; Scheier et al., 1974) to explicit experimental instructions (Carver, 1974; Wicklund & Duval, 1971). In each case, self-attention caused more conformity to the value.

Hierarchical Organization

These studies suggest that feedback processes might be involved in behavior. But a single feedback loop is too simple. Some of the needed complexity is added by the idea that feedback systems can be ordered in a hierarchy of layers. William Powers (1973) has argued that this type of organization is what makes physical behavior possible. Related arguments have been made by others (e.g., Broadbent, 1977; Dawkins, 1976a; Gallistel, 1980; Rosenbaum, 1987, 1990; Vallacher & Wegner, 1987).

The notion of a **feedback hierarchy** is based on the idea that people have both high-level and low-level goals. For example, you may have the goal of attaining a particular possible self, but you may also have the goal of having clean clothes to wear and the goal of making it to your psychology class on time. Recall the structure of the feedback loop from Figure 17.3. Powers says that in a hierarchical system the *behavioral output* of a high-level loop consists of setting a goal for a lower-level loop (Figure 17.5). High-order loops don't "behave" by doing physical acts—they "behave" by providing guides to the loops below them. Only the very lowest loops actually produce physical acts, by controlling muscle groups (Rosenbaum, 1987, 1990).

Powers proposed that human action involves nine levels of control. He used them to account for self-regulation from the highest level of abstraction (e.g., your ideal sense of self, or of a relationship or a group) down to the lowest level of ab-

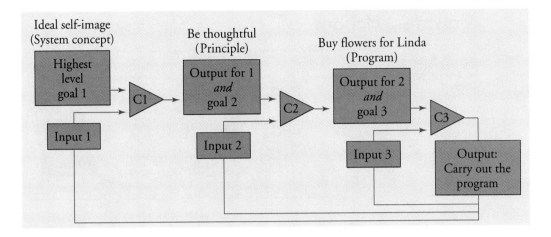

FIGURE 17.5

Diagram of a three-tiered hierarchy of feedback systems. This diagram shows the "cascade" of control that flows from higher-level loops to lower-level ones. High-level loops set the goals for the loops directly below them. The levels of control illustrated here are those at the top of the hierarchy proposed by Powers (1973). The diagram shows a cross section of the behavior of a young man who is actively attempting to (1) match his self-perceptions to his idealized self, by (2) following the principle of thoughtfulness, which is being manifested (3) in the programmatic activity of buying flowers for his wife.

straction (specific muscle tensions). The levels most relevant to personality are shown in Figure 17.5.

Powers chose the label *system-concept control* for the highest level in his theory. **System concepts** are very abstract qualities. The easiest example is the generalized sense of self that people try to maintain over time and place. Richard, the person whose behavior is displayed in Figure 17.5, is trying to live up to his idealized self-image in exactly that way. Self-regulation toward this value resembles the experience of self-actualization (Chapter 14), in promoting the sense of personal wholeness and integration that self-actualization brings.

People can't just go out and "be" their ideal selves, though. Trying to attain such an abstract quality means trying to live in accord with guiding **principles** specified by that ideal self. Thus, Powers gave the name *principle control* to the level directly below system-concept control. Principles are broad guidelines. They specify *overriding qualities* of behavior, which can be manifested in many ways. Principles help you decide what activities to undertake and what choices to make as you do them. These decisions are the behavioral outputs of loops that self-regulate principles.

As shown in Figure 17.5, Richard's ideal self specifies (in part) a principle of thoughtfulness. This principle can be used as a guide for action in many situations, including this opportunity to buy flowers. As another example, the principle of honesty would lead a person to ignore an opportunity to cheat on an exam. The principle of frugality would lead a person to choose a moderate restaurant over a more expensive one. If he was already at the expensive one, it would lead him toward inexpensive choices on the menu.

Calvin and Hobbes   by Bill Watterson

Though principles often have overtones of goodness and morality, that need not be the case. Principles can also be self-serving. What's necessary is that a principle must be abstract enough to apply to many kinds of behavior. Calvin and Hobbes copyright Watterson. Distributed by Universal Press Syndicate. Reprinted with permission. All rights reserved.

What defines a principle isn't its social acceptability, but rather its abstractness and broad applicability. Thus, expedience is a principle, though not necessarily a socially desirable one (see also cartoon above). Principles seem to be qualities that are describable by trait labels.

Just as people don't go out and "become" their ideal selves, neither do they "do" principles. Principles act by specifying what Powers called **programs,** or by specifying decisions within programs. Thus the third level in Figure 17.5 is called *program control*. What Powers called a program is similar to what Schank and Abelson (1977) called a script. It specifies a general course of action, but with many details left out. Enacting a program, or script, thus requires you to make many choices within a larger set of possibilities.

The principle of thoughtfulness led Richard in Figure 17.5 to enter the program of buying flowers. The program is partly specified: Stop at the florist, pick out flowers, and pay. But which flowers he gets will depend on what's available; he can pay with cash or a credit card; and he may or may not have to put money into a meter when he parks.

Note two more things about this example, both of which stem from the fact that there are several ways for Richard to conform to the principle of thoughtfulness. First, he might have chosen a *different* program to live up to this principle—for example, making a special dinner for Linda or washing her car. Choosing any of these programs would have matched his behavior to the *same* principle.

Second, matching the principle of thoughtfulness didn't have to mean *entering* a particular program—the principle might have come into play *during* a program, influencing his choices in it. For example, suppose Linda had asked him to pick up flowers on his way home. Given this request, he would be buying flowers anyway. The thoughtfulness principle might have become engaged in the midst of the buying-flowers program, leading him to decide to buy Linda's favorite kind of flower, even though it's out of season and thus expensive.

Much of what people do in their day-to-day lives seems programlike, or scriptlike. Most of the intentions you form in an average day involve programs. Doing the laundry, going to a store or the movies, preparing for an exam, fixing lunch, trying to get noticed by that person in class the other day—all these are programs. They all have general courses of predictable acts and subgoals, but exactly what you do at any given point can vary, depending on the situation.

Issues Concerning Hierarchical Organization

Several questions commonly come up in people's minds the first time they think about the idea of hierarchies of behavior. Let's consider some of them. For example, from what we've said so far, you may assume that all levels of this hierarchy are fully active all the time. This is not necessarily true. There are many times when self-regulation is guided not by the overall sense of self but by values at the program level (or even lower). To put it differently, lower levels of control may sometimes be *functionally superordinate.*

This seems to be what happens, for example, when people do the sort of routine "maintenance" activities that make up much of life—shopping for groceries, washing dishes, driving to school. During such times, people may lose sight of higher-order goals as they focus on the situations before them. Indeed, programs inherently require frequent decision making. This may cause this level to be functionally superordinate more often than other levels (Carver & Scheier, 1981). Interestingly enough, when people spontaneously describe themselves, they tend to describe things they *do*, rather than what they *are* (McGuire & McGuire, 1986). This suggests that the program level may be especially salient to people in thinking about their lives.

When low levels are functionally superordinate, active effort at higher levels is minimal. It's almost as though the higher layers were temporarily disconnected. The disconnection isn't complete, though. Goals at high levels can be affected by things that happen while lower levels are temporarily in charge. For example, a program of action (buying shoes that are on sale) can create conformity to a principle (frugality), even if that's not why you chose the program (you just liked the shoes the moment you saw them).

A program can also create a *discrepancy* for a principle if doing the program violates the principle. In such a case, the act is one you wouldn't have done if you'd been thinking about that principle. For example, health-conscious people sometimes have the principle of eating only low-fat foods. But if they get caught up in the action at a party (with lower levels of control in charge), they might eat lots of greasy food, which they'll later regret.

Much of what we do in our day-to-day lives, such as grocery shopping, has a programlike or scriptlike character.

There are several more points worth noting about this hierarchical view of self-regulation. As we said earlier, this view assumes that goals can often be achieved in diverse ways. This is particularly obvious at high levels, where the goals are abstract. Most principles can be realized in many ways by many kinds of behavior. Progress toward being the kind of person you want to be occurs not just in one aspect of your life, but in many.

In a complementary way, any concrete act can be performed in the service of diverse goals. For example, Richard in Figure 17.5 could have been buying flowers not to be thoughtful but to be manipulative—to get on Linda's good side. Precisely the same physical motions would be taking place, but they'd be aimed at reaching a very different higher-order goal.

A third point is that people often try to match several values at once. We don't mean just low-level values within higher-level values. Rather, people often have several goals in mind at the same time *at the same level*. In some cases, these values are compatible (e.g., being frugal while being conscientious). In other cases they're less so (e.g., being frugal while dressing fashionably; losing weight quickly while staying healthy; getting good grades while having an active social life). Matching one value can create a discrepancy for the other (cf. Emmons & King, 1988; Emmons, King, & Sheldon, 1993). From the self-regulation view, this is what defines **conflict** (see also Box 17.2).

Finally, this hierarchical approach accounts easily for a fact that's obvious but hard to explain: Very restricted and concrete acts (changes in muscle tension) are the basis by which people display abstract qualities in their behavior (e.g., being gracious to guests, delivering a speech with style, showing love for someone). It seems hard to account for this fact in many theoretical terms, but it's a natural consequence of the hierarchical approach.

Research on Hierarchies of Behavior

Is behavior organized hierarchically? Work by Robin Vallacher, Dan Wegner, and their colleagues suggests that it is (Vallacher & Wegner, 1985, 1987).

This research began by posing the question of how people think about their actions. Any given behavior can be given a wide variety of **action identifications.** For example, the very same activity (taking notes) can be thought of as "sitting in a room, making marks on paper with a pen," as "taking notes in a class," as "trying to do well in a course," as "getting an education," or even as "moving forward on my career path." Some of these identities are concrete, others are more abstract. Presumably the level at which you think about your actions indicates something about the goals you're using as reference points for the behavior.

Vallacher and Wegner assume that when both a low-order identification and a higher-order act identification are readily available, people tend to adopt the higher one. To put it another way, people tend to view (and regulate) their actions in as high-level a way as they can. For example, you're more likely to view your student behavior as "attending classes," "getting an education," or "listening to a lecture" than as "walking into a building, sitting down, and listening to another person talk."

There's also a second assumption: If people begin to struggle in performing an act at the high level, they tend to retreat to a lower-level identity for the act. In the terms used in the last section, difficulty at a high level causes the person to act such that a lower level is functionally superordinate. Using the lower-level identification, the person irons out the problem in its concrete elements. As the problem is resolved, the person tends to drift again to a higher-level identification.

BOX 17. 2

DISTINGUISHING AMONG THE VALUES THAT GUIDE BEHAVIOR: Public and Private Aspects of Self

Standards for behavior can vary in many ways. One division among human goals concerns whether the goals are personal or social (Fenigstein et al., 1975). Some goals are personal, reflections of private desires and aims that don't take into account needs or perceptions of others. Some goals are more public, social, or self-presentational in nature. In these goals the desires and perceptions of others play a significant role (Carver & Scheier, 1998).

In the hierarchy proposed by Powers (1973), this distinction seems most meaningful at the level of principles. Regulating with respect to private aspects of the self means relying on your own judgments and opinions ("To thine own self be true"). Regulating with respect to public aspects of the self means adopting the principle that others' opinions should be taken into account ("Put your best foot forward," or "Make your mother proud").

At the lowest levels of the hierarchy, the distinction is meaningless. The same low-order reference values are matched when you move your arm in a certain way, regardless of why you're moving it. Even engaging in a program of action would seem to be essentially the same, whether you're doing it for personal or for social reasons.

The distinction between public and private selves also loses meaning at the highest level of control. Presumably the idealized self is holistic, incorporating both private and public aspects (cf. Tesser & Paulhus, 1983). At that level, a success or failure at self-regulation is "personal" whether it relates mainly to private goals or relates, instead, to adequate social self-portrayal.

This private-public distinction forces us to qualify an aspect of what we said earlier in the chapter about the self-regulatory effects of self-awareness. In particular, focusing attention on a specific *aspect* of the self—private versus public—causes goals pertaining to *that self-aspect* to be used to guide behavior. Because these two aspects of the self sometimes call for different kinds of behavior, conflict can arise if both aspects of the self become salient at the same time.

For example, focusing on private self-aspects causes less conformity to the incorrect opinion of a unanimous group. In contrast, focusing on public self-aspects causes *more* conformity to that incorrect opinion (Froming & Carver, 1981; Santee & Maslach, 1982). As another example, focusing on private self-aspects causes people to act in line with personally held values. Focusing on public self-aspects causes people to act in line with what they think "most people" value (Froming, Walker, & Lopyan, 1982). In sum, reflecting on one's behavior clearly matters to self-regulation. Just as clearly, however, it matters what facet of the self you're reflecting on.

As an example, if you're in class taking notes and you're having trouble understanding the material, you may stop thinking of your behavior as "getting an education" and start thinking of it as "writing down as much as I possibly can so I can try to figure it out later." If the lecture gets easier to follow after a while, you may be able to start thinking of your note-taking in more abstract terms again.

As another example, imagine you just met someone you're interested in and you're starting to talk. You're more likely to see what you're doing as "conveying the impression of someone who's cool and worth knowing" than as "saying sentences and asking questions." On the other hand, if you find yourself struggling to carry off "acting cool," you may retreat to focusing on specific things to say and ask. If things start to go better again, you can then drift back to the higher-order identification.

What kinds of behavioral qualities do Vallacher and Wegner use in their studies of act identification? Interestingly enough, the qualities seem to reflect three levels proposed by Powers: principle, program, and sequence control (the level just below program control). Thus, Vallacher and Wegner's evidence that people naturally think of their actions at these levels converges with Powers's theory in suggesting that these levels are important.

Emotion

The beginning of the chapter posed several questions about the analogy between humans and robots. One question was how such a view (as cold and analytical as it seems) could ever have a place in it for emotions.

An early statement bearing on this question came from Herbert Simon (1967), who suggested that emotions play a *crucial* role in information processing. Simon pointed out that people often have several goals, which they pursue sequentially (e.g., you go to a gas station, then stop somewhere for lunch, then drive to the beach, where you study for an upcoming exam while getting some sun, and then you go home and do some laundry, if there's time). The order in which you do things is partly a matter of their priorities—how important each goal is to you.

Priorities aren't fixed, but are subject to rearrangement. Simon suggested that emotions are an internal call to change priorities. They call for a change by becoming strong enough to interrupt what you're now doing. An emotion such as anxiety is a signal that you're not attending well to personal well-being (an important goal) and that you should do so. Anger seems to represent a signal that your autonomy (another goal that people tend to value) is threatened and needs to be given a higher priority.

It's implicit in Simon's theory that progress toward various goals is monitored outside awareness (while you're concentrating on something else) until there gets to be a real problem for one of them. At that point, the emotion becomes intense enough to interrupt you. For example, look back at the goals described two paragraphs earlier. If you decided to put off buying gas until after doing the other things, you might later start to feel anxious about the possibility of being stranded at the beach with an empty gas tank. If the anxiety got strong enough, you'd change your mind and stop for the gas after all.

Simon's theory is compatible with an idea of our own: that emotions arise from another feedback system that monitors your rate of "progress" toward goals (Carver & Scheier, 1990, 1998). When your progress is going well, you feel happy (cf. Stotland, 1969b). When progress is very rapid, the feeling is joy or even ecstasy. When progress is going poorly, on the other hand, you get negative feelings—anxiety, frustration, or sadness. If you're actually losing ground instead of just doing poorly at gaining ground, the negative feelings intensify. In all these cases the emotion (which can interrupt behavior, in line with Simon's theory) gives a kind of subjective read-out of how well you're doing at attaining a goal.

Findings consistent with this have been reported by Hsee and Abelson (1991). Research participants (Experiment 2) were asked to place themselves in hypothetical situations in which they'd bet money on a sports outcome. Each viewed a computer on which progress toward winning was shown at different rates. They indicated how satisfied they'd be with each event they observed. As predicted, participants reported more satisfaction with faster movement in the desired direction. Of special interest were comparisons between events in which the starting and ending points were identical, but the rate of change differed. Participants were more satisfied with the faster change than the slower one.

The *general* tone of people's feelings seems a product of the goodness or badness of progress. The *specific* qualities of the feelings are determined in other ways—for instance, by information about *why* you're doing well or poorly (Roseman, 1984; Weiner, 1982). If you think you're doing well because of your abilities or efforts, the feeling has overtones of pride. If it's because of the environment (helpful others, or a situation that works to your advantage), the feeling will be gratitude. If you're doing poorly because of personal inadequacies, you feel shame. If it's because of external influences (hostile others, or a situation with insurmountable obstacles), the feeling is likely to have overtones of anger and resentment.

Emotions thus convey a lot of information. This idea in itself is useful to theorists. For example, as noted in Chapter 16, it's been argued that anxiety interferes with performance by taking up space in consciousness. With less space available, performance deteriorates. Another theorist who thinks of emotions in terms of information is Bower (1981), who emphasizes that emotion qualities are stored in memory just as is other information (cf. Schwarz, 1990). The node simply happens to hold information about feelings rather than about something else. Bower and his colleagues have produced a good deal of evidence fitting this picture.

In sum, it would be a mistake to assume that the self-regulation view has no place for emotions. Certainly many questions remain to be answered. Yet the fact that these theorists are interested in emotions for several reasons makes it plain that emotions constitute an important topic within this framework.

Effects of Expectancies: Effort versus Disengagement

So far we've focused on people's behavior *when there are no major difficulties*. However, things don't always work so well. People often encounter obstacles when they try to carry out their intentions, attain goals. What happens then?

As suggested in the preceding section, obstacles can cause negative feelings. Obstacles also tend to cause an interruption of action (Carver & Scheier, 1981, 1990, 1998; Mandler & Watson, 1966; Simon, 1967). The interruption can be brief or long. It can occur before you start an action (if you anticipate trouble) or during it (if problems arise along the way). It may occur once or often. The interruption removes you from action temporarily and it leads you to assess how likely you are to reach your goal, given the situation you're in.

The expectancy of being successful or not is an idea that's come up in other chapters. We discussed expectancies in the context of social learning theory (Chapter 13) and touched on expectancies in describing Mischel's cognitive view of personality (Chapter 16). The expectancy concept, in fact, provides a major link between learning models and cognitive–self-regulation models.

The way expectancies function in self-regulation models is essentially the same as in the cognitive learning theories. Favorable expectations for overcoming the obstacle lead people back into self-regulatory effort. Indeed, the renewed effort is sometimes even stronger than the initial effort. With unfavorable expectations, the person is more likely to **disengage,** reduce effort toward goal attainment and perhaps even abandon the goal altogether, temporarily or even permanently (Klinger, 1975; Kukla, 1972; Wright, 1996).

Effort can be viewed as varying from very intense down to some zero point. It can be useful, though, to think of variations in effort as forming a rough dichotomy

When people confront difficulties in moving toward their goals, they sometimes interrupt their efforts to assess the likelihood of succeeding. Sufficient confidence leads to renewed efforts; sufficient doubt leads to giving up. All responses seem ultimately to fall into one or the other of these classes.

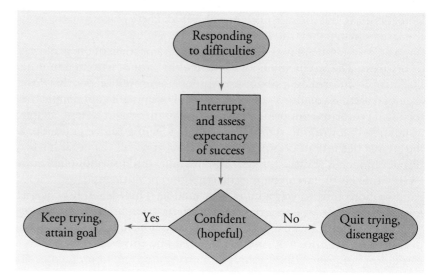

(Figure 17.6). Think of it as the question of whether or not you continue to pursue the goal. In many cases people really have only two options: to keep trying or quit (Carver & Scheier, 1998). This view of effort provides a way to talk about how people abandon one goal and turn to another. To use the metaphor of robotics, this view creates a way for the human robot who's walked into a corner to back out of it and take up another goal.

Different people emphasize somewhat different expectancy qualities in their theories. In our work, for instance, we've emphasized confidence versus doubt of attaining desired outcomes, without focusing on the *reason* for the confidence or doubt (Carver & Scheier, 1998). Bandura, in contrast (as described in Chapter 13), stresses self-efficacy expectancy—the belief that one has the personal capability of doing the action that needs to be done. He links confidence and doubt more explicitly to the person's own self-perceived capabilities.

Whatever variation you prefer, there's a good deal of evidence that expectancies play an important role in determining how hard people try and how well they do. People who are confident about reaching their goals (or who hold perceptions of high efficacy) are more persistent and perform better than doubtful people (or those with perceptions of low efficacy).

An interesting example of how confidence can influence behavior comes from a study by Ozer and Bandura (1990). Participants were women learning how to protect themselves against sexual assault. They were taught the physical skills needed to defend themselves. They were also taught verbal techniques for dealing with potentially dangerous situations before they escalate.

At several points in the study, the women made a series of ratings. For instance, they rated their confidence that they could execute each coping response—both the disabling maneuvers and the verbal tactics to deal with threats or harassment. They were also asked to rate their confidence that they could turn off thoughts about sexual assault and to rate the extent to which they had such thoughts. The behavioral outcome was ratings of the extent to which they engaged in (or avoided) a range of activities outside the home.

The results of this study are complex, but a broad theme shows through them. The sense of efficacy played an important role in participants' experiences. The women's confidence that they could use the coping skills they'd learned related to lowered perceptions of vulnerability, increased confidence that they could tell risky situations from safe ones, and ultimately their behavior. Confidence about using the coping skills also related to confidence about being able to control thoughts about assault, which related to lower incidence of such thoughts, which also related to behavior. In sum, confidence in these areas helped the women cope more effectively with their social world.

In discussing disengagement and giving up, we should point out that whether giving up is bad or good depends on the context. In some cases, disengagement is bad. It's an ineffective way of coping with the ordinary difficulties of life. These are cases where persistence would pay off in success. In such cases, the goal shouldn't be abandoned so easily.

On the other hand, it's often sensible to give up or defer goals when circumstances make it hard or impossible to reach them. For example, it's senseless to continue to shop for groceries once you realize you've left your money and credit cards at home. This sort of example makes it easy to see why giving up is sometimes the right response. But in some cases where giving up might be the right answer, it doesn't happen. There are times when it feels as though a goal *can't* be abandoned, when it seems so important that it can't be left behind. In this case, the failure to disengage results in continuing distress. We'll return to this point later on, when we consider problems in behavior.

Assessment

The self-regulation view on personality is fairly new. It's been primarily theoretical rather than applied. Nevertheless, it offers a few suggestions concerning personality assessment.

Assessment of Self-Regulatory Qualities

The view on behavior presented in this chapter emphasizes the existence of several processes. This emphasis on process suggests that it might be useful to measure *individual differences in self-regulatory processes* (Williams, Moore, Pettibone, & Thomas, 1992).

For example, the Self-Consciousness Scale (Fenigstein et al., 1975) measures a tendency to be self-reflective—that is, to think about your feelings, motives, actions, and so on. (The term *self-conscious* as used here doesn't imply embarrassment, by the way—just self-focus.) As was said earlier in the chapter, self-focus seems to engage the comparator of a feedback system that's guiding behavior. The disposition to be self-focused acts in much the same way.

It's reasonable, then, to suggest that people high in self-consciousness are likely to be relatively "careful and thorough" self-regulators (or at an extreme even "obsessive-compulsive" ones). They notice when their actions don't match their intentions and they adjust the actions accordingly. People with lower self-consciousness are somewhat more random and less goal guided in their behavior (see also Box 17.3). Thus, the Self-Consciousness Scale is a measure of individual differences in the sensitivity of a process that's important in self-regulation.

THE REDUCTION OF SELF-REGULATION:
Effects of Deindividuation and Alcohol

Earlier in the chapter we described how self-focused attention causes better self-regulation toward salient standards. If greater self-focus causes behavior to become better regulated, it stands to reason that reduced self-focus causes behavior to become more *poorly* regulated. But what does this mean? It doesn't mean that the person stops acting altogether. It means that the behavior is more likely to fluctuate, to become random and less carefully thought out.

Two bodies of research have investigated the effects of reduced self-awareness. Their origins are different from each other, but the effects they've found are strikingly similar. One set of studies concerns deindividuation. The other concerns the effects of alcohol.

Deindividuation was discussed in the context of encounter groups (Chapter 14). It's an experience that people have when they become immersed in a group. In so doing, they often lose their sense of personal identity. This, in turn, makes them more likely to use obscenities (Festinger et al., 1952), to be aggressive (Mullen, 1986; Prentice-Dunn & Rogers, 1980, 1982), and to engage in childish and uninhibited acts such as playing in mud and sucking on baby bottles (Diener, 1979).

There's evidence that deindividuation involves loss of self-focus (Diener, 1979; Mullen, 1986; Prentice-Dunn & Rogers, 1982, 1989). It's easy to see its effects as reflecting poor self-regulation regarding programs and principles that normally guide behavior. Thus there's a tendency to act impulsively, to respond to cues of the moment rather than to use well-thought-out plans. In terms of the hierarchy presented earlier in the chapter, behavior becomes a string of sequences rather than being guided by higher-order values.

These effects of deindividuation are remarkably similar to some of the effects of alcohol intoxication. People who've been drinking are often inappropriately aggressive and overly responsive to cues of the moment. Alcohol is widely regarded as a releaser of inhibitions, and it's sometimes used intentionally for precisely that purpose. Taken as a group, the behavioral manifestations of alcohol intoxication seem to reflect a loss of careful self-regulation regarding programs and principles. As with deindividuation, the result seems to be a string of sequences of spontaneous acts, rather than carefully planned activity.

Furthermore, behavioral effects of alcohol and deindividuation seem to have at least one process in common. That is, alcohol appears to act on behavior (at least partly) by reducing self-awareness (Hull, 1981; Hull & Rielly, 1986). As self-awareness diminishes, you stop monitoring your values and intentions. As a result, behavior becomes more disorganized, impulsive, and fragmented. Thus, two distinct sets of phenomena—deindividuation and alcohol intoxication—can be interpreted by a single principle. Both seem to involve interference with a process that underlies the normal self-regulation of behavior.

Note that differences in self-focus are relatively content-free. That is, the self-regulatory effect of self-consciousness is largely independent of the goal for behavior. For example, an athlete who's self-focused should be obsessive about working out. A self-conscious biology major should be sure she's always up to date in her biology homework. A self-conscious musician should be closely focused on reaching the music-related goals she's set for herself.

Other self-regulatory functions can also be assessed. For example, it might be useful to know whether a person tends to think about his or her behavior in terms of high-level goals or in terms of lower-level goals. Vallacher and Wegner (1989) developed a measure called the Behavior Identification Form, intended to assess exactly that quality. They argue that two people—even if they have similar trait patterns—can be notably different from each other if they consistently think of their goals at two different levels of abstraction.

Just as with the measure of self-consciousness, this measure of action identification tendencies is relatively independent of behavioral content. People who identify their actions at high levels tend to have a "big picture" view of what's going on—whether they're focused on socializing, studying, or making music. People who identify their actions at lower levels tend to take a more "nuts and bolts" view of what's going on, no matter the domain of the behavior.

Assessment of Goals

These two examples both reflect individual differences in self-regulatory qualities that don't depend on the content of the behavior. We don't mean to imply, though, that the content of behavior doesn't matter to this viewpoint. It does.

The self-regulation view suggests a way of thinking about the content of behavior that differs from ways derived from other perspectives. As we said earlier, the self-regulation view emphasizes people's goals (life tasks, personal projects, personal strivings, current concerns). It would seem useful, then, to assess people's goals (Emmons, 1986; Pervin, 1983) and the nature of the organization among them. One might even want to assess what sort of "possible selves" the person has in mind (Markus & Nurius, 1986). Knowing what goals are salient to a person might be more informative than knowing other aspects of what the person is "like."

An example of this is the technique that Emmons (1986) used to assess personal strivings. He asked people to describe themselves in terms of recurring personal goals in four areas: work/school, home/family, social relationships, and leisure/recreation. People listing their strivings are asked to think about their own intentions and goals and not to compare themselves with other people. Within these guidelines, they're free to write down any striving that seems important to them. This produces an individualized picture of the goal values that occupy the person's mind over a given span of time.

Problems in Behavior, and Behavior Change

Given how new the self-regulation point of view is, one might expect it to have had little or no impact on attempts to understand problems in behavior or the process of therapy. However, this isn't the case (for broader discussions see Hamilton, Greenberg, Pyszczynski, & Cather, 1993; Ingram, 1986; Merluzzi, Rudy, & Glass, 1981). The self-regulation approach suggests several ways to view problems in self-management (see also Box 17.4).

Problems as Conflicts among Goals, and Lack of Goal Specifications

One view on problems stems from the hierarchical model. That model suggests at least three ways for problems in self-regulation to arise (Carver & Scheier, 1990, 1998).

The simplest way stems from the idea of a deeply rooted conflict between goals. Conflict occurs when a person is committed to two goals that can't be attained easily at the same time (e.g., being a successful attorney while being a good wife and

BOX 17.4

REGULATING WITH THE WRONG FEEDBACK

The central theme of this chapter is that people act, monitor the effects of the actions, and check to see whether they're doing what they intended to do. Just how fundamental is this principle? Research from health psychology suggests that informational feedback matters so much that people will seek it out and rely on it *even when it doesn't tell them anything.* They'll rely on it even when they're *told* it doesn't tell them anything. They'll rely on it even though relying on it creates *problems.*

The studies that show this are studies of the behavior of people being treated for hypertension—high blood pressure (Baumann & Leventhal, 1985; Meyer, Leventhal, & Gutmann, 1985). Most people with hypertension have no reliable symptoms. Yet most people who enter treatment for hypertension quickly come to believe that they *can* isolate a symptom of it. Indeed, the longer they're in treatment, the more likely they are to think they can tell when their blood pressure is up. More than 90% of those in treatment for more than 3 months claim to be able to tell (Meyer et al., 1985).

Can they? By and large, no. In one study (Baumann & Leventhal, 1985), self-reports of elevated blood pressure were well correlated with self-reports of symptoms and (somewhat less well) with self-reported moods. Unfortunately, self-reported blood pressure elevation was virtually unrelated to actual elevation.

Why unfortunately? Because people with hypertension use their symptoms as a guide to whether their blood pressure's up. They then make important decisions on the basis of those symp-toms. In particular, they use the symptom to tell them whether to take their medication. If they think their blood pressure isn't up (because the symptom isn't there), they don't take the medication. When they feel no symptoms, they often drop out of treatment altogether. This can lead to serious medical problems—all because the people are relying on a particular kind of feedback information to guide their decisions and actions.

This example concerns a physical problem rather than a psychological one. But the same pattern can also be seen in cases where people misinterpret others' reactions to them, or rely on the wrong kinds of cues from others. If you take someone's frown as a sign of rejection, when it's really his remembering he forgot to put the cat out, you may behave in ways that create problems for you rather than help you attain your desired ends.

These examples also illustrate how much people rely on feedback to guide behavior. If the people with hypertension perceive a discrepancy between present state (symptom) and standard (no symptoms), they act in a way they think will reduce the discrepancy (take their medication). They're using feedback, just as the self-regulation approach suggests people do all the time. The problem is that the input channel is faulty. One interpretation of such phenomena is that people *need* feedback. The natural bias to use feedback apparently is so strong that people will continue to do so even when the feedback they're using is actually unrelated to what they're trying to control.

---

mother; having a close relationship while being emotionally independent). You may alternate between the goals, but this can be exhausting. It requires considerable effort to keep the conflict from reemerging. Another solution is to decide that one goal contributes more to your higher-order values than the other and to reorganize your hierarchy accordingly.

Consistent with the view that conflict is maladaptive, there's evidence that conflict among goals creates problems. Emmons and King (1988) had participants report the personal strivings that motivate their lives, then make some further ratings. These included ratings of the extent to which success in one striving tended to create problems for another one. Emmons and King found that conflicts between personal strivings were related to psychological distress and to physical symptoms.

Another idea suggested by the hierarchical model is that people sometimes want abstract goals, but lack the know-how to reach them. That is, the hierarchical view says that people regulate toward high-level values by specifying values at the next lower level, and so on. If specifications are missing at some level, self-regulation falls apart. Thus, many people want to be "fulfilled," "well liked," or "successful"—many even have more-specific goals, such as "not arguing with my wife" or "being more assertive"—but don't know how to go about attaining them. They can't specify the concrete pieces of behavior that would move them in the right direction, so they can't make any progress and end up distressed.

Problems from an Inability to Disengage

A third source of problems suggested by the hierarchical model stems from the idea that people who expect bad outcomes experience distress and quit trying. As noted earlier, sometimes disengaging is the right response to difficulties (when you realize you've forgotten your money, you quit shopping). Sometimes, however, this response can't really be made. There are some goals from which complete disengagement isn't feasible, even if you have extreme doubts about reaching them.

Goals such as doing well in your chosen work or having a good and fulfilling relationship with another person fall into this category. Why is it so hard to give up on these goals? The hierarchical view says it's hard because these goals are paths to attaining yet *higher* goals. Giving up creates gaps at the higher level. Sometimes you can't abandon a concrete goal, because it means giving up on who you want to be as a person. To put it more simply, some goals are too important to give up.

When people have serious doubts about attaining goals that are important to them, they show a predictable pattern. They stop trying, but given the structure of their lives they confront that goal again. For example, having decided to give up on having a fulfilling relationship, you see a movie about relationships, which reminds you that you really want one. Having given up trying to get along with a coworker, you find you're assigned to work on a project together. Having given up on your calculus assignment, you realize it's time for calculus class. The result of deep doubt about reaching an important goal can be a repeated cycle of sporadic effort, doubt, distress, disengagement, and reconfrontation with the goal.

This line of reasoning began with the idea that people try to quit from goals they think they can't reach. When most people fail, they want to ignore it or put it behind them and move on. Indeed, after a failure most people avoid self-focus, whereas after a success they seek out self-focus (Gibbons & Wicklund, 1976; Greenberg & Musham, 1981). Self-focus here presumably means focusing on the success (or the domain where the success occurred). Avoidance of self-focus means trying to avoid thinking about the failure.

In contrast to this pattern, however, Tom Pyszczynski and Jeff Greenberg (1985, 1987) found that people who are depressed show the *opposite* pattern. Depressed people are more likely to self-focus after a *failure* than after a success. What's going on? Apparently people who are depressed have difficulty giving up on goals they haven't reached. Given a failure, they tend to perseverate on it, even if the failure wasn't important. They have the opposite orientation to success. They let it slide by without enjoying it.

It's not always bad to keep thinking about a failure—doing this can motivate you to try harder next time (if there is a next time), and sometimes it leads to ideas about how to do things differently next time (Martin & Tesser, 1996). But Pyszczynski and Greenberg (1985, 1987) argue that it's dangerous to do this when the failure (or loss) is one that can't be compensated for or undone. When people lose a central source of self-worth and focus too long on trying to regain what's been lost, serious distress results. More important, doing this for too long makes the pattern settle in and become stable. Focusing on failure and ignoring success not only maintain the depressive symptoms, but also cause the pattern to become self-perpetuating.

A similar point is made by Susan Nolen-Hoeksema and her colleagues. She argues that people who are prone to depression focus much of their attention on their sad feelings. This rumination acts to prolong the depressed state (Nolen-Hoeksema, Morrow, & Frederickson, 1993; Nolen-Hoeksema, Parker, & Larson, 1994).

Self-Regulation and the Process of Therapy

Control-process ideas have been used by several theorists in addressing therapy issues. Most notable is the work of Fred Kanfer and his colleagues (e.g., Kanfer & Busemeyer, 1982; Kanfer & Hagerman, 1985; Kanfer & Schefft, 1988; see also Semmer & Frese, 1985). Kanfer has depicted the therapy process in a way that's compatible with the self-regulatory ideas presented throughout this chapter (as well as with the cognitive principles discussed in Chapter 16).

One point that Kanfer and his colleagues make about therapy is that much of human behavior isn't well monitored but occurs automatically to certain cues, a point made by many cognitive theorists as well (e.g., Beck, 1972, 1976; Dodge, 1986; Semmer & Frese, 1985). Therapy is partly an effort to break down the automaticity. The person needs to engage in more "controlled" or monitored processing of what's going on. Doing this should yield responses that are more carefully thought out.

The idea that much behavior is automatic has additional implications. People in therapy aren't ordinarily expected to spend the rest of their lives carefully monitoring their actions (although this *has* been suggested—see Kirschenbaum, 1987). If the person is to avoid lifelong monitoring, though, therapy must include a way to make the desired responses automatic, in place of the problem responses.

How do you substitute one set of automatic responses for another? Presumably the existing responses are automatic because they're so thoroughly coded in memory. Kanfer and his colleagues argue that other responses become automatic by building them into memory with equivalent redundancy. This, in turn, makes it more likely that this information will be used later, when the person's on "automatic pilot." They further suggest that techniques already in widespread use—such as imagery, role play, and practicing the therapeutic changes in real-life situations—do exactly this.

Another general point made by Kanfer and Busemeyer (1982) is that the long-term process of therapy is a dynamic feedback system. It's a series of stages in which clients repeatedly use feedback, both from therapy sessions and from actions outside therapy, to adjust their "movement" through a long-term plan of change.

Let's expand on this point a little, starting with the nature of the feedback. When a client makes decisions in therapy and acts on them, feedback occurs both in and outside the therapy setting. For instance, suppose you have the goal of making a relationship more evenhanded, serving the broader goal of making your life happier. You decide to be more assertive in the relationship as a way of making it more evenhanded. This decision may be viewed favorably in therapy, as a step forward in your growth. Your relationship partner, however. may react with disapproval.

Either or both sources of feedback can be used in deciding where to go from here. For example, your partner's disapproval may cause you to suspend your present goal (making the relationship more evenhanded) and consider a broader question—whether this is a relationship that makes you happy, and whether it should continue or not.

Therapy Is Dynamic

This example also illustrates that the process of therapy is dynamic. That is, the goals and questions that are guiding the process of changing your behavior keep changing, rather than being fixed. As you proceed in therapy, you must keep checking to make sure the specific goals you're working toward remain consistent with your higher-order goals. In the example above, the goal of making your relationship more evenhanded was adopted in service of the broader goal of making your life more satisfying. If you decide that the relationship no longer seems a way to reach that higher goal, it's time to abandon the goal of making the relationship more evenhanded.

A third point made by Kanfer and Busemeyer is that a good deal of therapy is (and should be) directed toward making the client a better problem solver, a person who will be better able to deal with unforeseen problems in the future (see also D'Zurilla & Goldfried, 1971; Nezu, 1987; Schefft & Lehr, 1985). Problem solving (knowing how to generate alternative behavior choices) and decision making (knowing how to select one of the choices) are important skills to develop, whether through therapy or on your own.

In this context, Kanfer and Busemeyer favor what's termed **means–end analysis** (Newell & Simon, 1972). You begin a means–end analysis by determining the difference between your present state and your desired state (the desired "end"). You then think of an action that would reduce the difference (a "means"). At first, the things that come to mind are usually abstract, involving large-scale goals. You then examine each of these large steps and break it down into more-restricted subgoals. If you keep breaking things down long enough, the means–end paths become sufficiently complete and concrete to get you from here to there.

Indeed, there's evidence that it helps to form specific intentions concerning the concrete behaviors. Particularly effective are links that tie a particular situational context to a specific act (Gollwitzer & Brandstätter, 1997). People who form such links are far more likely to attain their desired goals than people who haven't done so.

It's good to have goals broken down enough to be concrete and well specified. On the other hand, it's also possible to break things down too far (Kirschenbaum, 1985). In particular, too rigid a timetable may cause you to lose motivation. People seem to do best when they have flexibility. By being able to choose when to try to move forward, people can recognize better when certain kinds of efforts are counterproductive. They're also able to be "opportunistic," that is, take advantage of unexpected opportunities (Hayes-Roth & Hayes-Roth, 1979).

Finally, Kanfer and Busemeyer emphasize the importance of seeking accurate feedback about the consequences of your actions. If you can get accurate feedback, it isn't necessary to make perfect choices. If you make continual adjustments according to the feedback you get, you keep moving in the right direction. This principle, which is basic to the self-regulation approach, yields an important kind of freedom—the freedom from having to be right the first time.

Self-Regulation Theories: Problems and Prospects

As is true of the cognitive view, the self-regulation view on personality has been some-what controversial. It shares some loose ends and unanswered questions with the cognitive view, and it remains unclear whether these are fatal problems or just gaps remaining to be filled.

One criticism of this view derives from the computer and robot metaphor. The criticism holds that such artificial systems can't possibly be adequate models for human behavior, because they have limitations that humans don't have. Humans have free will and make their own decisions. Computers and robots rely on the programs they've been given.

One response to this criticism is that it rests on the assumption that *people* have free will, and not everyone shares that assumption. Further, the behavior of "intelligent" artificial systems moves farther every year in the direction of what looks suspiciously like self-determination. It seems clear that how humans and artificial systems resemble and differ from each other will continue to be debated well into the future. But as the behavior of artifacts becomes more and more person-like, the debate appears likely to focus on increasingly subtle points.

Another criticism that's made of the self-regulation approach is that a model of human behavior based on feedback principles is merely a model of *homeostasis* (which literally means "steady state"). Homeostatic mechanisms make sense when you're talking about controlling body temperature, or the levels of various elements in the blood. But how much sense does it make when talking about something we know is always changing? Human behavior isn't about steady states. Doesn't the self-regulation view imply that people should be immobile, or just do the same thing over and over?

Actually, no. People do regulate some of their experiences in a recurrently homeostatic way (e.g., the amount of affiliation they engage in across time—O'Connor & Rosenblood, 1996), but that isn't always the case. Many of the goals behind self-regulation involve process rather than constancy. As we noted earlier, many human goals are dynamic (e.g., going on a vacation trip, having an interesting conversation with someone). Being dynamic doesn't make these goals any less goal-like. It just means that the whole process of matching behavior to the goal must be dynamic as well. If the goal is to create a flow of experiences rather than a state, the qualities of behavior being monitored will also have this changing quality. Thus there's no contradiction between the fact that humans keep changing what they're doing and the idea that behavior is embedded within a system of feedback control.

Greater difficulty is posed by another criticism of feedback ideas—that they fail to deal effectively with the "homunculus" problem. *Homunculus,* a term once used to explain how people act, refers to a hypothetical tiny man who sits inside your head and tells you what to do. That explains *your* behavior. But who tells the *little man* what to do? To return to the robot metaphor, robots are pretty stupid. When they do something, it's because an instruction has told them to. But if people are just fancy robots, where does the instruction come from? What tells the person what to do? To reframe this issue in terms of the hierarchy described earlier, the question is this: Where do the *highest* goals come from, the ones that specify all the lower goals?

One response is that information-processing models often assume an "executive," or superordinate system, which coordinates other activities, makes decisions, and so on. The executive is manifest in subjective experience as consciousness. The executive presumably has control over other systems and thus is the analogue of the homunculus. This reasoning is plausible, but it isn't altogether satisfying.

Another response is that people have built-in goals of survival, personal coherence, and so on. These goals are vague enough that they rarely appear in consciousness, but they're pervasive enough that they constantly influence in subtle ways people's decisions about what goals to take up. Thus, behavior is being guided by values that are built into the organism, but which aren't always apparent to the person. This line of reasoning is plausible too, but it's also less than fully satisfying. The homunculus problem thus remains a real one.

A final criticism of the self-regulation view (and the cognitive view of Chapter 16) is similar to a criticism made of the learning perspective: All of this seems too mechanistic, too much a description from the outside looking in, with too little of the feel of what it means to *have* a personality. This approach describes the "self-regulation of behavior," but what does this really say about personality? This approach emphasizes structure and process, rather than content. For this reason, some see the ideas as dealing with an empty shell, programmed in ways that aren't well specified, for purposes and goals that are largely arbitrary (e.g., Ryan & Deci, 1999).

There is some merit to this criticism. We note, however, that these ideas weren't devised to focus directly on the concept of personality. Rather, they were intended to focus on issues that stand off at a slight tangent from personality. Although these ideas don't form a full theory of personality, they do provide a window on the nature of human experience, a view that seems to have implications for personality. Is the window truly informative? Will these ideas evolve into a more complete picture of personality? It's too early to be sure.

Despite these criticisms, the self-regulation view on personality has proven to have some merit. It's had heuristic value, suggesting new places to look for information about how things work. Indeed, it makes some predictions that aren't intuitively suggested by other views. This value alone makes it likely that it will be around for some years to come. Only the test of time and further investigation will tell whether this approach will continue to emerge as a viable perspective on personality.

SUMMARY

Self-regulation models assume that behavior is directed from within the person. Behavior relies on motor schemas, information about how to execute acts. These can be cued by interpretive schemas, if an interpretation is closely tied to an action quality. More commonly, actions depend on forming intentions. Intentions are products of a mental algebra in which personally desired outcomes and social considerations are weighed to yield a likelihood of acting.

Theory concerning self-regulation emphasizes the importance of goals. The goals underlying behavior have a variety of labels, including life tasks, personal strivings, personal projects, and current concerns. This view treats the structure of the self as an organization among goals. Some goals are fairly neutral, but others imply a standard of excellence. In the latter case, setting higher goals results in higher performances. This is because committing oneself to a more demanding goal focuses one's efforts more fully.

Once a goal for behavior has been evoked, self-regulation reflects a process of feedback control. A reference value (or goal) is compared against present behavior. If the two differ, behavior is adjusted, leading to a new perception and comparison. Given that many goals are dynamic and evolving, this view emphasizes that self-regulation is a never-ending process. A feedback loop is too simple to account for the diversity in people's actions alone, but greater complexity is given by the fact that feedback systems can be organized in a hierarchy, in which one system acts by providing reference values to the system directly below it.

Emotions have been viewed within this framework as interrupters of behavior and as calls for reprioritizing one's goals. Emotions are also viewed as providing a subjective reading of how well you're progressing toward a goal. Emotion thus conveys information, which is stored in memory in the same way as any information.

When people encounter obstacles in their efforts, self-regulation is interrupted and the people consider whether success or failure is likely. If expectancies are positive enough, the person keeps trying; if not, the person may disengage from effort and give up. Disengagement is sometimes the adaptive response, but people sometimes give up too quickly.

Assessment from this view is partly a matter of assessing individual differences in self-regulatory functions, such as self-reflectiveness or the level of abstraction at which people think about their goals. This view also suggests the value of assessing goals themselves. There are several ways in which problems can be conceptualized from this view. One possibility focuses on conflict between incompatible goals, and another points to a lack of specification of mid-level behavioral reference values to guide behavior. Another view emphasizes that people sometimes are unable to disengage from behaviors that are necessary for the attainment of higher-order goals. There's evidence that people who are depressed display an exaggerated inability to disengage.

Just as behavior can be construed in terms of a hierarchy of feedback systems, so can the process of behavior change induced by therapy. People in therapy use feedback from decisions they've put into practice to make further decisions. They monitor the effects of changes in behavior to determine whether the changes have produced the desired effects. One long-term goal of therapy is to make people better problem solvers through techniques such as means—end analysis, so that they can make their own adjustments when confronting new problems.

GLOSSARY

Action identification The way one thinks of or labels whatever action one is performing.

Attitude A personal evaluation of the desirability of an action.

Comparator A mechanism that compares two values to each other.

Conflict An attempt to self-regulate toward two incompatible goals at the same time.

Disengage To cease and put aside self-regulation with regard to some goal.

Feedback hierarchy An organization of feedback loops in which superordinate loops act by providing reference values to subordinate loops.

Feedback loop A self-regulating system that maintains conformity to some comparison value.

Means–end analysis The process of creating a plan to attain an overall goal (end) by breaking it into successively more-concrete goals (means).

Motor schema A mental organization of information providing instructions for acting.

Principle A broad, abstract action quality that could be displayed in any of several programs.

Program A guideline for the actions that take place in some category of events (as a script).

Subjective norm A person's impression of how other people value an action.

System Concept A very abstract guide for behavior, such as ideal sense of self.

PART nine

Personality in Perspective

18

Overlap and Integration

■   Six blind men of Indostan heard of a creature called an elephant. They went to it, to determine its nature. One of them bumped into the elephant's side, and concluded that elephants resemble walls. The second encountered a tusk, and decided that elephants are much like spears. The third, grasping the wriggling trunk, decided that elephants are like large snakes. Placing his arms around one of its legs, the fourth man concluded that elephants resemble trees. The fifth felt a floppy ear, and surmised that elephants are a type of fan. Coming upon its tail, the sixth decided that elephants are like ropes.

Each of these men was sure his investigation had led him to the truth. And indeed each was partly right. But all were also partly wrong.

—Hindu fable

In the preceding chapters you encountered a series of viewpoints on the nature of personality. Each of them was rooted in its own assumptions about how best to view human nature. Each had its own way of thinking about how people function. Each had its own view of the sources of individual differences, as well as their meaning and importance. Though we emphasized it less, each approach also had its drawbacks, places where things were left unexplained or even unexamined.

In writing about these various perspectives on personality, we tried to give you a sense of what each one was like, from inside that perspective. In that process, our emphasis tended to be on what makes each approach special, distinct from other approaches. The views do differ in important ways, and some points of conflict seem hard to resolve. For example, how can you reconcile the belief that people have free will (from the phenomenological perspective) with the belief that behavior is determined by patterns of prior outcomes (from the learning perspective) or the belief that behavior is determined by the pressure of internal impulses (from the psychoanalytic perspective)?

Our emphasis on each theory's uniqueness may have led you to see the theories as being quite different from one another. The diversity may even have led you to wonder whether the theorists were describing the same *creature*. (This would also be true, of course, for anyone who listened to the blind men describe the elephant.) The diversity of ideas in earlier chapters raises questions. Do the various perspectives have anything in common? Is one perspective right, or better than the others? If so, which one? Let's consider these questions in order.

Do the theories you've read about have anything in common? Despite the differences, there's more in common than may have been apparent. In the first part of this chapter we describe several commonalities we think are interesting. You may have noticed some of them already, but others are more subtle and difficult to spot.

The question of which view is "best" or "right" is harder to answer. One answer is that even big differences among theories may not mean that one is right and the others are wrong. It often happens that some issue, or some element of personality, seems very important from the view of one theory but less important or even irrelevant from the view of another theory. As with the blind men, one theory grapples closely with an issue, but the other theory doesn't even touch on it. To borrow Kelly's phrase, each theory has a "focus of convenience" that differs from those of other theories.

It seems reasonable to suggest, then, that the various perspectives on personality may actually reflect facets of a bigger picture. From this point of view, the perspectives would complement, rather than contradict, each other. Each may have some truth, but none by itself has the entire truth. The idea that different perspectives represent facets of a broader picture is developed more fully in the last part of the chapter.

Similarities among Perspectives

Let's first consider some specific similarities among the views described earlier in the book. Be forewarned that we won't indicate every single similarity there is. Rather, we want simply to give you a sense of what kinds of connections can be made among perspectives.

We begin with commonalities between psychoanalysis and other views. Psychoanalysis is a natural starting point. It's been around for a very long time, and many people regard it as the only really comprehensive theory of personality. For both of these reasons, it stands as a comparison point for every other approach.

On the other hand, psychoanalysis is also a particularly *unusual* theory. This suggests it should be hard to find similarities between it and other approaches. As we noted earlier in the book, even neoanalytic theories—which *derive* from psychoanalysis—don't seem to share a lot with it. Despite the unusual character of psychoanalysis, however, there are several similarities worth noting between it and other theories. In fact, parallels have been suggested between psychoanalytic ideas and ideas in at least three other perspectives: biological, learning, and cognitive self-regulation.

Psychoanalysis and Evolutionary Psychology: The Structural Model

How does psychoanalysis relate to the biological approach? Often overlooked is how strongly Freud was influenced by Darwin's view of evolution. Psychoanalytic theory is about beings that are deeply concerned with biological necessities—survival and reproduction. It's critical to attain these goals, because that's what biological life is all about. It should be no surprise, then, that the core of personality focuses closely on these goals. On the other hand, because humans live in a dangerous world, it's necessary to deal with complexities imposed by reality. Because we live in groups, it's eventually important to deal with another issue as well: the fact that people other than us also have needs.

This is the general line of thought that lies behind an attempt by Leak and Christopher (1982) to interpret Freud's ideas about three personality components within the framework of evolutionary psychology. They note that the evolutionary view sees behavior as fundamentally self-serving (with one exception, to which we turn momentarily). This self-serving quality in genetically determined behavior resembles the selfish nature of Freud's concept of id. The id is animalistic, primitive, and single-minded about its desires. The id represents the self-interested animal that our genes cause us to be, as the genes attempt to continue their existence.

Neither the id nor the genes is rational. Freud tied rationality to the ego, a mechanism to mediate between id and external reality. Leak and Christopher suggest that the genes also need something to mediate between them and the complexities of reality. They argue that the cortex of the brain evolved to serve this purpose. This evolution in the species would parallel the evolution of the ego in the individual. Both structures—cortex and ego—permit greater planfulness and care in decision making. Both are adaptations that foster survival.

What about the superego? This is the most complex part of Leak and Christopher's argument. To view the superego in evolutionary terms requires one more idea. Specifically, survival isn't just an individual matter. Humans evolved as highly social beings, living and surviving in groups. Because we're so interdependent, we sometimes do better for ourselves in the long run by letting group interests override personal interests in the short run. As noted in Chapter 6, it's been argued that people living in groups evolved mechanisms for inducing—and even forcing—reciprocal altruism (Trivers, 1971). A genetic mechanism to do this is desirable evolutionarily, because it enhances the adaptive success of the group.

In psychological terms, evolving such a mechanism looks like developing a capacity to have a superego. Thus, having a superego confers an evolutionary advantage. People who take up the values of their social group and act by those values are likely to be accepted as members of the group. They're more likely to enjoy the benefits that follow from group membership (for example, having other members take care of you if you're sick). These benefits in turn confer survival value.

In sum, Leak and Christopher suggest that the ego (conscious rationality) is a behavioral management system, for which the id and the superego provide motivation. There are two types of motivation—selfish and group-related—but both have adaptive value. The id adapts to the nonsocial environment, where competition for resources is intense and selfish. The superego is the tendencies that evolved in response to pressures that arose when our ancestors took up group living.

Psychoanalysis and Evolutionary Psychology: Fixations and Mating Patterns

We see one more similarity between psychoanalytic and evolutionary views, which is quite different from the points made by Leak and Christopher. Think back to the Oedipal conflict and the fixations that emerge in this stage. Fixation in the phallic stage for a male is believed to cause an exaggerated attempt to demonstrate that he hasn't been castrated, by having sex with as many women as possible and by seeking power and status. Female fixation in this stage involves a seductiveness that doesn't necessarily lead to sex.

These effects on personality that Freud traced to an Oedipal conflict look remarkably similar to the mating strategies that evolutionary psychologists argue are part of our species. Recall from Chapter 6 the idea that men and women have different reproductive strategies, based on differences in their investment in offspring (Trivers, 1972). The male mating tactic is to create the appearance of power and status and to mate as frequently as possible. The female tactic is to appear highly desirable to males, but to hold out for the best mate available.

These tactics are quite similar to the fixations just described. We can't help but wonder whether Freud noticed a phenomenon that's biologically based, and ascribed psychodynamic properties to it in order to fit it better into his theory.

Psychoanalysis and Conditioning

Let's now turn to the relationship between psychoanalysis and the learning perspective. We noted this relationship in Chapter 12, in passing, when discussing Miller and Dollard's (1941) effort to describe personality in terms of conditioning. In doing so, they were trying to translate psychoanalytic concepts into the ideas of learning. Thus there's a built-in link between aspects of Freud's theory and Miller and Dollard's theory.

Of particular relevance is Miller and Dollard's analysis of repression. This concept is important in Freud's theory, and it therefore was something of a focus for Miller and Dollard. They saw repression as a conditioned tendency to "*not-think*" about things that are distressing. By not-thinking about them, you avoid the pain. Escaping the pain reinforces the tendency to not-think. It thereby builds this tendency in more completely. In this way Miller and Dollard were able to account for a phenomenon that's central to a psychodynamic understanding of behavior, using a very different language.

Though it may not be obvious, development of the not-thinking tendency also is a special case of extinction. That is, learning to "not-think" means that the tendency to "think" is getting weaker. If you're learning to not-think about a distressing topic, whatever stimulus formerly cued the thought no longer does so. Thus the conditioned response (thinking) is extinguishing. It's only one more step to suggest that there may be a connection between *all* instances of extinction and repression, or anticathexis.

Freud said an anticathexis uses energy to keep an impulse or thought out of consciousness. If the restraining force isn't strong enough, the response leaks out and is expressed. Recall that in Chapter 12 we described a phenomenon called spontaneous recovery after extinction. This phenomenon suggests that the behavioral tendency is still there. This in turn suggests that, at some level, extinction may involve creating an active restraint. Because a restraint presumably requires energy, it may be the same process as an anticathexis.

Thinking about *anti*cathexes in conditioning terms leads us to consider *cathexes* as well. We noted in Chapter 8 that psychoanalytic theory distinguishes between id cathexes and ego cathexes. An id cathexis is binding energy in an activity or object that satisfies a need. An ego cathexis doesn't satisfy a need directly. Rather, it binds energy in an object or activity that's *associated* with the satisfying of a need.

There's a similarity between these ideas and conditioning concepts. Primary reinforcers in operant conditioning are substances that directly satisfy a need (e.g., food or water). Obtaining a primary reinforcer might be equivalent to having an id cathexis. Secondary reinforcers are stimuli *associated* with primary reinforcers or which provide a way to *get* primary reinforcers. Getting (or anticipating) a secondary reinforcer seems similar to forming an ego cathexis.

A final similarity between conditioning and psychoanalytic views concerns the role of the unconscious in determining behavior. To behaviorists, behavior stems from prior conditioning. Conditioning occurs outside consciousness. This says, in effect, that behavior results from unconscious influences. In this particular learning view, people do things for reasons they may not be aware of. This is very consistent with one of Freud's beliefs. Obviously Freud had different dynamics in mind. Nonetheless, it's a potentially important link between the views.

Psychoanalysis and Self-Regulation: The Structural Model

The psychoanalytic approach to personality also has certain similarities to the cognitive self-regulation approach. One similarity derives from the notion of a self-regulatory hierarchy. The behavioral qualities involved range from very limited movements, through organized sequences, to abstract higher-level qualities. As pointed out in Chapter 17, attention can be pulled away from the higher levels. When this happens, behavior becomes more spontaneous and responsive to cues of the moment. It's as though low-level action sequences, once triggered, run off by themselves. In contrast to this impulsive style of behavior, actions being regulated according to higher-order values (programs or principles) have a more carefully managed character.

Aspects of this description hint at similarities to Freud's three-part view of personality. Consider the spontaneity and responsiveness to situational cues in the self-regulation model when higher-level control isn't being exerted. This resembles certain characteristics of id functioning. An obvious difference is Freud's assumption that id impulses are primarily sexual or aggressive. The self-regulation model, in contrast, makes no such assumption. It's worth noting, though, that intoxication and deindividuation, which seem to involve loss of control at high levels (Chapter 17), often lead to sexual and/or destructive activity.

The link between id processes and low-level control is tenuous. There's a far stronger resemblance, though, between program control in the self-regulation approach and ego functioning in the psychoanalytic approach. Program control involves planning, decision making, and behavior that's pragmatic, as opposed to either impulsive or principled. These qualities also characterize the ego's functioning.

The levels higher than program control resemble in some ways the functioning of the superego. Engaging in principle control, in some cases at least, causes people to conform to moral principles. Control at the highest level involves an effort to conform to your idealized sense of self. These efforts resemble in some respects the attempt to fit your behavior to the principles of the ego ideal and to avoid a guilty conscience for violating these principles.

The fit between models at this high level isn't perfect, partly because not all principles are moralistic. Yet here's a question: Why did Freud focus on morality and ignore other kinds of ideals? Was it perhaps because morality was so salient an issue in his society at that historical period? If this were so, and if the superego actually pushes behavior toward *other* principles as well as moral ones, the similarity between models would be even greater.

Psychoanalysis and Cognitive Processes

Several links exist between psychoanalytic themes and ideas from cognitive psychology (e.g., Westen, 1998). Matthew Erdelyi (1985) has even suggested that Freud's theory was in large part a theory of cognition. Indeed, he said that Freud was straining toward an analogy between mind and computer, but never got there because the computer wasn't invented yet.

Erdelyi argued that cognitive psychologists essentially reinvented many psychodynamic concepts, though using different names and having different purposes in mind for them. For example, Freud assumed a process that keeps threats out of awareness. This resembles in some ways the filtering process by which the mind "preattentively" selects information to process more fully. Freud's concept of ego becomes "executive control processes." The strength of a cathexis is the amount of attention devoted to something. The topography of the mind becomes a matter of "levels of processing," and distortions become "biases in processing."

As an example of Erdelyi's approach, consider repression and denial (see also Paulhus & Suedfeld, 1988). When there are ideas, thoughts, or perceptions that are painful or threatening, repression and denial prevent them from reaching consciousness. This protective reaction can occur before a threatening stimulus is even experienced (a phenomenon termed *perceptual defense*), or it can involve forgetting an event after it's been experienced.

FIGURE 18.1

An information-processing picture of repression and denial. Input information (top)—whether perceptual or from a suppressed memory—is judged preattentively for its anxiety-inducing value. Then comes a series of implicit decisions. First, does the anxiety the information would create (x) exceed a criterion of "unbearability" (u)? If so, processing stops; if not, the material goes to a memory area corresponding to the preconscious. Next does the predicted anxiety exceed a "serious discomfort" criterion (v)? If so, processing ceases and the information stays in memory; if not, the information moves to consciousness. The final decision is whether to acknowledge openly the information that's now conscious, depending on whether the anxiety from doing so will exceed a final criterion (w). This sequence provides for information never to be stored in memory, to be stored but not reach consciousness, to reach consciousness but be suppressed, or to be acknowledged openly (adapted from Erdelyi, 1985).

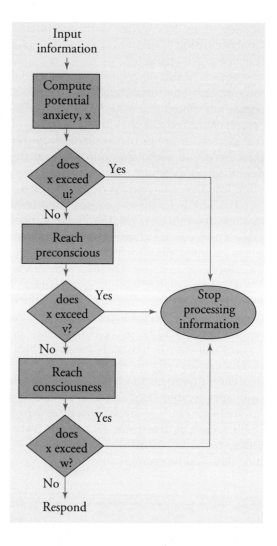

Erdelyi (1985) argued that these phenomena represent a sequence of information-processing decisions, most of them preattentive (Figure 18.1). He says incoming information (or partly activated information from memory) is analyzed preattentively. This yields (among other things) an estimate of how much anxiety would arise if the information were in awareness. If the estimate exceeds a level that's "unbearable," processing stops and the information never goes beyond that point. If the estimate is lower than that, the material goes to a memory area corresponding to the preconscious. Similar decisions are made at other stages, with lower and lower criteria for moving to the next level of processing. This model treats repression, response suppression, and self-deception more generally (Chapter 9) as reflecting checks at several stages of information processing.

The cognitive unconscious.   As implied by the preceding description, today's cognitive view assumes that part of the mind is unconscious. Indeed, the study of unconscious processes is an active area of work, known by such terms as preattentive processes (Dixon, 1981; see also Kihlstrom, 1987). As this term suggests, today's cognitive view tends to equate consciousness with attention. Events that are unconscious are those that get little or no attention.

There are several reasons why an event might get little attention. It may be tagged preattentively as having too much potential for anxiety. Another possibility is that the event is in a part of the nervous system that attentional processes can't reach. Many cognitive scientists think of the nervous system as a set of special-purpose components, only some of which can be examined consciously (Gardner, 1985). Thus the basic "wiring" of the system renders some aspects of experience inaccessible. To put it in the terms of cognitive psychology (Bower, 1970), the information is *available* (it's in the nervous system somewhere) but not *retrievable* (not accessible to consciousness).

Another way for events to be unconscious derives from the fact that certain behaviors are highly preprogrammed and automatic. Acts that are automatic require little or no monitoring. Highly automated sequences can be triggered by stimuli that are noted by the nervous system at some level but never reach consciousness (Bargh, 1997; Norman, 1981). Even elaborate actions drop mostly out of awareness as they become routine (which all experienced drivers discover at one time or other, as they arrive at home with no memory of how they got there). The result is that a person does things, but at the time is unaware of doing them and can't recall having done them even immediately afterward (Bargh, 1997).

These descriptions obviously differ in important ways from Freud's treatment of the unconscious. Only the case involving preattentive estimates of anxiety implies

Highly programmed acts, such as walking, can occur with little awareness. This suggests a possible point of contact between cognitive self-regulation ideas and psycho-dynamic theory.

the sort of process that Freud assumed. All these ideas, however, suggest ways in which information can fail to reach consciousness.

Schemas and transference. Another body of work has linked cognitive processes to the psychoanalytic concept of transference. Transference occurs when a person in therapy displaces emotional reactions onto the therapist. Presumably these reactions were initially stimulated by significant others in the person's earlier life. Recent studies provide a cognitive explanation for such a turn of events (Andersen, Glassman, Chen, & Cole, 1995).

Specifically, the schemas people have of significant others seem chronically to be partially active (thus accessible). As with other instances of partial activation, this makes it easier for the schema to emerge and be used in perceiving and interpreting other stimuli. As a result, you may view many people through the lens of that schema, and not even realize it. If someone does something that reminds you vaguely of your mother's way of inducing guilt, you may use your mother schema and perceive that person as like your mother.

Indeed, when such schemas pop up, self-aspects relating to those significant others emerge as well (Hinkley & Andersen, 1996). Thus, if someone tends to induce guilt as your mother did, you may react just as you did to your mother (e.g., by becoming irrationally angry), even if the reaction isn't appropriate to the present. All this can happen in therapy—or anywhere.

Social Learning and Cognitive Self-Regulation Views

As newer theories were created over the years, personality psychologists were often influenced by ideas that were being used in other areas of psychology. Indeed, this cross-fertilization has become increasingly common. Among the sources of ideas for personality psychologists during the past several decades were learning psychology and cognitive psychology. To a considerable extent, people who sampled from these sources sampled from both rather than just one.

One result of this pattern is a set of similarities between the social-cognitive learning approach (Chapter 13) and the cognitive self-regulation approaches (Chapters 16 and 17). One of these similarities is also shared with Kelly's personal construct theory (Chapter 15). These approaches have diverse historical backgrounds, but their central concepts resemble one another more than just a little. Indeed, as you may have noticed, the work of several researchers pertains not just to one of these views but to two or more of them.

One area of overlap concerns the importance that these approaches ascribe to cognitive processes in creating and organizing representations of the world and of the self. The differences among theories on this issue stem largely from the fact that each has different *reasons* for emphasizing cognition.

In discussing cognition from the point of view of the social learning approach, Mischel (1973) said that if we want to understand how learning takes place, we have to look at people's mental representations of stimuli, rather than the stimuli themselves. People learn from what *they* think is there, not what an outsider thinks is there. The meanings conveyed, and the way the stimuli are mentally transformed, determine how people will respond to them (see also Bandura, 1977a, 1986).

From the learning perspective, these statements emphasize that human learning is more complicated than it seems. An event doesn't lead automatically to conditioning that's the same for everyone. From the learning perspective, such statements are elaborations, or qualifications, on theories of learning. They say to other learning theorists that the *person* has to be considered in analyzing learning. That's the point of statements like this—*when they're made from the learning perspective.*

When embedded in Kelly's theory of personal constructs or today's cognitive view on personality, however, ideas about the role of cognition take on a broader life. From these views, cognitive processes are central to an understanding of *everything* about personality. When he's taking the cognitive view on personality, Mischel focuses not on the subtleties of learning but on how people organize their understanding. Note the difference of emphasis. In the cognitive view, the idea that people organize experience is an important principle regarding the essence of personality. Learning per se is more peripheral, and may even be disregarded altogether. Cognitive processes are also critical to the self-regulation view on personality, although once again there's a slight difference of emphasis. The focus in the self-regulation approach is mostly on the role cognitions play in creating behavior.

Another similarity between the social learning and cognitive self-regulation viewpoints concerns expectancies. (Indeed, expectancies also appear in the need-and-motive approach, and are implicit in feelings of personal competence in ego psychology.) All these approaches see expectancies as determinants of how hard people try to reach their goals. Many people—Rotter (1954, 1966), Bandura (1977a, 1986), Kanfer (1977), Kirsch (1985, 1990), Mischel (1973, 1979), Carver and Scheier (1981, 1990, 1998), and others—have pointed out that people hold expectancies about the effect their actions are likely to have and expectancies about whether they can do the things they want to do. These expectations can influence how much effort a person puts out, and what the person learns from an event.

The social learning and cognitive self-regulation approaches also resemble each other in the structure they assume within behavior. (At this point Kelly's theory becomes less relevant, because Kelly didn't say much about behaving, as opposed to construing.) The social learning view assumes people have incentives, which draw them forward into action. Incentives are virtually the same as goals, a concept that plays a large role in the cognitive self-regulation perspective. In the self-regulation view, people have images of goals, which they use as guides for action. Indeed, other perspectives also have constructs that serve a comparable role in guiding behavior (see Table 18.1).

There is, however, an important difference of emphasis here between the learning and self-regulation views. It concerns the concept of reinforcement. The social learning view explicitly uses this concept, which is basic to the principle of instrumental learning. As we noted in Chapter 13, however, one prominent theorist of the social learning view—Bandura—has consistently used the concept differently than

TABLE 18.1

Comparable behavioral concepts taken from four perspectives on personality.	
Concept	**Theoretical perspective**
Incentive	Social learning
Goal, reference value	Self-regulation
Motive	Need and motive
Ego cathexis	Psychoanalytic

did earlier theorists. To Bandura, reinforcers create mental representations of future incentives. They cause people to learn expectancies about what actions are useful in what situations. But reinforcers don't directly increase the tendency to do the acts that preceded them. The way Bandura used this concept raises questions about whether its meaning is compatible with that assumed by other learning theorists.

Keep in mind, though, that Bandura stands with one foot in the learning perspective and one in the cognitive self-regulation perspective. His view on reinforcement may reflect Bandura the self-regulation theorist more than it does Bandura the learning theorist. As we noted in Chapter 17, self-regulation theorists are more divided than learning theorists on the issue of reinforcement. Some assume that people engage in self-reinforcement after success and self-punishment after failure (the functions Bandura assumes). Others see this idea as less useful.

This may be one of those points where the personal histories of the theorists play a role in how their theories are constructed. Most self-regulation theorists who assume a role for self-reinforcement began their work in the learning perspective. Only gradually did they become identified with the emerging cognitive self-regulation view. Perhaps they retain a role for self-reinforcement from a kind of psychological inertia. That is, maybe they retain it primarily because it represents a comfortable tie to the past.

In considering this question, it's also of interest that these theorists are more likely to talk about *self*-reinforcement than external reinforcement (e.g., Kanfer, 1977). It's the person's own goal representations that matter, after all, and only *you* can decide whether or not your goal's been met. Thus self-reinforcement, rather than external reinforcement, is at the heart of these discussions.

To other people, introducing self-reinforcement as a concept simply raises more questions. Certainly people often feel a sense of pride after success and sadness after failure. But do these reactions create the learning? Or are they just emotional reactions to informational events, with the informational events being what's really important? This is an issue that hasn't been settled within the self-regulation perspective (or to some extent even within the learning perspective—see Timberlake, 1993; Viken & McFall, 1994).

Neoanalytic and Cognitive Self-Regulation Perspectives

The learning and cognitive self-regulation perspectives arose in the context of academic psychology, with an emphasis on controlled research. Early neoanalytic psychology, in contrast, derived primarily from the clinical experiences of the theorists. Despite this difference, there's a surprising convergence across these views (cf. Westen, 1991).

Consider, for example, a series of conceptual similarities between self-regulation ideas and Adler's ideas. Recall that Adler saw people as motivated by feelings of inferiority, which make them strive for superiority. He referred to the continual struggle for greater competence as a great upward drive. As we said in Chapter 10, Adler believed that feelings of inferiority cause healthy people to work throughout life toward greater integration and perfection.

Adler also believed that people established long-term goals for their lives. He referred to this as the principle of *fictional finalism*. This term conveys the sense that people are motivated by views of their final outcomes and that those views are invented, or fictional. Future goals are always fictional in the sense that they aren't yet real. People act, however, as though they're headed toward these end points, and use them as guides for their efforts. To Adler these future-oriented goals (which he also called guiding self-ideals) are more important determinants of behavior than are events in the person's past.

These ideas resemble ideas from the cognitive self-regulation perspective in two ways. First, Adler's thinking placed considerable emphasis on goals, which are also a cornerstone of the self-regulation view of personality. Indeed, Adler's fictional life plans seem especially similar to the possible selves discussed by Markus and her colleagues.

The other similarity relates to the structure of people's strivings. Adler's account resembles the self-regulation approach in one respect here, while differing from it in another. The similarity is Adler's belief that shifts in behavior are prompted by discrepancies between where you are and where you want to be. When the person notices an inferiority (as Adler called it), there's an effort to overcome it. The structure of this process is very similar to the structure of the feedback loop described in Chapter 17. The difference is that Adler emphasized the role of subjective feelings of inferiority. The self-regulation model doesn't assume such feelings, but simply assumes that when goals have been set, the person tries to meet them.

Maslow's Hierarchy and Hierarchies of Self-Regulation

There are also similarities between elements of the phenomenological perspective and the cognitive self-regulation perspective. We noted earlier a strong thematic resemblance between Kelly's theory of personal constructs and today's cognitive theories. But this isn't the only similarity. Consider Maslow's hierarchy of motives (Chapter 14). There are at least two similarities between that hierarchy and the self-regulation hierarchy.

First, Maslow conceived of the motive qualities at the top of the hierarchy as more abstract and subtle in their influence, but also as more integrative, than those lower. The levels of the hierarchy of control also have this character. Second, Maslow saw the lower motives as more demanding than the higher ones, in the sense that a deficit or a problem lower in the hierarchy draws the person's attention to it and forces the person to deal with it. Similarly, in the control hierarchy, if a problem develops at a low level, attention is brought to that level in an attempt to resolve the problem.

There are, however, big differences between these views, as well. The biggest difference concerns the "content" of the hierarchies. Maslow's analysis was explicitly an analysis of *motives,* intended to incorporate both biological needs and psychological motives. The control hierarchy, in contrast, focuses on the structure of *action,* with goals that relate to qualities of behavior. This difference means that the two hierarchies are very different at their low levels. Maslow's hierarchy points to survival needs, the other hierarchy points to muscle movements.

At higher levels, though, the two hierarchies are more similar. The highest level of control in the self-regulation view seems roughly equivalent to the concept of self-actualization used by Maslow and Rogers. There's still one difference, however. Woven through the writings of Maslow and Rogers on this topic is the sense that self-actualization is something that happens *to* you, if you can free yourself from the demands of motives at lower levels and just let yourself sense what your body is saying is right for you. It shouldn't involve an effort. If you're *trying* to self-actualize, you probably *aren't* self-actualizing.

The nature of self-regulation in the control hierarchy is ambiguous in that regard. It's by no means clear that such high-level self-regulation is free of effort. On the other hand, the nature of the goal at the highest level—an ideal self that relates to the many principles in force at the next lower level—is quite diffuse. It's so diffuse, in fact, that it isn't too hard to imagine that self-regulation toward it might also feel diffuse. Thus the subjective experience of self-regulation at the highest level might *not* feel effortful in the same way as does self-regulation at lower levels.

Self-Actualization and Self-Regulation

Three other similarities between these two views of personality go beyond Maslow's hierarchy. One similarity is that both viewpoints use concepts corresponding to idealized and experienced qualities of self. The labels *real self* and *ideal self* are explicit in the phenomenological view of Rogers. The sense of an idealized self is also involved at the top of the control hierarchy, as is the experienced actual self that's compared with it.

The comparison process itself is also similar between the approaches. Rogers emphasized that people compare their current selves with their ideal selves and that they experience anxiety when there's incongruity between them. The comparison between a sensed condition and a standard, or reference point, is also intimately involved in the self-regulation perspective—not just with respect to an ideal self but at all levels of the hierarchy.

Finally, both approaches place an emphasis on conscious experience, though for different reasons. The phenomenologists emphasize it because consciousness is the searchlight of your will. It's the point where you experience the flow of life. Self-regulation theorists emphasize it because they see conscious experience as reflecting the operation of control mechanisms behind behavior. The question of will is rarely dealt with by most cognitive or self-regulation theorists, but on occasion it's been addressed indirectly via the concept of attention. Norman and Shallice (1986) suggested that attention is involved in behavior mostly when a plan must be changed or when a decision must be monitored. When viewed this way, attention begins to resemble will.

Dispositions and Their Equivalents in Other Models

Another resemblance among theories brings us full circle to an idea with which we began this book. We started with the concept of dispositions, and we now return to it. As we noted in Chapter 1, a major theme of personality psychology is how people differ from one another—not just temporarily, but in an enduring way. This theme provides a basis for the dispositional perspective on personality. Dispositions take a variety of forms—traits, enduring motive qualities, and (in a biological extension of this view) inherited temperaments.

The essence of dispositions, if not the concept itself, is also prominent in at least two more views on personality. The psychoanalytic view assumes that people derive stable personality qualities from childhood psychosexual crises. The neoanalytic view holds that early experience influences personality in other ways. Erikson assumed that childhood psychosocial crises shape adult personality, and object relations and attachment theories make similar assumptions.

These theories have a good deal of diversity about the source of dispositions. Yet the theories share two assumptions: that something is stamped or etched into the individual early in life, and that this characteristic continues to influence the person from then on. The disposition has been viewed as a biological temperament, a transformation of sexual drives, a reflection of a psychosocial crisis, a learned motive quality, and simply a trait. Yet all these theories treat the disposition as having an enduring impact on the person's life experiences. This similarity among approaches, which is often overlooked, is not a trivial one.

Indeed, the disposition concept also has a place in other views. For example, one version of the learning approach assumes that people differ in locus of control and that these differences help determine how and what people learn. One aspect of the self-regulation approach assumes that people vary in the disposition to be self-reflective and thus carefully self-regulated. In both of these cases (and many others as well), it's assumed that individual differences are stable dispositions that influence a broad range of the person's experiences.

Recurrent Themes, Viewed from Different Angles

Our emphasis in the preceding section has been on the possibility that certain ideas in one theoretical perspective resemble ideas from another perspective. We also want to note another kind of similarity across perspectives. This is a similarity in issues considered by the theories. We said earlier in this chapter that different theories often address different issues. That's true in many respects. But at least a couple of themes seem to recur, either strongly or in a more muted way, across a wide range of perspectives.

Impulse and Restraint

One of these themes concerns what seems to be a basic distinction between *acting* (perhaps impulsively) and *restraint* from acting. One place where this issue clearly emerges is delay of gratification, where a choice must be made between a small reward now versus a larger reward later. In earlier chapters we discussed delay of gratification from the angle of psychoanalysis (where we said that the ego restrains id impulses), ego psychology (where we described variations in ego-control and ego-resiliency), social learning theory (where we considered the effect of models), and the cognitive view (where the focus was on mental images that can foster restraint).

However, the issue of impulse versus restraint also arises in other approaches to personality. It comes up in trait psychology, where conscientiousness is defined partly by restraint in the face of temptation. It comes up in temperament theory, where activity and maybe impulsiveness are thought to be genetically based. It comes up in biological process models, where impulsiveness and behavioral inhibition relate to nervous system functioning. The question of how and why a person chooses to act quickly versus hold back from acting is basic. It's no wonder that many theories say something or other about this question.

Individual versus Group Needs

Another fundamental issue concerns the competing pressure of individualistic self-interest versus the needs implied by being involved in groups (or couples). In specific examples, this issue is often tangled up with the issue of action versus restraint. This is because the needs of others are often what urge restraint. Conceptually, however, it's a separate issue.

Earlier in this chapter we noted that psychoanalytic theory and evolutionary psychology both confront the contrast between these pressures. In psychoanalysis, the ego deals with social reality as well as physical reality, and the superego reflects certain aspects of social needs. In evolutionary psychology, people have individualistic needs—survival, competition for mates. But they also have group-based needs—cooperation with a mate and with the larger society.

This distinction between individualistic and social goals also appears in other approaches. In trait psychology it emerges in the nature of agreeableness and of introversion versus extraversion. In the motive approach, it shows up in motives to achieve and exert power versus affiliate and attain intimacy. It's in the biological process approach, in the dimension of unsocialized sensation seeking; it's in the psychosocial approach, in the issue of separation-individuation versus merger; it's in the self-actualization approach, in the balance between the self-actualizing tendency and the need for positive regard. In the self-regulation approach, the same issue appears in the effects of attending to private versus public aspects of the self.

In all of these cases, people confront the need to balance these two competing pressures. Both are important, in different ways. Given all this attention from theorists of so many different perspectives, this issue appears to be critically important in human experience.

Combining Perspectives

As is now apparent, similarities do exist between seemingly unrelated approaches to personality. These similarities may, in time, allow an integration of these approaches with one another. It's probably safe to say, though, that most personality psychologists view such integration as a distant goal. One reason for this is the sheer size and complexity of the job.

Theorists do sometimes try to integrate across boundaries. For example, Cattell (1985) tried to merge psychoanalytic elements of id, ego, and superego with physiological qualities of temperament and cognitive variables such as expectancy, all in a factor-analytic framework. It's hard, however, to fit all these pieces together in a way that people can easily use.

Theorists such as Eysenck and Zuckerman have attempted to integrate across two or three perspectives. In describing Eysenck's work in earlier chapters, we treated it as two sets of ideas with separate focuses of convenience. Some of the ideas are biological, dealing with individual differences in brain function (and to a lesser extent the heritability of these differences). Others form a hierarchical model of the relations among acts, habits, traits, and supertraits. Though we presented these ideas as separate subtheories, Eysenck viewed them as an integrated model with multiple facets. Zuckerman (1991a, 1994) has made a similar kind of statement, binding together—in a single model—trait, inheritance, and biological-process views.

Eclecticism

Another option, exercised by many psychologists, is to take an eclectic approach to personality. This involves drawing useful ideas from many theories, rather than being tied to just one or two. Essentially, it means saying that different ideas are useful for different purposes, and that there may be no approach that's best for all purposes. To understand a phenomenon, you may need to look at it from the angle of a theory that focuses on it, rather than a theory that doesn't. As Scarr (1985, p. 511) put it, "There is no need to choose a single lens for psychology when we can enjoy a kaleidoscope of perspectives."

This sort of approach suggests that views of personality from the various perspectives may be mutually supportive. It may not be necessary to integrate them into a single set of constructs or principles. As we said earlier, the "focus of convenience" of one theory differs from those of other theories. By taking bits of theory across several focuses of convenience, perhaps we can obtain a more well-rounded picture of what personality is really like.

Thus, many personality psychologists today accept the idea that personality was shaped by evolutionary pressures. Most assume there are inherited temperaments, and that the processes by which personality is reflected are biological. Several psychoanalytic ideas are also widely accepted—for example, that determinants of behavior are sometimes outside awareness, and that mechanisms exist protecting us from things we don't want to deal with. Many personality psychologists accept the idea that early experiences have a big impact on what people are like. (Indeed, there's even evidence from the learning lab that associations conditioned first to a stimulus are more permanent than associations conditioned later—Bouton, 1994.) Obviously learning has an impact on personality, and people do appear to organize the experiences of their lives in idiosyncratic ways. People may well have an inner voice of self-actualization. Behavior may even reflect the operation of feedback loops.

All of these ideas may be true, or only some of them. All of them may be useful, or perhaps only some of them. Many psychologists pick and choose bits from various perspectives and use them where they seem reasonable. The choice among the array of available elements is an individual one.

Perhaps the simplest illustration of this eclectic approach is that psychologists almost universally acknowledge the importance to personality of both biology and learning. Everyone does this—people who focus on biology, people who focus on learning, and people who focus on some other part of personality. To show just how sensible this particular eclecticism is, let's note more closely a couple of examples of the interweaving of biology and learning.

An Example: Biology and Learning as Complementary Influences on Personality

The first example comes from the work of theorists whose focus lies in the study of temperaments—Buss and Plomin (1975, 1984). Temperaments are genetically based dispositions that appear early in life and influence many different behaviors. They influence people's transactions with their world throughout life.

Despite this emphasis on built-in behavioral tendencies, however, Buss and Plomin point out that the expression of temperaments can be modified. Behavior can be shaped—even in ways that run contrary to the temperament's "natural" bias. This heavily biological theory thus includes the assumption that learning processes make important contributions to personality.

Buss and Plomin began with an interest in biological tendencies and added a role for learning. Other theorists began with an interest in learning and added a role for biological influences. Early learning theorists tended to see the human mind as a "blank slate" on which any kind of personality can be sketched, depending only on the person's experiences. It's clear, however, that this isn't true. There are biological constraints on learning.

For example, some associations are learned more easily than others. A term often used to describe this is **preparedness.** This term refers to the idea that organisms are prepared for certain links to occur by conditioning more easily than others

Both biological and learning principles are needed to understand fully the phenomenon of preparedness—such as the biological readiness that chimps and people show in learning to use tools.

(Seligman & Hager, 1972). Preparedness isn't an all-or-nothing matter. Rather it's a dimension of ease versus difficulty in creating learned connections. Presumably this variable is biologically influenced.

As an example, if you get sick to your stomach, a conditioned aversive response could develop toward any number of stimuli. If conditioning depended just on association between stimuli, you should get conditioned aversions to *all* neutral stimuli at the aversive event. Research shows, though, that you're more likely to develop an aversion to a *flavor* experienced just before getting sick than to other stimuli. Even rats are more likely to associate getting sick with something they ate or drank rather than something they saw or heard (Garcia & Koelling, 1966). Apparently the links are just easier to create in the nervous system for some pairs of events than others.

Preparedness also seems to be involved in instrumental learning. That is, some kinds of actions are easier for animals to learn than others, even if the same reward follows both. For example, rats learn more quickly to avoid a foot shock by jumping than by pressing a bar (Wickelgren, 1977). Pigeons quickly learn to peck a spot to obtain food, but it's hard to get them to learn to *refrain* from pecking to get food.

Thus, an eclectic acceptance of both biology and learning as important influences on personality seems well-founded. Perhaps other combinations will prove in the future to be similarly well-founded.

Which Theory Is Best?

As we said a little earlier, one answer to the question of which theory is best is that no theory is perfect, and you may benefit from using bits and pieces of many theories. We should point out, though, that this question is sometimes answered in another way. This answer returns us to a point we made in the book's opening chapter. It may provide a fitting way to end, as well.

Over a century ago, William James wrote that theories must account reasonably well for the phenomena that people experience as real, but to be successful a theory needs to do more than that. He wrote (James, 1890, p. 312) that people will believe those theories which " . . . are most interesting, those which appeal most urgently to our aesthetic, emotional, and active needs." Put more simply, the theory that's best is the one you *like* best. The one that's best—for you—is the one that appeals to you most, the one you find most interesting and engaging. Edward Tolman (1959, p. 152) also put it pretty simply: "I have liked to think about psychology in ways that have proved congenial to me . . . . In the end, the only sure criterion is to have fun. And I have had fun."

SUMMARY

Although various perspectives on personality differ from one another in important ways, there are also similarities among theories. The psychoanalytic perspective has similarities to at least three alternative views. First, ideas about biological evolution in the species parallel Freud's ideas about the evolution of personality in the individual. That is, in each case a primitive force (the genes, the id) needs another force to help it deal with reality (the cortex, the ego), and eventually it also needs a force to keep it in contact with the social world (inherited sensitivity to social influence, the superego). Second, one branch of the conditioning view was devised to create a link between psychoanalytic concepts and the language of learning. Third, the psychoanalytic view and the cognitive self-regulation view resemble each other in two ways. The notion of a hierarchy of control echoes psychoanalytic theory's three components of personality. Work on cognition has also developed concepts that resemble in some ways those postulated years earlier by Freud.

A substantial overlap exists between the social learning and the cognitive self-regulation viewpoints. They share an emphasis on mental representations of the world (as does Kelly's theory of personal constructs), although the theories have somewhat different rationales for the emphasis. They also have similar views of the importance of people's expectancies and similar views on the basic structure of behavior.

A similarity also exists between self-regulation ideas and Adler's neoanalytic theory. Both assume that behavior is aimed at reducing discrepancies, and both emphasize the importance of people's long-term goals. The notion of a hierarchy in self-regulation also suggests a similarity between that view and the phenomenological view, especially Maslow's. Maslow's motive hierarchy deals with several motives that are ignored in the control hierarchy, but at their upper levels the models resemble each other more closely. The principle of self-actualization also resembles the self-regulation model in the concepts of ideal and actual self and the desire for congruity between them.

Another similarity among approaches concerns the concept of disposition. Obviously, this construct is central to the dispositional perspective. It's also important in the psychoanalytic and neoanalytic views. In all these cases (and by implication in others as well), the assumption is made that people have qualities that endure over time and circumstances and that influence their behaviors, thoughts, and feelings.

Although the various theories differ in their focus, certain issues do seem to recur across many of them. This represents another kind of similarity among the theories. One issue that many different theories address is the polarity between action and restraint. Another is the competing pressures of individual self-interest and communal interest.

Thus, there are areas of overlap among theories. Yet the theories also differ. Which, then, is right? One answer is that all perspectives seem to have something of value to offer. Many psychologists prefer an eclectic position, taking elements and ideas from several views, rather than just one. At a minimum, people who operate within the framework of a given theory must take into account limitations imposed by other views. For example, temperament theorists believe much of personality is determined by genetics. Yet they also assume that temperaments are modified by learning. Learning theorists believe that personality is a product of a learning history. Yet it's clear that some kinds of learning are easier than others. Perhaps the future will see greater emphasis on this eclecticism, the sharing of ideas from one perspective to another.

GLOSSARY

Preparedness The idea that some conditioning is easy because the animal is biologically "prepared" for it to happen.

references

Abramson, L. Y., Alloy, L. B., & Metalsky, G. I. (1995). Hopelessness depression.Zn G. M. Buchanan & M. E. P. Seligman (Eds.), *Explanatory style* (pp. 113–134). Hillsdale, NJ: Erlbaum.

Abramson, L. Y., Metalsky, G. I., & Alloy, L. B. (1989). Hopelessness depression: A theory-based subtype of depression. *Psychological Review, 96,* 358–372.

Abramson, L. Y., Seligman, M. E. P., & Teasdale, J. D. (1978). Learned helplessness in humans: Critique and reformulation. *Journal of Abnormal Psychology, 87,* 49–74.

Adams, G. R., & Shea, J. A. (1979). The relationship between identity status, locus of control, and ego development. *Journal of Youth and Adolescence, 8,* 81–89.

Adams, J. A. (1976). Issues for a closed-loop theory of motor learning. In G. E. Stelmach (Ed.), *Motor control: Issues and trends* (pp. 87–107). New York: Academic Press.

Adams-Webber, J. R. (1979). *Personal construct theory: Concepts and applications.* New York: Wiley.

Adler, A. (1917). *Study of organ inferiority and its psychical compensation.* New York: Nervous and Mental Diseases Publishing Company.

Adler, A. (1927). *Practice and theory of individual psychology.* New York: Harcourt, Brace, & World.

Adler, A. (1929). *The science of living.* New York: Greenberg.

Adler, A. (1930). Individual psychology. In C. Murchison (Ed.), *Psychologies of 1930.* Worcester, MA: Clark University Press.

Adler, A. (1931). *What life should mean to you.* Boston: Little, Brown.

Adler, A. (1956). *The individual psychology of Alfred Adler: A systematic presentation of selections from his writings.* H. L. Ansbacher & R. R. Ansbacher (Eds.). New York: Basic Books.

Adler, A. (1958). *What life should mean to you.* New York: Capricorn Books. (Originally published, 1931)

Adler, A. (1964). *Social interest: A challenge to mankind.* New York: Capricorn Books. (Originally published, 1933)

Agostinelli, G., Sherman, S. J., Presson, C. C., & Chassin, L. (1992). Self-protection and self-enhancement biases in estimates of population prevalence. *Personality and Social Psychology Bulletin, 18,* 631–642.

Agronick, G. S., & Duncan, L. E. (1998). Personality and social change: Individual differences, life path, and importance attributed to the women's movement. *Journal of Personality and Social Psychology, 74,* 1545–1555.

Ahadi, S., & Diener, E. (1989). Multiple determinants and effect size. *Journal of Personality and Social Psychology, 56,* 398–406.

Ainsworth, M. D. S. (1983). Patterns of infant-mother attachment as related to maternal care. In D. Magnusson & V. Allen (Eds.), *Human development: An interactional perspective.* New York: Academic Press.

Ainsworth, M. D. S. (1989). Attachments beyond infancy. *American Psychologist, 44,* 709–716.

Ainsworth, M. D. S., Blehar, M. C., Waters, E., & Wall, T. (1978). *Patterns of attachment.* Hillsdale, NJ: Erlbaum.

Ajzen, I. (1985). From intentions to actions: A theory of planned behavior. In J. Kuhl & J. Beckmann (Eds.), *Action control: From cognition to behavior.* Heidelberg & New York: Springer-Verlag.

Ajzen, I. (1988). *Attitudes, personality, and behavior.* Chicago: Dorsey Press.

Ajzen, I., & Fishbein, M. (1980). *Understanding attitudes and predicting social behavior.* Englewood Cliffs, NJ: Prentice-Hall.

Alexander, R. (1979). *Darwinism and human affairs.* Seattle: University of Washington Press.

Alicke, M. D. (1985). Global self-evaluation as determined by the desirability and controllability of trait adjectives. *Journal of Personality and Social Psychology, 49,* 1621–1630.

Allen, J. J., Iacono, W. G., Depue, R. A., Arbisi, P. (1993). Regional electroencephalographic asymmetries in bipolar seasonal affective disorder before and after exposure to bright light. *Biological Psychiatry, 33,* 642–646.

Allen, L. S., & Gorski, R. A. (1992). Sexual orientation and the size of the anterior commissure in the human brain. *Proceedings of the National Academy of Sciences of the U. S. A., 89,* 7199–7202.

Allen, M. G. (1976). Twin studies of affective illness. *Archives of General Psychiatry, 33,* 1476–1478.

Alloy, L. B., & Abramson, L. Y. (1988). Depressive realism: Four theoretical perspectives. In L. B. Alloy (Ed.), *Cognitive processes in depression* (pp. 223–265). New York: Guilford Press.

Allport, G. W. (1937). *Personality: A psychological interpretation.* New York: Holt.

Allport, G. W. (1961). *Pattern and growth in personality.* New York: Holt, Rinehart, & Winston.

Allport, G. W., & Odbert, H. S. (1936). Trait-names: A psycho-lexical study. *Psychological Monographs, 47* (1, Whole No. 211).

Almagor, M., Tellegen, A., & Waller, N. G. (1995). The Big Seven model: A cross-cultural replication and further exploration of the basic dimensions of natural language trait descriptors. *Journal of Personality and Social Psychology, 69,* 300–307.

Amabile, T. M. (1985). Motivation and creativity: Effects of motivational orientation on creative writers. *Journal of Personality and Social Psychology, 48,* 393–399.

Amsel, A. (1967). Partial reinforcement effects on vigor and persistence: Advances in frustration theory derived from a variety of within-subject experiments. In K. W. Spence & J. T. Spence (Eds.), *The psychology of learning and motivation* (Vol. 1). New York: Academic Press.

Anastasi, A. (1988). *Psychological testing* (6th ed.). New York: Macmillan.

Andersen, S. M., & Cole, S. W. (1990). "Do I know you?": The role of significant others in general social perception. *Journal of Personality and Social Psychology, 59,* 384–399.

Andersen, S. M., Glassman, N. S., Chen, S., & Cole, S. W. (1995). Transference in social perception: The role of chronic accessibility in significant-other representations. *Journal of Personality and Social Psychology, 69,* 41–57.

Anderson, C. A., & Weiner, B. (1992). Attribution and attributional processes in personality. In G. Caprara & G. Heck (Eds.), *Modern personality psychology: Critical reviews and new directions* (pp. 295–324). New York: Harvester Wheatsheaf.

Anderson, J. R. (1976). *Language, memory and thought.* Hillsdale, NJ: Erlbaum.

Anderson, J. R. (1985). *Cognitive psychology and its implications* (2nd ed.). New York: Freeman.

Anderson, J. R. (1991). The adaptive nature of human categorization. *Psychological Review, 98,* 409–429.

Anderson, J. W. (1988). Henry Murray's early career: A psychobiographical exploration. *Journal of Personality, 56,* 138–171.

Anderson, R. C., & Pichert, J. W. (1978). Recall of previously unrecallable information following a shift in perspective. *Journal of Verbal Learning and Verbal Behavior, 17,* 1–12.

Ardrey, R. (1966). *The territorial imperative.* New York: Dell.

Arkin, R. M., & Baumgardner, A. H. (1985). Self-handicapping. In J. H. Harvey & G. Weary (Eds.), *Attribution: Basic issues and applications.* New York: Academic Press.

Arkin, R. M., Lake, E. A., & Baumgardner, A. H. (1986). Shyness and self-presentation. In W. H. Jones, J. M. Cheek, & S. R. Briggs (Eds.), *A sourcebook on shyness: Research and treatment.* New York: Plenum.

Arnett, P. A., Smith, S. S., & Newman, J. P. (1997). Approach and avoidance motivation in psychopathic criminal offenders during passive avoidance. *Journal of Personality and Social Psychology, 72,* 1413–1428.

Aron, E. N., & Aron, A. (1997). Sensory-processing sensitivity and its relation to introversion and emotionality. *Journal of Personality and Social Psychology, 73,* 345–368.

Asendorpf, J. B., & Wilpers, S. (1998). Personality effects on social relationships. *Journal of Personality and Social Psychology, 74,* 1531–1544.

Aserinsky, E., & Kleitman, N. (1953). Regularly occurring periods of eye motility, and concomitant phenomena during sleep. *Science, 118,* 273.

Atkinson, J. W. (1957). Motivational determinants of risk-taking behavior. *Psychological Review, 64,* 359–372.

Atkinson, J. W., & Birch, D. (1970). *The dynamics of action.* New York: Wiley.

Atkinson, J. W., & Birch, D. (1978). *Introduction to motivation* (2nd ed.). New York: D. Van Nostrand.

Atkinson, J. W., Heyns, R. W., & Veroff, J. (1954). The effect of experimental arousal of the affiliation motive on thematic apperception. *Journal of Abnormal and Social Psychology, 49,* 405–410.

Atkinson, J. W., & McClelland, D. C. (1948). The projective expression of needs II. The effect of different intensities of the hunger drive on thematic apperception. *Journal of Experimental Psychology, 38,* 643–658.

Atkinson, J. W., & Raynor, J. O. (Eds.). (1974). *Motivation and achievement.* Washington, DC: V. H. Winston.

Austin, J. T., & Vancouver, J. B. (1996). Goal constructs in psychology: Structure, process, and content. *Psychological Bulletin, 120,* 338–375.

Avery, R. R., & Ryan, R. M. (1988). Object relations and ego development: Comparison and correlates in middle childhood. *Journal of Personality, 56,* 547–569.

Avia, M. D., & Kanfer, F. H. (1980). Coping with aversive stimulation: The effects of training in a self-management context. *Cognitive Therapy and Research, 4,* 73–81.

Axelrod, R., & Hamilton, W. D. (1981). The evolution of cooperation. *Science, 211,* 1390–1396.

Axline, V. M. (1947). *Play therapy.* Boston: Houghton-Mifflin.

Axline, V. M. (1964). *Dibs: In search of self.* Boston: Houghton Mifflin.

Ayllon, T., & Azrin, N. H. (1965). The measurement and reinforcement of behavior of psychotics. *Journal of the Experimental Analysis of Behavior, 8,* 357–383.

Ayllon, T., & Azrin, N. H. (1968). *The token economy.* New York: Appleton-Century-Crofts.

Babad, E. Y. (1973). Effects of informational input on the "social deprivation-satisfaction effect." *Journal of Personality and Social Psychology, 27,* 1–5.

Bailey, J. M., Gaulin, S., Agyei, Y., & Gladue, B. A. (1994). Effects of gender and sexual orientation on evolutionarily relevant aspects of human mating psychology. *Journal of Personality and Social Psychology, 66,* 1081–1093.

Bailey, J. M., & Pillard, R. C. (1991). A genetic study of male sexual orientation. *Archives of General Psychiatry, 48,* 1089–1096.

Bailey, J. M., Pillard, R. C., Neale, M. C., & Agyei, Y. (1993). Heritable factors influence sexual orientation in women. *Archives of General Psychiatry, 50,* 217–223.

Bain, A. (1859). *The emotions and the will.* London: Longmans.

Baker, J. W., II, & Schaie, K. W. (1969). Effects of aggressing "alone" or "with another" on physiological and psychological arousal. *Journal of Personality and Social Psychology, 12,* 80–86.

Balay, J., & Shevrin, H. (1988). The subliminal psychodynamic activation method: A critical review. *American Psychologist, 43,* 161–174.

Baldwin, J. M. (1902). *Social and ethical interpretations in mental development* (3rd ed.). New York: Macmillan.

Baldwin, M. W. (1992). Relational schemas and the processing of social information. *Psychological Bulletin, 112,* 461–484.

Baldwin, M. W., Carrell, S. E., & Lopez, D. F. (1990). Priming relationship schemas: My advisor and the Pope are watching me from the back of my mind. *Journal of Experimental Social Psychology, 26,* 435–454.

Balmary, M. (1979). *Psychoanalyzing psychoanalysis: Freud and the hidden fault of his father.* Baltimore, MD: Johns Hopkins University Press.

Baltes, P. B., & Staudinger, U. M. (1993). The search for a psychology of wisdom. *Current Directions in Psychological Science, 2,* 75–80.

Bandura, A. (1965). Influence of models' reinforcement contingencies on the acquisition of imitative response. *Journal of Personality and Social Psychology, 1,* 589–595.

Bandura, A. (1969). *Principles of behavior modification.* New York: Holt, Rinehart, & Winston.

Bandura, A. (1971). Vicarious and self-reinforcement processes. In R. Glaser (Ed.), *The nature of reinforcement.* New York: Academic Press.

Bandura, A. (1973). *Aggression: A social learning analysis.* Englewood Cliffs, NJ: Prentice-Hall.

Bandura, A. (1976). Self-reinforcement: Theoretical and methodological considerations. *Behaviorism, 4,* 135–155.

Bandura, A. (1977a). *Social learning theory.* Englewood Cliffs, NJ: Prentice-Hall.

Bandura, A. (1977b). Self-efficacy: Toward a unifying theory of behavioral change. *Psychological Review, 84,* 191–215.

Bandura, A. (1978). The self system in reciprocal determinism. *American Psychologist, 33,* 344–358.

Bandura, A. (1982a). Self-efficacy mechanism in human agency. *American Psychologist, 37,* 122–147.

Bandura, A. (1982b). The psychology of chance encounters and life paths. *American Psychologist, 37,* 747–755.

Bandura, A. (1986). *Social foundations of thought and action: A social cognitive theory.* Englewood Cliffs, NJ: Prentice-Hall.

Bandura, A. (1997). *Self-efficacy: The exercise of control.* New York: Freeman.

Bandura, A., Adams, N. E., & Beyer, J. (1977). Cognitive processes mediating behavioral change. *Journal of Personality and Social Psychology, 35,* 125–139.

Bandura, A., Adams, N. E., Hardy, A. B., & Howells, G. N. (1980). Tests of the generality of self-efficacy theory. *Cognitive Therapy and Research, 4,* 39–66.

Bandura, A., Grusec, J. E., & Menlove, F. L. (1967). Vicarious extinction of avoidance behavior. *Journal of Personality and Social Psychology, 5,* 16–23.

Bandura, A., & Jeffery, R. W. (1973). Role of symbolic coding and rehearsal processes in observational learning. *Journal of Personality and Social Psychology, 26,* 122–130.

Bandura, A., Jeffery, R., & Bachicha, D. L. (1974). Analysis of memory codes and cumulative rehearsal in observational learning. *Journal of Research in Personality, 7,* 295–305.

Bandura, A., & Menlove, F. L. (1968). Factors determining vicarious extinction of avoidance behavior through symbolic modeling. *Journal of Personality and Social Psychology, 8,* 99–108.

Bandura, A., & Mischel, W. (1965). Modification of self-imposed delay of reward through exposure to live and symbolic models. *Journal of Personality and Social Psychology, 2,* 698–705.

Bandura, A., & Rosenthal, T. L. (1966). Vicarious classical conditioning as a function of arousal level. *Journal of Personality and Social Psychology, 3,* 54–62.

Bandura, A., & Schunk, D. H. (1981). Cultivating competence, self-efficacy, and intrinsic interest through proximal self-motivation. *Journal of Personality and Social Psychology, 41,* 586–598.

Bandura, A., & Walters, R. (1963). *Social learning and personality development.* New York: Holt, Rinehart, & Winston.

Bannister, D. (Ed.). (1970). *Perspectives in personal construct theory.* London: Academic Press.

Bannister, D. (1985). *Issues and approaches in personal construct theory.* London: Academic Press.

Barash, D. P. (1977). *Sociobiology and human behavior.* New York: Elsevier.

Barash, D. P. (1986). *The hare and the tortoise: Culture, biology, and human nature.* New York: Penguin.

Barber, J. P., & DeRubeis, R. J. (1989). On second thought: Where the action is in cognitive therapy for depression. *Cognitive Therapy and Research, 13,* 441–457.

Bargh, J. A. (1997). The automaticity of everyday life. In R. S. Wyer, Jr. (Ed.), *Advances in social cognition* (Vol. 10, pp. 1–61). Mahwah, NJ: Erlbaum.

Bargh, J. A., Chen, M., & Burrows, L. (1996). Automaticity of social behavior: Direct effects of trait construct and stereotype activation on action. *Journal of Personality and Social Psychology, 71,* 230–244.

Bargh, J. A., Lombardi, W. J., & Higgins, E. T. (1988). Automaticity of chronically accessible constructs in person X situation effects on person perception: It's just a matter of time. *Journal of Personality and Social Psychology, 55,* 599–605.

Bargh, J. A., & Pratto, F. (1986). Individual construct accessibility and perceptual selection. *Journal of Experimental Social Psychology, 22,* 293–311.

Barkow, J. H., Cosmides, L., & Tooby, J. (1992). *The adapted mind: Evolutionary psychology and the generation of culture.* New York: Oxford University Press.

Barlow, D. H. (Ed.). (1981). *Behavioral assessment of adult disorders.* New York: Guilford.

Baron, R. A. (1974a). The aggression-inhibiting influence of heightened sexual arousal. *Journal of Personality and Social Psychology, 30,* 318–322.

Baron, R. A. (1974b). Sexual arousal and physical aggression: The inhibiting influence of "cheesecake" and nudes. *Bulletin of the Psychonomic Society, 3,* 337–339.

Baron, R. A. (1979). Heightened sexual arousal and physical aggression: An extension to females. *Journal of Research in Personality, 13,* 91–102.

Baron, R. A., & Bell, P. A. (1977). Sexual arousal and aggression by males: Effects of type of erotic stimuli and prior provocation. *Journal of Personality and Social Psychology, 35,* 79–87.

Baron, R. A., & Kempner, C. R. (1970). Model's behavior and attraction toward the model as determinants of adult aggressive behavior. *Journal of Personality and Social Psychology, 14,* 335–344.

Baron, R. A., & Richardson, D. R. (1994). *Human aggression* (2nd ed.). New York: Plenum.

Barron, F. (1953). An ego-strength scale which predicts response to psychotherapy. *Journal of Consulting Psychology, 17,* 327–333.

Bartholomew, K. & Horowitz, L. M. (1991). Attachment styles among young adults: A test of a four-category model. *Journal of Personality and Social Psychology, 61,* 226–244.

Batson, C. D. (1990). How social an animal? The human capacity for caring. *American Psychologist, 45,* 336–346.

Batson, C. D. (1991). *The altruism question: Toward a social-psychological answer.* Hillsdale, NJ: Erlbaum.

Batson, C. D., Bolen, M. H., Cross, J. A., & Neuringer-Benefiel, H. E. (1986). Where is the altruism in the altruistic personality? *Journal of Personality and Social Psychology, 50,* 212–220.

Batson, C. D., Dyck, J. L., Brandt, J. R., Batson, J. G., Powell, A. L., McMaster, M. R., & Griffitt, C. (1988). Five studies testing two new egoistic alternatives to the empathy-altruism hypothesis. *Journal of Personality and Social Psychology, 55,* 52–77.

Batson, C. D., Fultz, J., & Schoenrade, P. A. (1987). Distress and empathy: Two qualitatively distinct vicarious emotions with different motivational consequences. *Journal of Personality, 55,* 19–39.

Batson, C. D., Sympson, S. C., Hindman, J. L., Decruz, P., Todd, R. M., Weeks, L. J., Jennings, G., & Burris, C. T. (1996). "I've been there, too": Effect on empathy of prior experience with a need. *Personality and Social Psychology Bulletin, 22,* 474–482.

Battle, E., & Rotter, J. B. (1963). Children's feelings of personal control as related to social class and ethnic groups. *Journal of Personality, 31,* 482–490.

Baumann, L. J., & Leventhal, H. (1985). "I can tell when my blood pressure is up, can't I?" *Health Psychology, 4,* 203–218.

Baumeister, R. F. (1989). The problem of life's meaning. In D. M. Buss & N. Cantor (Eds.), *Personality psychology: Recent trends and emerging directions* (pp. 138–148). New York: Springer-Verlag.

Baumeister, R. F. (1994). The crystallization of discontent in the process of major life changes. In T. F. Heatherton & J. L. Weinberger (Eds.), *Can personality change?* (pp. 281–297). Washington, DC: American Psychological Association.

Baumeister, R. F., Bratslavsky, E., Muraven, M., & Tice, D. M. (1998). Ego depletion: Is the active self a limited resource? *Journal of Personality and Social Psychology, 74,* 1252–1265.

Baumeister, R. F., & Leary, M. R. (1995). The need to belong: Desire for interpersonal attachments as a fundamental human motivation. *Psychological Bulletin, 117,* 497–529.

Baumeister, R. F., & Tice, D. M. (1988). Metatraits. *Journal of Personality, 56,* 571–598.

Beck, A. T. (1972). *Depression: Causes and treatments.* Philadelphia: University of Pennsylvania Press.

Beck, A. T. (1976). *Cognitive therapy and the emotional disorders.* New York: International Universities Press.

Beck, A. T. (1991). Cognitive therapy: A 30-year retrospective. *American Psychologist, 46,* 368–375.

Beck, A. T., Rush, A. J., Shaw, B. F., & Emery, G. (1979). *Cognitive therapy of depression: A treatment manual.* New York: Guilford Press.

Beer, R. D. (1995). A dynamical systems perspective on agent-environment interaction. *Artificial Intelligence, 72,* 173–215.

Bell, M., Billington, R., & Becker, B. (1986). A scale for the assessment of object relations: Reliability, validity, and factorial invariance. *Journal of Clinical Psychology, 42,* 733–741.

Belmont, L., & Marolla, F. A. (1973). Birth order, family size, and intelligence. *Science, 182,* 1096–1101.

Bem, D. J., & Allen, A. (1974). On predicting some of the people some of the time: The search for cross-situational consistencies in behavior. *Psychological Review, 81,* 506–520.

Bem, S. L. (1974). The measurement of psychological androgyny. *Journal of Consulting and Clinical Psychology, 42,* 155–162.

Bem, S. L. (1975). Sex role adaptability: One consequence of psychological androgyny. *Journal of Personality and Social Psychology, 31,* 634–643.

Bem, S. L. (1981). Gender schema theory: A cognitive account of sex-typing. *Psychological Review, 88,* 354–364.

Benet, V., & Waller, N. G. (1995). The Big Seven factor model of personality description: Evidence for its cross-cultural generality in a Spanish sample. *Journal of Personality and Social Psychology, 69,* 701–718.

Benjamin, J., Li, L., Patterson, C., Greenberg, B. D., Murphy, D. L., & Hamer, D. H. (1996). Population and familial association between the D4 dopamine receptor gene and measures of novelty seeking. *Nature Genetics, 12,* 81–84.

Bentler, P. M. (1990). Comparative fit indexes in structural models. *Psychological Bulletin, 107,* 238–246.

Benton, C., Hernandez, A., Schmidt, A., Schmitz, M., Stone, A., & Weiner, B. (1983). Is hostility linked with affiliation among males and with achievement among females? A critique of Pollak and Gilligan. *Journal of Personality and Social Psychology, 45,* 1167–1171.

Berenbaum, S. A., & Hines, M. (1992). Early androgens are related to childhood sex-typed toy preferences. *Psychological Science, 3,* 203–206.

Berg, I. A. (Ed.). (1967). *Response set in personality assessment.* Chicago: Aldine.

Bergeman, C. S., Chipuer, H. M., Plomin, R., Pedersen, N. L., McClearn, G. E., Nesselrode, J. R., Costa,

P. T., Jr., & McCrae, R. R. (1993). Genetic and environmental effects on openness to experience, agreeableness, and conscientiousness: An adoption/twin study. *Journal of Personality, 61,* 159–179.

Berger, S. M. (1961). Incidental learning through vicarious reinforcement. *Psychological Reports, 9,* 477–491.

Berger, S. M. (1962). Conditioning through vicarious instigation. *Psychological Review, 69,* 450–466.

Berglas, S., & Jones, E. E. (1978). Drug choice as an internalization strategy in response to noncontingent success. *Journal of Personality and Social Psychology, 36,* 405–417.

Bergmann, M. S. (1980). Symposium on object relations theory and love: On the intrapsychic function of falling in love. *Psychoanalytic Quarterly, 49,* 56–77.

Berkowitz, L., & Alioto, J. T. (1973). The meaning of an observed event as a determinant of its aggressive consequences. *Journal of Personality and Social Psychology, 28,* 206–217.

Berkowitz, L., & Holmes, D. S. (1960). A further investigation of hostility generalization to disliked objects. *Journal of Personality, 28,* 427–442.

Berkowitz, L., & Knurek, D. A. (1969). Label-mediated hostility generalization. *Journal of Personality and Social Psychology, 13,* 200–206.

Berman, J. S., & Kenny, D. A. (1976). Correlational bias in observer ratings. *Journal of Personality and Social Psychology, 34,* 263–273.

Bernhardt, P. C., Dabbs, J. M., Jr., Fielden, J., & Lutter, C. (1998). Testosterone changes during vicarious experiences of winning and losing among fans at sporting events. *Physiology and Behavior, 65,* 59–62.

Bernstein, D. A. (1973). Situational factors in behavioral fear assessment: A progress report. *Behavior Therapy, 4,* 41–48.

Bernstein, I. L. (1985). Learning food aversions in the progression of cancer and its treatment. *Annals of the New York Academy of Sciences, 443,* 365–380.

Bernstein, W. M., Stephenson, B. O., Snyder, M. L., & Wicklund, R. A. (1983). Causal ambiguity and heterosexual affiliation. *Journal of Experimental Social Psychology, 19,* 78–92.

Bertrand, S., & Masling, J. M. (1969). Oral imagery and alcoholism. *Journal of Abnormal Psychology, 74,* 50–53.

Berzonsky, M. D., & Neimeyer, G. J. (1994). Ego identity status and identity processing orientation: The moderating role of commitment. *Journal of Research in Personality, 28,* 425–435.

Bettelheim, B. (1982). Reflections: Freud and the soul. *New Yorker, 58,* 52–93.

Binswanger, L. (1963). *Being-in-the-world: Selected papers of Ludwig Binswanger.* New York: Basic Books.

Blackburn, R. (1968a). Emotionality, extraversion and aggression in paranoid and non-paranoid schizophrenic offenders. *British Journal of Psychiatry, 115,* 1301–1302.

Blackburn, R. (1968b). Personality in relation to extreme aggression in psychiatry offenders. *British Journal of Psychiatry, 114,* 821–828.

Blake, R. R., & Mouton, J. S. (1980). *The versatile manager: A grid profile.* Homewood, IL: Dow Jones-Irwin.

Blanchard, E. B., & Epstein, L. H. (1978). *A biofeedback primer.* Reading, MA: Addison-Wesley.

Blanck, R., & Blanck, G. (1986). *Beyond ego psychology: Developmental object relations theory.* New York: Columbia University Press.

Blatt, S. J., Wein, S. J., Chevron, E., & Quinlan, D. M. (1979). Parental representations and depression in normal young adults. *Journal of Abnormal Psychology, 88,* 388–397.

Blatt, S. J., & Zuroff, D. C. (1992). Interpersonal relatedness and self-definition: Two prototypes for depression. *Clinical Psychology Review, 12,* 527–562.

Block, J. (1971). *Lives through time.* Berkeley, CA: Bancroft.

Block, J. (1977). Advancing the science of personality: Paradigmatic shift or improving the quality of research? In D. Magnusson & N. S. Endler (Eds.), *Personality at the crossroads: Current issues in interactional psychology* (pp. 37–63). Hillsdale, NJ: Erlbaum.

Block, J. (1982). Assimilation, accommodation, and the dynamics of personality development. *Child Development, 53,* 281–295.

Block, J. (1995). A contrarian view of the five-factor approach to personality assessment. *Psychological Bulletin, 117,* 187–215.

Block, J., & Kremen, A. M. (1996). IQ and ego-resiliency: Conceptual and empirical connections and separateness. *Journal of Personality and Social Psychology, 70,* 349–361.

Block, J., von der Lippe, A., & Block, J. H. (1973). Sex-role and socialization patterns: Some personality concomitants and environmental antecedents. *Journal of Consulting and Clinical Psychology, 41,* 321–341.

Block, J., Weiss, D. S., & Thorne, A. (1979). How relevant is a semantic similarity interpretation of personality ratings? *Journal of Personality and Social Psychology, 37,* 1055–1074.

Block, J. H. (1961). *The Q-sort method in personality assessment and psychiatric research.* Springfield, IL: Charles C Thomas.

Block, J. H. (1973). Conceptions of sex role: Some cross-cultural and longitudinal perspectives. *American Psychologist, 28,* 512–526.

Block, J. H. (1979). Another look at sex differentiation in the socialization behaviors of mothers and fathers. In F. L. Denmark & J. Sherman (Eds.), *Psychology of women: Future directions for research.* New York: Psychological Dimensions.

Block, J. H., & Block, J. (1980). The role of ego-control and ego-resiliency in the organization of behavior. In W. A. Collins (Ed.), *Development of cognition, affect, and social relations* (Minnesota symposia on child psychology, Vol. 13, pp. 39–101). Hillsdale, NJ: Erlbaum.

Blum, G. S., & Miller, D. (1952). Exploring the psychoanalytic theory of the "oral character." *Journal of Personality, 20,* 287–304.

Blumer, H. (1969). *Symbolic interactionism: Perspective and method.* Englewood Cliffs, NJ: Prentice-Hall.

Bohman, M., Cloninger, R., Sigvardsson, S., & von Knorring, A.-L. (1987). The genetics of alcoholism and related disorder. *Journal of Psychiatric Research, 21,* 447–452.

Bolles, R. C. (1972). Reinforcement, expectancy, and learning. *Psychological Review, 79,* 394–409.

Bonarius, H., Holland, R., & Rosenberg, S. (Eds.). (1980). *Personal construct theory: Recent advances in theory and practice.* London: Macmillan.

Booth, A., & Dabbs, J. M., Jr. (1993). Testosterone and men's marriages. *Social Forces, 72,* 463–477.

Borgatta, E. F. (1964). The structure of personality characteristics. *Behavioral Science, 12,* 8–17.

Borkenau, P., & Liebler, A. (1992). The cross-modal consistency of personality: Inferring strangers' traits from visual or acoustic information. *Journal of Research in Personality, 26,* 183–204.

Borkenau, P., & Liebler, A. (1993). Convergence of stranger ratings of personality and intelligence with self-ratings, partner ratings, and measured intelligence. *Journal of Personality and Social Psychology, 65,* 546–553.

Bornstein, R. F., & Masling, J. (1985). Orality and latency of volunteering to serve as experimental subjects: A replication. *Journal of Personality Assessment, 49,* 306–310.

Boss, M. (1963). *Psychoanalysis and Daseinsanalysis.* New York: Basic Books.

Bottome, P. (1939). *Alfred Adler: A biography.* New York: Putnam's.

Botwin, M. D., & Buss, D. M. (1989). Structure of act-report data: Is the five-factor model of personality recaptured? *Journal of Personality and Social Psychology, 56,* 988–1001.

Bouchard, T. J., Jr., Lykken, D. T., McGue, M., Segal, N. L., & Tellegen, A. (1990). Sources of human psychological differences: The Minnesota study of twins reared apart. *Science, 250,* 223–228.

Bouchard, T. J., Jr., & McGue, M. (1990). Genetic and rearing environmental influences on adult personality: An analysis of adopted twins reared apart. *Journal of Personality, 58,* 263–292.

Bourne, E. (1978a). The state of research on ego identity: A review and appraisal. Part I. *Journal of Youth and Adolescence, 7,* 223–251.

Bourne, E. (1978b). The state of research on ego identity: A review and appraisal. Part II. *Journal of Youth and Adolescence, 7,* 371–392.

Bouton, M. E. (1994). Context, ambiguity, and classical conditioning. *Current Directions in Psychological Science, 3,* 49–53.

Bower, G. H. (1970). Organizational factors in memory. *Cognitive Psychology, 1,* 18–46.

Bower, G. H. (1981). Mood and memory. *American Psychologist, 36,* 129–148.

Bower, J. E., Kemeny, M. E., Taylor, S. E., & Fahey, J. L. (1998). Cognitive processing, discovery of meaning, CD4 decline, and AIDS-related mortality among bereaved HIV seropositive men. *Journal of Consulting and Clinical Psychology. 66,* 979–986.

Bowlby, J. (1969). *Attachment and loss: Vol. 1, Attachment.* New York: Basic Books.

Bowlby, J. (1988). *A secure base: Parent—child attachment and healthy human development.* New York: Basic Books.

Boyatzis, R. E. (1973). Affiliation motivation. In D. C. McClelland & R. S. Steele (Eds.), *Human motivation: A book of readings.* Morristown, NJ: General Learning Press.

Bradburn, N. M., & Berlew, D. E. (1961). Need for achievement and English industrial growth. *Economic Development and Cultural Change, 10,* 8–20.

Bradley, G. W. (1978). Self-serving biases in the attribution process: A reexamination of the fact or fiction question. *Journal of Personality and Social Psychology, 36,* 56–71.

Brady, J. P. (1972). Systematic desensitization. In W. S. Agras (Ed.), *Behavior modification: Principles and clinical applications.* Boston: Little, Brown.

Bramel, D., Taub, B., & Blum, B. (1968). An observer's reaction to the suffering of his enemy. *Journal of Personality and Social Psychology, 8,* 384–392.

Brandstätter, H. (1983). Emotional responses to other persons in everyday life situations. *Journal of Personality and Social Psychology, 45,* 871–883.

Bransford, J. D., & Franks, J. J. (1971). The abstraction of linguistic ideas. *Cognitive Psychology, 2,* 331–350.

Bransford, J. D., & Johnson, M. K. (1972). Contextual prerequisites for understanding: Some investigations of comprehension and recall. *Journal of Verbal Learning and Verbal Behavior, 11,* 717–726.

Breedlove, S. M. (1992). Sexual dimorphism in the vertebrate nervous system. *Journal of Neuroscience, 12,* 4133–4142.

Breedlove, S. M. (1994). Sexual differentiation of the human nervous system. *Annual Review of Psychology, 45,* 389–418.

Brehm, J. W. (1966). *A theory of psychological reactance.* New York: Academic Press.

Brehm, S. S., & Brehm, J. W. (1981). *Psychological reactance: A theory of freedom and control.* New York: Academic Press.

Breland, H. M. (1974). Birth order, family constellation, and verbal achievement. *Child Development, 45,* 1011–1019.

Breland, K., & Breland, M. (1961). The misbehavior of organisms. *American Psychologist, 16,* 681–684.

Brenner, C. (1957). *An elementary textbook of psychoanalysis.* Garden City, NY: Doubleday.

Breuer, J., & Freud, S. (1955). Studies on hysteria. In J. Strachey (Ed.), *The standard edition of the complete psychological works of Sigmund Freud* (Vol. 2). London: Hogarth Press. (Originally published, 1895)

Brewer, M. B., Dull, V., & Lui, L. (1981). Perceptions of the elderly: Stereotypes as prototypes. *Journal of Personality and Social Psychology, 41,* 656–670.

Brewer, W. F. (1974). There is no convincing evidence for operant or classical conditioning in adult humans. In W. B. Weimer & D. S. Palermo (Eds.), *Cognition and the symbolic processes.* Hillsdale, NJ: Erlbaum.

Brewer, W. F., & Treyens, J. C. (1981). Role of schemata in memory for places. *Cognitive Psychology, 13,* 207–230.

Bridger, W. H., & Mandel, I. J. (1964). A comparison of GSR fear responses produced by threat and electric shock. *Journal of Psychiatric Research, 2,* 31–40.

Briggs, S. R. (1989). The optimal level of measurement for personality constructs. In D. M. Buss & N. Cantor (Eds.), *Personality psychology: Recent trends and emerging directions* (pp. 246–260). New York: Springer-Verlag.

Britt, T. W. (1993). Metatraits: Evidence relevant to the validity of the construct and its implications. *Journal of Personality and Social Psychology, 65,* 554–562.

Broadbent, D. E. (1977). Levels, hierarchies, and the locus of control. *Quarterly Journal of Experimental Psychology, 29,* 181–201.

Brody, N. (1970). Information theory, motivation, and personality. In H. M. Schroder & P. Suedfeld (Eds.), *Personality theory and information processing.* New York: Ronald Press.

Brody, N. (Ed.). (1987). Special issue on the unconscious. *Personality and Social Psychology Bulletin, 13,* 293–429.

Brokaw, D. W., & McLemore, C. W. (1983). Toward a more rigorous definition of social reinforcement: Some interpersonal clarifications. *Journal of Personality and Social Psychology, 44,* 1014–1020.

Brown, I., Jr., & Inouye, D. K. (1978). Learned helplessness through modeling: The role of perceived similarity in competence. *Journal of Personality and Social Psychology, 36,* 900–908.

Brown, J. S. (1948). Gradients of approach and avoidance responses and their relation to level of motivation. *Journal of Comparative and Physiological Psychology, 41,* 450–465.

Brown, J. S. (1957). Principles of intrapersonal conflict. *Journal of Conflict Resolution, 1,* 135–154.

Bruhn, A. R., & Schiffman, H. (1982). Prediction of locus of control stance from the earliest childhood memory. *Journal of Personality Assessment, 46,* 380–390.

Bruhn, A. R., & Schiffman, H. (1982). Prediction of locus of control stance from the earliest childhood memory. *Journal of Personality Assessment, 46,* 380–390.

Bruner, J. S. (1957). On perceptual readiness. *Psychological Review, 64,* 123–152.

Bruner, J. S., & Tagiuri, R. (1954). The perception of people. In G. Lindzey (Ed.), *Handbook of social psychology* (Vol. 2). Cambridge, MA: Addison-Wesley.

Brunswik, E. (1951). The probability point of view. In M. H. Marx (Ed.), *Psychological theory.* New York: Macmillan.

Buchanan, G. M. (1995). Explanatory style and coronary heart disease. In G. M. Buchanan & M. E. P. Seligman (Eds.), *Explanatory style* (pp. 225–232). Hillsdale, NJ: Erlbaum.

Burger, J. M. (1989). Negative reactions to increases in perceived personal control. *Journal of Personality and Social Psychology, 56,* 246–256.

Burns, M. O., & Seligman, M. E. P. (1989). Explanatory style across the life span: Evidence for stability over 52 years. *Journal of Personality and Social Psychology, 56,* 471–477.

Burnstein, E., Crandall, C., & Kitayama, S. (1994). Some neo-Darwinian decision rules for altruism: Weighing cues for inclusive fitness as a function of the biological importance of the decision. *Journal of Personality and Social Psychology, 67,* 773–789.

Burroughs, W. J., & Drews, D. R. (1991). Rule structure in the psychological representation of physical settings. *Journal of Experimental Social Psychology, 27,* 217–238.

Bursik, K. (1991). Adaptation to divorce and ego development in adult women. *Journal of Personality and Social Psychology, 60,* 300–306.

Bushman, B. J., & Baumeister, R. F. (1998). Threatened egotism, narcissism, self-esteem, and direct and displaced aggression: Does self-love or self-hate lead to violence? *Journal of Personality and Social Psychology, 75,* 219–229.

Buss, A. H. (1983). Social rewards and personality. *Journal of Personality and Social Psychology, 44,* 553–563.

Buss, A. H. (1989). Personality as traits. *American Psychologist, 44,* 1378–1388.

Buss, A. H. (1995). *Personality: Temperament, social behavior, and the self.* Boston: Allyn & Bacon.

Buss, A. H., & Plomin, R. (1975). *A temperament theory of personality development.* New York: Wiley-Interscience.

Buss, A. H., & Plomin, R. (1984). *Temperament: Early developing personality traits.* Hillsdale, NJ: Erlbaum.

Buss, D. M. (1984). Toward a psychology of person-environment correlation: The role of spouse selection. *Journal of Personality and Social Psychology, 47,* 361–377.

Buss, D. M. (1985). Human mate selection. *American Scientist, 73,* 47–51.

Buss, D. M. (1988). The evolution of human intrasexual competition: Tactics of mate attraction. *Journal of Personality and Social Psychology, 54,* 616–628.

Buss, D. M. (1989). Sex differences in human mate preferences: Evolutionary hypotheses tested in 37 cultures. *Behavioral and Brain Sciences, 12,* 1–49.

Buss, D. M. (1991). Evolutionary personality psychology. *Annual Review of Psychology, 42,* 459–491.

Buss, D. M. (1994a). *The evolution of desire: Strategies of human mating.* New York: Basic Books.

Buss, D. M. (1994b). The strategies of human mating. *American Scientist, 82,* 238–249.

Buss, D. M. (1995). Evolutionary psychology: A new paradigm for psychological science. *Psychological Inquiry, 6,* 1–30.

Buss, D. M., Gomes, M., Higgins, D. S., & Lauterbach, K. (1987). Tactics of manipulation. *Journal of Personality and Social Psychology, 52,* 1219–1229.

Buss, D. M., Larsen, R. J., Westen, D., & Semmelroth, J. (1992). Sex differences in jealousy: Evolution, physiology, and psychology. *Psychological Science, 3,* 251–255.

Buss, D. M., & Schmitt, D. P. (1993). Sexual strategies theory: An evolutionary perspective on human mating. *Psychological Review, 100,* 204–232.

Buss, D. M., & Shackelford, T. K. (1997). From vigilance to violence: Mate retention tactics in married couples. *Journal of Personality and Social Psychology, 72,* 346–361.

Bussey, K., & Bandura, A. (1984). Influence of gender constancy and social power on sex-linked modeling. *Journal of Personality and Social Psychology, 47,* 1292–1302.

Butcher, J. N. (Ed.). (1996). *International adaptations of the MMPI-2: Research and clinical applications.* Minneapolis: University of Minnesota Press.

Butcher, J. N., Dahlstrom, W., Graham, J., Tellegen, A., & Kaemmer, B. (1989). *Manual for administering and scoring the MMPI-2.* Minneapolis: University of Minnesota Press.

Butler, J. M., & Haigh, G. V. (1954). Changes in the relation between self-concepts and ideal concepts consequent upon client-centered counseling. In C. R. Rogers & R. F. Dymond (Eds.), *Psychotherapy and personality change: Co-ordinated research studies in the client-centered approach.* Chicago: University of Chicago Press.

Byrne, D., McDonald, R. D., & Mikawa, J. (1963). Approach and avoidance affiliation motives. *Journal of Personality, 31,* 21–37.

Cacioppo, J. T., & Petty, R. E. (1980). The effects of orienting task on differential hemispheric EEG activation. *Neuropsychologia, 18,* 675–683.

Cacioppo, J. T., & Petty, R. E. (1982). The need for cognition. *Journal of Personality and Social Psychology, 42,* 116–131.

Cacioppo, J. T., & Petty, R. E. (1983). *Social psychophysiology.* New York: Guilford Press.

Cacioppo, J. T., & Petty, R. E. (1984). The need for cognition: Relationship to attitudinal processes. In

R. P. McGlynn, J. E. Maddux, C. Stoltenberg, & J. H. Harvey (Eds.), *Social perception in clinical and counseling psychology.* Lubbock: Texas Tech Press.

Cacioppo, J. T., Petty, R. E., Feinstein, J. A., & Jarvis, W. B. G. (1996). Dispositional differences in cognitive motivation: The life and times of individuals varying in need for cognition. *Psychological Bulletin, 119,* 197–253.

Cacioppo, J. T., Petty, R. E., Kao, C. F., & Rodriguez, R. (1986). Central and peripheral routes to persuasion: An individual difference perspective. *Journal of Personality and Social Psychology, 51,* 1032–1043.

Cacioppo, J. T., Petty, R. E., & Morris, K. J. (1983). Effects of need for cognition on message evaluation, recall, and persuasion. *Journal of Personality and Social Psychology, 45,* 805–818.

Cacioppo, J. T., & Sandman, C. A. (1981). Psychophysiological functioning, cognitive responding, and attitudes. In R. E. Petty, T. M. Ostrom, & T. C. Brock (Eds.), *Cognitive responses in persuasion.* Hillsdale, NJ: Erlbaum.

Campbell, D. T. (1960). Recommendations for the APA test standards regarding construct, trait, and discriminant validity. *American Psychologist, 15,* 546–553.

Campbell, D. T., & Fiske, D. W. (1959). Convergent and discriminant validation by the multitrait-multimethod matrix. *Psychological Bulletin, 56,* 81–105.

Cannon, D. S., Baker, T. B., Gino, A., & Nathan, P. E. (1986). Alcohol-aversion therapy: Relation between strength of aversion and abstinence. *Journal of Consulting and Clinical Psychology, 54,* 825–830.

Cannon, W. B. (1932). *The wisdom of the body.* New York: Norton.

Cantor, N. (1990). From thought to behavior: "Having" and "doing" in the study of personality and cognition. *American Psychologist, 45,* 735–750.

Cantor, N., & Kihlstrom, J. F. (Eds.). (1981). *Personality, cognition, and social interaction.* Hillsdale, NJ: Erlbaum.

Cantor, N., & Kihlstrom, J. F. (1987). *Personality and social intelligence.* Englewood Cliffs, NJ: Prentice-Hall.

Cantor, N., & Mischel, W. (1977). Traits as prototypes: Effects on recognition memory. *Journal of Personality and Social Psychology, 35,* 38–48.

Cantor, N., Mischel, W., & Schwartz, J. C. (1982). A prototype analysis of psychological situations. *Cognitive Psychology, 14,* 45–77.

Cantor, N., Smith, E. E., French, R., & Mezzich, J. (1980). Psychiatric diagnosis as prototype categorization. *Journal of Abnormal Psychology, 89,* 181–193.

Carey, G., Goldsmith, H. H., Tellegen, A., & Gottesman, I. I. (1978). Genetics and personality inventories: The limits of replication with twin data. *Behavior Genetics, 8,* 299–313.

Carlston, D. E., & Skowronski, J. J. (1994). Savings in the relearning of trait information as evidence for spontaneous inference generation. *Journal of Personality and Social Psychology, 66,* 840–856.

Carnelley, K. B., Pietromonaco, P. R., & Jaffe, K. (1994). Depression, working models of others, and relationship functioning. *Journal of Personality and Social Psychology, 66,* 127–140.

Carroll, B. J. (1982). The dexamethasone suppression test for melancholia. *British Journal of Psychiatry, 140,* 292–304.

Carroll, B. J. (1985). Dexamethasone suppression test: A review of contemporary confusion. *Journal of Clinical Psychiatry, 46,* 13–24.

Carroll, L. (1987). A study of narcissism, affiliation, intimacy, and power motives among students in business administration. *Psychological Reports, 61,* 355–358.

Carver, C. S. (1974). Facilitation of physical aggression through objective self-awareness. *Journal of Experimental Social Psychology, 10,* 365–370.

Carver, C. S. (1975). Physical aggression as a function of objective self awareness and attitudes toward punishment. *Journal of Experimental Social Psychology, 11,* 510–519.

Carver, C. S. (1989). How should multifaceted personality constructs be tested? Issues illustrated by self-monitoring, attributional style, and hardiness. *Journal of Personality and Social Psychology, 56,* 577–585.

Carver, C. S. (1996). Emergent integration in contemporary personality psychology. *Journal of Research in Personality, 30,* 319–334.

Carver, C. S. (1997a). Adult attachment and personality: Converging evidence and a new measure. *Personality and Social Psychology Bulletin, 23,* 865–883.

Carver, C. S. (1997b). The Internal–External scale confounds internal locus of control with expectancies of positive outcomes. *Personality and Social Psychology Bulletin, 23,* 580–585.

Carver, C. S. (1998). Generalization, adverse events, and development of depressive symptoms. *Journal of Personality, 66,* 609–620.

Carver, C. S., & Baird, E. (1998). The American dream revisited: Is it *what* you want or *why* you want it that matters? *Psychological Science, 9,* 289–292.

Carver, C. S., & Ganellen, R. J. (1983). Depression and components of self-punitiveness: High standards, self-criticism, and overgeneralization. *Journal of Abnormal Psychology, 92,* 330–337.

Carver, C. S., Ganellen, R. J., Froming, W. J., & Chambers, W. (1983). Modeling: An analysis in terms of category accessibility. *Journal of Experimental Social Psychology, 19,* 403–421.

Carver, C. S., LaVoie, L., Kuhl, J., & Ganellen, R. J. (1988). Cognitive concomitants of depression: A further examination of the roles of generalization, high standards, and self-criticism. *Journal of Social and Clinical Psychology, 7,* 350–365.

Carver, C. S., Lawrence, J. W., & Scheier, M. F. (in press). Self-discrepancies and affect: Incorporating the role of feared selves. *Personality and Social Psychology Bulletin.*

Carver, C. S., & Scheier, M. F. (1981). *Attention and self-regulation: A control-theory approach to human behavior.* New York: Springer-Verlag.

Carver, C. S., & Scheier, M. F. (1986). Functional and dysfunctional responses to anxiety: The interaction between expectancies and self-focused attention. In R. Schwarzer (Ed.), *Self-related cognitions in anxiety and motivation.* Hillsdale, NJ: Erlbaum.

Carver, C. S., & Scheier, M. F. (1990). Principles of self-regulation: Action and emotion. In E. T. Higgins & R. M. Sorrentino (Eds.), *Handbook of motivation and cognition: Foundations of social behavior* (Vol. 2, pp. 3–52). New York: Guilford.

Carver, C. S., & Scheier, M. F. (1998). *On the self-regulation of behavior.* New York: Cambridge University Press.

Carver, C. S., & White, T. L. (1994). Behavioral inhibition, behavioral activation, and affective responses to impending reward and punishment: The BIS/BAS scales. *Journal of Personality and Social Psychology, 67,* 319–333.

Caspi, A., Begg, D., Dickson, N., Herringbone, H., Largely, J., Miff, T. E., & Silver, P. A. (1997). Personality differences predict health-risk behaviors in young adulthood: Evidence from a longitudinal study. *Journal of Personality and Social Psychology, 73,* 1052–1063.

Caspi, A., Elder, G. H., Jr., & Bem, D. J. (1987). Moving against the world: Life-course patterns of explosive children. *Developmental Psychology, 23,* 308–313.

Caspi, A., Elder, G. H., Jr., & Bem, D. J. (1988). Moving away from the world: Life-course patterns of shy children. *Developmental Psychology, 24,* 824–831.

Caspi, A., & Herbener, E. S. (1990). Continuity and change: Assortative marriage and the consistency of

personality in adulthood. *Journal of Personality and Social Psychology, 58,* 250–258.

Catania, A. C., & Harnad, S. (Eds.). (1988). *The operant behaviorism of B. F. Skinner: Comments and consequences.* New York: Cambridge University Press.

Cattell, H. E. P. (1993). Comment on Goldberg. *American Psychologist, 48,* 1302–1303.

Cattell, R. B. (1947). Confirmation and clarification of primary personality factors. *Psychometrica, 12,* 197–220.

Cattell, R. B. (1965). *The scientific analysis of personality.* Baltimore: Penguin Books.

Cattell, R. B. (1978). *The scientific use of factor analysis.* New York: Plenum.

Cattell, R. B. (1979). *Personality and learning theory, Volume 1. The structure of personality in its environment.* New York: Springer.

Cattell, R. B. (1985). *Human motivation and the dynamic calculus.* New York: Praeger.

Cattell, R. B., Eber, H. W., & Tatsuoka, M. M. (1977). *Handbook for the 16 personality factor questionnaire.* Champaign, IL: IPAT.

Cattell, R. B., & Kline, P. (1977). *The scientific analysis of personality and motivation.* New York: Academic Press.

Cervone, D. (1997). Social-cognitive mechanisms and personality coherence: Self-knowledge, situational beliefs, and cross-situational coherence in perceived self-efficacy. *Psychological Science, 8,* 43–50.

Chambliss, C. A., & Murray, E. J. (1979). Efficacy attribution, locus of control, and weight loss. *Cognitive Therapy and Research, 3,* 349–354.

Chapman, L. J. (1967). Illusory correlations in observational report. *Journal of Verbal Learning and Verbal Behavior, 6,* 151–155.

Chatterjee, B. B., & Eriksen, C. W. (1962). Cognitive factors in heart rate conditioning. *Journal of Experimental Psychology, 64,* 272–279.

Cheek, J. (1982). Aggregation, moderator variables, and the validity of personality tests: A peer-rating study. *Journal of Personality and Social Psychology, 43,* 1254–1269.

Chew, S. L., Larkey, L. S., Soli, S. D., Blount, J., & Jenkins, J. J. (1982). The abstraction of musical ideas. *Memory & Cognition, 10,* 413–423.

Chomsky, N. (1959). Review of *Verbal behavior* by B. F. Skinner. *Language, 35,* 26–58.

Church, A. T., & Burke, P. J. (1994). Exploratory and confirmatory tests of the big five and Tellegen's three- and four-dimensional models. *Journal of Personality and Social Psychology, 66,* 93–114.

Cialdini, R. B., Schaller, M., Houlihan, D., Arps, K., & Fultz, J. (1987). Empathy-based helping: Is it selflessly or selfishly motivated? *Journal of Personality and Social Psychology, 52,* 749–758.

Ciminero, A. R., Calhoun, K. S., & Adams, H. E. (Eds.). (1977). *Handbook of behavioral assessment.* New York: Wiley.

Claridge, G. S. (1967). *Personality and arousal.* New York: Pergamon.

Clark, R. A., & McClelland, D. C. (1956). A factor analytic integration of imaginative and performance measures of the need for achievement. *Journal of General Psychology, 55,* 73–83.

Clark, R. D., & Hatfield, E. (1989). Gender differences in receptivity to sexual offers. *Journal of Psychology and Human Sexuality, 2,* 39–55.

Clark, W. R. (1996). *Sex and the origins of death.* New York: Oxford University Press.

Clausen, J. A. (1981). Men's occupational careers in the middle years. In D. H. Eichorn, J. A. Clausen, N. Haan, M. P. Honzik, & P. H. Mussen (Eds.), *Present and past in middle life* (pp. 321–351). New York: Academic Press.

Cline, V. B., Croft, R. G., & Courrier, S. (1973). Desensitization of children to television violence. *Journal of Personality and Social Psychology, 27,* 360–365.

Cloninger, C. R. (1987). A systematic method of clinical description and classification of personality variants: A proposal. *Archives of General Psychiatry, 44,* 573–588.

Cloninger, C. R. (1988). A unified biosocial theory of personality and its role in the development of anxiety states: A reply to commentaries. *Psychiatric Developments, 2,* 83–120.

Cloninger, C. R., Svrakic, D. M., & Przybeck, T. R. (1993). A psychobiological model of temperament and character. *Archives of General Psychiatry, 50,* 975–990.

Cohen, A. R. (1957). Need for cognition and order of communication as determinants of opinion change. In C. I. Hovland (Ed.), *The order of presentation in persuasion.* New Haven, CT: Yale University Press.

Cohen, A. R., Stotland, E., & Wolfe, D. M. (1955). An experimental investigation of need for cognition. *Journal of Abnormal and Social Psychology, 51,* 291–294.

Cohn, L. D. (1991). Sex differences in the course of personality development: A meta-analysis. *Psychological Bulletin, 109,* 252–266.

Collaer, M. L., & Hines, M. (1995). Human behavioral sex differences: A role for gonadal hormones during early development? *Psychological Bulletin, 118,* 55–107.

Collins, N. L., & Read, S. J. (1990). Adult attachment, working models, and relationship quality in dating couples. *Journal of Personality and Social Psychology, 58,* 644–663.

Colvin, C. R., & Block, J. (1994). Do positive illusions foster mental health? An examination of the Taylor and Brown formulation. *Psychological Bulletin, 116,* 3–20.

Comrey, A. L. (1973). *A first course in factor analysis.* New York: Academic Press.

Conley, J. J. (1985). Longitudinal stability of personality traits: A multitrait-multimethod-multioccasion analysis. *Journal of Personality and Social Psychology, 49,* 1266–1282.

Constantian, C. A. (1981). Attitudes, beliefs, and behavior in regard to spending time alone. Unpublished doctoral dissertation, Harvard University, Cambridge, MA.

Converse, J., & Presser, S. (1986). *Survey questions: Handcrafting the standardized questionnaire.* Newbury Park, CA: Sage.

Conway, M., & Giannopoulos, C. (1993). Dysphoria and decision making: Limited information use for evaluations of multiattribute targets. *Journal of Personality and Social Psychology, 64,* 613–623.

Cook, M. L., & Peterson, C. (1986). Depressive irrationality. *Cognitive Therapy and Research, 10,* 293–298.

Cooley, C. H. (1902). *Human nature and the social order.* New York: Scribner's.

Cooley, E. J., & Spiegler, M. D. (1980). Cognitive versus emotional coping responses as alternatives to test anxiety. *Cognitive Therapy and Research, 4,* 159–166.

Corr, P. J., Pickering, A. D., & Gray, J. A. (1997). Personality, punishment, and procedural learning: A test of J. A. Gray's anxiety theory. *Journal of Personality and Social Psychology, 73,* 337–344.

Cortes, J. B., & Gatti, F. M. (1965). Physique and self-descriptions of temperament. *Journal of Consulting Psychology, 29,* 432–439.

Cosmides, L. (1989). The logic of social exchange: Has natural selection shaped how we reason? *Cognition, 31,* 187–276.

Cosmides, L., & Tooby, J. (1989). Evolutionary psychology and the generation of culture, Part II. *Ethology and Sociobiology, 10,* 51–97.

Costa, P. T., Jr., & McCrae, R. R. (1980). Influence of extraversion and neuroticism on subjective well-being: Happy and unhappy people. *Journal of Personality and Social Psychology, 38,* 668–678.

Costa, P. T., Jr., & McCrae, R. R. (1985). *The NEO Personality Inventory manual.* Odessa, FL: Psychological Assessment Resources.

Costa, P. T., Jr., & McCrae, R. R. (1988a). From catalog to classification: Murray's needs and the five-factor model. *Journal of Personality and Social Psychology, 55,* 258–265.

Costa, P. T., Jr., & McCrae, R. R. (1988b). Personality in adulthood: A six-year longitudinal study of self-reports and spouse ratings on the NEO personality inventory. *Journal of Personality and Social Psychology, 54,* 853–863.

Costa, P. T., Jr., & McCrae, R. R. (1989). Personality continuity and the changes of adult life. In M. Storandt & G. R. VandenBos (Eds.), *The adult years: Continuity and change* (pp. 45–77). Washington, DC: American Psychological Association.

Costa, P. T., Jr., & McCrae, R. R. (1990). Personality disorders and the five-factor model of personality. *Journal of Personality Disorders, 4,* 362–371.

Costa, P. T., Jr., & McCrae, R. R. (1992). *Revised NEO Personality Inventory (NEO-PI-R) and NEO Five-Factor Inventory (NEO-FFI) professional manual.* Odessa, FL: Psychological Assessment Resources.

Costa, P. T., Jr., & McCrae, R. R. (1995). Domains and facets: Hierarchical personality assessment using the revised NEO Pesonality Inventory. *Journal of Personality Assessment, 64,* 21–50.

Costa, P. T., Jr., & Widiger, T. A. (1994). *Personality disorders and the five factor model of personality.* Washington, DC: American Psychological Association.

Couch, A., & Keniston, K. (1960). Yeasayers and naysayers: Agreeing response set as a personality variable. *Journal of Abnormal and Social Psychology, 60,* 151–174.

Coursey, R. D., Buchsbaum, M. S., & Frankel, B. L. (1975). Personality measures and evoked responses in chronic insomniacs. *Journal of Abnormal Psychology, 84,* 234–244.

Cozzarelli, C. (1993). Personality and self-efficacy as predictors of coping with abortion. *Journal of Personality and Social Psychology, 65,* 1224–1236.

Craig, K. D., & Weinstein, M. S. (1965). Conditioning vicarious affective arousal. *Psychological Reports, 17,* 955–963.

Craighead, W. E., Kazdin, A. E., & Mahoney, M. J. (1981). *Behavior modification: Principles, issues, and applications.* Boston: Houghton Mifflin.

Crandall, R., McCown, D. A., & Robb, Z. (1988). The effects of assertiveness training on self-actualization. *Small Group Behavior, 19,* 134–145.

Crawford, C. B. (1989). The theory of evolution: Of what value to psychology? *Journal of Comparative Psychology, 103,* 4–22.

Crawford, C. B., Smith, M. S., & Krebs, D. (Eds.). (1987). *Sociobiology and psychology: Ideas, issues and applications.* Hillsdale, NJ: Erlbaum.

Crews, F. (1996). The verdict on Freud. *Psychological Science, 7,* 63.

Crick, N. R., & Dodge, K. A. (1994). A review and reformulation of social information-processing mechanisms in children's social adjustment. *Psychological Bulletin, 115,* 74–101.

Crocker, J. (1981). Judgment of covariation by social perceivers. *Psychological Bulletin, 90,* 272–292.

Cronbach, L. J., & Meehl, P. E. (1955). Construct validity in psychological tests. *Psychological Bulletin, 52,* 281–302.

Crouse, B. B., & Mehrabian, A. (1977). Affiliation of opposite-sexed strangers. *Journal of Research in Personality,* 11, 38–47.

Crowne, D. P., & Marlowe, D. (1964). *The approval motive: Studies in evaluative dependence.* New York: Wiley.

Csikszentmihalyi, M. (1975). *Beyond boredom and anxiety.* San Francisco: Jossey-Bass.

Csikszentmihalyi, M. (1978). Attention and the holistic approach to behavior. In K. S. Pope & J. L. Singer (Eds.), *The stream of consciousness: Scientific investigations into the flow of human experience.* New York: Plenum.

Csikszentmihalyi, M. (1982). Toward a psychology of optimal experience. In L. Wheeler (Ed.), *Review of personality and social psychology* (Vol. 3, pp. 13–36). Beverly Hills, CA: Sage.

Csikszentmihalyi, M. (1990). *Flow: The psychology of optimal experience.* New York: Harper & Row.

Csikszentmihalyi, M., & Csikszentmihalyi, I. S. (Eds.). (1988). *Optimal experience: Psychological studies of flow in consciousness.* New York: Cambridge University Press.

Cunningham, M. R., Barbee, A. P., & Pike, C. L. (1990). What do women want? Facialmetric assessment of multiple motives in the perception of male facial physical attractiveness. *Journal of Personality and Social Psychology, 59,* 61–72.

Cutter, H. S. G., Boyatzis, R. E., & Clancy, D. D. (1977). The effectiveness of power motivation training in rehabilitating alcoholics. *Journal of Studies on Alcohol, 38,* 131–141.

Dabbs, J. M., Jr. (1992a). Testosterone and occupational achievement. *Social Forces, 70,* 813–824.

Dabbs, J. M., Jr. (1992b). Testosterone measurements in social and clinical psychology. *Journal of Social and Clinical Psychology, 11,* 302–321.

Dabbs, J. M., Jr. (1997). Testosterone, smiling, and facial appearance. *Journal of Nonverbal Behavior, 21,* 45–55.

Dabbs, J. M., Jr. (1998). Testosterone and the concept of dominance. *Behavioral and Brain Sciences, 21,* 370–371.

Dabbs, J. M., Jr., Alford, E. C., & Fielden, J. A. (1998). Trial lawyers: Blue collar talent in a white collar world. *Journal of Applied Social Psychology, 28,* 84–94.

Dabbs, J. M., Jr., de La Rue, D., & Williams, P. M. (1990). Testosterone and occupational choice: Actors, ministers, and other men. *Journal of Personality and Social Psychology, 59,* 1261–1265.

Dabbs, J. M., Jr., Frady, R. L., Carr, T. S., & Besch, N. F. (1987). Saliva testosterone and criminal violence in young adult prison inmates. *Psychosomatic Medicine, 49,* 174–182.

Dabbs, J. M., Jr., Hargrove, M. F., & Heusel, C. (1996). Testosterone differences among college fraternities: Well-behaved vs. rambunctious. *Personality and Individual Differences, 290,* 157–161.

Dabbs, J. M., Jr., Jurkovic, G. J., & Frady, R. L. (1991). Salivary testosterone and cortisol among late adolescent male offenders. *Journal of Abnormal Child Psychology, 19,* 469–478.

Dabbs, J. M., Jr., & Mohammed, S. (1992). Male and female salivary testosterone concentrations before and after sexual activity. *Physiology and Behavior, 52,* 195–197.

Dabbs, J. M., Jr., & Morris, R. (1990). Testosterone, social class, and antisocial behavior in a sample of 4,462 men. *Psychological Science, 1,* 209–211.

Dabbs, J. M., Jr., Ruback, R. B., Frady, R. L., Hopper, C. H., & Sgoutas, D. S. (1988). Saliva testosterone and criminal violence among women. *Personality and Individual Differences, 9,* 269–275.

Daitzman, R., & Zuckerman, M. (1980). Disinhibitory sensation seeking, personality and gonadal hormones. *Personality and Individual Differences, 1,* 103–110.

Daly, M., & Wilson, M. I. (1988). *Homicide.* New York: Aldine de Gruyter.

Daly, M., & Wilson, M. I. (1990). Killing the competition: Female/female and male/male homicide. *Human Nature, 1,* 81–107.

Daly, M., & Wilson, M. I. (1996). Violence agianst stepchildren. *Current Directions in Psychological Science, 5,* 77–81.

D'Andrade, R. G. (1974). Memory and the assessment of behavior. In H. Blalock (Ed.), *Measurement in the social sciences.* Chicago: Aldine.

Daniels, D. (1986). Differential experiences of siblings in the same family as predictors of adolescent sibling personality differences. *Journal of Personality and Social Psychology, 51,* 339–346.

Daniels, D., & Plomin, R. (1985). Differential experience of siblings in the same family. *Developmental Psychology, 21,* 747–760.

Darley, J. M., & Goethals, G. R. (1980). People's analyses of the causes of ability-linked performances. In L. Berkowitz (Ed.), *Advances in experimental social psychology* (Vol. 13). New York: Academic Press.

Davidson, M. A., McInnes, R. G., & Parnell, R. W. (1957). The distribution of personality traits in seven-year-old children: A combined psychological, psychiatric, and somatotype study. *British Journal of Educational Psychology, 27,* 48–61.

Davidson, R. J. (1984). Affect, cognition, and hemispheric specialization. In C. E. Izard, J. Kagan, & R. Zajonc (Eds.), *Emotion, cognition, and behavior.* New York: Cambridge University Press.

Davidson, R. J. (1988). EEG measures of cerebral asymmetry: Conceptual and methodological issues. *International Journal of Neuroscience, 39,* 71–89.

Davidson, R. J. (1992a). Anterior cerebral asymmetry and the nature of emotion. *Brain and Cognition, 20,* 125–151.

Davidson, R. J. (1992b). Prolegomenon to the structure of emotion: Gleanings from neuropsychology. *Cognition and Emotion, 6,* 245–268.

Davidson, R. J. (1995). Cerebral asymmetry, emotion, and affective style. In R. J. Davidson, & K. Hugdahl (Eds.), *Brain asymmetry* (pp. 361–387). Cambridge, MA: MIT Press.

Davidson, R. J., Ekman, P., Saron, C. D., Senulis, J. A., & Friesen, W. V. (1990). Approach–withdrawal and cerebral asymmetry: Emotional expression and brain physiology I. *Journal of Personality and Social Psychology, 58,* 330–341.

Davidson, R. J., & Sutton, S. K. (1995). Affective neuroscience: The emergence of a discipline. *Current Opinion in Neurobiology, 5,* 217–224.

Davis, P. J. (1987). Repression and the inaccessibility of affective memories. *Journal of Personality and Social Psychology, 53,* 585–593.

Davis, P. J., & Schwartz, G. E. (1987). Repression and the inaccessibility of affective memories. *Journal of Personality and Social Psychology, 52,* 155–162.

Davis, W. N. (1969). Drinking: A search for power or for nurturance? Unpublished doctoral dissertation, Harvard University, Cambridge, MA.

Davison, G. C., & Wilson, G. T. (1973). Processes of fear reduction in systematic desensitization: Cognitive and social reinforcement factors in humans. *Behavior Therapy, 4,* 1–21.

Dawkins, R. (1976a). Hierarchical organisation: A candidate principle for ethology. In P. P. G. Bateson & R. A. Hinde (Eds.), *Growing points in ethology* (pp. 7–54). Cambridge, England: Cambridge University Press.

Dawkins, R. (1976b). *The selfish gene.* New York: Oxford University Press.

Dawson, M. E., & Furedy, J. J. (1976). The role of awareness in human differential autonomic classical conditioning: The necessary-gate hypothesis. *Psychophysiology, 13,* 50–53.

Deaux, K., & Lewis, L. L. (1984). Structure of gender stereotypes: Interrelationships among components and gender label. *Journal of Personality and Social Psychology, 46,* 991–1004.

Deaux, K., & Major, B. (1987). Putting gender into context: An interactive model of gender-related behavior. *Psychological Review, 94,* 369–389.

Deci, E. L. (1971). Effects of externally mediated rewards on intrinsic motivation. *Journal of Personality and Social Psychology, 18,* 105–115.

Deci, E. L. (1975). *Intrinsic motivation.* New York: Plenum.

Deci, E. L., & Ryan, R. M. (1980). The empirical exploration of intrinsic motivational processes. In L. Berkowitz (Ed.), *Advances in experimental social psychology* (Vol. 13). New York: Academic Press.

Deci, E. L., & Ryan, R. M. (1985). *Intrinsic motivation and self-determination in human behavior.* New York: Plenum.

Deci, E. L., & Ryan, R. M. (1987). The support of autonomy and the control of behavior. *Journal of Personality and Social Psychology, 53,* 1024–1037.

Deci, E. L., & Ryan, R. M. (1991). A motivational approach to self: Integration in personality. In R. Dienstbier (Ed.), *Nebraska symposium on motivation: Perspectives on motivation* (Vol. 38, pp. 237–288). Lincoln: University of Nebraska Press.

Deci, E. L., & Ryan, R. M. (1995). Human autonomy: The basis for true self-esteem. In M. Kernis (Ed.), *Efficacy, agency, and self-esteem* (pp. 31–49). New York: Plenum.

Deffenbacher, J. L., Story, D. A., Brandon, A. D., Hogg, J. A., & Hazaleus, S. L. (1988). Cognitive and cognitive-relaxation treatments of anger. *Cognitive Therapy and Research, 12,* 167–184.

Deluty, R. H. (1985). Consistency of assertive, aggressive, and submissive behavior for children. *Journal of Personality and Social Psychology, 49,* 1054–1065.

Denney, D. R. (1974). Active, passive, and vicarious desensitization. *Journal of Counseling Psychology, 21,* 369–375.

Depue, R. A. (1979). *The psychobiology of the depressive disorders: Implications for the effect of stress.* New York: Academic Press.

Depue, R. A. (in press). *A neurobehavioral model of temperament and personality.* New York: Springer-Verlag.

Depue, R. A., & Collins, P. F. (in press). Neurobiology of the structure of personality: Dopamine, facilitation of incentive motivation, and extraversion. *Behavioral and Brain Sciences.*

Depue, R. A., & Iacono, W. G. (1989). Neurobehavioral aspects of affective disorders. *Annual Review of Psychology, 40,* 457–492.

Depue, R. A., Krauss, S. P., & Spoont, M. R. (1987). A two-dimensional threshold model of seasonal bipolar affective disorder. In D. Magnusson & A. Öhman (Eds.), *Psychopathology: An interactional perspective* (pp. 95–123). Orlando, FL: Academic Press.

Depue, R. A., Luciana, M., Arbisi, P., Collins, P., & Leon, A. (1994). Dopamine and the structure of personality: Relation of agonist-induced dopamine cativity to positive emotionality. *Journal of Personality and Social Psychology, 67,* 485–498.

Detera-Wadleigh, S. D., Berrettini, W. H., Goldin, L. R., Boorman, D., Anderson, S., & Gershon, E. S. (1987). Close linkage of c-harvey-ras-1 and the insulin gene to affective disorder is ruled out in three North American pedigrees. *Nature, 325,* 806–808.

Deutsch, F. M., Ruble, D. N., Fleming, A., Brooks-Gunn, J., & Stangor, C. (1988). Information-seeking and maternal self-definition during the transition to motherhood. *Journal of Personality and Social Psychology, 55,* 420–431.

DeVellis, R. F., DeVellis, B. M., & McCauley, C. (1978). Vicarious acquisition of learned helplessness. *Journal of Personality and Social Psychology, 36,* 894–899.

DeVito, A. J. (1985). Review of Myers-Briggs Type Indicator. In J. V. Mitchell (Ed.), *The ninth mental measurements yearbook* (pp. 1029–1032). Lincoln, NE: Buros Institute of Mental Measurements.

Diamond, M. J., & Shapiro, J. L. (1973). Changes in locus of control as a function of encounter group experiences: A study and replication. *Journal of Abnormal Psychology, 82,* 514–518.

DiClemente, C. C. (1981). Self-efficacy and smoking cessation. *Cognitive Therapy and Research, 5,* 175–187.

Diener, C. I., & Dweck, C. S. (1978). An analysis of learned helplessness: Continuous changes in performance, strategy, and achievement cognitions following failure. *Journal of Personality and Social Psychology, 36,* 451–462.

Diener, E. (1977). Deindividuation: Causes and consequences. *Social Behavior and Personality, 5,* 143–155.

Diener, E. (1979). Deindividuation, self-awareness, and disinhibition. *Journal of Personality and Social Psychology, 37,* 1160–1171.

Diener, E. (1980). Deindividuation: The absence of self-awareness and self-regulation in group members. In P. B. Paulus (Ed.), *The psychology of group influence.* Hillsdale, NJ: Erlbaum.

Diener, E., Sandvik, E., Pavot, W., & Fujita, F. (1992). Extraversion and subjective well-being in a U.S. national probability sample. *Journal of Research in Personality, 26,* 205–215.

Diener, E., & Wallbom, M. (1976). Effects of self-awareness on antinormative behavior. *Journal of Research in Personality, 10,* 413–423.

Digman, J. M. (1990). Personality structure: Emergence of the five-factor model. *Annual Review of Psychology, 41,* 417–440.

Digman, J. M. (1997). Higher-order factors of the Big Five. *Journal of Personality and Social Psychology, 73,* 1246–1256.

Digman, J. M., & Inouye, J. (1986). Further specification of the five robust factors of personality. *Journal of Personality and Social Psychology, 50,* 116–123.

Digman, J. M., & Shmelyov, A. G. (1996). The structure of temperament and personality in Russian children. *Journal of Personality and Social Psychology, 71,* 341–351.

Digman, J. M., & Takemoto-Chock, N. K. (1981). Factors in the natural language of personality: Re-analy-sis, comparison, and interpretation of six major studies. *Multivariate Behavioral Research, 16,* 149–170.

DiLalla, L. F., & Gottesman, I. I. (1991). Biological and genetic contributors to violence—Widom's untold tale. *Psychological Bulletin, 109,* 125–129.

Diven, K. (1936). Certain determinants in the conditioning of anxiety reactions. *Journal of Psychology, 3,* 291–308.

Dixon, N. F. (1981). *Preconscious processing.* Chichester, England: Wiley.

Dodge, K. A. (1986). A social information processing model of social competence in children. In M. Perlmutter (Ed.), *Minnesota symposium on child psychology* (Vol. 18). Hillsdale, NJ: Erlbaum.

Dodge, K. A., & Crick, N. R. (1990). Social information-processing bases of aggressive behavior in children. *Personality and Social Psychology Bulletin, 16,* 8–22.

Dollard, J., & Miller, N. E. (1950). *Personality and psychotherapy: An analysis in terms of learning, thinking, and culture.* New York: McGraw-Hill.

Dollinger, S. J., & Orf, L. A. (1991). Personality and performance in "personality": Conscientiousness and openness. *Journal of Research in Personality, 25,* 276–284.

Donahue, E. M. (1994). Do children use the big five, too? Content and structural form in personality description. *Journal of Personality, 62,* 45–66.

Donahue, E. M., & Harary, K. (1998). The patterned inconsistency of traits: Mapping the differential effects of social roles on self-perceptions of the Big Five. *Personality and Social Psychology Bulletin, 24,* 610–619.

Donnerstein, E. (1980). Aggressive erotica and violence against women. *Journal of Personality and Social Psychology, 39,* 269–277.

Donnerstein, E. (1983). Erotica and human aggression. In R. G. Geen & E. Donnerstein (Eds.), *Aggression: Theoretical and empirical reviews.* New York: Academic Press.

Donnerstein, E., & Berkowitz, L. (1981). Victim reactions in aggressive erotic films as a factor in violence against women. *Journal of Personality and Social Psychology, 41,* 710–724.

Donnerstein, E., Donnerstein, M., & Evans, R. (1975). Erotic stimuli and aggression: Facilitation or inhibition. *Journal of Personality and Social Psychology, 32,* 237–244.

Donnerstein, E., & Hallam, J. (1978). The facilitating effects of erotica on aggression toward females. *Journal of Personality and Social Psychology, 36,* 1270–1277.

Donovan, J. M. (1975). Identity status and interpersonal style. *Journal of Youth and Adolescence, 4,* 37–55.

Doob, A. N. (1970). Catharsis and aggression: The effect of hurting one's enemy. *Journal of Experimental Research in Personality, 4,* 291–296.

Dosamantes-Alperson, E., & Merrill, N. (1980). Growth effects of experiential movement psychotherapy. *Psychotherapy: Theory, Research, and Practice, 17,* 63–68.

Douglas, C. (1993). *Translate this darkness: The life of Christiana Morgan.* New York: Simon & Schuster.

Drabman, R. S., & Spitalnik, R. (1973). Training a retarded child as a behavioral teaching assistant. *Journal of Behavior Therapy and Experimental Psychiatry, 4,* 269–272.

Duck, S. W. (1973). *Personal relationships and personal constructs.* London: Wiley.

Duck, S. W. (1977). Inquiry, hypothesis, and the quest for validation: Personal construct systems in the development of acquaintance. In S. W. Duck (Ed.), *Theories of interpersonal attraction.* London: Academic Press.

Duck, S. W., & Allison, D. (1978). I liked you but I can't live with you: A study of lapsed friendships. *Social Behavior and Personality, 8,* 43–47.

Dulany, D. E. (1968). Awareness, rules and propositional control: A confrontation with S-R behavior theory. In T. R. Dixon & D. L. Horton (Eds.), *Verbal behavior and general behavior theory.* Englewood Cliffs, NJ: Prentice-Hall.

Dunn, J., & Plomin, R. (1990). *Separate lives: Why siblings are so different.* New York: Basic Books.

Dunnette, M. D. (1969). People feeling: Joy, more joy, and the "slough of despond." *Journal of Applied Behavioral Science, 5,* 25–44.

Dunning, D., & McElwee, R. O. (1995). Idiosyncratic trait definitions: Implications for self-description and social judgment. *Journal of Personality and Social Psychology, 68,* 936–946.

Dweck, C. S., & Leggett, E. L. (1988). A social-cognitive approach to motivation and personality. *Psychological Review, 95,* 256–273.

Dykman, B. M. (1998). Integrating cognitive and motivational factors in depression: Initial tests of a goal-orientation approach. *Journal of Personality and Social Psychology, 74,* 139–158.

D'Zurilla, T., & Goldfried, M. (1971). Problem-solving and behavior modification. *Journal of Abnormal Psychology, 78,* 107–126.

Eagle, M. N. (1984). *Recent developments in psychoanalysis: A critical evaluation.* New York: McGraw-Hill.

Eagly, A. (1987). *Sex differences in social behavior: A social-role interpretation.* Hillsdale, NJ: Erlbaum.

Eaves, L. J., Eysenck, H. J., & Martin, N. G. (1989). *Genes, culture, and personality: An empirical approach.* San Diego: Academic Press.

Ebbesen, E. B., Duncan, B., & Konečni, V. J. (1975). Effects of content of verbal aggression on future verbal aggression: A field experiment. *Journal of Experimental Social Psychology, 11,* 192–204.

Ebstein, R. P., Novick, O., Umansky, R., Priel, B., Osher, Y., Blaine, D., Bennett, E. R., Nemanov, L., Katz, M., & Belmaker, R. H. (1996). Dopamine D4 receptor (D4DR) exon III polymorphism associated with the human personality trait of novelty seeking. *Nature Genetics, 12,* 78–80.

Edwards, A. L. (1957). *The social desirability variable in personality assessment and research.* New York: Dryden.

Edwards, A. L. (1959). *Edwards Personal Preference Schedule manual.* New York: The Psychological Corporation.

Egeland, J. A., Gerhard, D. S., Pauls, D. L., Sussex, J. N., & Kidd, K. K. (1987). Bipolar affective disorders linked to DNA markers on chromosome 11. *Nature, 325,* 783–787.

Eisenberg, N., Fabes, R. A., Murphy, B., Karbon, M., Maszk, P., Smith, M., O'Boyle, C., & Suh, K. (1994). The relations of emotionality and regulation to dispositional and situational empathy-related responding. *Journal of Personality and Social Psychology, 66,* 776–797.

Eisenberger, R. (1992). Learned industriousness. *Psychological Review, 99,* 248–267.

Eisenberger, R., Armeli, S., & Pretz, J. (1998). Can the promise of reward increase creativity? *Journal of Personality and Social Psychology, 74,* 704–714.

Eisenberger, R., & Selbst, M. (1994). Does reward increase or decrease creativity? *Journal of Personality and Social Psychology, 66,* 1116–1127.

Ekehammar, B. (1974). Interactionism in personality from a historical perspective. *Psychological Bulletin, 81,* 1026–1048.

Elder, G. H., Jr., Caspi, A., & Downey, G. (1986). Problem behavior and family relationships: Life course and intergenerational themes. In A. B. Sorenson, F. Weinert, & L. R. Sherrod (Eds.), *Human development and the life course: Multidisciplinary perspectives* (pp. 293–340). Hillsdale, NJ: Erlbaum.

Elder, G. H., Jr., & MacInnis, D. J. (1983). Achievement imagery in women's lives from adolescence to adulthood. *Journal of Personality and Social Psychology, 45,* 394–404.

Ellenberger, H. F. (1970). *The discovery of the unconscious.* New York: Basic Books.

Elliot, A. J., & Harackiewicz, J. M. (1994). Goal setting, achievement orientation, and intrinsic motivation: A mediational analysis. *Journal of Personality and Social Psychology, 66,* 968–980.

Elliott, A. J., & Sheldon, K. M. (1997). Avoidance achievement motivation: A personal goals analysis. *Journal of Personality and Social Psychology, 73,* 171–185.

Elliott, E. S., & Dweck, C. S. (1988). Goals: An approach to motivation and achievement. *Journal of Personality and Social Psychology, 54,* 5–12.

Ellis, A. (1962). *Reason and emotion in psychotherapy.* Secaucus, NJ: Lyle Stuart.

Ellis, A. E. (1987). The impossibility of achieving consistently good mental health. *American Psychologist, 42,* 364–375.

Elmore, A. M., & Tursky, B. (1981). A comparison of two psychophysiological approaches to the treatment of migraine. *Headache, 21,* 93–101.

Emmons, R. A. (1986). Personal strivings: An approach to personality and subjective well-being. *Journal of Personality and Social Psychology, 51,* 1058–1068.

Emmons, R. A., & Diener, E. (1986). Situation selection as a moderator of response consistency and stability. *Journal of Personality and Social Psychology, 51,* 1013–1019.

Emmons, R. A., Diener, E., & Larsen, R. J. (1986). Choice and avoidance of everyday situations and affect congruence: Two models of reciprocal interactionism. *Journal of Personality and Social Psychology, 51,* 815–826.

Emmons, R. A., & King, L. A. (1988). Conflict among personal strivings: Immediate and long-term implications for psychological and physical well-being. *Journal of Personality and Social Psychology, 54,* 1040–1048.

Emmons, R. A., King, L. A., & Sheldon, K. (1993). Goal conflict and the self-regulation of action. In D. M. Wegner & J. W. Pennebaker (Eds.), *Handbook of mental control* (pp. 528–551). Englewood Cliffs, NJ: Prentice-Hall.

Endler, N. S., & Magnusson, D. (1976). *Interactional psychology and personality.* Washington, DC: Hemisphere.

Entwisle, D. R. (1972). To dispel fantasies about fantasy-based measures of achievement motivation. *Psychological Bulletin, 77,* 377–391.

Epstein, L. H., Saelens, B. E., Myers, M. D., & Vito, D. (1997). Effects of decreasing sedentary behaviors on activity choice in obese children. *Health Psychology, 16,* 107–113.

Epstein, S. (1979). The stability of behavior: I. On predicting most of the people much of the time. *Journal of Personality and Social Psychology, 37,* 1097–1126.

Epstein, S. (1980). The stability of behavior: II. Implications for psychological research. *American Psychologist, 35,* 790–806.

Epstein, S. (1983). The unconscious, the preconscious, and the self-concept. In J. Suls & A. G. Greenwald (Eds.), *Psychological perspectives on the self* (Vol. 2). Hillsdale, NJ: Erlbaum.

Epstein, S. (1986). Does aggregation produce spuriously high estimates of behavior stability? *Journal of Personality and Social Psychology, 50,* 1199–1210.

Epstein, S. (1994). Integration of the cognitive and the psychodynamic unconscious. *American Psychologist, 49,* 709–724.

Epting, F. R. (1972). The stability of cognitive complexity in construing social issues. *British Journal of Social and Clinical Psychology, 11,* 122–125.

Epting, F. R. (1980). *Personal construct theory psychotherapy.* New York: Wiley.

Erdelyi, M. H. (1985). *Psychoanalysis: Freud's cognitive psychology.* New York: Freeman.

Erikson, E. H. (1950). *Childhood and society* (1st ed.). New York: Norton.

Erikson, E. H. (1963). *Childhood and society* (2nd ed.). New York: Norton.

Erikson, E. H. (1964). *Insight and responsibility.* New York: Norton.

Erikson, E. H. (1968). *Identity: Youth and crisis.* New York: Norton.

Erikson, E. H. (1974). *Dimensions of a new identity.* New York: Norton.

Erikson, E. H. (Ed.). (1978). *Adulthood.* New York: Norton.

Erikson, E. H. (1982). *The life cycle completed: A review.* New York: Norton.

Ernst, C., & Angst, J. (1983). *Birth order: Its influence on personality.* Berlin: Springer-Verlag.

Esterton, A. (1993). *Seductive mirage: An exploration of the work of Sigmund Freud.* Chicago: Open Court.

Esterton, A. (1998). Jeffrey Masson and Freud's seduction theory: A new fable based on old myths. *History of the Human Sciences, 11,* 1–21.

Evans, R. I. (1989). *Albert Bandura: The man and his ideas—A dialogue.* New York: Praeger.

Ewart, C. K. (1978). Self-observation in natural environments: Reactive effects of behavior desirability and goal-setting. *Cognitive Therapy and Research, 2,* 39–56.

Exner, J. E., Jr. (1974). *The Rorschach systems.* New York: Grune & Stratton.

Exner, J. E., Jr. (1993). *The Rorschach: A comprehensive system:* Vol. 1. Basic foundations (3rd ed.). New York: Wiley.

Exner, J. E., Jr. (1996). A comment on "The comprehensive system for the Rorschach: A critical examination." *Psychological Science, 7,* 11–13.

Eysenck, H. J. (1952). *The scientific study of personality.* New York: Macmillan.

Eysenck, H. J. (1961). The effects of psychotherapy. In H. J. Eysenck (Ed.), *Handbook of abnormal psychology.* New York: Basic Books.

Eysenck, H. J. (1964a). Involuntary rest pauses in tapping as a function of drive and personality. *Perceptual and Motor Skills, 18,* 173–174.

Eysenck, H. J. (1964b). *Crime and personality.* Boston: Houghton Mifflin.

Eysenck, H. J. (1967). *The biological basis of personality.* Springfield, IL: Charles C Thomas.

Eysenck, H. J. (1970). *The structure of human personality* (3rd ed.). London: Methuen.

Eysenck, H. J. (1971). *Readings in extraversion-introversion: 3. Bearings on basic psychological processes.* New York: Wiley-Interscience.

Eysenck, H. J. (1975). *The inequality of man.* San Diego: EdITS.

Eysenck, H. J. (Ed.). (1981). *A model for personality.* Berlin: Springer-Verlag.

Eysenck, H. J. (1983). Psychopharmacology and personality. In W. Janke (Ed.), *Response variability to psychotropic drugs.* London: Pergamon.

Eysenck, H. J. (1986). Models and paradigms in personality research. In A. Angleitner, A. Furnham, & G. Van Heck (Eds.), *Personality psychology in Europe, Vol. 2: Current trends and controversies* (pp. 213–223). Lisse, Holland: Swets & Zeitlinger.

Eysenck, H. J. (1992). Four ways five factors are *not* basic. *Personality and Individual Differences, 13,* 667–673.

Eysenck, H. J. (1993). Comment on Goldberg. *American Psychologist, 48,* 1299–1300.

Eysenck, H. J., & Eysenck, M. W. (1985). *Personality and individual differences: A natural science approach.* New York: Plenum.

Eysenck, H. J., & Eysenck, S. B. G. (1975). *Manual of the Eysenck Personality Questionnaire.* San Diego, CA: EdITS.

Eysenck, H. J., & Eysenck, S. B. G. (1976). *Psychoticism as a dimension of personality.* London: Hodder & Stoughton.

Fagot, B. I. (1977). Consequences of moderate cross-gender behavior in preschool children. *Child Development, 48,* 902–907.

Fairbairn, W. R. D. (1952). *Psycho-analytic studies of the personality.* New York: Basic Books.

Fairbairn, W. R. D. (1954). *An object relations theory of personality.* New York: Basic Books.

Falbo, T. (1981). Relationships between birth category, achievement, and interpersonal orientation. *Journal of Personality and Social Psychology, 41,* 121–131.

Feather, N. T. (1961). The relationship of persistence at a task to expectations of success and achievement related motivation. *Journal of Abnormal and Social Psychology, 63,* 552–561.

Feather, N. T. (1968). Change in confidence following success and failure as a predictor of subsequent task performance. *Journal of Personality and Social Psychology, 9,* 38–46.

Feather, N. T. (Ed.). (1982). *Expectations and actions: Expectancy-value models in psychology.* Hillsdale, NJ: Erlbaum.

Feeney, J. A., & Noller, P. (1990). Attachment style as a predictor of adult romantic relationships. *Journal of Personality and Social Psychology, 58,* 281–291.

Feij, J. A., Orlebeke, J. F., Gazendam, A., & van Zuilen, R. W. (1985). Sensation seeking: Measurement and psychophysiological correlates. In J. Strelau, F. H. Farley, & A. Gale (Eds.), *The biological bases of personality and behavior. Vol. 1. Theories, measurement techniques, and development.* Washington, DC: Hemisphere.

Feingold, A. (1992). Gender differences in mate selection preferences: A test of the parental investment model. *Psychological Bulletin, 112,* 125–139.

Fekken, G. C., & Holden, R. R. (1992). Response latency evidence for viewing personality traits as schema indicators. *Journal of Research in Personality, 26,* 103–120.

Feldman, F. (1968). Results of psychoanalysis in clinic case assignments. *Journal of the American Psychoanalytic Association, 16,* 274–300.

Feldman, M. P., & MacCulloch, M. J. (1971). *Homosexual behavior: Therapy and assessment.* Oxford: Pergamon.

Fenichel, O. (1945). *The psychoanalytic theory of neurosis.* New York: Norton.

Fenigstein, A., & Buss, A. H. (1974). Association and affect as determinants of displaced aggression. *Journal of Research in Personality, 7,* 306–313.

Fenigstein, A., Scheier, M. F., & Buss, A. H. (1975). Public and private self-consciousness: Assessment and theory. *Journal of Consulting and Clinical Psychology, 43,* 522–527.

Fernando, C. K., & Basmajian, J. V. (1978). Biofeedback in physical medicine and rehabilitation. *Biofeedback and Self-regulation, 3,* 435–455.

Festinger, L., Pepitone, A., & Newcomb, T. (1952). Some consequences of deindividuation in a group. *Journal of Abnormal and Social Psychology, 47,* 382–389.

Findley, M. J., & Cooper, H. M. (1983). Locus of control and academic achievement: A literature review. *Journal of Personality and Social Psychology, 44,* 419–427.

Finkelhor, D., & Dziuba-Leatherman, J. (1994). Victimization of children. *American Psychologist, 49,* 173–183.

Fisher, S. (1973). *The female orgasm.* New York: Basic Books.

Fisher, S., & Greenberg, R. P. (1977). *The scientific credibility of Freud's theories and therapy.* New York: Basic Books.

Fiske, A. P. (1992). The four elementary forms of sociality: Framework for a unified theory of social relations. *Psychological Review, 99,* 689–723.

Fiske, D. W. (1949). Consistency of the factorial structures of personality ratings from different sources. *Journal of Abnormal and Social Psychology, 44,* 329–344.

Fiske, S. T., & Taylor, S. E. (1984). *Social cognition.* Reading, MA: Addison-Wesley.

Flanders, J. P. (1968). A review of research on imitative behavior. *Psychological Bulletin, 69,* 316–337.

Fletcher, G. J. O., Danilovics, P., Fernandez, G., Peterson, D., & Reeder, G. D. (1986). Attributional complexity: An individual differences measure. *Journal of Personality and Social Psychology, 51,* 875–884.

Flink, C., Boggiano, A. K., & Barrett, M. (1990). Controlling teaching strategies: Undermining children's self-determination and performance. *Journal of Personality and Social Psychology, 59,* 916–924.

Floderus-Myrhed, B., Pedersen, N., & Rasmuson, I. (1980). Assessment of heritability for personality, based on a short form of the Eysenck Personality Inventory: A study of 12,898 twin pairs. *Behavior Genetics, 10,* 153–162.

Fodor, E. M. (1984). The power motive and reactivity to power stresses. *Journal of Personality and Social Psychology, 47,* 853–859.

Ford, D. H. (1987). *Humans as self-constructing living systems: A developmental perspective on behavior and personality.* Hillsdale, NJ: Erlbaum.

Ford, J. G. (1991a). Inherent potentialities of actualization: An initial exploration. *Journal of Humanistic Psychology, 31,* 65–88.

Ford, J. G. (1991b). Rogerian self-actualization: A clarification of meaning. *Journal of Humanistic Psychology, 31,* 101–111.

Fowles, D. C. (1980). The three arousal model: Implications of Gray's two-factor learning theory for heart rate, electrodermal activity, and psychopathy. *Psychophysiology, 17,* 87–104.

Fox, J., Knapp, R. R., & Michael, W. B. (1968). Assessment of self-actualization of psychiatric patients: Validity of the Personal Orientation Inventory. *Educational and Psychological Measurement, 28,* 565–569.

Fox, N. A., & Davidson, R. J. (1988). Patterns of brain electrical activity during facial signs of emotion in 10-month old infants. *Developmental Psychology, 24,* 230–236.

Frank, L. K. (1939). Projective methods for the study of personality. *Journal of Psychology, 8,* 389–413.

Frank, S., & Quinlan, D. M. (1976). Ego development and female delinquency: A cognitive-developmental approach. *Journal of Abnormal Psychology, 85,* 505–510.

Frankel, A., & Snyder, M. L. (1978). Poor performance following unsolvable problems: Learned helplessness or egotism? *Journal of Personality and Social Psychology, 36,* 1415–1423.

Frankl, V. E. (1969). *The doctor and the soul.* New York: Bantam.

Fransella, F. (1972). *Personal change and reconstruction.* New York: Academic Press.

Freedman, J. L. (1986). Television violence and aggression: A rejoinder. *Psychological Bulletin, 100,* 372–378.

French, E. G. (1955). Some characteristics of achievement motivation. *Journal of Experimental Psychology, 50,* 232–236.

French, E. G., & Lesser, G. S. (1964). Some characteristics of the achievement motive in women. *Journal of Abnormal and Social Psychology, 68,* 119–128.

Freud, A. (1966). *The ego and the mechanisms of defense* (Rev. ed.). New York: International Universities Press.

Freud, S. (1933). *New introductory lectures on psychoanalysis.* New York: Norton. (Translated by W. J. H. Sprott)

Freud, S. (1936). *The problem of anxiety.* New York: Norton. (Translated by H. A. Bunker; originally published, 1926)

Freud, S. (1949). *An outline of psychoanalysis.* New York: Norton. (Translated by J. Strachey; originally published, 1940)

Freud, S. (1953a). Three essays on sexuality. In J. Strachey (Ed.), *The standard edition of the complete psychological works of Sigmund Freud* (Vol. 7). London: Hogarth Press. (Originally published, 1905)

Freud, S. (1953b). The interpretation of dreams. In J. Strachey (Ed.), *The standard edition of the complete psychological works of Sigmund Freud* (Vols. 4 and 5). London: Hogarth Press. (Originally published, 1900)

Freud, S. (1955). Beyond the pleasure principle. In J. Strachey (Ed.), *The standard edition of the complete psychological works of Sigmund Freud* (Vol. 18). London: Hogarth Press. (Originally published, 1920)

Freud, S. (1959). Inhibitions, symptoms and anxiety. In J. Strachey (Ed.), *The standard edition of the complete psychological works of Sigmund Freud* (Vol. 20). London: Hogarth Press. (Originally published, 1926)

Freud, S. (1960a). *Jokes and their relation to the unconscious.* New York: Norton. (Translated by J. Strachey, originally published, 1905)

Freud, S. (1960b). Psychopathology of everyday life. In J. Strachey (Ed.), *The standard edition of the complete psychological works of Sigmund Freud* (Vol. 6). London: Hogarth Press. (Originally published, 1901)

Freud, S. (1961). The unconscious. In J. Strachey (Ed.), *The standard edition of the complete psychological works of Sigmund Freud* (Vol. 14). London: Hogarth Press. (Originally published, 1915)

Freud, S. (1962). *The ego and the id.* New York: Norton. (Originally published, 1923)

Friendly, M. L., & Glucksberg, S. (1970). On the description of subcultural lexicons: A multidimensional approach. *Journal of Personality and Social Psychology, 14,* 55–65.

Fritz, H. L., & Helgeson, V. S. (1998). Distinctions of unmitigated communion from communion: Self-neglect and overinvolvement with others. *Journal of Personality and Social Psychology, 75,* 121–140.

Frodi, A. (1977). Sexual arousal, situational restrictiveness, and aggressive behavior. *Journal of Research in Personality, 11,* 48–58.

Froming, W. J., & Carver, C. S. (1981). Divergent influences of private and public self-consciousness in a compliance paradigm. *Journal of Research in Personality, 15,* 159–171.

Froming, W. J., Walker, G. R., & Lopyan, K. J. (1982). Public and private self-awareness: When personal attitudes conflict with societal expectations. *Journal of Experimental Social Psychology, 18,* 476–487.

Fultz, J., Schaller, M., & Cialdini, R. B. (1988). Empathy, sadness, and distress: Three related but distinct vicarious affective responses to another's suffering. *Personality and Social Psychology Bulletin, 14,* 312–325.

Funder, D. C. (1991). Global traits: A neo-Allportian approach to personality. *Psychological Science, 2,* 31–39.

Funder, D. C., & Block, J. (1989). The role of ego-control, ego-resiliency, and IQ in delay of gratification in adolescence. *Journal of Personality and Social Psychology, 57,* 1041–1050.

Funder, D. C., Block, J. H., & Block, J. (1983). Delay of gratification: Some longitudinal personality correlates. *Journal of Personality and Social Psychology, 44,* 1198–1213.

Funder, D. C., & Colvin, C. R. (1991). Explorations in behavioral consistency: Properties of persons, situations, and behaviors. *Journal of Personality and Social Psychology, 60,* 773–794.

Funder, D. C., & Ozer, D. J. (1983). Behavior as a function of the situation. *Journal of Personality and Social Psychology, 44,* 107–112.

Gacsaly, S. A., & Borges, C. A. (1979). The male physique and behavioral expectancies. *Journal of Psychology, 101,* 97–102.

Gallagher, W. (1994). How we become what we are. *The Atlantic Monthly, 274,* 39–55.

Gallistel, C. R. (1980). *The organization of action: A new synthesis.* Hillsdale, NJ: Erlbaum.

Ganellen, R. J. (1996a). *Integrating the Rorschach and MMPI-2 in personality assessment.* Hillsdale, NJ: Erlbaum.

Ganellen, R. J. (1996b). Comparing the diagnostic efficiency of the MMPMI, MCMI-II, and Rorschach: A review. *Journal of Personality Assessment, 67,* 219–243.

Gangestad, S., & Snyder, M. (1985). "To carve nature at its joints": On the existence of discrete classes in personality. *Psychological Review, 92,* 317–349.

Garcia, J., & Koelling, R. A. (1966). Relation of cue to consequence in avoidance learning. *Psychonomic Science, 4,* 123–124.

Gardner, H. (1985). *The mind's new science: A history of the cognitive revolution.* New York: Basic Books.

Gauthier, J., & Ladouceur, R. (1981). The influence of self-efficacy reports on performance. *Behavior Therapy, 12,* 436–439.

Geen, R. G. (1981). Behavioral and physiological reactions to observed violence: Effects of prior exposure to aggressive stimuli. *Journal of Personality and Social Psychology, 40,* 868–875.

Geen, R. G. (1984). Preferred stimulation levels in introverts and extraverts: Effects on arousal and performance. *Journal of Personality and Social Psychology, 46,* 1303–1312.

Geen, R. G. (1998). Aggression and antisocial behavior. In D. T. Gilbert, S. T. Fiske, & G. Lindzey (Eds.). *The handbook of social psychology* (Vol. 2, 4th ed., pp. 317–356). Boston: McGraw-Hill.

Geen, R. G., Stonner, D., & Shope, G. L. (1975). The facilitation of aggression by aggression: Evidence against the catharsis hypothesis. *Journal of Personality and Social Psychology, 31,* 721–726.

Gerst, M. S. (1971). Symbolic coding processes in observational learning. *Journal of Personality and Social Psychology, 19,* 7–27.

Gibbons, F. X. (1978). Sexual standards and reactions to pornography: Enhancing behavioral consistency through self-focused attention. *Journal of Personality and Social Psychology, 36,* 976–987.

Gibbons, F. X., & Wicklund, R. A. (1976). Selective exposure to self. *Journal of Research in Personality, 10,* 98–106.

Gibson, H. B. (1981). *Hans Eysenck: The man and his work.* London: Peter Owen.

Gigerenzer, G., & Goldstein, D. G. (1996). Reasoning the fast and frugal way: Models of bounded rationality. *Psychological Review, 103,* 650–669.

Gill, M. M. (1959). The present state of psychoanalytic theory. *Journal of Abnormal and Social Psychology, 58,* 1–8.

Gilovich, T. (1990). Differential construal and the false consensus effect. *Journal of Personality and Social Psychology, 59,* 623–634.

Glueck, S., & Glueck, E. (1956). *Physique and delinquency.* New York: Harper.

Goldberg, A. (Ed.). (1985). *Progress in self psychology (Vol. 1).* New York: Guilford Press.

Goldberg, L. R. (1981). Language and individual differences: The search for universals in personality lexicons. In L. Wheeler (Ed.), *Review of personality and social psychology* (Vol. 2, pp. 141–165). Beverly Hills, CA: Sage.

Goldberg, L. R. (1982). From ace to zombie: Some explorations in the language of personality. In C. D. Spielberger & J. N. Butcher (Eds.), *Advances in personality assessment* (Vol. 1). Hillsdale, NJ: Erlbaum.

Goldberg, L. R. (1993a). The structure of phenotypic personality traits. *American Psychologist, 48,* 26–34.

Goldberg, L. R. (1993b). The structure of personality traits: Vertical and horizontal aspects. In D. C. Funder, R. Parke, C. Tomlinson-Keasey, & K. Widaman (Eds.), *Studying lives through time: Approaches to personality and development* (pp. 169–188). Washington, DC: American Psychological Association.

Goldfried, M. R. (1971). Systematic desensitization as training in self-control. *Journal of Consulting and Clinical Psychology, 37,* 228–234.

Goldfried, M. R., & Davison, G. C. (1976). *Clinical behavior therapy.* New York: Holt, Rinehart, & Winston.

Goldfried, M. R., & Merbaum, M. (Eds.). (1973). *Behavior change through self-control.* New York: Holt, Rinehart, & Winston.

Goldiamond, I. (1976). Self-reinforcement. *Journal of Applied Behavior Analysis, 9,* 509–514.

Goldstein, J. H., & Arms, R. L. (1971). Effects of observing athletic contests on hostility. *Sociometry, 34,* 90–93.

Gollwitzer, P. M. (1990). Action phases and mind-sets. In E. T. Higgins & R. M. Sorrentino (Eds.), *Handbook of motivation and cognition: Foundations of social behavior* (Vol. 2, pp. 53–92). New York: Guilford.

Gollwitzer, P. M., & Brandstätter, V. (1997). Implementation intentions and effective goal pursuit. *Journal of Personality and Social Psychology, 73,* 186–199.

Goranson, R. E. (1970). Media violence and aggressive behavior: A review of experimental research. In L. Berkowitz (Ed.), *Advances in experimental social psychology* (Vol. 5). New York: Academic Press.

Gormly, J. (1983). Predicting behavior from personality trait scores. *Personality and Social Psychology Bulletin, 9,* 267–270.

Gotlib, I. H. (1983). Perception and recall of interpersonal feedback: Negative bias in depression. *Cognitive Therapy and Research, 7,* 399–412.

Gottesman, I. I., Carey, G., & Hanson, D. R. (1983). Pearls and perils in epigenetic psychopathology. In S. B. Guze, E. J. Earls, & J. E. Barrett (Eds.), *Childhood psychopathology and development* (pp. 287–300). New York: Raven Press.

Gottesman, I. I., Goldsmith, H. H., & Carey, G. (1997). A developmental *and* a genetic perspective on aggression. In N. L. Segal, G. E. Weisfeld, & C. C. Weisfeld

(Eds.), *Uniting psychology and biology: Integrative perspectives on human development* (pp. 107–130). Washington, DC: American Psychological Association.

Gottesman, I. I., & Shields, J. (1972). *Schizophrenia and genetics.* New York: Academic Press.

Gough, H. G. (1956). *California Psychological Inventory.* Palo Alto, CA: Consulting Psychologists Press.

Gough, H. G. (1960). Theory and measurement of socialization. *Journal of Consulting Psychology, 24,* 23–30.

Gough, H. G. (1968). An interpreter's syllabus for the California Psychological Inventory. In P. McReynolds (Ed.), *Advances in psychological assessment* (Vol. 1). Palo Alto, CA: Science and Behavior Books.

Gough, H. G. (1987). *The California Psychological Inventory administrator's guide.* Palo Alto, CA: Consulting Psychologists Press.

Gould, R. L. (1980). Transformations during early and middle adult years. In N. J. Smelser & E. H. Erikson (Eds.), *Themes of work and love in adulthood* (pp. 213–237). Cambridge, MA: Harvard University Press.

Grammer, K., & Thornhill, R. (1994). Human facial attractiveness and sexual selection: The role of symmetry and averageness. *Journal of Comparative Psychology, 108,* 233–242.

Gray, J. (1992). *Men are from Mars, women are from Venus: A practical guide for improving communication and getting what you want in your relationships.* New York: HarperCollins.

Gray, J. A. (1981). A critique of Eysenck's theory of personality. In H. J. Eysenck (Ed.), *A model for personality.* Berlin: Springer-Verlag.

Gray, J. A. (1982). *The neuropsychology of anxiety: An enquiry into the functions of the septo-hippocampal system.* New York: Oxford University Press.

Gray, J. A. (1987). Perspectives on anxiety and impulsivity: A commentary. *Journal of Research in Personality, 21,* 493–509.

Gray, J. A. (1990). Brain systems that mediate both emotion and cognition. *Cognition and Emotion, 4,* 269–288.

Gray, J. A. (1991). The neuropsychology of temperament. In J. Strelau & A. Angleitner (Eds.), *Explorations in temperament: International perspectives on theory and measurement* (pp. 105–128). New York: Plenum.

Gray, J. A. (1994a). Personality dimensions and emotion systems. In P. Ekman & R. J. Davidson (Eds.), *The nature of emotion: Fundamental questions* (pp. 329–331). New York: Oxford University Press.

Gray, J. A. (1994b). Three fundamental emotion systems. In P. Ekman, & R. J. Davidson (Eds.), *The nature of emotion: Fundamental questions* (pp. 243–247). New York: Oxford University Press.

Gray, J. D., & Silver, R. C. (1990). Opposite sides of the same coin: Former spouses' divergent perspectives in coping with their divorce. *Journal of Personality and Social Psychology, 59,* 1180–1191.

Graziano, W. G., Jensen-Campbell, L. A., & Hair, E. C. (1996). Perceiving interpersonal conflict and reacting to it: The case for agreeableness. *Journal of Personality and Social Psychology, 70,* 820–835.

Greenberg, J. (1980). Attentional focus and locus of performance causality as determinants of equity behavior. *Journal of Personality and Social Psychology, 38,* 579–585.

Greenberg, J., & Musham, C. (1981). Avoiding and seeking self-focused attention. *Journal of Research in Personality, 15,* 191–200.

Greenberg, J., Pyszczynski, T., & Paisley, C. (1984). Effect of extrinsic incentives on use of test anxiety as an anticipatory attributional defense: Playing it cool when the stakes are high. *Journal of Personality and Social Psychology, 47,* 1136–1145.

Greenberg, J., Pyszczynski, T., & Solomon, S. (1982). The self-serving attributional bias: Beyond self-presentation. *Journal of Experimental Social Psychology, 18,* 56–67.

Greene, D. L., & Winter, D. G. (1971). Motives, involvements, and leadership among Black college students. *Journal of Personality, 39,* 319–332.

Greenfield, N. S., & Sternbach, R. A. (1972). *Handbook of psychophysiology.* New York: Holt, Rinehart, & Winston.

Greenwald, A. G., & Banaji, M. R. (1989). The self as a memory system: Powerful, but ordinary. *Journal of Personality and Social Psychology, 57,* 41–54.

Greenwald, A. G., & Pratkanis, R. A. (1984). The self. In R. S. Wyer, Jr., & T. K. Srull (Eds.), *Handbook of social cognition* (Vol. 3). Hillsdale, NJ: Erlbaum.

Griffin, D., & Bartholomew, K. (1994). Models of the self and other: Fundamental dimensions underlying measures of adult attachment. *Journal of Personality and Social Psychology, 67,* 430–445.

Grings, W. W. (1973). The role of consciousness and cognition in autonomic behavior change. In F. J. McGuigan & R. Schoonover (Eds.), *The psychophysiology of thinking.* New York: Academic Press.

Grolnick, W. S., & Ryan, R. M. (1989). Parent styles associated with children's self-regulation and competence in school. *Journal of Educational Psychology, 81,* 143–154.

Gruen, R. J., & Mendelsohn, G. (1986). Emotional responses to affective displays in others: The distinction between empathy and sympathy. *Journal of Personality and Social Psychology, 51,* 609–614.

Guisinger, S., & Blatt, S. J. (1994). Individuality and relatedness: Evolution of a fundamental dialectic. *American Psychologist, 49,* 104–111.

Gur, R. C., & Sackeim, H. A. (1979). Self-deception: A concept in search of a phenomenon. *Journal of Personality and Social Psychology, 37,* 147–169.

Gurin, P., Gurin, G., Lao, R. C., & Beattie, M. (1969). Internal-external control in the motivational dynamics of Negro youth. *Journal of Social Issues, 25,* 29–53.

Haaga, D. A. F., Dyck, M. J., & Ernst, D. (1991). Empirical status of cognitive theory of depression. *Psychological Bulletin, 110,* 215–236.

Haan, N. (1981). Common dimensions of personality development: Early adolescence to middle life. In D. H. Eichorn, J. A. Clausen, N. Haan, M. P. Honzik, & P. H. Mussen (Eds.), *Present and past in middle life* (pp. 117–151). New York: Academic Press.

Hackett, G., & Horan, J. J. (1979). Partial component analysis of a comprehensive smoking program. *Addictive Behaviors, 4,* 259–262.

Haemmerlie, F. M., & Montgomery, R. L. (1984). Purposefully biased interactions: Reducing heterosocial anxiety through self-perception theory. *Journal of Personality and Social Psychology, 47,* 900–908.

Hall, C. S., & Van de Castle, R. L. (1963). An empirical investigation of the castration complex in dreams. *Journal of Personality, 33,* 20–29.

Hall, J. F. (1966). *The psychology of learning.* New York: Lippincott.

Hall, R. V., Lund, D., & Jackson, D. (1968). Effects of teacher attention on study behavior. *Journal of Applied Behavior Analysis, 1,* 1–12.

Halpern, J. (1977). Projection: A test of the psychoanalytic hypothesis. *Journal of Abnormal Psychology, 86,* 536–542.

Halverson, C. F. Jr., Kohnstamm, G. A., & Martin, R. P. (Eds.) (1994). *The developing structure of temperament and personality from infancy to adulthood.* Hillsdale, NJ: Erlbaum.

Hamer, D. H., Hu, S., Magnuson, V. L., Hu, N., & Pattatucci, A. M. L. (1993). A linkage between DNA markers on the X chromosome and male sexual orientation. *Science, 261,* 321–327.

Hamilton, D. L. (1979). A cognitive-attributional analysis of stereotyping. In L. Berkowitz (Ed.), *Advances in experimental social psychology* (Vol. 12). New York: Academic Press.

Hamilton, J. C., Greenberg, J., Pyszczynski, T., & Cather, C. (1993). A self-regulatory perspective on psychopathology and psychotherapy. *Journal of Psychotherapy Integration, 3,* 205–248.

Hamilton, W. D. (1964). The genetical evolution of social behavior. *Journal of Theoretical Biology, 7,* 1–52.

Harackiewicz, J. M. (1979). The effects of reward contingency and performance feedback on intrinsic motivation. *Journal of Personality and Social Psychology, 37,* 1352–1363.

Hardaway, R. A. (1990). Subliminally activated symbiotic fantasies: Facts and artifacts. *Psychological Bulletin, 107,* 177–195.

Hardy, K. R. (1957). Determinants of conformity and attitude change. *Journal of Abnormal and Social Psychology, 54,* 289–294.

Harmon-Jones, E., & Allen, J. J. (1997). Behavioral activation sensitivity and resting frontal EEG asymmetry: Covariation of putative indicators related to risk for mood disorders. *Journal of Abnormal Psychology, 106,* 159–163.

Harris, J. R. (1995). Where is the child's environment? A group socialization theory of development. *Psychological Review, 102,* 458–489.

Hart, D., Keller, M., Edelstein, W., & Hofmann, V. (1998). Childhood personality influences on social-cognitive development: A longitudinal study. *Journal of Personality and Social Psychology, 74,* 1278–1289.

Hartmann, H. (1958). *Ego psychology and the problem of adaptation.* New York: International Universities Press. (Originally published, 1939)

Hartmann, H. (1964). *Essays on ego psychology: Selected problems in psychoanalytic theory.* New York: International Universities Press.

Haslam, N. (1994). Mental representation of social relationships: Dimensions, laws, or categories? *Journal of Personality and Social Psychology, 67,* 575–584.

Hathaway, S. R., & McKinley, J. C. (1943). *MMPI manual.* New York: Psychological Corporation.

Haugtvedt, C. P., & Petty, R. E. (1992). Personality and persuasion: Need for cognition moderates the persistence and resistance of attitude changes. *Journal of Personality and Social Psychology, 63,* 308–319.

Hauser, S. T. (1976). Loevinger's model and measure of ego development: A critical review. *Psychological Bulletin, 83,* 928–955.

Haviland, J. M., McGuire, T. R., & Rothbaum, P. A. (1983). A critique of Plomin and Foch's "A twin study of objectively assessed personality in childhood." *Journal of Personality and Social Psychology, 45,* 633–640.

Hayes, S. C., Rincover, A., & Volosin, D. (1980). Variables influencing the acquisition and maintenance of aggressive behavior: Modeling versus sensory reinforcement. *Journal of Abnormal Psychology, 89,* 254–262.

Hayes-Roth, B., & Hayes-Roth, F. (1979). A cognitive model of planning. *Cognitive Science, 3,* 275–310.

Hazan, C., & Shaver, P. (1987). Romantic love conceptualized as an attachment process. *Journal of Personality and Social Psychology, 52,* 511–524.

Hazan, C., & Shaver, P. (1990). Love and work: An attachment-theoretical perspective. *Journal of Personality and Social Psychology, 59,* 270–280.

Hazan, C., & Shaver, P. R. (1994). Attachment as an organizational framework for research on close relationships. *Psychological Inquiry, 5,* 1–22.

Hazen, N. L., & Durrett, M. E. (1982). Relationship of security of attachment to exploration and cognitive mapping abilities in 2-year-olds. *Developmental Psychology, 18,* 751–759.

Heath, A. C., Neale, M. C., Kessler, R. C., Eaves, L. J., & Kendler, K. S. (1992). Evidence for genetic influences on personality from self-reports and informant ratings. *Journal of Personality and Social Psychology, 63,* 85–96.

Heckhausen, H. (1967). *The anatomy of achievement motivation.* New York: Academic Press.

Heckhausen, H., Schmalt, H. D., & Schneider, K. (1985). *Achievement motivation in perspective.* New York: Academic Press.

Heiby, E. M. (1982). A self-reinforcement questionnaire. *Behaviour Research and Therapy, 20,* 397–401.

Heider, F. (1944). Social perception and phenomenal causation. *Psychological Review, 51,* 358–374.

Heider, F. (1958). *The psychology of interpersonal relations.* New York: Wiley.

Heilbrun, K. S. (1980). Silverman's psychodynamic activation: A failure to replicate. *Journal of Abnormal Psychology, 89,* 560–566.

Helgeson, V. S. (1994). Relation of agency and communion to well-being: Evidence and potential explanations. *Psychological Bulletin, 116,* 412–428.

Helgeson, V. S., & Fritz, H. L. (1998). A theory of unmitigated communion. *Personality and Social Psychology Review, 2,* 173–183.

Helgeson, V. S., & Fritz, H. L. (in press). Unmitigated agency and unmitigated communion: Distinctions from agency and communion. *Journal of Research in Personality.*

Helgeson, V. S., & Sharpsteen, D. J. (1987). Perceptions of danger in achievement and affiliation situations: An extension of the Pollak and Gilligan versus Benton et al. debate. *Journal of Personality and Social Psychology, 53,* 727–733.

Heller, M. S., & Polsky, S. (1975). *Studies in violence and television.* New York: American Broadcasting Companies.

Helmreich, R. L., LeFan, J. H., Bakeman, R., Wilhelm, J., & Radloff, R. (1972). The Tektite 2 human behavior program. *JSAS Catalog of Selected Documents in Psychology, 2,* 13 (MS no. 70).

Helson, R., & Moane, G. (1987). Personality change in women from college to midlife. *Journal of Personality and Social Psychology, 53,* 176–186.

Helson, R., & Roberts, B. W. (1994). Ego development and personality change in adulthood. *Journal of Personality and Social Psychology, 66,* 911–920.

Henriques, J. B., & Davidson, R. J. (1990). Asymmetrical brain electrical activity discriminates between previously depressed subjects and healthy controls. *Journal of Abnormal Psychology, 99,* 22–31.

Henriques, J. B., & Davidson, R. J. (1991). Left frontal hypoactivation in depression. *Journal of Abnormal Psychology, 100,* 535–545.

Herr, P. M., Sherman, S. J., & Fazio, R. H. (1983). On the consequences of priming: Assimilation and contrast effects. *Journal of Experimental Social Psychology, 19,* 323–340.

Hersch, P. D., & Scheibe, K. E. (1967). Reliability and validity of internal-external control as personality dimensions. *Journal of Consulting Psychology, 31,* 609–613.

Hersen, M., & Bellack, A. (Eds.). (1976). *Behavioral assessment.* New York: Pergamon.

Hess, E. H. (1973). *Imprinting.* New York: Van Nostrand Reinhold.

Hewitt, P. L., & Genest, M. (1990). The ideal self: Schematic processing of perfectionistic content in dysphoric university students. *Journal of Personality and Social Psychology, 59,* 802–808.

Higgins, E. T. (1987). Self discrepancy: A theory relating self and affect. *Psychological Review, 94,* 319–340.

Higgins, E. T. (1990). Personality, social psychology, and person-situation relations: Standards and knowledge activation as a common language. In L. A. Pervin (Ed.), *Handbook of personality: Theory and research* (pp. 301–338). New York: Guilford Press.

Higgins, E. T. (1997). Beyond pleasure and pain. *American Psychologist, 52,* 1280–1300.

Higgins, E. T., & Bargh, J. A. (1987). Social cognition and social perception. *Annual Review of Psychology, 38,* 369–425.

Higgins, E. T., Bond, R. N., Klein, R., & Strauman, T. (1986). Self-discrepancies and emotional vulnerability: How magnitude, accessibility and type of discrepancy influence affect. *Journal of Personality and Social Psychology, 51,* 1–15.

Higgins, E. T., & Brendl, C. M. (1995). Accessibility and applicability: Some "activation rules" influencing judgment. *Journal of Experimental Social Psychology, 31,* 218–243.

Higgins, E. T., King, G. A., & Mavin, G. H. (1982). Individual construct accessibility and subjective impressions and recall. *Journal of Personality and Social Psychology, 43,* 35–47.

Higgins, E. T., Rholes, W. S., & Jones, C. R. (1977). Category accessibility and impression formation. *Journal of Experimental Social Psychology, 13,* 141–154.

Higgins, R. L., Snyder, C. R., & Berglas, S. (Eds.). (1990). *Self-handicapping: The paradox that isn't.* New York: Plenum.

Hilgard, E. R., & Hilgard, J. R. (1983). *Hypnosis in the relief of pain* (Rev. ed.). Los Altos, CA: Kaufman.

Hill, C. A. (1987). Affiliation motivation: People who need people . . . but in different ways. *Journal of Personality and Social Psychology, 52,* 1008–1018.

Hill, C. A. (1991). Seeking emotional support: The influence of affiliative need and partner warmth. *Journal of Personality and Social Psychology, 60,* 112–121.

Hill, T., Lewicki, P., Czyzewska, M., & Boss, A. (1989). Self-perpetuating development of encoding biases in person perception. *Journal of Personality and Social Psychology, 57,* 373–387.

Hillix, W. A., & Marx, M. H. (1960). Response strengthening by information and effect on human learning. *Journal of Experimental Psychology, 60,* 97–102.

Hinkley, K., & Andersen, S. M. (1996). The working self-concept in transference: Significant-other activation and self change. *Journal of Personality and Social Psychology, 71,* 1279–1295.

Hiroto, D. S., & Seligman, M. E. P. (1975). Generality of learned helplessness in man. *Journal of Personality and Social Psychology, 31,* 311–327.

Hobfoll, S. E., Rom, T., & Segal, B. (1989). Sensation seeking, anxiety, and risk taking in the Israeli context. In S. Einstein (Ed.), *Drugs and alcohol use: Issues and factors* (pp. 53–59). New York: Plenum.

Hobson, J. A. (1988). *The dreaming brain.* New York: Basic Books.

Hodgins, H. S., Koestner, R., & Duncan, N. (1996). On the compatibility of autonomy and relatedness. *Personality and Social Psychology Bulletin, 22,* 227–237.

Hodgkinson, S., Sherrington, R., Gurling, H., Marchbanks, R., & Reeders, S. (1987). Molecular genetic evidence for heterogeneity in manic depression. *Nature, 325,* 805–806.

Hoffman, E. (1988). *The right to be human: A biography of Abraham Maslow.* Los Angeles: Jeremy P. Tarcher.

Hoffman, E. (1994). *The drive for self: Alfred Adler and the founding of individual psychology.* Reading, MA: Addison-Wesley.

Hoffman, L. W. (1991). The influence of the family environment on personality: Accounting for sibling differences. *Psychological Bulletin, 110,* 187–203.

Hofstee, W. K. B., de Raad, B., & Goldberg, L. R. (1992). Integration of the big five and circumplex approaches to trait structure. *Journal of Personality and Social Psychology, 63,* 146–163.

Hogan, R., DeSoto, C. B., & Solano, C. (1977). Traits, tests, and personality research. *American Psychologist, 32,* 255–264.

Hogan, R., & Nicholson, R. A. (1988). The meaning of personality test scores. *American Psychologist, 43,* 621–626.

Hokanson, J. E., & Burgess, M. (1962a). The effects of status, type of frustration, and aggression on vascular processes. *Journal of Abnormal and Social Psychology, 65,* 232–237.

Hokanson, J. E., & Burgess, M. (1962b). The effects of three types of aggression on vascular processes. *Journal of Abnormal and Social Psychology, 64,* 446–449.

Hokanson, J. E., Burgess, M. & Cohen, M. F. (1963). Effects of displaced aggression on systolic blood pressure. *Journal of Abnormal and Social Psychology, 67,* 214–218.

Hokanson, J. E., & Edelman, R. (1966). Effects of three social responses on vascular processes. *Journal of Personality and Social Psychology, 3,* 442–447.

Hokanson, J. E., & Shetler, S. (1961). The effect of overt aggression on physiological arousal. *Journal of Abnormal and Social Psychology, 63,* 446–448.

Hokanson, J. E., Willers, K. R., & Koropsak, E. (1968). The modification of autonomic responses during aggressive interchanges. *Journal of Personality, 36,* 386–404.

Holden, K. B., & Rotter, J. B. (1962). A nonverbal measure of extinction in skill and chance situations. *Journal of Experimental Psychology, 63,* 519–520.

Holmes, D. (1972). Aggression, displacement and guilt. *Journal of Personality and Social Psychology, 21,* 296–301.

Holmes, D. S. (1981). Existence of classical projection and the stress-reducing function of attribution projection: A reply to Sherwood. *Psychological Bulletin, 90,* 460–466.

Holmes, D. S., & Houston, B. K. (1974). Effectiveness of situational redefinition and affective isolation in coping with stress. *Journal of Personality and Social Psychology, 29,* 212–218.

Holt, R. (1966). Measuring libidinal and aggressive motives and their controls by means of the Rorschach test. In D. Levine (Ed.), *Nebraska symposium on motivation.* Lincoln: University of Nebraska Press.

Holt, R. R. (1980). Loevinger's measure of ego development: Reliability and national norms for male and female short forms. *Journal of Personality and Social Psychology, 39,* 909–920.

Holtzworth-Munroe, A. (1992). Social skill deficits in maritally violent men: Interpreting the data using a social information processing model. *Clinical Psychology Review, 12,* 605–617.

Holyoak, K. J., Koh, K., & Nisbett, R. E. (1989). A theory of conditioning: Inductive learning within rule-based default hierarchies. *Psychological Review, 96,* 315–340.

Hopkin, K. (1995). Programmed cell death: A switch to the cytoplasm? *The Journal of NIH Research, 7,* 39–41.

Hoppe, C. (1972). *Ego development and conformity behavior.* Unpublished doctoral dissertation, Washington University, St. Louis.

Hormuth, S. E. (1990). *The ecology of the self: Relocation and self-concept change.* Cambridge, England: Cambridge University Press.

Horner, M. S. (1973). A psychological barrier to achievement in women: The motive to avoid success. In D. C. McClelland & R. S. Steele (Eds.), *Human motivation: A book of readings.* Morristown, NJ: General Learning Press.

Horney, K. (1937). *Neurotic personality of our times.* New York: Norton.

Horney, K. (1939). *New ways in psychoanalysis.* New York: Norton.

Horney, K. (1942). *Self-analysis.* New York: Norton.

Horney, K. (1945). *Our inner conflicts.* New York: Norton.

Horney, K. (1950). *Neurosis and human growth.* New York: Norton.

Horney, K. (1967). *Feminine psychology.* New York: Norton.

Horowitz, M. J. (1986). *Stress response syndromes* (2nd ed.). New York: Aronson.

Horvath, P., & Zuckerman, M. (1993). Sensation seeking, risk appraisal, and risky behavior. *Personality and Individual Differences, 14,* 41–52.

Hovland, C. I. (1937). The generalization of conditioning responses. I. The sensory generalization of conditioned responses with varying frequencies of tone. *Journal of General Psychology, 17,* 125–148.

Howard, G. S. (1990). On the construct validity of self-reports: What do the data say? *American Psychologist, 45,* 292–294.

Howard, G. S., Maxwell, S. E., Weiner, R. L., Boynton, K. S., & Rooney, W. M. (1980). Is a behavioral measure the best estimate of behavioral parameters? Perhaps not. *Applied Psychological Measurement, 4,* 293–311.

Hsee, C. K., & Abelson, R. P. (1991). The velocity relation: Satisfaction as a function of the first derivative of outcome over time. *Journal of Personality and Social Psychology, 60,* 341–347.

Hubbard, R. (1995). Genomania and health. *American Scientist, 83,* 8–10.

Huesmann, L. R. (1988). An information processing model for the development of aggression. *Aggressive Behavior, 14,* 13–24.

Hull, C. L. (1943). *Principles of behavior.* New York: Appleton-Century-Crofts.

Hull, J. G. (1981). A self-awareness model of the causes and effects of alcohol consumption. *Journal of Abnormal Psychology, 90,* 586–600.

Hull, J. G., & Rielly, N. P. (1986). An information processing approach to alcohol use and its consequences. In R. E. Ingram (Ed.), *Information processing approaches to clinical psychology.* New York: Academic Press.

Humphreys, L. G. (1939). The effect of random alteration of reinforcement on the acquisition and extinction of conditioned eyelid reactions. *Journal of Experimental Psychology, 15,* 141–158.

Hurlburt, R. T. (1979). Random sampling of cognitions and behavior. *Journal of Research in Personality, 13,* 103–111.

Hy, L. X., & Loevinger, J. (1996). *Measuring ego development (2nd ed.).* Mahwah, NJ: Erlbaum.

Hyman, I. E., Husband, T. H., & Billings, F. J. (1995). False memories of childhood experiences. *Applied Cognitive Psychology, 9,* 181–197.

Hymbaugh, K., & Garrett, J. (1974). Sensation seeking among skydivers. *Perceptual and Motor Skills, 38,* 118.

Ingram, R. E. (Ed.). (1986). *Information processing approaches to clinical psychology.* New York: Academic Press.

Isaacs, E. A., & Clark, H. H. (1987). References in conversation between experts and novices. *Journal of Experimental Psychology: General, 116,* 26–37.

Isabella, R. A., Belsky, J., & von Eye, A. (1989). Origins of infant-mother attachment: An examination of interactional synchrony during the infant's first year. *Developmental Psychology, 25,* 12–21.

Jacklin, C. N., Maccoby, E. E., & Doering, C. H. (1983). Neonatal sex-steroid hormones and timidity in 6–18-month-old boys and girls. *Developmental Psychobiology, 16,* 163–168.

Jackson, D. N. (1984). *Personality Research Form manual* (3rd ed.). Port Huron, MI: Research Psychologists Press.

Jackson, D. N., & Messick, S. (Eds.). (1967). *Problems in assessment.* New York: McGraw-Hill.

James, W. (1890). *The principles of psychology* (Vol. 2). New York: Holt.

Jang, K. L., Livesley, W. J., & Vernon, P. A. (1996). Heritability of the big five personality dimensions and their facets: A twin study. *Journal of Personality, 64,* 577–591.

Jang, K. L., McCrae, R. R., Angleitner, A., Riemann, R., & Livesley, W. J. (1998). Heritability of facet-level traits in a cross-cultural twin sample: Support for a hierarchical model of personality. *Journal of Personality and Social Psychology, 74,* 1556–1565.

Janoff-Bulman, R. (1992). *Shattered assumptions: Towards a new psychology of trauma.* New York: Free Press.

Jaroff, L. (1989). The gene hunt. *Time, 133,* 62–67.

Jeffery, R. W. (1976). The influence of symbolic and motor rehearsal on observational learning. *Journal of Research in Personality, 10,* 116–127.

Jenkins, H. M. (1962). Resistance to extinction when partial reinforcement is followed by regular reinforcement. *Journal of Experimental Psychology, 64,* 441–450.

Jenkins, S. R. (1987). Need for achievement and women's careers over 14 years: Evidence for occupa-

tional structure effects. *Journal of Personality and Social Psychology, 53,* 922–932.

Jenkins, S. R. (1994). Need for power and women's careers over 14 years: Structural power, job satisfaction, and motive change. *Journal of Personality and Social Psychology, 66,* 155–165.

Jensen-Campbell, L. A., Graziano, W. G., & West, S. G. (1995). Dominance, prosocial orientation, and female preferences: Do nice guys really finish last? *Journal of Personality and Social Psychology, 68,* 427–440.

Jessor, R., Costa, F., Jessor, L., & Donovan, J. E. (1983). Time of first intercourse: A prospective study. *Journal of Personality and Social Psychology, 44,* 608–626.

Jessor, S. L., & Jessor, R. (1975). Transition from virginity to nonvirginity among youth: A social-psychological study over time. *Developmental Psychology, 11,* 473–484.

Jockin, V., McGue, M., & Lykken, D. T. (1996). Personality and divorce: A genetic analysis. *Journal of Personality and Social Psychology, 71,* 288–299.

John, O. P. (1990). The big-five factor taxonomy: Dimensions of personality in the natural language and in questionnaires. In L. Pervin (Ed.), *Handbook of personality theory and research* (pp. 66–100). New York: Guilford Press.

John, O. P., & Robins, R. W. (1994). Accuracy and bias in self-perception: Individual differences in self-enhancement and the role of narcissism. *Journal of Personality and Social Psychology, 66,* 206–219.

Johnson, D. J., & Rusbult, C. E. (1989). Resisting temptation: Devaluation of alternative partners as a means of maintaining commitment in close relationships. *Journal of Personality and Social Psychology, 57,* 967–980.

Johnson, G. B. (1966). Penis envy? Or pencil needing? *Psychological Reports, 19,* 758.

Johnson, J. A., & Ostendorf, F. (1993). Clarification of the five-factor model with the abridged big five dimensional circumplex. *Journal of Personality and Social Psychology, 65,* 563–576.

Johnson, J. A., Germer, C. K., Efran, J. S., & Overton, W. F. (1988). Personality as the basis for theoretical predilections. *Journal of Personality and Social Psychology, 55,* 824–835.

Johnson, W., & Kieras, D. (1983). Representation-saving effects of prior knowledge in memory for simple technical prose. *Memory & Cognition, 11,* 456–466.

Jones, A., & Crandall, R. (1986). Validation of a short index of self-actualization. *Personality and Social Psychology Bulletin, 12,* 63–73.

Jones, E. E., & Berglas, S. (1978). Control of attributions about the self through self-handicapping strategies: The appeal of alcohol and the role of underachievement. *Personality and Social Psychology Bulletin, 4,* 200–206.

Jones, E. E., & Nisbett, R. E. (1971). The actor and the observer: Divergent perceptions of the causes of behavior. In E. E. Jones et al. (Eds.), *Attribution: Perceiving the causes of behavior.* Morristown, NJ: General Learning Press.

Jones, E. E., & Pittman, T. S. (1982). Toward a general theory of strategic self-presentation. In J. Suls (Ed.), *Psychological perspectives on the self* (Vol. 1). Hillsdale, NJ: Erlbaum.

Jones, M. C. (1924). A laboratory study of fear. *Pedagogical Seminar, 31,* 308–315.

Jones, M. C. (1968). Personality correlates and antecedents of drinking patterns in adult males. *Journal of Consulting and Clinical Psychology, 32,* 2–12.

Jones, M. C. (1971). Personality antecedents and correlates of drinking patterns in women. *Journal of Consulting and Clinical Psychology, 36,* 61–69.

Jones, W. H., Hobbes, S. A., & Hockenberg, D. (1982). Loneliness and social skills deficits. *Journal of Personality and Social Psychology, 42,* 682–689.

Jöreskog, K. G., & Sörbom, D. (1979). *Advances in factor analysis and structural equations.* Cambridge, MA: Abt Associates.

Jorm, A. F., Henderson, A. S., Jacomb, P. A., Christensen, H., Korten, A. E., Rodgers, B., Tan, X., & Easteal, S. (1998). An association study of a functional polymorphism of the serotonin transporter gene with personality and psychiatric symptoms. *Molecular Genetics, 1,* 1–4.

Jourard, S. M. (1974). *Healthy personality: An approach from the viewpoint of humanistic psychology.* New York: Macmillan.

Jung, C. G. (1933). *Psychological types.* New York: Harcourt, Brace, & World.

Jung, C. G. (1960). *The structure and dynamics of the psyche, Collected works* (Vol. 8). Princeton, NJ: Princeton University Press. (Originally published in German, 1926)

Jung, C. G. (1968). *Analytical psychology: Its theory and practice.* New York: Pantheon.

Juni, S. (1981). Maintaining anonymity vs. requesting feedback as a function of oral dependency. *Perceptual and Motor Skills, 52,* 239–242.

Juni, S., & Fischer, R. E. (1985). Religiosity and preoedipal fixation. *Journal of Genetic Psychology, 146,* 27–35.

Juni, S., & Lo Cascio, R. (1985). Preference for counseling and psychotherapy as related to preoedipal fixation. *Psychological Reports, 56,* 431–438.

Juni, S., Masling, J., & Brannon, R. (1979). Interpersonal touching and orality. *Journal of Personality Assessment, 43,* 235–237.

Juni, S., & Rubenstein, V. (1982). Anality and routine. *Journal of Personality Assessment, 46,* 142.

Jussim, L. (1991). Social perception and social reality: A reflection-construction model. *Psychology Review, 98,* 54–73.

Kagan, J. (1994). *Galen's prophecy: Temperament in human nature.* New York: Basic Books.

Kahn, S., Zimmerman, G., Csikszentmihalyi, M., & Getzels, J. W. (1985). Relations between identity in young adulthood and intimacy at midlife. *Journal of Personality and Social Psychology, 49,* 1316–1322.

Kamin, L. J. (1968). Attention-like processes in classical conditioning. In M. R. Jones (Ed.), *Miami symposium on the prediction of behavior: Aversive stimuli* (pp. 9–32). Coral Gables, FL: University of Miami Press.

Kanfer, F. H. (1977). The many faces of self-control, or behavior modification changes its focus. In R. B. Stuart (Ed.), *Behavioral self-management: Strategies, techniques, and outcomes.* New York: Brunner/Mazel.

Kanfer, F. H., & Busemeyer, J. R. (1982). The use of problem-solving and decision-making in behavior therapy. *Clinical Psychology Review, 2,* 239–266.

Kanfer, F. H., & Hagerman, S. (1981). The role of self-regulation. In L. P. Rehm (Ed.), *Behavior therapy for depression: Present status and future directions.* New York: Academic Press.

Kanfer, F. H., & Hagerman, S. M. (1985). Behavior therapy and the information-processing paradigm. In S. Reiss & R. R. Bootzin (Eds.), *Theoretical issues in behavior therapy.* New York: Academic Press.

Kanfer, F. H., Karoly, P., & Newman, A. (1975). Reduction of children's fear of the dark by competence-related and situational threat-related verbal cues. *Journal of Consulting and Clinical Psychology, 43,* 251–258.

Kanfer, F. H., & Marston, A. R. (1963). Human reinforcement: Vicarious and direct. *Journal of Experimental Psychology, 65,* 292–296.

Kanfer, F. H., & Saslow, G. (1965). Behavioral analysis: An alternative to diagnostic classification. *Archives of General Psychiatry, 12,* 519–538.

Kanfer, F. H., & Schefft, B. K. (1988). *Guiding the process of therapeutic change.* Champaign, IL: Research Press.

Kaplan, A. G., & Bean, J. P. (1976). *Beyond sex-role stereotypes: Readings toward a psychology of androgyny.* Boston: Little, Brown.

Kaplan, A. G., & Sedney, M. A. (1980). *Psychology and sex roles: An androgynous perspective.* Boston: Little, Brown.

Karylowski, J. J. (1990). Social reference points and accessibility of trait-related information in self—other similarity judgments. *Journal of Personality and Social Psychology, 58,* 975–983.

Kasser, T., & Ryan, R. M. (1993). A dark side of the American dream: Correlates of financial success as a central life aspiration. *Journal of Personality and Social Psychology, 65,* 410–422.

Kazdin, A. E. (1974). Effects of covert modeling and reinforcement on assertive behavior. *Journal of Abnormal Psychology, 83,* 240–252.

Kazdin, A. E. (1975). Covert modeling, imagery assessment, and assertive behavior. *Journal of Consulting and Clinical Psychology, 43,* 716–724.

Kazdin, A. E. (1977). *The token economy: A review and evaluation.* New York: Plenum.

Keane, T. M., Kolb, L. C., Kaloupek, D. G., Orr, S. P., Blanchard, E. B., Thomas, R. G., Hsieh, F. Y., & Lavori, P. W. (1998). Utility of psychophysiological measurement in the diagnosis of posttraumatic stress disorder: Results from a Department of Veteran Affairs cooperative study. *Journal of Consulting and Clinical Psychology, 66,* 914–923.

Kelly, G. A. (1955). *The psychology of personal constructs* (Vols. 1 and 2). New York: Norton.

Kelly, G. A. (1962). Europe's matrix of decisions. In M. R. Jones (Ed.), *Nebraska symposium on motivation* (Vol. 10). Lincoln: University of Nebraska Press.

Kelly, G. A. (1969). In whom confide: On whom depend for what? In B. Maher (Ed.), *Clinical psychology and personality.* New York: Wiley.

Kelso, J. A. S. (Ed.). (1982). *Human motor behavior: An introduction.* Hillsdale, NJ: Erlbaum.

Kenrick, D. T., & Funder, D. C. (1988). Profiting from controversy: Lessons from the person-situation debate. *American Psychologist, 43,* 23–34.

Kenrick, D. T., Groth, G. E., Trost, M. R., & Sadalla, E. K. (1993). Integrating evolutionary and social exchange perspectives on relationships: Effects of gender, self-appraisal, and involvement level on mate selection criteria. *Journal of Personality and Social Psychology, 64,* 951–969.

Kenrick, D. T., & Keefe, R. C. (1992). Age preferences in mates reflect sex differences in human reproductive strategies. *Behavioral and Brain Sciences, 15,* 75–91.

Kenrick, D. T., Neuberg, S. L., Zierk, K. L., & Krones, J. M. (1994). Evolution and social cognition: Contrast effects as a function of sex, dominance, and physical attractiveness. *Personality and Social Psychology Bulletin, 20,* 210–217.

Kenrick, D. T., Sadalla, E. K., Groth, G., & Trost, M. R. (1990). Evolution, traits, and the stages of human courtship: Qualifying the parental investment model. *Journal of Personality, 58,* 97–116.

Kenrick, D. T., & Stringfield, D. O. (1980). Personality traits and the eye of the beholder: Crossing some traditional philosophical boundaries in the search for consistency in all of the people. *Psychological Review, 87,* 88–104.

Kernberg, O. (1976). *Borderline conditions and pathological narcissism.* New York: Jason Aronson.

Kernberg, O. (1980). *Internal world and external reality.* New York: Jason Aronson.

Kernis, M. H., & Reis, H. T. (1984). Self-consciousness, self-awareness, and justice in reward allocation. *Journal of Personality, 52,* 58–70

Kessler, R. C., Kendler, K. S., Heath, A., Neale, M. C., & Eaves, L. J. (1992). Social support, depressed mood, and adjustment to stress: A genetic epidemiologic investigation. *Journal of Personality and Social Psychology, 62,* 257–272.

Kevles, D. J., & Hood, L. (Eds.). (1992). *The code of codes: Scientific and social issues in the human genome project.* Cambridge, MA: Harvard University Press.

Kihlstrom, J. F. (1987). The cognitive unconscious. *Science, 237,* 1445–1452.

Kirkpatrick, L. A., & Davis, K. E. (1994). Attachment style, gender, and relationship stability: A longitudinal analysis. *Journal of Personality and Social Psychology, 66,* 502–512.

Kirsch, I. (1985). Response expectancy as a determinant of experience and behavior. *American Psychologist, 40,* 1189–1202.

Kirsch, I. (1990). *Changing expectations: A key to effective psychotherapy.* Pacific Grove, CA: Brooks/Cole.

Kirsch, I., Mearns, J., & Catanzaro, S. J. (1990). Mood-regulation expectancies as determinants of dysphoria in college students. *Journal of Counseling Psychology, 37,* 306–312.

Kirschenbaum, D. S. (1985). Proximity and specificity of planning: A position paper. *Cognitive Therapy and Research, 9,* 489–506.

Kirschenbaum, D. S. (1987). Self-regulatory failure: A review with clinical implications. *Clinical Psychology Review, 7,* 77–104.

Kitcher, P. (1987). Précis of *Vaulting ambition: Sociobiology and the quest for human nature. Behavioral and Brain Sciences, 10,* 61–100.

Klein, G. S. (1970). *Perception, motives, and personality.* New York: Knopf.

Klein, G. S. (1972). The vital pleasures. In R. R. Holt & E. Peterfreund (Eds.), *Psychoanalysis and contemporary science: An annual of integrative and interdisciplinary studies* (Vol. I). New York: Macmillan.

Klein, J. (1987). *Our need for others and its roots in infancy.* London: Tavistock.

Klein, M. (1935). *The psychoanalysis of children.* New York: Norton.

Klein, M. (1955a). The psychoanalytic play technique. *American Journal of Orthopsychiatry, 112,* 418–422.

Klein, M. (1955b). The psychoanalytic play technique, its history and significance. In M. Klein, P. Heiman, & R. Money-Kyrle (Eds.), *New directions in psychoanalysis: The significance of infant conflict in the pattern of adult behavior.* New York: Basic Books.

Kleitman, N. (1963). *Sleep and wakefulness.* Chicago: University of Chicago Press.

Klinger, E. (1975). Consequences of commitment to and disengagement from incentives. *Psychological Review, 82,* 1–25.

Klinger, E. (1977). *Meaning and void.* Minneapolis: University of Minnesota Press.

Klinger, E. (1987). Current concerns and disengagement from incentives. In F. Halisch & J. Kuhl (Eds.), *Motivation, intention, and volition* (pp. 337–347). Berlin: Springer-Verlag.

Klion, R. E., & Leitner, L. M. (1991). Impression formation and construct system organization. *Social Behavior and Personality, 19,* 87–98.

Klohnen, E. C. (1996). Conceptual analysis and measurement of the construct of ego-resiliency. *Journal of Personality and Social Psychology, 70,* 1067–1079.

Klohnen, E. C., Vandewater, E. A., & Young, A. (1996). Negotiating the middle years: Ego-resiliency and successful midlife adjustment in women. *Psychology and Aging, 11,* 431–442.

Knapp, R. R. (1976). *Handbook for the Personal Orientation Inventory.* San Diego: EdITS.

Knutson, B., Wolkowitz, O. M., Cole, S. W., Chan, T., Moore, E. A., Johnson, R. C., Terpstra, J., Turner, R. A., & Reus, V. I. (1998). Selective alteration of personalty and social behavior by serotonergic intervention. *American Journal of Psychiatry, 155,* 373–379.

Kobak, R. R., & Hazan, C. (1991). Attachment in marriage: Effects of security and accuracy of working models. *Journal of Personality and Social Psychology, 60,* 861–869.

Koestner, R., Zuckerman, M., & Koestner, J. (1987). Praise, involvement, and intrinsic motivation. *Journal of Personality and Social Psychology, 53,* 383–390.

Koffka, K. (1935). *Principles of Gestalt psychology.* New York: Harcourt, Brace.

Köhler, W. (1947). *Gestalt psychology.* New York: Liveright.

Kohut, H. (1977). *The restoration of the self.* New York: International Universities Press.

Konečni, V. J. (1975). Annoyance, type and duration of postannoyance activity, and aggression: The "cathartic effect." *Journal of Experimental Psychology: General, 104,* 76–102.

Kornhaber, R. C., & Schroeder, H. E. (1975). Importance of model similarity on extinction of avoidance behavior in children. *Journal of Consulting and Clinical Psychology, 43,* 601–607.

Kotre, J. (1984). *Outliving the self: Generativity and the interpretation of lives.* Baltimore: Johns Hopkins University Press.

Kowaz, A. M., & Marcia, J. E. (1991). Development and validation of a measure of Eriksonian industry. *Journal of Personality and Social Psychology, 60,* 390–396.

Kramer, P. D. (1993). *Listening to Prozac: A psychiatrist explores anti-depressant drugs and the remaking of the self.* New York: Viking.

Krasner, L. (1970). Token economy as an illustration of operant conditioning procedures with the aged, with youth, and with society. In D. J. Lewis (Ed.), *Learning approaches to therapeutic behavior change.* Chicago: Aldine.

Kretschmer, E. (1925). *Physique and character.* New York: Harcourt, Brace.

Krieger, S. R., Epting, F. R., & Leitner, L. (1974). Personal constructs and attitudes toward death. *Omega, 5,* 299.

Kriegman, D., & Knight, C. (1988). Social evolution, psychoanalysis, and human nature. *Social Policy, 19,* 49–55.

Krueger, R. F., Schmutte, P. S., Caspi, A., Moffitt, T. E., Campbell, K., & Silva, P. A. (1994). Personality traits are linked to crime among men and women: Evidence from a birth cohort. *Journal of Abnormal Psychology, 103,* 328–338.

Kuhl, J. & Helle, P. (1986). Motivational and volitional determinants of depression: The degenerated-intention hypothesis. *Journal of Abnormal Psychlogy, 95,* 247–251.

Kuiper, N. A., & Derry, P. A. (1981). The self as a cognitive prototype: An application to person perception and depression. In N. Cantor & J. Kihlstrom (Eds.), *Cognition, social interaction, and personality.* Hillsdale, NJ: Erlbaum.

Kukla, A. (1972). Foundations of an attributional theory of performance. *Psychological Review, 79,* 454–470.

Kulhavy, R. W., & Stock, W. A. (1989). Feedback in written instruction: The place of response certitude. *Educational Psychology Review, 1,* 279–308.

La Greca, A. M., & Santogrossi, D. A. (1980). Social skills training with elementary school students: A behavioral group approach. *Journal of Consulting and Clinical Psychology, 48,* 220–227.

La Greca, A. M., Stone, W. L., & Bell, C. R. III (1983). Facilitating the vocational-interpersonal skills of mentally retarded individuals. *American Journal of Mental Deficiency, 88,* 270–278.

Lakoff, G. (1987). *Women, fire, and dangerous things: What categories reveal about the mind.* Chicago: University of Chicago Press.

Lamiell, J. T. (1981). Toward an idiothetic psychology of personality. *American Psychologist, 36,* 276–289.

Landers, P. (1993, March 2). When science can play God, there are new questions for humans. *Miami Herald,* p. 1E.

Landreth, G. L. (1991). *Play therapy: The art of the relationship.* Muncie, IN: Accelerated Development Publishers.

Landy, F. J. (1986). Stamp collecting versus science: Validation as hypothesis testing. *American Psychologist, 41,* 1183–1192.

Lang, P. J., & Lazovik, A. D. (1963). Experimental desensitization of a phobic. *Journal of Abnormal and Social Psychology, 66,* 519–525.

Langston, C., & Cantor, N. (1989). Social anxiety and social constraint: When "making friends" is hard. *Journal of Personality and Social Psychology, 56,* 649–661.

Lanning, K. (1994). Dimensionality of observer ratings on the California Adult Q-set. *Journal of Personality and Social Psychology, 67,* 151–160.

Lansing, J. B., & Heyns, R. W. (1959). Need affiliation and frequency of four types of communication. *Journal of Abnormal and Social Psychology, 58,* 365–372.

Larsen, R. J., & Diener, E. (1985). A multitrait-multimethod examination of affect structure: Hedonic level and emotional intensity. *Personality and Individual Differences, 6,* 631–636.

Larsen, R. J., & Diener, E. (1987). Affect intensity as an individual difference characteristic: A review. *Journal of Research in Personality, 21,* 1–39.

Larsen, R. J., Diener, E., & Emmons, R. A. (1986). Affect intensity and reactions to daily life events. *Journal of Personality and Social Psychology, 51,* 803–814.

Larsen, R. J., & Ketelaar, T. (1991). Personality and susceptibility to positive and negative emotional states. *Journal of Personality and Social Psychology, 61,* 132–140.

Lassiter, G. D., Briggs, M. A., & Bowman, R. E. (1991). Need for cognition and the perception of ongoing behavior. *Personality and Social Psychology Bulletin, 17,* 156–160.

Lassiter, G. D., Briggs, M. A., & Slaw, R. D. (1991). Need for cognition, causal processing, and memory for behavior. *Personality and Social Psychology Bulletin, 17,* 694–700.

Lau, R. R. (1989). Construct accessibility and electoral choice. *Political Behavior, 11,* 5–32.

Lauer, R. H., & Handel, W. H. (1983). *Social psychology: The theory and application of symbolic interactionism.* Englewood Cliffs, NJ: Prentice-Hall.

Laurenceau, J-P., Barrett, L. F., & Pietromonaco, P. R. (1998). Intimacy as an interpersonal process: The importance of self-disclosure, partner disclosure, and perceived partner responsiveness in interpersonal exchanges. *Journal of Personality and Social Psychology, 69,* 1238–1251.

Lazarus, R. S. (1966). *Psychological stress and the coping process.* New York: McGraw-Hill.

Lazarus, R. S., & Folkman, S. (1984). *Stress, appraisal, and coping.* New York: Springer.

Leak, G. K., & Christopher, S. B. (1982). Freudian psychoanalysis and sociobiology: A synthesis. *American Psychologist, 37,* 313–322.

Leary, T. (1957). *Interpersonal diagnosis of personality.* New York: Ronald Press.

LeBon, G. (1896). *Psychologie des foules.* London: Unwin.

Lee, L., & Snarey, J. (1988). The relationship between ego and moral development: A theoretical review and empirical analysis. In D. K. Lapsley & F. C. Power

(Eds.), *Self, ego, and identity: Integrative approaches* (pp. 151–178). New York: Springer-Verlag.

Lefcourt, H. M. (1976). *Locus of control: Current trends in theory and research.* Hillsdale, NJ: Erlbaum.

Lefcourt, H. M. (Ed.). (1981). *Research with the locus of control construct. Vol. 1, Assessment methods.* New York: Academic Press.

Lefcourt, H. M., & Ludwig, G. W. (1965). The American Negro: A problem in expectancies. *Journal of Personality and Social Psychology, 1,* 377–380.

Lefcourt, H. M., Martin, R. A., Fick, C. M., & Saleh, W. E. (1985). Locus of control for affiliation and behavior in social interactions. *Journal of Personality and Social Psychology, 48,* 755–759.

Lefcourt, H. M., Von Baeyer, C. I., Ware, E. E., & Cox, D. J. (1979). The Multidimensional-Multiattributional Causality scale: The development of a goal specific locus of control scale. *Canadian Journal of Behavioral Science, 11,* 286–304.

Leitner, L. M., & Cado, S. (1982). Personal constructs and homosexual stress. *Journal of Personality and Social Psychology, 43,* 869–872.

Lemann, N. (1994). Is there a science of success? *The Atlantic Monthly, 273,* 83–98.

Lepper, M. R., & Greene, D. (1975). Turning play into work: Effects of adult surveillance and extrinsic rewards on children's intrinsic motivation. *Journal of Personality and Social Psychology, 31,* 479–486.

Lepper, M. R., & Greene, D. (1978). *The hidden costs of reward.* Hillsdale, NJ: Erlbaum.

Lesch, K-P., Bengel, D., Heils, A., Sabol, S. Z., Greenberg, B. D., Petri, S., et al. (1996). Association of anxiety-related traits with a polymorphism in the serotonin transporter gene regulatory region. *Science, 274,* 1527–1531.

Lesser, G. S. (1973). Achievement motivation in women. In D. C. McClelland & R. S. Steele (Eds.), *Human motivation: A book of readings.* Morristown, NJ: General Learning Press.

Le Vay, S. (1991). A difference in hypothalamic structure between heterosexual and homosexual men. *Science, 253,* 1034–1037.

Le Vay, S. (1993). *The sexual brain.* Cambridge, MA: MIT Press.

Levenson, H. (1973). Multidimensional locus of control in psychiatric patients. *Journal of Consulting and Clinical Psychology, 41,* 397–404.

Levenson, H. (1981). Differentiating among internality, powerful others, and chance. In H. F. Lefcourt (Ed.), *Research with the locus of control construct. Vol. 1, Assessment methods.* New York: Academic Press.

Levenson, R. W., & Ruef, A. M. (1992). Empathy: A physiological substrate. *Journal of Personality and Social Psychology, 63,* 234–246.

Levinson, D. J. (1978). *The seasons of a man's life.* New York: Alfred A. Knopf.

Lewin, D. I. (1990). Gene therapy nears starting gate. *The Journal of NIH Research, 2,* 36–38.

Lewin, K. (1951a). *Field theory in social science.* New York: Harper.

Lewin, K. (1951b). The nature of field theory. In M. H. Marx (Ed.), *Psychological theory.* New York: Macmillan.

Lewinsohn, P. M., Mischel, W., Chaplin, W., & Barton, R. (1980). Social competence and depression: The role of illusory self-perceptions. *Journal of Abnormal Psychology, 89,* 203–212.

Lewis, D. J., & Duncan, C. P. (1956). Effect of different percentages of money reward on extinction of a lever pulling response. *Journal of Experimental Psychology, 52,* 23–27.

Lewontin, R. C., Rose, S., & Kamin, L. J. (1984). *Not in our genes: Biology, ideology, and human nature.* New York: Penguin.

Lichtenstein, E., & Danaher, B. G. (1976). Modification of smoking behavior: A critical analysis of theory, research, and practice. In M. Hersen, R. M. Eisler, & P. M. Miller (Eds.), *Progress in behavior modification* (Vol. 3). New York: Academic Press.

Liebert, R. M., & Baron, R. A. (1972). Some immediate effects of televised violence on children's behavior. *Developmental Psychology, 6,* 469–475.

Liebert, R. M., & Fernandez, L. E. (1970). Effects of vicarious consequences on imitative performance. *Child Development, 41,* 841–852.

Linden, W., Paulhus, D. L., & Dobson, K. S. (1986). The effects of response styles on the report of psychological and somatic distress. *Journal of Consulting and Clinical Psychology, 54,* 309–313.

Linder, D. E., & Crane, K. A. (1970). Reactance theory analysis of predecisional cognitive processes. *Journal of Personality and Social Psychology, 15,* 258–264.

Linder, D. E., Wortman, C. B., & Brehm, J. W. (1971). Temporal changes in predecision preferences among choice alternatives. *Journal of Personality and Social Psychology, 19,* 282–284.

Linville, P. W. (1987). Self-complexity as a cognitive buffer against stress-related illness and depression. *Journal of Personality and Social Psychology, 52,* 663–676.

Litt, M. D. (1988). Self-efficacy and perceived control: Cognitive mediators of pain tolerance. *Journal of Personality and Social Psychology, 54,* 149–160.

Little, B. R. (1983). Personal projects: A rationale and methods for investigation. *Environment and Behavior, 15,* 273–309.

Little, B. R. (1989). Personal projects analysis: Trivial pursuits, magnificent obsessions, and the search for coherence. In D. M. Buss & N. Cantor (Eds.), *Personality psychology: Recent trends and emerging directions* (pp. 15–31). New York: Springer-Verlag.

Lobel, T. E. (1994). Sex typing and the social perception of gender stereotypic and nonstereotypic behavior: The uniqueness of feminine males. *Journal of Personality and Social Psychology, 66,* 379–385.

Lockard, J. S., & Paulhus, D. L. (1988). *Self-deception: An adaptive mechanism?* Englewood Cliffs, NJ: Prentice-Hall.

Locke, E. A., & Latham, G. P. (1990). *A theory of goal setting and task performance.* Englewood Cliffs, NJ: Prentice-Hall.

Locksley, A., & Colten, M. E. (1979). Psychological androgyny: A case of mistaken identity. *Journal of Personality and Social Psychology, 37,* 1017–1031.

Locurto, C. M., Terrace, H. S., & Gibbon, J. (Eds.). (1980). *Autoshaping and conditioning theory.* New York: Academic Press.

Loehlin, J. C. (1992). *Genes and environment in personality development.* Newbury Park, CA: Sage.

Loehlin, J. C. (1997). A test of J. R. Harris's theory of peer influences on personality. *Journal of Personality and Social Psychology, 72,* 1197–1201.

Loehlin, J. C., & Nichols, R. C. (1976). *Heredity, environment, and personality.* Austin: University of Texas Press.

Loehlin, J. C., Willerman, L., & Horn, J. M. (1985). Personality resemblances in adoptive families when the children are late-adolescent or adult. *Journal of Personality and Social Psychology, 48,* 376–392.

Loehlin, J. C., Willerman, L., & Horn, J. M. (1988). Human behavior genetics. *Annual Review of Psychology, 38,* 101–133.

Loevinger, J. (1966). The meaning and measurement of ego development. *American Psychologist, 21,* 195–206.

Loevinger, J. (1969). Theories of ego development. In L. Breger (Ed.), *Clinical-cognitive psychology: Models and integrations.* Englewood Cliffs, NJ: Prentice-Hall.

Loevinger, J. (1976). *Ego development: Conceptions and theories.* San Francisco: Jossey-Bass.

Loevinger, J. (1987). *Paradigms of personality.* New York: W. H. Freeman.

Loevinger, J., & Knoll, E. (1983). Personality: Stages, traits, and the self. *Annual Review of Psychology, 34,* 195–222.

Loevinger, J., & Wessler, R. (1970). *Measuring ego development 1. Construction and use of a sentence-completion test.* San Francisco: Jossey-Bass.

Loftus, E. (Ed.). (1992). Science watch [Special section on the unconscious]. *American Psychologist, 47,* 761–809.

Loftus, E. F. (1993). The reality of repressed memories. *American Psychologist, 48,* 518–537

Loftus, E. F. (1994). The repressed memory controversy. *American Psychologist, 49,* 443–445.

Loftus, E. F. (1997). Creating false memories. *Scientific American, 277,* 70–75.

Loftus, E. F., Coan, J. A., & Pickrell, J. E. (1996). Manufacturing false memories using bits of reality. In L. Reder (Ed.), *Implicit memory and metacognition* (pp. 195–220). Mahwah, NJ: Erlbaum.

Loftus, E. F., & Pickrell, J. E. (1995). The formation of false memories. *Psychiatric Annals, 25,* 720–725.

Lord, C. G. (1982). Predicting behavioral consistency from an individual's perception of situational similarities. *Journal of Personality and Social Psychology, 42,* 1076–1088.

Lovaas, O. I., Freitag, G., Gold, V. J., & Kassorla, I. C. (1965). Recording apparatus for observation of behaviors of children in free play settings. *Journal of Experimental Child Psychology, 2,* 108–120.

Lowell, E. L. (1952). The effect of need for achievement on learning and speed of performance. *Journal of Psychology, 33,* 31–40.

Lumsden, C., & Wilson, E. O. (1981). *Genes, mind, and culture.* Cambridge, MA: Harvard University Press.

Lundin, R. W. (1961). *Personality.* New York: Macmillan.

Lundy, A. C. (1985). The reliability of the Thematic Apperception Test. *Journal of Personality Assessment, 49,* 141–145.

Lurigio, A. J., & Carroll, J. S. (1985). Probation officers' schemata of offenders: Content, development, and impact on treatment decisions. *Journal of Personality and Social Psychology, 48,* 1112–1126.

Lütkenhaus, P., Grossmann, K. E., & Grossmann, K. (1985). Infant-mother attachment at twelve months and style of interaction with a stranger at the age of three years. *Child Development, 56,* 1538–1542.

Lykken, D. T., & Tellegen, A. (1993). Is human mating adventitious or the result of lawful choice? A twin study of mate selection. *Journal of Personality and Social Psychology, 65,* 56–68.

Lynn, S. J., Myers, B., & Malinoski, P. (1997). Hypnosis, pseudomemories, and clinical guidelines: A sociocognitive perspective. In J. D. Read & D. S. Lindsay (Eds.), *Recollections of trauma: Scientific studies and clinical practice.* New York: Plenum Press.

Maccoby, E. E., & Wilson, W. C. (1957). Identification and observational learning from films. *Journal of Abnormal and Social Psychology, 55,* 76–87.

MacKay, D. M. (1963). Mindlike behavior in artefacts. In K. M. Sayre & F. J. Crosson (Eds.), *The modeling of mind: Computers and intelligence.* Notre Dame, IN: University of Notre Dame Press.

MacKay, D. M. (1966). Cerebral organization and the conscious control of action. In J. C. Eccles (Ed.), *Brain and conscious experience.* Berlin: Springer-Verlag.

Macrae, C. N., Milne, A. B., & Bodenhausen, G. V. (1994). Stereotypes as energy-saving devices: A peek inside the cognitive toolbox. *Journal of Personality and Social Psychology, 66,* 37–47.

Maddi, S. R. (1980). *Personality theories: A comparative analysis.* Homewood, IL: Dorsey Press.

Madsen, D. (1985). A biochemical property relating to power seeking in humans. *American Political Science Review, 79,* 448–457.

Maes, P. (Ed.). (1990). *Designing autonomous agents: Theory and practice from biology to engineering and back.* Cambridge, MA: MIT Press.

Maes, P. (1994). Modeling adaptive autonomous agents. *Artificial Life, 1,* 135–162.

Magnus, K., Diener, E. Fujita, F., & Pavot, W. (1993). Extraversion and neuroticism as predictors of objective life events: A longitudinal analysis. *Journal of Personality and Social Psychology, 65,* 1046–1053.

Magnusson, D., & Endler, N. S. (Eds.). (1977). *Personality at the crossroads: Current issues in interactional psychology.* Hillsdale, NJ: Erlbaum.

Mahler, M. S. (1968). *On human symbiosis and the vicissitudes of individuation: Infantile psychosis.* New York: International Universities Press.

Mahler, M. S. Pine, F., & Bergman, A. (1975). *The psychological birth of the human infant: Symbiosis and individuation.* New York: Basic Books.

Mahone, C. H. (1960). Fear of failure and unrealistic vocational aspiration. *Journal of Abnormal and Social Psychology, 60,* 253–261.

Mahoney, M. J. (1977). Some applied issues in self-monitoring. In J. D. Cone & R. P. Hawkins (Eds.), *Behavioral assessment: New directions in clinical psychology.* New York: Brunner/Mazel.

Main, M., & Cassidy, J. (1988). Categories of response to reunion with the parent at age 6: Predictable from infant attachment classifications and stable over a 1-month period. *Developmental Psychology, 24,* 415–426.

Main, M., & Hesse, E. (1990). Parents' unresolved traumatic experiences are related to infant disorganized attachment status. In M. T. Greenberg, D. Cicchetti, & E. M. Cummings (Eds.), *Attachment in the preschool years: Theory, research, and intervention* (pp. 161–182). Chicago: University of Chicago Press.

Main, M., & Solomon, J. (1986). Discovery of an insecure-disorganized/disoriented attachment pattern. In T. B. Brazelton & M. W. Yogman (Eds.), *Affective development in infancy* (pp. 95–124). Norwood, NJ: Ablex.

Major, B., Cozzarelli, C., Sciacchitano, A. M., Cooper, M. L., Testa, M., & Mueller, P. M. (1990). Perceived social support, self-efficacy, and adjustment to abortion. *Journal of Personality and Social Psychology, 59,* 452–463.

Major, B., Richards, C., Cooper, M. L., Cozzarelli, C., & Zubek, J. (1998). Personal resilience, cognitive appraisals, and coping: An integrative model of adjustment to abortion. *Journal of Personality and Social Psychology, 74,* 735–752.

Malamuth, N. M., & Donnerstein, E. (Eds.). (1984). *Pornography and sexual aggression.* New York: Academic Press.

Malec, J., Park, T., & Watkins, J. T. (1976). Modeling with role playing as a treatment for test anxiety. *Journal of Consulting and Clinical Psychology, 44,* 679.

Mallick, S. K., & McCandless, B. R. (1966). A study of catharsis of aggression. *Journal of Personality and Social Psychology, 4,* 591–596.

Maltzman, I. (1968). Theoretical conceptions of semantic conditioning and generalization. In T. R. Dixon & D. L. Horton (Eds.), *Verbal behavior and general behavior theory.* Englewood Cliffs, NJ: Prentice-Hall.

Mancuso, J. C., & Adams-Webber, J. R. (Eds.) (1982). *The construing person.* New York: Praeger.

Mandler, G., & Watson, D. L. (1966). Anxiety and the interruption of behavior. In C. D. Spielberger (Ed.), *Anxiety and behavior* (pp. 263–288). New York: Academic Press.

Manning, M. M., & Wright, T. L. (1983). Self-efficacy expectancies, outcome expectancies, and the persistence of pain control in childbirth. *Journal of Personality and Social Psychology, 45,* 421–431.

Mansfield, E. D., & McAdams, D. P. (1996). Generativity and themes of agency and communion in adult autobiography. *Personality and Social Psychology Bulletin, 22,* 721–731.

Marangoni, C., Garcia, S., Ickes, W., & Teng, G. (1995). Empathic accuracy in a clinically relevant setting. *Journal of Personality and Social Psychology, 68,* 854–869.

Marcia, J. E. (1966). Development and validation of ego identity statuses. *Journal of Personality and Social Psychology, 3,* 551–558.

Marcia, J. E. (1976). Identity six years after: A follow-up study. *Journal of Youth and Adolescence, 5,* 145–160.

Marcia, J. E. (1980). Identity in adolescence. In J. Adelson (Ed.), *Handbook of adolescent psychology.* New York: Wiley.

Marcus, G. F. (1996). Why do children say "breaked"? *Current Directions in Psychological Science, 5,* 81–85.

Markus, H. (1977). Self-schemata and processing information about the self. *Journal of Personality and Social Psychology, 35,* 63–78.

Markus, H., & Nurius, P. (1986). Possible selves. *American Psychologist, 41,* 954–969.

Markus, H., & Sentis, K. (1982). The self and social information processing. In J. Suls (Ed.), *Psychological perspectives on the self* (Vol. 1, pp. 41–70). Hillsdale, NJ: Erlbaum.

Markus, H., Smith, J., & Moreland, R. L. (1985). Role of the self-concept in the perception of others. *Journal of Personality and Social Psychology, 49,* 1494–1512.

Markus, H., & Wurf, E. (1987). The dynamic self-concept: A social psychological perspective. *Annual review of psychology, 38,* 299–337.

Marlatt, G. A., & Gordon, J. R. (1979). Determinants of relapse: Implications for the maintenance of behavior change. In P. O. Davidson (Ed.), *Behavioral medicine: Changing health lifestyles.* New York: Brunner/Mazel.

Marsden, G. (1971). Content analysis studies of psychotherapy: 1954 through 1968. In A. E. Bergin & S. L. Garfield (Eds.), *Handbook of psychotherapy and behavior change.* New York: Wiley.

Martin, L. L., & Tesser, A. (1996). Some ruminative thoughts. In R. S. Wyer, Jr. (Ed.), *Advances in social cognition* (Vol. 9, pp. 1–47). Mahwah, NJ: Erlbaum.

Masling, J. M., & Bornstein, R. F. (Eds.). (1994). *Empirical perspectives on object relations theory.* Washington, DC: American Psychological Association.

Masling, J., Johnson, C., & Saturansky, C. (1974). Oral imagery, accuracy of perceiving others, and performance in Peace Corps training. *Journal of Personality and Social Psychology, 30,* 414–419.

Masling, J., O'Neill, R., & Jayne, C. (1981). Orality and latency of volunteering to serve as experimental subjects. *Journal of Personality Assessment, 45,* 20–22.

Masling, J., O'Neill, R., & Katkin, E. S. (1982). Autonomic arousal, interpersonal climate, and orality. *Journal of Personality and Social Psychology, 42,* 529–534.

Masling, J., Price, J., Goldband, S., & Katkin, E. S. (1981). Oral imagery and autonomic arousal in social isolation. *Journal of Personality and Social Psychology, 40,* 395–400.

Masling, J., Rabie, L., & Blondheim, S. H. (1967). Obesity, level of aspiration, and Rorschach and TAT measures of oral dependence. *Journal of Consulting Psychology, 31,* 233–239.

Masling, J., Weiss, L., & Rothschild, B. (1968). Relationships of oral imagery to yielding behavior and birth order. *Journal of Consulting and Clinical Psychology, 32,* 38–81.

Maslow, A. H. (1955). Deficiency motivation and growth motivation. In M. R. Jones (Ed.), *Nebraska symposium on motivation.* Lincoln: University of Nebraska Press.

Maslow, A. H. (1962). *Toward a psychology of being.* Princeton, NJ: Van Nostrand.

Maslow, A. H. (1968). *Toward a psychology of being* (2nd ed.). New York: Van Nostrand.

Maslow, A. H. (1970). *Motivation and personality* (Rev. ed.). New York: Harper & Row.

Maslow, A. H. (1971). *The farther reaches of human nature.* New York: Viking.

Maslow, A. H. (1979). *The journals of A. H. Maslow* (2 vols.). R. J. Lowry (Ed.). Monterey, CA: Brooks/Cole.

Mason, A., & Blankenship, V. (1987). Power and affiliation motivation, stress, and abuse in intimate relationships. *Journal of Personality and Social Psychology, 52,* 203–210.

Masson, J. M. (1984). *The assault on truth.* New York: Farrar, Straus, & Giroux.

Matarazzo, J. D., & Wiens, A. N. (1972). *The interview: Research on its anatomy and structure.* Chicago: Aldine-Atherton.

Matas, L., Arend, R. A., & Sroufe, L. A. (1978). Continuity of adaptation in the second year: The relationship between quality of attachment and later competence. *Child Development, 49,* 547–556.

Matthews, K. A., Batson, C. D., Horn, J., & Rosenman, R. (1981). "Principles in his nature which interest him in the fortune of others . . . ": The heritability of empathic concern for others. *Journal of Personality, 49,* 237–247.

May, R. (1953). *Man's search for himself.* New York: Norton.

May, R. (1958). The origins and significance of the existential movement in psychology. In R. May, E. Angel, & H. F. Ellenberger (Eds.), *Existence: A new dimension in psychiatry and psychology.* New York: Basic Books.

May, R. (Ed.). (1969). *Existential psychology* (2nd ed.). New York: Random House.

Mazur, A. (1985). A biosocial model of status in face-to-face primate groups. *Social Forces, 64,* 377–402.

Mazur, A., & Booth, A. (1998). Testosterone and dominance in men. *Behavior and Brain Sciences; 21,* 353–397.

Mazur, A., Booth, A., & Dabbs, J. M., Jr. (1992). Testosterone and chess competition. *Social Psychology Quarterly, 55,* 70–77.

McAdams, D. P. (1982). Experiences of intimacy and power: Relationships between social motives and autobiographical memory. *Journal of Personality and Social Psychology, 42,* 292–302.

McAdams, D. P. (1984). Human motives and personal relationships. In V. J. Derlaga (Ed.), *Communication, intimacy, and close relationships.* New York: Academic Press.

McAdams, D. P. (1985). *Power, intimacy, and the life story: Personological inquiries into identity.* New York: Guilford Press.

McAdams, D. P. (1989). *Intimacy: The need to be close.* New York: Doubleday.

McAdams, D. P. (1992). The five-factor model *in* personality: A critical appraisal. *Journal of Personality, 60,* 329–361.

McAdams, D. P., & Bryant, F. B. (1987). Intimacy motivation and subjective mental health in a nationwide sample. *Journal of Personality, 55,* 395–413.

McAdams, D. P., & Constantian, C. A. (1983). Intimacy and affiliation motives in daily living: An experience sampling analysis. *Journal of Personality and Social Psychology, 45,* 851–861.

McAdams, D. P., & de St. Aubin, E. (1992). A theory of generativity and its assessment through self-report, behavioral acts, and narrative themes in autobiogra-phy. *Journal of Personality and Social Psychology, 62,* 1003–1015.

McAdams, D. P., Diamond, A., de St. Aubin, E., & Mansfield, E. (1997). Stories of commitment: The psychosocial construction of generative lives. *Journal of Personality and Social Psychology, 72,* 678–694.

McAdams, D. P., Healy, S., & Krause, S. (1984). Social motives and patterns of friendship. *Journal of Personality and Social Psychology, 47,* 828–838.

McAdams, D. P., Jackson, R. J., & Kirshnit, C. (1984). Looking, laughing, and smiling in dyads as a function of intimacy motivation and reciprocity. *Journal of Personality, 52,* 261–273.

McAdams, D. P., & Powers, J. (1981). Themes of intimacy in behavior and thought. *Journal of Personality and Social Psychology, 40,* 573–587.

McAdams, D. P., & Vaillant, G. E. (1982). Intimacy motivation and psychosocial adjustment: A longitudinal study. *Journal of Personality Assessment, 46,* 586–593.

McArthur, L. Z. (1981). The role of attention in impression formation and causal attribution. In E. T. Higgins, C. P. Herman, & M. P. Zanna (Eds.), *Social cognition: The Ontario Symposium* (Vol. 1). Hillsdale, NJ: Erlbaum.

McCardel, J., & Murray, E. J. (1974). Nonspecific factors in weekend encounter groups. *Journal of Consulting and Clinical Psychology, 42,* 337–345.

McClelland, D. C. (1961). *The achieving society.* Princeton, NJ: Van Nostrand.

McClelland, D. C. (1965). Toward a theory of motive acquisition. *American Psychologist, 20,* 321–333.

McClelland, D. C. (1975). *Power: The inner experience.* New York: Halsted-Wiley.

McClelland, D. C. (1977). The impact of power motivation training on alcoholics. *Journal of Studies on Alcohol, 38,* 142–144.

McClelland, D. C. (1979). Inhibited power motivation and high blood pressure in men. *Journal of Abnormal Psychology, 88,* 182–190.

McClelland, D. C. (1984). *Human motivation.* Glenview, IL: Scott, Foresman.

McClelland, D. C. (1985). How motives, skills, and values determine what people do. *American Psychologist, 40,* 812–825.

McClelland, D. C. (1989). Motivational factors in health and disease. *American Psychologist, 44,* 675–683.

McClelland, D. C., Atkinson, J. W., Clark, R. A., & Lowell, E. L. (1953). *The achievement motive.* New York: Appleton-Century-Crofts.

McClelland, D. C., & Boyatzis, R. E. (1982). Leadership motive pattern and long-term success in management. *Journal of Applied Psychology, 67,* 737–743.

McClelland, D. C., Davis, W. N., Kalin, R., & Wanner, E. (Eds.). (1972). *The drinking man.* New York: Free Press.

McClelland, D. C., Koestner, R., & Weinberger, J. (1989). How do self-attributed and implicit motives differ? *Psychological Review, 96,* 690–702.

McClelland, D. C., & Winter, D. G. (1969). *Motivating economic achievement.* New York: Free Press.

McClelland, J. L., & Rumelhart, D. E. (1986). *Parallel distributed processing* (Vol. 2). Cambridge, MA: MIT Press.

McCrae, R. R. (1993). Moderated analyses of longitudinal personality stability. *Journal of Personality and Social Psychology, 65,* 577–585.

McCrae, R. R. (1996). Social consequences of experiential openness. *Psychological Bulletin, 120,* 323–337.

McCrae, R. R., & Costa, P. T., Jr. (1987). Validation of the five-factor model of personality across instruments and observers. *Journal of Personality and Social Psychology, 52,* 81–90.

McCrae, R. R., & Costa, P. T., Jr. (1989a). Reinterpreting the Myers-Briggs type indicator from the perspective of the five-factor model of personality. *Journal of Personality, 57,* 17–40.

McCrae, R. R., & Costa, P. T., Jr. (1989b). The structure of interpersonal traits: Wiggins's circumplex and the five-factor model. *Journal of Personality and Social Psychology, 56,* 586–595.

McCrae, R. R., & Costa, P. T., Jr. (1989c). Different points of view: Self-reports and ratings in the assessment of personality. In J. P. Forgas & J. M. Innes (Eds.), *Recent Advance in Social Psychology: An International perspective* (pp. 429–439). Amsterdam: Elsevier North-Holland.

McCrae, R. R., & Costa, P. T., Jr. (1997). Personality trait structure as a human universal. *American Psychologist, 52,* 509–516.

McCrae, R. R., Costa, P. T., Jr., & Busch, C. M. (1986). Evaluating comprehensiveness in personality systems: The California Q-Set and the five factor model. *Journal of Personality, 54,* 430–446.

McCrae, R. R., Costa, P. T., Jr., & Piedmont, R. L. (1993). Folk concepts, natural language, and psychological constructs: The California Psychological Inventory and the five-factor model. *Journal of Personality, 61,* 1–26.

McCrae, R. R., & John, O. P. (1992). An introduction to the five-factor model and its implications. *Journal of Personality, 60,* 175–215.

McCrae, R. R., Zonderman, A. B., Costa, P. J., Jr., Bond, M. H., & Paunonen, S. V. (1996). Evaluating replicability of factors in the Revised NEO Personality Inventory: Confirmatory factor analysis versus procrustes rotation. *Journal of Personality and Social Psychology, 70,* 552–566.

McFall, R., & Twentyman, C. T. (1973). Four experiments on relative contributions of rehearsal, modeling and coaching to assertion training. *Journal of Abnormal Psychology, 81,* 199–218.

McGue, M., & Lykken, D. T. (1992). Genetic influence on risk of divorce. *Psychological Science, 3,* 368–373.

McGuffin, P. (1987). The new genetics and childhood psychiatric disorder. *Journal of Child Psychology and Psychiatry, 28,* 215–222.

McGuire, W. (Ed.). (1974). *The Freud/Jung letters: The correspondence between Sigmund Freud and C. G. Jung.* Princeton, NJ: Princeton University Press.

McGuire, W. J., & McGuire, C. V. (1986). Differences in conceptualizing self versus conceptualizing other people as manifested in contrasting verb types used in natural speech. *Journal of Personality and Social Psychology, 51,* 1135–1143.

McKeachie, W. J. (1961). Motivation, teaching methods, and college learning. In M. R. Jones (Ed.), *Nebraska symposium on motivation.* Lincoln: University of Nebraska Press.

McMahan, I. D. (1973). Relationships between causal attributions and expectancy of success. *Journal of Personality and Social Psychology, 28,* 108–114.

Mead, G. H. (1934). *Mind, self, and society.* Chicago: University of Chicago Press.

Medin, D. L. (1989). Concepts and conceptual structure. *American Psychologist, 44,* 1469–1481.

Meehl, P. E. (1962). Schizotaxia, schizotypy, schizophrenia. *American Psychologist, 17,* 827–838.

Meehl, P. E. (1992). Factors and taxa, traits and types, differences of degree and differences in kind. *Journal of Personality, 60,* 117–174.

Megargee, E. I. (1966). Undercontrolled and overcontrolled personality types in extreme antisocial aggression. In E. I. Megargee & J. E. Moranson (Eds.), *Psychological Monographs.* New York: Harper & Row.

Megargee, E. I. (1971). The role of inhibition in the assessment and understanding of violence. In J. L. Singer (Ed.), *The control of aggression and violence.* New York: Academic Press.

Megargee, E. I., Cook, P. E., & Mendelsohn, G. A. (1967). Development and evaluation of an MMPI scale of assaultiveness in overcontrolled individuals. *Journal of Abnormal Psychology, 72,* 519–528.

Meichenbaum, D. (1971). Examination of model characteristics in reducing avoidance behavior. *Journal of Personality and Social Psychology, 17,* 298–307.

Meichenbaum, D. (1972). Cognitive modification of test anxious college students. *Journal of Consulting and Clinical Psychology, 39,* 370–379.

Meichenbaum, D. (1974). *Cognitive behavior modification.* Morristown, NJ: General Learning Press.

Meichenbaum, D. (1977). *Cognitve-behavior modification: An integrative approach.* New York: Plenum.

Meichenbaum, D. (1985). *Stress inoculation training.* New York: Pergamon.

Meichenbaum, D., & Goodman, J. (1971). Training impulsive children to talk to themselves: A means of developing self-control. *Journal of Abnormal Psychology, 77,* 115–126.

Melamed, B. G., & Siegel, L. J. (1975). Reduction of anxiety in children facing hospitalization and surgery by use of filmed modeling. *Journal of Consulting and Clinical Psychology, 43,* 511–521.

Melamed, B. G., Weinstein, D., Hawes, R., & Katin-Borland, M. (1975). Reduction of fear-related dental management problems using filmed modeling. *Journal of the American Dental Association, 90,* 822–826.

Meltzoff, A. N. (1985). Immediate and deferred imitation in fourteen- and twenty-four-month-old infants. *Child Development, 56,* 62–72.

Mendola, R., Tennen, H., Affleck, G., McCann, L., & Fitzgerald, T. (1990). Appraisal and adaptation among women with impaired fertility. *Cognitive Therapy and Research, 14,* 79–93.

Merluzzi, T. V., Glass, C. R., & Genest, M. (Eds.). (1981). *Cognitive assessment.* New York: Guilford Press.

Merluzzi, T. V., Rudy, T. E., & Glass, C. R. (1981). The information-processing paradigm: Implications for clinical science. In T. V. Merluzzi, C. R. Glass, & M. Genest (Eds.), *Cognitive assessment.* New York: Guilford Press.

Mershon, B., & Gorsuch, R. L. (1988). Number of factors in the personality sphere: Does increase in factors increase predictability of real-life criteria? *Journal of Personality and Social Psychology, 55,* 675–680.

Meyer, D., Leventhal, H., & Gutmann, M. (1985). Common-sense models of illness: The example of hypertension. *Health Psychology, 4,* 115–135.

Meyer, J. P. (1980). Causal attribution for success and failure: A multivariate investigation of dimensionality, formation, and consequences. *Journal of Personality and Social Psychology, 38,* 708–718.

Meyer, J. P., & Pepper, S. (1977). Need compatibility and marital adjustment in young married couples. *Journal of Personality and Social Psychology, 35,* 331–342.

Mickelson, K. D., Kessler, R. C., & Shaver, P. R. (1997). Adult attachment in a nationally representative sample. *Journal of Personality and Social Psychology, 73,* 1092–1106.

Mikulincer, M. (1998). Attachment working models and the sense of trust: An exploration of interaction goals and affect regulation. *Journal of Personality and Social Psychology, 74,* 1209–1224.

Mikulincer, M., Florian, V., & Weller, A. (1993). Attachment styles, coping strategies, and posttraumatic psychological distress: The impact of the Gulf War in Israel. *Journal of Personality and Social Psychology, 64,* 817–826.

Mikulincer, M., & Nachshon, O. (1991). Attachment styles and patterns of self-disclosure. *Journal of Personality and Social Psychology, 61,* 321–331.

Mill, J. S. (1962). "On liberty." In M. Warnock (Ed.), *John Stuart Mill: Utilitarianism, On liberty, Essay on Bentham, together with selected writings of Jeremy Bentham and John Austin.* Cleveland, OH: World Publishing Company. (Originally published, 1859)

Miller, G. A., Galanter, E., & Pribram, K. H. (1960). *Plans and the structure of behavior.* New York: Holt, Rinehart, & Winston.

Miller, I. W., & Norman, W. H. (1979). Learned helplessness in humans: A review and attribution-theory model. *Psychological Bulletin, 86,* 93–119.

Miller, N. E. (1944). Experimental studies of conflict. In J. McV. Hunt (Ed.), *Personality and the behavior disorders* (Vol. 1, 431–465). New York: Ronald Press.

Miller, N. E. (1948). Theory and experiment relating psychoanalytic displacement to stimulus-response generalization. *Journal of Abnormal and Social Psychology, 43,* 155–178.

Miller, N. E. (1951). Learnable drives and rewards. In S. S. Stevens (Ed.), *Handbook of experimental psychology.* New York: Wiley.

Miller, N. E., & Dollard, J. (1941). *Social learning and imitation.* New Haven: Yale University Press.

Miller, R. S. (1987). Empathic embarrassment: Situational and personal determinants of reactions to the embarrassment of another. *Journal of Personality and Social Psychology, 53,* 1061–1069.

Miller, S., Saccuzzo, D., & Braff, D. (1979). Information processing deficits in remitted schizophrenics. *Journal of Abnormal Psychology, 88,* 446–449.

Mirels, H. (1970). Dimensions of internal versus external control. *Journal of Consulting and Clinical Psychology, 34,* 226–228.

Mischel, W. (1961). Delay of gratification, need for achievement, and acquiescence in another culture. *Journal of Abnormal and Social Psychology, 62,* 543–552.

Mischel, W. (1966). Theory and research on the antecedents of self-imposed delay of reward. In B. A. Maher (Ed.), *Progress in experimental personality research* (Vol. 3). New York: Academic Press.

Mischel, W. (1968). *Personality and assessment.* New York: Wiley.

Mischel, W. (1970). Sex typing and socialization. In P. H. Mussen (Ed.), *Carmichael's manual of child psychology* (Rev. ed.). New York: Wiley.

Mischel, W. (1973). Toward a cognitive social learning reconceptualization of personality. *Psychological Review, 80,* 252–283.

Mischel, W. (1974). Processes in delay of gratification. In L. Berkowitz (Ed.), *Advances in experimental social psychology* (Vol. 7). New York: Academic Press.

Mischel, W. (1977). The interaction of person and situation. In D. Magnusson & N. S. Endler (Eds.), *Personality at the crossroads: Current issues in interactional psychology.* Hillsdale, NJ: Erlbaum.

Mischel, W. (1979). On the interface of cognition and personality: Beyond the person-situation debate. *American Psychologist, 34,* 740–754.

Mischel, W. (1990). Personality dispositions revisited and revised: A view after three decades. In L. A. Pervin (Ed.), *Handbook of personality: Theory and research* (pp. 111–134). New York: Guilford Press.

Mischel, W., & Baker, N. (1975). Cognitive transformations of reward objects through instructions. *Journal of Personality and Social Psychology, 31,* 254–261.

Mischel, W., & Ebbesen, E. (1970). Attention in delay of gratification. *Journal of Personality and Social Psychology, 16,* 329–337.

Mischel, W., Ebbesen, E., & Zeiss, A. (1973). Selective attention to the self: Situational and dispositional determinants. *Journal of Personality and Social Psychology, 27,* 129–142.

Mischel, W., & Liebert, R. M. (1966). Effects of discrepancies between observed and imposed reward criteria on their acquisition and transmission. *Journal of Personality and Social Psychology, 3,* 45–53.

Mischel, W., & Metzner, R. (1962). Preference for delayed reward as a function of age, intelligence, and length of delay interval. *Journal of Abnormal and Social Psychology, 64,* 425–431.

Mischel, W., & Moore, B. (1973). Effects of attention to symbolically presented rewards upon self-control. *Journal of Personality and Social Psychology, 28,* 172–179.

Mischel, W., & Peake, P. K. (1982). Beyond déjà vu in the search for cross-situational consistency. *Psychological Review, 89,* 730–755.

Mischel, W., & Shoda, Y. (1995). A cognitive-affective system theory of personality: Reconceptualizing situations, dispositions, and invariance in personality structure. *Psychological Review, 102,* 246–268.

Monmaney, T. (1987). Are we led by the nose? *Discover, 8,* 48–56.

Monson, T., Hesley, J., & Chernick, L. (1982). Specifying when personality traits can and cannot predict behavior: An alternative to abandoning the attempt to predict single-act criteria. *Journal of Personality and Social Psychology, 43,* 385–399.

Moore, B., Mischel, W., & Zeiss, A. (1976). Comparative effects of the reward stimulus and its cognitive representation in voluntary delay. *Journal of Personality and Social Psychology, 34,* 419–424.

Moore, J. W. (1972). Stimulus control: Studies of auditory generalization in rabbits. In A. H. Black & W. F. Prokasy (Eds.), *Classical conditioning II: Current research and theory.* New York: Appleton-Century-Crofts.

Morf, C. C., & Rhodewalt, F. (1993). Narcissism and self-evaluation maintenance: Explorations in object relations. *Personality and Social Psychology Bulletin, 19,* 668–676.

Morgan, C. D., & Murray, H. A. (1935). A method for investigating fantasies. *Archives of Neurology and Psychiatry, 34,* 289–306.

Morris, J. L. (1966). Propensity for risk taking as a determinant of vocational choice: An extension of the theory of achievement motivation. *Journal of Personality and Social Psychology, 3,* 328–335.

Morris, L. W., Davis, M. A., & Hutchings, C. H. (1981). Cognitive and emotional components of anxiety: Literature review and a revised worry-emotionality scale. *Journal of Educational Psychology, 73,* 541–555.

Moskowitz, D. S. (1994). Cross-situational generality and the interpersonal circumplex. *Journal of Personality and Social Psychology, 66,* 921–933.

Moskowitz, G. B. (1993). Individual differences in social categorization: The influence of personal need for structure on spontaneous trait inferences. *Journal of Personality and Social Psychology, 65,* 132–142.

Motley, M. T. (1985). Slips of the tongue. *Scientific American, 253,* 116–127.

Mowrer, O. H., & Mowrer, W. M. (1938). Enuresis—A method for its study and treatment. *American Journal of Orthopsychiatry, 8,* 436–459.

Mueller, C. M., & Dweck, C. S. (1998). Praise for intelligence can undermine children's motivation and performance. *Journal of Personality and Social Psychology, 75,* 33–52.

Mullen, B. (1986). Atrocity as a function of lynch mob composition: A self-attention perspective. *Personality and Social Psychology Bulletin, 12,* 187–197.

Muraven, M., Tice, D. M., & Baumeister, R. F. (1998). Self-control as a limited resource: Regulatory depletion patterns. *Journal of Personality and Social Psychology, 74,* 774–789.

Murray, E. J. (1985). Coping and anger. In T. M. Field, P. M. McCabe, & N. Schneiderman (Eds.), *Stress and coping.* Hillsdale, NJ: Erlbaum.

Murray, H. A. (1938). *Explorations in personality.* New York: Oxford University Press.

Murray, S. L., & Holmes, J. G. (1993). Seeing virtues in faults: Negativity and the transformation of interpersonal narratives in close relationships. *Journal of Personality and Social Psychology, 65,* 707–722.

Myers, M. B., & McCaulley, M. H. (1985). *Manual: A guide to the development and use of the Myers-Briggs Type Indicator.* Palo Alto, CA: Consulting Psychologists Press.

Myers, T. I., & Eisner, E. J. (1974). *An experimental evaluation of the effects of karate and meditation.* (Report No. 43800[P-391X-1–29]). Washington, DC: American Institutes for Research.

Nasby, W. (1985). Private self-consciousness, articulation of the self-schema, and the recognition memory of trait adjectives. *Journal of Personality and Social Psychology, 49,* 704–709.

Neale, M. C., & Stevenson, J. (1989). Rater bias in the EASI temperament scales: A twin study. *Journal of Personality and Social Psychology, 56,* 446–455.

Neary, R. S., & Zuckerman, M. (1976). Sensation seeking, trait and state anxiety, and the electrodermal orienting reflex. *Psychophysiology, 13,* 205–211.

Neimeyer, G. J., & Neimeyer, R. A. (1981). Personal construct perspectives on cognitive assessment. In T. V. Merluzzi, C. R. Glass, & M. Genest, Eds., *Cognitive assessment.* New York: Guilford Press.

Neimeyer, R. A. (1985). Personal constructs in clinical practice. In P. C. Kendall (Ed.), *Advances in cognitive-behavioral research and therapy* (Vol. 4, pp. 275–339). New York: Academic Press.

Nelson, R. O. (1977). Methodological issues in assessment via self-monitoring. In J. D. Cone & R. P. Hawkins (Eds.), *Behavioral assessment: New directions in clinical psychology.* New York: Brunner/Mazel.

Netter, P., Hennig, J., & Roed, I. S. (1996). Serotonin and dopamine as mediators of sensation seeking behavior. *Neuropsychobiology, 34,* 155–165.

Neuberg, S. L., & Newsom, J. T. (1993). Personal need for structure: Individual differences in the desire for simple structure. *Journal of Personality and Social Psychology, 65,* 113–131.

Newcomb, M. D., & McGee, L. (1991). Influence of sensation seeking on general deviance and specific problem behaviors from adolescence to young adulthood. *Journal of Personality and Social Psychology, 61,* 614–628.

Newell, A. (1990). *Unified theories of cognition.* Cambridge, MA: Harvard University Press.

Newell, A., & Simon, H. A. (1972). *Human problem solving.* Englewood Cliffs, NJ: Prentice-Hall.

Newman, D. L., Tellegen, A., & Bouchard, T. J. Jr. (1998). Individual differences in adult ego development: Sources of influence in twins reared apart. *Journal of Personality and Social Psychology, 74,* 985–995.

Newman, J. P., Wallace, J. F., Strauman, T. J., Skolaski, R. L., Oreland, K. M., Mattek, P. W., Elder, K. A., & McNeeley, J. (1993). Effects of motivationally significant stimuli on the regulation of dominant responses. *Journal of Personality and Social Psychology, 65,* 165–175.

Newman, L. S., Duff, K. J., & Baumeister, R. F. (1997). A new look at defensive projection: Thought suppression, accessibility, and biased person perception. *Journal of Personality and Social Psychology, 72,* 980–1001.

Newtson, D., & Engquist, G. (1976). The perceptual organization of ongoing behavior. *Journal of Experimental Social Psychology, 12,* 436–450.

Newtson, D., Engquist, G., & Bois, J. (1977). The objective basis of behavior units. *Journal of Personality and Social Psychology, 35,* 847–862.

Newtson, D., Rindner, R., Miller, R., & LaCross, K. (1978). Effects of availability of feature changes on behavior segmentation. *Journal of Experimental Social Psychology, 14,* 379–388.

Nezu, A. M. (1987). A problem-solving formulation of depression: A literature review and proposal of a pluralistic model. *Clinical Psychology Review, 7,* 121–144.

Nicholls, J. G. (1984). Achievement motivation: Conceptions of ability, subjective experience, task choice, and performance. *Psychological Review, 91,* 328–346.

Niedenthal, P. M., Setterlund, M. B., & Wherry, M. B. (1992). Possible self-complexity and affective reactions to goal-relevant evaluation. *Journal of Personality and Social Psychology, 63,* 5–16.

Nisbett, R. E. (1980). The trait construct in lay and professional psychology. In L. Festinger (Ed.), *Retrospections on social psychology.* New York: Oxford University Press.

Nisbett, R. E., & Cohen, D. (1996). *Culture of honor.* Boulder, CO: Westview Press.

Nisbett, R. E., & Ross, L. (1980). *Human inference: Strategies and shortcomings of social judgment.* Englewood Cliffs, NJ: Prentice-Hall.

Nisbett, R. E., & Wilson, T. D. (1977). Telling more than we can know: Verbal reports on mental processes. *Psychological Review, 84,* 231–259.

Nolen-Hoeksema, S., Morrow, J., & Frederickson, B. L. (1993). Response styles and the duration of episodes of depressed mood. *Journal of Abnormal Psychology, 102,* 20–28.

Nolen-Hoeksema, S., Parker, L., & Larson, J. (1994). Ruminative coping with depressed mood following loss. *Journal of Personality and Social Psychology, 67,* 92–104.

Norman, D. A. (1981). Categorization of action slips. *Psychological Review, 88,* 1–15.

Norman, D. A., & Shallice, T. (1986). Attention to action: Willed and automatic control of behavior. In R. J. Davidson, G. E. Schwartz, & D. Shapiro (Eds.), *Consciousness and self-regulation: Advances in research and theory* (Vol. 4, pp. 1–18). New York: Plenum.

Norman, W. T. (1963). Toward an adequate taxonomy of personality attributes: Replicated factor structure in peer nomination personality ratings. *Journal of Abnormal and Social Psychology, 66,* 574–583.

Novaco, R. W. (1978). Anger and coping with stress: Cognitive behavioral interventions. In J. P. Foreyt & D. P. Rathjen (Eds.), *Cognitive behavior therapy: Research and application.* New York: Plenum.

Nunnally, J. C., Duchnowski, A. J., & Parker, R. K. (1965). Association of neutral objects and rewards: Effects on verbal evaluation, reward expectancy, and selective attention. *Journal of Personality and Social Psychology, 1,* 270–274.

O'Connor, S. C., & Rosenblood, L. K. (1996). Affiliation motivation in everyday experience: A theoretical comparison. *Journal of Personality and Social Psychology, 70,* 513–522.

O'Leary, K. D., & Becker, W. C. (1967). Behavior modification of an adjustment class: A token reinforcement program. *Exceptional Children, 33,* 637–642.

Ogilvie, D. M. (1987). The undesired self: A neglected variable in personality research. *Journal of Personality and Social Psychology, 52,* 379–385.

Oliver, M. B., & Hyde, J. S. (1993). Gender differences in sexuality: A meta-analysis. *Psychological Bulletin, 114,* 29–51.

Oring, E. (1984). *The jokes of Sigmund Freud: A study in humor and Jewish identity.* Philadelphia: University of Pennsylvania Press.

Orlofsky, J. L., Marcia, J. E., & Lesser, I. M. (1973). Ego identity states and the intimacy versus isolation crisis of young adulthood. *Journal of Youth and Adolescence, 27,* 211–219.

Orr, S. P., Lasko, N. B., Metzger, L. J., Berry, N. J., Ahern, C. E., & Pitman, R. K. (1998). Psychophysiologic assessment of women with posttraumatic stress disorder resulting from childhood sexual abuse. *Journal of Consulting and Clinical Psychology, 66,* 906–913.

Oshman, H. P., & Manosevitz, M. (1976). Father absence: Effects of stepfathers upon psychosocial development in males. *Developmental Psychology, 12,* 479–480.

Overmier, J. B., & Seligman, M. E. P. (1967). Effects of inescapable shock upon subsequent escape and avoidance learning. *Journal of Comparative and Physiological Psychology, 63,* 28–33.

Ozer, D. J. (1986). *Consistency in personality: A methodological framework.* New York: Springer-Verlag.

Ozer, D. J., & Gjerde, P. F. (1989). Patterns of personality consistency and change from childhood through adolescence. *Journal of Personality, 57,* 483–507.

Ozer, D. J., & Reise, S. P. (1994). Personality assessment. *Annual Review of Psychology, 45,* 357–388.

Ozer, E. M., & Bandura, A. (1990). Mechanisms governing empowerment effects: A self-efficacy analysis. *Journal of Personality and Social Psychology, 58,* 472–486.

Parke, R. D. (1969). Effectiveness of punishment as an interaction of intensity, timing, agent nurturance, and cognitive structuring. *Child Development, 40,* 211–235.

Parkes, C. M., Stevenson-Hinde, J., & Marris, P. (Eds.). (1991). *Attachment, bonding, and psychiatric problems after bereavement.* London: Tavistock/Routledge.

Parnell, R. W. (1957). Physique and mental breakdown in young adults. *British Medical Journal, 1,* 1485–1490.

Passini, F. T., & Norman, W. T. (1966). A universal conception of personality structure? *Journal of Personality and Social Psychology, 4,* 44–49.

Patterson, C. M., & Newman, J. P. (1993). Reflectivity and learning from aversive events: Toward a psychological mechanism for the syndromes of disinhibition. *Psychological Review, 100,* 716–776.

Paul, G. L. (1966). *Insight vs. desensitization in psychotherapy: An experiment in anxiety reduction.* Stanford, CA: Stanford University Press.

Paulhus, D. L. (1983). Sphere-specific measures of perceived control. *Journal of Personality and Social Psychology, 44,* 1253–1265.

Paulhus, D. L. (1984). Two-component models of socially desirable responding. *Journal of Personality and Social Psychology, 46,* 598–609.

Paulhus, D. L. (1998). Interpersonal and intrapsychic adaptiveness of trait self-enhancement: A mixed blessing? *Journal of Personality and Social Psychology, 74,* 1197–1208.

Paulhus, D. L., & Christie, R. (1981). Spheres of control: An interactionist approach to assessment and perceived control. In H. F. Lefcourt (Ed.), *Research with the locus of control construct. Vol. 1, Assessment methods.* New York: Academic Press.

Paulhus, D. L., & Levitt, K. (1987). Desirable responding triggered by affect: Automatic egotism? *Journal of Personality and Social Psychology, 52,* 245–259.

Paulhus, D. L., & Reid, D. B. (1991). Enhancement and denial in socially desirable responding. *Journal of Personality and Social Psychology, 60,* 307–317.

Paulhus, D. L., & Suedfeld, P. (1988). A dynamic complexity model of self-deception. In J. S. Lockard & D. L. Paulhus (Eds.), *Self-deception: An adaptive mechanism?* Englewood Cliffs, NJ: Prentice-Hall.

Paunonen, S. V. (1989). Consensus in personality judgments: Moderating effects of target-rater acquaintanceship and behavior observability. *Journal of Personality and Social Psychology, 56,* 823–833.

Paunonen, S. V. (1998). Hierarchical organization of personality and prediction of behavior. *Journal of Personality and Social Psychology, 74,* 538–556.

Paunonen, S. V., Jackson, D. N., Trzebinski, J., & Forsterling, F. (1992). Personality structure across cultures: A multimethod evaluation. *Journal of Personality and Social Psychology, 62,* 447–456.

Pavlov, I. P. (1927). *Conditioned reflexes.* Oxford, England: Oxford University Press.

Pavlov, I. P. (1955). *Selected works.* New York: Foreign Languages.

Peabody, D. (1984). Personality dimensions through trait inferences. *Journal of Personality and Social Psychology, 46,* 384–403.

Peabody, D., & Goldberg, L. R. (1989). Some determinants of factor structures from personality-trait descriptors. *Journal of Personality and Social Psychology, 57,* 552–567.

Pedersen, N. L., Plomin, R., McClearn, G. E., & Friberg, L. (1988). Neuroticism, extraversion, and related traits in adult twins reared apart and reared together. *Journal of Personality and Social Psychology, 55,* 950–957.

Pelham, B. W. (1993). The idiographic nature of human personality: Examples of the idiographic self-concept. *Journal of Personality and Social Psychology, 64,* 665–677.

Pennebaker, J. W. (1989). Confession, inhibition, and disease. In L. Berkowitz (Ed.), *Advances in Experimental Social Psychology* (Vol. 22, pp. 211–244). San Diego: Academic Press.

Pennebaker, J. W. (1993). Putting stress into words: Health, linguistic, and therapeutic implications. *Behaviour Research and Therapy, 31,* 539–548.

Pennebaker, J. W., & Beall, S. K. (1986). Confronting a traumatic event: Toward an understanding of inhibition and disease. *Journal of Abnormal Psychology, 95,* 274–281.

Pennebaker, J. W., Kiecolt-Glaser, J. K., & Glaser, R. (1988). Disclosure of traumas and immune function: Health implications for psychotherapy. *Journal of Consulting and Clinical Psychology, 56,* 239–245.

Peplau, L. A. (1976). Impact of fear of success and sex-role attitudes on women's competitive achievement. *Journal of Personality and Social Psychology, 34,* 561–568.

Peplau, L. A., & Perlman, D. (Eds.). (1982). *Loneliness: A sourcebook of current theory, research, and therapy.* New York: Wiley.

Perls, F. S. (1969). *Gestalt therapy verbatim.* Lafayette, CA: Real People Press.

Pervin, L. A. (1983). The stasis and flow of behavior: Toward a theory of goals. In M. M. Page & R. Dienstbier (Eds.), *Nebraska symposium on motivation* (Vol. 31). Lincoln: University of Nebraska Press.

Pervin, L. A. (1985). Personality: Current controversies, issues, and directions. *Annual review of psychology, 36,* 83–114.

Pervin, L. (Ed.). (1989). *Goal concepts in personality and social psychology.* Hillsdale, NJ: Erlbaum.

Pervin, L. A. (1994). A critical analysis of current trait theory. *Psychological Inquiry, 5,* 103–113.

Peterson, C. (1995). Explanatory style and health. In G. M. Buchanan & M. E. P. Seligman (Eds.), *Explanatory style* (pp. 233–246). Hillsdale, NJ: Erlbaum.

Peterson, C., & Seligman, M. E. P. (1984). Causal explanations as a risk factor for depression: Theory and evidence. *Psychological Review, 91,* 347–374.

Peterson, L. M. (1980). Why men have pockets in their pants: A feminist insight (or, If Freud had been a woman). *Society for the Advancement of Social Psychology Newsletter, 6,* 19.

Petri, H. L., & Mishkin, M. (1994). Behaviorism, cognitivism, and the neuropsychology of memory. *American Scientist, 82,* 30–37.

Phares, E. J. (1957). Expectancy changes in skill and chance situations. *Journal of Abnormal and Social Psychology, 54,* 339–342.

Phares, E. J. (1976). *Locus of control in personality.* Morristown, NJ: General Learning Press.

Piedmont, R. L., McCrae, R. R., & Costa, P. T., Jr. (1992). An assessment of the Edwards Personal Preference Schedule from the perspective of the five-factor model. *Journal of Personality Assessment, 58,* 67–78.

Pietromonaco, P. R., & Carnelley, K. B. (1994). Gender and working models of attachment: Consequences for perception of self and romantic relationships. *Personal Relationships, 1,* 3–26.

Plomin, R. (1974). *A temperament theory of personality development: Parent-child interactions.* Unpublished doctoral dissertation, University of Texas at Austin.

Plomin, R. (1981). Ethnological behavioral genetics and development. In K. Immelmann, G. W. Barlow, L. Petrinovich, & M. Main (Eds.), *Behavioral development: The Bielefeld interdisciplinary project.* Cambridge, England: Cambridge University Press.

Plomin, R. (1983). Developmental behavioral genetics. *Child Development, 54,* 253–259.

Plomin, R. (1989). Environment and genes: Determinants of behavior. *American Psychologist, 44,* 105–111.

Plomin, R. (1995). Molecular genetics and psychology. *Current Directions in Psychological Science, 4,* 114–117.

Plomin, R. (1997). *Behavioral Genetics.* New York: Freeman.

Plomin, R., & Daniels, D. (1987). Why are children in the same family so different from one another? *Behavioral and Brain Sciences, 10,* 1–60.

Plomin, R., DeFries, J. C., & Loehlin, J. C. (1977). Genotype-environment interaction and correlation in the analysis of human behavior. *Psychological Bulletin, 84,* 309–322.

Plomin, R., DeFries, J. C., & McClearn, G. E. (1990). *Behavioral genetics: A primer* (2nd ed.). New York: W. H. Freeman.

Plomin, R., & Foch, T. T. (1980). A twin study of objectively assessed personality in childhood. *Journal of Personality and Social Psychology, 39,* 680–688.

Plomin, R., & Rende, R. (1991). Human behavioral genetics. *Annual Review of Psychology, 42,* 161–190.

Plomin, R., & Rowe, D. C. (1977). A twin study of temperament in young children. *Journal of Psychology, 97,* 107–113.

Pollak, S., & Gilligan, C. (1982). Images of violence in Thematic Apperception Test stories. *Journal of Personality and Social Psychology, 42,* 159–167.

Pool, R. (1993). Evidence for homosexuality gene. *Science, 261,* 291–292

Postman, L. (1951). Toward a general theory of cognition. In J. H. Rohrer & M. Sherif (Eds.), *Social psychology at the crossroads.* New York: Harper.

Powell, J., & Azrin, N. (1968). The effects of shock as a punisher for cigarette smoking. *Journal of Applied Behavior Analysis, 1,* 63–71.

Powell, R. A., & Boer, D. P. (1994). Did Freud mislead patients to confabulate memories of abuse? *Psychological Reports, 74,* 1283–1298.

Powers, W. T. (1973). *Behavior: The control of perception.* Chicago: Aldine.

Prager, K. J. (1982). Identity development and self-esteem in young women. *Journal of Genetic Psychology, 141,* 177–182.

Prentice-Dunn, S., & Rogers, R. W. (1980). Effects of deindividuating situational cues and aggressive models on subjective deindividuation and aggression. *Journal of Personality and Social Psychology, 39,* 104–113.

Prentice-Dunn, S., & Rogers, R. W. (1982). Effects of public and private self-awareness on deindividuation and aggression. *Journal of Personality and Social Psychology, 43,* 503–513.

Prentice-Dunn, S., & Rogers, R. W. (1989). Deindividuation and the self-regulation of behavior. In P. B. Paulus (Ed.), *Psychology of group influence* (2nd ed., pp. 87–109). Hillsdale, NJ: Erlbaum.

Privette, G., & Landsman, T. (1983). Factor analysis of peak performance: The full use of potential. *Journal of Personality and Social Psychology, 44,* 195–200.

Pyszczynski, T., & Greenberg, J. (1985). Depression and preference for self-focusing stimuli after success and failure. *Journal of Personality and Social Psychology, 49,* 1066–1075.

Pyszczynski, T., & Greenberg, J. (1987). Self-regulatory perseveration and the depressive self-focusing style: A self-awareness theory of reactive depression. *Psychological Bulletin, 102,* 122–138.

Quarti, C., & Renaud, J. (1964). A new treatment of constipation by conditioning: A preliminary report. In C. M. Franks (Ed.), *Conditioning techniques in clinical practice and research.* New York: Springer.

Quinn, S. (1987). *A mind of her own: The life of Karen Horney.* New York: Summit Books.

Rabin, A. I., Zucker, R. A., Emmons, R. A., & Frank, S. (Eds.). (1990). *Studying persons and lives.* New York: Springer.

Rachlin, H. (1977). Reinforcing and punishing thoughts. *Behavior Therapy, 8,* 659–665.

Rachman, J., & Teasdale, J. (1969). *Aversion therapy and behaviour disorders: An analysis.* Coral Gables, FL: University of Miami Press.

Rachman, S. (Ed.). (1978). *Advances in behaviour research and therapy* (Vol. 1). Oxford: Pergamon Press.

Rapaport, D. (1960). *The structure of psychoanalytic theory: A systematizing attempt* (Psychological Issues Monograph 6). New York: International Universities Press.

Raskin, P. A., & Israel, A. C. (1981). Sex-role imitation in children: Effects of sex of child, sex of model, and sex-role approriateness of modeled behavior. *Sex Roles, 7,* 1067–1076.

Razran, G. (1961). The observable unconscious and the inferable conscious in current Soviet psychophysiology: Interoceptive conditioning, semantic conditioning, and the orienting reflex. *Psychological Review, 68,* 81–147.

Razran, G. H. S. (1940). Conditioned response changes in rating and appraising sociopolitical slogans. *Psychological Bulletin, 37,* 481.

Read, S. J. (1987). Constructing causal scenarios: A knowledge structure approach to causal reasoning. *Journal of Personality and Social Psychology, 52,* 288–302.

Read, S. J., Jones, D. K., & Miller, L. C. (1990). Traits as goal-based categories: The importance of goals in the coherence of dispositional categories. *Journal of Personality and Social Psychology, 58,* 1048–1061.

Reason, J., & Mycielska, K. (1982). *Absent-minded? The psychology of mental lapses and everyday errors.* Englewood Cliffs, NJ: Prentice-Hall.

Redmore, C., & Waldman, K. (1975). Reliability of a sentence completion measure of ego development. *Journal of Personality Assessment, 39,* 236–243.

Reese, E. P. (1966). The analysis of human operant behavior. In J. A. Vernon (Ed.), *Introduction to psychology: A self-selection textbook.* Dubuque, IA: Brown.

Reinisch, J. M. (1981). Prenatal exposure to synthetic progestins increases potential for aggression in humans. *Science, 211,* 1171–1173.

Rescorla, R. A. (1972). Informational variables in Pavlovian conditioning. In G. H. Bower (Ed.), *The psychology of learning and motivation* (Vol. 6, pp. 1–46). New York: Academic Press.

Rescorla, R. A. (1987). A Pavlovian analysis of goal-directed behavior. *American Psychologist, 42,* 119–129.

Rescorla, R. A. (1988). Pavlovian conditioning: It's not what you think it is. *American Psychologist, 43,* 151–160.

Rescorla, R. A. (1997). Response-inhibition in extinction. *Quarterly Journal of Experimental Psychology: Comparative and Physiological Psychology, 50B,* 238–252.

Rescorla, R. A. (1998). Instrumental learning: Nature and persistence. In M. Sabourin, F. Craik, et al. (Eds.), *Advances in psychological science, Vol. 2: Biological and cognitive aspects* (pp. 239–257). Hove, England: Psychology Press.

Rhawn, J. (1980). Awareness, the origin of thought, and the role of conscious self-deception in resistance and repression. *Psychological Reports, 46,* 767–781.

Rhodewalt, F., & Morf, C. C. (1998). On self-aggrandizement and anger: A temporal analysis of narcissism and affective reactions to success and failure. *Journal of Personality and Social Psychology, 74,* 672–685.

Riedel, W. (1970). An investigation of personal constructs through nonverbal tasks. *Journal of Abnormal Psychology, 76,* 173–179.

Riordan, C. A., & Tedeschi, J. T. (1983). Attraction in aversive environments: Some evidence for classical conditioning and negative reinforcement. *Journal of Personality and Social Psychology, 44,* 683–692.

Risley, T. R. (1968). The effects and side effects of punishing the autistic behaviors of a deviant child. *Journal of Applied Behavior Analysis, 1,* 21–34.

Ritvo, L. B. (1990). *Darwin's influence on Freud: A tale of two sciences.* New Haven: Yale University Press.

Roberts, J. E., Gotlib, I. H., & Kassel, J. D. (1996). Adult attachment security and symptoms of depression: The mediating roles of dysfunctional attitudes and low self-esteem. *Journal of Personality and Social Psychology, 70,* 310–320.

Roberts, J. E., & Monroe, S. M. (1994). A multidimensional model of self-esteem in depression. *Clinical Psychology Review, 14,* 161–181.

Robins, R. W., John, O. P., Caspi, A., Moffitt, T. E., & Stouthamer-Loeber, M. (1996). Resilient, overcontrolled, and undercontrolled boys: Three replicable personality types. *Journal of Personality and Social Psychology, 70,* 157–171.

Robinson, F. G. (1992). *Love's story told: A life of Henry A. Murray.* Cambridge, MA: Harvard University Press.

Rogers, C. R. (1951). *Client-centered therapy: Its current practice, implications and theory.* Boston: Houghton Mifflin.

Rogers, C. R. (1954). The case of Mrs. Oak: A research analysis. In C. R. Rogers & R. F. Dymond (Eds.), *Psychotherapy and personality change: Co-ordinated research studies in the client-centered approach* (pp. 259–348). Chicago: University of Chicago Press.

Rogers, C. R. (1959). A theory of therapy, personality and interpersonal relationships, as developed in the client-centered framework. In S. Koch (Ed.), *Psychology: A study of a science* (Vol. 3). New York: McGraw-Hill.

Rogers, C. R. (1961). *On becoming a person.* Boston: Houghton Mifflin.

Rogers, C. R. (1965). *Client-centered therapy: Its current practice, implication, and theory.* Boston: Houghton Mifflin.

Rogers, C. R. (1970). *Carl Rogers on encounter groups.* New York: Harper & Row.

Rogers, C. R. (1980). *A way of being.* Boston: Houghton Mifflin.

Rogers, C. R., & Dymond, R. F. (Eds.). (1954). *Psychotherapy and personality change: Co-ordinated research studies in the client-centered approach.* Chicago: University of Chicago Press.

Rogers, C. R., & Stevens, B. (1967). *Person to person: The problem of being human.* New York: Simon & Schuster.

Rogers, R. W., & Prentice-Dunn, S. (1981). Deindividuation and anger-mediated inter-racial aggression: Unmasking regressive racism. *Journal of Personality and Social Psychology, 41,* 63–73.

Rogers, T. B. (1981). A model of the self as an aspect of the human information processing system. In N. Cantor & J. F. Kihlstrom (Eds.), *Personality, cognition and social interaction.* Hillsdale, NJ: Erlbaum.

Rogers, T. B., Kuiper, N. A., & Kirker, W. S. (1977). Self-reference and the encoding of personal information. *Journal of Personality and Social Psychology, 35,* 677–688.

Rorer, L. G. (1965). The great response-style myth. *Psychological Bulletin, 63,* 129–156.

Rorschach, H. (1942). *Psychodiagnostics.* Berne, Switzerland: Huber.

Rosch, E., & Mervis, C. (1975). Family resemblances: Studies in the internal structure of categories. *Cognitive Psychology, 7,* 573–605.

Rose, R. J. (1995). Genes and human behavior. *Annual Review of Psychology, 46,* 625–654.

Rosekrans, M. A. (1967). Imitation in children as a function of perceived similarity and vicarious reinforcement. *Journal of Personality and Social Psychology, 7,* 307–315.

Roseman, I. J. (1984). Cognitive determinants of emotions: A structural theory. In P. Shaver (Ed.), *Review of personality and social psychology* (Vol. 5, pp. 11–36). Beverly Hills, CA: Sage.

Roseman, I. J. (1991). Appraisal determinants of discrete emotions. *Cognition and Emotion, 5,* 161–200.

Rosen, C. M. (1987). The eerie world of reunited twins. *Discover, 8,* 36–46.

Rosenbaum, D. A. (1987). Hierarchical organization of motor programs. In S. Wise (Ed.), *Neural and behaviorial approaches to higher brain function* (pp. 45–66). New York: Wiley.

Rosenbaum, D. A. (1990). *Human motor control.* San Diego: Academic Press.

Rosenfield, D., Folger, R., & Adelman, H. F. (1980). When rewards reflect competence: A qualification of the overjustification effect. *Journal of Personality and Social Psychology, 39,* 368–376.

Rosenthal, T. L., & Reese, S. L. (1976). The effects of covert and overt modeling on assertive behavior. *Behavior Research and Therapy, 14,* 463–469.

Rosenwald, G. C. (1972). Effectiveness of defenses against anal impulse arousal. *Journal of Consulting and Clinical Psychology, 39,* 292–298.

Ross, D. M., Ross, S. A., & Evans, T. A. (1971). The modification of extreme social withdrawal by modeling with guided participation. *Journal of Behavior Therapy and Experimental Psychiatry, 2,* 273–279.

Ross, M. (1989). Relation of implicit theories to the construction of personal histories. *Psychological Review, 96,* 341–357.

Ross, M., & Fletcher, G. J. O. (1985). Attribution and social perception. In G. Lindzey & E. Aronson (Eds.),

The handbook of social psychology (3rd. ed., pp. 73–122). Reading, MA: Addison-Wesley.

Roth, S. (1980). A revised model of learned helplessness in humans. *Journal of Personality, 48,* 103–133.

Rotter, J. B. (1954). *Social learning and clinical psychology.* New York: Prentice-Hall.

Rotter, J. B. (1966). Generalized expectancies for internal versus external control of reinforcement. *Psychological Monographs, 80* (1, Whole No. 609).

Rotter, J. B. (1982). *The development and applications of social learning theory: Selected papers.* New York: Praeger.

Rotter, J. B. (1990). Internal versus external control of reinforcement: A case history of a variable. *American Psychologist, 45,* 489–493.

Rotter, J. B., Liverant, S., & Crowne, D. P. (1961). The growth and extinction of expectancies in chance controlled and skill tasks. *Journal of Psychology, 52,* 165–177.

Rotter, J. B., Seeman, M., & Liverant, S. (1962). Internal versus external control of reinforcement: A major variable in behavior theory. In N. F. Washburne (Ed.), *Decisions, values, and groups* (Vol. 2). New York: Pergamon.

Rowe, D. C. (1994). *The limits of family influence: Genes, experience, and behavior.* New York: Guilford.

Rozsnafszky, J. (1981). The relationship of level of ego development to Q-sort personality ratings. *Journal of Personality and Social Psychology, 41,* 99–120.

Rubin, R. T., Reinisch, J. M., & Haskett, R. F. (1981). Postnatal gonadal steroid effects on human behavior. *Science, 211,* 1318–1324.

Runck, B. (1980). *Biofeedback—Issues in treatment assessment.* Rockville, MD: National Institute of Mental Health.

Rushton, J. P. (1988). Genetic similarity, mate choice, and fecundity in humans. *Ethology and Sociobiology, 9,* 329–335.

Rushton, J. P. (1989a). Genetic similarity, human altruism, and group selection. *Behavioral and Brain Sciences, 12,* 503–559.

Rushton, J. P. (1989b). Genetic similarity in male friendships. *Ethology and Sociobiology, 10,* 361–373.

Rushton, J. P., Brainerd, C. J., & Pressley, M. (1983). Behavioral development and construct validity: The principle of aggregation. *Psychological Bulletin, 94,* 18–38.

Rushton, J. P., Fulker, D. W., Neale, M. C., Nias, D. K. B., & Eysenck, H. J. (1986). Altruism and aggression: The heritability of individual differences. *Journal of Personality and Social Psychology, 50,* 1192–1198.

Rushton, J. P., Russell, R. J. H., & Wells, P. A. (1984). Genetic similarity theory: Beyond kin selection. *Behavior Genetics, 14,* 179–193.

Ryan, R. M. (1982). Control and information in the intrapersonal sphere: An extension of cognitive evaluation theory. *Journal of Personality and Social Psychology, 43,* 450–461.

Ryan, R. M. (1993). Agency and organization: Intrinsic motivation, autonomy, and the self in psychological development. In J. Jacobs (Ed.), *Nebraska symposium on motivation: Developmental perspectives on motivation* (Vol. 40, pp. 1–56). Lincoln: University of Nebraska Press.

Ryan, R. M., & Deci, E. L. (1999). Approaching and avoiding self-determination: Comparing cybernetic and organismic paradigms of motivation. In R. S. Wyer, Jr. (Ed.), *Advances in social cognition* (Vol. 12). Mahwah, NJ: Erlbaum.

Ryan, R. M., Rigby, S., & King, K. (1993). Two types of religious internalization and their relations to religious orientations and mental health. *Journal of Personality and Social Psychology, 65,* 586–596.

Ryan, R. M., Sheldon, K. M., Kasser, T., & Deci, E. L. (1996). All goals are not created equal: An organismic perspective on the nature of goals and their regulation. In P. M. Gollwitzer & J. A. Bargh (Eds.), *The psychology of action: Linking cognition and motivation to behavior* (pp. 7–26). New York: Guilford.

Sackeim, H. A. (1983). Self-deception, self-esteem, and depression: The adaptive value of lying to oneself. In J. Masling (Ed.), *Empirical studies of psychoanalytic theories.* Hillsdale, NJ: Erlbaum.

Sackeim, H. A., & Gur, R. C. (1985). Voice recognition and the ontological status of self-deception. *Journal of Personality and Social Psychology, 48,* 1365–1368.

Sadalla, E. K., Kenrick, D. T., & Vershure, B. (1987). Dominance and heterosexual attraction. *Journal of Personality and Social Psychology, 52,* 730–738.

St. Clair, M. (1986). *Object relations and self psychology: An introduction.* Monterey, CA: Brooks/Cole.

St. Clair, S., & Day, H. D. (1979). Ego identity status and values among high school females. *Journal of Youth and Adolescence, 8,* 317–326.

Salmoni, A. W., Schmidt, R. A., & Walter, C. B. (1984). Knowledge of results and motor learning: A review and critical reappraisal. *Psychological Bulletin, 95,* 355–386.

Santee, R. T., & Maslach, C. (1982). To agree or not to agree: Personal dissent amid social pressure to conform. *Journal of Personality and Social Psychology, 42,* 690–700.

Sarason, I. G. (1975). Test anxiety and the self-disclosing coping model. *Journal of Consulting and Clinical Psychology, 43,* 148–153.

Saucier, G. (1992). Benchmarks: Integrating affective and interpersonal circles with the big-five personality factors. *Journal of Personality and Social Psychology, 62,* 1025–1035.

Saudino, K. J., McGuire, S., Reiss, D., Hetherington, E. M., & Plomin, R. (1995). Parent ratings of EAS temperaments in twins, full siblings, half siblings, and step siblings. *Journal of Personality and Social Psychology, 68,* 723–733.

Saudino, K. J., Pedersen, N. L., Lichtenstein, P., McClearn, G. E., & Plomin, R. (1997). Can personality explain genetic influences on life events? *Journal of Personality and Social Psychology, 72,* 196–206.

Scarr, S. (1985). Constructing psychology: Making facts and fables for our time. *American Psychologist, 40,* 499–512.

Scarr, S., & Carter-Saltzman, L. (1979). Twin method: Defense of a critical assumption. *Behavior Genetics, 9,* 527–542.

Scarr, S., & McCartney, K. (1983). How people make their own environments: A theory of genotype → environment effects. *Child Development, 54,* 424–435.

Schank, R. C., & Abelson, R. P. (1977). *Scripts, plans, goals, and understanding.* Hillsdale, NJ: Erlbaum.

Scheff, B. K., & Lehr, B. K. (1985). A self-regulatory model of adjunctive behavior change. *Behavior Modification, 9,* 458–476.

Scheier, M. F., & Carver, C. S. (1983). Self-directed attention and the comparison of self with standards. *Journal of Experimental Social Psychology, 19,* 205–222.

Scheier, M. F., & Carver, C. S. (1988). A model of behavioral self-regulation: Translating intention into action. In L. Berkowitz (Ed.), *Advances in experimental social psychology* (Vol. 21, pp. 303–346). New York: Academic Press.

Scheier, M. F., & Carver, C. S. (1992). Effects of optimism on psychological and physical well-being: Theoretical overview and empirical update. *Cognitive Therapy and Research, 16,* 201–228.

Scheier, M. F., & Fenigstein, A., & Buss, A. H. (1974). Self-awareness and physical aggression. *Journal of Experimental Social Psychology, 10,* 264–273.

Scheier, M. F., Weintraub, J. K., & Carver, C. S. (1986). Coping with stress: Divergent strategies of optimists and pessimists. *Journal of Personality and Social Psychology, 51,* 1257–1264.

Scheirer, M. A., & Kraut, R. E. (1979). Increasing educational achievement via self concept change. *Review of Educational Research, 49,* 131–150.

Schiedel, D. G., & Marcia, J. E. (1985). Ego identity, intimacy, sex role orientation, and gender. *Journal of Personality and Social Psychology, 21,* 149–160.

Schlenker, B. R., Dlugolecki, D. W., & Doherty, K. (1994). The impact of self-presentations on self-appraisals and behavior: The power of public commitment. *Personality and Social Psychology Bulletin, 20,* 20–33.

Schmidt, D. P., & Buss, D. M. (1996). Strategic self-promotion and competitor derogation: Sex and context effects on the perceived effectiveness of mate attraction tactics. *Journal of Personality and Social Psychology, 70,* 1185–1204.

Schmidt, R. A. (1976). The schema as a solution to some persistent problems in motor learning theory. In G. E. Stelmach (Ed.), *Motor control: Issues and trends.* New York: Academic Press.

Schmidt, R. A. (1988). *Motor control and learning: A behavioral emphasis* (2nd ed.). Champaign, IL: Human Kinetics Publishers.

Schmitt, D. P., & Buss, D. M. (1996). Strategic self-promotion and competitor derogation: Sex and context effects on the perceived effectiveness of mate attraction tactics. *Journal of Personality and Social Psychology, 70,* 1185–1204.

Schneider, D. J. (1973). Implicit personality theory: A review. *Psychological Bulletin, 73,* 294–309.

Schneider, D. J. (1991). Social cognition. *Annual Review of Psychology, 42,* 527–561.

Schneiderman, N., & Gormezano, I. (1964). Conditioning of the nictitating membrane of the rabbit as a function of the CS-US interval. *Journal of Comparative and Physiological Psychology, 57,* 188–195.

Schober, M. F., & Clark, H. H. (1989). Understanding by addressees and overhearers. *Cognitive Psychology, 21,* 211–232.

Schouten, P. G. W., & Handelsman, M. M. (1987). Social basis of self-handicapping: The case of depression. *Personality and Social Psychology Bulletin, 13,* 103–110.

Schriesheim, C. A., & Hill, K. D. (1981). Controlling acquiescence response bias by item reversals: The effect on questionnaire validity. *Educational and Psychological Measurement, 41,* 1101–1114.

Schuckit, M. A., & Rayses, V. (1979). Ethanol ingestion: Differences in blood acetaldehyde concentrations in relatives of alcoholics and controls. *Science, 203,* 54–55.

Schuengel, C., Bakermans-Kranenburg, M. J., & Van IJzendoorn, M. H. (1999). Frightening maternal behavior linking unresolved loss and disorganized infant attachment. *Journal of Consulting and Clinical Psychology, 67,* 54–63.

Schultz, C. B., & Pomerantz, M. (1976). Achievement motivation, locus of control, and academic achievement behavior. *Journal of Personality, 44,* 38–51.

Schutte, N. S., Kenrick, D. T., & Sadalla, E. K. (1985). The search for predictable settings: Situational prototypes, constraint, and behavioral variation. *Journal of Personality and Social Psychology, 49,* 121–128.

Schutz, W. C. (1967). *Joy: Expanding human awareness.* New York: Grove Press.

Schwartz, B. (1989). *Psychology of learning and behavior* (3rd ed.). New York: Norton.

Schwarz, N. (1990). Feelings as information: Informational and motivational functions of affective states. In E. T. Higgins and R. M. Sorrentino (Eds.), *Handbook of motivation and cognition: Foundations of social behavior* (Vol. 2, pp. 527–561). New York: Guilford.

Sears, D. O. (1986). College sophomores in the laboratory: Influences of a narrow data base on social psychology's view of human nature. *Journal of Personality and Social Psychology, 51,* 515–530.

Sears, R. R. (1943). *Survey of objective studies of psychoanalytic concepts* (Bulletin 51). New York: Social Sciences Research Council.

Sears, R. R., Rau, L., & Alpert, R. (1965). *Identification and child rearing.* Stanford: Stanford University Press.

Sechrest, L. (1977). Personal constructs theory. In R. J. Corsini (Ed.), *Current personality theories.* Itasca, IL: Peacock.

Sederer, L., & Seidenberg, R. (1976). Heiress to an empty throne: Ego-ideal problems of contemporary women. *Contemporary Psychoanalysis, 12,* 240–251.

Segal, N. L. (1993). Twin, sibling, and adoption methods: Tests of evolutionary hypotheses. *American Psychologist, 48,* 943–956.

Segal, Z. V. (1988). Appraisal of the self-schema construct in cognitive models of depression. *Psychological Bulletin, 103,* 147–162.

Seifer, R., Sameroff, A. J., Barrett, L. C., & Krafchuk, E. (1994). Infant temperament measured by multiple observations and mother report. *Child Development, 65,* 1478–1490.

Seligman, M. E. P., & Hager, J. L. (Eds.). (1972). *Biological boundaries of learning.* New York: Appleton-Century-Crofts.

Seligman, M. E. P., & Maier, S. F. (1967). Failure to escape traumatic shock. *Journal of Experimental Psychology, 74,* 1–9.

Seltzer, R. A. (1973). Simulation of the dynamics of action. *Psychological Reports, 32,* 859–872.

Semmer, N., & Frese, M. (1985). Action theory in clinical psychology. In M. Frese & J. Sabini (Eds.), *Goal directed behavior: The concept of action in psychology.* Hillsdale, NJ: Erlbaum.

Shagass, C., & Kerenyi, A. B. (1958). Neurophysiological studies of personality. *Journal of Nervous and Mental Diseases, 126,* 141–147.

Shapiro, D. (1965). *Neurotic styles.* New York: Basic Books.

Shapiro, D., & Surwit, R. S. (1979). Biofeedback. In O. F. Pomerleau & J. P. Brady (Eds.), *Behavioral medicine: Theory and practice.* Baltimore: Williams & Wilkins.

Shaver, P. R., & Brennan, K. A. (1992). Attachment styles and the "big five" personality traits: Their connections with each other and with romantic relationship outcomes. *Personality and Social Psychology Bulletin, 18,* 536–545.

Shaver, P., & Rubenstein, C. (1980). *Childhood attachment experience and adult loneliness.* In L. Wheeler (Ed.), *Review of personality and social psychology* (Vol. 1, pp. 42–73). Beverly Hills, CA.: Sage.

Shaver, P., Schwartz, J., Kirson, D., & O'Connor, C. (1987). Emotion knowledge: Further exploration of a prototype approach. *Journal of Personality and Social Psychology, 52,* 1061–1086.

Shedler, J., & Block, J. (1990). Adolescent drug use and psychological health: A longitudinal inquiry. *American Psychologist, 45,* 612–630.

Shedler, J., Mayman, M., & Manis, M. (1993). The *illusion* of mental health. *American Psychologist, 48,* 1117–1131.

Sheehy, G. (1976). *Passages: Predictable crises of adult life.* New York: E. P. Dutton.

Shekelle, R. B., Gale, M., Ostfeld, A. M., & Paul, O. (1983). *Psychosomatic Medicine, 45,* 109–114.

Sheldon, W. H. (with the collaboration of S. S. Stevens) (1942). *The varieties of temperament: A psychology of constitutional differences.* New York: Harper.

Sherwood, G. G. (1981). Self-serving biases in person perception: An examination of projection as a mechanism of defense. *Psychological Bulletin, 90,* 445–459.

Shibutani, T. (1961). *Society and personality: An interactionist approach to social psychology.* Englewood Cliffs, NJ: Prentice-Hall.

Shipley, T. E., & Veroff, J. (1952). A projective measure of need for affiliations. *Journal of Experimental Psychology, 43,* 349–356.

Shoda, Y., Mischel, W., & Wright, J. C. (1989). Intuitive interactionism in person perception: Effects of situation-behavior relations on dispositional judgments. *Journal of Personality and Social Psychology, 56,* 41–53.

Shoda, Y., Mischel, W., & Wright, J. C. (1993). The role of situational demands and cognitive competencies in behavior organization and personality coherence. *Journal of Personality and Social Psychology, 65,* 1023–1035.

Shoda, Y., Mischel, W., & Wright, J. C. (1994). Intraindividual stability in the organization and patterning of behavior: Incorporating psychological situations into the idiographic analysis of personality. *Journal of Personality and Social Psychology, 67,* 674–687.

Shostrom, E. L. (1964). An inventory for the measurement of self-actualization. *Educational and Psychological Measurement, 24,* 207–218.

Shostrom, E. L. (1974). *Manual for the Personal Orientation Inventory.* San Diego: EdITS.

Shostrom, E. L., & Knapp, R. R. (1966). The relationship of a measure of self-actualization (POI) to a measure of pathology (MMPI) and to therapeutic growth. *American Journal of Psychotherapy, 20,* 193–202.

Showers, C. (1992a). Compartmentalization of positive and negative self-knowledge: Keeping bad apples out of the bunch. *Journal of Personality and Social Psychology, 62,* 1036–1049.

Showers, C. (1992b). Evaluatively integrated thinking about characteristics of the self. *Personality and Social Psychology Bulletin, 18,* 719–729.

Showers, C. J., & Ryff, C. D. (1996). Self-differentiation and well being in a life transition. *Personality and Social Psychology Bulletin, 22,* 448–460.

Shubsachs, A. P. W. (1975). To repeat or not to repeat? Are frequently used constructs more important to the subject? *British Journal of Medical Psychology, 48,* 31–37.

Shweder, R. A. (1975). How relevant is an individual difference theory of personality? *Journal of Personality, 43,* 455–485.

Shweder, R. A. (1982). Fact and artifact in trait perception: The systematic distortion hypothesis. In B. A. Maher & W. B. Maher (Eds.), *Progress in experimental personality research* (Vol. 11). New York: Academic Press.

Shweder, R. A., & D'Andrade, R. G. (1979). Accurate reflection or systematic distortion? A reply to Block, Weiss, and Thorne. *Journal of Personality and Social Psychology, 37,* 1075–1084.

Sidanius, J., Pratto, F., & Bobo, L. (1994). Social dominance orientation and the political psychology of gender: A case of invariance? *Journal of Personality and Social Psychology, 67,* 998–1011.

Siegel, J., & Driscoll, P. (1996). Recent developments in an animal model of visual evoked potential augmenting/reducing and sensation seeking behavior. *Neuropsychobiology, 34,* 130–135.

Silverman, L. H. (1976). Psychoanalytic theory: "The reports of my death are greatly exaggerated." *American Psychologist, 31,* 621–637.

Silverman, L. H. (1983). The subliminal psychodynamic activation method: Overview and comprehensive listing of studies. In J. Masling (Ed.), *Empirical studies of psychoanalytic theories* (Vol. 1, pp. 69–100). Hillsdale, NJ: Erlbaum.

Silverman, L. H., Ross, D. L., Adler, J. M., & Lustig, D. A. (1978). Simple research paradigm for demonstrating subliminal psychodynamic activation: Effects of Oedipal stimuli on dart-throwing accuracy in college men. *Journal of Abnormal Psychology, 87,* 341–357.

Simon, H. A. (1967). Motivational and emotional controls of cognition. *Psychological Review, 74,* 29–39.

Simons, G. (1986). *Is man a robot?* Chichester, England: Wiley.

Simpson, J. A. (1990). Influence of attachment styles on romantic relationships. *Journal of Personality and Social Psychology, 59,* 971–980.

Simpson, J. A., & Rholes, W. S. (Eds.). (1997). *Attachment theory and close relationships.* New York: Guilford.

Simpson, J. A., Rholes, W. S., & Nelligan, J. S. (1992). Support seeking and support giving within couples in an anxiety-provoking situation: The role of attachment styles. *Journal of Personality and Social Psychology, 62,* 434–446.

Singh, D. (1995). Female judgment of male attractiveness and desirability for relationships: Role of waist-to-hip ratio and financial status. *Journal of Personality and Social Psychology, 69,* 1089–1101.

Skinner, B. F. (1938). *The behavior of organisms.* New York: Appleton-Century-Crofts.

Skinner, B. F. (1948). "Superstition" in the pigeon. *Journal of Experimental Psychology, 38,* 168–172.

Skinner, B. F. (1953). *Science and human behavior.* New York: Macmillan.

Skinner, B. F. (1974). *About behaviorism.* New York: Knopf.

Skinner, B. F. (1987). Whatever happened to psychology as the science of behavior? *American Psychologist, 42,* 780–786.

Skinner, B. F. (1989). The origins of cognitive thought. *American Psychologist, 44,* 13–18.

Skolnick, A. (1986). Early attachment and personal relationships across the life course. In P. B. Baltes, D. L. Featherman, and R. M. Lerner (Eds.), *Life-span development and behavior* (pp. 173–206). Hillsdale, NJ: Erlbaum.

Skowronski, J. J., Carlston, D. E., Mae, L., & Crawford, M. T. (1998). Spontaneous trait transference: Communicators take on the qualities they describe in others. *Journal of Personality and Social Psychology, 74,* 837–848.

Small, M. F. (1993). *Female choices: Sexual behavior of female primates.* Ithaca, NY: Cornell University Press.

Smith, A. (1969). *The theory of moral sentiments.* New Rochelle, NY: Arlington House. (Originally published in 1759)

Smith, C. P. (Ed.). (1992). *Motivation and personality: Handbook of thematic content analysis.* New York: Cambridge University Press.

Smith, E. E., Adams, N., & Schorr, D. (1978). Fact retrieval and the paradox of interference. *Cognitive Psychology, 10,* 438–464.

Smith, E. E., Shoben, E. J., & Rips, L. J. (1974). Structure and process in semantic memory: A featural model for semantic decisions. *Psychological Review, 81,* 214–241.

Smith, G. M. (1967). Usefulness of peer ratings of personality in educational resarch. *Educational and Psychological Measurement, 27,* 967–984.

Smith, K. D., Keating, J. P., & Stotland, E. (1989). Altruism reconsidered: The effect of denying feedback on a victim's status to empathic witnesses. *Journal of Personality and Social Psychology, 57,* 641–650.

Smith, M. L., & Glass, G. V. (1977). Meta-analysis of psychotherapy outcome studies. *American Psychologist, 32,* 752–760.

Smith, M. L., Glass, G. V., & Miller, T. I. (1980). *The benefits of psychotherapy.* Baltimore: Johns Hopkins Press.

Smith, R. E. (1989). Effects of coping skills training on generalized self-efficacy and locus of control. *Journal of Personality and Social Psychology, 56,* 228–233.

Smith, T. W., Snyder, C. R., & Handelsman, M. M. (1982). On the self-serving function of an academic wooden leg: Test anxiety as a self-handicapping strategy. *Journal of Personality and Social Psychology, 42,* 314–321.

Smith, T. W., Snyder, C. R., & Perkins, S. C. (1983). The self-serving function of hypochondriacal complaints: Physical symptoms as self-handicapping strategies. *Journal of Personality and Social Psychology, 44,* 787–797.

Snyder, C. R., & Higgins, R. L. (1988). Excuses: Their effective role in the negotiation of reality. *Psychological Bulletin, 104,* 23–35.

Snyder, C. R., Smith, T. W., Augelli, R. W., & Ingram, R. E. (1985). On the self-serving function of social anxiety: Shyness as a self-handicapping strategy. *Journal of Personality and Social Psychology, 48,* 970–980.

Snyder, M. (1974). The self-monitoring of expressive behavior. *Journal of Personality and Social Psychology, 30,* 526–537.

Snyder, M. (1987). *Public appearances/private realities: The psychology of self-monitoring.* New York: W. H. Freeman.

Snyder, M. L., Stephan, W. G., & Rosenfield, D. (1976). Egotism and attribution. *Journal of Personality and Social Psychology, 33,* 435–441.

Snyder, M. L., Stephan, W. G., & Rosenfield, D. (1978). Attributional egotism. In J. H. Harvey, W. Ickes, & R. F. Kidd (Eds.), *New directions in attributional research* (Vol. 2). Hillsdale, NJ: Erlbaum.

Snyder, M., & Gangestad, S. (1982). Choosing social situations: Two investigations of the self-monitoring process. *Journal of Personality and Social Psychology, 43,* 123–135.

Sobotka, S. S., Davidson, R. J., & Senulis, J. A. (1992). Anterior brain electrical asymmetries in response to reward and punishment. *Electroencephalography and Clinical Neurophysiology, 83,* 236–247.

Solomon, R. L. (1964). Punishment. *American Psychologist, 19,* 239–253.

Sorg, B. A., & Whitney, P. (1992). The effect of trait anxiety and situational stress on working memory capacity. *Journal of Research in Personality, 26,* 235–241.

Sorrentino, R. M., & Field, N. (1986). Emergent leadership over time: The functional value of positive motivation. *Journal of Personality and Social Psychology, 50,* 1091–1099.

Spacapan, S., & Cohen, S. (1983). Effects and after-effects of stressor expectations. *Journal of Personality and Social Psychology, 45,* 1243–1254.

Spangler, W. D., & House, R. J. (1991). Presidential effectiveness and the leadership motive profile. *Journal of Personality and Social Psychology, 60,* 439–455.

Spanos, N. P. (1996). *Multiple identities and false memories.* Washington, DC: American Psychological Association.

Spence, J. T., Helmreich, R., & Stapp, J. (1975). Ratings of self and peers on sex role attributes and their relation to self-esteem and conceptions of masculinity and femininity. *Journal of Personality and Social Psychology, 32,* 29–39.

Sperling, M. B., & Berman, W. H. (Eds.). (1994). *Attachment in adults: Clinical and developmental perspectives.* New York: Guilford.

Spetch, M. L., Wilkie, D. M., & Pinel, J. P. J. (1981). Backward conditioning: A reevaluation of the empirical evidence. *Psychological Bulletin, 89,* 163–175.

Spielberger, C. D., & DeNike, L. D. (1966). Descriptive behaviorism versus cognitive theory in verbal operant conditioning. *Psychological Review, 73,* 309–326.

Spooner, A., & Kellogg, W. N. (1947). The backward conditioning curve. *American Journal of Psychology, 60,* 321–334.

Sprecher, S., Sullivan, Q., & Hatfield, E. (1994). Mate selection preferences: Gender differences examined in a national sample. *Journal of Personality and Social Psychology, 66,* 1074–1080.

Sroufe, L. A., & Fleeson, J. (1986). Attachment and the construction of relationships. In W. W. Hartup & Z. Rubin (Eds.), *Relationships and development* (pp. 51–71). Hillsdale, NJ: Erlbaum.

Srull, T. K., & Wyer, R. S., Jr. (1979). The role of category accessibility in the interpretation of information about persons: Some determinants and implications. *Journal of Personality and Social Psychology, 37,* 1660–1672.

Staats, A. W. (1996). *Behavior and personality: Psychological behaviorism.* New York: Springer.

Staats, A. W., & Burns, G. L. (1982). Emotional personality repertoire as cause of behavior. *Journal of Personality and Social Psychology, 43,* 873–881.

Staats, A. W., & Staats, C. K. (1958). Attitudes established by classical conditioning. *Journal of Abnormal and Social Psychology, 57,* 37–40.

Staats, A. W., Staats, C. K., & Crawford, H. L. (1962). First-order conditioning of meaning and the parallel conditioning of a GSR. *Journal of General Psychology, 67,* 159–167.

Staats, C. K., & Staats, A. W. (1957). Meaning established by classical conditioning. *Journal of Experimental Psychology, 54,* 74–80.

Steele, C. M. (1988). The psychology of self-affirmation: Sustaining the integrity of the self. In L. Berkowitz (Ed.), *Advances in experimental social psychology,* (Vol. 21, pp. 261–302). New York: Academic Press.

Stephenson, W. (1953). *The study of behavior: Q-technique and its methodology.* Chicago: University of Chicago Press.

Sternberg, R. J. (Ed.). (1982). *Handbook of human intelligence.* New York: Cambridge University Press.

Sternberg, R. J. (1985). Implicit theories of intelligence, creativity, and wisdom. *Journal of Personality and Social Psychology, 49,* 607–627.

Steronko, R. J., & Woods, D. J. (1978). Impairment in early stages of visual information processing in nonpsychotic schizotypic individuals. *Journal of Abnormal Psychology, 87,* 481–490.

Stevens, R. (1983). *Erik Erikson: An introduction.* New York: St. Martin's Press.

Stevenson, H. W. (1965). Social reinforcement of children's behavior. In L. P. Lipsitt & C. C. Spiker (Eds.), *Advances in child development* (Vol. 2). New York: Academic Press.

Stevenson, H. W., Hale, G. A., Hill, K. T., & Moely, B. E. (1967). Determinants of children's preferences for adults. *Child Development, 38,* 1–14.

Stewart, A. J. (1980). Personality and situation in the prediction of women's life patterns. *Psychology of Women Quarterly, 5,* 195–206.

Stolar, D., & Fromm, E. (1974). Activity and passivity of the ego in relation to the superego. *International Review of Psycho-Analysis, 1,* 297–311.

Stolberg, S. (1994, March 27). Genetic bias: Held hostage by heredity. *Los Angeles Times,* p. 1A.

Stone, L. J., & Hokanson, J. E. (1969). Arousal reduction via self-punitive behavior. *Journal of Personality and Social Psychology, 12,* 72–79.

Stotland, E. (1969a). Exploratory investigation of empathy. In L. Berkowitz (Ed.), *Advances in experimental social psychology* (Vol. 4). New York: Academic Press.

Stotland, E. (1969b). *The psychology of hope.* San Francisco: Jossey-Bass.

Strauman, T. J. (1989). Self-discrepancies in clinical depression and social phobia: Cognitive structures that underlie emotional disorders? *Journal of Abnormal Psychology, 53,* 14–22.

Strauman, T. J., & Higgins, E. T. (1987). Automatic activation of self-discrepancies and emotional syndromes: When cognitive structures influence affect. *Journal of Personality and Social Psychology, 53,* 1004–1014.

Strube, M. J. (1989). Evidence for the *type* in Type A behavior: A taxometric analysis. *Journal of Personality and Social Psychology, 56,* 972–987.

Stumpf, H. (1993). The factor structure of the Personality Research Form: A cross-national evaluation. *Journal of Personality, 61,* 27–48.

Stumphauzer, J. S. (1972). Increased delay of gratification in young prison inmates through imitation of high delay peer models. *Journal of Personality and Social Psychology, 21,* 10–17.

Suppes, P., Pavel, M., & Falmagne, J-Cl. (1994). Representations and models in psychology. *Annual Review of Psychology, 45,* 517–544.

Sutton, S. K., & Davidson, R. J. (1997). Prefrontal brain asymmetry: A biological substrate of the behavioral approach and inhibition systems. *Psychological Science, 8,* 204–210.

Swann, W. B., Jr. (1987). Identity negotiation: Where two roads meet. Journal of Personality and Social Psychology, 53, 1038–1051.

Swann, W. B., Jr. (1990). To be adored or to be known: The interplay of self-enhancement and self-verification. In E. T. Higgins & R. M. Sorrentino (Eds.), *Handbook of motivation and cognition* (Vol. 2, pp. 408–448). New York: Guilford Press.

Swann, W. B., Jr., Pelham, B. W., & Krull, D. S. (1989). Agreeable fancy or disagreeable truth? Reconciling self-enhancement and self-verification. *Journal of Personality and Social Psychology, 57,* 782–791.

Swann, W. B., Jr., Wenzlaff, R. M., & Tafarodi, R. W. (1992). Depression and the search for negative evaluations: More evidence of the role of self-verification strivings. *Journal of Abnormal Psychology, 101,* 314–317.

Tajfel, H., & Turner, J. C. (1986). The social identity theory of intergroup behavior. In S. Worchel & W. G. Austin (Eds.), *Psychology of intergroup relations* (2nd ed., pp. 7–24). Chicago: Nelson-Hall.

Tannen, D. (1990). *You just don't understand: Women and men in conversation.* New York: Ballantine Books.

Tarde, G. (1903). *The laws of imitation.* New York: Holt, Rinehart, & Winston.

Tavris, C., & Wade, C. (1984). *The longest war: Sex differences in perspective* (2nd ed.). New York: Harcourt Brace Jovanovich.

Taylor, M. C., & Hall, J. A. (1982). Psychological androgyny: Theories, methods and conclusions. *Psychological Bulletin, 92,* 347–366.

Taylor, S. E. (1983). Adjustment to threatening events: A theory of cognitive adaptation. *American Psychologist, 38,* 1161–1173.

Taylor, S. E., & Brown, J. D. (1988). Illusion and well-being: A social psychological perspective on mental health. *Psychological Bulletin, 103,* 193–210.

Taylor, S. E., & Brown, J. D. (1994). Positive illusions and well-being revisited: Separating fact from fiction. *Psychological Bulletin, 116,* 21–27.

Taylor, S. E., & Crocker, J. (1981). Schematic bases of social information processing. In E. T. Higgins, C. P. Herman, & M. P. Zanna (Eds.), *Social cognition: The Ontario symposium* (Vol. 1). Hillsdale, NJ: Erlbaum.

Taylor, S. E., & Fiske, S. T. (1978). Salience, attention, and attribution: Top of the head phenomena. In L. Berkowitz (Ed.), *Advances in experimental social psychology* (Vol. 11). New York: Academic Press.

Tedeschi, R. G., & Calhoun, L. G. (1995). *Trauma and transformation: Growing in the aftermath of suffering.* Thousand Oaks, CA: Sage.

Tellegen, A. (1985). Structure of mood and personality and their relevance to assessing anxiety, with an emphasis on self-report. In A. H. Tuma & J. D. Maser (Eds.), *Anxiety and the anxiety disorders* (pp. 681–706). Hillsdale, NJ: Erlbaum.

Tellegen, A., Lykken, D. T., Bouchard, T. J., Jr., Wilcox, K. J., Segal N. L., & Rich, S. (1988). Personality similarity in twins reared apart and together. *Journal of Personality and Social Psychology, 54,* 1031–1039.

Tesch, S. A., & Whitbourne, S. K. (1982). Intimacy status and identity status in young adults. *Journal of Personality and Social Psychology, 43,* 1041–1051.

Tesser, A. (1971). Evaluative and structural similarity of attitudes as determinants of interpersonal attraction. *Journal of Personality and Social Psychology, 18,* 92–96.

Tesser, A. (1986). Some effects of self-evaluation maintenance on cognition and action. In R. M. Sorrentino & E. T. Higgins (Eds.), *The handbook of motivation and cognition: Foundations of social behavior.* New York: Guilford Press.

Tesser, A. (1988). Toward a self-evaluation maintenance model of social behavior. In L. Berkowitz (Ed.), *Advances in experimental social psychology,* (Vol. 21, pp. 181–227). New York: Academic Press.

Tesser, A. (1991). Social vs. clinical approaches to self psychology: The self evaluation maintenance model and Kohutian object relations theory. In R. Curtis (Ed.), *The relational self: Theoretical convergences in psychoanalysis and social psychology* (pp. 257–281). New York: Guilford.

Tesser, A. (1993). The importance of heritability in psychological research: The case of attitudes. *Psychological Review, 100,* 129–142.

Tesser, A., & Campbell, J. (1983). Self-definition and self-evaluation maintenance. In J. Suls & A. G. Greenwald (Eds.), *Psychological perspectives on the self* (Vol. 2). Hillsdale, NJ: Erlbaum.

Tesser, A., & Paulhus, D. (1983). The definition of self: Private and public self-evaluation management strategies. *Journal of Personality and Social Psychology, 44,* 672–682.

Theios, J. (1962). The partial reinforcement effect sustained through blocks of continuous reinforcement. *Journal of Experimental Psychology, 64,* 1–6.

Thelen, M. H., & Rennie, D. L. (1972). The effect of vicarious reinforcement on imitation: A review of the literature. In B. Maher (Ed.), *Progress in experimental personality research* (Vol. 6). New York: Academic Press.

Thiessen, D., & Gregg, B. (1980). Human assortative mating and genetic equilibrium: An evolutionary perspective. *Ethology and Sociobiology, 1,* 111–140.

Thomas, A., & Chess, S. (1977). *Temperament and development.* New York: Brunner/Mazel.

Thomas, M. H., Horton, R. W., Lippincott, E. C., & Drabman, R. S. (1977). Desensitization to portrayals of real-life aggression as a function of exposure to television violence. *Journal of Personality and Social Psychology, 35,* 450–458.

Thompson, G. C. (1968). George Alexander Kelly (1905–1967). *Journal of General Psychology, 79,* 19–24.

Thompson, S. C. (1985). Finding positive meaning in a stressful event and coping. *Basic and Applied Social Psychology, 6,* 279–295.

Thompson, S. C. (1991). The search for meaning following a stroke. *Basic and Applied Social Psychology, 12,* 81–96.

Thompson, S. C., & Janigian, A. S. (1988). Life schemes: A framework for understanding the search for meaning. *Journal of Social and Clinical Psychology, 7,* 260–280.

Thorndike, E. L. (1898). Animal intelligence: An experimental study of the associative processes in animals. *Psychological Monographs, 2* (Whole No. 8).

Thorndike, E. L. (1905). *The elements of psychology.* New York: A. G. Seiler.

Thorndike, E. L. (1933). *An experimental study of rewards.* New York: Columbia University Teachers College Press.

Thorne, A. (1987). The press of personality: A study of conversations between introverts and extraverts. *Journal of Personality and Social Psychology, 53,* 718–726.

Thronquist, M. H., Zuckerman, M., & Exline, R. V. (1991). Loving, liking, looking, and sensation seeking in unmarried college couples. *Personality and Individual Differences, 12,* 1283–1292.

Timberlake, W. (1993). Behavior systems and reinforcement: An integrative approach. *Journal of the Experimental Analysis of Behavior, 60,* 105–128.

Tolman, E. C. (1932). *Purposive behavior in animals and men.* New York: Appleton-Century-Crofts.

Tolman, E. C. (1959). Principles of purposive behavior. In S. Koch (Ed.), *Psychology: A study of a science* (Vol. 2, pp. 92–157). New York: McGraw-Hill.

Toner, I. J., & Smith, R. A. (1977). Age and overt verbalization in delay-maintenance behavior in children. *Journal of Experimental Child Psychology, 24,* 123–128.

Tooby, J., & Cosmides, L. (1989). Evolutionary psychology and the generation of culture, Part I. *Ethology and Sociobiology, 10,* 29–49.

Tooby, J., & Cosmides, L. (1990). On the universality of human nature and the uniqueness of the individual. *Journal of Personality, 58,* 17–67.

Trapnell, P. D., & Wiggins, J. S. (1990). Extension of the interpersonal adjective scales to include the big five dimensions of personality. *Journal of Personality and Social Psychology, 59,* 781–790.

Tresemer, D. W. (1977). *Fear of success.* New York: Plenum.

Triandis, H. C., Hui, H., Albert, R. D., Leung, S., Lisansky, J., Diaz-Loving, R., Plascencia, L., Marin, G., Betancourt, H., & Loyola-Cintron, L. (1984). Individual models of social behavior. *Journal of Personality and Social Psychology, 46,* 1389–1404.

Trickett, P. K., & Putnam, F. W. (1993). Impact of child sexual abuse on females: Toward a developmental, psychobiological integration. *Psychological Science, 4,* 81–87.

Trivers, R. L. (1971). The evolution of reciprocal altruism. *Quarterly Review of Biology, 46,* 35–57.

Trivers, R. L. (1972). Parental investment and sexual selection. In B. Campbell (Ed.), *Sexual selection and the descent of man: 1871–1971* (pp. 136–179). Chicago: Aldine.

Trope, Y. (1975). Seeking information about one's own ability as a determinant of choice among tasks. *Journal of Personality and Social Psychology, 32,* 1004–1013.

Trope, Y. (1979). Uncertainty-reducing properties of achievement tasks. *Journal of Personality and Social Psychology, 37,* 1505–1518.

Trope, Y. (1980). Self-assessment, self-enhancement, and task preference. *Journal of Experimental Social Psychology, 16,* 116–129.

Truax, C. B., & Mitchell, K. M. (1971). Research on certain therapist interpersonal skills in relation to process and outcome. In A. E. Bergin & S. L. Garfield (Eds.), *Handbook of psychotherapy and behavior change.* New York: Wiley.

Tsuang, M. T., & Faraone, S. V. (1990). *The genetics of mood disorders.* Baltimore: Johns Hopkins Press.

Tulving, E. (1972). Episodic and semantic memory. In E. Tulving & W. Donaldson (Eds.), *Organization of memory.* New York: Academic Press.

Tulving, E. (1993). What is episodic memory? *Current Directions in Psychological Science, 2,* 67–70.

Turk, D. (1978). Cognitive behavioral techniques in the management of pain. In J. P. Foreyt & D. P. Rathjen (Eds.), *Cognitive behavior therapy: Research and application.* New York: Plenum.

Turner, J. L., Foa, E. B., & Foa, U. G. (1971). Interpersonal reinforcers: Classification, interrelationship, and some differential properties. *Journal of Personality and Social Psychology, 19,* 168–170.

Tversky, B., & Hemenway, K. (1983). Categories of environmental scenes. *Cognitive Psychology, 15,* 121–149.

Udry, J. R., & Talbert, L. M. (1988). Sex hormone effects on personality at puberty. *Journal of Personality and Social Psychology, 54,* 291–295.

Uleman, J. S., & Bargh, J. A. (1989). *Unintended thought.* New York: Guilford.

Vaillant, G. E. (1977). *Adaptation to life.* Boston: Little, Brown.

Vallacher, R. R., & Wegner, D. M. (1985). *A theory of action identification.* Hillsdale, NJ: Erlbaum.

Vallacher, R. R., & Wegner, D. M. (1987). Action identification theory: The representation and control of behavior. *Psychological Review, 94,* 3–15.

Vallacher, R. R., & Wegner, D. M. (1989). Levels of personal agency: Individual variation in action identification. *Journal of Personality and Social Psychology, 57,* 660–671.

Vandenberg, S. G., Singer, S. M., & Pauls, D. L. (1986). *The heredity of behavior disorders in adults and children.* New York: Plenum.

Vandewater, E. A., Ostrove, J. M., & Stewart, A. J. (1997). Predicting women's well-being in midlife: The importance of personality development and social role involvements. *Journal of Personality and Social Psychology, 72,* 1147–1160.

Van Maanen, J. (1973). Observations on the making of policemen. *Human Organization, 32,* 407–418.

Van Maanen, J. (1975). Police socialization: A longitudinal examination of job attitudes in an urban police department. *Administrative Science Quarterly, 20,* 207–228.

Vaughan, K. B., & Lanzetta, J. T. (1980). Vicarious instigation and conditioning of facial expressive and autonomic responses to a model's expressive display of pain. *Journal of Personality and Social Psychology, 38,* 909–923.

Vernon, D. T. A. (1974). Modeling and birth order in responses to painful stimuli. *Journal of Personality and Social Psychology, 29,* 794–799.

Vernon, P. E. (1964). *Personality assessment: A critical survey.* New York: Wiley.

Veroff, J. (1957). Development and validation of a projective measure of power motivation. *Journal of Abnormal and Social Psychology, 54,* 1–8.

Verplanken, B. (1991). Persuasive communication of risk information: A test of cue versus message processing effects in a field experiment. *Personality and Social Psychology Bulletin, 17,* 188–193.

Viken, R. J., & McFall, R. M. (1994). Paradox lost: Implications of contemporary reinforcement theory for behavior therapy. *Current Directions in Psychological Science, 3,* 121–125.

Viken, R. J., Rose, R. J., Kaprio, J., & Koskenvuo, M. (1994). A developmental genetic analysis of adult personality: Extraversion and neuroticism from 18 to 59 years of age. *Journal of Personality and Social Psychology, 66,* 722–730.

Wagner, A. R., Siegel, S., Thomas, E., & Ellison, G. D. (1964). Reinforcement history and the extinction of a conditioned salivary response. *Journal of Comparative and Physiological Psychology, 58,* 354–358.

Wahlsten, D. (1990). Insensitivity of the analysis of variance to heredity-environment interaction. *Behavioral and Brain Sciences, 13,* 100–161.

Walker, E. F., & Diforio, D. (1997). Schizophrenia: A neural diathesis-stress model. *Psychological Review, 104,* 667–685.

Walker, R. N. (1962). Body build and behavior in young children. Body build and nursery school teacher ratings. *Monographs of the Society for Research on Child Development, 27* (Serial No. 84).

Waller, N. G., Lilienfeld, S. O., Tellegen, A., & Lykken, D. T. (1991) The tridimensional personality questionnaire: Structural validity and comparison with the multidimensional personality questionnaire. *Multivariate Behavioral Research, 26,* 1–23.

Walls, R. T., & Cox, J. (1971). Expectancy of reinforcement in chance and skills tasks under motor handicaps. *Journal of Clinical Psychology, 27,* 436–438.

Wallston, B. S., & Wallston, K. A. (1978). Locus of control and health: A review of the literature. *Health Education Monographs, 6,* 107–117.

Wallston, K. A., & Wallston, B. S. (1981). Health locus of control scales. In H. F. Lefcourt (Ed.), *Research with the locus of control construct. Vol. 1, Assessment methods.* New York: Academic Press.

Walters, R. H., & Parke, R. D. (1964). Influence of response consequences to a social model on resistance to deviation. *Journal of Experimental Child Psychology, 1,* 269–280.

Waterman, A. S. (1982). Identity development from adolescence to adulthood: An extension of theory and a review of research. *Developmental Psychology, 18,* 341–358.

Watson, D. (1989). Strangers' ratings of the five robust personality factors: Evidence of a surprising convergence with self-report. *Journal of Personality and Social Psychology, 57,* 120–128.

Watson, D., & Clark, L. A. (1984). Negative affectivity: The disposition to experience aversive emotional states. *Psychological Bulletin, 96,* 465–490.

Watson, D., & Clark, L. A. (1994). Introduction to the special issue on personality and psychopathology. *Journal of Abnormal Psychology, 103,* 3–5.

Watson, D., Clark, L. A., McIntyre, C. W., & Hamaker, S. (1992). Affect, personality, and social activity. *Journal of Personality and Social Psychology, 63,* 1011–1025.

Watson, D., & Tellegen, A. (1985). Toward a consensual structure of mood. *Psychological Bulletin, 98,* 219–235.

Watson, J. B., & Raynor, R. (1920). Conditioned emotional reactions. *Journal of Experimental Psychology, 3,* 1–14.

Watt, J. D., & Blanchard, M. J. (1994). Boredom proneness and the need for cognition. *Journal of Research in Personality, 28,* 44–51.

Wegner, D. M. (1989). *White bears and other unwanted thoughts: Suppression, obsession, and the psychology of mental control.* New York: Viking Penguin.

Wegner, D. M. (1994). Ironic processes of mental control. *Psychological Review, 101,* 34–52.

Wegner, D. M., Schneider, D. J., Carter, S. R., III, & White, T. L. (1987). Paradoxical effects of thought suppression. *Journal of Personality and Social Psychology, 53,* 5–13.

Wegner, D. M., Shortt, J. W., Blake, A. W., & Page, M. S. (1990). The suppression of exciting thoughts. *Journal of Personality and Social Psychology, 58,* 409–418.

Weinberger, D. A., Schwartz, G. E., & Davidson, R. J. (1979). Low-anxious, high-anxious, and repressive coping styles: Psychometric patterns and behavioral and physiological responses to stress. *Journal of Abnormal Psychology, 88,* 369–380.

Weinberger, J. L., & Hardaway, R. (1990). Separating science from myth in subliminal psychodynamic activation. *Clinical Psychology Review, 10,* 727–756.

Weinberger, J. L., & Silverman, L. H. (1987). Subliminal psychodynamic activation: A method for studying psychoanalytic dynamic propositions. In R. Hogan & W. H. Jones (Eds.), *Perspectives in personality* (Vol. 2, pp. 251–287). Greenwich, CT: JAI Press.

Weiner, B. (1979). A theory of motivation for some classroom experiences. *Journal of Educational Psychology, 71,* 3–25.

Weiner, B. (1982). The emotional consequences of causal ascriptions. In M. S. Clark & S. T. Fiske (Eds.), *Affect and cognition: The 17th annual Carnegie symposium on cognition.* Hillsdale, NJ: Erlbaum.

Weiner, B. (1986). *An attributional theory of motivation and emotion.* New York: Springer-Verlag.

Weiner, B. (1990). Attribution in personality psychology. In L. A. Pervin (Ed.), *Handbook of personality: Theory and research* (pp. 465–485). New York: Guilford Press.

Weiner, B., Heckhausen, H., Meyer, W., & Cook, R. E. (1972). Causal ascriptions and achievement behaviors: A conceptual analysis of effort and reanalysis of locus of control. *Journal of Personality and Social Psychology, 21,* 239–248.

Weiner, B., & Litman-Adizes, T. (1980). An attributional, expectancy-value analysis of learned helplessness and depression. In J. Garber & M. E. P. Seligman (Eds.), *Human helplessness: Theory and applications.* New York: Academic Press.

Weiner, B., Nierenberg, R., & Goldstein, M. (1976). Social learning (locus of control) versus attributional (causal stability) interpretations of expectancy of success. *Journal of Personality, 44,* 52–68.

Weinstein, N. D. (1989). Optimistic biases about personal risks. *Science, 246,* 1232–1233.

Weisberg, P., & Waldrop, P. B. (1972). Fixed-interval work habits of congress. *Journal of Applied Behavioral Analysis, 5,* 93–97.

Weiss, D. S., & Mendelsohn, G. A. (1986). An empirical demonstration of the implausibility of the semantic similarity explanation of how trait ratings are made and what they mean. *Journal of Personality and Social Psychology, 50,* 595–601.

Weiss, L., & Masling, J. (1970). Further validation of a Rorschach measure of oral imagery: A study of six clinical groups. *Journal of Abnormal Psychology, 76,* 83–87.

Weiss, R. S. (Ed.). (1973). *Loneliness: The experience of emotional and social isolation.* Cambridge, MA: MIT Press.

Wenzlaff, R. M., Wegner, D. M., & Roper, D. W. (1988). Depression and mental control: The resurgence of unwanted negative thoughts. *Journal of Personality and Social Psychology, 55,* 1–11.

Westen, D. (1991). Social cognition and object relations. *Psychological Bulletin, 109,* 429–455.

Westen, D. (1998). The scientific legacy of Sigmund Freud: Toward a psychodynamically informed psychological science. *Psychological Bulletin, 124,* 333–371.

Westenberg, P. M., & Block, J. (1993). Ego development and individual differences in personality. *Journal of Personality and Social Psychology, 65,* 792–800.

Wheeler, R. E., Davidson, R. J., & Tomarken, A. J. (1993). Frontal brain asymmetry and emotional reactivity: A biological substrate of affective style. *Psychophysiology, 30,* 82–89.

Whitam, F. L., Diamond, M., & Martin, J. (1993). Homosexual orientation in twins: A report on 61 pairs and three triplet sets. *Archives of Sexual Behavior, 22,* 187–206.

Whitbeck, L. B., Hoyt, D. R., Simons, R. L., Conger, R. D., Elder, G. H., Jr., Lorenz, F. O., & Huck, S. (1992). Intergenerational continuity of parental rejection and depressed affect. *Journal of Personality and Social Psychology, 58,* 644–663.

Whitbourne, S. K., Zuschlag, M. K., Elliot, L. B., & Waterman, A. S. (1992). Psychosocial development in adulthood: A 22-year sequential study. *Journal of Personality and Social Psychology, 63,* 260–271.

White, K. M., Houlihan, J., Costos, D., & Speisman, J. C. (1990). Adult development in individuals and relationships. *Journal of Research in Personality, 24,* 371–386.

White, R. W. (1959). Motivation reconsidered: The concept of competence. *Psychological Review, 66,* 297–333.

White, R. W. (1963). *Ego and reality in psychoanalytic theory: A proposal regarding independent ego energies* (Psychological Issues Monograph 11). New York: International Universities Press.

Wickelgren, W. A. (1977). *Learning and memory.* Englewood Cliffs, NJ: Prentice-Hall.

Wicker, F. W., Brown, G., Wiehe, J. A., Hagen, A. S., & Reed, J. L. (1993). On reconsidering Maslow: An examination of the deprivation/domination proposition. *Journal of Research in Personality, 27,* 118–133.

Wicklund, R. A., & Duval, S. (1971). Opinion change and performance facilitation as a result of objective self-awareness. *Journal of Experimental Social Psychology, 7,* 319–342.

Wiedenfeld, S. A., O'Leary, A., Bandura, A., Brown, S., Levine, S., & Raska, K. (1990). Impact of perceived self-efficacy in coping with stressors on components of the immune system. *Journal of Personality and Social Psychology, 59,* 1082–1094.

Wiener, N. (1948). *Cybernetics: Control and communication in the animal and the machine.* Cambridge, MA: MIT Press.

Wiggins, J. S. (1973). *Personality and prediction: Principles of personality assessment.* Reading, MA: Addison-Wesley.

Wiggins, J. S. (1979). A psychological taxonomy of trait-descriptive terms: The interpersonal domain. *Journal of Personality and Social Psychology, 37,* 395–412.

Wiggins, J. S. (Ed.). (1996). *The five-factor model of personality: Theoretical perspectives.* New York: Guilford.

Wiggins, J. S., Phillips, N., & Trapnell, P. (1989). Circular reasoning about interpersonal behavior: Evidence concerning some untested assumptions underlying diagnostic classification. *Journal of Personality and Social Psychology, 56,* 296–305.

Wiggins, J. S., & Pincus, A. L. (1989). Conceptions of personality disorders and dimensions of personality. *Psychological Assessment: A Journal of Consulting and Clinical Psychology, 1,* 305–316.

Willerman, L., Loehlin, J. C., & Horn, J. M. (1992). An adoption and a cross-fostering study of the Minnesota Multiphasic Personality Inventory (MMPI) Psychopathic Deviate scale. *Behavior Genetics, 22,* 515–529.

Williams, G. C., & Deci, E. L. (1996). Internalization of biopsychosocial values by medical students: A test of self-determination theory. *Journal of Personality and Social Psychology, 70,* 767–779.

Williams, G. C., Grow, V. M., Freedman, Z. R., Ryan, R. M., & Deci, E. L. (1996). Motivational predictors of weight loss and weight-loss maintenance. *Journal of Personality and Social Psychology, 70,* 115–126.

Williams, R. L., Moore, C. A., Pettibone, T. J., & Thomas, S. P. (1992). Construction and validation of a brief self-report scale of self-management practices. *Journal of Research in Personality, 26,* 216–234.

Wilson, E. O. (1975). *Sociobiology: The new synthesis.* Cambridge, MA: Harvard University Press.

Wilson, J. Q., & Herrnstein, R. J. (1985). *Crime and human nature.* New York: Simon & Schuster.

Wilson, M. I., & Daly, M. (1985). Competitiveness, risk-taking, and violence: The young male syndrome. *Ethology and Sociobiology, 6,* 59–73.

Wilson, M. I., & Daly, M. (1996). Male sexual proprietariness and violence against wives. *Current Directions in Psychological Science, 5,* 2–7.

Wine, J. D. (1982). Evaluation anxiety: A cognitive-attentional construct. In H. W. Krohne & L. C. Laux (Eds.), *Achievement, stress, and anxiety.* Washington, DC: Hemisphere.

Wink, P., & Helson, R. (1993). Personality change in women and their partners. *Journal of Personality and Social Psychology, 65,* 597–605.

Winson, J. (1985). *Brain and psyche: The biology of the unconscious.* Garden City, NY: Doubleday.

Winson, J. (1990). The meaning of dreams. *Scientific American, 263,* 86–96.

Winter, D. G. (1972). The need for power in college men: Action correlates and relationship to drinking. In D. C. McClelland, W. N. Davis, R. Kalin, & E. Wanner (Eds.), *The drinking man.* New York: Free Press.

Winter, D. G. (1973). *The power motive.* New York: Free Press.

Winter, D. G. (1988). The power motive in women—and men. *Journal of Personality and Social Psychology, 54,* 510–519.

Winter, D. G. (1993). Power, affiliation, and war: Three tests of a motivational model. *Journal of Personality and Social Psychology, 65,* 532–545.

Winter, D. G. (1996). *Personality: Analysis and interpretation of lives.* New York: McGraw-Hill.

Winter, D. G., & Barenbaum, N. B. (1985). Responsibility and the power motive in women and men. *Journal of Personality, 53,* 335–355.

Winter, D. G., John, O. P., Stewart, A. J., Klohnen, E. C., & Duncan, L. E. (1998). Traits and motives: Toward an integration of two traditions in personality research. *Psychological Bulletin, 105,* 230–250.

Winter, D. G., Stewart, A. J., & McClelland, D. C. (1977). Husband's motives and wife's career level. *Journal of Personality and Social Psychology, 35,* 159–166.

Wispé, L. (1986). The distinction between sympathy and empathy: To call forth a concept, a word is needed. *Journal of Personality and Social Psychology, 50,* 314–321.

Woike, B. A. (1995). Most-memorable experiences: Evidence for a link between implicit and explicit motives and social cognitive processes in everyday life. *Journal of Personality and Social Psychology, 68,* 1081–1091.

Wolberg, L. R. (1967). *The technique of psychotherapy.* New York: Grune & Stratton.

Wolfe, J. B. (1936). Effectiveness of token-rewards for chimpanzees. *Comparative Psychology Monographs, 12* (Whole No. 60).

Wolfe, R. N., & Kasmer, J. A. (1988). Type versus trait: Extraversion, impulsivity, sociability, and preferences for cooperative and competitive activities. *Journal of Personality and Social Psychology, 54,* 864–871.

Wolpe, J. (1961). The systematic desensitization treatment of neuroses. *Journal of Nervous and Mental Disorders, 132,* 189–203.

Wolpe, J. (1981). Behavior therapy versus psychoanalysis: Therapeutic and social implications. *American Psychologist, 36,* 159–164.

Wong, M. M., & Csikszentmihalyi, M. (1991). Affiliation motivation and daily experience: Some issues on gender differences. *Journal of Personality and Social Psychology, 60,* 154–164.

Wood, J. M., Nezworski, M. T., & Stejskal, W. J. (1996a). The comprehensive system for the Rorschach: A critical examination. *Psychological Science, 7,* 3–10.

Wood, J. M., Nezworski, M. T., & Stejskal, W. J. (1996b). Thinking critically about the comprehensive system for the Rorschach: A reply to Exner. *Psychological Science, 7,* 14–17.

Wood, R., & Bandura, A. (1989). Impact of conceptions of ability on self-regulatory mechanisms and complex decision making. *Journal of Personality and Social Psychology, 56,* 407–415.

Woodruffe, C. (1985). Consensual validation of personality traits: Additional evidence and individual differences. *Journal of Personality and Social Psychology, 48,* 1240–1252.

Wortman, C. B., & Brehm, J. W. (1975). Responses to uncontrollable outcomes: An integration of reactance theory and the learned helplessness model. In L. Berkowitz (Ed.), *Advances in experimental social psychology* (Vol. 8). New York: Academic Press.

Wright, J. C., & Mischel, W. (1988). Conditional hedges and the intuitive psychology of traits. *Journal of Personality and Social Psychology, 55,* 454–469.

Wright, R. A. (1996). Brehm's theory of motivation as a model of effort and cardiovascular response. In P. M. Gollwitzer & J. A. Bargh (Eds.), *The psychology of action: Linking cognition and motivation to behavior* (pp. 424–453). New York: Guilford.

Wyer, R. S., Jr., & Srull, T. K. (Eds.). (1984). *Handbook of social cognition* (Vols. 1–3). Hillsdale, NJ: Erlbaum.

Wyer, R. S., Jr., & Srull, T. K. (1986). Human cognition in its social context. *Psychology Review, 93,* 322–359.

Wylie, R. (1979). *The self concept* (Vol. 2). Lincoln: University of Nebraska Press.

Yates, A. J. (1970). *Behavior theory.* New York: Wiley.

Yates, B. T., & Mischel, W. (1979). Young children's preferred attentional strategies for delaying gratification. *Journal of Personality and Social Psychology, 37,* 286–300.

Yates, J., & Taylor, J. (1978). Stereotypes for somatotypes: Shared beliefs about Sheldon's physiques. *Psychological Reports, 43,* 777–778.

York, K. L., & John, O. P. (1992). The four faces of Eve: A typological analysis of women's personality at midlife. *Journal of Personality and Social Psychology, 63,* 494–508.

Young, J. E., & Klosko, J. S. (1993). *Reinventing your life.* New York: Plume.

Young, P. A., Eaves, L. J., & Eysenck, H. J. (1980). Intergenerational stability and change in the causes of variation in personality. *Personality and Individual Differences, 1,* 35–55.

Zadeh, L. (1965). Fuzzy sets. *Information and Control, 8,* 338–353.

Zajonc, R. B., Markus, H., & Markus, G. B. (1979). The birth order puzzle. *Journal of Personality and Social Psychology, 37,* 1325–1341.

Zanna, M. P., Kiesler, C. A., & Pilkonis, P. A. (1970). Positive and negative attitudinal affect established by classical conditioning. *Journal of Personality and Social Psychology, 14,* 321–328.

Zeisel, H., & Kalven, H., Jr. (1977). Parking tickets and missing women: Statistics and the law. In J. M. Tanur et al. (Eds.), *Statistics: A guide to political and social issues.* Oakland, CA: Holden Day.

Zeldow, P. B., Daugherty, S. R., & McAdams, D. P. (1988). Intimacy, power, and psychological well-being in medical students. *The Journal of Nervous and Mental Disease, 176,* 182–187.

Zener, K. (1937). The significance of behavior accompanying conditioned salivary secretion for theories of the conditioned response. *American Journal of Psychology, 50,* 384–403.

Zentall, T. R., Sutton, J. E., & Sherburne, L. M. (1996). True imitative learning in pigeons. *Psychological Science, 7,* 343–346.

Zern, D. (1973). Competence reconsidered: The concept of secondary process development as an explanation of "competence" phenomena. *The Journal of Genetic Psychology, 122,* 135–162.

Zillmann, D. (1971). Excitation transfer in communication-mediated aggressive behavior. *Journal of Experimental Social Psychology, 7,* 419–434.

Zillmann, D. (1998). *Connections between sexuality and aggression* (2nd ed.). Mahwah, NJ: Erlbaum.

Zimbardo, P. G. (1969). The human choice: Individuation, reason, and order versus deindividuation, impulse, and chaos. In W. J. Arnold & D. Levine (Eds.), *Nebraska symposium on motivation.* Lincoln: University of Nebraska Press.

Zimmerman, B. J., & Rosenthal, J. T. (1974). Observational learning of rule governed behavior by children. *Psychological Bulletin, 81,* 29–42.

Zimmerman, D. W. (1957). Durable secondary reinforcement: Method and theory. *Psychological Review, 14,* 373–383.

Zinbarg, R. E., & Mohlman, J. (1998). Individual differences in the acquisition of affectively valenced associations. *Journal of Personality and Social Psychology, 74,* 1024–1040.

Zuckerman, M. (1971). Dimensions of sensation seeking. *Journal of Consulting and Clinical Psychology, 36,* 45–52.

Zuckerman, M. (1979). *Sensation seeking: Beyond the optimal level of arousal.* Hillsdale, NJ: Erlbaum.

Zuckerman, M. (1985). Biological foundations of the sensation-seeking temperament. In J. Strelau, F. H. Farley, & A. Gale (Eds.), *The biological bases of personality and behavior. Vol. 1. Theories, measurement techniques, and development.* Washington, DC: Hemisphere.

Zuckerman, M. (1991a). *The psychobiology of personality.* New York: Cambridge University Press.

Zuckerman, M. (1991b). Biotypes for basic personality dimensions? "The twilight zone" between genotype and social phenotype. In J. Strelau & A. Angleitner

(Eds.), *Explorations in temperament: International perspectives on theory and measurement* (pp. 129–146). New York: Plenum.

Zuckerman, M. (1992). What is a basic factor and which factors are basic? Turtles all the way down. *Personality and Individual Differences, 13,* 675–681.

Zuckerman, M. (1993). P-impulsive sensation seeking and its behavioral, psychophysiological and biochemical correlates. *Neuropsychobiology, 28,* 30–36.

Zuckerman, M. (1994). *Behavioral expression and biosocial bases of sensation seeking.* New York: Cambridge University Press.

Zuckerman, M. (1995). Good and bad humors: Biochemical bases of personality and its disorders. *Psychological Science, 6,* 325–332.

Zuckerman, M. (1996). The psychobiological model for impulsive unsocialized sensation seeking: A comparative approach. *Neuropsychobiology, 34,* 125–129.

Zuckerman, M., Bernieri, F., Koestner, R., & Rosenthal, R. (1989). To predict some of the people some of the time: In search of moderators. *Journal of Personality and Social Psychology, 57,* 279–293.

Zuckerman, M., Kieffer, S. C., & Knee, C. R. (1998). Consequences of self-handicapping: Effects on coping, academic performance, and adjustment. *Journal of Personality and Social Psychology, 74,* 1619–1628.

Zuckerman, M., Koestner, R., DeBoy, T., Garcia, T., Maresca, B. C., & Sartoris, J. M. (1988). To predict some of the people some of the time: A reexamination of the moderator variable approach in personality theory. *Journal of Personality and Social Psychology, 54,* 1006–1019.

Zuckerman, M., Kuhlman, D. M., & Camac, C. (1988). What lies beyond E and N? Factor analyses of scales believed to measure basic dimensions of personality. *Journal of Personality and Social Psychology, 54,* 96–107.

Zuckerman, M., Kuhlman, D. M., Joireman, J., Teta, P., & Kraft, M. (1993). A comparison of three structural models for personality: The big three, the big five, and the alternative five. *Journal of Personality and Social Psychology, 65,* 757–768.

Zuckerman, M., Murtaugh, T. M., & Siegel, J. (1974). Sensation seeking and cortical augmenting-reducing. *Psychophysiology, 11,* 535–542.

Zuckerman, M., & Neeb, M. (1980). Demographic influences in sensation seeking and expressions of sensation seeking in religion, smoking, and driving habits. *Personality and Individual Differences, 1,* 197–206.

Zuckerman, M., Schultz, D. P., & Hopkins, T. R. (1967). Sensation seeking and volunteering for sensory deprivation and hypnosis experiments. *Journal of Consulting Psychology, 31,* 358–363.

Zuckerman, M., Ulrich, R. S., & McLaughlin, J. (1993). Sensation seeking and reactions to nature paintings. *Personality and Individual Differences, 15,* 563–576.

Zuroff, D. C. (1986). Was Gordon Allport a trait theorist? *Journal of Personality and Social Psychology, 51,* 993–1000.

name index

575

subject index

photo credits